The Last Centuries
of Byzantium

The Last Centuries
of Byzantium

1261-1453

Donald M. Nicol

Rupert Hart-Davis   London

Granada Publishing Limited
First published in Great Britain 1972 by Rupert Hart-Davis Ltd
3 Upper James Street, London W1R 4BP

Copyright © 1972 by Donald M. Nicol

ISBN 0 246 10559 3

Printed in Great Britain by
Northumberland Press Limited
Gateshead

Contents

PART 4: BYZANTIUM AS A VASSAL OF THE TURKS: THE LAST
HUNDRED YEARS—1354-1453

Preface

The historian of the Byzantine Empire is in the rare position of being able to study an institution which endured for more than a millennium and which, whenever it may be thought to have begun, came to a certain end on a well-defined date in the year 1453. It forms a compact unit of history, much of it well documented by its own records and by its own sophisticated historians. It can therefore be analysed, dissected, criticized, or admired in a dispassionate manner; and it might, as Byzantine historians themselves often hoped, provide guiding principles, warnings and exemplary lessons for future generations of humanity. The English-speaking public have been understandably slow to awaken from the spell of Edward Gibbon, who saw in Byzantium little to admire and much to criticize, who narrated its history as a prolonged decline from a golden age, and who could only conclude that he had borne witness to 'the triumph of barbarism and religion'.

In recent years Byzantine history, whether or not it affords warnings or lessons for the present, has become an object of deeper and more reflective study. General histories of the Byzantine Empire have been produced, notably by G. Ostrogorsky and A. A. Vasiliev, which present a picture less dramatic but more objective and sympathetic than that of Gibbon. Several more or less scholarly books written in or translated into English already exist to guide the student or the general reader through the early and the middle periods of the Empire's long history. The last period of Byzantium, however, is in a special case. For long it was less closely studied than the earlier centuries, and it still contains many secrets in the way of unpublished documents and manuscripts. It is now attracting more and more attention from scholars writing in specialist publications and periodicals in a babel of languages. But to discover the course of events in the years between 1261 and 1453 one has at present to turn to the rather sparse accounts given in the final chapters of the general histories of the Empire; for hardly anyone has yet attempted a more extended work of synthesis in any language. In the existing state of research and of the evidence it is doubtless rash and premature to make the attempt. But it is my hope that even an interim report may be useful, before the specialized studies of experts proliferate to such an extent that their subject sinks beneath the weight of their contributions, and their readers fall back exhausted and dispirited from the effort of trying to distinguish the wood from the trees. The need for having such a book to hand has constantly been brought home to me when teaching Byzantine history to students. It was partly to fill this need that I embarked on writing this book.

This is a dry and perhaps mundane motive, however. I must also confess that I find in the last two hundred years of Byzantium a special fascination. They were not the halcyon days of a young society, nor were they the golden age of a mature civilization. But they were the years in which the Byzantines, whose forefathers had so often had to live in a state of nervous apprehension and impending catastrophe, were put to the final test. If I have described this experience in terms of the failing strength and mortal illness of an invalid, it is with reference to the institution rather than to its people. The structure of the Empire was old and perhaps past saving by the fourteenth century. It only needed a vigorous and determined enemy such as the Ottomans to deliver the *coup de grâce*. But its people, bred in a state of emergency, seemed to thrive on the excitement of their insecurity. There were more new developments of old ideas in politics, in religion and in philosophy in the last two centuries of Byzantium than there had been in the previous two hundred years. In this book I have tried to present a narrative of what took place in those centuries, so that those who have little Latin and less Greek may gain some clearer idea of the stages by which the institution of the Byzantine Empire came to its lingering end.

The footnotes and bibliographies are intended to indicate material for more detailed study of particular periods or topics. Where recent monographs on the reigns of individual Emperors already exist, as in the cases of Michael VIII, Andronikos III, or Manuel II, I have as often as not referred the reader to them for the source material. Where no such monographs existed at the time of writing, as in the case of Andronikos II, I have been more generous with references to the original sources. I am aware that I have paid scant attention to the social, intellectual and artistic life of the period; but a proper treatment of these aspects of the subject would require the space of another volume, and I have thought it best to confine myself to providing simply the historical framework in which they must be set. The affairs of the Church, however, have been recorded, sometimes at length, since the line between things spiritual and things temporal in the Byzantine world was never so clearly drawn as in the West, and the course of political life and of imperial policy was frequently affected or determined by ecclesiastical or theological considerations.

My debt to those who have already explored greater or lesser parts of the history of this relatively unfamiliar age will be evident and is expressed in the footnotes. But my greatest debt is to the Greek historians of the fourteenth and fifteenth centuries, whose works have for too long been neglected. Where I have misread or misinterpreted my authorities, medieval or modern, the fault is my own.

D.M.N.
November 1971

Note on Abbreviations

The following abbreviations are used for periodicals, collections of documents and standard works:

B	=	*Byzantion*
BNJ	=	*Byzantinisch-neugriechische Jahrbücher*
Bréhier, *Vie et Mort*		L. Bréhier, *Le monde byzantin*, I: *Vie et Mort*
	=	*de Byzance* (new edition: Paris, 1969)
BS	=	*Byzantinoslavica*
BZ	=	*Byzantinische Zeitschrift*
CMH, IV	=	*Cambridge Medieval History*, IV: *The Byzantine Empire*. Part 1: *Byzantium and its Neighbours*; Part 2: *Government, Church and Civilisation*. Edited by J. M. Hussey (Cambridge, 1966, 1967).
CSHB	=	*Corpus Scriptorum Historiae Byzantinae* (Bonn, 1828-97)
Diehl, *L'Europe orientale*		
	=	C. Diehl, R. Guilland, L. Oeconomos and R. Grousset, *L'Europe orientale de 1081 à 1453* (=*Histoire Générale*, ed. G. Glotz: *Histoire du Moyen Âge*, IX, 1: Paris, 1945)
Dölger, *Regesten*		
	=	F. Dölger, *Regesten der Kaiserurkunden des oströmischen Reiches*, part III: 1204-82; part IV: 1282-1341; part V: 1341-1453 (Munich and Berlin, 1931-65)
DOP	=	*Dumbarton Oaks Papers*
EEBS	=	*Epeteris Hetaireias Byzantinon Spoudon* (Annual of the Society for Byzantine Studies: Athens)
MM	=	F. Miklosich and J. Müller, *Acta et Diplomata graeca medii aevi sacra et profana*, 6 vols. (Vienna, 1860-90)
OCP	=	*Orientalia Christiana Periodica*

Ostrogorsky, *History*

 = G. Ostrogorsky, *History of the Byzantine State*, translated by Joan Hussey, 2nd edition (Oxford, 1968)

PG = J. P. Migne, *Patrologiae cursus completus. Series graeco-latina*

REB = *Revue des Etudes Byzantines*

Vasiliev, *History*

 = A. A. Vasiliev, *History of the Byzantine Empire* (Madison, 1952)

VV = *Vizantijskij Vremennik* (Leningrad)

Zbornik Radova

 = *Zbornik Radova Vizantološkog Instituta* (Recueil des travaux de l'Académie Serbe des Sciences, Institut d'Etudes Byzantines : Belgrade)

One

The Byzantine Empire after the Fourth Crusade

In April 1204 the city of Constantinople was stormed and occupied by the soldiers of the Fourth Crusade. It was the greatest sack of a city that anyone could remember. It was the greatest city that any of the crusaders had ever seen. To its inhabitants and to all the millions who lived within its orbit it was simply the City, or the Queen of Cities. It was the centre and focal point of the Roman Empire, an institution divinely-ordained and capable of infinite expansion and infinite survival as God's last word on the order of the world. Byzantine is a convenient term to describe the culture of the medieval world that centred on Constantinople. It was not a word that the inhabitants of that world were in the habit of employing. They saw themselves as Roman or *Romaioi*, and their empire as that eastern portion of the Greco-Roman world of antiquity which had, by God's grace, survived all the catastrophes and changes that had afflicted the western part of the old Roman Empire.

The Greco-Roman tradition and the mystique of the *imperium Romanum* of the ancient world never died east of the Adriatic Sea. The myth of the immortality of the Roman Empire was sustained rather than weakened by the Christian faith, so foreign to the mind of ancient Rome. The blood of the ruling families of the Byzantine Empire and the stock of its farmers and soldiers were enriched rather than adulterated by integration with races such as the Syrians, Armenians and Slavs, which the true Greeks and Romans of old would have regarded as barbarous. The Byzantine armies which ensured the survival and expansion of the Empire in the middle ages were very far from being either Greek or Roman. The emperors and officers who commanded them were as often as not of Macedonian or Armenian family and were not concerned to claim descent from Pericles or Augustus. The Byzantine Empire was a multiracial and multilingual society. Yet Greek in its spoken form was the *lingua franca*, and Greek in its highly elaborate literary form was the language of the court, the church and the law of Constantinople,

I

and of the *literati*, the poets, historians, theologians and essayists.

The commonly accepted knowledge of Greek was one of the binding forces of the Empire, at least in its later years. Another was the common acceptance of the Christian faith in the form for ever defined as Orthodox by the early councils of the Church. But the most visible symbol of the continuity and perpetuation of the Christian Roman Empire was the city of Constantinople itself, the New Jerusalem of the Byzantine world. Its foundation by Constantine the Great in A.D. 330 had marked the culmination of antiquity and the beginning of a new era. The city was the enduring advertisement for the ancient tradition of urban civilization and the guardian of the Christian religion which had grown up in urban environments. Though many times besieged, blockaded and assaulted, Constantinople had never fallen to its enemies until the soldiers of the Fourth Crusade broke in. The event of April 1204 was thus the most shattering break with their past that the Byzantines had ever experienced. They could not conceive how their God, under whose special protection they lived, could have allowed such a thing to happen, unless it were in retribution for their sins. They could not imagine how their way of life could survive so long as their city remained in alien hands. For no matter what happened to the provinces of the Empire, the possession of Constantinople was nine-tenths of God's law. An Orthodox emperor seated on his throne in Constantinople and an Orthodox patriarch celebrating the liturgy in the Great Church of St Sophia—such were the symbols of immortality for the Byzantines.

How then had the disaster come about, and who were the culprits? The sins of the Byzantines, so far as concerned the material welfare of their empire, were sins of omission and neglect. In the tenth and early eleventh centuries the Empire had been a well-integrated structure covering southern Italy, the Balkans, Greece and Asia Minor. Its defence and its administration were centrally controlled from the headquarters in Constantinople. Its soldiers had, for the most part, become native to the soil on which they lived and were therefore interested in its defence and cultivation. The agriculture and the economy were prosperous and apparently stable, and the Byzantine gold coin was the standard of monetary value from one end of the civilized world to the other. The emerging powers of western Europe, the Holy Roman Empire and the Papacy, were regarded by the Byzantine emperors of the tenth century sometimes with contempt and sometimes with tolerance, but seldom with great interest except as wayward cousins in the great Christian fraternity. There seemed no reason why

2

this state of affairs should ever change, though there was always the hope that the westerners might wake up to the fact of their waywardness and return to the Roman Empire.

But in the course of the eleventh century Byzantine complacency suffered a number of shocks. In 1054 the emancipation of the western Christian world from its last ties with the ancient order of things was manifested in the schism between the Churches of Rome and Constantinople. The reformed Papacy was no longer prepared to be treated with contempt or even with tolerance; and the schism between the Churches was one of the first symptoms of the new shifting of the balance of power in the Mediterranean world. At about the same time, the eastern and western extremities of the Byzantine Empire were threatened by new enemies—in the west the Normans, in the east the Seljuq Turks. It had always been the fate of the emperors in Constantinople to have to fight on two sides at once. But now their ingenuity and their resources were unequal to the task. In 1071 the Normans captured the last remaining Byzantine possession in southern Italy, and in the same year the imperial armies in the east were massacred by the Seljuq Turks at Manzikert in Asia Minor. The consequent loss of most of Asia Minor was to have far more serious effects than the loss of southern Italy. For the Byzantine province in southern Italy was merely part of the *damnosa haereditas* of Justinian's universal Roman Empire. But Asia Minor was the largest and most productive land mass in the whole imperial structure and the greatest source of native troops for its defence.

The Emperor Alexios I Komnenos, who came to the throne in 1081, therefore did well to cut his losses in the west and look to the strengthening of the battered eastern frontiers. Much territory had already been lost, but at least Alexios contrived to fix a new boundary between Byzantines and Turks in Asia Minor. These were short-term measures. In the long run the real problem was how the ancient organization of the Byzantine Empire could stand up to the new and vigorous forces of its hostile neighbours to east and west. And it is here that the sins of the Byzantines were visited upon their own heads. For in the eleventh century the centralized and integrated system of administration and defence which had sustained the Empire against many worse foes than the Normans and the Turks had broken up. The aristocracy of Constantinople and the other cities of the Empire, blinded by the splendour of their own civilization, fed on the legacy of their great past and were lulled into a sense of false security. The landlords of the provinces, many of whom were soldiers by breeding

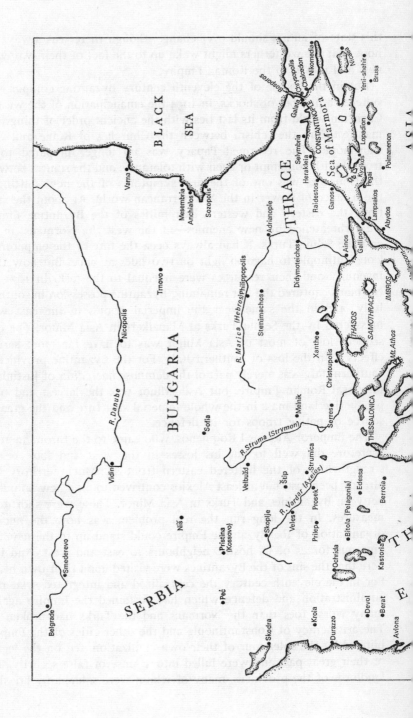

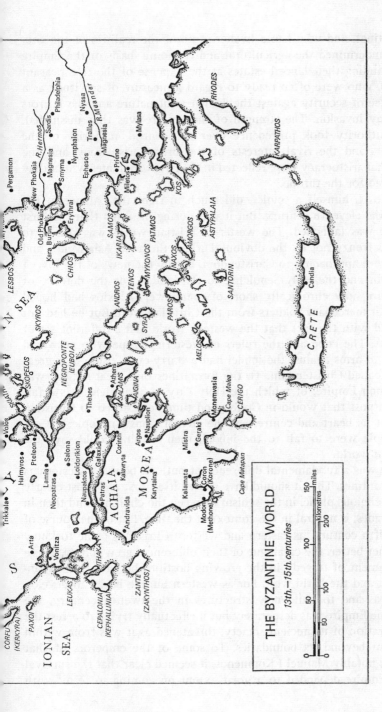

THE BYZANTINE WORLD
13th.–15th. centuries

Pergamon

New Phokaia
Old Phokaia
Kara Burun
Smyrna
Sardis
Magnesia
Philadelphia
Nyssa
Nymphaion
Tralles
Magnesia
R. Hermos
R. Maander
Ephesos
Priene
Erythrai
Miletos
Mylasa

RHODES

KARPATHOS

LESBOS

SAMOS

CHIOS

IKARIA

SKYROS

PATMOS

KOS

ASTYPALAIA

MYKONOS

TENOS

ANDROS

NAXOS

AMORGOS

SANTORIN

PAROS

SYRA

MELOS

AIGINA
PSALAMIS

CRETE

Candia

NEGROPONTE
(EUBOIA)

SKOPELOS

Volos
Halmyros
Trikkala
Preleon
Lamia

Athens
Thebes

Salona
Neopatras
Loidorikion
Naupaktos
Galaxidi
Patras
Corinth
Argos
Nauplion

Monemvasia
Cape Malea
CERIGO

Mistra
Geraki

MOREA
ACHAIA

Kalamata
Coron
(Korone)
Modon
(Methone)
Karytaina
Kalavryta
Andravida

Cape Matapan

Arta
Jonitza

CORFU
(KERKYRA)

PAXOI

IONIAN
SEA

LEUKAS

CEPALONIA
(KEFHALLINIA)

ITHAKA

ZANTE
(IZAKYNTHOS)

AN SEA

and instinct, and who had a livelier sense of the realities of the situation, undermined the agricultural and economic basis of the Empire by expanding their landed estates at the expense of the free peasant farmers, who were often ready to regard a measure of servitude as a guarantee of security against the fickleness of nature and the horrors of enemy invasion. The strength of the Empire was thus dissipated, local authority took precedence over the central authority of the Emperor, and the rival interests of the urban aristocracy and the provincial aristocracy were reflected in the rival candidates whom they supported for the throne.

Alexios I, himself a soldier, did much to right the balance at the end of the eleventh century. But it was during his reign that the First Crusade was launched. The western Christian world was stirred to religious frenzy not by the obvious Turkish threat to Asia Minor and the eastern approaches to Christendom, but by the news of the loss of Jerusalem and the Holy Sepulchre to the infidel. For the defence of an empire now chronically short of manpower, Alexios had hoped to recruit mercenary soldiers from the Christian west. But he had not reckoned with the fact that the western world had a different set of priorities. The Pope and the rulers of western Europe who answered the call to arms against the infidel had a starry-eyed vision of a great society called Christendom. To the Byzantines that great society was the Roman Empire, of which the Holy City of Jerusalem was a far-flung outpost that would in God's good time be restored to Christian rule. But its heart and centre was the city of Constantinople; if Constantinople were to fall to the infidel, then nothing could save the Christian world.

There was a fundamental difference of outlook between westerners and Byzantines. That it should have shown itself first and most clearly on the religious plane, in the schism between the churches and then in the crusades, is natural in the context of the time. But in the course of the twelfth century, as eastern and western Christians came to know each other better, the catalogue of their differences grew longer. There is an element of tragedy in the growing hostility between the Byzantine east and the Latin west. For as western Europe began to develop new ideas and to build new structures in the twelfth century, the Byzantine Empire was desperately but ineffectually trying to arrest the disintegration of its ancient society, threatened as it was from within and from beyond its boundaries. To some of the emperors of that century, notably Manuel I Komnenos, it seemed clear that the survival of the Empire depended to a great extent on coming to terms with the new political, commercial and ecclesiastical forces in the west. Western merchants, especially those of the expanding commercial republic of Venice, who were ready to police the seas on behalf of the emperors, should be encouraged to trade and to settle in Constantinople and the harbours of the Empire. Western kings like Frederick Barbarossa should be humoured and not ridiculed when they laid claim to the exclusive title of Emperor of the Romans. It was even possible that the westerners had something to teach the Byzantines in the way of culture and civilization. In general terms, a policy of active co-operation with the west might prove more profitable than one of isolation.

Manuel I may have been right, but his views were far from popular with his subjects. The more enlightened of the Byzantines were prepared to overlook the fact that the westerners were mainly a rather uncouth, belligerent and avaricious lot, whose own stupidity and arrogance kept them beyond the pale of the Orthodox Christian world. After all, they were not technically barbarians nor infidels like the Arabs and Turks. They were even, in some sense, Christians, for all their failure to realize that the great society of the Christian faith was governed and protected by the Roman Emperor in Constantinople and that their part of the church had strayed far from the paths laid down by the early fathers and councils. One day they might see the error of their ways and return to the fold, acknowledging the fact that their kings and 'emperors' were but the agents of the one true Emperor of the Romans, and that their pope was but one of the five patriarchs of the undivided Christian church. On these terms peaceful co-existence was possible. But all too often the activities of western soldiers and western merchants in the Empire taxed Byzantine tolerance and patience to their limits; and the majority of Byzantines, born with the superiority complex of heirs to a civilization older and finer than any in western Europe, were not disposed to be tolerant to upstart foreigners who mocked their traditions and exploited their markets. They made little distinction between the Normans and the Venetians, the French and the Germans. The westerners were collectively known and indiscriminately disliked as the 'Latins'. The Byzantine historian Niketas Choniates, writing about the year 1200, summed up the feelings of the ordinary Byzantines in these words:

Between us and the Latins is set the widest gulf. We are poles apart. We have not a single thought in common. They are stiff-necked, with a proud affection of an upright carriage, and love to

7

sneer at the smoothness and modesty of our manners. But we look on their arrogance and boasting as a flux of the snivel which keeps their noses in the air; and we tread them down by the might of Christ, who giveth unto us the power to trample upon the adder and upon the scorpion.[1]

In 1171 anti-Latin feeling resulted in the arrest of the Venetian merchants in Constantinople and the major cities of the Empire. In 1182 it reached its horrifying climax in the brutal massacre of all foreigners in Constantinople, the destruction of their property and the proclamation of an emperor known to hold violently anti-western opinions. The feeling of bitterness was mutual; but on the Latin side it was compounded by greed and ambition. The Venetians never forgot the episode of 1171. They had learnt to value the wealth of Byzantium and the eastern Mediterranean. They came to feel that the only certain way to secure their interests there was to put Constantinople under western control. In 1185 the Normans crossed over from Italy to Greece and sacked Thessalonica, the second largest city in the Byzantine Empire. The Holy Roman Emperor Frederick Barbarossa, who already claimed the imperial title held by the emperors in Constantinople, threatened to substantiate that claim by turning his crusading army against the Byzantines. Under his successor, Henry VI, the ambition of the Normans was united with the imperial claims of the German emperors by the union of the Norman kingdom of Sicily with the Holy Roman Empire.

By the end of the twelfth century the internal rot of the administration and economy of the Byzantine Empire was aggravated by the external threat to its survival, from the Christians on one side and the Turks on the other. If the Empire was doomed to suffer from the sins of its inhabitants it was because their rulers and statesmen had no constructive policy either with regard to their new western enemies or with regard to the dissipation of their authority and the disintegration of their territories. The Empire was reduced in size to a small state with a disproportionately large and wealthy capital city. In the few remaining provinces, in western Asia Minor, in Thrace, Macedonia, Greece and the Greek islands, the land was largely in the hands of members of the aristocracy lording it over their own domains and almost independent of the central government in Constantinople. They were prepared to defend only their own immediate interests and properties. The situation which had developed in the eleventh century was now widespread and beyond cure or control. The Empire's defence system had long since ceased to be under unified command; it relied on armies of foreign mercenaries, many of them westerners, or on isolated armies commanded by local lords, fighting in defence of their own territories. In this way the island of Cyprus had become completely independent of Constantinople under Isaac Komnenos, a grand-nephew of the Emperor Manuel I. Isaac had publicly declared his independence and assumed the title of Emperor. There were others like him in other parts of the provinces, who enjoyed their autonomy without troubling to declare it.

The emperors of the family of Angelos, who held the throne from 1185 to 1204, were unable to halt the process of disintegration. In the Balkans, where Manuel I had recently managed to reassert control, everything was breaking down again. Hungary was a separate king-dom, no longer even pretending to be a client state of Byzantium. But the nearer northern neighbours of Constantinople, the Serbs and the Bulgars, profited more directly from the feebleness of the Empire to which they had reluctantly belonged. The Serbs, supported by Hun-gary, had broken away from Byzantine control and united themselves into a new kingdom under Stephen Nemanja; their country would never again be a part of the Byzantine Empire. In 1186, following the lead of the Serbs, the Bulgars chose the moment to organize themselves once again into a free kingdom for the first time since their conquest in 1018 by Basil II, the Bulgar-slayer. Two Bulgarian nobles, Peter and Asen, began the formation of what was to become the Second Bul-garian Empire. On the eastern frontier, in Asia Minor, the situation was beyond repair. The best that could be done was to try to hold the line. The principalities founded by the crusaders in Syria and Palestine still maintained their foothold on the coast. But by the end of the twelfth century they were cut off from Constantinople by the advance of the Seljuq Turks in Asia Minor, and their existence was threatened by Saladin from Egypt.

The outlook was gloomy for the Byzantines. Their historians could still remind them that they had survived more dire emergencies in the past; and so long as their city remained in their hands they could still hope that the tide would turn as it had turned so many times before. But they had an uneasy feeling that the threat to their existence now came not from their age-old and familiar enemies, the Turks or the Bulgars, but in an unfamiliar and more nebulous form from western Europe. It was not that the west presented any real coalition or united front against Byzantium. It was rather that there had grown up in the west a consensus of opinion, not very clearly expressed but ominously deep, that Constantinople stood in the way of the development of western interests. The popes had made themselves believe that Byzantium had betrayed the cause of the Crusade against the infidel, and that the Holy War would never be successful until the schismatic Greeks had been brought into the fold of the Roman Church. The Holy Roman Emperor in the west had openly voiced his belief that what he rudely called 'the Kingdom of Greece' should be exterminated by conquest; the Normans, his allies, had made several incursions into Byzantine territory and plundered the city of Thessalonica. The Venetians were ready to support any power that would help them to regain and to strengthen their hold on the trade of Constantinople and the eastern Mediterranean. A climate of opinion had been created in western Europe in which the eventual capture of Constantinople and conquest of the Byzantine Empire seemed a quite logical and natural development. When the event occurred, in April 1204, it cannot have been entirely unexpected by the Byzantines.[2]

On the other hand, the event of the Fourth Crusade vindicated all the forebodings and bigotries of the anti-western faction in Byzantium. To them it was the work of the 'Latin dogs', and the burden of guilt rested on the shoulders of every inhabitant of western Europe collectively. Pope Innocent III, the architect of the enterprise in its original form, might justifiably complain that the leaders of his crusade had perverted and exceeded his orders. But to the Byzantines this was no excuse, for to them such a division of the responsibilities of Church and State was incomprehensible. The Roman Church and all the 'soldiers of Christ' who fought for it stood condemned.

It is not the purpose of this book to tell again the story of the Fourth Crusade or to assess the causes or apportion the blame for one of the most disastrous episodes in the history of Europe.[3] It is enough to recall that Constantinople was attacked, captured and devastated in April 1204 by an army of French, Flemings, Lombards, Germans and Venetians. The villains of the piece were undoubtedly the Venetians, led by that formidable champion of private enterprise, the Doge, Enrico Dandolo, blind and aged eighty-three. But Dandolo was ably supported by Boniface, the Marquis of Montferrat in Lombardy and official leader of the crusade, and by Baldwin, Count of Flanders. It was this triumvirate who laid the foundations of the so-called Latin Empire of Constantinople. The Byzantine Emperor and the Orthodox Patriarch both fled from their capital. The crown of the Empire fell 'by the grace of God' to Baldwin of Flanders. The Doge of Venice contented himself with appointing a trusted Venetian as Patriarch;

while Boniface of Monferrat, who had hoped for the greater glory of the Emperor's crown, accepted by way of compensation the invented title of King of Thessalonica. Pope Innocent III, who was quick to condemn the horrors of the sack of Constantinople by his disobedient crusaders, soon came round to the view that the conquest of the Byzantine Empire by the west must be part of God's plan for the reunification of Christendom.

It was the professed intention of the crusaders to conquer and divide the provinces as well as the two chief cities of the Empire; and to this end they drew up a document known as the Treaty of Partition. The provinces in Greece, the Greek islands and Asia Minor were to be parcelled out among the Venetians and the crusading knights and barons. The Venetians, wise from the long experience of their merchants in the eastern Mediterranean, appropriated most of the red meat of the carcass of the Empire. The dry bones were left for the crusaders to fight over. The Venetians claimed their share as their inalienable property. The crusaders, however, agreed to hold their prospective conquests by terms of feudal tenure, acknowledging the Latin Emperor in Constantinople as their sovereign lord.

The Latin Empire of Constantinople lasted for 57 years, from 1204 to 1261. In retrospect it is possible to say that it was doomed to failure from the start. The Venetians alone knew the terrain and knew what they meant to get out of it. The crusaders had no clear idea of where they were or what they were doing. But to the Byzantines they represented an alien régime which had imposed its will on the queen of cities, usurped the title and authority of the Emperor of the Romans, desecrated the Great Church of St Sophia, and installed a foreign and heretical Patriarch of Constantinople. Refugees left the capital in large numbers in 1204, either for Greece or for Asia Minor. But life had to go on, and once the first shock had worn off, there were those who found that it was after all possible to tolerate the unfamiliar régime, or even to collaborate with its representatives. There were others, perhaps more out of self-interest than patriotism, who took it upon themselves to organize resistance to the Latin conquerors in the provinces. Their centres of operation became rallying points for refugees from the capital, for those who had lost their livelihood and property, for the disaffected, and particularly for the clergy and monks of the Byzantine Church, who refused to compromise their faith by accepting the creed of Rome or the jurisdiction of foreign bishops whom they believed to be in heresy. But the prospect of overthrowing the Latin conquerors and restoring Constantinople and the Empire to its rightful owners seemed for a long time to be unlikely.

It is hard to see what the crusaders hoped to gain by invading the provinces of the Empire. When Boniface of Montferrat set out from Thessalonica in 1204 to conquer his allotted domains of Greece, it was into almost unknown country that he led his army. The inhabitants of northern Greece had cause to remember the Norman invasions in the previous century, and the Ionian islands of Corfu, Cephalonia and Zante had already been partly appropriated by freelance buccaneers from Italy. But central and southern Greece were unexplored territory. Here, as in the eastern Byzantine provinces, the imperial government had ceased to command much obedience in recent years. Land was held and estates administered by aristocratic Greek landlords, many of them related to the imperial families in Constantinople. They enjoyed tenure of their estates technically at the emperor's pleasure or in *pronoia*, but in practice they ruled as autonomous princes or archons. A few were already connected by marriage with French or Italian families, and some found it convenient to throw in their lot with the new invaders. But others preferred to take refuge in north-western Greece, behind the barrier of the Pindos mountains. Here, in Epiros and Akarnania, a lackland bastard of the ruling aristocracy called Michael Doukas seized the opportunity of the Latin conquest to carve out for himself a domain centred around the city of Arta on the Ambracian Gulf. Whatever Michael's original intentions may have been, Arta was to become one of the focal points of resistance to the Latin conquerors. But the rest of Greece soon fell before them. Thebes and Athens were granted as fiefs by Boniface of Montferrat to a Burgundian knight, Otto de la Roche, while the Peloponnese, or the Morea (the 'mulberry bush') as they called it, was eventually acquired by Geoffrey of Villehardouin, a nephew of the chronicler of the Fourth Crusade. As time went on the conquerors adopted more glorious titles and fought each other over their feudal rights and boundaries. The lord of Attica became the Duke of Athens; Geoffrey of Villehardouin entitled himself Prince of Achaia. The feudal ascendancy imposed on Greece by the knights of the Fourth Crusade lasted in some districts until the conquest of the whole country by the Ottoman Turks in the fifteenth century. Most of the Morea was in due course to be re-established as a Byzantine Greek province. But the city of Athens never again reverted to Byzantine rule after 1204.

While Boniface and his knights invaded Greece, Baldwin of Flanders set about the conquest of Byzantine Asia Minor. Here the going was harder. For the Byzantines of the east, already harried by the Seljuqs, were less ready to submit to a new invader than those of the west. The great landed estates of Asia Minor, as well as the walled cities such as Nicaea, Brusa or Philadelphia, were better organized for defence than those in Greece. At Trebizond, on the southern shore of the Black Sea, an independent principality had already been set up by two brothers of the family of Komnenos even before the crusaders occupied Constantinople; and like Isaac Komnenos in Cyprus, Alexios Komnenos in Trebizond claimed the Byzantine imperial title. The crusaders hardly ventured as far east as Trebizond. But nearer to the capital they early encountered fierce and organized resistance. Theodore Laskaris, a son-in-law of the Byzantine Emperor Alexios III, had fled from Constantinople to Asia Minor in April 1204. Like his western Greek counterpart Michael Doukas, Theodore gathered together a following of refugees and sympathizers and organized an army of resistance. In due course, having established a headquarters and capital in the city of Nicaea in north-western Asia Minor, he adopted the title of Emperor of the Byzantine Empire in exile. A new Orthodox Patriarch was appointed in Nicaea, and in 1208 he placed the imperial crown on the head of Theodore Laskaris. The Byzantine church and state were reborn in Nicaea.[4]

The Latin Empire was thus faced with Byzantine resistance from two sides. But the Emperor Baldwin of Flanders, a stranger in a strange land, provoked a third and more dangerous enemy in the north. The revived Empire of Bulgaria had passed to the rule of Kalojan, brother of Peter and Asen, in 1197. Kalojan, as the natural enemy of the Byzantines, had regarded the crusaders as his potential allies and sought an alliance with them as an equal partner. But his offer was rudely refused by the Emperor Baldwin; Kalojan, in his resentment, turned from butchering the Greeks in Thrace and Macedonia to inciting them against the common enemy. Thenceforth the rulers of Bulgaria sided now with the Byzantines in Epiros and now with those in Nicaea to the detriment of the Latin Empire.

The first to suffer from his tactlessness was Baldwin himself. Kalojan advanced on Constantinople in 1205 and inflicted severe casualties on the Latins. Baldwin was captured by the Bulgars and never seen again. It was the Doge of Venice who collected the remnants of the army and retreated to safety. But the effort proved too much for an octogenarian, and he died soon afterwards. The Latin Emperor was lost, the Doge dead, and only a year later Boniface of Montferrat also perished in the defence of his kingdom of Thessalonica against the

Bulgars. The Latin Empire was barely two years old when it was deprived of the three leaders who had been its main inspiration. Thessalonica passed to the infant son of Boniface; Constantinople to Baldwin's brother Henry.

Of all the line of Latin Emperors, Henry of Flanders was by far the most capable and intelligent. His task was made easier at the start of his reign by the sudden death of Kalojan of Bulgaria. The Bulgarian Empire was temporarily weakened by dynastic disputes; Henry was able at least to maintain communications between Constantinople and Thessalonica. But the death of Boniface led to further trouble in the administration of the Empire. The Lombard nobles of Thessalonica, who owed their position to Boniface, refused to give allegiance to Henry and rebelled; and for two years the strength of the Empire, which might have discouraged its enemies, was turned against its own members. By 1210 Henry had suppressed the rebellion and asserted his authority as sovereign. But the Greeks in Epiros and Nicaea had been allowed a breathing-space in which to consolidate their positions. Theodore Laskaris in Nicaea defended his infant empire against both Turks and Latins, and the Latin emperor was soon obliged to fix a boundary between his own territories and those of the Byzantine Empire in exile. In the west, Michael Doukas of Epiros extended his rule into Thessaly, thus severing the land route between Thessalonica and Athens.

Henry of Flanders died in 1216. There was no immediate successor to maintain even the precarious balance of power that he had achieved. His brother-in-law, Peter of Courtenay, then in France, was elected Emperor of Constantinople and set out for his capital, stopping at Rome to receive his crown from the Pope. His wife Yolanda was to continue her journey by sea, while Peter made his way overland through Epiros and Macedonia. This foolhardy plan was inspired by Venice, who hoped to have her paper claim to the coast towns of Epiros substantiated free of charge. But the Latins had under-estimated the resources of the ruler of Epiros, Theodore Doukas, who had recently succeeded his brother Michael at Arta. Peter of Courtenay and several of his company were ambushed and captured in the mountains of Epiros by Theodore, and their army was scattered. The ultimate fate of the new Latin emperor is as mysterious as that of his predecessor Baldwin, but his capture was a triumph for the Byzantine cause.

The Empress Yolanda arrived at Constantinople in 1217 and for two years reigned as regent for her eldest son, Philip of Namur, who

14

obstinately refused to leave France. Her only act of diplomacy was to give her daughter in marriage to Theodore Laskaris of Nicaea, which temporarily pacified the eastern Byzantines. But in the north a nephew of the great Kalojan, John Asen, was re-assembling the pieces of the Bulgarian Empire; and in the west Theodore Doukas was fast increasing his power at the expense of the Latin kingdom of Thessalonica. From the Latin point of view it was disastrous that both Constantinople and Thessalonica should be bereft of male rulers so soon after their acquisition.

When Yolanda died her younger son, Robert of Courtenay, became emperor. Robert was young and self-indulgent. He had none of the adventurous spirit which, however misdirected, had guided the crusaders. His accession marks the beginning of the decline and fall of the Latin Empire, though the process was to be prolonged for 40 years. It may truly be said of its latter stages that the Latin régime survived not because of the weakness but because of the strength of its enemies. As the spirit of the Latins waned the ambitions of the exiled Greeks rose. The recovery of Constantinople became for them an attainable and an acknowledged aim. But the prize was so great that the rivalry was intense, and the Byzantines of Epiros and Nicaea could never sink their pride and jealousy sufficiently to join forces. They were divided not only by their geographical separation, but also by mutual envy and hostility which had finally to be resolved in open warfare.

Robert of Courtenay reigned from 1221 to 1228. Those years saw the loss of the Kingdom of Thessalonica, the first of the crusader establishments to fall, and the loss of the last Latin footholds in Asia Minor. In 1224 Theodore Doukas of Epiros ended a chapter of campaigns fought against Bulgars as well as Latins in western Macedonia by capturing Thessalonica; much to the chagrin of the Byzantines in Nicaea, he rewarded himself with the title and the crown of Emperor of the Romans. In the same year John III Vatatzes, who had succeeded Theodore Laskaris at Nicaea in 1222, routed the armies of the Latin Empire in Asia Minor. Pope Honorius III, much concerned for the fate of the Catholic cause, organized a crusade for the defence of Thessalonica. But the response was poor and ineffective. Barely 20 years after its foundation, the Latin Empire was almost confined to the walls of its capital. Only the Morea and some of the Aegean islands remained; and Venetian ships maintained communications.

When Robert of Courtenay died in 1228 on his way back from a visit to Italy to seek assistance, the throne passed to his ten-year-old brother, Baldwin II. A regent had to be found. John Asen of Bulgaria

15

kindly offered his services, but the barons turned him down and appointed instead the aged but bellicose John of Brienne, titular King of Jerusalem, who was summoned from France. For a second time the Latins had slighted the dignity of the ruler of Bulgaria. They were given no third chance.

The chief danger to the Latins in Constantinople then came from Theodore Doukas, the new Byzantine Emperor in Thessalonica. But in 1230, when his army was already in sight of the city, Theodore brought disaster on himself by rashly provoking the Bulgars to war. He was utterly defeated and much of his territory was appropriated. The Bulgarian Empire was extended, in a lightning campaign, from the Black Sea to the Adriatic. The initiative now lay with its ruler, John Asen, who proposed a grand alliance of the Orthodox states against their common enemy. In 1235 Asen joined forces with John Vatatzes of Nicaea in a resolute attack on Constantinople. Pope Gregory IX appealed to the western world for help against this counter-crusade of 'schismatics, allied in impiety'. But the west had lost interest in a dying cause. Still the city was saved, as it had been conquered, by Venetian ships, spurred on by the vigour of John of Brienne. The Orthodox alliance of Greeks and Bulgars broke up; and for a little longer the Latin Empire eked out its existence.

John of Brienne died two years later, and the young Emperor Baldwin, driven to despair, left his capital for western Europe. He took with him a choice selection of the treasures and relics of the Byzantine Church. In Rome, and more especially in France at the court of St Louis, he found a ready sale for his wares, and in 1240 he returned to Constantinople with substantial reinforcements. The empire enjoyed a brief moment of renewed glory. But Baldwin could no more pay his augmented army than he could direct its operations, and in 1243 he set out again to tour the courts of Europe cap in hand.

In its last years the Latin Empire was supported only by Venetian economic aid and by occasional outbursts of papal zeal. The emperor was reduced first to craving an alliance with the Seljuq Turks, and then to stripping the lead from the roofs of churches to make money. Finally he pawned his own son, and the Venetians shamelessly acted as brokers. The Pope issued appeals on behalf of the Latin patriarch who 'through the malice of the Greeks had lost almost all his income and property, and spent his all, so that he had not enough to live on'. Latterly even the popes lost heart, and a patriarch was again appointed by the Doge of Venice. The wheel had come a full circle. Only the Venetians at the end were interested in maintaining this ghost of an empire. But the fighting spirit of the crusaders who won and defended that empire for them was long since dead and could not now be revived. The initiative passed more and more to the Byzantines in exile in Epiros and Nicaea. Their rulers found themselves befriended by all the western powers who, for reasons of their own, wished the destruction of a colonial project supported only by Venice and the Papacy. The Hohenstaufen Emperor Frederick II gave his daughter in marriage to the Emperor John Vatatzes of Nicaea. His successor Manfred struck up an alliance with the ruler of Epiros, Michael II Doukas, who had come into his father's inheritance at Arta. The French prince in the Morea, William of Villehardouin, the only competent soldier left among the Latins, threw in his lot with the Greeks; and finally the Genoese offered their services to the Emperor in Nicaea in the hope of taking over where Venice might soon be obliged to leave off.

That the Latin Empire survived at all is remarkable. Still more remarkable is the long drawn out hostility between the rival Byzantine states which made its survival possible. In campaign after campaign the rulers of Nicaea and Epiros disputed each other's claim to the Empire while the Latins watched in bewilderment from the walls of its capital. The issue was not resolved until 1259, when the ruler of Epiros, supported by Manfred of Sicily and William of Villehardouin, was defeated by the army of Nicaea. Two years later the Emperor of Nicaea, Michael Palaiologos, made a treaty with the Republic of Genoa. The Genoese were to supply him with ships to drive the Venetians out of Constantinople. But in the event their help was not required. An unexpected stroke of good fortune delivered the city to the Byzantines of Nicaea in July 1261. The Latin Emperor Baldwin escaped to the west, and there ended his days busily conferring empty titles on those whom he hoped to tempt into a crusade for his restoration. Venice, business-like to the end, bought from the new Byzantine emperor the recognition of her claim to many of the towns and islands she had appropriated.[5]

The recovery of Constantinople by the Byzantines of Nicaea in 1261 seemed to many contemporaries to be clear evidence of divine favour. To the statesman and historian of Nicaea, George Akropolites, it appeared that the history of the Roman Empire had in fact continued in unbroken continuity during the years of exile for the Byzantine church and state. The restoration of Constantinople simply set the seal of legitimacy on the Empire of Nicaea. The era of the Latin Empire had been nothing more than an unfortunate interlude. But the

Byzantines, purged of their sins by the fire of suffering and exile, would now bring their empire to new heights of glory under the rule of a new Constantine. This was wishful thinking. The general effect of the Fourth Crusade and the Latin régime had been to accelerate the process of disintegration and separatism in the once unified structure of the Byzantine Empire to the point of no return. It might be possible to restore a measure of grandeur and brilliance to the city of Constantinople, burnt, desolated, dilapidated, impoverished and empty as it was after the years of Latin rule. But it would need more than a new Constantine to knit together again the dismembered provinces and make the Empire anything like commensurate with the size and grandeur of its capital city.

In 1261, when the Emperor of Nicaea moved to Constantinople, the territory that he commanded was restricted to the western fringes of Asia Minor and some of the Aegean islands offshore and, on the European side, to Byzantine Thrace and Macedonia, including Thessalonica. In Asia Minor a frontier several hundred miles long had to be defended against Turks and Mongols. The remaining European provinces lay under the shadow of the now fully independent kingdoms of Serbia and Bulgaria. It was idle to pretend that the boundaries of the Byzantine Empire in Europe would ever again extend to the Danube. Central and southern Greece, Athens and the Morea were still French colonies whose princes were naturally hostile to the revived Byzantine Empire. The trade routes from east to west of the Mediterranean were firmly in the control of Italian merchants from Venice or Genoa, who put their own interests before those of any empire whether Greek or Latin. Worse still, there were now separatist Byzantine principalities whose rulers refused to acknowledge that the Empire in any real sense had been re-established. In Epiros in northwestern Greece and in Trebizond on the Black Sea the spirit of independence had grown too strong to be eradicated. The rulers of Epiros, descended from Michael and Theodore Doukas, were for long to go on fighting the emperors in Constantinople for what they still believed to be their own right to the throne. The emperors in Trebizond, the heirs of the first Alexios Komnenos, continued to employ the imperial title and maintained their own Byzantine Empire in miniature in defiance of the emperors in Constantinople. The problems of a disintegrating political structure which had existed before 1204 were found to exist in a much more aggravated form after 1261. If it had not proved possible to restore the Empire's unity and solidarity in the twelfth

18

century, the chances of doing so in the thirteenth century were even more remote.

The economic consequences of the Fourth Crusade were also disastrous. The city of Constantinople, standing at the junction of Europe and Asia and of the trade routes between the Black Sea and the Mediterranean, continued to be an international market and a centre of world commerce. But the routes and the market and the profits were in the hands of Italian sailors and business men. The Byzantine gold coinage soon ceased to be the standard currency of the world. During the years of exile the emperors in Nicaea and the rulers of Epiros had minted their own gold and silver coins for trade with the Seljuq Turks or with the Latins. But such coinage had never commanded great respect, and neither state had possessed a fleet with which to challenge the control of Byzantine waters by the Venetians. The reconstruction of a Byzantine navy and merchant fleet would be one of the most urgent tasks for the restored Empire. But nothing could save the Byzantine economy when it had to compete with new ideas in banking, credit and capitalism from the western world. Here again, the developments foreshadowed in the eleventh and twelfth centuries had gone too far to be arrested or modified. It was the business enterprise of Venice that had turned the Fourth Crusade against Byzantium, and in the end it was the Venetians, and their rivals the Genoese, who continued to reap the only substantial benefits from the affair.

The miraculous recovery of their city doubtless led the Byzantines to feel that, with God's help, the unity and prosperity of the Roman Empire would eventually be restored. The political and economic effects of the catastrophe would be overcome. But the catastrophe had itself made a deep psychological impact on the Byzantine people. Their mistrust and dislike of the Latins, which had shown itself so savagely in Constantinople in 1182, had by 1261 become a more rational and obsessive hatred. It had been proved beyond any doubt that the Latins were a different race with a different set of values. The Byzantines, whom they had treated as an inferior and subject people, emerged with an even more inflated superiority complex. To be a Byzantine or a 'Roman' was now seen to be a mark of distinction that set a man apart from the lesser breeds in the western world. There were even some intellectuals who began to toy with the fancy that the remnants of the Empire, reduced as it was to its purely Greek-speaking provinces, had some special Greek or Hellenic character, and that the particular virtue that marked off Byzantines from Latins was the legacy of Hellenic culture. The Fourth Crusade engendered in the Byzantines a form of nationalistic sentiment that was new and indeed hardly consonant with their inherited concept of a universal world empire.

This sentiment was fostered especially by the Church. In a society where the line between things spiritual and things temporal was so faintly drawn, theology and religious feeling were apt to be political forces. Before 1204 it was generally believed in Byzantium that the western or Roman Catholic Church was in heresy on a matter of dogma and misguided in many of its doctrines and practices. Its attitude towards the Byzantine Church during the years of the Latin Empire had amply proved its lack of understanding and tolerance of the Orthodox tradition. Pope Innocent III had regarded the establishment of the Latin Empire as a heaven-sent opportunity to unite the Byzantine Church under Rome, if necessary by force, since the Byzantines were perverse enough not to perceive the nature of the opportunity. In a letter to Theodore Laskaris of Nicaea, the Pope had asserted that the Latins were the tools of providence in punishing the Greeks for their refusal to accept the supremacy of the see of Rome. All Orthodox bishops had been obliged to sign a declaration of their undying obedience to the apostolic see of St Peter and to its infallible incumbent. It is not surprising that very few saw fit to accept such terms of submission. The majority preferred exile or persecution to the abandonment of their traditional faith or the compromise of their principles. The Lateran Council summoned by Innocent III in 1215 was boycotted by the Byzantine hierarchy. The Bishop of Corfu replied to the Pope's invitation by asking him to consider the likelihood of any members of the Orthodox clergy, whom he himself had evicted and replaced by adulterers of the faith, attending a church council in Rome. The efforts of the succeeding popes to make triumph out of disaster did little to ease the tension between Byzantine and Latin clergy.

In these circumstances Orthodoxy became more and more synonymous with Byzantine nationalism. Orthodox bishops in exile fanned the flames of anti-Latin prejudice in the hearts of their flocks, until by the time that an Orthodox patriarch was reinstated in Constantinople it had come to be believed that God had restored the city to its rightful owners because of their steadfast adherence to the true faith. What the Empire lost in political strength after 1204 it gained in religious fervour. The Byzantine Church, always a potent force in social and political affairs, was more influential than ever in the last centuries of the Empire. Its spiritual resources gave it greater powers of recuperation than the ancient machinery of the state.

The recovery of Constantinople in 1261 was therefore, to the majority of the Byzantines, an event that restored their confidence and gave them new hope for the future. The western attitude to the event, on the other hand, was one of bitterness and resentment. To the interested parties in western Europe and to the Roman Church the collapse of the Latin Empire spelt failure. A great prize had been lost through negligence. The cause of the crusade against the infidel, the cause of the union of the churches, the cause of the security of Christendom were all, it was said, in jeopardy. Each of these causes had in fact been retarded rather than advanced as a result of the Fourth Crusade. But they were deeply felt by the Papacy, and above all they made good moral cover for the less idealistic causes inspired by greed, ambition and trade. Almost as soon as the news of the loss of Constantinople was reported in the west, plans were being laid for its recovery and for the re-incorporation of the Byzantine Empire and Church in the western fold. In the early years of its existence the restored Byzantine Empire had to fight for survival not against the barbarians of the north or the infidels of the east, but against the Christians of the west.

NOTES

1 Niketas Choniates, *Historia* (*CSHB*), 391; translated by R. J. H. Jenkins, *CMH*, IV, 2, 81.

2 The events leading up to the Fourth Crusade are described and analysed by C. M. Brand, *Byzantium Confronts the West, 1180-1204* (Cambridge, Mass, 1968). Cf. Ostrogorsky, *History*, 401-14.

3 Accounts of the Fourth Crusade and the Latin Empire of Constantinople are numerous. Among the most recent are: S. Runciman, *A History of the Crusades*, III (Cambridge, 1954), 107-31; R. L. Wolff, 'The Latin Empire of Constantinople, 1204-1261', in *A History of the Crusades*, ed. K. M. Setton, II (*The Later Crusades, 1189-1311*, ed. R. L. Wolff and H. W. Hazard: Philadelphia, 1962), 187-233; D. M. Nicol, 'The Fourth Crusade and the Greek and Latin Empires, 1204-1261', *CMH*, IV, 1, 275-330; E. Bradford, *The Great Betrayal. Constantinople 1204* (London, 1967).

4 Ostrogorsky, *History*, 422-8. The histories of the Byzantine successor states in Nicaea, Epiros and Trebizond are described by: A. Gardner, *The Lascarids of Nicaea* (London, 1912); D. M. Nicol, *The*

Despotate of Epiros (Oxford, 1957); W. Miller, *Trebizond. The Last Greek Empire* (London, 1926); E. Janssens, *Trébizonde en Colchide* (Brussels, 1969). On the Latin conquest of the Morea, see W. Miller, *The Latins in the Levant* (London, 1908); J. Longnon, *L'empire latin de Constantinople et la principauté de Morée* (Paris, 1949); A. Bon, *La Morée franque*, 2 vols (Paris, 1969).

5 Ostrogorsky, *History*, 428-50; *CMH*, IV, 1, 288-330.

Two

The Empire in Exile and its Restoration

The fact that Constantinople was recovered in 1261 by the emperor in exile at Nicaea was due to a combination of good luck, patience and long-term planning. It was the conceit of the Emperor himself and of his historian George Akropolites that the history and development of the Empire in Nicaea had been guided to this conclusion by the hand of God. The rival contenders for the goal had been nothing but rebels against the divinely-appointed authority of the legitimate successors of the last Byzantine emperors. This explanation ignored the claims and achievements of the Byzantine rulers in Epiros and Thessalonica, who twice within the years between 1204 and 1261 came very near to toppling the Latin régime.

It was evident from the start, however, that Nicaea, a city only some 40 miles from Constantinople, lay nearer the heart of the Byzantine world than Arta or Trebizond; it was also nearer to the eastern frontier of the Empire. Once Theodore Laskaris had established himself there as emperor and defeated or assimilated his neighbouring rivals, he was faced with the problem of fighting on two sides at once. But to Byzantine emperors this was almost second nature; and, as events were to prove, Nicaea was if anything better placed than Constantinople for fighting the Seljuq Turks in Asia Minor. The Latin Emperor Baldwin and his brother Henry of Flanders waged a bitter struggle to stifle the Empire of Nicaea at birth, even calling on the help of the Seljuqs. But by 1214 Henry had been forced to recognize that that empire had come to stay. The Seljuq Sultans too were soon obliged to acknowledge that their Greek neighbours were now more united and better organized than for many generations. The growing strength of Nicaea as the centre of the continuing Byzantine and Orthodox tradition in the east gave the lie to the pretensions of the emperors in Trebizond. Theodore Laskaris was able to annex much of the territory that they had originally claimed and to extend his own boundaries up to the Black Sea. Trebizond shrank to a small Greek principality hemmed

23

in on its landward side by the Byzantines of Nicaea and by the Seljuq Turks. It ceased to count for much in the struggle between Byzantines and Latins.

The early successes of the Byzantine resistance movements in Epiros as well as Nicaea were facilitated by the embarrassments of the Latins in other quarters. The campaigns of Kalojan of Bulgaria and the revolt of the Lombard nobles in Greece probably did more harm to the Latin régime in its early years than all the efforts of Theodore Laskaris in Asia and Michael Doukas in Europe. But with the death of Henry of Flanders in June 1216 and the death of Pope Innocent III only a month later, the Latin Empire lost its ablest ruler and its most enthusiastic supporter. It was the ruler of Epiros, Theodore Doukas, who had just succeeded his half-brother Michael, who gained the immediate glory from the troubles of the Latins by capturing the newly-crowned Latin Emperor, Peter of Courtenay. And it was Theodore Doukas who, in the following years, made the most of the temporary weakness of the Serbian and Bulgarian kingdoms to the north of his dominions. In 1218 he launched the campaigns, first against the Latins in Thessaly and then against the Bulgars in Macedonia, which were to lead to the encirclement and re-conquest of Thessalonica from the Latins in 1224.

Thessalonica provided for the Byzantines in Europe what Nicaea had provided for those in Asia; it was a capital city and a headquarters from which the recapture of Constantinople might be planned and directed. The people of northern Greece who had helped Theodore Doukas to his victory were in no doubt that the master of Thessalonica, the second city of the Byzantine Empire, had a better claim to the title Emperor of the Romans than the self-styled Emperor in Nicaea. The bishops of the Orthodox Church in Greece, who had tasted more of the bitterness of Latin occupation than their colleagues at Nicaea, loudly supported the proclamation of Theodore Doukas as rightful Emperor, and belittled the status of the Patriarch at Nicaea. Theodore Doukas was crowned as Emperor in Thessalonica by the Archbishop of Ochrida, perhaps in 1228. The intention was clear, for it was an axiom of Byzantine political thought that there could be only one true Emperor. A rival empire had thus been born in Europe. It had a short material life, for Theodore Doukas was defeated in battle by the Bulgars in 1230. The collapse of his empire left a vacuum into which the Bulgars, led by John Asen, were quickly swept; and although Thessalonica was allowed to remain in Greek hands, the political pattern of Byzantine Europe was changed. But the memory of Theodore's victories and of his title to the Byzantine crown lived on in northern Greece and in the hearts of his descendants for many generations to come.

The tactics of war and conquest were less applicable to the circumstances of the Empire of Nicaea than to those of the Empire in Greece. The conquest of Thessalonica had been a necessity for the rulers of Epiros if ever they were to be in the running for the prize of Constantinople. But to the rulers of Nicaea Constantinople was the first, the nearest, and the only objective. But none knew better than they the immense strength of the city's fortifications. An outright attack would be doomed to failure without elaborate and expensive naval and military preparations. Theodore Laskaris therefore did not pin all his hopes on a violent solution. In the best Byzantine tradition he used the weapon of diplomacy, encouraging the Latins to feel that the two empires could co-exist, at least for a time. In 1218 he married the daughter of the dowager Latin Empress, Yolanda of Courtenay, and in 1219 he signed a commercial agreement with the Venetian colony in Constantinople, allowing the merchants of Venice free access to Nicaea and its dependencies on very favourable terms. Such overtures to the enemy were regarded by the Byzantines in Greece as the blackest treachery. But to those in Nicaea they were practical measures. They brought peace to the exiled Empire; they fostered its economic viability; they gave it time to strengthen the foundations of an administration that might one day be called upon to move to Constantinople; and intermarriage with the Latins might make it possible for the Emperor at Nicaea to keep a foot in the door before the move took place. The Empire of Nicaea thus gained greater stability than the fragile structure of its rival in Thessalonica, built in a blaze of war and glory.[1]

Theodore Laskaris died in 1222 and was succeeded by his son-in-law John Vatatzes, or John III. It was he who, building on the foundations laid by his predecessor, raised the Empire of Nicaea to the status of a great power able to hold its own and to dictate terms to Latins and Turks alike, but also capable of taking back the city of Constantinople whenever the moment seemed ripe. During his reign of 32 years the balance of power between Latins and Byzantines in the east turned decisively in favour of Nicaea. In 1225 he compelled the Latins to make a treaty by terms of which their forces evacuated almost all their conquests in Asia Minor. At the same time, however, the Latins were being deprived of their conquests in Europe by Theodore Doukas, now master of Thessalonica.

25

In the year 1230, on what had once been Byzantine territory, there were in fact three empires in existence, two Greek and one Latin. But hovering on the side lines was the ruler of Bulgaria, John Asen, who fancied his own chances of mastering Constantinople. And in the event, by humiliating the Empire of Thessalonica, it was John Asen who saved the Latin Empire from premature extinction and wrested the initiative on the European scene.

In the succeeding years the rulers of Bulgaria and Nicaea twice joined forces in assaults on Constantinople. But about 1237 John Asen allowed Theodore Doukas, who had been his prisoner since 1230, to return to the scene of his former triumphs in Thessalonica, and a ghost of the Byzantine Empire in Europe was made to walk again. Theodore invested his young and reluctant son with the trappings of an emperor. John Vatatzes in Nicaea was annoyed if not alarmed by this re-appearance of his old rival. But he was a patient and methodical man. In 1241 John Asen of Bulgaria, who had seemed to be favouring the cause of Theodore Doukas, died leaving only an infant son. In 1242 Vatatzes crossed over to Europe with his army and marched on Thessalonica. Theodore's son John was persuaded to lay aside his imperial crown and to accept instead the rank and title of Despot, graciously conferred upon him by the one true Emperor. The settlement was not as secure as Vatatzes would have wished. But in the end it had to be concluded in a hurry because of news reaching the Emperor from Nicaea, which necessitated his immediate return to Asia; and not for another four years was he able to come back.

The news that reached the Emperor in 1242 was that the Mongols had invaded the territory of the Seljuq Sultan and that the Empire of Nicaea was in danger. The Mongol invasions of the Near East and eastern Europe in the thirteenth century were on a scale which must make the battles and rivalries of Greeks and Latins over the possession of Constantinople seem like the squabbles of naughty children. Masters of an empire that stretched from Korea to Persia, from the Indian Ocean to Siberia, the successors of Genghis Khan, who died in 1227, could doubtless have swept the Byzantine as well as the Latin and Bulgar Empires out of existence had the mood so taken them. As it was, one branch of their army swept north of the Caspian and Aral seas into Russia. Kiev fell to the Mongols in 1240. They then pressed on through Poland, Bohemia and Moravia to Hungary and up to the Adriatic coast, before withdrawing through Serbia and Bulgaria leaving a wake of desolation. Only in Russia, in the lower valleys of the Volga and the Don, did they pitch camp permanently. And for about 200 years thereafter the Russians were subject to the leaders of the Golden Horde.

The Mongol invasion convulsed and devastated most of the developing countries of eastern Europe. But it had little immediate effect on the fate of Constantinople and the eastern Mediterranean. Of the countries within the Byzantine sphere of influence only Bulgaria suffered the attentions of the Mongols. But at the same time another branch of their army had stormed westwards out of Persia into Asia Minor, threatening the Seljuq Turkish Sultanate and so ultimately its western neighbour, the Empire of Nicaea, as well as the Empire of Trebizond. In 1243 the Sultan Kaykhusraw II was defeated in battle by the Mongol general Baichu. He turned for help to his natural enemy, the Emperor of Nicaea; and in the face of the common danger John Vatatzes and the Sultan signed a treaty of alliance. The Emperor of Trebizond, after one defeat, discreetly elected to pay tribute to the Khan of the Mongols and became his vassal. The Seljuqs were soon obliged to do the same to preserve what was left of their identity. The Mongols, who had many larger fish to fry in the Far East, did not measure the little Empires of Trebizond or Nicaea, or even the Seljuq Sultanate, with the same yardstick as the Byzantines and the Turks themselves. The Sultanate never really rallied after its defeat and humiliation by the Mongols. But the Empire of Nicaea, protected from the horrors of the Mongol invasion by the Turks, survived unscathed and indeed stronger and more secure than before as a result of the damage done to its eastern neighbour.[2]

Once the storm had blown itself out therefore John Vatatzes was able to turn his mind to the unresolved problems of the Byzantine world with even greater confidence. In 1246 he crossed over to Europe once again, and within twelve months his army had restored a large part of southern Bulgaria to Byzantine rule and completed the work earlier begun at Thessalonica. The city was now deprived of its last vestige of independence from the Empire of Nicaea. An imperial governor was appointed as the Emperor's deputy. His name was Andronikos Palaiologos, and at the same time his more famous son, Michael Palaiologos, the future emperor, was given a command in Macedonia. In Thessalonica it had been proved that there was a faction in favour of incorporation into the Empire of Nicaea. But elsewhere in northern Greece there was still a hope that all the labours and sacrifices of Michael and Theodore Doukas had not been in vain, and that the real Byzantine Empire would yet be reconstituted in Greece and not in Asia Minor.

In Epiros, the original centre of Greek resistance to the Latins, Michael II, a bastard son of the first Michael Doukas, had taken over what he regarded as his heritage and set up his capital at Arta. He assumed or had acquired from the Emperor in Thessalonica the title of Despot, and the territory over which he ruled came to be called the Despotate of Epiros. Michael II contrived to add Thessaly to Epiros and so to extend his rule over the whole of northern Greece, and he exploited the weakness of the Bulgars to win back much of the country that they had taken over in 1230. It did not at first seem that the Emperor in Nicaea had much to fear from this new arrival on the scene. Thessalonica was now firmly attached to his empire and protected from possible attack by a chain of fortresses in western Macedonia. But Vatatzes proposed to make sure by arranging an alliance with the Despot of Epiros. In 1249 the eldest son of Michael II, Nikephoros, was betrothed to the Emperor's granddaughter Maria.

Two years later warfare broke out between Epiros and Nicaea. Michael II crossed his frontier in Macedonia and advanced towards Thessalonica. It should have been clear to John Vatatzes that all the thwarted ambitions of the Byzantines in Europe were now being centred in the person of Michael II of Epiros. But he tended to regard the Despot of Epiros merely as a rebel in a remote province who could either be coaxed into alliance or bullied into submission by a show of force. In 1252 or 1253 he brought an army over to Europe again and persuaded the rebel to come to terms. A frontier was fixed between the western limits of the Empire of Nicaea and the eastern limits of the Despotate of Epiros. It was hoped that this would serve to satisfy the Despot and protect Thessalonica until such time as the Emperor of Nicaea had made himself Emperor of Constantinople. For by 1253 the position of the Latin Empire in Constantinople was so desperate that it could hardly survive a concentrated attack.

John Vatatzes surely deserved to crown his achievements by mounting that attack. But he died on 3 November 1254, and the crowning achievement of the Empire of Nicaea was delayed for seven years more. But it was Vatatzes who laid the ground and made that achievement possible. In the long course of his reign he had doubled the size of his empire, so that now, like the Byzantine Empire proper, it straddled the straits between Asia and Europe. Only the city of

Constantinople was lacking as the connecting link between the two continents; but the Latins, who now held little but that city, were incapable of hindering communications or the passage of armies to and from Nicaea and Thessalonica. The imperial pretensions of the Byzantines in Europe seemed to have been stifled, the Bulgars had been put out of the race, and on the Asiatic side the Seljuq Turks had ceased to present any serious threat.

The eastern frontier of the Byzantine world was indeed now protected more effectively than it had been since the great days of the tenth century. New fortifications were built and a standing frontier-defence force was maintained. It was composed of soldiers whose families farmed their own plots of land allotted to them by the state. Refugees from the Mongols, among them the savage Cumans, were wisely enlisted for the defence of the Empire and granted settlements along the remoter frontiers in Thrace and Macedonia, and in the Meander valley in Asia Minor. The attractions of military service in the Empire of Nicaea were so competitive that mercenary troops were never lacking. Many of them were westerners who despaired of making a livelihood out of serving the impoverished Latin Empire and its colonies; and the Latin mercenaries came to form a special corps in the army of Nicaea, commanded by a Byzantine officer with the title of Grand Constable.

But the achievements of John Vatatzes are not to be measured only in military terms. His predecessor Theodore Laskaris had shown that the Empire in exile could uphold the traditions of Byzantium. Vatatzes proved that it could in many ways do even better. The very fact that his empire lacked the great city of Constantinople, on whose upkeep and defence so much of its wealth might have been consumed, seemed to make for a more even distribution of the resources available. The economy was based not on the needs and the traffic of great cities but upon the land, on agriculture and the breeding of cattle. The Emperor himself encouraged his subjects to be self-sufficient by taking a personal interest in the management of his imperial estates. He liked to point out that careful running of his own chicken-farm had realized a profit large enough for him to be able to buy a new coronet for his wife. The economy of the Empire of Nicaea was healthier in the reign of Vatatzes than that of the Byzantine Empire had been for centuries. But self-sufficiency did not mean the end of trade. Especially after the devastation of the Seljuq Sultanate by the Mongols there was much traffic in produce and cattle between Nicaea and the Turks, from which the Empire made a handsome profit. On the other hand, Vatatzes legislated for the protection of native products as against the importation of foreign luxuries. For he was determined that the dependence upon foreign, and particularly Venetian, trade which had begun to cripple the Byzantine economy in the twelfth century, should not undermine his own empire. It would have been tactless to single out the Venetian merchants for special tariffs, for they had been granted trading concessions in Nicaea by Theodore Laskaris. But the Emperor could and did enact sumptuary laws aimed at protecting his people from the consequences of their own extravagance.

Nor did self-sufficiency mean isolationism. Vatatzes maintained diplomatic contacts with all his actual and potential enemies and friends—Latins, Bulgars, Turks, Mongols and Greeks. He gave his only son Theodore in marriage to the daughter of the Bulgarian tsar John Asen; his grand-daughter Maria married the son of Michael II of Epiros. He exchanged gifts and embassies with the Khan of the Mongols, and his agents kept careful watch on the movements of the Latins in Constantinople and elsewhere. But he was also in direct communication with the two great powers of the time in the western world, the Holy Roman Emperor and the Pope. For either might be of service to Nicaea in the restoration of the Byzantine Empire. His relationship with the Hohenstaufen Emperor Frederick II added greatly to the prestige of the Empire of Nicaea. Frederick, the enemy of the Papacy, felt sympathetic towards the Byzantines who had been dispossessed of their empire and its capital. He was on friendly terms with the rulers of Epiros, but as time went on he concluded that the initiative lay rather with the Byzantines at Nicaea. A correspondence took place between the two Emperors, Frederick II and John Vatatzes. An alliance was made, and in 1244 Vatatzes married as his second wife Constance of Hohenstaufen, Frederick's illegitimate daughter. The marriage was not a success, but the friendship between Frederick and Vatatzes survived unbroken until Frederick's death in 1250.

In his diplomatic relations with the Pope, Vatatzes acted on the principle that the Papacy was the institution most likely to be able to influence the fate of the Latin Empire of Constantinople. The union of the churches was a cause always dear to the hearts of the popes. It had been discussed under unpromising circumstances by representatives of both churches during the reign of Theodore Laskaris, but to no avail. Vatatzes was prepared to re-open the discussions on the understanding that if he recognized the fact of papal supremacy, the Pope would acknowledge him as Emperor of Constantinople and allow a Greek patriarch to be reinstated in his rightful see. So long as there was any life left in the Latin Empire such terms were unacceptable to the Papacy. But it became ever clearer that the régime was dying, and Pope Innocent IV resumed negotiations with John Vatatzes in 1250. The Pope had heard the facts about Constantinople from the Latin Emperor Baldwin II and had drawn his own conclusions. He agreed to lend his support to the now thriving Empire of Nicaea and to recognize the Byzantine patriarchate if Vatatzes would guarantee the submission of the Orthodox Church to Rome. It was a realistic political bargain. But it could hardly have been put into practice. For it left out of account not only the prejudices but also the theological and doctrinal differences which separated the Orthodox from the Catholics. And, as later Byzantine Emperors were soon to discover, the theological differences were always dearer to the hearts of their clergy than any political advantages, however desirable, that might be gained from the union of the churches. Not even the prospect of the restoration of Constantinople could persuade the Byzantine Church to compromise the articles of its faith. The negotiations dragged on inconclusively until both Vatatzes and Innocent IV died in 1254. Pope Alexander IV attempted to reopen them in 1256, but the new Emperor declined to receive the papal legate. For by that time the state of the Latin Empire was such that it was no longer necessary to make any concessions to the west to bring it to an end. Time was on the side of the Byzantines.[3]

The survival of the Latin Empire in its final years was indeed only made possible by the division and rivalry between its Byzantine enemies. After the death of John Vatatzes the Despotate of Epiros rose from strength to strength, until its position became comparable to that of the Empire of Thessalonica before 1230. If Michael II of Epiros could capture Thessalonica he would be well on the way to Constantinople. The fate of Constantinople could not be decided until the issue between its rival liberators had been settled. The son who succeeded John Vatatzes as Emperor in Nicaea was not the man to grapple with this problem. Theodore II Laskaris was a scholar and a theologian, but not a soldier or a statesman. It was to his credit that he gathered men of similar tastes at his court and made Nicaea a centre of culture and scholarship. Art and literature flourished. But the foreign policy of the Empire suffered, and its internal affairs were affected by the vacillations of the Emperor. Theodore II was an epileptic. His illness made him the prey of his moods, and he compensated for his nervousness by an autocratic and obstinate temper. He had a morbid suspicion of the aristocracy who had served his father's administration. He preferred to appoint his own officials from the lower ranks of society. To the patriarchate, which fell vacant in 1254, he secured the election of a pious but narrow-minded monk called Arsenios. Such men were grateful to accept his orders and do his bidding. For in Theodore's view of things, and perhaps because he had lived in the shadow of a father who was a great emperor, it was an emperor's duty to order and control all departments of church and state. He neither sought nor commanded the respect of the aristocracy of Nicaea who had helped to bring the Empire to greatness. They were soon to show their resentment in violent form.

Theodore II Laskaris reigned for only four years. It was a period in which nothing was lost in the way of territory or prestige by the Empire of Nicaea, though much was gained by the Empire's principal rival, the Despot of Epiros. The Bulgars tried to benefit from the death of Vatatzes by crossing the limits that he had imposed on them in Macedonia and Thrace. They were driven back in 1256 after two expensive campaigns. Michael II of Epiros, who had also thought to take advantage of the change of emperors in Nicaea, was bullied into making an alliance. The wedding of his son Nikephoros to the Emperor's daughter Maria, arranged seven years before, was finally celebrated in October 1256. But here Theodore Laskaris overreached himself by demanding the surrender of two key fortresses of the Despotate of Epiros as a condition of the marriage. It was an ill-considered tactic which shattered any hope of understanding or of co-operation between Epiros and Nicaea.

In 1257 Michael of Epiros, assisted by his friends in Serbia and Albania, began a systematic campaign to encircle and capture the city of Thessalonica. The fortified towns to the west and north of the city, which had been garrisoned by imperial troops of Nicaea for ten years, fell one by one. Michael II pushed his frontiers as far east as the Vardar valley. But a new slant was given to the situation when Michael cast his net further afield for allies and supporters. Manfred, the bastard son of the late Frederick II, had now come into the possession of the kingdom of Sicily. Like earlier rulers of Sicily and southern Italy, Manfred had his own designs on Greece and Constantinople, and he had personal reasons for disliking the Empire of Nicaea. His half-sister, Constance of Hohenstaufen, now the young widow of John Vatatzes, was being held at Nicaea against her will. Manfred was therefore willing to give support to Michael of Epiros in his struggle to the death against the Emperor in Nicaea. It was arranged that he should marry Michael's eldest daughter Helena; her dowry was to consist of the island of Corfu and several other places on the mainland of Epiros, which Manfred could not but regard as having valuable strategic potential.

The other foreign ally whose help Michael II enlisted was William of Villehardouin, the French Prince of Achaia and descendant of Geoffrey of Villehardouin, who had first carved out that principality in southern Greece. William was a highly successful soldier who had made himself overlord of Athens and Euboia as well as the Morea. This alliance too was to be secured by a marriage contract. In the summer of 1258 Michael of Epiros gave his second daughter in marriage to Prince William. It seemed as if the whole continent of Greece, backed by the strength of the King of Sicily and further supported by the ruler of Serbia, was now ranged against the Empire of Nicaea.

The last months of the reign of Theodore II Laskaris were darkened by the military and diplomatic victories of his rival in Greece, and by the increasing tension between himself and the aristocracy of Nicaea who supplied most of the commanders of his armies. Provided with insufficient troops by an emperor who constantly suspected their motives, the officers naturally felt aggrieved; and their grievances were aggravated by the accusations and charges of treason which the Emperor took to levelling against their families and relatives in Nicaea. Theodore II might well have been removed by revolution. But in August 1258 he died of the illness which had clouded his vision. He left his empire to his eight-year-old son, John Laskaris, under the regency of the Patriarch Arsenios and his own trusted administrator, George Mouzalon. Mouzalon was not one of the blue-blooded aristocrats of Byzantine society to whom the office of regent might have seemed second nature. He was one of the upstarts whom the late Emperor had raised from humble status. The aristocracy had been summoned to the Emperor's deathbed and made to swear an oath of loyalty to a regent they despised. Only ten days later their pent-up bitterness broke out. A conspiracy was formed and, during a memorial service for the Emperor in September 1258, George Mouzalon and his brother were murdered at the altar.[4]

By common consent of the disprized nobility the regency for the infant John Laskaris now passed to a young and vigorous member of their own class, Michael Palaiologos. The Palaiologos family had moved in high circles in Byzantium since the eleventh century. Though

33

it could boast no direct claim to the throne, its members had inter-married with the imperial families of Doukas, Angelos and Kom-nenos. Michael's mother was a grand-daughter of the Emperor Alexios III Angelos. His father Andronikos Palaiologos had been sent to govern Thessalonica and had then been appointed Grand Domestic or commander-in-chief of the armies of Nicaea by John Vatatzes, in whose palace Michael had been brought up. Michael advertised in his person and in his character all the features of the gilded aristo-cracy which the suspicious Theodore Laskaris had so mistrusted. George Akropolites, who was his tutor for a while, observed how easily the young man could suit his character to his company, playing the sweet, gay and clever youth with those of his own age, and the mature, wise and responsible man with his elders. He was ambitious, but his charm and versatility made him popular among his own class, and his respectable piety assured him the influential friendship and support of the Church. Michael soon showed himself to be a brilliant soldier and a courageous leader on the field of battle. He was liked by his troops, not least by the Latin mercenaries whose pay had been docked by Theodore Laskaris and whose ranks he came to command as Grand Constable. But there was something mercurial about his temperament which perhaps explains, if it does not justify, the special mistrust with which Theodore Laskaris regarded him.

It was in 1246, when he was just over 21, that Michael Palaiologos was given his first public office, as a commander in Macedonia, which was then under the general governorship of his father Andronikos; and it was there, seven years later, that he first fell under suspicion of conspiring against the throne. By a mixture of bluff and bravado he restored himself to favour, married a grand-niece of the Emperor John Vatatzes, and was appointed Grand Constable. It is hinted that the Emperor Vatatzes had planned a marriage for the young Michael Palaiologos to his own grand-daughter, which would have brought him even nearer to the throne. But if so sober an emperor as Vatatzes found it hard to trust Michael, his successor Theodore Laskaris was obsessed with suspicions. The mistrust was mutual. In 1256 Michael anticipated his probable arrest on a charge of treason by escaping to the court of the Seljuq Sultan. But less than two years later he was back at Nicaea, begging forgiveness and swearing eternal loyalty to the house of Laskaris. The Emperor could not afford to waste the talents of such a soldier and packed him off to Macedonia to fight the Despot of Epiros. But as his morbid fantasies gained hold on his mind, Laskaris complained that he was the victim of magic spells woven by Michael Palaiologos and his family. Michael was arrested, brought before the Emperor and put in prison. But the Emperor's mind was now unhinged and his days were numbered. And at the end, in August 1258, Michael Palaiologos was again at liberty and bound by a new oath of loyalty to the crown. It was even suggested that, in the event of the Emperor's death, Michael should become guardian of the orphaned imperial family. In the event he became not only guardian but also regent for the young John Laskaris, and finally Emperor.

There are many strands still unravelled in the story of Michael's rise to power. The Byzantine historians who tell the tale were all living under the rule of Michael himself or of his direct descendants and successors in Constantinople. It is therefore remarkable that they tell as much of the truth as they do. But to have told the whole truth might have been for them injudicious, for the ease and swiftness of Michael's ascent to the top suggests that he knew what he wanted and had prepared the ground well in advance. His part in the conspiracy to murder the regent George Mouzalon is difficult to assess but easy to surmise. The agents of the deed were, after all, the Latin mercenaries whose commander was Michael himself. Nor were the assassins punished for their crime by the new regent of the Empire. For as soon as the deed was done an assembly of the aristocracy was hastily summoned at Nicaea under the presidency of the Patriarch Arsenios, and Michael Palaiologos was elected regent and guardian of the boy Emperor. The choice was hailed by the army, by the church and by the common people, for Michael was evidently the man best qualified to defend the Empire of Nicaea against its enemies. But among the aristocracy, notably those who were related to the Laskaris family, there were some who reserved judgment. In the last four months of 1258 Michael was elevated to the more exalted rank of Grand Duke, and then, having been careful to win the approval of the Patriarch and bishops, to that of Despot, which was next in order to that of Emperor. Finally, in December, when he had persuaded the majority that the Empire might succumb to its enemies before John Laskaris had come of age, Michael was proclaimed Emperor. A few days later, perhaps on Christmas Day 1258, the Patriarch performed the double coronation of Michael VIII Palaiologos and John IV Laskaris. It did not pass unnoticed that Michael was crowned first.[5]

In the last months of 1258 it was certainly true that the Empire of Nicaea needed an experienced soldier at its head. The coalition of Michael of Epiros with William of Achaia and Manfred of Sicily seemed likely to threaten not only the possession of Thessalonica but even of Constantinople itself. As soon as he became regent Michael Palaiologos posted reinforcements to Thessalonica under the command of his own brother John, whom he had promoted in rank. In an effort to break up the coalition he sent separate embassies to each of the three parties concerned. But they had by then made their plans and the prospect before them was too promising to be laid aside. The rivalry between the Byzantine claimants to the throne in Constantinople would have to be resolved at the end by war.

Early in 1259, equipped now with all the authority of a Byzantine emperor, Michael made preparation for war on a scale that would have been beyond the imagination of his predecessor. In March a great army was assembled in Thrace. It included mercenary contingents from Hungary, Serbia and Bulgaria, as well as Turkish and Cuman horsemen. By the time it reached Thessalonica, however, the advance guard under John Palaiologos had already struck the first blow against the enemy by surprising Michael of Epiros and his army in the region of Kastoria and driving them across the mountains to the coast. The fortified town of Berat in Albania had been captured. The Despot of Epiros, surprised but not defeated, reassembled his forces at Avlona on the Albanian coast. He then called on the help of his ally across the water. Arrangements were hurriedly concluded for the marriage of his daughter Helena to Manfred of Sicily, and an escort arrived to take her over to Trani in Apulia, where the wedding took place on 2 June 1259. Manfred quickly honoured his agreement by sending over 400 German knights to fight for his father-in-law.

Meanwhile his other ally, William of Achaia, had brought his own feudal levy over from the Morea, and the Despot's son John Doukas had collected an army in Thessaly. The combined forces of the coalition gathered in southern Macedonia and met the army of Nicaea under John Palaiologos in the plain of Pelagonia in the Monastir Gap. There, towards the end of July 1259, was fought the battle that was to determine which of the rival Byzantine states should have the privilege of restoring the Byzantine Empire in Constantinople. The sources give varying accounts of what took place. But it is clear that the army of Nicaea, disciplined and united under the single command of the new Emperor's brother, was a sounder instrument of war than the allied armies of Greeks, French and Germans, each under separate leadership. Personal jealousy and

36

mutual hostility between Greeks and Latins played their part in disrupting the coalition on the field. The Despot Michael's son John was provoked to anger by some of the French knights and then taunted as a low-born bastard by William of Villehardouin. He deserted to the enemy. Michael himself, and his other son Nikephoros, abandoned their allies in the night. What battle there was at Pelagonia, apart from the preliminary skirmishes, was fought between John Palaiologos on the one side and the French and German cavalry of Villehardouin and Manfred on the other. They fought with the desperation of men betrayed, but they were outclassed. Some escaped but many were captured. Manfred's knights were rounded up and surrendered. Villehardouin was found hiding near Kastoria and taken prisoner. John Palaiologos followed up his victory by marching into Thessaly, while his colleague, Alexios Strategopoulos, invaded Epiros and captured Arta. Michael of Epiros with his son Nikephoros took refuge in the offshore island of Cephalonia.[6]

It looked as if the Despotate of Epiros was no more. The battle of Pelagonia seemed to have settled the issue. But it was also the prelude to the recovery of Constantinople from the Latins. For the victory of the army of Nicaea had cut the Latin Empire off from any effective military support from the western world, and the capture of William of Villehardouin had deprived it of its only capable defender. The Latins in Constantinople knew that their days were numbered. They had already begged for a truce from the new Emperor in Nicaea and offered to bargain away their few remaining assets to play for time. But time seemed now, more than ever, to be on the side of their enemies. The Latin Emperor Baldwin II could not elicit much but sympathy from the west. The Pope was absorbed with the problems of Italy. The Venetians were absorbed in war with Genoa and could spare no more ships. But so long as the Venetian fleet guarded the Bosporos it would be hard for Michael Palaiologos to fight his way into the city.

In the spring of 1260 there seemed a chance that the city might be delivered to him by treachery. One of Baldwin's knights who had been captured at Pelagonia offered to have a postern gate in the walls opened in exchange for his freedom. Michael took an army over to Thrace and up to the outskirts of the city, but the promise was never fulfilled. The attempt ended in a skirmish between Byzantine and Latin soldiers at the suburb of Galata across the Golden Horn, and Baldwin seized the occasion to arrange a truce for another year. A sense of urgency was introduced into the situation by the news from Greece that the Despot of Epiros had already managed to undo much of the work done at Pelagonia. Rejoined by his repentant son John Doukas he had found his way back to his capital at Arta in 1260. His other son Nikephoros had collected a company of Italian soldiers from Manfred of Sicily. The inhabitants of Epiros had hailed the return of their native ruler with joy and enthusiasm, and the fallen fortunes of the Despotate were beginning to revive. The Emperor Michael VIII took the precaution of sending his brother John, now dignified with the title of Despot, back to Thessalonica to keep guard again over the western approaches.[7]

In the winter of 1260 Michael VIII applied all his very considerable diplomatic and military talents to the recovery of Constantinople. Every frontier must be secured, every possible enemy pacified, and every contingency foreseen. Treaties were signed with the Seljuq Turks, the Mongols and the Bulgars. But Michael's greatest triumph was to discover allies who could help him break the Venetian defences of Constantinople by sea. The Genoese, ever the rivals of Venice in the trade of the eastern Mediterranean, had only in 1258 been expelled from their profitable market in Acre. They were desperate to find new markets and eager to score over the Venetians in any quarter. If their own chroniclers are to be believed, it was the Genoese themselves who took the initiative in offering their services to the Emperor Michael. Had they not done so it seems probable that he would have invited them in any case. For an alliance of Nicaea and Genoa at this juncture was clearly of great potential benefit to both parties. Negotiations took place in secret, and on 13 March 1261 a treaty was drawn up at Nymphaion where the Emperor had been spending the winter. It was ratified at Genoa on 10 July.

The Treaty of Nymphaion postulated a permanent alliance between Byzantines and Genoese directed against Venice. Genoa was to put up to 50 ships at the Emperor's disposal. In return, assuming victory over the Venetian fleet at Constantinople, the merchants of Genoa were to inherit all the concessions formerly enjoyed by the Venetians in Byzantine waters. They would have the right to trade duty-free in all parts of the Byzantine Empire; they would have a monopoly of access to the ports of the Black Sea; they would be granted their own commercial quarter in Constantinople, in Thessalonica and in the other major ports of the Empire; and they would be given absolute possession of the city of Smyrna. All this was a heavy price to pay for the hire of 50 ships. But at the time the Emperor, if he considered the cost at all, privately set it against the possibility of modifying the terms when, as master of Constantinople, he could argue from a position of greater strength. Nevertheless, the Treaty of Nymphaion proved to be a document of the most far-reaching significance for the future of the Byzantine Empire. For it laid the foundations of the Genoese commercial empire in the eastern Mediterranean and the Black Sea, and so for the interminable conflict between Venice and Genoa that was to be fought out over the body of the Byzantine Empire until its very last days. After 1261 the trade and economy of Byzantium was to be at the mercy not of one Italian republic but of two, until the resources of the Empire were drained dry and its resistance was at an end.[8]

It was an irony of history that the alliance between Nicaea and Genoa, designed to furnish the necessary ships for an attack on Constantinople, should ever have been concluded. For only a few weeks after it had been signed Constantinople fell without the help or the use of any fleet at all. The recovery of the capital, which had become the *raison d'être* of the Empire of Nicaea, was achieved in the end almost by accident. In July 1261, when his latest truce with the Emperor Baldwin had still a month to run, Michael VIII had sent his general Alexios Strategopoulos with a small army over to Thrace. They were to patrol the Bulgarian frontier and spy out the defences of Constantinople on the land side. When he reached Selymbria on the coast some 30 miles west of the city, Strategopoulos learnt from some of the local farmers that almost all the Latin garrison and the Venetian fleet were at that moment away on a raiding party in the Black Sea. The city lay undefended, except by its massive walls. But Strategopoulos was told of a secret passage under the walls and of a spot where scaling-ladders could probably be erected. The opportunity seemed too good to miss, and in the dead of night Strategopoulos and some of his soldiers made their way, guided by the locals, under or over the walls. They surprised the guard at the Gate of the Fountain and hacked it open from inside before the alarm could be raised. On 25 July 1261 a Byzantine army was once again in possession of a part of Constantinople. It took some anxious hours to establish control, for at any moment the Latin troops and Venetian ships might return, and Strategopoulos was understandably apprehensive of winning not the crown of glory but the punishment due to a general who had exceeded his orders.

There was some fighting in the streets, but by the break of day it was seen that the Byzantines had taken control of the land walls.

The Latin Emperor Baldwin was asleep in the Blachernai Palace at the northern end of the walls. He was roused by the noise and confusion, and as the Byzantine troops advanced upon him he gave up all hope and ran down to the harbour, where he boarded a Venetian merchant ship and sailed away to Euboia. His escape was so abrupt that he had no time to pack his crown and sceptre; they were found abandoned in the palace. To forestall the return of the Latins from the Black Sea, Strategopoulos acted on the advice of one of the Greek inhabitants of the city and set fire to the buildings and warehouses of the Venetians along the Golden Horn; and when the Venetians, hearing of the disaster, came hurrying back with the garrison, they found their homes and properties in flames. Their wives and families stood crowded on the shore like smoked-out bees, asking nothing more than to be rescued. All that the Venetians could do was to salvage what was left from the flames and sail away. Refugees swarmed aboard the ships and the fleet made off for the Venetian island of Euboia. But the ships, perhaps about 30 in number, were so overcrowded that many of their passengers died of hunger and thirst before they reached safety. The Latin inhabitants of the city who were left behind feared the worst. Their terror was magnified by the sudden shock of the event and they ran panic-stricken into hiding in holes in the walls, in passage ways, even in the sewers. Others thought to save themselves in churches and monasteries. Some dressed up like Orthodox monks to escape detection. Few can have remembered the awful manner in which their fathers had celebrated the capture of Constantinople in 1204. But they could expect neither gratitude nor mercy from the owners of the city who had now returned to claim possession.[9]

The Emperor Michael VIII was asleep in his camp at Meteorion some 200 miles away when the good news was brought to him. The first to hear it was his sister Eulogia. She woke him gently by tickling his toes with a feather and announced that he was master of Constantinople. At first Michael refused to believe the story. But when a courier arrived bringing the captured crown and sceptre of the Latin Emperor, he joyfully accepted the fact that God had delivered the city to him. At once he summoned an assembly of the people and in their hearing gave thanks to God for what must surely be accounted a miracle of divine favour to the Empire of Nicaea. 'Many times', he told them, 'have we tried and failed to win back Constantinople. For God wished to show us that the possession of this city was in his gift and his alone.

The gift has been reserved for our reign, a fact for which we must be eternally thankful.'[10] Michael had special cause to play the line that God was on his side; for the possession of Constantinople would clearly help to establish him as legitimate Emperor in the eyes of the Byzantine people.

Not until three weeks later, when he had made fitting preparations for moving the seat of the Byzantine government back to its proper home, did Michael make the journey to Constantinople. On 15 August 1261, the Feast of the Dormition of the Virgin, he entered the Golden Gate at the south-west corner of the city, and from there, after a prayer of thanksgiving, walked in solemn procession to the cathedral of St Sophia. It was through the Golden Gate that emperors returning in triumph from war were accustomed to re-enter their capital. But the entry of Michael Palaiologos, an emperor who had been born in exile and who had never seen the city, was of a different nature. It was a solemn and religious occasion symbolizing a moral victory. The procession through the streets was led not by a triumphant soldier but by the ancient icon of the Virgin Hodegetria, protectress of the city, held on high. When the liturgy had been celebrated in St Sophia, the Patriarch Arsenios performed a second coronation ceremony. Michael and his wife Theodora were crowned Emperor and Empress, and their son, aged two, was proclaimed heir-presumptive to the throne. The legitimate Emperor, the young John IV Laskaris, had been left neglected in Nicaea. Within a few months he was to be blinded and confined to a castle on the Sea of Marmora. Tradition had it that blindness disqualified a man for the role of Byzantine Emperor. Michael Palaiologos, the grateful recipient of God's special favour in the restoration of the Byzantine Empire, thus made sure that God would not go back on his word. The dynasty of Laskaris, which had held the pass for 57 years, was to be replaced by the dynasty of Palaiologos.[11]

NOTES

1 *CMH*, IV, 1, 290-309; Ostrogorsky, *History*, 422-34.

2 *CMH*, IV, 1, 309-16.

3 *CMH*, IV, 1, 316-21; Ostrogorsky, 434-44; Nicol, *Despotate of Epiros*, 128-56.

4 *CMH*, IV, 1, 321-4; Ostrogorsky, 444-7; Nicol, *Despotate of Epiros*, 157-68.

5 On the early career of Michael VIII Palaiologos, see C. Chapman, *Michel Paléologue, restaurateur de l'empire byzantin* (1261-82) (Paris, 1926), 25-38; D. J. Geanakoplos, *Emperor Michael Palaeologus and the West*, 1258-82 (Cambridge, Mass, 1959), 16-46; Ostrogorsky, 447.

6 On the battle of Pelagonia, see D. J. Geanakoplos, 'Greco-Latin relations on the eve of the Byzantine restoration: The Battle of Pelagonia—1259', *DOP*, VII (1953), 99-141. Cf. Nicol, *Despotate of Epiros*, 169-85; Geanakoplos, *Emperor Michael*, 47-74; *CMH*, IV, 1, 324-5; Ostrogorsky, 447-8.

7 Nicol, *Despotate of Epiros*, 186-90.

8 On the Treaty of Nymphaion, see Geanakoplos, *Emperor Michael*, 81-91 and references.

9 Geanakoplos, *Emperor Michael*, 92-115.

10 George Pachymeres, *De Michaele Palaeologo* (CSHB), 155.

11 Geanakoplos, *Emperor Michael*, 119-22.

Part One

The Problems of the Restored Empire: The Reign of Michael VIII Palaiologos—1261-82

The principal narrative sources for the period 1261-82 are the Byzantine historians: George Pachymeres, *De Michaele Palaeologo*, ed. I. Bekker, I (*CSHB*, 1835); Nikephoros Gregoras, *Byzantina Historia*, ed. L. Schopen, I (*CSHB*, 1829), 78-155.

Modern accounts: Ostrogorsky, *History*, 450-65; Vasiliev, *History*, 591-603 and *passim*; Bréhier, *Vie et Mort*, 321-34; Diehl, *L'Europe orientale*, 198-221; Chapman, *Michel Paléologue*; Geanakoplos, *Emperor Michael*.

Three

The Price of Survival

The long-term consequences of the events of July and August 1261 were not made clear for some time to come. In the excitement of the moment all that mattered was that Constantinople had been liberated from foreign rule. The city churches, now at length cleansed from the Latin abomination, were thronged with people giving thanks. An air of festivity reigned for a day and a night. But there was no witch-hunt for the westerners who remained, and they were soon able to come out of hiding and go about their business unmolested. Even collaborators were forgiven; and indeed the Emperor was glad to be able to employ some of them as ambassadors or interpreters because of their acquired knowledge of western languages. The inauguration of the restored Byzantine Empire was not marked, like that of the Latin Empire, by an orgy of bloodshed and violence. Alexios Strategopoulos, the general to whom the victory was due, was given the exceptional privilege of a triumph, and for a whole year his name was associated with that of the Emperor Michael in prayers throughout the churches. But the 'new Constantine', the second founder of Constantinople, was the Emperor himself.

These were titles by which Michael liked to be addressed, and it is only fair to say that he tried hard to live up to them. The city of Constantinople as he found it in August 1261 was desolate and in ruins. Whole districts had been destroyed by fire, and even the imperial palaces were so dilapidated as to be scarcely habitable. The palace of the Blachernai, where the Latin emperors had resided, was a smoke-blackened ruin. Michael preferred at first to move in to the more ancient buildings of the Great Palace on the Bosporos. But the Latin Emperor Baldwin, in his extremity, had stripped and sold the lead and even the timber from the roofs of many of the churches and public buildings, and the great walls that defended the city were badly in need of repair and attention. The city had an air not only of poverty and neglect but also of emptiness, for under the Latin régime the population had dwindled. Many descendants of noble families who had formerly owned urban properties now returned to claim their rights and Michael made it his business to see that their claims were met, for he could not afford to fall out with the aristocracy. But unclaimed property was taken over for distribution by the crown. Some of it was assigned to the refugees, who were encouraged to return, and a special quarter of the city was made over to a colony of Tzakonians from the southeast region of the Morea, who were to form an important part of the new Byzantine navy.

Great efforts were made to repair and re-endow the city's churches and monasteries, for the restoration of the Orthodox faith was the sign and symbol of the rebirth of the Empire. Particular attention was paid to repairing and strengthening the walls, especially those along the coast, on the Golden Horn and on the side of the Sea of Marmora. For some time there was no telling whether the Venetian fleet might return to the attack. If it did, the attack would certainly be made on the walls along the Golden Horn, where it had succeeded before. Against such a possibility Michael took care also to implement the letter of his treaty with Genoa. The Genoese merchants were welcomed into the city and given possession of the converted monastery which the Venetians had used as their headquarters. By the end of 1261 there were at least 46 Genoese ships cruising off Constantinople and the Venetians kept their distance, restricting their activities to protecting their colonies in Greece and the islands. In time, however, Michael managed to recreate a Byzantine imperial navy so that the defence of the city and Empire would not have to depend wholly on foreign aid. The crews and marines were drawn partly from the Tzakonians of southern Greece, born sailors, who were paid well to move to the capital. But some, especially oarsmen, were recruited from among the rootless population of the city, the offspring of mixed marriages between Greeks and Latins. They were commonly known and despised as the Gasmouli, though some said that they combined the martial qualities of both races. To provide an adequate and defensible harbour for the new fleet, Michael had the old harbour called the Kontoskalion dredged and refortified. It lay on the Sea of Marmora, on the south side of the city, where the sea currents gave natural protection against attack. The city garrison too was strengthened and food and provisions were stockpiled in the warehouses to be used in the event of a siege. But there was no shortage of food, for the empty spaces in the city were so great that it was possible for herds of cattle to be pastured and fields of corn to be cultivated within the city walls.[1]

All these measures for rehabilitation and defence were vastly expensive. The reserves that had been built up by the careful management of John Vatatzes in Nicaea were being eaten away. One method of making the money go further was to devalue the currency. Michael VIII decreed that the Byzantine gold coin or *hyperpyron* was to be lowered in value by one carat, so that it was composed of fifteen parts pure gold to nine of alloy. This was a remedy unworthy of an emperor who posed as the new Constantine. It was the beginning of a steady and rapid depreciation of the Byzantine currency in the thirteenth and fourteenth centuries, as the gold coinage of the Italian republics usurped the place of the bezant in international trade. The Emperor could not bar the Italian traders from the city altogether, for their activities helped to restore prosperity. The Genoese were in a favoured position, and their merchants flocked to Constantinople after 1261 to make the most of the favours showered upon them. Merchants from the smaller republic of Pisa were also accorded special privileges. But even the remaining Venetians, who had been specifically excluded by terms of Michael's treaty with Genoa, could not be sent home. The best that the Emperor could do to prevent Byzantine trade from being once again monopolized by foreign competitors was to try to limit their operations by law, and above all to prevent them from uniting or conspiring together. He therefore made independent agreements with each of the separate colonies of Italians in the city and insisted that each should be administered according to its own laws by a governor appointed from its mother city. The Genoese in Constantinople should have their Podestà, the Venetians their Baillie, and the Pisans their Consul, answerable to the Emperor for the conduct of his people. The Empire disliked them but it could hardly do without them, and by dividing and controlling their operations it might even be possible to play them off one against the other. It was a dangerous game and one at which Michael VIII's successors proved to be the losers.[2]

To commemorate his victory and to serve as a perpetual reminder to his subjects of the man to whom that victory had been granted by God, Michael had a column erected in front of the church of the Holy Apostles. On its top was a bronze statue of his patron saint, the Archangel Michael, towering over the smaller figure of the Emperor holding the city in his hands. Some of his coins bore a picture of the city protected by the Virgin. But the Byzantines had little need of propaganda to impress upon them that the old order of things had returned, that God was again in His heaven and that all would shortly be right with the world. For they knew that an Orthodox emperor once more sat in the Great Palace and an Orthodox patriarch presided in the Great Church.[3]

The possession of Constantinople made the Byzantine Empire once again a great power to be reckoned with in the affairs of the world and the church. But the Empire was now a top-heavy structure. The balance between the European and Asiatic cities of Thessalonica and Nicaea was thrown out by the massive added weight of Constantinople. The maintenance and defence of the capital city taxed the resources of the few remaining provinces; and yet the possession of that city was constantly threatened by the western powers who sought to recover it, and challenged by the continuing rivalry of the separatist Byzantine rulers in northern Greece and in Trebizond. Constantinople was better placed than Nicaea for holding the frontiers against the Bulgars and the Tartars, but it was less well oriented for defending the frontiers in Asia. Those who were left in Nicaea after 1261, and in the other Byzantine cities of Asia Minor such as Brusa, Nikomedia, Ephesos, or Philadelphia, began to feel neglected and aggrieved. The people of Byzantine Asia Minor watched the concentrated riches of their former Empire of Nicaea being dissipated in Constantinople. The sympathies of many of them continued to be with the family of Laskaris rather than with that of the usurper Palaiologos. For it was the Laskarids who had maintained the Empire in exile, and it was they who had brought prosperity to Asia Minor.

Thus from the outset the restored Empire was faced with internal as well as external problems. Michael VIII's coronation in Constantinople in 1261, at which his own infant son Andronikos had been proclaimed co-Emperor, appeared to exclude the legitimate heir John Laskaris from the succession. The appearance became a fact when, in December of the same year, John Laskaris was blinded. The matter was hushed up, but the secret got out, and the Patriarch Arsenios excommunicated Michael. It was not his first disagreement with the Emperor whom he had crowned. But now he had the strongest moral argument for condemning a barbaric deed. At the same time it was discovered that the Emperor had deliberately arranged for the three sisters of John Laskaris to marry foreigners. Two of them became wives of Italians and the third married a Bulgarian noble. Michael must have regretted that two other daughters of the late Theodore II Laskaris were already married, one to Nikephoros, son of Michael

II of Epiros, the other to Constantine Tich, who had made himself ruler of Bulgaria. But no one could doubt that the new Emperor was doing his best to ensure that all the surviving members of the Laskaris family were put out of the running for the throne in Constantinople. The restoration of the Empire necessitated a rewriting of history. The Laskarids were to be relegated to the status of mere provincial rulers like the Despots of Epiros.[4]

There was an immediate wave of hostile reaction. A pretender impersonating John Laskaris gained such a following in Nicaea that Michael had to send an army to quell the riots and scotch the rumour. The Patriarch Arsenios flatly refused to receive the Emperor back into the church, except on impossible conditions. Michael was convinced that his Patriarch was hand-in-glove with the Laskarid sympathizers. He lost his patience, and tried to frighten the old man into submission by threatening to appeal to the more distant authority of the Pope. But not until 1264 did he find it possible to bring any charges against Arsenios to justify removing him from office. A synod of bishops was convened, Arsenios was deposed and, towards the end of May 1264, sent into exile. Almost a year elapsed before a successor was appointed as Patriarch in the person of Germanos III. But he too could not find it in his heart to absolve the Emperor, and he too was bullied into resigning. Finally, in December 1266, a monk called Joseph was enthroned as Patriarch, and on 2 February 1267, after much deliberation, he accepted the Emperor back into the church.[5]

Such were the lengths to which Michael VIII was led by his ambition to found a new imperial dynasty and to cut off the new régime completely from the past of the Empire of Nicaea. For the first five years of his reign in Constantinople he was denied the sacraments of the Orthodox Church. He was even forbidden to enter the cathedral of St Sophia; and it is reported that on one occasion he tried to force a decision by sneaking into the church clutching the Patriarch's robe from behind. Any other emperor in this situation would have found himself in serious danger in the capital. There were indeed rumours of plots against Michael's life; and in 1265 an organized conspiracy was revealed in Constantinople whose ringleader, under torture, implicated the Patriarch in his plans. But the ordinary people of the city had known no other emperor and were for the most part loyal to the man who had liberated them from Latin domination. It was in Asia Minor and in the church itself that the opposition was strongest. A large number of bishops in

Asia Minor, and especially the monks, denounced Michael's cruelty to John Laskaris and ranged themselves on the side of the Patriarch Arsenios. The deposition of Arsenios and of his successor made matters worse; for many years thereafter the peace of the church and of the state was troubled by a deviationist party calling themselves the Arsenites, who remained loyal to the memory of the patriarch who had defied the Emperor and refused to recognize the authority of his appointed successors. The motives of the Arsenites were mixed. High ideals of canon law, of moral scruple and of the precedence of church over state were confused with loyalty to the house of Laskaris and antipathy to the policies of Michael VIII. But the Arsenite schism, as it came to be called, disrupted Byzantine society no less than it divided the Orthodox Church, for the reason that the Byzantines found it unnatural to distinguish religious from political issues.[6]

The opposition to Michael VIII within the Empire was a great encouragement to his enemies beyond the frontiers. The uncertain state of affairs and the neglect of administration and defence in Byzantine Asia Minor played into the hands of the Seljuq Turks. Constantine Tich of Bulgaria, incited by his Laskarid wife, went to war against Michael. His fingers were badly burnt by the Byzantine army and he had to surrender some important places on the Black Sea coast in 1263. But he awaited his opportunity for revenge and joined forces with the Mongols of the Golden Horde in South Russia. An even more natural enemy of Michael VIII as a usurper was the Despot of Epiros who, though not involved in the Arsenite or Laskarid causes, was happy to foster all forms of opposition to the new Emperor, whether native or foreign. Even before 1261 Michael II of Epiros, supported by his sons Nikephoros and John, had returned to the attack in northern Greece and driven out the troops that had invaded his territories after the battle of Pelagonia. For a brief moment he accepted a diplomatic settlement after the recapture of Constantinople. But in 1262 war broke out again.[7]

But the most dangerous enemies of the restored Empire were the westerners who hoped to re-establish the Latin Empire. The last effective champion of the Latin cause on what was strictly Byzantine territory was William of Villehardouin, the French Prince of Achaia. William had been taken prisoner at Pelagonia in 1259 and became a hostage for the return of southern Greece to the Byzantine Empire. In 1262 he bought his release by agreeing to hand over to the Emperor certain fortresses in his principality, among them Mistra and the rock and harbour of Monemvasia. These would provide valuable bases for the eventual Byzantine reconquest of the rest of Greece. The agreement was confirmed by solemn oaths; William acted as godfather to one of the Emperor's sons, and he was granted the Byzantine title of Grand Domestic before returning to Greece. But the agreement was scrapped within the year. For in July 1262 Pope Urban IV absolved Prince William from his pledges on the ground that they had been made to a Greek who was in schism from the Roman Church. The Venetians were quick to rush in with a helping hand to defend their interests in Greece, and Michael VIII was forced into war.

It was a campaign fought on two western fronts against enemies who had been allies on the field of Pelagonia, the Despot of Epiros and the Prince of Achaia. On neither front did the Emperor have more than a limited success. His armies were commanded in northern Greece by his brother John and in the south by his brother Constantine. But they were largely composed of Latin and Turkish mercenaries, and it was hard to keep their pay up to date. In 1264 the Turkish troops deserted to the enemy in the Morea, and much of the work of reconquest that had been achieved there was lost in a battle at Makry Plagi. In the north, however, in the same year, the Despot Michael was forced to submit, though only after some bitter and costly fighting. A treaty was signed; the town of Ioannina in northern Epiros was made over to the Empire, and it was agreed that the Despot's son Nikephoros, recently widowed of his Laskarid wife, should marry the Emperor's niece Anna Palaiologina. For a time there was peace between the Despotate and the Empire. But the defeat of the Emperor's hopes in the south of Greece was a bitter blow. Moreover the Genoese, who had supplied ships for the enterprise, were roundly beaten by a Venetian fleet near the island of Spetsai (Settepozzi) off the coast of the Morea in 1263. It was their first encounter with their rivals since 1261. Michael VIII concluded that they were unreliable if not useless as allies, revoked his agreement with them and turned instead to Venice. The Venetians can hardly have thought that they would so easily resume their dominant position in the Byzantine world, and they were wary of taking advantage of the offer. But the Genoese were temporarily turned out of their quarter in Constantinople and their fleet was sent home. They expressed their bitterness by conspiring with the western enemies of Byzantium whose designs were conceived and planned on a grander scale.[8]

51

For the enemies of the restored Byzantine Empire in Greece did not stand alone. Their hostility derived some of its nourishment from further west. Michael VIII with his armies and ships could hold his own against the outposts of western colonialism in the Morea and in the Aegean islands; and he could for a time at least play off Venetians against Genoese. But he was well aware that the real danger to Constantinople came not from the outposts but from the centres of power in Italy, from the Papacy and from King Manfred of Sicily. The last Latin emperor, Baldwin II, had escaped by way of Euboia first to the court of King Manfred, then to Venice, and finally to the papal Curia. The restoration of a schismatic emperor to the throne in Constantinople seemed particularly galling to the Papacy, which had once had such high hopes of the good that would come out of the evil of the Fourth Crusade. Pope Urban IV, who was elected only a month after the event, was naturally sympathetic to the dispossessed Emperor Baldwin, and in August 1261, while Michael VIII was being crowned in Constantinople, the new Pope was preaching a crusade for the reconquest of the city and the reinstatement of Baldwin. At the time the response was small. The only western ruler actively interested in such a project was Manfred of Sicily. His kingdom was well placed for an invasion of the Byzantine Empire; he was a son-in-law of the Despot of Epiros, and he already possessed forward bases in Albania and northern Greece. But Pope Urban could not bring himself to nominate Manfred, the rebellious and excommunicated bastard of Frederick II, as leader of a crusade for the unity of Christendom.

The agents of the Byzantine Foreign Office kept Michael VIII well informed about Baldwin's movements and about the Pope's intentions. Like his great predecessor John Vatatzes, Michael hoped that he could forestall his political enemies in the west by appealing to the highest ideal of the Papacy, the peace and unity of the Church. To remove the threat of a crusade he would show his willingness to remove the schism or, as the Byzantines called it, the scandal that divided the Church. Michael VIII was no doubt as sincere as all Orthodox Christians in his desire to see that scandal abolished. But in the circumstances of the time he felt it politic to concede the first point by taking the initiative. In June 1262 he wrote to Pope Urban reminding him of the numerous wrongs done to the Empire by the Latins, but expressing the hope that diplomatic relations between Rome and Byzantium might now be resumed, and that papal legates might be sent to Constantinople. The peace of the Church would surely follow once temporal peace had been established. The Pope was pleased but noncommittal. In his eyes the real Emperor of Constantinople was still Baldwin II; Michael Palaiologos was simply 'Emperor of the Greeks'. In fact so long as Michael continued to make war on the remaining Latin colonies in Greece, Urban continued to favour the idea of a crusade against him. But the Pope had his own hands tied by domestic affairs. The situation in Italy was delicate. The King of Sicily was rather more the enemy of the Papacy than he was of the Greeks, and in the end Pope Urban, seconded by King Louis IX of France, decided to be rid of him. By July 1263 Louis' brother, Charles of Anjou, had been nominated as the champion of the Pope against Manfred of Sicily.

In the same month the Pope wrote to Michael VIII promising to send four Franciscans to Constantinople to discuss the union of the churches, and even suggesting that he might recognize Michael as true Emperor if only he would withdraw his troops from Latin territory in Greece. To show his good intent Michael had already invited Nicholas of Cotrone, a Greek Catholic bishop from southern Italy, to come to Constantinople to expound the Roman faith. As a Greek-speaker Nicholas was more sympathetic than the many legates from the west who in times past had had to present their case through interpreters. Early in 1264 the Emperor sent him to Rome with a glowing report on the possibilities of reconciling the differences between Orthodox and Catholics; and in the summer the four Franciscans also returned to Italy from Constantinople bearing a proposal from the Emperor that a council should be convened to debate the problems of the schism.[9]

There matters rested for more than two years. Pope Urban IV died in October 1264. His successor Clement IV was preoccupied with the events in Italy which Urban had set in motion. On 26 February 1266 Charles of Anjou defeated Manfred of Sicily at the battle of Benevento. Charles inherited not only Manfred's title to the kingdom of Naples and Sicily, but also his ambitions with regard to Byzantium. Manfred had never lost control of the strategic points across the Adriatic which he had hoped to use as bases for his campaign against Constantinople, and when he died they were quickly taken over by Charles's agents. By 1267 the new King of Sicily was in possession of the island of Corfu and much of the adjacent mainland of Greece.

To Michael VIII it soon became clear that Charles of Anjou presented a new and a more formidable version of the threat to his western provinces and ultimately to the survival of his empire. Manfred had been the enemy of the Papacy, but Charles was its protector and a much more plausible candidate for the leadership of a crusade to restore the Latin Empire. Michael thought that the time had come to reopen negotiations with the Papacy. He wrote to Clement IV reminding him of the embassies which had already been exchanged and begging him to use his influence to restrain the King of Sicily from attacking his fellow Christians. He repeated his proposal that a council of the church should be held, preferably in one of the cities of Byzantium.

Pope Clement was naturally in favour of promoting the unity of Christendom, but it would be on his own terms; and with Charles of Anjou at hand, ready and willing to lead a crusade against the schismatic Greeks, Clement could confidently dictate those terms to the Emperor and Patriarch in Constantinople. Michael VIII, who had hoped to confine the matter to generalities, found himself presented with a detailed profession of faith to which he was ordered to subscribe. There was to be no debate and no council. The Greek Church must simply submit to the terms laid down in Clement's reply. Then and then only could the Emperor in Constantinople be assured of the support of the Papacy against his enemies. Michael hastened to write again, hoping to win the Pope's sympathy by offering to take part in a crusade against the Turks, if only he could be assured that he would not be leaving his western provinces open to attack by the Latins. But Pope Clement was arguing from a position of strength. He replied that he could give no assurances to the Emperor until the reunion of the Greek Church with Rome had been accomplished on the terms already stated.

The Pope seemed now to have concluded that there was only one way of bringing the Greeks back to the fold. In May 1267 he was responsible for promoting a series of alliances and treaties between Charles of Anjou and the Latin Emperor Baldwin, which legitimized the proposed reconquest of Constantinople. At the papal court at Viterbo it was arranged that Baldwin's son Philip, heir presumptive to the title of Emperor of Constantinople, should marry Charles's daughter. One of Charles's sons was to marry the daughter of William of Villehardouin, who would cede to the King of Sicily the suzerainty over the Principality of Achaia; and Charles promised to prepare an army of 2000 knights within six or at most seven years for the 'sacred task' of rescuing the imperial city from the schismatic Greeks and restoring it to the Holy Roman Church.[10]

The treaty of Viterbo in May 1267 united against Byzantium most of the interested parties in the west, the Papacy, the Kingdom of Sicily, the claimant to the Latin Empire, and the Prince of Achaia. From that date almost to the moment of his death in December 1282 the reign of Michael VIII was a long battle of wits to stave off the threat of this alliance and to persuade his subjects that the methods he employed to this end were, however unpalatable, the only possible methods in the circumstances. If Charles of Anjou's invasion of the Byzantine Empire could be made acceptable to the Papacy as a just and holy war, then the forces at Michael's disposal could hardly prevent its success. The only way to ensure that the Popes would withhold their moral sanction from the enterprise was to remove the moral pretext for it by voluntarily submitting the Byzantine Church to their authority. In the bitter atmosphere following the Latin occupation this was not a policy likely to win much approval from the Greeks. But Michael carefully calculated the concessions that it would be necessary to make to the Popes and tried hard to persuade his people into making them. That such a policy should have entailed some double dealing is not surprising. What is strange is that, while Michael seemed ready to lean over backwards to satisfy the Popes' demands, the Popes themselves had a remarkable faith in his ability to fulfil all his promises. Michael seemed prepared to believe that the Popes in fact exercised the authority over secular rulers that they claimed, while the Popes were led to believe that the Byzantine Emperor actually wielded the kind of authority over his church which, in other contexts, they were so quick to deplore as Caesaropapism.

Michael's correspondence with Pope Clement IV gave little hope of encouragement, although he continued to send embassies to the Curia, some with presents for the cardinals who might be induced to influence papal policy. But Clement IV died in November 1268, and for three years the Holy See was vacant. There was no higher moral authority to whom the Emperor could appeal to restrain Charles of Anjou from fulfilling the agreements he had made at Viterbo. Michael did what he could by writing to Charles's brother, King Louis of France. King Louis, though in other respects a saint, considered the Byzantines to be wayward schismatics; but he was more interested in the destruction of the infidel than in the forcible salvation of heretics. He was in the midst of preparations for a crusade in North Africa, and he felt that his brother's intention to invade the Byzantine Empire involved a misuse of valuable military resources. He managed to persuade Charles to postpone his plans for the conquest of Constantinople and to lend his support for the worthier cause of fighting the infidel. Michael VIII was gratified that Louis had taken the hint and sent envoys to greet him in North Africa. By the time they arrived at Carthage, Louis had been taken ill and was barely able to receive them. He died on 25 August 1270. The envoys from Constantinople had at least the satisfaction of witnessing the safe arrival in Africa of their enemy, for Charles of Anjou sailed in on the very day that his brother died. But the envoys had to make their way home empty-handed.

The campaign in Tunis, of which he assumed command, kept Charles occupied for several months. But early in 1271 he was back in Italy and ready to resume plans for his Byzantine expedition. He was fortunate to gain control of the city and harbour of Durazzo or Dyrrachion on the Adriatic coast. The local Albanians proclaimed him their King, and he was able to send troops across to Albania and to Greece. The rulers of Serbia and Bulgaria were also both ready to join in a campaign whose goal was Constantinople. It was even put about in the Kingdom of Sicily that the young John Laskaris had escaped from prison and arrived there as a refugee. The story was mere propaganda, but it lent a colour of legality to Charles's enterprise. The leaders of the Fourth Crusade had similarly posed as champions of a refugee Byzantine prince against a usurper in Constantinople. Michael VIII did all he could to prevent the building up of a massive coalition of his Slav and Latin enemies. But now that King Louis was dead and so long as the Papal throne remained unoccupied there seemed no means by which he could bring moral pressure to bear on Charles. He could only hope that the cardinals would find a suitable candidate for the Papacy as soon as possible. Charles of Anjou, though for different reasons, hoped the same.[11]

In September 1271 the Holy See was at last filled by the election of Pope Gregory X. The choice was as disappointing to Charles as it was encouraging to Michael. For Gregory's policy was ruled by his passion for the Holy Land, and he hoped that the Christians of the east might see the error of their ways so that they too could join in a great crusade to Jerusalem. From such a Pope, Michael VIII might reasonably expect the assurances of protection against Charles of Anjou which Clement IV had been unwilling to provide. Gregory was enthroned at the end of March 1272, and four days later he announced that a general council of the church would be held in two years' time. The main items on its agenda would be the reform of the church, the union of the churches of Rome and Constantinople, and the crusade. Not long afterwards Michael VIII sent a formal letter of greeting to the new Pope, expressing his sincere desire to promote peace between the churches and to assist in the war against the infidel.

The response was disappointing. Michael and his Patriarch Joseph were indeed invited to attend or to send legates to the Pope's forthcoming council, but only on condition of subscribing to a written and oral profession of the Roman faith and after acknowledging obedience to the See of Rome as head of all the churches. The terms remained precisely the same as they had been stated by Pope Clement IV. The only difference was that where Clement had arrogantly demanded submission, Gregory invited the Emperor to return to Rome like the Prodigal Son. But, much as he desired the unity of Christendom, he was not prepared to make any compromise. Michael was in no position to argue. Charles of Anjou had promised at Viterbo to have his army and navy ready for the invasion by 1273 or 1274. Time was running short. Michael had already gone out of his way to explain to the Patriarch and his synod the material dangers that threatened the Empire. But they had not been greatly impressed. They agreed that the unity of the church was highly desirable, but they did not suppose, in the light of past experience, that it could be effected in a moment, as their Emperor appeared to believe. Michael had therefore been driven to conduct his negotiations more or less in secret, in the hope that when it came to the point he would be able to offer reasonably acceptable terms to his clergy.[12]

Pope Gregory's reply changed the situation, for it seemed like an ultimatum. The moment had now come for the Emperor to bring the matter into the open and to try to convince his people that formal acceptance of the Pope's terms was the only way of saving the Empire. He launched a campaign of propaganda in Constantinople, sweetening the pill by assuring the Byzantine clergy that what they might say in Rome they need not necessarily do in Byzantium. They could take comfort in the thought that Rome was separated from Constantinople by a vast extent of sea, which the Pope was not likely to traverse. There was thus no harm in paying lip service to his conditions. Above all, Michael tried to steer the thoughts of his patriarch and bishops away from the theological issues, which were so dear to the Byzantine mind. But this proved impossible, for the bishops were well aware that the Pope required adherence not only to the western form of the Creed, but also to many alien forms of doctrine and ritual; and these were matters of deepest significance to the Orthodox.

The opposition was loud and strong. Its spokesman was at first John Bekkos, the archivist of St Sophia, a priest of great intelligence and integrity, who had been one of the envoys to King Louis two years before. Bekkos was no rabble-rouser, but he voiced his opinion that union with the Latin Christians was undesirable because their faith was suspect; and though it might be impolite to say so, they were technically in heresy. The Patriarch Joseph thought that this expressed the case very well. But the Emperor, seeing his plans going awry, was furious. John Bekkos was arrested and thrown into prison. Michael VIII's relations with his church were difficult enough without the added complication of an anti-unionist party. The Arsenite faction were still in open schism with the Patriarch Joseph, and among the monks especially there were many extremists quick to detect any sign of imperial dictation to the church. But matters had now gone too far. The opposition rallied round the Patriarch, and its numbers grew among the laity as well as the clergy as the news got about. The Emperor's favourite sister Eulogia, hitherto one of his most ardent supporters, professed herself readier to contemplate her brother's ruin than to compromise her Orthodox faith. Michael sent her into exile, but she soon escaped and joined her daughter Maria in Bulgaria. The Bulgarian court became a hive of anti-unionist activities. Several other members of the imperial family joined the ranks of the opposition, and even the Arsenites threw in their lot with the Orthodox to prevent the worse evil of union with Rome. The Patriarch made a public statement denouncing the Church of Rome for its 'innovations' in the Creed; and in June 1273 he composed an encyclical to the faithful to strengthen their powers of resistance to imperial pressure. In his position as Patriarch, Joseph felt it his duty to remind the Emperor that only an ecumenical council was empowered to take decisions affecting the whole church. The Patriarch of Constantinople alone could not act in so weighty a matter without consulting the opinion of his colleagues in the other patriarchates of Alexandria, Antioch and Jerusalem.

The Emperor began to foresee that it might be necessary to get rid of Joseph and appoint a more tractable patriarch. Charles of Anjou was temporarily involved in trouble in the north of Italy. But he had recently been able to send more troops over to Greece, and his army was known to be assembling at Durazzo, which was evidently to be the base for his advance through Macedonia. Moreover, the wedding of his daughter to Baldwin's son Philip, arranged at Viterbo, had just taken place, and Baldwin died a few weeks afterwards in December 1273, so that Charles found himself not only King of Albania and lord of all the French colonies in Greece, but also father-in-law of the new Latin Emperor of Constantinople. Somehow the Pope must be convinced that the Byzantines were willing to fulfil his conditions. For otherwise he would not much longer undertake to hold Charles of Anjou back from his invasion of the Empire. Michael therefore cast about for a respected spokesman for the cause of union with Rome to counter-balance the statements of the Patriarch. He picked on John Bekkos, who was still under arrest. Bekkos was plied with select translated passages from the Latin fathers to while away his hours in prison. The quotations were carefully chosen to illustrate the basic identity of belief between Orthodox and Catholics; and before long Bekkos had come to the conclusion that the Latins were not, after all, heretics, and that therefore the union of the churches was, in the political circumstances, both permissible and desirable, so long as the customs and ritual of the Orthodox church remained unchanged. He was then released and encouraged to impart his findings to others. Some of the more moderate of the clergy were thus induced to come out in favour of the Emperor's policy, and an official unionist party was formed in opposition to the Patriarch and his supporters.[13]

The Byzantine church and society were now divided even more sharply into two camps. But at least it became possible for the Emperor to send a hopeful reply to the Pope's invitation to a council. Pope Gregory was happy to hear such welcome news. It had been rumoured in Italy, a rumour no doubt fostered by Charles of Anjou, that the negotiations were being deliberately prolonged by the Emperor in order to play for time and to force the Pope to withhold his sanction from the projected invasion of the Empire. The rumour had seemed to gain substance from the Emperor's long delay in replying. It was now clear that such was not the case. But Michael VIII had to make all haste to complete his arrangements to send legates to the council, now scheduled for May 1274, at which the union of the churches would be effected. Pope Gregory was determined that his council should have every chance of success. He instructed Charles of Anjou to postpone for one year the fulfilment of the obligations he had undertaken at Viterbo, and to allow the legates from Constantinople safe passage through his dominions. William of Villehardouin was also instructed to observe a truce with the Byzantine forces in the Morea.

Pope Gregory had done his bit. It was now up to the Emperor to fulfil his part of the bargain. Throughout the winter of 1273 to 1274 Michael, helped by John Bekkos, waged ceaseless propaganda for the cause of union with Rome. In January 1274 the Patriarch Joseph was confined to a monastery pending the outcome of the Pope's council. The opposition was thus bereft of its leader. But for all his efforts it was clear that the Emperor would never be able to bring more than a small minority of his clergy to the point of declaring or signing the full profession of the Roman faith required by the Pope. In the end he prevailed upon a few of the more moderate and favourable of the bishops to draft a statement of their own submission to the Pope. It was phrased in the most general terms, but reinforced by a detailed profession of faith signed by the Emperor himself and by his son and co-Emperor Andronikos.

These documents were entrusted to the imperial legates who were to attend the Pope's council, which was to be held at Lyons in the south of France. The Emperor's personal representative was his Grand Logothete, George Akropolites, an accomplished diplomat, a scholar, and something of a theologian. The Orthodox Church was to be represented by the former Patriarch Germanos III and by Theophanes, Bishop of Nicaea. Neither had any special qualifications or commanded any great respect; and Theophanes at least had private doubts about the whole affair. But they were the best that the Emperor could find in the circumstances. The delegation set out from Constantinople in two ships early in March 1274. Towards the end of the month, when they had got no further than the Morea, they ran into a storm off Cape Malea. The ship carrying the cargo of treasures and icons which were to be presented to the Pope was lost. There was only one survivor. But Akropolites, with the ex-patriarch and the Bishop of Nicaea managed, after a short delay, to reach Italy.

The council had meanwhile been opened in the cathedral of St John at Lyons by Pope Gregory in person on 7 May 1274. It was a brilliant assembly of representatives of all the rulers of church and state in the western world. But one ruler, Charles of Anjou, was not seen to be present. At the beginning of the second session, on 18 May, the Pope announced that he had received word that the delegation was on its way from Constantinople; and on 24 June the Byzantine legates arrived to be greeted with the kiss of peace from the Pope and all his cardinals. They presented the Pope with the documents of submission from the Emperor Michael and his son Andronikos. Thomas Aquinas was to have been present at the council. He had rather tactlessly been commissioned to deliver a speech on the errors of the Greeks, but he died on his way to Lyons. Cardinal Bonaventura preached a sermon on the unity of Christendom, and on 6 July 1274 the reunion of the churches of Rome and Constantinople was formally celebrated. The documents from the Emperor and his bishops were read out in Latin translation. George Akropolites, in the name of the Emperor, swore an oath of loyalty to the See of Rome and of adherence to the Roman Creed; and at the end of the ceremony Pope Gregory X preached a sermon telling of his joy and thanksgiving that the Greeks had returned to the fold of their own free-will and without seeking any material reward. This last statement was rather an extenuation of the truth; for the Pope can hardly have been blind to the political motives that had prompted the Byzantine Emperor to his action. But it underlines the fact that while the Union of Lyons was a spiritual triumph for Pope Gregory, it was a diplomatic triumph for Michael VIII.[14]

NOTES

1 Geanakoplos, *Emperor Michael*, 121-30; Chapman, *Michel Paléologue*, 46-9.

2 Geanakoplos, 131-7. On the depreciation of the gold coinage, see Pachymeres, *De Andronico Palaeologo*, II (*CSHB*), 493. Cf. D. A. Zakythinos, *Crise monétaire et crise économique à Byzance du XIIᵉ au XVᵉ siècle* (Athens, 1948), 8; Ostrogorsky, *History*, 484.

3 W. Wroth, *Catalogue of the Imperial Byzantine Coins in the British Museum*, II (London, 1908), 608-9, Plates LXXIV, 1 and 2.

4 Pachymeres, I, 35-6, 180-1, 190-2; Gregoras, 92-3. Cf. F. Dölger, 'Die dynastische Familienpolitik des Kaisers Michael Palaiologos', in *PARASPORA* (Ettal, 1961), 178-88.

5 Pachymeres, I, 193-204, 257-71. V. Laurent, 'La chronologie des patriarches de Constantinople au XIIIᵉ siècle (1208-1309)', *REB*, XXVII (1969), 142-4.

6 On the Arsenites, see L. Petit, 'Arsène Autorianus et les Arsénites', in *Dictionnaire de théologie catholique*, I, ii, cols. 1991-4; I. Sykoutres, 'On the schism of the Arsenites' (in Greek), *Hellenika*, II (1929), 267-

332; V. Laurent, 'Les grandes crises religieuses à Byzance. La fin du schisme arsénite', *Académie Roumaine. Bulletin de la section historique*, XXVI (1945), 225-313.

7 Geanakoplos, *Emperor Michael*, 181; Nicol, *Despotate of Epiros*, 192-4.

8 Geanakoplos, 147-59, 171-5, 182-4.

9 Geanakoplos, 139-47, 175-80; S. Runciman, *The Sicilian Vespers* (Cambridge, 1958), 66-70.

10 Geanakoplos, 192-200; Runciman, *Sicilian Vespers*, 136-7; Longnon, *L'empire latin de Constantinople*, 236-7; B. Roberg, *Die Union zwischen der griechischen und der lateinischen Kirche auf dem II. Konzil von Lyon (1274)* (Bonn, 1964), 58-64.

11 Geanakoplos, 200-6, 216-18, 223-28; Runciman, *Sicilian Vespers*, 140-7.

12 Geanakoplos, 237-45; Roberg, *Die Union*, 95-102.

13 D. M. Nicol, 'The Greeks and the Union of the Churches. The Preliminaries to the Second Council of Lyons, 1261-1274', in *Medieval Studies presented to A. Gwynn* (Dublin, 1961), 464-72.

14 Geanakoplos, 258-64; Runciman, 163-7. The Latin versions of the submissions of the Byzantine Emperor and clergy have been re-edited by Roberg, *Die Union*, 235-47.

Four

The Battle of Wits between East and West

In the eyes of the western world the Union of Lyons meant that the Byzantine Emperor Michael Palaiologos must now be accepted not merely as a Catholic prince against whom no just war could be waged, but also as the legitimate heir to the throne in Constantinople. Charles of Anjou and his son-in-law the Latin Emperor Philip found it hard to subscribe to this view. But Michael had outwitted them and, trusting that the Pope would now identify all enemies of Byzantium with the enemies of Christendom, he took the offensive which was directed against Charles of Anjou's bases in Albania. In the spring of 1274, while his envoys were still on their way to Lyons, Michael's army in Macedonia advanced towards the coast from the fortress of Berat and closed in on Durazzo, the headquarters of Charles's Albanian kingdom. Charles, preoccupied as he was with affairs in Sicily and Italy, could send few reinforcements; and for two years his garrisons in Albania were constantly on the defensive.

At the same time, however, the Emperor had to guard against the possibility that the separatist rulers of northern Greece might be seduced into giving help or comfort to Charles. The Despot of Epiros, Michael II, had died in 1268, and his dominions were now divided between his sons Nikephoros and John. Nikephoros had inherited the southern portion of Epiros with his capital at Arta, and was the neighbour of the Angevin Kingdom of Albania. John had taken possession of Thessaly and had his capital at Neopatras or Hypati, not far from Lamia. Both brothers were on good terms with the French princes of Athens and the Morea. Both were naturally hostile to the restored Empire in Constantinople. Nikephoros of Epiros had been brought within the imperial orbit by his marriage to the Emperor's niece Anna in 1265. Michael VIII tried the same tactics with John of Thessaly; John's daughter was to marry another relative of the Emperor, and he was granted the imperial title of *sebastokrator*. But John was less ready to accommodate himself than his brother.[1]

In 1274 Michael sent ambassadors to both rulers to persuade them to accept the Union of Lyons. It was a forlorn hope. The Emperor's negotiations with the Papacy had made it possible for the heirs of the Despotate of Epiros to pose even more convincingly as the champions of Orthodoxy and of the true Byzantine tradition. John of Thessaly in particular kept open house for all who were in disagreement with the Emperor's policies. But the Union of Lyons, by relieving the Empire of the immediate threat of invasion from the west, gave the Emperor a chance to deal with his enemies nearer home. He embarked on a campaign of reconquest first from the rebel Greeks and then from the Latins in Greece and the islands. To begin with, an army and a fleet were sent across to Thessaly to bring the rebel to heel. The army was commanded by Michael VIII's brother John Palaiologos, a soldier of great experience. But it was roundly defeated by John of Thessaly who called on the help of his friend, the French Duke of Athens. The navy had an unexpected success. But the shock of defeat was too much for the Emperor's brother, who resigned his command and retired into private life. He died before the end of the year 1274.

The victory of the Byzantine fleet, however, encouraged Michael to think in terms of expelling the Latins from all the Greek islands that they still controlled. It was his practice to exploit the grievances of any disgruntled westerners who offered him their services. One such was an adventurer from Verona called Licario who had fallen out with the Venetian and Lombard governors of the island of Negroponte or Euboia. Negroponte was the most important naval base held by Venice in the Aegean Sea, protecting central Greece and also the Morea from attacks by the Byzantines. When Licario offered to help the Emperor recover the island he was given every encouragement. About 1273 Michael made Licario his vassal, in western style. Licario succeeded in occupying the town of Karystos in the south of Negroponte and from there extended his operations to other islands with equal success. The Emperor promoted him to the rank of Grand Duke and granted him the title to the island of Negroponte as an imperial fief. Licario's victories were not very enduring, but they did much to enhance the prestige of Michael VIII in the eyes of the Latins.[2]

Other western adventurers contrived to secure more lasting possessions by making themselves useful to the Emperor. Two brothers from Genoa, Benedetto and Manuele Zaccaria, were granted the port of Phokaia as an imperial fief about 1275. Phokaia lay to the north of the gulf of Smyrna on the coast of Asia Minor. The Zaccaria brothers made their family fortune by exploiting the local alum mines, whose produce was in great demand for the dyeing of cloth. They built a fleet to protect their trade from pirates, and for long they defended Smyrna from attacks by other Latins and by the Turks from the interior of the country. They also served the Emperor as ambassadors to the west, and the fame of their success lured other Italian freebooters to join the imperial cause and fight for Byzantium in the hope of winning similar rewards.[3]

For a few years in the reign of Michael VIII it might have been true to say that the Byzantine navy and its agents had control over the Aegean Sea. But it never proved possible to re-establish Byzantine rule over all the islands. Those nearest to the Asiatic shore such as Lesbos, Chios, Samos and Rhodes, which had been included in the Empire of Nicaea, remained for some time longer within the Empire. But Negroponte quickly reverted to Venetian control after the death of Licario. The island of Crete, which had passed to Venice by terms of the Partition Treaty of 1204, was never recovered by the Byzantines. While the Cyclades and Sporades islands of the Archipelago remained in the possession of the Venetian family of Marco Sanudo, who had captured Naxos in 1207 and established there the seat of a duchy comprising a number of the neighbouring islands. Some of them were temporarily captured by Licario, but the line of the Sanudo family ruling over the Duchy of Naxos lasted well into the fourteenth century.

The major western beneficiaries of Byzantine imperial policy, however, were not the free-lance businessmen but the great commercial republics of Genoa and Venice. In 1267, when the threat from Charles of Anjou first became clear, Michael VIII had taken up the broken thread of his contacts with the Genoese. A new treaty was drawn up, confirming and supplementing that signed at Nymphaion in 1261. It was to have even greater consequences, for it was now agreed that the Genoese merchants returning to Constantinople should be allowed to establish their own settlement beyond the walls. They were allotted land across the water from the city, in the district known as Galata or Pera on the other side of the Golden Horn. This arrangement might have the merit of obviating tension between Genoese and Byzantines within the city. The Emperor took care to impress upon the Genoese that their presence in Galata was dependent on his favour and on their behaviour. Their Podestà was required to act out his allegiance by doing obeisance when granted audience by the Emperor, and their ships were supposed to salute when sailing past the palace on the Golden Horn. But these formalities were forgotten with the passing of the years, and the Genoese colony at Galata, increasingly independent of Byzantine control, was soon to become a thorn in the flesh to succeeding emperors and a natural target for the envy of the Venetians.[4]

However, the Doge of Venice himself took the initiative in working out a new agreement with Byzantium. The Venetians were alarmed by the outcome of the treaty of Viterbo and the consequent encroachment of Charles of Anjou on the Adriatic coast. In April 1268 they signed a treaty with Michael VIII. It was to run for five years, and although it did not yet allow to Venetian merchants the preferential treatment granted to the Genoese, it gave them exemption from the payment of customs duties in all parts of the Byzantine Empire. The Venetians were to be much coveted by Charles of Anjou in the following years as potential allies. But so long as Charles's eastern plans were thwarted they held to their agreement with Michael VIII. After the Union of Lyons in 1274, Venice again took the initiative in seeking to extend the terms of her treaty of 1268. In March 1277 Venetian merchants were once again granted a free commercial quarter in Constantinople for their own use, as well as similar facilities in Thessalonica and other ports of the Empire. The agreement was to run for a trial period of two years. It remained to be seen whether they would continue to be satisfied with this arrangement if and when Charles of Anjou was in a position to resume his offensive against Constantinople. But at the time Michael VIII could congratulate himself on having gained the upper hand over both of the maritime republics of Italy.[5]

So long as Pope Gregory X was alive Charles of Anjou was kept at bay, for Michael VIII continued to convince the Pope that the Byzantine Church and people would eventually come round to accepting the Union of Lyons. The Patriarch Joseph thought otherwise, but he was removed and his place was taken by the unionist John Bekkos. There was even talk of a combined Greek and Latin crusade against the Turks. But Gregory X died in January 1276, and his successors became increasingly sceptical about the nature of the Union and more and more exacting in their demands. Pope Innocent V kept the door open for negotiations; he required certain assurances, but he seemed willing to trust the good intentions of the Emperor Michael. John XXI, who succeeded to the Papacy in the same year

1276, was gratified to learn that the Union had at length been officially ratified in Constantinople. For in the winter of 1276 the Patriarch John Bekkos held a synod of clergy and laity in the capital at which the union of the churches was solemnly proclaimed and the sentence of excommunication was pronounced against all who refused to accept it. In April 1277, at a ceremony in the Blachernai palace, Michael VIII and Andronikos publicly swore to recognize the supremacy of the Holy See and the Roman Creed; documents confirming the Union of Lyons and sealed with the Emperor's golden bull were prepared and forwarded to the Pope.[6]

On paper, and from a distance, all seemed to be well. No pope could authorize a crusade against Byzantium so long as the Empire was governed by a Catholic emperor and its church by a Catholic patriarch. But the popes must soon discover that the reality was far different from the appearance. The Patriarch Joseph, deposed for his loyalty to Orthodoxy, had become the hero and the martyr of the anti-unionists. The 'Josephites' joined forces with the Arsenites in fanatical opposition to an emperor whom they deemed to be in heresy, and many members of the aristocracy refused to sacrifice the principles of their Orthodox faith. The Emperor's explanations fell on deaf ears, and when persuasion failed he resorted to persecution. The anti-unionists were declared to be traitors. Their property was confiscated. The prisons were crowded with monks, priests and laymen arrested on evidence or on suspicion of treason, and many of the opposition leaders were blinded, mutilated, or banished. Refugees from the reign of terror in the capital found their way almost by instinct to the separatist Byzantine states in Trebizond or in northern Greece, where the rulers of Epiros and Thessaly welcomed them with open arms. John of Thessaly broadcast his reputation for unsullied Orthodoxy by convening an anti-unionist synod at Neopatras in the winter of 1276-77. It was attended by about 100 monks and abbots with eight bishops, who almost unanimously anathematized the Pope, the Emperor and the Patriarch. The Emperor found it especially embarrassing that so many of his own relatives were actively engaged in plotting against him. His sister Eulogia encouraged her daughter to give asylum to refugees in Bulgaria. His niece Anna, another daughter of Eulogia, and wife of the Despot Nikephoros of Epiros, encouraged her husband to make friends with the Emperor's enemies. Both John of Thessaly and Nikephoros of Epiros were excommunicated by the Patriarch John Bekkos at a synod held in St Sophia on 16 July 1277. But their political manoeuvrings were more worrying to the Emperor than the state of their souls. For both were known to be in friendly communication not only with the French in Athens and the Morea, but also with Charles of Anjou.[7]

John of Thessaly was engaged in various commercial transactions with the Kingdom of Sicily at least from 1273. Nikephoros of Epiros, who was next-door neighbour of the Angevin Kingdom of Albania, entered into diplomatic relations with Charles of Anjou in 1276; and in April 1279, if not before, he formally became a vassal of Charles, making over certain territories in northern Epiros which were of the greatest strategic value to an invader from Italy. This alliance helped to persuade Charles more firmly than ever that his route to Constantinople lay overland through Albania and Macedonia and not by sea. The way was still barred by the Byzantine army stationed in western Macedonia, particularly at the impregnable mountain fortress of Berat behind Durazzo. But sheer force of numbers might prevail, and Charles took pains to see that his forward bases in Albania were well manned and supplied.[8]

It became more than ever imperative for Michael VIII to maintain the fiction of union with the Roman Church to prevent Charles of Anjou from gaining the blessing of the Pope. Pope Nicholas III, who was appointed in November 1277, was no great friend or admirer of Charles, and explicitly forbade him to attack the Byzantine Empire. But at the same time the reports that he received from Constantinople led him to feel that the Greeks were not taking the Union of Lyons as seriously as they should, and he demanded more adequate and concrete evidence of their conversion and of their total conformity to the Roman Creed and doctrine. Nicholas instructed his legates to Constantinople to secure unconditional and unequivocal professions of the Roman faith not only from the Emperor and his son but also from the Patriarch and from every member of the Orthodox clergy individually and by word of mouth. There was to be no concession to the Greeks in the matter of ritual, no hair-splitting about matters of dogma, and no evading the fact of the absolute primacy of the Holy See. Worst of all the Emperor was to admit a cardinal-legate to reside permanently in Constantinople, and the Byzantine clergy were to beg the favour of absolution from Rome for the schism and confirmation from Rome of their orders. These demands took the matter much further than Michael had ever intended it to go. But he could not see his way to turn back. The best that he could do was to impress upon the Pope the heroic efforts that he was making in the cause of union and the difficulties that he was encountering.[9]

When he had interviewed the Pope's messengers in Constantinople in 1278 Michael sent back with them a written record of what he had said. It was in the form of a memorandum taken down during the interview by the imperial protonotary and interpreter Ogerius. The Emperor complained of the activities of the rulers of Epiros, Thessaly and Trebizond, and of the help given to them by the Latins. He lamented that the number of his enemies in high places and among his own family was so great that he was hard pressed to find officers and administrators whom he could trust. A number of his commanders, among them two of the Emperor's own cousins, who had been sent to make war on John of Thessaly in the previous year, had actually declared themselves to be of like mind with the rebel concerning the heresy of their emperor and his union with the Pope, and changed sides. It was useless to give command of armies to generals who were already secretly hand-in-glove with the enemy. In short, the Emperor wished the Pope to know that, though he was working without pause to fulfil the obligations that he had undertaken at Lyons, his efforts were being constantly undermined by the operations of enemies who were the common foes of himself and of the Church of Rome.[10]

In 1279 Pope Nicholas III sent another delegation to Constantinople. The situation in the capital had by then deteriorated so far that even the unionist Patriarch Bekkos had fallen foul of his Emperor and withdrawn into a monastery. But the Emperor was so anxious to provide the Pope's legates with visible proof of his persecution of the enemies of the church that he sent them on a conducted tour of the state prison. There they were able to see with their own eyes several members of the imperial family bound in chains as traitors. And so that Pope Nicholas should be under no illusions, Michael insisted that the legates take back with them to Italy two of the leading anti-unionist monks. John Bekkos was induced to resume his office as Patriarch in August 1279, and the Emperor then caused another synod of bishops and clergy to be convened in the capital. He harangued them on the need to exercise tact in the presence of the Pope's legates. But the demands of Pope Nicholas were more than most of them could stomach, for each was now asked to take an oath of obedience to the Roman Church in person. This they refused to do; the Emperor had to be content with a declaration phrased once again in general terms, which very few would sign. It is said that the Emperor, in his desperate anxiety to convince the Pope, had a long list of forged signatures of non-existent bishops appended to this document. On September 1 of the same year Michael himself and his son Andronikos signed and sealed yet another declaration of submission to Rome, and the papal legates returned to Italy with these two pieces of documentary evidence.[11]

Pope Nicholas was far from satisfied, and in the meantime Charles of Anjou, with the connivance of the Despot of Epiros, had been quietly shipping great quantities of troops and supplies over the Adriatic to Albania. In August 1279 Charles had appointed as commander-in-chief of all his territories in Albania and Epiros a Burgundian knight, Hugues le Rousseau de Sully. He was reputed to be a giant of a man with flaming red hair and tireless energy. Throughout 1279 and 1280 he supervised the reception of boatloads of soldiers, arms, money, horses and siege-engines sent across from Italy in preparation for the great offensive. The objective was to be first Thessalonica and then Constantinople. In August 1280 Pope Nicholas died and Charles was given a free hand. It was to be six months before the contending Italian and French parties in the college of cardinals elected a successor. But by that time the offensive in the Balkans had begun.

In the autumn of 1280 Hugues de Sully led his army of about 8000 men inland from Durazzo to lay siege to the fortress of Berat, the gateway to the road through Macedonia. The Byzantine commander of Berat at once sent word to Constantinople to announce that the storm had broken. Reinforcements must be rushed westwards. It was a moment of crisis for the restored Byzantine Empire. If the western defences collapsed the flood gates would be open. Michael VIII rose to the occasion and sent an army post-haste to hold the road and relieve the siege of Berat. It was led by two of his most experienced generals, the Grand Domestic Michael Tarchaniotes and the Grand Stratopedarches John Synadenos. With them went Michael Doukas, a younger brother of Nikephoros of Epiros and John of Thessaly, who had recently defected to the imperial side and married a daughter of Michael VIII. His experience of war was limited, but he knew the terrain and might be in a position to prevent his brothers collaborating with the enemy. Before the army left the capital the Patriarch and his bishops blessed the troops, and prayers were offered for the safety of the Empire.

The siege of Berat continued through the winter of 1280. Tarchaniotes and his army came to its relief in the spring of 1281. They contrived to smuggle food in to the starving inhabitants by loading it on to rafts and floating them down the river by night. The Byzantine generals hoped if possible to avoid an open battle, but the impetuous Sully longed for a fight. He decided to spy out the land for himself and rode towards the Byzantine camp with a small bodyguard. Some of the Turkish mercenaries in the imperial army sprang out from an ambush, shot his horse and captured him. At the news that their commander was taken, the Angevin army turned and fled in panic, with the Byzantine troops in hot pursuit. Tarchaniotes and his men rounded up most of Sully's generals and collected a vast amount of booty, before chasing the remnants of the great expedition as far as the Adriatic coast.

The prisoners were taken to Constantinople to be led in triumph through the streets. The Emperor watched the procession from a hill near the palace, where he could see and be seen by all. The sight of the huge figure of Hugues de Sully bound in chains roused the people to a frenzy of excitement and rage. But the triumph was also an occasion of jubilation. For the almost effortless victory at Berat in 1281 restored Byzantine morale and confidence. It proved that when it came to a direct encounter the imperial army was still master of the situation. Doubtless there were those who felt that the victory also demonstrated the futility of all the Emperor's concessions to the Papacy. But the Emperor himself characteristically regarded it as yet further evidence of divine favour to his cause, and to commemorate it he had scenes of the battle painted on the walls of the Blachernai palace along with pictures of other victories granted to him by God.[12]

Important as it was the victory at Berat was by no means the end of the danger to Byzantium presented by Charles of Anjou. It prompted him to reconsider his tactics and to plan a second attempt by a different route; but his objective remained the same, and his chances of achieving it soon began to seem greater than ever before. In February 1281 Charles had contrived to secure the election of a French pope, Martin IV, who could be relied upon to identify the interests of the church with the interests of the house of Anjou. Pope Martin conveniently reverted to the view that the Greeks could only be cured of their religious errors by force, and he announced that Charles of Anjou was the man to lead a crusade for that purpose. The defeat of Sully in Albania, on the other hand, convinced Charles that his second attempt on Constantinople must be made by sea and not overland. His own navy was not adequate. But Venice might now be induced to lend him her help. The Venetians were not displeased by the collapse of Charles's venture in Albania, which had seemed to threaten their own interests in the Adriatic. Their trade agreement with Byzantium, last signed in 1277, expired in March 1279. It had brought them little profit, and they were envious of the privileged position of the

71

Genoese who had settled so firmly in Galata. Venice required little persuasion now to join forces with Charles of Anjou in an assault on Constantinople.

So it came about that Charles was able to satisfy the material as well as the spiritual requirements for a second and grander attack on Byzantium. On 3 July 1281, in the city of Orvieto which Pope Martin IV had chosen for his residence, Charles signed a treaty with Venice. A third party to the treaty was Charles's son-in-law, Philip of Courtenay, titular Latin Emperor of Constantinople. The object of the alliance was nothing less than the restoration of Philip to the throne once occupied by his father Baldwin. The Venetians were promised rich rewards for providing at least 40 warships and troop-carriers to transport some 8,000 men and horses to Constantinople. The date of the expedition was fixed at not later than April 1283. While Venice supplied the ships, Pope Martin supplied the moral sanction to convert the campaign into what was now described as a crusade for the glory of the faith, the mending of the schism, and the recovery of the Empire usurped from the Latins by Michael Palaiologos. A few weeks after the signing of the treaty of Orvieto the Pope excommunicated Michael, and so undid at one stroke all the work of the Council of Lyons and all Michael's efforts of the previous 20 years to avert a repetition of the Fourth Crusade. The union of the Churches was no more. Two Greek bishops whom Michael had sent to the new Pope were rudely treated and dismissed with his anathema of their emperor ringing in their ears. The Byzantine Emperor was no longer to be considered in any sense a Catholic prince. The Pope re-affirmed his excommunication in November 1282, and went so far as to declare him deposed from his throne unless he repented.

For his final assault Charles of Anjou seemed to have united not only Venice and the Papacy, but also almost all the Balkan powers against Byzantium. Nikephoros of Epiros, though probably not a direct party to the treaty of Orvieto, concluded a new treaty of his own with Charles, the Latin Emperor, and the Doge of Venice in September 1281. John of Thessaly was in sympathy if not in alliance with Charles, while in the south of Greece, the Morea had passed under the personal rule of Charles himself upon the death of William of Villehardouin in 1278. But further afield, the rulers of Bulgaria and Serbia, sensing the drift of the political tide, were quick to enlist on what looked like the winning side. In Bulgaria, George Terter, who was proclaimed Emperor by the nobility in 1280, declared himself to be the ally of Charles in 1281. In Serbia, Stephen Milutin or Uroš II, who came to the throne in 1282, invaded Byzantine Macedonia and captured the town of Skoplje. He too declared his support for Charles. It is no wonder that contemporaries should have thought the King of Sicily was about to make himself monarch of the world and to unite east and west under his sway.[13]

The situation of the Byzantine Empire was indeed even more critical than it had been in 1280. Michael VIII's western policy seemed to have failed, and there were ominous developments in his eastern provinces that seemed to portend catastrophe in Asia Minor at the same time. When the news of his excommunication by Pope Martin reached him, the harassed Emperor was not in his capital but at Brusa in Asia Minor, desperately striving to fortify his eastern frontier, which had been penetrated by the Turks. As in so many crises of the Empire, Constantinople was beset by enemies on two sides at once. It was the kind of emergency in which previous emperors had sometimes distinguished themselves. Michael VIII was no exception. But the weapons that he employed were those of diplomacy not of war. He induced the Mamluk Sultan of Egypt, with whom he had often exchanged embassies, to lend him ships for the defence of Constantinople. The Tartars of the Golden Horde in South Russia, whose khan Nogaj had married a daughter of Michael VIII, kept a watchful eye on the movement of the Bulgars. While the king of Hungary, whose daughter Anne had married the Byzantine heir-presumptive Andronikos, was prevented from joining the Serbs in their alliance with Charles of Anjou.

But there were still other allies whom Michael could employ to counterbalance the coalition built up by Charles. There were the Genoese, eager to protect their interests in Galata and the Byzantine market from Venetian intervention. But further west than Genoa there was one ruler who was known to have personal reasons for detesting Charles of Anjou. King Peter III of Aragon was a son-in-law of the late Manfred of Sicily, whom Charles had dispossessed. He had a fleet which he would have dearly loved to use for an invasion of Sicily. He had the services of a number of refugees from Angevin rule in Sicily, among them his trusted secretary and chancellor, John of Procida. Peter of Aragon needed little encouragement to stab Charles of Anjou in the back. Lastly there were the inhabitants of Sicily. Taxed to the hilt to pay for Charles's imperialist schemes, the Sicilians were in a mood to rebel against their French overlords. The King of Aragon was ready to help them. The Byzantine Emperor had the means to under-

73

write a revolt in Sicily and an invasion of the island by the Aragonese.[14]

Charles had agreed at Orvieto to launch his crusade against Constantinople by 1283. By the beginning of 1282 his preparations were far advanced. But when he was at the height of his glory, on 30 March 1282, the citizens of Palermo broke out in rebellion and massacred all the French in the city. The rebellion was ignited by an incident outside the Church of the Holy Spirit at Palermo when the people were gathering for the evening service; and from this it acquired the name of the Sicilian Vespers. It spread like wild-fire throughout the island, as though by pre-arranged signals. The great fleet which Charles had assembled at Messina was completely destroyed. In August, Peter of Aragon arrived in Sicily at the head of his own fleet. The French were driven out. Charles's empire and his dream were shattered, and Pope Martin IV, who had been deeply involved in trying to make that dream come true, solaced himself by preaching a crusade against the Aragonese. But when the dust began to settle, one monarch was seen to be set more securely than ever on his throne. Michael VIII had emerged triumphant at the end in the long battle of wits between Latins and Greeks.[15]

Shortly after the event Michael was to boast that he had played no small part in promoting the Sicilian Vespers. In his autobiography he writes: 'Should I dare to claim that God brought (the Sicilians) their freedom and that he did it through me, I should only be telling the truth.'[16] This claim can hardly be without foundation, difficult though it now is to find the facts that would support it. The nature and extent of Michael's implication in the Sicilian Vespers has for long been a matter for dispute among historians. Documentary and other evidence certainly exists for negotiations between Byzantium and Aragon between 1280 and 1282. The only contemporary Byzantine historian, George Pachymeres, omits to mention them. But Nikephoros Gregoras, writing in the fourteenth century, preserves at least a garbled memory of the way in which Michael VIII incited the King of Aragon to war against Charles of Anjou. It was a diplomatic achievement, according to Gregoras, which gave the Emperor more pride and satisfaction than any of his other successes, for it had the effect of diverting the Angevin fleet to a domestic conflict.[17] The part played by John of Procida, secretary to King Peter of Aragon, as a ubiquitous emissary between Constantinople, Sicily, Aragon and the Papacy, seems to have been inflated by legend. But it is certain that Byzantine agents were active at the court of Aragon and that they were empowered to subsidize the cost of an invasion of Sicily by King Peter. The Italian chronicler Sanudo has it that Michael VIII promised to underwrite the expedition to the cost of 60,000 *hyperpyra* a year. The Genoese lord of Phokaia, Benedetto Zaccaria, Michael VIII's vassal, is said by another contemporary source to have negotiated the agreement between Michael and Peter III after a sum of money had been sent from Constantinople to Aragon.[18]

That Byzantine gold changed hands is clear enough. It helped to persuade Peter of Aragon that the moment had come to go to war with Charles of Anjou. Michael VIII was so lavish with his subsidies that he had to devalue the Byzantine gold coinage for a second time in 1282. How much gold was infiltrated into Sicily to help the inhabitants to organize their conspiracy is another question, and one which cannot now be answered. An element of mystery will perhaps always obscure the facts of Michael's dealings with Aragon and more especially with Sicily before the Sicilian Vespers. For Byzantine diplomacy was still the most efficient in the world precisely because it worked in conditions of secrecy. The Sicilians might well have rebelled against the French in any case. The Aragonese might well have invaded the island in due course. But to the Byzantine Emperor, faced with an overwhelming invasion in 1283, the timing of these events was all-important. His boast to have been God's agent in the liberation of the Sicilians may be exaggerated, but the timing of the Sicilian Vespers seems to be further proof of the Emperor Michael's undoubted talent for influencing God to act in the manner and at the moment when divine intervention was most required. In this, as in other respects, Michael could lay a modest claim to being the agent and the instrument of providence. For, as Gregoras was later to observe, 'the Empire of the Romans would easily have succumbed to Charles King of Italy had not such an Emperor been then in charge of its affairs'.[19]

The humiliation of Charles of Anjou and the Papacy was the climax of Michael VIII's diplomacy. A few months later he was dead. But even before his death it was becoming clear that the effort to outwit the western powers had given rise to almost intolerable tensions within the Empire and overtaxed its limited resources. Far from being united against the common enemy, the Byzantines had become more than ever divided among themselves. The separatist states in Greece and Trebizond had gained rather than lost in power and prestige and their rulers continued to resist all attempts to reincorporate them in the Empire. The Balkan kingdoms of Serbia and Bulgaria had failed to respond to the diplomatic and military treatment of Michael VIII.

75

Some territorial gains had been made in the Morea after the death of William of Villehardouin in 1278. But the sensational victories of Licario over the Italians in the Aegean islands had proved to be ephemeral, and the Emperor had had to give up his hope of making the Aegean Sea a Byzantine lake. It was true that Constantinople had been saved from a determined enemy, and so long as the city remained in Byzantine hands there was always the hope that the rest of the Empire would eventually fall into place. For the myth of its immortality was still strong in the thirteenth century. But the most disruptive factor in the capital as in the provinces of the Empire was the disloyalty and treachery among its inhabitants, of which the Emperor complained; and for that he had only himself to blame. For many of his subjects had a deep sense that the real traitor in their midst was the Emperor Michael himself.

NOTES

1 Pachymeres, I, 307-9; Gregoras, 109-11. On the date of the death of the Despot Michael II, see B. Ferjančić, in *Zbornik Radova*, IX (1966), 29-32.

2 Geanakoplos, *Emperor Michael*, 235-7, 279-85, 295-9; Runciman, *Sicilian Vespers*, 176-8; Longnon, *L'empire latin*, 242-5.

3 Geanakoplos, 210-13.

4 Geanakoplos, 206-9.

5 Geanakoplos, 213-16, 300-4.

6 Geanakoplos, 285-94, 305-9; Roberg, *Die Union*, 170f., 196f.

7 See D. M. Nicol, 'The Byzantine reaction to the Second Council of Lyons, 1274', in *Studies in Church History*, VII (Cambridge, 1971), 113-46 (especially 129f.), and references there cited.

8 Geanakoplos, 231, 279-80, 328.

9 Geanakoplos, 309-17.

10 R.-J. Loenertz, 'Mémoire d'Ogier, protonotaire, pour Marco et Marchetto nonces de Michel VIII Paléologue auprès du Pape Nicholas III', *OCP*, XXXI (1965), 374-408; D. M. Nicol, 'The Greeks and the Union of the Churches. The Report of Ogerius, Protonotarius of Michael VIII Palaiologos', *Proceedings of the Royal Irish Academy*, 63, Sect. C, 1 (1962), 1-16.

11 Geanakoplos, 322-5; Nicol, 'The Byzantine reaction . . .', 131-2.

12 Geanakoplos, 329-34; Runciman, *Sicilian Vespers*, 195-6; Longnon, *L'empire latin*, 258-9. The battle of Berat is described at length by

Pachymeres, I, 515-19; cf. Gregoras, 146-8, and the eye-witness account of the triumph in one of the letters of Maximos Planoudes, *Epistulae*, ed. M. Treu (Breslau, 1890), no. CXIII, 151-2.

13 Geanakoplos, 335-44, 363-4; Runciman, *Sicilian Vespers*, 194-5; Roberg, *Die Union*, 214f.; Ostrogorsky, *History*, 463-4.

14 Geanakoplos, 344-58; Runciman, 201f.

15 Geanakoplos, 364-7; Runciman, 214f.

16 'Imperatoris Michaelis Palaeologi De Vita Sua', ed. H. Grégoire, *B*, XXIX-XXX (1959-60), 461, 462.

17 Gregoras, 146.

18 Marino Sanudo Torsello, *Istoria del Regno di Romania*, ed. C. Hopf, *Chroniques gréco-romanes* (Berlin, 1873), 133; cf. Geanakoplos, 347.

19 Gregoras, 144.

Five

The Byzantine Dilemma in the Thirteenth Century

In the tenth century it had been an article of faith among the Byzantines that their empire, the Roman Empire, was a divinely-ordained institution destined to endure until the Second Coming. God might for a time permit other kings and princes to emerge from the wreckage of the Empire in western Europe, but in due course their dominions would inevitably be reintegrated into the imperial structure. They might call themselves kings. They could never legally call themselves emperors. For there was but one emperor and he reigned in Constantinople, the capital of the Christian world. Pending the process of reintegration, the kings and princes of the 'nations' or the 'gentiles', as the Byzantines were pleased to call those outside the charmed circle of their society, could be given honorary status in the imperial hierarchy. The most illustrious and successful, such as Charlemagne, might be granted the dignity of 'spiritual brothers' of the emperor. Lesser rulers were designated as his 'sons' or 'nephews'. But the paterfamilias, the head of the Christian family or *oikoumene*, was the emperor in Constantinople.[1]

The emperor was chosen by God, crowned by God, and guarded by God. The fact of his election by the senate, the army, the people, and the church at once translated him, whatever his social origins, to a higher order of being. Hereditary succession to the throne was a custom or a convenience in Byzantium, but not an inviolable principle. Emperors, particularly in the later period, would take pains to nominate their sons as co-emperors, for the rule of a dynasty made for stability and continuity. But in theory the road to the throne was a *carrière ouverte aux talents*, as Basil I, the palace stable boy who murdered his way to the throne in 867, had demonstrated. Once elected, however, the emperor became the regent of God on earth. As early as the fourth century, in the days of Constantine the Great, Christian apologists had formulated the theory that the Christian Roman Emperor was the earthly image of the Logos of God, and that the empire over which he reigned was the earthly reflexion of the

Kingdom of Heaven. Just as there was only one God, so there was only one Basileus or Emperor, through whom God spoke and acted for the good of all Christians. And just as the Kingdom of Heaven was eternal, so also was the Christian Empire which was its image. The conceit was developed as the years went on. Even the loss of the western provinces in the fifth century, which seemed to western Christians like St Augustine to show that all earthly institutions were transient when compared to the City of God, could be explained away by Byzantine apologists. For their empire survived and flourished. It was argued that this must be so, since the birth of the Roman Empire had coincided in time with the birth of Christ himself; the Empire therefore participated in the majesty and immortality of Christ.[2]

In the tenth century this myth bore some relation to the reality. Constantinople was manifestly the greatest city in the world, and all those gentiles or barbarians who had challenged the might of the Empire, Persians, Arabs, Slavs or Bulgars, had been beaten back. The claims of the Holy Roman Emperors in Germany were regarded by the true emperors in Byzantium with angry contempt or amused disdain. The reintegration of the western provinces of the old Roman Empire was still very much in the minds of the emperors. Justinian had shown the way in the sixth century. Basil II was preparing the reconquest of Sicily and Italy at the moment of his death in 1025. In the thirteenth century, however, and especially after the experience of the Fourth Crusade, an even greater act of faith was needed to believe that the Byzantine Empire was still the mirror image of the heavenly kingdom. So many concessions had been made over the years. So many shocks had been inflicted on Byzantine sensibilities. The existence of other kingdoms and even empires had been perforce acknowledged, not merely in western Europe, but even in the Slav lands of Serbia and Bulgaria which had always been within the Byzantine orbit. Even the existence of the Papacy as an independent institution exercising sovereignty over the whole of the Latin Church had been tacitly, if not overtly, recognized.[3]

The Byzantines had a face-saving device for dealing with small discrepancies between the real and the ideal. When it became necessary, for diplomatic reasons, to make some minor concession in political or ecclesiastical matters, they would appeal to the principle of *oikonomia* or economy. When Michael VIII was trying to persuade his bishops that union with the Church of Rome was vital to the security of the Empire, he begged them to regard it as a case for economy or compromise. He reminded them of the many occasions in the past when the fathers of the church had 'economized' over small points so that greater good might occur. He even suggested that the Incarnation of God in the person of Christ was a notable example of economy on a divine scale.[4] The Byzantines were therefore quite capable of making minor adjustments to their outlook. But in the thirteenth century some of them felt that the process of adjustment to a changing world had gone far enough. They were alarmed at the extent to which their inherited ideals were being debased by the accumulation of compromises that they were asked to make. In the old days an emperor such as Nikephoros Phokas had exploded in anger when an envoy from the backwoods of Germany had addressed him as 'Emperor of the Greeks' instead of Emperor of the Romans. Michael VIII, on the other hand, made no protest when the popes addressed him as Emperor of the Greeks, or worse still 'Emperor of Constantinople'. In the old days no emperor would have contemplated marrying any of his relatives to a barbarian or an infidel. But Michael VIII gave one of his daughters to the Ilkhan of the Mongols, and another to the Khan of the Golden Horde. Both daughters were his illegitimate offspring, but it was the thin end of the wedge. The concessions that Michael was prepared to make to the temporal and spiritual rulers of the west qualified him, in the eyes of his more conservative subjects, for the derogatory title of 'Latinophron' or Latin-minded. He had ceased to be a Byzantine in the proper sense, for he had conceded too much of the Byzantine ideal to the demands of the west.

No concessions could be made, of course, to Greeks who claimed the imperial title or indeed any rank not granted to them by the Emperor himself. The rulers of Epiros and of Thessaly were supposed to be bound to the crown by the titles of Despot and *sebastokrator* that the Emperor had been pleased to confer upon them. When they went to war against Byzantium they were considered not as foreign enemies but simply as rebels. Michael VIII made this point crystal clear to the Emperor of Trebizond towards the end of his life. John II Komnenos, who came to the throne as a young man in June 1280, was encouraged to think of himself as Emperor by his own subjects and also by the anti-unionists who had taken refuge in his city. In the last years of his reign Michael VIII sent at least three embassies to John telling him that he might govern his dominions in any way he chose, provided he recognized the fact that there was only one true Emperor in the world. John protested that his imperial title was hereditary and that he had not invented it. But Michael persisted in his purpose of making the rulers of Trebizond acknowledge their dependence on Constantinople; in 1282 John II was finally persuaded to accept the hand of Michael's third daughter Eudokia in marriage. The wedding was in Constantinople in September 1282, and the Emperor of Trebizond meekly divested himself of his imperial trappings and insignia before entering the city and accepted the rank and title of Despot from his father-in-law. The arrangement satisfied Michael VIII if no one else. But John II died in 1285, and his successors had no compunction about styling themselves emperors, though the Byzantine historians, always conscious of protocol, regularly refer to them merely as rulers or tyrants.[5]

The rightful emperors in Constantinople had their own methods of dealing with Greeks or Byzantines who pretended to be their equals in rank. But the same principles could no longer be realistically applied to the western, Latin world. Michael VIII has sometimes been compared with his great predecessor Manuel I Komnenos in the twelfth century. Manuel too was accused of being Latin-minded, not only because he introduced some western ideas and practices into his empire, but also because he seemed dangerously near to recognizing the western powers as equal partners with Byzantium. In this sense both Manuel and Michael might be classed as realists. For in the thirteenth century, if not in the twelfth, it was surely more realistic to negotiate with the rulers of the west on equal terms than to ignore their existence, or talk down to them from Olympian heights. The days when the Byzantines could afford to be complacently superior or aloof were long past. It is true that Michael VIII had Latin-mindedness forced upon him by pressure of events to an even greater extent than Manuel I. But to the conservatives and to the idealists of Byzantium it was all the same. There was a point at which they called a halt to concessions, compromises and re-evaluations of their ideas.

Michael VIII and his policies came under fire from many quarters and for many reasons. Some condemned him as a usurper of the throne; others as a criminal who had blinded the rightful heir. But there had been usurpers before, some of them, like the soldier emperors of the tenth century, among the greatest of all Byzantine rulers. Other emperors had reached their thrones by violence too. But to the more conservative it must have seemed that no emperor before had so greatly betrayed all their ideals. The most conservative element in Byzantine society was the Orthodox Church. The Church was conservative in a dynamic and not a static fashion. Its priests, monks and laymen considered their faith to be worth conserving and worth protecting from the deviations and innovations in belief that had gained

81

currency in other branches of the Christian Church. An emperor who tampered with the Orthodox faith ceased to be the elect of God, and an empire governed by such an emperor was in danger of forfeiting God's special protection. These were extreme views, but the extremists in the Church, or the zealots (as they were called), were always at hand and quick to detect a lapse from Orthodox standards on the part of an Orthodox emperor. And Michael VIII, by forcing union with Rome on his church, had lapsed far. The union itself was objectionable to the zealots on religious grounds. But the methods that the Emperor employed to make it work raised the fundamental question of the nature and extent of imperial authority over the Church. It was a question that the Byzantines usually fought shy of solving by definitions, though it was dear to the minds of the zealots and especially of the monks. The Patriarch Photios had answered it thus in the ninth century: 'As the constitution consists, like man, of parts and members, the greatest and most necessary parts are the Emperor and the Patriarch. Wherefore the peace and felicity of subjects, in body and soul, lies in the agreement and concord of the kingship and the priesthood in all things.' The twelfth-century canonist Theodore Balsamon declared that, while the Emperor should serve his subjects both in soul and in body, the Patriarch's concern was only with the welfare of their souls.[6] The emphasis varied. Lawyers might concede that since the emperor had the last word in the election of a patriarch and gave him his staff of office at his consecration, then it was in the power of an emperor to depose a patriarch. But the grounds for his so doing must be valid, and he should not make a habit of it. Michael VIII deposed three patriarchs in the course of his reign, two because they refused to subscribe to the Union of Lyons. The zealots in the Church had cause to regard Michael as a ruler who put the kingship before the priesthood in all things. The Arsenites, who upheld the principles for which the Patriarch Arsenios had suffered, and the Josephites, who remained loyal to the Orthodox Patriarch Joseph, were united in their hatred of Michael VIII.

But even the more moderate element in the Church, who might wink at the Emperor's Caesaropapism, were appalled at the mounting number of concessions that it became necessary to make to satisfy the popes that the Union of Lyons was being enforced. The Emperor had hoped all along that the matter could be kept to superficialities and settled with the minimum of fuss. Above all, he had hoped to avoid any discussion about the controversial issues of dogma and doctrine that separated the Orthodox from the Catholics. He had begun by assuring his clergy that he would never submit to a demand from any pope that the Orthodox should change the form of their ritual or the wording of their Creed. The popes would be satisfied with mere formal recognition of their primacy and their privileges, but not one jot or tittle would be altered in the Creed. This soon turned out to be a gross underestimate of the popes' demands. And if there was one thing on which zealots and moderates in the Byzantine Church were agreed it was that the form of the Orthodox Creed was untouchable and unchangeable. For the Creed had been determined by the seven œcumenical councils of the church, and, as the Patriarch Joseph had reminded his emperor, any further clarifications or definitions of Orthodoxy in the sense of right belief would necessitate the convening of another œcumenical council, at which all five patriarchs of the whole Church would have to be present. The Second Council of Lyons in 1274 fell far short of these requirements. Part of the Byzantine objection to the Roman form of the Creed was that it had been sanctioned by the fiat of the Pope alone, without reference to his colleagues in the Pentarchy of Patriarchs. The main bone of contention on theological grounds was the Roman inclusion of the word *filioque*, indicating as it does, that the Holy Spirit proceeds not from the Father alone, but from the Father and the Son. Byzantine theologians considered that this addition, or 'innovation' as they termed it, upset the delicate balance between the persons of the Trinity. Any innovation in the Creed was technically heresy, and no innovation was possible in any case on the authority of one bishop alone, however exalted his see. The Latins therefore stood condemned, and no political or military threat to his material welfare would persuade an Orthodox Byzantine to endanger the salvation of his soul by subscribing to a heretical doctrine. This was irrational, and irrelevant to the political situation. But Byzantine man was a religious animal in whom belief, however irrational or irrelevant, usually prevailed over fact.

This is not to say that the Emperor Michael had no supporters in his western policy. There were men, particularly among the educated classes, who saw their way either conscientiously or as time-servers to declare that union with Rome was harmless and necessary in the circumstances. George Akropolites, the Grand Logothete, who had in former times written tracts denouncing the errors of the Latins, came round to accepting union, and indeed went to the Council of Lyons as the Emperor's deputy. Among the clergy there were men like Constantine Meliteniotes, successor to John Bekkos as archivist or *char-tophylax* of St Sophia, and the archdeacon George Metochites, both of whom served as imperial ambassadors to the west. George of Cyprus, later to become Patriarch of Constantinople, was at first a unionist, though people said that his mind had been turned by his upbringing in the French kingdom of Cyprus. John Bekkos himself was a notable convert to the unionist cause. But Bekkos displeased his emperor by labouring the theological issues and by begging him to be more merciful to his opponents, for Michael's persecution of the anti-unionists increased in cruelty and savagery in proportion to the ever more exacting demands of the popes.

George Pachymeres, in his history of the age, has some horrifying tales to tell of the reign of terror in Constantinople. Manuel Holobolos, the public orator of St Sophia, who when still a youth had been mutilated for expressing sympathy with John Laskaris, was flogged with ten others who defied the Emperor. Theodore Mouzalon, a member of the family brought to prominence by Theodore II Laskaris at Nicaea, declined to go on an embassy to the Pope and was submitted to a flogging at the hands of his own brother until he yielded to the Emperor's will.[7] The report to the Pope of the imperial protonotary Ogerius in 1278 confirms many of the facts given by Pachymeres about the persecution of high-ranking members of the Byzantine aristocracy. The brothers Manuel and Isaac Raoul, who were closely related both to the Emperor Michael and to the Empress Theodora, were imprisoned and later blinded for refusing to renounce their faith. Two of the Emperor's nephews, John Cantacuzene and John Palaiologos, were arrested and threatened with the same penalty. Andronikos Palaiologos, a cousin of the Emperor, who had held the high military rank of *protostrator*, died in prison.[8] The monks, however, were the victims of particularly vicious treatment. Their appeal to the ordinary people carried more weight than the reasoned arguments of intellectuals, and they inflamed popular opinion against the Emperor. Many of them were no doubt, as Gregoras scathingly reports, hair-shirted quacks who stirred up the rabble with their nonsense and false prophecies, notably in the Morea, in Thessaly and in Trebizond, where they were out of reach of the Emperor.[9] But in the capital the monks, in the words of Pachymeres, counted the days until they should be rid not of their emperor (for they could no more live without an emperor than a body without a heart), but of their current misfortunes. When forbidden to address the people they secretly circulated pamphlets condemning the Emperor's policy and ridiculing the beliefs and practices of the Roman Church. Those caught with such pamphlets in their possession were put to death if they refused to burn them.

Many of the monks were, in any case, devoted Arsenites and so had prior reasons for their fanatical hatred of the Emperor. One of their leading champions, Meletios of the monastery on Mount Galesios near Ephesos, went so far as to call the Emperor a second Julian the Apostate. Meletios was put in prison and later had his tongue cut out. His monkish colleague Galaktion was blinded. The fortunate ones were those who were merely sent into exile.[10]

Michael VIII was pleased to regard himself as the instrument of providence in saving the Empire from its western enemies. But he did the Empire irreparable damage in the process, and the damage is not to be measured only in economic or strategic terms. Economically his policy of appeasing the western powers and bribing their enemies was ruinous. His military policy, though successful from the short-term point of view, as witnessed by his victory at Berat, had dreadful consequences in Asia Minor and on the eastern frontier. But the upheaval that he created in Byzantine society and the church undermined the general will of the people to co-operate with their government for a true restoration of the Empire. For, to quote Pachymeres, apart from the Emperor and the Patriarch and a few of their close associates, everyone loathed the peace that the Emperor had laboured to bring about, enforced as it was with such outrageous penalties.[11] Even the Patriarch Bekkos had no illusions about the general dislike of the union with the west. Every man, woman and child, he wrote, regarded it as war rather than peace, separation rather than unity.[12] Michael VIII may have been a political realist. It has been argued that his western policy was a 'calculated risk', which would be vindicated by its success and by the salvation of the Empire. But he seems to have been blind to the fact that his people were for the most part less realistic than himself. The myth of the invincibility and immortality of the Empire still clouded their vision of the harsh realities. They saw no future in saving the body of the Empire by selling its soul to appease the Latins. God would still defend his city of Constantinople if its inhabitants remained true to the faith which he had revealed to their fathers. But he would surely abandon it if they abandoned or adulterated their faith. In one sense, therefore, Michael VIII fortified the Byzantine myth by alienating his people still further from the hated gentiles of the west. He drove them too far and too fast in accommodating their traditions to the changing scene of the thirteenth century. They reacted by withdrawing into an even more stubborn isolationism from the rest of the Christian world. Nearly 50 years elapsed after Michael VIII's death before an emperor dared to propose that relationships with the Papacy might be resumed. The tragedy was that, during those years and in the years to follow, it became ever clearer that Byzantium needed the help and co-operation of the western world if it was to survive at all.

This tragedy too was in large measure a consequence of the policies of Michael VIII. Even some of his contemporaries were uneasily aware that the long-term threat to the Empire's existence and survival came from the east and not from western Europe. The Emperor himself seems to have realized as much towards the end of his life. But for most of his reign the danger from the west was more vivid and immediately recognizable. To an emperor born in Nicaea the problems on the eastern frontiers seemed more familiar and more predictable. Michael VIII may perhaps be excused for not foreseeing that the arrival of the Mongols would radically and decisively change the old pattern of war and diplomacy between Byzantines and Seljuqs in Asia Minor. He had made it his business to keep on diplomatic terms with the new as well as the old powers in the east. The Mamluk Sultans of Egypt, who had overthrown the Arab dynasty there in 1250, were left in no doubt of the Byzantine Emperor's interest. Seven embassies passed between Constantinople and the Sultan Baibars in Cairo before 1275, and Michael signed a treaty with his successor Kelaun in 1281. The Seljuq Turks, on the other hand, could be safely ignored: since the loss of Baghdad in 1258 they had become mere vassals of the Mongols. But their overlords, the Ilkhan Hulagu and his son Abaga, had to be treated with respect. Michael VIII had taken care very early in his reign to enter into alliance with Hulagu. In 1265 it was arranged that Hulagu should marry one of the Emperor's illegitimate daughters, Maria. The Ilkhan died before Maria reached his court, but she stayed there and married his son Abaga instead. The Mongols tended to favour the Christian cause as against Islam; and they were the natural enemies of the Muslim Mamluks of Egypt, as well as of the Seljuq Turks, whose Sultans they made and unmade at will. But the Mamluks maintained friendship with the Mongols or Tartars of the Golden Horde in South Russia, who were nearer neighbours of the Byzantine world than the Mongols of Persia and inclined to side with the Bulgars against Constantinople. The Emperor Michael, caught between two fires, eventually found it expedient to negotiate with the Khan of the Golden Horde himself. In 1265, and again about 1268 he was in communication with the 'Sultan of Kipchak' or the Golden Horde, Nogaj; and about 1272, Nogaj married another of Michael's illegitimate daughters, Euphrosyne. Thus, for most of his reign Michael could rely upon the valuable support of the Golden Horde to the north and the Mamluks to the south.[13]

But these alliances, like so much of Michael VIII's diplomacy, were directed towards protecting Byzantium from the west. They cost him the friendship of the eastern Mongols, and so contributed to weakening the Byzantine position in Asia Minor. The emperors in Nicaea had established a well-defined boundary between Byzantine and Turkish territory. So long as the seat of Empire had remained in Asia Minor the balance of power had been in favour of Byzantium, for the Mongol invasion had humbled the Seljuq Turks. But when the capital was moved to Constantinople, and when it became necessary to concentrate the Empire's resources on the west, then the balance of power was upset. Conditions were created which left the eastern frontiers open to attack. The true nature of the new threat from the east was at first barely understood. It was obscured by the fact that the Byzantine province of Asia Minor, the old nucleus of the Empire of Nicaea, was a centre of disaffection and intrigue against the new Emperor in Constantinople. But this in itself was a symptom of the danger, for it reflected a feeling among the inhabitants of Asia Minor that they were being neglected and impoverished by their government. They had a natural inclination to uphold the cause of the disinherited Laskarid family. The Patriarch Arsenios, who had excommunicated Michael VIII, retired to a monastery in Bithynia in north-western Asia Minor, and this district became a rallying point for all the Arsenites and supporters of the Laskarids. It was here that the false Laskaris had appeared in 1261 and stirred up a local rebellion.

It was unfortunate that these demonstrations of unrest and disloyalty to the restored Byzantine government in Constantinople coincided with the first advances of new enemies across the eastern frontier. The Mongol invasion had caused a great upheaval in Asia. Numerous tribes and families of Turks or Turkoman nomads from further east had migrated westwards to escape from the Mongol conquerors. The Seljuq Sultans found these refugees an embarrassment and diverted them into the areas along the Byzantine frontier. When the Seljuq Sultanate succumbed to the Mongols, the new arrivals were left to fend for themselves. They were joined by more bands of refugees who brought their families and their flocks to settle in the no-man's-land between Seljuq and Byzantine territory. Uprooted from their homes and cut off from the controlling authority of the old Sultanate, they found their means of livelihood and their prospect of improvement in making raids over the Byzantine border. The warriors among them were their natural leaders, and they soon began to justify and glorify their deeds by recalling the ancient Muslim traditions of holy war against the infidel Christians. Their enthusiasm was whipped up by dervishes and holy men who had also been driven from their homes further east, and whose fanatical exhortations inspired the new Turkish immigrants with the spirit of the Ghazis or 'warriors for the faith'.[14]

By 1261 they were to be numbered in their thousands. They presented no united front and their military operations were on a small scale. But they made their raids with the zeal of religious fanatics and with the desperation of men for whom there was no chance of retreat. Their future depended on plundering and on the hope of advancing westwards into the fertile valleys and plains nearer the coast of Asia Minor. The ghazi leaders of these scattered tribes directed their attacks at different points along the border that had been established by the emperors of Nicaea. The natural limits of that frontier had for long been the valley of the Sangarios river in the north, which flows down into the Black Sea, and the valley of the Meander river in the south, running down to the Aegean Sea at the ancient city of Miletos. Before 1261 it had been well defended by soldiers native to the soil, whose families farmed their own land, and by the *akritai* or frontier defence troops stationed in the border marches. These troops had vivid memories of the great days when the Emperor John Vatatzes had relied upon them and rewarded them well to protect the Empire in exile. Their loyalties were with his descendants and not with the usurper Michael Palaiologos. They complained that the new government in faraway Constantinople had fallen behind with their pay.

The defence of Byzantine Asia Minor was also affected by the change in the economic and social structure that followed on the transference of government from Nicaea to Constantinople. Michael VIII at first found it politic to favour the interests of the aristocratic families of Nicaea who had helped him to power. Many of the great landlords as well as the great monasteries that flourished in the areas of Bithynia and in the Meander valley were granted, or assumed, immunity from taxation. It is true that, once installed in Constantinople, Michael did not hesitate to remind them of their obligations in the way of military service and taxation on their estates. But the burdens fell most heavily on the peasantry and the smaller proprietors who were struggling to maintain their independence; and the fact that most of the money that they were obliged to contribute to the state was spent on the defence of Constantinople and in the European pro vinces of the Empire did not inspire in them a sense of security or of loyalty. The wealth of the old Empire of Nicaea was thus concentrated in the hands of a few or drained away to Europe. Its army vanished and its system of defences broke down.

The Ghazi warriors of the Turkish tribes massed along the eastern frontier of the Empire therefore found the going much easier than they expected. The Byzantine historian, George Pachymeres, lived through the early stages of the events which were ultimately to bring ruin to the Empire. He describes the mounting disaster in the district of Paphlagonia, east of the Sangarios river, in the years immediately after 1261, and he lays the blame for it on the Emperor Michael VIII. 'For the Emperor', he writes, 'had exhausted the treasury and bankrupted the Empire by his subsidies to the "nations", and he had imposed crushing taxation on the people of these areas to make up the deficiencies. He seems also to have supposed that, by depriving them of the necessities of life, he would weaken their powers of resistance; for he feared that these people were the most prone to rebel against him because of their loyalties to the house of Laskaris and to the Patriarch Arsenios. He appointed to the task of fleecing them by taxation, vile creatures of no distinction ... and the farmers of Paphlagonia and further afield, unable to find the tax in currency, which they were required to do, gave up the hopeless task and went over to the Turks day by day, regarding them as better masters than the Emperor. The trickle of defectors became a flood, and the Turks employed them as guides and allies to lead them the other way and to ravage the land of those who remained loyal to the Emperor, at first by way of raiding parties, but soon as permanent settlers taking over the land. The Emperor meanwhile turned a deaf ear to all appeals for help, and spent all his energies on the west, disregarding what was at his own feet.'[15]

Nikephoros Gregoras describes how piratical bands of Turkish warriors descended upon the Byzantine frontier towns only to find many of them undefended, for the garrison troops had left their posts because their pay from the imperial treasury was in arrears. 'What to begin with seemed a matter of small importance was later seen to be the origin of disaster for the Romans.' For the Turks began to pour into Byzantine territory not only in Paphlagonia but also further south. There were almost continuous skirmishes in the frontier areas, and apparently one encounter on a larger scale which Gregoras takes to mark the beginning of the catastrophe. It resulted in an overwhelming defeat for the Byzantine army. The army was badly led and made up of mercenary troops, for the native soldiers who might have been protecting their own soil had been drafted to Europe to fight the Bulgars and the Greeks of Thessaly and Epiros. 'The barbarians were thus able to occupy the citadels of our frontier towns and to divide up their conquered territory into provinces.'[16]

The general state of insecurity is illustrated by the tale that Pachymeres tells of an event at Nicaea in 1267. A report was spread in the city that the Mongols had encircled, attacked and penetrated the walls in broad daylight. It was nothing but a rumour, but mass hysteria broke out. Some of the citizens leapt off the walls, others hid themselves in the cemeteries, and there was wild panic and confusion until the city guards showed that the alarm was false. The Emperor wrote a letter to the people of Nicaea telling them that it was their duty to show more courage.[17] But their anxieties were understandable. For as the Turks were emboldened to settle in the countryside, communications between the Byzantine cities began to break down. Before long the towns on the Black Sea coast to the east of the Sangarios river, such as Herakleia and Amastris, were isolated. Commerce was no longer possible, agriculture was abandoned, and refugees from the interior of the country swarmed into the coastal cities or fled to Constantinople.

In the southern part of Asia Minor the tale was much the same, though here the flood was held back for a time. The Emperor's brother John Palaiologos, who had commanded the Byzantine army at Pelagonia in 1259, was a soldier of great experience. Since 1261 he had been mainly concerned with the attempt to pacify the separatist rulers of northern Greece. But in 1264 he forced the Despot Michael II to sign a treaty. As soon as he could be spared from that front, the Emperor recalled him from his headquarters at Thessalonica and appointed him to lead an army to the area of the Meander river. Reports had been reaching Constantinople of increasingly devastating Turkish raids into the rich country round the city of Tralles. John Palaiologos was loyal to his brother's cause and eager to cover himself with glory. He also had a personal interest in the defence of Asia Minor since he owned a great deal of property on the mainland and in the islands of Lesbos and Rhodes, which had been granted to him in *pronoia* by the Emperor. The Meander valley was then famous for its numerous large and wealthy monasteries, which also owned much property in the district. John took these establishments under his personal protection. But the Turks had already begun to make themselves at home in some places and it proved impossible to dislodge them. The best that John could do was to strengthen the fortifications of Tralles and the smaller towns on both sides of the Meander valley and to see that the local troops, whose will to resist had been undermined when so many of them were drafted to fight in Europe, were paid in full and encouraged to man the defences. The Turks were evidently impressed by these counter-measures and sent envoys to John offering to release their prisoners and come to terms. For a while therefore the Byzantines regained the initiative in the south of Asia Minor; and so long as John Palaiologos was available to take command the Turks respected the agreement that they had made with him.

But this was only a temporary relief. The Emperor's brother, posted back to northern Greece, resigned his command and died in 1274. There was no general of comparable ability to strike fear into the Turks, and within a year or two the Meander valley also was devastated and depopulated. The monks made their own terms with the conquerors. The farmers who had cultivated the monastic estates went over to the Turks or joined the crowds of refugees making for the coast or the capital. The district of Karia to the south of the river was completely lost. Tralles was destroyed, and the Turks penetrated as far as the sea around Priene and Miletos, and down the valley of the Kayster river further north. The Emperor Michael nourished a pious hope that out of the Union of Lyons there might come a crusade for the liberation of Asia Minor. In 1275 his ambassador to the Pope, George Metochites, proposed a scheme and an itinerary that would lead the crusaders from the west overland through Asia Minor on their way to Syria. He even suggested that the Pope and the Emperor should meet together to work out the details. So long as Gregory X was Pope there was a chance that such a crusade might materialize. But after Gregory's death in 1276 the hope of a combined Byzantine and Latin crusade faded, and the Emperor was left to his own resources.

In 1278 he appointed his son Andronikos to command an army for the liberation and restoration of the stricken provinces in the south of Asia Minor. Andronikos was then about 19 years of age. He had been crowned as co-Emperor with his father in 1272, but he had never before commanded an army. However, he was accompanied by the Grand Domestic Michael Tarchaniotes, who was later to distinguish himself in battle against Hugues de Sully at Berat, and by a number of subordinate officers. The size of their army is not told, but they contrived to drive the Turks out of the Meander valley. Andronikos then conceived the idea of rebuilding the ruins of Tralles and repopulating the city. It was to be renamed Andronikopolis or Palaiologopolis. The Grand Domestic was ordered to proceed with the work, and once the walls had been rebuilt, inhabitants to the number of 36,000 were collected from the surrounding districts. The idea was good, but the new city was poorly supplied with water and provisions. The Turks were never far away. The Byzantine commander at Nyssa higher up the river was defeated and taken prisoner after Andronikos had left, and before long Tralles was in a state of siege. The inhabitants resisted bravely and many died of hunger and thirst before they were compelled to surrender. 20,000 of them were taken away into captivity. Byzantine rule over the south-eastern portion of Asia Minor was now at an end. The Turks swarmed in to settle on the land and in the towns that they had conquered, and the Ghazi warriors began to organize small principalities or emirates. Tralles was incorporated into the dominions of the emir of Menteshe.

It is hard to be certain about the limits of the Turkish conquests before 1282. Such places as the important harbours of Smyrna and Ephesos and the cities of Magnesia and Philadelphia between the Meander and the Hermos rivers seem still to have been in Byzantine control. But whatever happened in the south, the safety of Constantinople itself depended upon holding the frontier in the north-west, where other Turkish tribes were pressing hard on the Byzantine defences at the Sangarios river. The Emperor had given orders for the river bank to be fortified with several castles, for fear that the Turks would cross over and make themselves masters of the province of Bithynia. In 1280 he went to inspect these new defences for himself. But at the other end of his empire the forces of Charles of Anjou were then being massed for the invasion of Albania; when that invasion began Michael VIII had to turn all his attention to holding the western approaches. Not until the summer of 1281, after the victory of his army at Berat, was the Emperor free to collect what troops he could find and hurry back to Bithynia. It was almost the first time in his reign that Michael was able to devote his undivided attention to the eastern problem. It was almost too late. For by then the constant raids of the Turks had reduced the border areas to a desert. The Emperor, who recalled what the district had once been like, was appalled at the desolation. He dedicated himself to the rigours of a hard campaign to drive the Turks back, sacrificing all his luxuries and comforts and living like a soldier. When he had pursued the Turks as far as he could he took measures to fortify and garrison the border on both sides of the Sangarios river before withdrawing to Brusa. It was there, towards the end of 1281, that the news reached him that the Pope had excommunicated him and that a new invasion of the Empire from the west was being planned.

Michael had great hopes of returning to fight what he foretold would be a decisive battle with the Turks. He had plans also for re-establishing and strengthening the frontier in the south. But it was not to be. He seems to have made another tour of the Sangarios frontier in 1282, after the Sicilian Vespers had finally removed the threat of invasion from the west. But he felt obliged to return to Constantinople in September, when it was reported that John Doukas of Thessaly had renounced his treaty and taken up arms again. It seemed particularly galling that, at a time when the Empire was losing ground to the new barbarians in the east, a Greek prince who called himself a Christian should prove so perfidious. Michael did not hesitate to call on the help of his son-in-law, Nogaj, the Khan of the Golden Horde. Nogaj willingly sent him 4000 Tartars to march on Thessaly, and if necessary, exterminate all its male inhabitants. Pachymeres expresses pious horror at this scheme to turn sacrilegious heathens against Christians.[18] But Michael had lost patience with his Greek enemy. He was determined to lead the campaign himself, and he spent the month of October 1282 equipping an army which was to join forces with his Tartar allies in Thrace. The Empress tried to dissuade him from going, for he was exhausted and had complained of feeling unwell. He compromised by telling her that he would go no further than Thrace; and so it turned out. Towards the end of November he travelled to Selymbria on the northern shore of the Sea of Marmora, where he took a boat and sailed through a fearful storm, as far as Raidestos, some 20 miles further along the coast. There he disembarked and rode to a village called Allagē. By then his illness had become much worse. He was able to review the troops sent by Nogaj, but only from his sick bed. He declined rapidly, until on Friday 11 December 1282, he died. The village in which he died lay in or near a place called Pachomios, and it was said that this fulfilled a prophecy made by one of the Emperor's political prisoners whose name was Pachomios, and who had been blinded for his pains.

His son Andronikos was present at his deathbed, and Michael had time to proclaim him as his successor. The dynasty of Palaiologos, which he had founded in such a mixture of crime and glory, would not now die out. For Andronikos already had two sons of his own. Michael was 58 years old at his death and had reigned for the space of 24 years all but 20 days. His passing was mourned by those present when he died, by the Tartars no less than the Greeks. But there were some doubts as to how the news would be received in the capital and in the Empire at large; the question of holding a state funeral was ruled out, for Michael had never formally renounced the Roman faith which he had forced upon his Orthodox subjects. To forestall a scandal Andronikos acted quickly. He ordered that his father's corpse be taken in the dead of night to a deserted spot far from the camp and there be covered with a mound of earth to protect it from wild animals. But no grave was dug, and there was no burial service. These things, says Gregoras, Andronikos did not out of disrespect for his father, for no son was ever more dutiful, but from hatred of his father's deeds.[19] The Emperor who had surrendered to all the demands of the Church of Rome and saved his Empire from its most persistent enemy died excommunicated by the Pope and denied the last rites of the Orthodox Church.

Some years later his remains were placed in a coffin and moved to a safer resting place in a monastery at Selymbria, though it was not suggested that they should be brought to Constantinople. But the Orthodox Church never forgave Michael VIII, and dreadful tales were put about. The flesh of his corpse was said to be incorruptible, a sure sign that a man had died in heresy.[20] No doubt, had he lived longer, Michael would have tried to win the forgiveness and the support of his church. For after the Sicilian Vespers and the humiliation of his Catholic enemies there was no longer any political necessity to maintain even a fiction of unity with the Church of Rome. Was he not in any case excommunicated by the head of that Church? But the dissension and confusion that his policy had created could not, as he saw it, be settled in a moment. His only reaction to the Pope's anathema was to remark bitterly that this was a poor reward for all the unpopularity that he had courted among his subjects on the Pope's behalf; and he forbade any further commemoration of the Pope's name in the liturgy.[21] But when it came to revoking his own confession of the Roman faith he hesitated. For he felt that to go back on his word at that stage would be to cause even greater confusion; and to reinstate the Patriarch Joseph would probably endanger his own position as Emperor because of the influence of the Patriarch's supporters. He therefore postponed his decision until it was too late.

It is quite possible that some spectacular victory on the eastern frontier, or some great act of reparation to the victims of his persecution, might have presented Michael with an occasion to gain the hearts of his people by a public confession of his sins and a renewed declaration of Orthodoxy. For there seems no evidence to support the view that he died, or indeed had ever lived, as a convinced Roman Catholic. But he was not given time to find or to prepare for the occasion, and at the end he died universally misunderstood, officially condemned and not much lamented. Almost as soon as he was gone the attempt was begun to heal the wounds that he had inflicted on the spirit of his people. But from the material point of view the principal sufferers from his policy were without doubt the inhabitants of Asia Minor. Pachymeres was surely justified in accusing Michael of neglecting the Empire's interests in this quarter.[22] But it is hard to see what alternative he had during most of his reign. Some modern historians have accused him of pursuing a deceptive policy of glory.[23] This seems an unfair judgment. It is true that Michael's diplomacy succeeded in putting Constantinople on the map again as far as the western world was concerned, and this may be accounted some glory. But his policy towards the west was defensive rather than aggressive, and it was dictated more by harsh necessity than by ambition. If, as a result, the eastern provinces of his empire were impoverished and on the way to being lost when Michael died, the fault was not entirely his. A large part of the blame must lie with the western powers, temporal and spiritual, whose own ambitions gave the restored Byzantine Empire so little rest and so little peace in which to fulfil its ancient role as protector not just of Constantinople but of all Europe against the might of Asia.

NOTES

1 F. Dölger, 'Die Familie der Könige im Mittelalter', in Dölger, *Byzanz und die europäische Staatenwelt* (Ettal, 1953), 34-69; G. Ostrogorsky, 'The Byzantine Empire and the Hierarchical World Order', *Slavonic and East European Review*, XXXV, 84 (1956), 1-14.

2 N. H. Baynes, 'The Byzantine State', and 'Eusebius and the Christian Empire', in Baynes, *Byzantine Studies and Other Essays* (London, 1955), 47-66, 168-72; W. Ensslin, 'The Government and Administration of the Byzantine Empire', in *CMH*, IV, 2, 1ff.

3 D. M. Nicol, 'The Byzantine view of Western Europe', *Greek, Roman and Byzantine Studies*, VIII (1967), 315-39.

4 Pachymeres, I, 387.

5 Pachymeres, I, 519-24; Gregoras, 148-9. A. Vasiliev, 'Foundation of the Empire of Trebizond', *Speculum*, XI (1936), 32-4.

6 E. Barker, *Social and Political Thought in Byzantium* (Oxford, 1957), 92, 106. Cf. D. J. Geanakoplos, 'Church and State in the Byzantine Empire: A Reconsideration of the Problem of Caesaropapism', in Geanakoplos, *Byzantine East and Latin West* (Oxford, 1966), 55-83.

7 Pachymeres, I, 394, 496.

8 Loenertz, 'Mémoire d'Ogier ...', *OCP*, XXXI (1965), 390; Nicol, 'Report of Ogerius ...', 11-16.

9 Gregoras, I, 127-8.

10 Pachymeres, I, 462, 489-90. Nicol, 'Byzantine reaction ...', 132-5.

11 Pachymeres, I, 505.

12 John Bekkos (Veccus), *De Depositione Sua Orationes*, in *PG*, CXLIII, 952-3.

13 Chapman, *Michel Paléologue*, 146-51; Ostrogorsky, *History*, 458-9.

14 C. Cahen, *Pre-Ottoman Turkey* (London, 1968), 303f.; P. Wittek, *The Rise of the Ottoman Empire* (London, 1938), 26-32.

15 Pachymeres, I, 221-3.

16 Gregoras, 137-42.

17 Pachymeres, I, 244-50. Cf. G. G. Arnakis, 'Byzantium's Anatolian provinces', *Actes du XIIᵉ Congrès International des Etudes byzantines* (Belgrade, 1963), 41, who dates the event to 1264.

18 Pachymeres, I, 525.

19 Gregoras, 150-55.

20 Nicol, 'Byzantine reaction ...', 137-8.

21 Pachymeres, I, 505-6.

22 Pachymeres, I, 223, 311.

23 e.g. S. Vryonis, *Byzantium and Europe* (London, 1967), 167.

Part Two

Byzantium as a Second-Rate Power: The Reign of Andronikos II Palaiologos 1282-1321

Narrative sources: Pachymeres, *De Andronico Palaeologo*, ed. I. Bekker, II (*CSHB*, 1835), 11-652 (for the years 1282 to 1307); Gregoras, *Byzantina Historia*, I (*CSHB*), 158-312 (for the years 1282 to 1321). Modern works: The first modern monograph on the reign of Andronikos II Palaiologos will be that by Angelike E. Laiou, *Constantinople and the Latins. The foreign policy of Andronicus II (1282-1328)*, to be published by the Harvard University Press (Cambridge, Mass, 1972). General surveys of the period are given by: Ostrogorsky, *History*, 478-98; Bréhier, *Vie et Mort*, 335-47; Diehl, *L'Europe orientale*, 221-36.

Six

The Restoration of Orthodoxy

The long reign of Andronikos II Palaiologos saw the Byzantine Empire decline to the status of a second-rate power. Andronikos has been blamed for failing to arrest this process. The charge is not entirely justified. As an emperor he did not possess the character, the ruthlessness or the diplomatic ability of his father. But neither did his administration command the resources that had been available to Michael VIII. Michael had spent them, and he bequeathed to his son an empire that already had many symptoms of decay. Andronikos tried to alleviate those symptoms by cutting down the empire's commitments, in foreign affairs, in commerce and in defence. For this too he has been blamed, since it was a policy that left the empire more and more at the mercy of foreign aid and foreign exploitation. But in principle the intention was good. Above all, Andronikos tried to restore in the Byzantine people a sense of unity and common purpose by healing the wounds inflicted on them by Michael VIII's insensitivity. It was not his fault that the wounds had festered too long and gone too deep.

Andronikos was barely 24 when he became Emperor of the Romans. The fact of his ultimate succession to the throne had not been left in doubt, for he had been co-Emperor with his father since 1272, and his eldest son Michael had already been nominated as the next heir-presumptive. Andronikos had married Anne, a daughter of King Stephen V of Hungary, in 1272. The marriage, arranged for political purposes by his father, was none the less a happy one, and Andronikos was miserable when Anne died in 1281. She left him with two sons, Michael and Constantine. Michael was born in 1277. He was proclaimed co-Emperor when he was only five, but his coronation did not take place until he was 17, in May 1294. Constantine, called Porphyrogenitus, was in due course honoured with the rank and title of Despot. The new Emperor therefore came to his throne with every appearance of entering upon his rightful inheritance and with every hope that his line would be perpetuated. But he well knew that the history of his father's rise to power had discredited the name of Palaiologos in the eyes of many people; and his father's actions, not least as they had affected the Orthodox Church, had led many to hope that the dynasty of Palaiologos would end with the death of its founder. It was therefore vital for Andronikos to assert his authority and state his policy as Emperor without delay.

He was in camp at Selymbria when his father died in December 1282. But he realized that he could not for the moment proceed with the proposed campaign to Thessaly. He must get to Constantinople as soon as possible. However, the 4000 Tartar troops whose services his father had engaged had to be found some alternative employment. Andronikos put them under the command of Michael Glabas Tarchaniotes, whom he raised to the rank of Grand Constable, and sent them off to fight the Serbs who were encroaching on Macedonia. He then wrote to the patriarch to inform him of Michael VIII's death, and a few days later the new Emperor arrived in his capital.

His first official act was to renounce the Union of Lyons and proclaim the restoration of Orthodoxy. The historians of the time, Pachymeres and Gregoras, devote many pages to describing this act and its consequences.[1] But this is not to say that they were obsessed with ecclesiastical affairs or that their historical sense was unbalanced. They recorded what seemed to them and to their audiences to be the most significant aspects of their age. Both were highly educated and intelligent men writing for sophisticated people like themselves. But the affairs of the Church were the affairs of their society, and they saw little distinction between religious and political issues. The new Emperor's solemn repudiation of the enforced union of the Orthodox Church with Rome was, at the time, a matter of no less importance than the inroads of the Turks on the eastern frontier. For the disunity among the Byzantines themselves played into the hands of all their foreign enemies.

Andronikos was under very strong pressure from many quarters to make a public renunciation of the promises that his father had obliged him to make to the Popes. His aunt Eulogia, who had latterly been confined in exile, was most insistent that he should be seen and heard to confess his sins and recant. She even persuaded the widowed Empress Theodora to abandon any hope that her late husband's soul might be saved from damnation. Another of Michael VIII's victims, Theodore Mouzalon, who had now been promoted to the position of Grand Logothete, also strongly advised the young

Emperor to break with the bad past. Andronikos did not require much persuasion. He was a devout Christian with a deep interest in theology. He hesitated only because he was very attached to the Patriarch John Bekkos, whom it would now be necessary to remove from office. For the former Patriarch Joseph, though now elderly and an invalid, would have to be reinstated. But Andronikos could not afford to let his personal feelings override the wish of most of his subjects, and on 26 December 1282, barely a fortnight after Michael VIII's death, John Bekkos was arrested and taken to a monastery in Constantinople. He went quietly and the Emperor's agents were careful to offer no violence to him. A few days later Joseph was carried back to the patriarchate on a stretcher. The streets were thronged with cheering crowds and the church bells were ringing.

The prisoners and the survivors of Michael VIII's reign of terror were now set free and became the heroes of the hour. The monks Meletios and Galaktion, the one rendered dumb, the other blind in the cause of the Orthodox faith, were paraded as martyrs. The zealots and the monks made the most of the occasion. The cathedral of St Sophia was purified with holy water and re-dedicated, as it had been when the Latins left the city in 1261. The monks took it upon themselves to impose various penances on those, both lay and religious, who had favoured union with Rome or worse still taken communion with the Latins and their supporters. A monk called Gennadios denounced them in prophetic tones as violators of the Scriptures. The Patriarch Joseph was too ill to be able to take much part in these cathartic proceedings, but he was prevailed upon to decree that all unionist bishops and priests must abstain from the sacrament for three months. Priests like Constantine Meliteniotes and George Metochites, who had served as envoys to the Pope and attended Mass with him, were unfrocked. The Emperor allowed these things to happen even against his better judgment so that, as Pachymeres puts it, 'the storms of yesterday might be stilled and peace be restored, and that his own conscience, which had been sorely troubled by having to support his father's policy, might be set at rest'.[2]

But the excitement mounted and the storms were not stilled. The Patriarch gave his tacit approval to the idea that prominent unionists should be brought to trial as traitors; and a campaign was whipped up for the prosecution of John Bekkos, not simply as a Latin-minded prelate but also as a usurper of the patriarchal throne. A synod of bishops was convened in Constantinople in January 1283. The

Patriarch was too weak to preside, but the presence of the Patriarch of Alexandria lent it some authority. The Grand Logothete Theodore Mouzalon proposed that all documents attesting the Union of the Churches should be burnt. The bishops then formally charged John Bekkos with heresy, his own arguments in favour of Latin theology being turned against him by his accusers. He refused to come and face the synod on trial until he had an assurance that he would be protected from the mob. Finally he was condemned and told that there was now no place for him, since the lawful patriarch had resumed his office. Bekkos was sent into exile in Brusa. But he was not, as yet, otherwise victimized. The Emperor saw to it that he was made as comfortable as possible in his exile. But the zealots had won the first round.

The Emperor confirmed in writing all the decisions made by the synod. One of them related to his deceased father. Michael VIII was not to be honoured by any memorial or requiem, nor to be given a Christian burial. Andronikos did well to raise no protest, for he was uneasily aware that, having allowed the zealots and the monks to take command of the situation, the question of his own right to the throne was once again very near the surface of some men's minds. For the restoration of Orthodoxy was by no means the end of the story. The various enemies of Michael VIII, who had sunk their differences in a common hatred of his unionist policy, now took up again the positions that they had held before the Council of Lyons. Andronikos found that, by agreeing to the recall of the Patriarch Joseph, he had fallen foul of the Arsenites, and the Arsenites presented a greater danger to his own person. They persisted in their loyalty to the long dead Patriarch Arsenios, who had excommunicated Michael VIII. To them the Patriarch Joseph was anathema, and they observed that it was he who, in 1272, had crowned the Emperor Andronikos. Andronikos, for all his Orthodoxy, stood condemned in the eyes of the Arsenites as the son of the excommunicated usurper, whose coronation was invalid. The Arsenites had been cruelly persecuted by Michael VIII, but they still had some influential leaders, among them Andronikos, Bishop of Sardis, and even some of the Emperor's own relatives, such as John Tarchaniotes. The Emperor went out of his way to be kind to them. He appointed the Bishop of Sardis as his own confessor, and he even granted their clergy the use of a special church in the capital where they could communicate separately.

On 23 March 1283 the Patriarch Joseph died. The Arsenites confidently expected that one of their number would be elected to succeed him. They were disappointed. The last word in the nomination lay with the Emperor, and Andronikos tried to steer a middle course between Josephites and Arsenites by choosing as Patriarch the eminent scholar George of Cyprus. He was a layman, which might be all to the good; and, though he had formerly favoured union with Rome, he had long since changed his theological views. Elaborate precautions were taken to ensure that he was consecrated by a bishop free of the taint of the Latin heresy, and on Palm Sunday, 28 March 1283, he was installed as the Patriarch Gregory II. But the Arsenites felt cheated, and the anti-unionists continued to call for the trial and conviction of those who had betrayed Orthodoxy. The new Patriarch convened another synod in Constantinople, in the church of the Blachernai near the palace. The dowager Empress Theodora was there required to recite a profession of her Orthodox faith, to repudiate her past, and to swear that she would never ask that her late husband Michael should be decently buried. The Patriarchs of Alexandria and Antioch were also called to account and ordered to renounce their unorthodox statements and deeds. The Patriarch of Antioch resigned for fear of reprisals and took refuge in Syria.[3]

These measures went some way towards satisfying the extremists of the Orthodox party. But the Arsenites were far from being appeased, and early in 1284 the Emperor made a determined effort to reconcile them to the church by summoning yet another synod. It was held at Adramyttion on the coast of Asia Minor, a concession to the Arsenites whose following was strong in the region of the old Empire of Nicaea. There was a great gathering of notables of church and state, but the show was stolen by the band of Arsenite monks who had been blinded, mutilated and ill-treated for their convictions by the late Emperor. The synod's deliberations were governed by passion rather than reason, and it proved impossible to come to any decisions. Both sides, however, agreed to accept the judgment of heaven. Documents were prepared setting out the rival cases and they were submitted to trial by fire. Both documents were reduced to ashes. The Arsenites at first conceded that this must be a sign that God was against them. They surrendered and agreed to recognize Gregory of Cyprus as Patriarch. But next day they felt that they had been deceived; and the Patriarch, who had been eavesdropping on their conversations, anathematized all who refused to accept him. The synod at Adramyttion was a costly operation for the Emperor, who provided the transport and paid the expense accounts of the attending bishops. At the end it achieved nothing. But it had its lighter moments. Andronikos of Sardis, who was known to fancy his chances for the Patriarchate, was accused of conspiring against the Emperor and was relegated to the status of a simple monk. One of the other bishops delighted the crowd by hoisting his colleague's mitre off his head with a string and dropping a monk's cowl down in its place. Andronikos threw it off in a rage leaving his head bare, which gave his enemies the joy of shouting that his head was now ready for the Patriarch's crown.[4]

When he got back to Constantinople from Adramyttion, the Emperor made one more gesture to placate the Arsenites. He allowed them to have the body of Arsenios, who had died in exile, disinterred and brought to the capital. It was received with great pomp and ceremony, and a shrine was built for it in the monastery of St Andrew. But the troubles in the church and society persisted. The anti-unionists would not rest until John Bekkos had been made to repent; the Arsenites clamoured for the resignation of the Patriarch Gregory. Bekkos, who rather wanted to have the chance to clear his name at a public hearing, was finally brought to trial again at another synod in the church of the Blachernai in 1285. Also in court were the former archdeacons Constantine Meliteniotes and George Metochites. Bekkos defended his theological position by producing a wealth of citations from the Fathers, and by so doing he showed himself to be wilfully unrepentant. He and his colleagues were convicted of heresy. The Emperor intervened personally to give them the option of making amends, but they remained defiant. And in the end they were removed to a prison on the Gulf of Astakos.

The synod of 1285 did more than any other act of reparation to salve the wounded conscience of the Orthodox Church. The Patriarch drew up for it a *Tomos* or formal condemnation of the heresies of John Bekkos concerning the Procession of the Holy Spirit, which the Emperor and the bishops were asked to sign. It was an unfortunate document, for by trying to define more closely the Orthodox position on the matter, the Patriarch raised yet another storm of protest and dissent. It soon appeared that there was a faction in the church that considered the Patriarch Gregory to be not much less of a heretic than Bekkos. Its spokesmen were the Bishops of Ephesos and Philadelphia, John Chilas and Theoleptos. The controversy that they aroused, however, might be said to have been on a higher plane than that between Josephites and Arsenites. For it was strictly about theology and less about personalities; and Theoleptos of Philadelphia at least was a figure of great integrity and spiritual stature. The argument raged for some years. The Patriarch Gregory retired into a monastery for a while. But the Emperor was bullied into bringing him to trial, and Gregory agreed that he would offer his resignation if he could first be declared innocent of the charge of heresy. In June 1289 a synod was held in the palace in the presence of the Emperor. Theoleptos proclaimed the Patriarch to be innocent except for the one point of theology, and on the next day Gregory resigned. For a few months there was no Patriarch of Constantinople.[5]

The Arsenite schism was more political in nature. The experience of the synod at Adramytion had caused some of the Arsenite leaders to take even more direct action against the Emperor. One of them, John Tarchaniotes, who had been recalled from exile as a token of goodwill, was discovered to have various crown jewels and imperial insignia in his possession. He was charged with conspiracy and arrested. The Emperor hoped to gratify the less violent of the Arsenites by making more concessions. He granted to their leader, a monk from the western provinces called Hyakinthos, the use of the monastery of Mosele in Constantinople. The monastery was to become a centre for the dissemination of Arsenite propaganda.

The most remarkable gesture that Andronikos made to his political enemies was to go and pay his respects to the last surviving member of the imperial family of Nicaea. John IV Laskaris, the first victim of Michael VIII's dynastic ambitions, and still, in the minds of many, the lawful heir to the Byzantine throne, had been languishing in prison in a castle at Dakibyze on the Sea of Marmora since 1261. He was now about 40 and for most of his life had lived in total blindness and total ignorance of the world around him. In 1290, when he was on his way to Asia Minor, the Emperor Andronikos broke his journey to interview John Laskaris. It was a somewhat furtive visit. Andronikos offered him whatever comforts he required, begged his forgiveness for what Michael VIII had done to him, and asked for his recognition as Emperor. The occasion must have been embarrassing for both parties, but especially for Andronikos who, after all, was the beneficiary of his father's crime against John Laskaris. But the propaganda value of the visit was high, and if Andronikos could say that Laskaris had in fact acknowledged him as Emperor then the effort had not been wasted.[6]

But these concessions and gestures of goodwill to his opponents seldom produced the desired effect. During the early years of the reign of Andronikos the Orthodox Church, divided though it was, proved itself to be the dominating influence in the Empire's internal affairs. This was partly the result of a powerful reaction against the Caesaropapism of Michael VIII. All parties in the Church were determined that no emperor should ever again be allowed to go so far. If Andronikos II had been a stronger character and less anxious about his own position he might have taken a firmer line with the Church and prevented its concerns from consuming so much of his own time and causing so much disturbance in the Empire. But Andronikos was too committed to the problem and too devoted to theology to be able to stand aside or direct the spiritual traffic with a firmer hand. And in the perennial debate over the relationship between things spiritual and things temporal, which lay at the root of all the problems, his piety generally inclined him to come down on the side of the Church. It is reported that on one occasion, when a bishop advised him that, as emperor, he could very well over-rule the Patriarch if he so wished. Andronikos replied that no emperor had the right to order the Patriarch about.[7] With such an emperor on the throne the power and influence of the Church naturally increased, and people noted that the life and ceremonial of the court as well took on an even more religious character.

But at the same time the pious Emperor had a less mundane vision of the meaning of Christianity than several of his clergy. In October 1289, four months after Gregory of Cyprus had resigned, he secured the election as Patriarch of Constantinople of a hermit called Athanasios. The monks and zealots might have rejoiced at the appointment to the patriarchate of one of their own number. But Athanasios was a zealot of a different kind. He was above the party politics of the Church. He had passed most of his life in the rarefied atmosphere of monastic communities or hermitages in Asia Minor, Palestine, and Mount Athos. He was a rigorous ascetic devoted to the precepts of primitive monasticism and concerned to reform the morals of Byzantine society by recalling the Church to the ideal of poverty and the people to the practice of Christian charity. Athanasios was a man of no education, and the intellectuals as well as the more worldly monks distrusted him. Pachymeres describes him as a hard and merciless ascetic, torn from his hermit existence to be placed at the head of the Church. Gregoras called him an ignoramus with unwashed feet, for the Patriarch was in the habit of walking the streets of Constantinople in hair shirt and sandals. But Gregoras at least admired his simple and frugal way of life.[8]

For Athanasios all the evils of the age were attributable to the contemporary lapse of Christian morals. The only remedy was repentance and a return to the godly life. The Church must lead the way by reforming itself and setting the example of practical Christianity by sacrificing much of its wealth and prestige. In the prevailing mood of euphoria and material power that the Church and the monasteries were enjoying at the end of the thirteenth century such counsels were not popular. But Athanasios denounced the avarice of priests whose thoughts seemed always to be turned to feathering their own nests. He abolished the permanent synod in Constantinople because it gave bishops the excuse to be absent from their dioceses and to spend their days intriguing in the capital. He lashed out at one bishop for drawing an annual income of 800 *hyperpyra* from church property, and at another for the extent of his real estate in Constantinople itself. He took steps to reform the monasteries and to relieve them of their excess of this world's goods. The proceeds were devoted to feeding the hungry in Constantinople. No one could doubt the high-mindedness of Athanasios, though some hinted that he deliberately courted the favour of the poor. But the agents of his reforms, often fanatical monks, behaved with the minimum of tact and charity.

The Emperor defended and supported these measures, partly no doubt because the hostility that they aroused diverted the minds of the clergy from political issues. But he was also deeply under the Patriarch's spell. A tale was told of how the Patriarch's footstool was stolen one day, and when it was replaced it was found to have a drawing on it of the Emperor as a horse with bit in mouth being goaded along by the Patriarch.[9] For much of this time the Emperor was in any case absent from the capital, seeing to the defence and administration of Asia Minor. Not until June 1293 did he return to Constantinople. He was met by a deputation complaining of the tyranny and injustice of the Patriarch. Athanasios had made himself so unpopular that he was insulted and even stoned in public places and had to ask for a bodyguard to protect himself. In October 1293, four years after his election, he resigned. But he made it plain that he did so under duress; and before leaving he drafted a document anathematizing his calumniators and everyone concerned in his resignation. This document, signed and sealed with his patriarchal bull, he hid under a pigeon's nest in the capital of a column in St Sophia. It was discovered some years later, as he had no doubt hoped, and caused a great sensation.[10]

Athanasios was replaced as patriarch by a monk of less violent and puritanical temperament called Kosmas, who came from Sozopolis on the Black Sea. He was installed as the Patriarch John XII on 1 January 1294. On 21 May of the same year he assisted at the coronation of the Emperor's son Michael IX as co-Emperor. But neither he nor the bishops would consent to the Emperor's proposal, made on this occasion, that anyone convicted of rebellion or conspiracy against the throne should be excommunicated. Only the year before, the Emperor's own brother Constantine had been caught plotting against him. But the Church was not prepared to employ its spiritual weapons to protect the dynasty of Palaiologos from its political enemies. The reform of abuses in the church, however, was allowed to continue, and the Emperor was supported by most of the bishops when he attacked the ancient tradition which permitted candidates for bishoprics to make gifts to their electors. A new law was carried forbidding this practice as being simoniacal.[11]

The coronation of Michael IX came at a time when the Emperor Andronikos was in a mood to divest himself of his worldly cares. Earlier in the same year his chief minister, Theodore Mouzalon, had died. Mouzalon's place in the councils of state was at once filled by one of the most urbane and sophisticated of the Emperor's courtiers, Nikephoros Choumnos. Choumnos had begun his diplomatic career under Michael VIII. Like others of his class, he had trimmed his theological sails to the prevailing wind and quickly joined in condemning the union of the churches which he had formerly defended. He composed a well-turned eulogy of the new Emperor Andronikos II, prudently emphasizing that Andronikos had never been a willing supporter of the Union of Lyons, which had in fact been detested by all classes of Byzantine society.[12] He gained rapid promotion in the civil service and, still better, succeeded in marrying off his daughter to the Despot John, eldest son of the Emperor by his second marriage. These things came later. But in 1294 Nikephoros Choumnos was already in charge of much of the imperial administration and ready to take still more responsibility off the Emperor's shoulders. Pachymeres reports that the Emperor entrusted all affairs of state to Choumnos while devoting more and more of his own time to constant prayer and fasting.[13] The call of the spiritual life was strong for Andronikos, as it was for many Byzantine Emperors. But the unceasing troubles in his church and the mounting disasters in his empire never left him the chance to respond to that call.

The Patriarch John XII fell out with Andronikos over a number of matters, political and ecclesiastical. In July 1302 he affected to resign, and the announcement caused another storm in the Church, from which the Arsenites were quick to make capital. The Emperor was then almost in despair at the news of the recent overwhelming victories of the Turks on the eastern frontiers. But he could always make time to attend to the affairs of the Church. It was his private opinion that order could only be restored by the strong hand of the former Patriarch Athanasios, if he could be induced to return to office. Helped by the followers of Athanasios, the Emperor skilfully built up the image and the reputation of the great patriarch as a man of God. From his monastic cell Athanasios sent a message to the palace predicting the imminent wrath of heaven against the people of Constantinople. That very night, 15 January 1303, there was a minor earthquake; two days later the whole city was shaken to its foundations. The Emperor revealed that he had been forewarned of these disasters by a monk whose name he would not yet disclose. He then assembled a great crowd of the people and clergy and commanded them to follow him in procession to bow down before so great a prophet. The procession made its way on foot to the monastery where Athanasios was living. The gates were flung open, and all at once recognized the mysterious messenger of God and fell on their knees before him, imploring him to return as their patriarch. John XII did not give in without a struggle, but in June 1303 Athanasios was finally led back in triumph to the patriarchate. Some of the hierarchy, mindful of his last term of office, refused to make their peace with him. But in March 1304 the Emperor induced most of them to acquiesce. The Patriarch of Alexandria, however, declined to join them and left Constantinople soon afterwards. He compared the case of Athanasios to that of the tailor's cat that fell into some black dye and so was supposed by the mice to have become a monk and ceased to be carnivorous.[14]

Athanasios indeed had not changed. Relying on the favour and support of the Emperor he re-imposed his ascetic régime on the Church and the monasteries. The opposition was again loud and strong. But the Emperor paid no heed, and he was pleased to point to further instances of the Patriarch's powers of prophecy and supernatural gifts, which were the sure marks of his sanctity. The second term of his patriarchate lasted from 1303 to September 1309. They were years of crisis for the Empire. It is to the credit of Athanasios that he took energetic measures to feed and comfort the homeless.

hungry crowds of refugees who came to Constantinople in growing numbers as the Turks swept westwards in Asia Minor. But, if Pachymeres is to be believed, he became even more ostentatious in his devotions and even more ardent in punishing those who objected or fell short of his high standards. He sat in judgment in his tribunal over laymen as well as clerics. He expropriated the property in Constantinople of his brother patriarchs of Alexandria, Antioch and Jerusalem, until the only patriarch allowed to be commemorated in the liturgy was Athanasios himself. Many of the monks in the city took refuge with the Italian friars across the water in Galata.[15]

In September 1309 Athanasios finally despaired of ever curing the Byzantines of their propensity for sin and retreated into the comfort of his monastic deprivations. His only fault, according to a modern commentator, was to look upon Byzantium as one vast monastery.[16] After some months a successor was found in Niphon, Bishop of Kyzikos, who became Patriarch on 9 May 1310. Niphon was noted for his administrative ability and his good living rather than for his mortifications. But he was an intelligent man of affairs, and he shared his emperor's longing to restore peace to the Church by putting an end to the Arsenite schism. In 1304 Andronikos had assembled the leaders of the Arsenites and implored them to bury the hatchet and not to stir up any more political trouble over spiritual matters. When they continued to create disturbances he ordered that the monastery of Mosele, their headquarters in Constantinople, should be surrounded by armed guards. The atmosphere in the capital, at that time was too tense for the Emperor to make any more concessions or to allow the Arsenites to go on spreading sedition. There were several plots and rumours of plots against the Emperor's life, and the refugees coming over from Asia Minor were not among his most grateful subjects. In the winter of 1305 a conspiracy was revealed in the heart of the city. It was led by one John Drimys, and the conspirators seem to have hatched their plot in the monastery of Mosele. Drimys may in fact have come from Epiros or Thessaly, but he claimed to be a descendant of the Laskarid Emperors of Nicaea pledged to the overthrow of the usurper Palaiologos. The Arsenites were deeply involved in the plot. They were evicted from their monastery and then from the city, and many arrests were made.[17]

This was the last attempt to stage a rebellion on behalf of the Laskarids. As the old centres of their Empire of Nicaea fell ever more rapidly to the Turks their cause lost much of its force. The cause of the Arsenites too, which was so closely linked to that of the Laskarid family, began to lose its appeal. The credit for the final resolution of the Arsenite schism belongs to the Patriarch Niphon. He made it possible for them to come to terms with the rest of the Orthodox Church without losing face or betraying their past. The terms of the settlement were committed to writing. The Emperor issued a chrysobull confirming them, as though a treaty were being signed at the end of a long war. It was composed by his counsellor Nikephoros Choumnos, a past-master at the arts of compromise and tactful diplomacy, and it proclaimed the reunion of the Arsenites and the Orthodox with the minimum of inconvenience or embarrassment to either side. It was agreed, among other matters, that neither Athanasios nor John XII should ever be recalled to the patriarchate. The name of the Patriarch Joseph was to be erased from the diptychs; but the text of the chrysobull included a eulogy of Joseph which suggested that the obliteration of his memory would have brought satisfaction rather than shame to one so modest and unassuming. In September 1310 the Patriarch Niphon celebrated the reunion of the Orthodox Church by publishing an encyclical.[18] There were still isolated fanatics. But the days of the Arsenites as a separate community and a schismatic church were over. It was the end of a conflict that had lasted for almost exactly 50 years.

Patriarchs of Constantinople continued to come and go during the remaining years of the reign of Andronikos II. Niphon was accused of simony and forced to abdicate in April 1314. After a year's vacancy his place was taken by John Glykys, a layman and civil servant of a scholarly turn of mind, who had to retire through ill-health in 1319. The Emperor then appointed an elderly monk called Gerasimos who was little more than a figurehead. He died in 1321 and no successor was elected until November 1323, when another monk, Esaias, became Patriarch.[19] The instability at the head of the Byzantine Church was, however, more apparent than real, and certainly reflected no lessening of ecclesiastical influence in the Empire. The patriarchs after Athanasios were not men of very strong character, but the powers and the jurisdiction of the office that they held were deliberately widened and reinforced by the Emperor Andronikos. In November 1312, while Niphon was Patriarch, Andronikos decreed that the monasteries of Mount Athos should come under the direct authority of the Patriarch of Constantinople. This was a great break with the past; for since the eleventh century Mount Athos had been directly under the jurisdiction of the Emperor. But now the Protos or Primate of all the monastic communities on the Holy Mountain was to be appointed by the Patriarch.[20] The future of the great monasteries in Asia Minor was, by 1312, very uncertain. Many were already in Turkish hands. The monasteries of Athos were consequently of even greater importance than before in the spiritual life of the Empire. Their monks were henceforth to play an increasingly active role in the life and administration of the Church in the fourteenth century.

Andronikos also recognized the need for a reorganization of the bishoprics of the Church to meet the sadly altered circumstances of the age. The official directory of bishops had last been drawn up in the tenth century and had ceased to bear much relationship to the facts. Andronikos prepared a completely revised list in 1299 or 1300. Several bishoprics which had gained in importance due to historical circumstances were now elevated to the status of metropolitan sees. Altogether the list accounted for a hierarchy of 112 metropolitans, of whom 13 were newly created. The parts of the Empire in Asia Minor and in Serbia and Bulgaria which were now politically detached from Constantinople were nevertheless still divided into bishoprics, which were held to be dependent upon the Patriarch of Constantinople. The Orthodox churches in the Caucasus, in Trebizond, and in Russia also still looked to the Patriarch as their spiritual head.[21] Thus, while the Emperor in Constantinople found it increasingly difficult to impose his single authority on his scattered provinces, the œcumenical patriarchs continued to command the respect, if not always the obedience, of most of the Orthodox Christian population of the world.

NOTES

1 Pachymeres, II, 14-66; Gregoras, I, 160-7.

2 Pachymeres, II, 22-3.

3 The text of the Empress Theodora's recantation has been published by, among others, J. Dräseke, in *Zeitschrift für wissenschaftliche Theologie*, XXXIV (1891), 353-4. Cf. Nicol, 'Byzantine reaction ...', 140-1.

4 Pachymeres, II, 60-6.

5 Pachymeres, II, 81-6, 88-102, 108-33.

6 Pachymeres, II, 103-5, 134-8; Gregoras, I, 173-4.

7 Pachymeres, II, 159.

8 Pachymeres, II, 140, 146-52; Gregoras, I, 180-2. See R. Guilland,

'La correspondance inédite d'Athanase, patriarche de Constantinople (1289-1293; 1304-1310)', in Guilland, *Etudes Byzantines* (Paris, 1959), 53-79; N. Banescu, 'Le patriarche Athanase Ier et Andronic II Paléologue —Etat religieux, politique et social de l'empire', *Académie Roumaine, Bulletin de la section historique*, XXIII (1942), 28-56; K. P. Matschke, 'Politik und Kirche im spätbyzantinischen Reich. Athanasios I, Patriarch von Konstantinopel 1289-1293; 1303-1309', *Wissenschaftliche Zeitschrift Universität Leipzig*, XV (1966), 479-86; J. Gill, 'Emperor Andronicus II and Patriarch Athanasius I', *Byzantina*, II (Thessalonike, 1970), 13-19.

9 Gregoras, I, 258-9.

10 Pachymeres, II, 166-78.

11 Pachymeres, II, 184-7, 195-200. The date of the coronation of Michael IX is confirmed by the *Short Chronicle of 1352*, ed. Loenertz, part I, 333, 346-7.

12 Nikephoros Choumnos, *Enkomion of Andronikos II*, ed. J. F. Boissonade, *Anecdota Graeca*, II (Paris, 1830), 1-56.

13 Pachymeres, II, 193-4. On Choumnos, see J. Verpeaux, *Nicéphore Choumnos, homme d'état et humaniste byzantin (ca 1250/1255-1327)* (Paris, 1959).

14 Pachymeres, II, 337-43, 347-77, 379-84, 409-10; Gregoras, I, 215-17.

15 Pachymeres, II, 518-21, 559-61, 579-80, 614-18, 642-50; Gregoras, I, 258-9.

16 Guilland, 'Correspondance inédite d'Athanase . . .', 75.

17 Pachymeres, II, 593. Cf. I. Ševčenko, 'Imprisonment of Manuel Moschopoulos in the year 1305 or 1306', *Speculum*, XXVII (1952), 149, 156.

18 Texts of chrysobull and encyclical in V. Laurent, 'Les grandes crises religieuses à Byzance . . .', *Académie Roumaine, Bulletin de la section historique*, XXVI (1945), 295-311.

19 Gregoras, I, 269-70, 289-92, 319, 360.

20 Ph. Meyer, *Die Haupturkunden für die Geschichte der Athosklöster* (Leipzig, 1894), 190-4. For other editions and commentaries on this document, see Dölger, *Regesten*, IV, no. 2342.

21 H. Gelzer, 'Ungedruckte und ungenügend veröffentlichte Texte der *Notitiae episcopatuum*', *Abhandlungen der Bayerischen Akademie der Wissenschaften*, XXI, Abh. 3 (Munich, 1903), 595f.

Seven

Symptoms and Causes of Decline

Many Byzantines living in the years after 1282 would have said that the revived spirit and influence of the Orthodox Church, torn though it was by divided loyalties, was the most hopeful sign for the future survival and prosperity of the Empire. Pachymeres admits that there were those who believed that, since the church had been restored to peace by the Emperor, God had rendered all the Empire's enemies powerless and ineffectual.[1] A modern historian, diagnosing the symptoms of material decline, would rather feel that the revival of Orthodoxy, at least as it was manifested in the intrigues and jealousies of Josephites and Arsenites, zealots and moderates, was a mixed blessing. He might also feel that the current pre-occupation with religious affairs betrayed a lack of proportion which portended ultimate disaster. For all the time that the Emperor Andronikos was striving to master the problems of the Church, the other domestic and foreign problems of his empire, which were no less a legacy from his father, accumulated until they became almost insoluble.

Andronikos early decided that the resources left to his empire were quite insufficient to maintain and defend the multifarious interests and scattered territories left to him by Michael VIII. This was a sensible decision, but Andronikos carried his economies too far. In later years the Byzantine army was so reduced in numbers that some contemporaries lost confidence in its ability to achieve anything. They contrasted the days when the Emperor had still been able to put sizeable armies into the field, whether in the Balkans or in Asia Minor. That the army should be largely composed of foreign mercenaries was nothing new. On the other hand, Andronikos may be blamed for trying to make do with the cheapest available fighting material, such as refugees from the Venetian occupation of Crete or Alans fleeing from the Tartars; for these were not always the most disciplined or efficient soldiers. He disbanded the navy altogether on the ground that, since the threat of invasion from Italy was now removed, the Empire could depend for its defence by sea on its maritime allies, the Genoese. The very great expense of equipping and manning a fleet could thus be saved for other purposes. The last occasion on which a Byzantine fleet was sent into action was in 1283, when about 80 ships sailed to support an army that had invaded Thessaly.[2]

To dispense with the navy was certainly a short-sighted policy. It played into the hands of the Genoese, who were given leave to defend not so much the Byzantine Empire as their own commercial interests in Constantinople and the Black Sea. It left the Aegean islands, which Michael VIII had once hoped to regain, at the mercy of Italian profiteers and pirates; and it left the crews of the derelict Byzantine warships unemployed. With no hope of alternative employment in the Empire, many of them took service with the Italians or even with the Turks rather than die of hunger. When the Turks reached the coast of Asia Minor and began to build ships of their own, as they did early in the fourteenth century, then the absence of a Byzantine fleet was seen to be disastrous, and the Emperor took emergency measures. Latterly he proposed to maintain a navy of 20 ships and a standing army of cavalry to the number of 3000, 2000 in Europe and 1000 in Asia. But these were token forces when compared with the fleets and armies that Michael VIII had controlled. The once invincible Byzantine army had, in the words of Gregoras, become the laughing stock of the world. This was one of the visible symptoms of the decline of Byzantium after 1282.[3]

Another was the economic distress of the Empire. The Emperor had reduced the defence forces to assist the economy. But the economy seemed to be beyond any ordinary kind of assistance. There was still very great wealth in the Empire, but it was mainly concentrated in the hands of a few, and much of it was in the form of landed estates. The Emperor's own brother Constantine Porphyrogenitus inherited 60,000 *hyperpyra* from his father and boasted of his intention to amass a fortune of nearly double that amount before he died.[4] But as the value of currency continued to decrease the safest form of investment was land. Landlords, both lay and religious, had contrived to evade taxation and to augment their properties during the troubled years of Michael VIII's reign. He had taken action to prevent the process. But he himself had connived at the increase of wealth among his own partisans in the nobility. He had further allowed them to treat such lands or possessions as they had been granted in *pronoia* or by imperial favour as heritable properties. Instead of reverting to the crown on the death of the beneficiary they now passed to his heir, and with them passed as goods and chattels the *paroikoi* or peasants who worked the land. It was still supposed that the *pronoiar* or beneficiary would render military service to the Emperor, but this obligation had become a dead letter by the end of the thirteenth century.[5]

The *pronoia* system had been intended to help in the supply of manpower for the Byzantine army by tying the possession of land or benefices to the rendering of military service. But even by the time of Michael VIII the system had backfired. There was seldom any lack of commanding officers among the aristocratic families, but there was a chronic shortage of native troops, and the only remedy was to hire mercenaries from beyond the frontiers. At the same time the growing feudalization of land tenure deprived the Empire of its principal source of revenue. *Pronoiars* who could prove title to their estates through two or more generations thought that they had a special right to manage their own affairs; and they resented any attempts at interference or expropriation by the central government. Among the largest and richest landowners were the monasteries. They were particularly resentful of any sign of governmental encroachment, and tended to side with the hereditary aristocracy in opposition to any suggestions that the wealth of the Empire might be more evenly distributed. Only the most confident of Byzantine Emperors ever dared to tamper with the property or the revenues of the church. Andronikos II had, for a time, the moral support of the Patriarch Athanasios for doing so. But even his tentative approaches to the problem of church property were bitterly contested and hardly successful.[6]

His attempts to levy taxes from secular landowners were no less resented and no more effective. It was too easy for the landlord to pass on the burden to his *paroikoi* or tenants. Such was the case in 1283, when the Emperor ordered a public levy for the equipment of a fleet to go to Thessaly. It took the form of a tithe on the produce of the estates of the *pronoiars*, to be collected on the spot. But Pachymeres comments that the tax was paid by the *paroikoi* and not by the landlords themselves.[7] Again, in 1296, when a similar tax was imposed on *pronoiars* to pay the Cretan refugees whom the Emperor took into service, it was the peasantry and not the landlords who had to find the money. 'And so', writes Pachymeres, 'the wretched people were oppressed by taxation and could see no end to their continual burdens; though, if they could have fore-

116

seen the later extent of their distress, they would have sacrificed all their livelihood on demand.'[8]

The effects of the Empire's economic depression were also noticeable in the cities of Constantinople and Thessalonica. The tentative raids of the Turkish ghazi warriors in Asia Minor produced the first influx of refugees into the capital and into the cities of Thrace. There was barely enough food to go round; and even if the newcomers found some form of employment they were forced to pay inflated prices for their commodities in a currency that was constantly decreasing in value. By 1304 the ratio of gold to alloy in the Byzantine *hyperpyron*, which in 1282 had stood at 14 to 10, had sunk to one half, or 12 parts gold to 12 parts alloy. Those who had gold hoarded it or put it into landed property. The wealth of some of the great courtiers in Constantinople in the thirteenth and fourteenth centuries was out of all proportion to the poverty of the great mass of the urban population.[9]

One of the causes of the disparity was the almost complete reliance upon Italian shipping and commerce for the import into the cities of the necessities of life. The Venetians had backed the wrong horse in the last years of Michael VIII's reign, leaving the Byzantine field once again clear for Genoa. The Genoese continued to reap the benefits of their settlement at Galata and monopolized the corn and fish markets of the Black Sea, on whose produce Constantinople was dependent. The Emperor's policy of relying on Genoese ships for defence as well as trade enriched them still further. The Venetians, however, managed to work their way back into the Emperor's confidence after a while. In June 1285 the agents of the Doge signed a new trade agreement with him. It was based on the treaty of 1277 and allotted Venetian merchants their own commercial quarter in Constantinople, as well as the privileges that they had enjoyed before. It was designed also to protect the Venetian title to the islands of Negroponte and Crete, as well as the rights of the Venetian landowners in the smaller islands, such as Marco Sanudo in the Duchy of Naxos and Bartolomaeo Ghisi in the islands of Tenos and Mykonos.[10] This confrontation of Genoese and Venetian interests in the Byzantine Empire was bound eventually to lead to war in which Constantinople would be forced to take sides. In 1291 the city of Acre fell to the Mamluk Sultan of Egypt. It was the end of the crusader states in Syria and Palestine. The Venetians were deprived of the last of their valuable markets in that quarter of the world. They began to move in to what had become Genoese waters further north in the Mediterranean.

In the summer of 1296 a series of earthquakes caused much damage in Constantinople and Asia Minor. The column bearing the bronze statue of the Archangel Michael, which Michael VIII had erected to the glory of his patron saint, crashed to the ground. It was taken to be an omen. On 22 July, less than a week after the last of the tremors, 75 Venetian ships sailed up to the Golden Horn and attacked Constantinople and Galata without warning. The Emperor at once placed all Venetian residents in the city under arrest as a precaution. Genoese women and children from across the water were allowed to take refuge behind the city walls. The Venetian sailors set fire to the Genoese warehouses and harbour buildings in Galata, and when imperial troops intervened they sailed over to burn the Greek houses along the shore outside the sea walls. They withdrew only after one of their commanders had been killed by the Genoese.

The Emperor was quick to lodge a formal complaint with Venice, pointing out that the action of her ships had violated the agreement of 1285. He also demanded that the Venetian residents in Constantinople should subscribe 80,000 *hyperpyra* in compensation for the damage done to Genoese property in Galata. But the Genoese were in no mood to wait for the formalities to be completed. In December 1296 they took the law into their own hands and massacred the leading Venetians in the city. The Emperor was unable to stop them. But, for fear that word might get about that he had been an accomplice in the horror, he promptly sent ambassadors to Venice to explain and apologize. The Venetians were not pleased. In the following summer 18 Venetian warships appeared in the Golden Horn. Their captain had orders to demand full compensation for the Venetian property which, it was alleged, the Emperor had allowed and incited the Genoese to destroy in Constantinople. When the Emperor refused to be bullied, the Venetians set fire to the buildings along the shore below the Blachernai palace so that the wind blew the smoke through the palace windows. Then they sailed off to plunder the coasts and islands of the Sea of Marmora. They came back with a number of prisoners whom they strung up from the masts of their ships, until their relatives agreed to pay for the ransom. In this way the Venetians collected far more even than was due to them by way of compensation for the loss of their property. Such, says Gregoras, were the evil effects of disbanding the Byzantine fleet. It was as if the Byzantines had deliberately set about the ruin of their own empire. 'For if they had still possessed a navy the Latins would never have behaved in this presumptuous fashion towards them, nor would the Turks ever have set eyes upon the sands of the sea shore.'[11]

What had begun as a commercial war between Venice and Genoa fought over the body of Constantinople had now developed into a war between Venice and Byzantium. The pattern was to be repeated many times in succeeding years. The Genoese made their own peace with Venice in 1299, leaving the Byzantines to sort out their own affairs with the Venetians. In the same year, while Andronikos was in Thessalonica, Venetian agents approached him to propose a new agreement. But the Emperor still refused to pay them their compensation. Venice then exerted pressure with a show of force. In July 1302 a Venetian fleet of 13 warships and seven pirate ships sailed into the Golden Horn and again set fire to Byzantine property opposite the palace. The Emperor ordered a bridge of merchant ships and cargo vessels to be built across the mouth of the Horn to hem them in. But the pirate ships slipped out by night to the island of Prinkipo. The island was then packed with refugees from the Turks. The Venetians threatened them all with slavery or death unless their emperor came up with a substantial ransom. Andronikos was thus cornered into paying 4000 *hyperpyra*. He then offered to negotiate with the Venetian commander, who protested that he was only carrying out the orders of the Doge. In September 1302 the Emperor signed a new treaty with the Venetians and meekly paid the sum that they demanded. The treaty was for a period of ten years, though it was renewed for a further 12 years in November 1310. Andronikos had held out against their blackmail for as long as he could. But by the autumn of 1302 he could hold out no longer. The Turks had just scored a resounding victory near Nikomedia, only some 50 miles from the capital.[12]

In this way peace was restored between Byzantium and Venice. But it was the Genoese who had come out of it best. To protect their settlement for the future the Genoese built a strong fortification wall around Galata. There was now an Italian fortress city in full view of Constantinople. Its existence and its rights were sanctioned by the Emperor in a number of agreements over the course of the next few years, in 1303, 1304 and 1308.[13] But it was no good pretending that the Genoese in Galata were henceforth in any real sense subject to Byzantine authority, as they had been said to be when Michael VIII first allowed them to settle there in 1267. Some 50 years later a patriotic Byzantine called Alexios Makrembolites wrote a short historical treatise to describe how this 'vile and murderous race' had prospered from the benefactions that the emperors had so generously showered upon them, and how they had then turned and bitten the hand that fed them. In his view their homeland of Genoa would be better described as the fire of Gehenna.[14]

At the same time there were other Genoese who, on their own account, made the most of the absence of a Byzantine navy and of the Empire's preoccupation with the Turks. The brothers Benedetto and Manuele Zaccaria of Genoa, to whom Michael VIII had granted possession of Phokaia near Smyrna, had turned some of their profits to building a new city just to the north-east of the old town. They called it New Phokaia. But in 1304 Benedetto managed to take over control of the nearby island of Chios. His excuse was that the island was inadequately defended by the Byzantines and was in danger of falling into the hands of Turkish pirates. It was a valid plea, for Pachymeres reports that by 1304 almost the entire coastline of Asia Minor was already in Turkish hands, save for the strip of land between Adramyttion and Phokaia.[15] The Emperor Andronikos had to agree to let Zaccaria hold the island as an imperial fief for a period of ten years, when it would revert to the Empire. But in fact the agreement was prolonged at five-yearly intervals after 1314, and the Zaccaria family remained in possession of Chios for another 25 years, until 1329.[16] A similar incident occurred some years later, when Domenico Cattaneo, the son of a Genoese pirate who had seized the cities of Phokaia, laid hold of the island of Lesbos. Another Genoese adventurer, Andrea Murisco, offered his services to the Emperor in 1304. He had only two ships but he made himself a great nuisance to the Venetians as well as the Turks. The Emperor rewarded him with a title. But in 1305 he attacked the island of Tenedos at the entrance to the Hellespont and, with the help of some Genoese ships that happened to be passing, evacuated the inhabitants and took over the island. Later still he is to be found again in the service of the Empire.[17] But the unpredictable behaviour of such allies did not make things easier for the Emperor. For ultimately the only interest that the Italians had in Constantinople and the Byzantine world was self-interest. They were there only for what they could make out of it.

It was an ancient maxim of Byzantine government that diplomacy was preferable to war. Having decided to economize on his army and navy, Andronikos II left himself little option. In 1284, two or three years after the death of his first wife, he married a daughter of the Marquis of Montferrat, William V, and his Spanish wife, Beatrice of

Castile. The Marquis was the claimant to the title of 'King of Thessalonica' which his ancestor had acquired out of the Fourth Crusade. He now relinquished it with the hand of his daughter in marriage to the Byzantine Emperor. Andronikos paid him a large sum of money and guaranteed to maintain a force of 500 soldiers in Lombardy, which he could ill afford to do, and the marriage had consequences which he had cause to regret. Yolanda, or as the Greeks called her, Eirene of Montferrat, was a headstrong and ambitious lady, who eventually quarrelled with her husband and went to settle in the city of Thessalonica. She bore Andronikos three sons who, to her western way of thinking, were each entitled to inherit an appanage or principality within the Empire. But these developments could not be foreseen in 1284. At the time of his marriage Andronikos probably felt that, although the claim of the house of Montferrat to Thessalonica had not been pressed for many years, it might do no harm to try to render it invalid for the future.[18]

There remained, however, the Byzantine claimants in the rest of northern Greece, the Greek rulers of Epiros and Thessaly. The death of the heretical Emperor Michael VIII had deprived them of one of their main pretexts for continuing to defy the government in Constantinople. Nikephoros, the Despot of Epiros, seemed ready enough to come to terms once Orthodoxy had been restored. His wife Anna set out for Constantinople as soon as she heard that her misguided uncle Michael had died. Anna's mother Eulogia, just released from prison at the end of 1282, was the prime mover in persuading her nephew Andronikos II to renounce the Union of Lyons. Anna of Epiros may well have attended the first of the synods of the Orthodox Church in Constantinople in 1283. She was certainly among those present at the synod at Adramyttion in 1284, in company with her mother Eulogia and her sister Theodora Raoulaina.

While she was in Constantinople the Emperor had words with her about the situation in Thessaly. John Doukas, the *sebastokrator* of Thessaly, unlike his brother Nikephoros of Epiros, saw no reason to change his plans because of the change of emperor in Byzantium. He remained defiant and pledged to carry on the fight against Andronikos which he had begun against Michael VIII. Moreover, he had three sons who, he hoped, would continue that fight after his death. Michael, the eldest of them, was already of an age to succeed his father. The Emperor Andronikos therefore suggested to Anna of Epiros while she was in Constantinople that she might care to perform a service for the Empire by kidnapping this troublesome youth and handing him over. Anna agreed to try, and it was in support of this plot that the Emperor sent his army and navy to Thessaly in 1283. The military operation was a failure, for its commander Michael Tarchaniotes, the victor at Berat in 1281, and many of his men died of malaria in the plains of Thessaly. But Anna and her husband Nikephoros carried out their part of the plan and later contrived to capture the young Michael of Thessaly. They sent him to Constantinople to be held there as a hostage for his father's conduct; and there he died in prison many years afterwards.[19]

This underhand piece of diplomacy brought some advantage to the Emperor if not to the Despot of Epiros. For it led to war between Thessaly and Epiros, which helped to relieve the Empire of anxiety in that quarter. The advantage might have been even greater. For Anna of Epiros and her husband proposed to strengthen their relationship with Constantinople by giving their daughter Thamar in marriage to the Emperor's son Michael. The offer would have reunited Epiros to Byzantium and made the future Michael IX effective ruler of Epiros after the death of Nikephoros. But the Patriarch objected to the marriage on canonical grounds and the opportunity was lost. The only outcome of the proposal was that the Emperor, by way of consolation, conferred the rank of Despot upon Thomas, the infant son and heir-presumptive of Nikephoros. But this was not very far-sighted diplomacy, for it could be construed as an encouragement to perpetuate the independence of the Despotate of Epiros from Constantinople.[20]

John of Thessaly died in or before 1289, leaving his dominions to his two younger sons, Constantine Doukas and Theodore Angelos.[21] At the time the rulers of Epiros were in alliance with Byzantium; and for a moment it looked as if the problem of the separatist states of northern Greece was solving itself. On the other hand, the claimants to the inheritance of Charles of Anjou and to the Latin Empire of Constantinople still cherished the hope that the great schemes of Charles might be revived. Charles died in 1285. His son, Charles II, was a prisoner of King Peter of Aragon until 1289. But once released and established as King of Naples, he began to reassemble the pieces of his father's territories in Greece and Albania. He had inherited suzerainty over the French principality in the Morea, which had devolved on Isabelle of Villehardouin, daughter of Prince William. She was the widow of Charles II's brother, Philip of Anjou. But in 1289 she took as her second husband a French knight, Florent of Hainault, whom Charles officially nominated as Prince of Achaia. In 1290 Florent signed a truce with the Byzantine Emperor. It gave peace to the Morea for seven years on the basis of a partition of territory between the Greeks and the French, which relieved the Emperor of anxiety in yet another quarter of his Empire.

But in 1291 Charles appointed Florent as his agent to resume diplomatic relations between the Kingdom of Naples and the Despotate of Epiros. An alliance was proposed, similar in nature to that which had bound Nikephoros to Charles's father. The princess Thamar of Epiros, who had been rejected as a wife for Michael IX, was to marry Charles II's son, Philip. Philip would thus become suzerain of the dominions in Epiros over which his grandfather had once ruled. This alliance represented the triumph of the anti-Byzantine faction in Epiros after the thwarted efforts of Nikephoros and Anna to make a lasting settlement with Constantinople. It reminded the Byzantine Emperor all too strongly of earlier alliances between Epiros and Italy which had nearly brought disaster in the western provinces.[22]

Andronikos at once sent an army to northern Greece under the command of Michael Glabas Tarchaniotes. At the same time a fleet sailed round to the Ambracian Gulf to attack Arta, the capital of the Despotate. The Byzantine historians are strangely silent about this campaign. But it is reported at length by the so-called Chronicles of the Morea; and the exploits of Michael Glabas were later to be celebrated in verse by the court poet of Constantinople, Manuel Philes. The Chronicles tell of a great Byzantine army of 14,000 knights and 30,000 infantry, which can hardly be the truth. But they are surely right in recording that the fleet, of 50 or 60 ships, was entirely Genoese, for the Byzantine navy was no more. The army scored some notable successes in northern Epiros, recovering Ioannina and, still more important, Durazzo on the Adriatic coast. But it was forced to withdraw in 1293, and the Genoese sailors, having plundered the coast near Arta, sailed off back to Constantinople.[23]

The Despot Nikephoros had saved most of Epiros from being forcibly incorporated into the Byzantine Empire. But he could not have done so without the help of his foreign allies. At the very start of the campaign, Florent of Hainault had come to his rescue with auxiliary troops from the Morea; and the Italian Count of Cephalonia, Richard Orsini, had also brought a small force over to the mainland. Both allies had their reward. Richard of Cephalonia was content to take one of the Despot's daughters, Maria, as a bride for his son John Orsini. The marriage was destined to have important consequences for the Despotate of Epiros. Florent of Hainault was given the satisfaction of arranging a more formal and more permanent alliance between his master and Nikephoros. In 1294 Charles II's son Philip was proclaimed Prince of Taranto and overlord of all his father's Greek possessions. His wedding to Thamar, daughter of Nikephoros, took place in Italy in August or September of that year. The Despotate of Epiros was henceforth to be held as a fief of the Kingdom of Naples. On paper it seemed that the Angevins had once again succeeded in building up a coalition of forces on Greek soil dedicated to the conquest of Constantinople.[24]

The appearance became even stronger when, in 1309, Philip divorced Thamar and married Catherine of Valois, great-grand-daughter of the last Latin Emperor of Constantinople and heiress to the title. But it was an illusion, and the Byzantines could see that it was so. In the early years of the fourteenth century the French principality of Achaia was bedevilled by internal squabbles over properties and titles, and the initiative in southern Greece passed more and more into the hands of the Greeks. Andronikos II felt confident enough about the Byzantine recovery there to change the system of government that had existed since 1261. In place of the annually appointed military governors who had defended and administered the Greek section of the Morea, Andronikos nominated imperial deputies or *epitropoi* who were given much wider jurisdiction and longer terms of office.[25]

The newly forged links between Epiros and Italy were also soon seen to be fragile. Nikephoros of Epiros died about 1294, leaving his wife Anna as regent for her son Thomas, who was barely ten years old. The rulers of Thessaly tried to profit from her bereavement by invading her territories, and for several years the strength of the separatist states in northern Greece was spent in warfare against each other. Anna of Epiros repeatedly called on the help of her French allies from the Morea. But when they became too demanding she changed her tactics and turned for support to Constantinople. In 1304 she proposed that her son Thomas should marry Anna Palaiologina, daughter of the co-Emperor Michael IX. Not until 1313 did this marriage take place. But by that time it was becoming clear to every-one that the destiny of northern Greece, and of the Balkan peninsula as a whole, was likely to be controlled not by the Greeks of Epiros and Thessaly, nor by the Angevins, but by the expanding kingdom of Serbia.[26]

The Serbs, like the Bulgars, regarded Constantinople with a mixture of envy and respect. As Orthodox Christians they were the godchildren of Byzantium. Their geographical position laid them open to Latin as well as Greek political and ecclesiastical influences; but their instincts made them look rather to Constantinople than to Rome. Byzantine officials who visited Serbia in the middle of the thirteenth century professed themselves appalled at the backward and barbaric state of the country. But by the end of that century things in Serbia had noticeably improved. Theodore Metochites, who went there as his Emperor's ambassador in 1298, was favourably impressed by the evidence of Byzantine influence and by the luxury of the Serbian court. The rulers of Bulgaria had more than once dreamt of the conquest of Byzantium and its replacement by a new form of Empire in which Constantinople or Tsargrad would become the capital of a community of Slavs and Greeks. It was this dream that had inspired Kalojan and John Asen in the early part of the thirteenth century. But the Second Bulgarian Empire which they had created never fully recovered from the treatment given to it by the Mongols of the Golden Horde in the 1240s. A hundred years later it became the turn of the ruler of Serbia to fancy his chances of taking over where the Bulgars had left off.

The Serbian people had achieved political independence from Byzantium under the rule of Stephen Nemanja and his son Stephen II, the 'first-crowned' king, who died in 1227. But not until the time of Stephen II's third son, Uroš I, did it begin to seem that a great future lay in store for the kingdom of Serbia. The reign of Uroš I, from 1243-76, coincided with the period of disintegration of the Empire set up by his neighbours in Bulgaria, which had dominated the Balkans for a generation. It was during these years that the silver mines of Serbia were first developed. Their resources enabled the Serbian kings to mint acceptable currency, and to pay for the hire of mercenary troops to supplement their armies. Serbia quickly became the richest state in the Balkans and rose to the rank of an international power. Both Uroš I and his successor Dragutin were sought after as valuable allies by Charles of Anjou.

Dragutin's brother Stephen Uroš II Milutin, who displaced him in 1282, took the first steps towards the Serbian conquest of Byzantine Macedonia. The town of Skoplje fell to him in 1282. Skoplje commands the Vardar valley and the route south from Serbia to Thessalonica and northern Greece. Milutin had gone through a form of marriage with a daughter of John Doukas of Thessaly. The alliance of Serbia and Thessaly placed Thessalonica and the Byzantine land route to the Adriatic in the greatest danger. It was doubtless for this reason that Andronikos II diverted the Tartars, whom Michael VIII had summoned to fight John of Thessaly in 1282, to direct their operations against the

Serbs instead. But the Serbian infiltration into northern Macedonia continued, and Milutin's army, in numbers and in efficiency, was more than a match for the Byzantines. In 1297 the Emperor ordered his Grand Constable Michael Glabas Tarchaniotes to take an army north from Thessalonica. Glabas had led the campaign against Nikephoros of Epiros in 1293. He was an able soldier, but he found it hard to bring the Serbs to open battle; he advised the Emperor that, in his opinion, it would be best to cut his losses in Macedonia and work for a diplomatic settlement with the Serbian king. It was a moment when all available troops were needed on the eastern frontiers, and the Emperor accepted his general's advice.[27]

A diplomatic settlement was easier said than achieved, however. Byzantine ambassadors to the Serbian court were kept coming and going. Milutin was well aware that he had the whip hand. But the Emperor knew that a barbarian king who was on the make could hardly resist the offer of a Byzantine princess in marriage. Milutin's married life had so far been somewhat irregular. But it was reported that the only one of his three wives to whom he was legally married had died. Andronikos proposed that his own sister Eudokia, recently widowed of her husband, John II of Trebizond, should become Milutin's lawful wife. Milutin was pleased and flattered. But nothing that Andronikos could do would influence his sister to entertain the prospect of life with a lecherous barbarian in the wilds of Serbia. Andronikos was at a loss. But, having offered Milutin the hand of a Byzantine princess, he could not now risk going back on his word. He therefore suggested that his own daughter Simonis should marry the Serbian king. Simonis, the child of the Emperor's second marriage to Eirene of Montferrat, was only five years old, and Milutin was about 40. But the proposal delighted him, and arrangements were made for the Emperor and the King to meet in Thessalonica. The Patriarch, John XII, was scandalized and raised all manner of objections. But for once Andronikos overruled the will of his church and left it until after the event to settle his account with the Patriarch. He spent Easter of 1299 in Thessalonica. It was the first time that he had visited the second city of his Empire. Milutin arrived from Serbia and handed over some hostages as earnest of his good intentions, and his wedding to little Simonis was then celebrated by Makarios, Archbishop of Ochrida. It had been agreed that she should be brought up with the other children of the Serbian royal family until she came of age to be regarded as a wife. The Emperor entertained Milutin in sumptuous fashion at Thessalonica before sending him home with his new wife, and even granted him a small body of soldiers which, at the time Byzantium could hardly afford to spare.[28]

The dowry that Simonis brought to her husband included all the Byzantine territory in Macedonia that he had already conquered. The southern boundary of the Serbian kingdom now lay just to the north of a line running from Ochrida east to Prilep and Stip. It had been a diplomatic marriage in the best or the worst sense of that term. The Patriarch of Constantinople at first refused to be consoled about it and offered his resignation. In his view it was a squalid and unchristian arrangement. Simonis was far too young, and in addition Milutin was already married and had been having an affair with his sister-in-law, who was a nun. The Emperor, however, interviewed his patriarch as soon as he got back to Constantinople. He explained that the marriage was peculiarly distasteful to him too, for he loved his daughter dearly and hated to give her to a loathsome barbarian when she might have been saved for one of the more respectable monarchs of western Europe. But he did not believe the marriage to be uncanonical, and he had gone through with it as a sacrifice of his own feelings on behalf of the common good and the security of the Empire. The Patriarch was slow to be convinced, but he was finally persuaded to resume his functions in time for the Feast of the Purification on 2 February 1300.[29]

Sacrifices had been made on both sides, for Milutin had had to overcome the objections of his nobles to signing any treaty with Byzantium, since they stood to gain by continuing warfare and conquest. But once a boundary had been fixed Milutin respected it, and until his death in 1321 relationships between Serbia and Constantinople remained friendly and fruitful. Both sides therefore benefited from their sacrifices. Byzantium was relieved of the fear that Thessalonica might fall to the Serbs; and Serbia became the richer by acquiring more of the benefits of Byzantine civilization, manners and art. The resulting assimilation of Byzantine culture by the Serbs helped to fortify the ideal of a Slavo-Byzantine Empire, which came to dominate the mind of Milutin's grandson, Stephen Dušan, later in the fourteenth century.

NOTES

1 Pachymeres, II, 69.

2 Pachymeres, II, 69-71. Hélène Ahrweiler, *Byzance et la Mer* (Paris, 1966), 374f.

3 Gregoras, I, 158, 174, 223, 317.

4 Pachymeres, I, 157.

5 Ostrogorsky, History, 481-3.

6 Zakythinos, Crise monétaire, 53f.

7 Pachymeres, II, 69.

8 Pachymeres, II, 208-9.

9 Pachymeres, II, 493-4. Zakythinos, Crise monétaire, 8-9; Ostrogorsky, 484.

10 Dölger, Regesten, IV, no. 2104.

11 Pachymeres, II, 232-4, 237-44; Gregoras, I, 207-10.

12 Pachymeres, II, 286-7, 322-7. Dölger, Regesten, IV, nos. 2247, 2325. Ostrogorsky, 490-1.

13 Dölger, Regesten, IV, nos. 2256, 2261, 2310.

14 Alexios Makrembolites, Historical Discourse, ed. A. Papadopoulos-Kerameus, Analekta Hierosolymitikes Stachyologias, I (1891), 144.

15 Pachymeres, II, 558.

16 P. Lemerle, L'Emirat d'Aydin. Byzance et l'Occident (Paris, 1957), 50f.

17 Pachymeres, II, 494, 556-7.

18 Pachymeres, II, 87-8, Gregoras, I, 167-8.

19 Pachymeres, II, 59, 67-77.

20 Pachymeres, II, 201-2.

21 D. M. Nicol, Meteora. The Rock Monasteries of Thessaly (London, 1963), 51.

22 Longnon, L'empire latin, 266-9.

23 Chronicle of the Morea, ed. P. P. Kalonaros (Athens, 1940), lines 8782-9235; Livre de la Conqueste de la Princée de l'Amorée. Chronique de Morée, ed. J. Longnon (Paris, 1911), 243-58; Libro de los Fechos et Conquistas del Principado de la Morea, ed. A. Morel-Fatio (Geneva, 1885), 456-68. Manuel Philes, Carmina, ed. E. Miller, II (Paris, 1857), 240-55.

24 Pachymeres, II, 450. Cf. E. Dade, Versuche zur Wiedererrichtung der lateinischen Herrschaft in Konstantinopel (Jena, 1938), 67-71; Longnon, L'empire latin, 269, 272-3; Ostrogorsky, 488.

25 D. A. Zakythinos, Le Despotat grec de Morée, I (Paris, 1932), 68; II (Athens, 1953), 63-4.

26 Longnon, L'empire latin, 283-4, 285-6. Pachymeres, II, 450-1; Gregoras, I, 283; John Cantacuzenus, Historiae, ed. L. Schopen, I (CSHB, 1828), 13.

27 Pachymeres, II, 271-7.
28 Pachymeres, II, 278-86; Gregoras, I, 202-4.
29 Pachymeres, II, 291-8. Cf. Ostrogorsky, 489-90. D. Obolensky, *The Byzantine Commonwealth* (London, 1971), 247-53.

Eight

The Failure to Find a Cure

When one reviews the problems with which the Emperor Andronikos had to contend at the end of the thirteenth century one may feel surprise that he achieved as much as he did. Politically and internally the Empire and the Church were divided into warring factions. There was never enough money, never enough troops. The Italians in Constantinople and the islands, and the Greeks in Epiros and Thessaly, were a constant embarrassment. The Serbs presented the greatest potential danger in Europe since the days of Charles of Anjou. But still Andronikos seemed able to meet, if only just, each emergency as it arose. What was difficult, if not impossible, for him in these circumstances was to formulate an overall policy for the Empire to cover every foreseeable contingency. The Empire seemed to live from crisis to crisis. There was an ideal but no comprehensive plan; there was a great tradition but the future seemed uncertain. A policy of living from day to day might serve in Europe, but it could not be applied in Asia Minor. It is here that Andronikos most signally failed. The experience of the last years of his father's reign might have taught him that it was of first importance to hold the eastern frontiers against the new forces of the Turks. But the lesson was lost on Andronikos.

In the first years of his own reign it may be said that he was too much occupied with other matters, domestic and foreign. But it appears that even by 1282 the Byzantines had still not grasped the real nature of the new problem in Asia. They continued to regard it as yet another temporary crisis which could be dealt with by emergency measures when the time seemed convenient to them. They seem to have ignored the fact that the Turkish tribes were beginning to settle on the soil that they conquered, and that the Greek peasants of the border areas, overburdened by taxation, were often ready enough to change their masters and come to terms with the invaders. The government in Constantinople perhaps preferred not to know that many of the sailors dismissed by the Emperor found alternative employment with the Turkish emirs on the south coast of Asia Minor. Andronikos had had his first taste of war in the Meander valley in 1278. He must have learnt the tactics of the Turks and the danger that they presented. But the Empire that his father left him still seemed to look towards Europe rather than Asia, and its immediate concerns appeared to lie to the west and not to the east of Constantinople.

In 1284 the situation in the north-western part of Asia Minor was still sufficiently secure for the Emperor to be able to convene a synod of his bishops at Adramyttion, at the head of the gulf opposite the island of Lesbos. Less than 20 years later the whole of this area had been overrun by the Turks. The frontier defences that Michael VIII had strengthened were presumably still manned. But Andronikos did not fulfil his father's promise of returning to wage an all-out campaign against the Turks. Indeed there is no record that Andronikos took any decisive action on the eastern frontiers during the first seven years of his reign. In 1290, however, he left Constantinople in charge of his eldest son Michael IX and crossed over to Bithynia. On his way down to Nikomedia at the eastern end of the Sea of Marmora he stopped to visit John Laskaris at Dakibyze. He had sent an army in advance led by his own brother Constantine Porphyrogenitus and the *protostrator* Michael Strategopoulos. They made their headquarters at Nymphaion. The Emperor seems to have stayed there for the best part of three years. He inspected the defences of the vital northern cities of Nicaea, Brusa and Lopadion. But much of his time was taken up with diplomatic affairs, and more especially with the discovery of a plot against him organized by his brother. Strategopoulos was also implicated in the conspiracy, as were many others, both lay and clerical. The ringleaders including Constantine were tried and condemned on the spot and were taken as prisoners to Constantinople when the Emperor returned there at the end of June 1293. Constantine had his own motives for conspiring against his brother. He was never released and died in prison on 5 May 1304. But the local people who had aided and abetted him had done so out of a sense of grievance against the government, which was no doubt exploited by the Arsenites and supporters of the Laskarid cause. The district was ripe either for revolt or for conquest by the Turks.[1]

In the years after 1293 the Emperor tried to reconstitute the *akritai* or frontier defence troops by settling Cretan refugees in military colonies along the border areas. But they too were soon to be infected by the prevailing spirit of discontent. They were answerable to Alexios

Philanthropenos, a son of Michael Tarchaniotes, who had been given command of the region of Nymphaion and Lydia, and to his subordinate Libadarios, whose headquarters were at Neokastra. Philanthropenos was a fine soldier and he scored some unexpected victories over the Turks. He even drove some of them back over the Meander river and advanced into the Turkish emirate of Menteshe in Karia, recapturing the city of Melanoudion. A vast amount of booty was collected. The local Greeks were overjoyed at this first evidence of successful intervention on their behalf, but they attributed it to the general Philanthropenos, and not to the Emperor in Constantinople who had appointed him. The Turks too were impressed, and some of them came over to his side to fight as mercenaries. His soldiers, who saw further prospects of booty, suggested that Philanthropenos should proclaim himself Emperor. The idea was enthusiastically taken up by the people of the district and particularly by the monks, who were evidently still numerous in the area. Philanthropenos hesitated. He even wrote to the Emperor asking to be posted to another command. Andronikos took no notice. In the autumn of 1295 Philanthropenos declared rebellion and was hailed as Emperor by his troops and followers; and, in the words of Pachymeres, 'in the many great monasteries of that part the name of the Emperor was no longer commemorated, but only that of Philanthropenos'.[2]

The revolt did not spread much further. Philanthropenos arrested the Emperor's youngest brother, Theodore Palaiologos, who was at Ephesos. But, though warmly supported by the local people, he was unable to win over all the other Byzantine commanders. His colleague Libadarios at Neokastra remained loyal to the crown. He was the father-in-law of Theodore Palaiologos; and it was he who talked or bribed the Cretan soldiers over to arresting their general. About Christmas 1295 Philanthropenos was blinded, and Libadarios then revealed the whole plot to the Emperor in Constantinople. The affair was smoothed over very efficiently and order was restored. But, as Pachymeres observes, this rebellion was symptomatic of a deeper malaise, and its effects greatly facilitated the subsequent Turkish occupation of the rest of western Asia Minor.[3]

In the following years the defence of the Byzantine frontiers in the east was continually weakened by political intrigues and personal jealousies. In 1298 the Emperor appointed John Tarchaniotes to take command in the southern sector. Tarchaniotes was a known Arsenite and had been in prison on and off for many years. But he came of one of the great military families; he was a soldier of distinction; and he

132

swore to be loyal to the Emperor if given the chance to lead an army against the Turks. The Emperor boldly decided to put the interest of the Empire above the interest of the Church. Tarchaniotes proved to be a great success and so competent that it became possible to increase the strength of his army and even to provide some ships to support it by sea. But the Patriarch never approved of his appointment because of his Arsenite past; and some of his own officers, who objected to a general who was unusually honest in financial affairs, made use of the Patriarch's disapproval to denounce Tarchaniotes to Theoleptos, Bishop of Philadelphia. A charge of treason was trumped up against him and he fled to the Emperor who was then in Thessalonica. His successors in the eastern command were feeble men by comparison. They allowed all his good work to be undone, and they were less scrupulous about seeing that the pay of the mercenary troops did not disappear into the pockets of their officers.[4]

In these circumstances Andronikos was soon at a loss not only for capable commanders but also for soldiers, since his mercenaries, including Turks who had come over, deserted and drifted away when their pay was in arrears. Early in 1302, however, a crowd of Alans streaming down from the Danube as refugees from the Mongols asked for asylum on Byzantine territory. They travelled with their wives and families and numbered between 10,000 and 16,000. The Emperor welcomed them as a providential addition to his armies and at once packed some of them off to join in the defence of the eastern frontiers. They proved to be a mixed blessing. To provide armour and horses for them Andronikos had to impose yet more taxes on his people, and the Alans resented being disciplined by Byzantine officers, whom they thought to be effeminate.[5]

In the spring of 1302 the Emperor sent his son Michael IX to take command in southern Asia Minor. He encamped at Magnesia on the Hermos river. It was his first experience of warfare, and his officers were determined to prevent him from being impetuous. The Turks were consequently encouraged to go in to the attack and hemmed Michael and his army in the region of Magnesia while they inflicted terrible devastation on the surrounding countryside. The Alans, who were unused to this kind of campaign, asked leave to be released from service; but the Greeks who had been fighting with the army, seeing the destruction of their property, had already deserted. Michael therefore begged the Alans to stay on for another three months, and wrote to his father in Constantinople to send more money with which to pay them. The money had to be raised by more taxation, and at the end of their three-month contract the Alans began to desert. Michael IX was left stranded in Magnesia, almost blockaded by thousands of Turkish warriors. Escape seemed the only solution, and the only route left open lay westwards to the coast. He left camp in secret one night. But the remnants of his army, as soon as they heard that their leader had absconded, abandoned their quarters with all their women and children, and marched through the night up to Pergamon. About 100 died on the way, for their march was harassed by the Turks. Their arrival at Pergamon created panic. Refugees crowded towards the coast thinking that the Turks were at their heels. Some made for Adramyttion, others for Lampsakos on the Hellespont; but most tried to get across the water to the European shore, where they arrived destitute and without hope, having left all behind them.

The Alans, who should at least have been holding the rearguard, had already made the crossing to Gallipoli; and once there they refused to lay down their arms. They had to be coerced into surrendering and begging the Emperor's forgiveness.[6] Almost at the same time, in July 1302, the rest of the Alans, who had been sent to help hold the frontier at the Sangarios river in Bithynia, were driven back by the Turks. They were commanded by one of the Mouzalon family, and the total strength of the Byzantine army was not above 2000. The Turks numbered some 5000 and they were led by a ghazi emir to whom Pachymeres, writing only about five years later, gives the name of Atman. This is the first mention in a contemporary source of Othman or Osman, the founder of the Ottoman or Osmanli state. Pachymeres describes how he and his warriors fought and won a great battle against the Byzantines at Bapheus near Nikomedia on 27 July 1302. The Byzantine troops were forced back and the Alans covered their retreat to the safety of the walled city of Nikomedia. But Osman and his Turks swept westwards and ravaged all the country from Nicaea to Brusa, up to the shore of the Sea of Marmora around Kyzikos, and even as far as the Aegean coast at Adramyttion. The fortified cities such as Nikomedia, Nicaea, Brusa and Lopadion were isolated from each other but intact; for the citizens brought all their belongings behind the walls and closed their gates. Nor was this first incursion of the Turks into Bithynia anything like a permanent settlement. But the peasants fled in terror to the coast. Their crops were ruined and their farms destroyed. Those in the coastal cities, secure behind their walls, refused to admit the refugees. Their only hope of salvation was to get across the Hellespont or the Bosporos; and there was to be seen a long line of people and animals threading its way towards the sea in the hope of reaching Constantinople. But even those in the cities were numbed by the extent of the catastrophe and took it as a sign of the wrath of God.[7]

The summer of 1302 brought disaster upon disaster for the Byzantines. One army was defeated at Magnesia, another near Nikomedia. A Venetian fleet lay in the Golden Horn holding the Emperor to ransom. It is no wonder that the Patriarch Athanasios held his audience when he predicted doom. Every day there came news of some fresh horror from Asia Minor. The Emperor clutched at every straw. He sought the help of the Ilkhan of the Mongols of Persia, offering him a daughter in marriage if he would use his influence on the Turks. He made a secret arrangement with a renegade Mongol chieftain called Kuzin Pasha. He was to take command of the district of Nikomedia and come to terms with the Turks by marrying the daughter of one of their emirs. But the plan failed. The situation was too confused and ill-defined for the Emperor to make agreements of his own with the leaders of the Turkish tribes. It was difficult to discover who they were; and it would in any case be an admission of defeat and morally distasteful to try to negotiate with them. This was a case where war was preferable to diplomacy.[8]

After the losses sustained in the summer of 1302 the army had to be reconstituted. To raise the money the Emperor now decreed that the proceeds from all ecclesiastical benefices, including the estates of the monasteries, should be diverted by their owners to military purposes. In this way, it was hoped, they could finance the immediate defence of their own properties. The Patriarch Athanasios, when consulted about this plan, is said to have replied by sending the Emperor an olive branch without comment. But the rest of the monks and clergy would not even give their tacit approval.[9] The plan was never put into practice, though some of the more energetic bishops took steps to protect their own sees. Niphon, Bishop of Kyzikos, who was later to become patriarch, repaired the fortifications of his city and gave shelter to refugees. Theoleptos, Bishop of Philadelphia, whose city was under siege by the Turks, took personal control of the administration and defence. Other places protected themselves as best they could. The city of Magnesia, abandoned by the imperial army and the Alans, was taken over by one of the Emperor's knights called Attaliotes, who defied the government as well as the Turks with the full support and co-operation of the inhabitants. The Emperor's son Michael IX held out in Pergamon for some months with the soldiers that he had left. In the summer of 1303, however, he withdrew to Pegai on the coast, where he succumbed to a serious illness aggravated by hope-lessness and despair. He was not fit to travel back to Constantinople until the following January.[10]

By that time his father had hit upon yet another plan for saving the Empire. Andronikos had had few contacts with the western world since 1282, but the Venetians and the Genoese had spread the word around in the western world that the Byzantine Empire was in des-perate trouble. The news reached the leader of the Catalan Company, a band of professional soldiers, in Sicily. They had been fighting for some years on the side of Frederick II, the Aragonese king of Sicily, against Charles II of Anjou. When that struggle was decided in favour of Frederick in 1302 the Catalans were paid off and began to look for some other theatre of war. Their commander, Roger de Flor, offered his services to the Emperor Andronikos. Roger had had a colourful career: thrown out of the Order of Knights Templars for embezzle-ment and misconduct, he had taken to piracy and formed his own company of knights. The mixed band of Spanish mercenaries, known as the Catalan Grand Company, which he now commanded had a well-earned reputation as fighting men. Pachymeres knew them as 'men who died hard in battle and were ready to gamble with their lives'.[11] They might not be so numerous as the Alans, but they would surely be more efficient and better disciplined. Once again Andronikos gave thanks to heaven for what seemed like a miracle and accepted the offer without hesitation.

Roger de Flor was a hard bargainer, but the Emperor gladly agreed to all his conditions. The Catalans were to be paid double the amount normally paid to mercenaries in Byzantine service and for four months in advance. Roger was to marry the Emperor's niece, Maria, and to be honoured with the title of Grand Duke. In September 1303 he arrived at Constantinople by sea, bringing his Company to the number of about 6500 and all their wives and children. Some of the ships were his own, some were supplied by Genoa. Roger married Maria and was for a time the favoured guest of the grateful Emperor. But Andronikos was anxious that the Catalans should leave the capital without too much delay. They were a restless lot. Within a few days of their arrival they became involved in murderous street fighting with the Genoese, who were expecting to be paid for the hire of their ships. The Emperor persuaded them to move over to Kyzikos for the winter. There too they spent their time plundering and looting.[12]

The Byzantines were soon made aware that there was a fatal differ-ence between the Catalan Company and the mercenary troops that they had employed before. The Alans, like the other foreigners who had been enlisted in the past, had fought under the command of Byzantine officers. The Latin mercenaries had their special commander, the Grand Constable, but he was not a westerner. The Alans may have despised their Byzantine officers, but they had to obey their orders. The Catalans on the other hand took their orders only from their leader Roger, and they fought as a separate unit. The Emperor, who was their employer, might suggest plans of campaign, but the conduct of those campaigns was in their own hands, and any marginal profits that they might make in the way of loot, whether at the expense of Greeks or Turks, were fair gain. Ramon Muntaner, the Spanish chronicler who was with the Company and recorded their exploits, presents them as misunderstood heroes constantly being deceived by the wily Greeks. The Byzantine historians, who had to live with the consequences of those exploits, take a different view and have therefore been accused of prejudice. It is true that the Catalans performed some remarkable feats of arms against the Turks and showed what could still be done in the way of reconquest by a small but efficient army. But their victories were limited to one area of Asia Minor and they did not stay long enough to make them of permanent value.

They drove back the Turks from Kyzikos early in 1304. But they caused so much damage to the city that even Roger de Flor felt bound to pay the inhabitants an indemnity; and fighting broke out when the Alan mercenaries discovered that the Catalans were being paid at a higher rate than themselves. The Alans, numbering about 500, refused to take orders from Roger and deserted. They roamed the district pillaging on their own account. The Catalans moved on to Pegai, but their reputation had gone before them. Michael IX, who was quartered there, would not let them enter the city. In April they marched on down to Philadelphia which was then blockaded and cut off by the Turks. The Turks were routed and Roger and his men entered the city in triumph.[13]

The relief of Philadelphia was almost the only practical service that the Catalans rendered to the Byzantine Empire in Asia Minor. Roger made no attempt to follow up his victory by marching south to the Meander valley. The town of Tripolis had just been taken by the Turks. The towns of Nyssa and Tralles were already in their control. But the Catalans left them to their fate. From Philadelphia Roger led his men west again to Magnesia on the Hermos river and thence down to the coast to Ephesos, where he could make contact with his fleet whose sailors had already occupied the islands of Chios, Lesbos and Lemnos.

The Catalans were later to boast of a long march that they made from Ephesos along the south coast of Asia Minor, driving all before them up to the borders of the kingdom of Armenia. The Turks fled from them in terror. But such heroics had no lasting consequences. Ephesos was captured by one of the Turkish emirs almost as soon as the Catalans had left it, in October 1304. Roger de Flor conceived it to be his duty, and perhaps it was, to punish all Byzantine officers and troops guilty of indiscipline or dereliction of duty wherever he found them. But some of his victims were priests and monks, and others were imperial officials whose principal crime was their wealth. Attaliotes, the Byzantine officer who had made himself master of Magnesia, at first came to terms with Roger when the Catalans came his way, and so saved himself and his city.

It was at Magnesia that Roger stored the booty that his men accumulated on their forays, and he began to think of using it as a base from which to establish and govern an independent Spanish principality in Asia Minor. But on one occasion, when coming back with more plunder, he found the gates of the city closed. The thought of losing so great an amount of treasure was almost more than the Catalans could bear. They laid siege to Magnesia, until the Emperor in Constantinople, hearing that matters had got out of hand, issued orders for them to return. For a while the orders were ignored; but the winter was coming on, and eventually the Catalans left Magnesia and marched up to Lampsakos on the Hellespont. They spent the winter of 1304 at Gallipoli. Word of their successful exploits and of the wealth they had amassed had meanwhile reached the west. King Frederick of Sicily had already seen that the Catalan Company might be the spearhead of an imperialist enterprise in the east over which he could exert some control. James II of Aragon, on the other hand, acting on information from Roger de Flor, appointed his own agent, Berenguer d'Entença, to go to Constantinople with what were called reinforcements for the Catalan Company. When Berenguer arrived Andronikos signed a contract with him, and Roger de Flor ceded to him his own title of Grand Duke.[14]

The Emperor had intended that some of the Catalans should be diverted to Thrace. For, as if to compound the sum of his troubles, the Bulgars had crossed the northern frontier and attacked the city of Adrianople. But Michael IX, who had been sent there with an army in 1304, had done better against the Bulgars than against the Turks. Michael disliked the Catalans and declared that he had no need of them in any case. They were rapidly becoming more of an embarrassment than a help. They refused to go back to Asia before they had been paid and compensated for the plunder that they had lost at Magnesia, and the Emperor was at his wits' end to find the money to satisfy their demands. When Michael IX had needed soldiers to fight the Bulgars he had been forced to have a great quantity of his own gold and silver plate converted into coin with which to pay them. Roger de Flor demanded the sum of 300,000 *hyperpyra* and then complained that the Emperor had nothing to offer him but base metal. He was right, for the Byzantine gold coinage had just been further devalued. Berenguer, on the other hand, quickly sized up the situation after a stormy interview with the Emperor and sailed away. To show the Greeks what he thought of them he threw his Grand Duke's bonnet into the sea as he went. He tried to engage the Genoese to join him in war against the Emperor, but they declined. There was a skirmish between the Catalan and the Genoese navies at the end of May 1305. All but one of Berenguer's ships were sunk and he himself was taken prisoner.

The loss of their fleet made things more difficult for the Catalans. But the Genoese reported to the Emperor that plans were being laid in the west for yet another Spanish expedition to Constantinople. Frederick of Sicily was said to have appointed his brother Ferdinand of Majorca as commander-in-chief of a great Spanish armada which was destined to set up a kingdom in the east. Meanwhile the Catalan Company had dug in at Gallipoli and refused to budge until every penny of their arrears had been paid. The Emperor tried to flatter Roger by giving him the title of Caesar. He paid him another instalment and made a new contract with him in February 1305. Roger then agreed to take his men back to Asia in the spring, but before leaving he expressed a wish to pay his respects to Michael IX, whom he had never met. Perhaps now that he held the rank of Caesar he felt that etiquette required him to make the acquaintance of the co-Emperor. Michael was in camp near Adrianople. He was surprised and cross, though he received his unwelcome guest with formal courtesy. But the Alans who were in camp with him had no time for good manners towards the Catalans. One of their leaders, whose son had been murdered by Roger's men at Kyzikos, took his personal revenge by stabbing Roger in the back. His colleagues then massacred the 300 Catalans whom Roger had brought with him as an escort.[15]

From that moment any semblance of control that the Emperor might have had over the Catalan Company vanished. The Catalans laid the blame for the murder of their leader not on the Alans but on the Byzantines. They ran berserk over the whole coast of Thrace, pillaging, destroying and slaughtering. They killed or enslaved all the inhabitants of the peninsula of Gallipoli and declared it to be Spanish soil. The soldiers elected as their new commander Berenguer de Rocafort. His seal of office advertised the rule of 'the army of the Franks over the kingdom of Macedonia'. The flag of St Peter flew from the walls of Gallipoli; and the Catalan army carried the banners of the kingdoms of Sicily and Aragon. Rocafort attracted a growing number of Turkish warriors to venture across the Hellespont as mercenaries. The Bulgars offered him their help as allies; and the Genoese of Galata were almost tempted to join in. For two and a half years Gallipoli was the capital of a hostile Catalan state on the very doorstep of Constantinople. Michael IX, who was given the task of containing their activities in Thrace, was utterly defeated in two battles in June 1305. In the second encounter, fought at Apros near Raidestos, he lost nearly all his army and only just escaped with his own life. He retired to shut himself up in Didymoteichos. The Catalans inflicted a terrible vengeance on the town of Raidestos: men, women and children were massacred. When they had made it empty of inhabitants they moved in to use it as their new headquarters. It was nearer to Constantinople and better placed for raiding the interior of the country. Ramon Muntaner, the chronicler of the enterprise, was appointed commander of Gallipoli, which the Catalans used as a slave market for the sale of their prisoners.[16]

The Genoese captain Andrea Murisco did valiant service for the Emperor by patrolling the Hellespont with his ships, intercepting the passage of the Turks to Gallipoli and bringing supplies to the beleaguered ports on the Sea of Marmora. The Emperor rewarded him with the rank of admiral. But before long Murisco was captured, and the Catalans were then able to bring over another 2000 Turkish soldiers. The Emperor appealed to the Genoese government to come to his rescue with a fleet, and in the spring of 1306 19 Genoese ships arrived at Constantinople. But they were cargo ships making for the Black Sea, and their captains demanded the sum of 300,000 gold coins for their services. This was much more than the Emperor could afford. He allowed most of them to go on their way, retaining only four ships to patrol the straits.

The Catalans were in no mood to negotiate a settlement. Success had gone to their heads and their demands were ever more exorbitant. As a counsel of despair the Emperor ordered that all the country between Selymbria and Constantinople should be evacuated and the crops destroyed. Refugees were now streaming into the capital from all sides, those from Thrace adding their numbers to those from Asia Minor, for all the rich land between the lower reaches of the Marica river and the suburbs of Constantinople had been turned into desert. The Thracian cities higher up the valley, however, especially Didymotei-chos and Adrianople, were too well fortified and guarded for the Catalans to be able to penetrate their defences. They made one attempt to besiege Adrianople and destroyed the vineyards and farms around its walls. But the city itself held out against them.

Unable to make any further headway either to the north or to the east the Catalans began to feel that they had, in the most literal sense, exhausted the possibilities of Thrace. They must move on if only to survive. As their provisions and their prospects shrank disagreement broke out amongst them. They split into three bands, one under Rocafort, another under Berenguer d'Entença who had been released by the Genoese, and a third under Fernand Ximenes de Arena, who had recently arrived with reinforcements. But in the summer of 1308 Ferdinand of Majorca arrived at Gallipoli to take overall command of the Company by order of Frederick II of Sicily. Rocafort refused to recognize him as leader; but it was Ferdinand who brought them all to agree that they should now move west in search of new territory and new plunder. They crossed the Marica river and set out along the road to Thessalonica. There were about 6000 Spaniards and some 3000 Turks, marching in two divisions and living off the land. They had no purpose but to enrich themselves and to carve out a kingdom in the empire which they had been engaged to protect.[17]

Their leaders continued to squabble. Berenguer d'Entença was murdered by Rocafort. Ximenes de Arena, fearing the same fate, deserted and surrendered to the commander of the Byzantine garrison in one of the towns on their route. He was taken to Constantinople where the Emperor was glad to have his services and in due course found a princess for him to marry and created him Grand Duke. Ferdinand of Majorca then abandoned the Company and went back to his master in Sicily, taking with him Ramon Muntaner. Rocafort, left in sole command, led the rest of them westwards into Macedonia. They fought their way through the passes of Christoupolis or Kavalla, crossed the peninsula of Chalkidike and occupied Kassandria, the ancient Potidaia, to the south of Thessalonica. There they spent the winter of 1308.

It was at this point that the historian George Pachymeres laid down his pen. He had traced the history of his time over the space of half a century, from the moment of the birth of the Emperor Andronikos II in 1259 up to the year 1308. He was himself 66 years of age. He had been born in the Empire of Nicaea; he had lived through and recorded the glorious restoration of the Empire in Constantinople in 1261 and the restoration of Orthodoxy in 1283. He had seen many changes in his lifetime, but they had not all been for the better, and the future seemed unpromising. The final pages of his history, however, show a guarded optimism: the news from the east, he writes, is slightly better; the Catalans have left Thrace and crossed the Marica river; some say they are making for home, others that they plan to attack Mount Athos. Their leaders have quarrelled among themselves. Some have reached Kassandria, others have set out for Thessaly. May these matters go as God wills them to go, and may God will them to go in accordance with our highest hopes and with the trust in him of our Emperor.[18]

The subsequent adventures of the Catalan Company are linked more with the history of Greece than with that of the Byzantine Empire. From Kassandria they plundered the monasteries of Athos and made several attacks on the neighbourhood of Thessalonica. Rocafort had dreams of reviving the Latin kingdom of Thessalonica and looked forward to the capture of so wealthy a city. But it was too well garrisoned and fortified. As time went on the Catalans found it increasingly difficult to maintain their position at Kassandria. Their retreat back to Thrace was cut off by a Byzantine army. Rocafort lost the confidence of his men, who appointed another leader, and in the spring of 1309 most of them decided to make a dash for Thessaly. Some of the Turks left the Company at the border of Macedonia, but the rest (about 9000 all told) entered the plain of Thessaly by way of the Vale of Tempe.[19]

The ruler of Thessaly was then John II Doukas. He had succeeded his father Constantine in 1303. But he was only a young man and he had not inherited the spirit of defiance that had inspired his father and grandfather. He had recently come to terms with Andronikos II and married one of the Emperor's daughters. In 1309 therefore Thessaly was the ally if not the subject of Constantinople. The alliance stood John II in good stead when the Catalans crossed his northern frontier and began to devastate his land. He appealed to the Emperor for help, and a Byzantine general, Chandrenos, was ordered to march south from Thessalonica. Between them the Byzantine and Thessalian armies obliged the Catalans to move on, and they agreed to withdraw south into Boeotia. John of Thessaly willingly supplied them with guides to show them the way and paid their expenses, and in the spring of 1310 they set off by way of Lamia.

In the meantime, however, the French Duke of Athens and Thebes, Walter of Brienne, had opened negotiations with the Catalans on his own account. He had made their acquaintance earlier in his career, and he hoped that he might now be able to employ them to conquer Thessaly for himself. He sent an intermediary to meet their leader near Lamia and gave them two months' pay in advance. As a result the Catalans turned back and overran Thessaly once again, capturing some 30 towns and castles. John II was forced to come to terms with them and with the Duke of Athens. But Walter of Brienne, like the Byzantine Emperor before him, found that it was easier to hire the Catalans than it was to dismiss them. They had served their purpose for him, but they now refused to go, and his attempt to disarm some of them by force led to war. The Catalans won a decisive victory over the French in a battle at the Kephissos river near Lake Kopais in March 1311. Walter and many of his knights were killed. The Catalans then marched south to conquer Thebes and Athens. The French Duchy, which had been set up there after the Fourth Crusade, passed into Catalan control, and what the Catalan Company had been unable to achieve at Magnesia, at Gallipoli, and at Kassandria, it finally achieved at Athens by establishing a principality of its own. The Catalan Duchy of Athens lasted for almost 80 years thereafter, until 1388.[20]

When the Catalans moved west from Thrace they left behind them what the Byzantine historians, in their pedantically archaic manner, were wont to call 'a Scythian desert'. They used the word Scythian to mean Mongol. The Catalans had been every bit as destructive as the Mongols. Their contribution to the ruin of the Byzantine Empire which they had been hired to save was indeed far greater than that of the Mongols. In some ways it was nearly as great as that of the Turks. It has been argued that the Emperor Andronikos should never have undertaken to employ them when he knew that he could barely afford to pay the rates that they demanded for their services. But if they had fulfilled the early promise of their victory at Philadelphia in 1304 and returned to the attack in the following year it is possible that the revenue of the Empire might have been increased. They could not reasonably complain of the Empire's poverty when they were busily impoverishing it by helping themselves to its riches. As it was, the Emperor strained every nerve to find the means to pay them.

143

It has been estimated that the Catalans received from the imperial treasury a total sum of 1,000,000 *hyperpyra* which, at the time, was rather more than the average annual income of the whole empire. It was the demands of the Catalans which led to the further debasement of the gold coinage in 1304, when the gold content of the *hyperpyron* was reduced to only 50 per cent. It was to satisfy them that the Emperor was forced to impose even more taxation on his over-burdened people. In the eastern provinces there was little left to tax. But in the western districts of Thrace and Macedonia one-third of all the estates and properties held in *pronoia* were appropriated by the state. It is not clear how this measure was put into practice, but it is certain that many who had formerly enjoyed exemption were now liable to payment of tax on their property; and it is a measure of the Emperor's need and determination that the regulations applied even to the great monasteries of Mount Athos. But this was not enough. In 1304 an entirely new form of levy was introduced. It was called the *sitokrithon* or wheat and barley tax. Every farmworker was bound to pay a portion of his produce in kind according to the acreage of his land. The collection of this tax must have produced problems of its own. But the proceeds were to be sold on the open market to realize gold and silver with which to pay the Catalans.[21]

Control of the open market was another matter. The influx of refugees into Constantinople, not only from Asia Minor but also from the parts of Thrace that had been occupied by the Catalans or deliberately devastated, produced a desperate shortage of food in the capital. Devaluation of the currency led to inflated prices for what food there was. There were quick profits to be made by unscrupulous dealers, Greeks as well as Italians. In 1303 the Patriarch John XII complained to the Emperor about the rising price of salt, the production of which was, after all, supposed to be a state monopoly. But the formidable Patriarch Athanasios did not stop short at complaints. He preached sermons denouncing the unchristian behaviour of profiteers; he threatened to excommunicate them from the pulpit; he badgered the Emperor to take action. In his letters Athanasios describes how, after the terrible Catalan 'vendetta' in 1305, there was famine in Constantinople. Some merchants made the most of it by running a black market in wheat; others were actually exporting wheat from the city to get higher prices elsewhere. Athanasios suggested that the Emperor should lay down new regulations and appoint a special commissioner to control and supervise the sale of wheat and the baking of bread in the city. The suggestion seems to have been adopted. An imperial order went out that strict watch was to be kept on bakers, on cargoes of wheat arriving in the Golden Horn, and on correct weights and measures in the markets. The Patriarch also denounced the Emperor's policy of reducing the already meagre food supply by evacuating and destroying the farmlands to the west of Constantinople. But the poor and the refugees had cause to be grateful to him, for he set up soup kitchens in various parts of the city where they could get hot gruel prepared from ears of corn. The Patriarch Athanasios loathed the Catalans as the enemies rather than the saviours of Constantinople. He was afraid of them only in so far as their Catholic faith might undermine still further the moral fibre of the Orthodox.[22]

Yet, for all the damage that the Catalans did to the Empire, there were a few Byzantines who hoped that they might represent the advance guard of a crusade against the Turks to be organized from western Europe. The Kings of Aragon and Sicily saw the Catalans as the agents of an imperialist venture in the east. Others in the west felt that they might be employed in the lost cause of restoring the Latin Empire. Charles of Valois, brother of Philip IV of France, had hopes that they might co-operate in a crusade for the reconquest of Constantinople. In 1301 Charles had married Catherine of Courtenay, grand-daughter of the last Latin Emperor Baldwin II. He was in alliance with Frederick of Sicily, with Venice and even with Serbia, and the Popes were ready to support him by preaching a holy war. In 1307 Pope Clement V, a firm supporter of the French, excommunicated Andronikos II and forbade all Catholics to have any dealings with him or render him any aid. Charles II of Anjou, and more especially his son Philip of Taranto, who had married the daughter of Nikephoros of Epiros, were naturally interested in any crusade that would fortify their claims in Greece.[23]

The intentions of these parties towards the Byzantine Empire were anything but altruistic. But there was evidently a small group of people in the Empire itself who thought that Charles of Valois might be able to direct the energies of all his friends and relations in the west to the larger purpose of a crusade against the Turks. Three of them wrote letters to Charles and to the Empress Catherine of Courtenay about 1307. One of the writers was John Monomachos, then governor of Thessalonica; another was Constantine Doukas Limpidaris or Libadarios, an imperial official in Asia Minor; the third was a monk called Sophronios. All three addressed Charles of

Valois as Emperor, or Emperor of the Romans, and looked forward to the day when he would lead his army to Byzantium to drive back the Turks. The day never came. Charles made some effort to secure the help of the Catalans when they reached Thessaly. But the Catalans were not interested in furthering any projects other than their own. The Venetians withdrew their support from the proposed crusade and renewed their trade agreement with Byzantium in November 1310, and the great plans of Charles of Valois and the Papacy were written off. By then Catherine of Courtenay had died, and her title of Latin Empress of Constantinople had passed to her daughter Catherine of Valois. It was through her, and through her Angevin husband Philip of Taranto, that the shadowy western claims to Constantinople were to be pressed in succeeding years.[24]

The Catalans were a transitory phenomenon, although the effects of their presence and their depredations were felt for many years to come. They came and went like a plague of locusts. But the Turks were a permanent feature. Those that were left behind by the Catalans in Thrace and Macedonia organized themselves into two bands. One, consisting of 1500 warriors, offered their services to Stephen Milutin of Serbia. He was glad to take them on. The other, led by one Halil, roamed the countryside of Thrace and made land communications between Constantinople and Thessalonica impossible. In 1310 Andronikos signed an agreement with Halil. He and his men, to the number of 1300 horsemen and 800 footsoldiers, were to be given free passage across the Hellespont with their booty so that they could return to Asia Minor. The Genoese were to supply the ships. The agreement was dishonoured, however, when one of the Emperor's officials tried to relieve the Turks of their booty; and Halil, far from going home, summoned reinforcements to come over and join him in Thrace. Michael IX tried to bring them to battle and was once more ignominiously defeated. It was said that Halil even captured Michael's imperial crown. For some two years much of Thrace was in Turkish hands. People in the cities did not venture out to cultivate their fields. In the end the Emperor managed to raise an army and confined the Turks to the peninsula of Gallipoli. Milutin of Serbia lent him 2000 cavalry. The Genoese prevented the enemy from escaping by sea, and about the end of 1312, hemmed in at Gallipoli and fighting to the last, Halil and his men were massacred. They were less than 2000 in number, but they had held the Empire at their mercy.[25]

After the Catalan disaster the Emperor's nerve seemed to have

146

broken and his inventiveness to have dried up. An added complication on the European front was the revival of Bulgarian power. The Mongol domination of Bulgaria was relaxed in 1299 when Nogaj, the Khan of the Golden Horde, was deposed. Theodore Svetoslav, the son of George Terter, who came to the Bulgarian throne in 1300, made the most of his relative freedom of action and of the feebleness of the Byzantine Empire. He attacked northern Thrace and occupied the Byzantine ports on the Black Sea, closing them to Genoese shipping and forbidding the export of wheat to Constantinople. The city was already desperately short of food. But the Emperor had no heart to threaten the Bulgars with reprisals. In 1307 he tamely signed a treaty allowing them to retain all their new conquests and gave one of his grand-daughters, a child of Michael IX, in marriage to Svetoslav.[26]

Andronikos could hardly cope with events on his own doorstep. The thought of driving back countless thousands of Turks in Asia Minor was beyond his powers of organization. Earlier on it had occured to him that the natural enemies of the Turks in Asia were not the Catalans, still less the princes of western Europe, but the Mongols of Persia. The Mongols were dangerous allies, and they were usually preoccupied by their own conflict with the Mamluks of Egypt, who controlled Syria and Palestine. But in the early fourteenth century the Ilkhan of the Mongols effectively controlled a very large part of Asia Minor. Andronikos had no wish to fall foul of such powerful potentates as the Mamluk Sultans; and, like his father Michael VIII, he too maintained at least diplomatic contacts with the Mamluks throughout his reign. But it seems to have been brought to his notice, somewhat late in the day, that the Mongols might be induced to provide him with soldiers for the defeat of the Turks in Asia. One wonders whether the idea was put to him by his half-sister Maria. Maria had been given as wife to the Ilkhan Abaga by Michael VIII. When Abaga died she returned to Constantinople. She was known to the Greeks as Despina Mougoulion or the Lady of the Mongols, and to the Mongols as Despina Khatoun; and she founded a convent in Constantinople dedicated to the Virgin of the Mongols.

In 1303 Andronikos appealed to the Ilkhan Gazan, the descendant of Abaga, for his help against the Turks. He offered him the hand in marriage of a princess who was reputed to be the Emperor's own natural daughter. Gazan was pleased to accept, and the mere rumour of an alliance between the Byzantines and the Mongols is said to have struck terror in the hearts of the Turks. But Gazan died in May 1304 leaving no offspring. He had rejected his nephew Tokhtu and nominated as his successor his own brother Öldjaitu or, as the Byzantines knew him, Charbadas. In the spring of 1305 the Emperor Andronikos sent an embassy to Öldjaitu with the same proposal that had been made to Gazan. The Khan promised to send him 40,000 men, 20,000 of whom were reported to be already in the district of Konya. The figures are those given by Pachymeres, and they betray the over-optimism of the Byzantines, hopeful of a great army coming out of the east to their rescue. The Emperor sent his sister Maria to Nicaea to rally the flagging resistance of the inhabitants by telling them of the help that the Mongols were about to send. Nicaea was then almost cut off by the warriors of Osman, who controlled all the surrounding country; but the news that the Mongols were upon him merely spurred Osman on to greater efforts. In 1307 he stormed and captured the fortress of Trikokkia, thus isolating Nicaea from Nikomedia. At the very end of his history George Pachymeres was able to report the heartening news that an army of Mongols, allegedly 30,000 strong, had been sent to Bithynia by Charbadas and had retrieved many of the places recently taken by the Turks. It may have been no more than a rumour or a hope. The friendship of the Mongols brought no further help or relief. No great army marched out of the east, and the Byzantines were left to fight their own losing battle against the Turks in western Asia Minor.[27]

NOTES

1 Pachymeres, II, 153-65, 424.   2 Pachymeres, II, 208-20.

3 Pachymeres, II, 220-32; Gregoras, I, 195-202.

4 Pachymeres, II, 258-62; cf. II, 38, 134f., 208 (for the earlier career of Tarchaniotes). See also P. Schreiner, Studien zu den BRAXEA XPONIKA (Munich, 1967), 181-5; and 'Zur Geschichte Philadelpheias im 14 Jh.', OCP XXXV (1969), 376-83; F. Tinnefeld, 'Pachymeres und Philes als Zeugen für ein Unternehmen gegen die Osmanen', BZ, LXIV (1971), 46-54.

5 Pachymeres, II, 307-10.

6 Pachymeres, II, 307-22; Gregoras, I, 204-7.

7 Pachymeres, II, 327-35. On the battle at Bapheus, see G. G. Arnakis, The Early Osmanlis (in Greek) (Athens, 1947), 127-30, who dates it on 27 July 1301; but cf. P. Wittek, 'Chroniques mineures byzantines', B, XII (1937), 321, who dates it to 1302.

8 Pachymeres, II, 345-7, 402-5.   9 Pachymeres, II, 389-90.

10 Pachymeres, II, 390-2, 428; Gregoras, I, 221.

11 Pachymeres, II, 562. The expedition of the Catalan Company to Greece is remarkably well documented in Greek as well as Spanish sources and has been the subject of much research and interest. See especially K. M. Setton, *Catalan Domination of Athens, 1311-88* (Cambridge, Mass, 1948), and in *CMH*, IV, 1, 411f., 908f., where the earlier literature is cited. For their preliminary exploits in Asia Minor, see Lemerle, *L'Emirat d'Aydin*, 15-18. In general, cf. G. Schlumberger, *Expédition des 'Almugavares' ou routiers catalans en Orient* (Paris, 1902); W. Miller, *The Latins in the Levant* (London, 1908), 211-34.

12 Pachymeres, II, 393-400; Gregoras, I, 217-20. Ramon Muntaner, *Chronicle*, translated by Lady Goodenough (Hakluyt Society, ser. 2, no. 50: London, 1921), II, 480-93.

13 Pachymeres, II, 415-27; Gregoras, I, 220-3; Muntaner, *Chronicle*, II, 494-7.

14 Pachymeres, II, 428-42, 450-1, 480-9; Gregoras, I, 223-4; Muntaner, II, 497-509.

15 Pachymeres, II, 445-8, 489-516, 521-8; Gregoras, I, 223-4; Muntaner, II, 509-15.

16 Pachymeres, II, 528-36, 539-56; Muntaner, II, 515-33.

17 Pachymeres, II, 556-7, 562-76, 578, 583-8, 597-600, 602-8. Gregoras, I, 224-33, 244-5; Muntaner, II, 533-52.

18 Pachymeres, II, 651-2; Muntaner, II, 553f.

19 Setton, *Catalan Domination of Athens*, 4-6.

20 Gregoras, I, 249-53. Setton, *Catalan Domination*, 7-14.

21 Pachymeres, II, 492-4. Cf. Zakythinos, *Crise monétaire*, 90-1; Ostrogorsky, *History*, 484-5.

22 Banescu, 'Le Patriarche Athanase ...', 49-53; Guilland, 'Correspondance inédite d'Athanase ...', 77-8. See A. Laiou, 'The provisioning of Constantinople during the winter of 1306-1307', *B*, XXXVII (1967), 91-113; J. Gill, 'Emperor Andronicus II and Patriarch Athanasius I', *Byzantina*, II (Thessalonike, 1970), 11-19.

23 Dade, *Versuche*, 72-8, 116-22, 138-46.

24 Dade, *Versuche*, 147-58. Hélène Constaninidi-Bibikou, 'Documents concernant l'histoire Byzantine déposés aux archives nationales de France', *Mélanges offerts à Octave et Melpo Merlier*, I (Athens, 1956), 119-32.

25 Gregoras, I, 254-5, 262-9.

26 Pachymeres, II, 628-9. Cf. Ostrogorsky, *History*, 494.

27 Pachymeres, II, 402-5, 456-60, 588-9, 620, 637-8, 650-1. S. Runciman, 'The Ladies of the Mongols', in *Eis Mnemen K. I. Amantou* (Athens, 1960), 46-53.

Nine

The Nature of the Enemy

By the turn of the thirteenth century the Byzantines were beginning to get a clearer picture of the true nature of their Turkish enemies in Asia Minor. By 1320 the picture was too clear for comfort. George Pachymeres knew at least a garbled version of the names of many of the tribes, although he was a little vague about their exact location. He writes of the devastation of the fields and farms of Bithynia, Mysia, Phrygia, Lydia and Asia by 'the Amourioi, Atmanes, Atinai, Alisurai, Mantachiai, Salampaxides, Alaides, Ameramanai, Lamisai, Sphondylai, Pagdinai, and other vile creatures with execrable names'. Nikephoros Gregoras, writing half a century later when the Turkish conquest of Byzantine Asia Minor was an accomplished fact, was able to fill in more of the details of the way in which it had come about.[1] The 'vile creatures' whose names Pachymeres only half understood were in fact the ruling families of the emirates or principalities set up by the ghazi warriors in central and western Anatolia. The Byzantine historians, never far from their classical models, were pleased to think of them in Herodotean terms as 'Persians', which is usually translated as 'Turks'. But the emirs and their warriors were not themselves conscious of belonging to one nation or race. They were inspired by the Muslim idea of holy war. But there was no central direction of their offensive and they seldom co-operated with each other.

The first of these new emirates came into being well to the east of the Byzantine frontiers, in the ruins of the old Seljuq Sultanate. The family of Karaman had invaded and settled in the area of Cilicia and the Taurus mountains in south-eastern Anatolia. They were friends of the Mamluk Sultans of Egypt and so the natural enemies of the Mongols of Persia. About 1308 they succeeded in capturing Konya, the capital of the Seljuq Sultans; this date is often taken to mark the end of the Seljuq Turkish state, although it had for many years been little more than an outlying province of the Mongol Empire. The Karamans were driven out of Konya by the Ilkhan Öldjaitu. But after Öldjaitu's death in 1316 the Mongols, distracted by their own domestic problems, began to relax their hold on Anatolia. The Karaman principality was left to develop into the greatest power in that part of Asia Minor. But it had little influence on the fortunes of the Byzantines, except in so far as it embarrassed the older Turkish enemies of Constantinople.

Nearer to the Byzantine frontier lay the emirate of the Germiyan which was founded at the end of the thirteenth century. It covered the area of Phrygia, the old border district of the Empire of Nicaea. Its centre was the once Byzantine city of Kotyaion, or Kütahya. Germiyan was the name of the tribe or people and not, as in other emirates, the name of their ruling family. Their emirs were descended from one Alishir, the 'Karmanos Alisourios' of Gregoras, the 'Alisuras' of Pachymeres. By 1300 they claimed possession of the land from Ankara in the east to the valley of the Meander in the south-west. Philadelphia and other Greek cities for a time paid tribute to the emirs of the Germiyan. But they had no access to the sea, and their strength declined as other emirs, some of them vassals of the Germiyan, began to establish their own little states on what was still Byzantine territory towards the west coast of Asia Minor.

In the disastrous years between 1282 and 1300 the pattern of Turkish conquest took shape as more and more ghazi warriors came down from the hills into the Byzantine frontier areas and explored the river valleys leading to the coast. In the very south-west corner of Asia Minor, in the district of Karia, the attack was led by an emir called Menteshe. The land that he occupied lay to the south of the Meander river, though his activities extended as far as Miletos. It was one of his relatives who besieged and captured the rebuilt city of Tralles in 1282. The emirs of Menteshe were the first to take to the sea as pirates. They profited greatly from the absence of a Byzantine fleet and also from the services of unemployed Byzantine sailors. About 1300 they attacked the offshore island of Rhodes. But here they met their first real opposition; for in 1308 the Knights of St John, who had vainly begged the Byzantine Emperor to let them have the island as a fief when they were turned out of Cyprus, took the law into their own hands and appropriated Rhodes as their new headquarters. The emirs of Menteshe were thus prevented from making piratical expeditions against other islands in the Aegean Sea.

North of the emirate of Menteshe lay that of Aydin, who was originally a vassal of the Germiyan. The sons of Aydin, or the Aydinoglou, seem to have made their earliest raids and conquests in collaboration with a relative of Menteshe called Sasa Beg. It was he who led them to the capture of Ephesos in October 1304; and it was to forestall them that Benedetto Zaccaria took over the island of Chios. But Sasa soon fell out with Mehmed, the eldest son of Aydin, and was killed in 1308. Mehmed Beg in due course proclaimed his independence from the Germiyan and established his own emirate. About 1317 his warriors captured the acropolis or upper citadel of Smyrna; and for some years he fought running battles off the coast against the navies of the Zaccaria family of Chios and the Knights of Rhodes. His more famous son Umur Beg received Smryna as his appanage and finally completed the Turkish conquest of the city by wresting the lower town and the harbour from the Latins in 1329.

The exploits of Umur of Aydin, whose principality was the most successful and the most troublesome of all the Turkish coastal emirates in the first half of the fourteenth century, were later to be celebrated in epic verse by a Turkish poet called Enveri. The *Destan* or the Achievements of Umur Pasha, committed to writing by Enveri in the 1460s, is a unique account of the history of one of the Turkish emirates of Asia Minor, written not from the Byzantine or Christian standpoint but from the Turkish side. The *Destan* covers the years from 1307 to 1348, the critical period between the collapse of Byzantine resistance in western Anatolia under Andronikos II and the foundation of the Osmanli or Ottoman emirate further north. It presents in dramatic and often entertaining form the story of the heroic raids and conquests of one of the ghazi states, that of Mehmed Beg Aydinoglou and his son Umur. It gives a vivid picture of a small but vigorous military society perpetually on the move, dependent for its survival on conquest, and inspired by the ideal of *djihad* or holy war. The ghazis or warriors for the faith had their own code of chivalry and gave allegiance to their emir in return for the livelihood which they obtained by plunder. The hero of the tale, the emir of Aydin, is described as Ghazi Umur and also as Umur Pasha, a title which in the fourteenth century had a religious as well as a military significance. Umur is the 'lion of God' leading a just and holy war of conquest against the 'miscreants' or infidel Christians.[2]

To the north of Smyrna lay the emirates of Saruchan and Karasi. Saruchan conquered the district of Lydia, with the cities of Magnesia and Pergamon; Karasi controlled the area of Mysia and the country to the south of the Hellespont. Neither of these principalities proved to be as successful as the emirates of Aydin and Menteshe. But both seemed at first to be rather more important than the emirate of Osman or Othman. One of the smallest of all the ghazi emirates at the end of the thirteenth century was that formed in the north-west of Asia Minor, behind the Byzantine frontier at the Sangarios river in eastern Bithynia. Its leader was Osman, known to the Byzantines as Atman. All that can safely be said about his origins is that he was the son of one Ertoghrul. In later times many myths and legends were invented to supply him with a longer and more glorious pedigree. For Osman was, after all, the founder of a dynasty that was to inherit the universal Empire of Constantinople and to terrorize western Europe in the fifteenth and sixteenth centuries. Later historians, European as well as Ottoman, therefore satisfied themselves and their readers with elaborate accounts of Osman's heroic past and ancestry, which was said to stretch right back to the Prophet or even to Noah. The legends are not without importance since there were no Turkish historians of Osman and his people before the fifteenth century. It has been said indeed that the Osmanlis have no history until they come in contact with the Byzantines. But the contemporary Byzantine historians have little to say about their origin or ancestry. They were more concerned with the deeds of Osman and his warriors on the frontier; nor could they be expected to know that Osman's descendants would eventually conquer the whole Byzantine Empire.[3]

Osman's father Ertoghrul is said to have commanded a band of ghazi warriors in the service of the last of the Seljuq Sultans. He defeated a Byzantine and Mongol army in the district of Dorylaion or Eskishehir on the Byzantine frontier. The Sultan rewarded him by granting him Eskishehir as a fief. Later legend has it that Ertoghrul was officially nominated as successor by the last Sultan, which made it possible for the genealogists to establish a legitimate connexion between the Osmanlis and the Seljuqs. Ertoghrul died in 1288 leaving most of his territory to Osman, or Ghazi Othman ibn Ertoghrul. In the next few years Osman slowly advanced into the Byzantine province of Bithynia, raiding the upper valley of the Sangarios river and the country between Busa and Nicaea. It was in this district that his name first became known to the Byzantines. In July 1302 Osman defeated a Byzantine army at Bapheus near Nikomedia. Soon afterwards he occupied the fortress of Melangeia or Yenishehir, the new city (as opposed to Eskishehir, the old city), and this became the base for his future operations. It lay between Brusa and Nicaea and so controlled the overland route from Constantinople to Bithynia. The Byzantine government could only communicate with Nicaea and the neighbouring cities by sea. In these circumstances it is hardly surprising that the Emperor Andronikos regarded the Catalans as a gift from heaven. The campaigns of the Catalan Company in 1304 had some effect on Osman's emirate, though their efforts were mainly directed further south, against the emirs of Aydin and Menteshe. The Mongol army sent to the relief of Nicaea in 1307 seems to have been more effective in clearing the Osmanlis out of the district. But as soon as it was gone Osman conquered all the surrounding area right up to the Sea of Marmora; and the cities of Nicaea, Brusa, Nikomedia and the rest were left isolated from each other and from Constantinople.

The fight for the possession of these cities was long and bitter, but their defence was mainly in their own hands. The Byzantine Emperor had too many troubles in Europe to be able to spare much thought for the defence of Asia Minor. The Empire was exhausted by the depredations of the Catalans and their aftermath. For some years it was as much as it could do to defeat a handful of Turks in Europe let alone trying to muster an army to cross over to fight the Turks in Asia. Something might have been done by an Emperor who was more energetic and resourceful. But Andronikos II was bereft of new ideas and past his prime. In 1321 some of the younger generation of the ruling class rose in rebellion against him and civil war broke out. For seven years the Byzantines were intermittently at war with each other and their foreign enemies had a free hand. During those crucial years Osman steadily enlarged his principality by overrunning the region between the Sangarios and the Bosporos and up to the shore of the Black Sea. On 6 April 1326 his son Orchan captured the city of Brusa. It had been under siege for a month but it had been virtually cut off from the Byzantine world for many years. In May of the same year the nearby city of Lopadion also fell to the Osmanlis after its walls had been damaged by an earthquake. The end of Byzantine rule in Bithynia was now in sight. Brusa became the new capital of the Osmanli emirate, and there Osman was buried when he died in 1326. He was succeeded by his son Orchan who set about the systematic conquest of the outstanding Byzantine cities and the foundation of a Turkish state that was soon to rival and to absorb all the other emirates in Asia Minor.[4]

How the Osmanlis rose from their humble origins to achieve greater fame and glory than any of the larger and more powerful ghazi emirates in Asia Minor is a question that has puzzled historians. Many answers have been suggested, but the simplest answer of all seems to contain much of the truth. The Osmanlis were the nearest of all the emirates to Constantinople. They therefore had to overcome the most stubborn resistance from the Byzantines. War and conquest were, as the *Destan* of Umur Pasha clearly demonstrates, the life blood of the ghazi warriors. When there was resistance to overcome they were fulfilled; when there was no further resistance and no possibility of further conquest they declined. The emirs of Menteshe and of Aydin found less and less opportunity for conquest in Asia Minor and less resistance once they had reached the sea. Umur of Aydin nourished the fighting spirit of his men in warfare against the Knights of Rhodes and their western allies, and in plundering the islands and the coast of Greece. But there was a limit to such activities; as the limits of conquest and plunder were exhausted in other emirates, their ghazis would join forces with the Osmanlis, whose fight to the death with the Byzantines, first in Asia and then in Europe, seemed to promise almost limitless prospects of holy war. The Osmanlis welcomed this development, for it added to the number of their people. For unlike most of the other Turkish princes the descendants of Osman very early conceived the idea of building a nation and of setting up stable and permanent institutions of government. The restless elements of the population could always be given work to do as ghazis on the frontiers. The old tradition of *djihad* could thus be upheld and the lust for plunder satisfied, but without prejudice to the establishment of an organized state at the centre.[5]

The Osmanlis did not therefore slaughter every Christian 'miscreant' in their path. Rather they encouraged the Christian inhabitants of the countryside and the towns to join them. Islamic law and tradition declared that enemies who surrendered on demand should be treated with tolerance. The Christians of Bithynia were obliged to pay the *haradj* or capitation tax for the privilege of being tolerated, but this was no more burdensome than the taxes they had paid to the Byzantine government which had neglected their interests. Once they had made the decision to surrender or defect the Byzantine population did not find the change of masters too distressing. The inducements were often strong for the Osmanlis wanted to increase their numbers. A band of Catalans even went over to them in 1304. Some Christians went all the way with the conquerors and were converted to Islam. But this was not demanded of them, for all who entered the service of Osman, Turks or Greeks, became part of the same nation and were collectively known as Osmanlis. It was because they began to look to the future instead of living from day to day that the Osmanlis prospered when the other emirates declined. In later years the only emirate comparable in government and organization was that of the Karamans. The Byzantine emperors often had cause to be grateful to the Karamans for diverting the attention of the Osmanlis. But the future to which the Osmanlis looked in the early fourteenth century can hardly have encompassed the conquest of Constantinople and of the whole Byzantine Empire.

NOTES

The subject of this Chapter is treated in the following modern works:
H. A. Gibbons, *The Foundation of the Ottoman Empire* (Oxford, 1916); P. Wittek, *Das Fürstentum Mentesche. Studie zur Geschichte Westkleinasiens im 13.-15. Jh.* (Istanbul, 1934); P. Wittek, *The Rise of the Ottoman Empire* (London, 1938); G. G. Arnakis, *The Early Osmanlis* [in Greek] (Athens, 1947); P. Lemerle, *L'Emirat d'Aydin. Byzance et l'Occident* (Paris, 1957); F. Taeschner, in *CMH*, IV, i, 749-52, 753-60; E. Werner, *Die Geburt einer Grossmacht—Die Osmanen (1300 bis 1481)* (Berlin, 1966); C. Cahen, *Pre-Ottoman Turkey* (London, 1968); H. Inalcik, 'The emergence of the Ottomans', in *Cambridge History of Islam*, I (Cambridge, 1970), 263-91.

1 Pachymeres, II, 388-9; Gregoras, I, 214-15.

2 *Le Destān d'Umūr Pacha (Düstūrnāme-i Enverī)*. Texte, traduction et notes par Irène Mélikoff-Sayar (Bibliothèque Byzantine, Documents, 2: Paris, 1954).

3 For the legends about Osman's birth and ancestry, see Gibbons, *Foundation of the Ottoman Empire*, 17-29.

4 The dates of the fall of Brusa and of Lopadion are provided by the *Short Chronicle of 1352*, ed. Loenertz, part I, 334, 352-4.

5 See especially Wittek, *Rise of the Ottoman Empire*, 33-51.

Part Three

The Mortal Illness of Byzantium: The Age of Civil Wars—1321-54

The history of the period 1321-54 is told in great detail by the contemporary historians Nikephoros Gregoras and John Cantacuzene. Cantacuzene (*Historiae*, 3 vols, *CSHB*) divided his narrative into four books, the first covering the years 1320-8, the second 1328-41, the third 1341-7, and the fourth describing the years of his own reign as Emperor, from 1347-54.

General accounts of the whole period may be found in: Ostrogorsky, *History*, 499-533; Bréhier, *Vie et Mort*, 347-64; Diehl, *L'Europe orientale*, 237-57.

Ten

The Question of the Succession and the First Civil War

Andronikos II had always intended that his eldest son Michael, the child of his first wife Anne of Hungary, should succeed to the throne. Michael had been crowned as co-Emperor in 1294. For a long time it was hoped that he would marry Catherine of Courtenay, the titular Latin Empress of Constantinople, thereby solving the problem of the western claim to the Byzantine title. There were many exchanges of embassies and courtesies between the interested parties over a number of years. But the proposal foundered on the rock of St Peter. For religious as well as political reasons the Popes objected to the Latin Empress marrying a heretical emperor. In 1301 Catherine made a much more satisfactory marriage to Charles of Valois, brother of the King of France. The same obstacle impeded Michael's marriage to a daughter of the French King of Cyprus; in the end, in 1295, he married a sister of the King of Armenia called Rita or Maria. She gave him two sons and two daughters. The elder of the sons was named, in the Byzantine custom, after his grandfather and became the Emperor Andronikos III; the younger was called Manuel. The Emperor's other son by his first marriage, Constantine, was given the rank of Despot. Only latterly was he considered for the succession to the throne, though he had an illegitimate son of his own called Michael Katharos to whom the old Emperor was devoted in his declining years.[1]

The Emperor's second wife Yolanda, or Eirene of Montferrat, whom he married in 1284, had great hopes for the three sons that she bore him, John, Theodore and Demetrios. She felt that they, as well as her stepson Michael IX whom she disliked, should have their share in the imperial heritage, and she proposed that the Empire should be partitioned among all the princes of the blood. This may have been western practice, but it was far from being in accord with Byzantine tradition. The historian Gregoras was deeply shocked by the idea. The Emperor refused to consider it and a family quarrel broke out. Andronikos tried to make it clear to his wife that 'no

159

Emperor had the power to turn the single monarchy of the Romans into a polyarchy'.[2] But Eirene saw his refusal simply as favouritism towards his first-born son and decided that she could no longer live with so stupid and stubborn a husband. She left Constantinople, taking her own three sons with her, and went to live in Thessalonica. There at least she could be nearer to her little daughter Simonis who had been sacrificed as bride to Stephen Milutin of Serbia in 1299. In Thessalonica, Eirene eased her frustrations by intriguing against her husband with Milutin and even with Charles of Valois and the Catalans; and it was at her summer retreat near Thessalonica that she died in 1317, an embittered but extremely wealthy woman. Her son Theodore inherited the marquisate of Montferrat, married a Genoese lady, and settled in Lombardy to found there a dynasty of the house of Palaiologos. He returned only occasionally to Byzantium to extort money from his parents. Eirene's son John, much against her wishes, married a daughter of the Emperor's minister Nikephoros Choumnos and died without issue. She tried to persuade her third son Demetrius to live at Milutin's court in Serbia on the chance of acquiring a Serbian principality. But Demetrios found the hardships and boredom of life in Serbia more than he could bear. He went back to live in Thessalonica where he married and produced three children.[3]

Michael IX, the heir-presumptive, had not been blessed with good fortune in his career. After his defeat by the Turks in Asia Minor he had settled in the Thracian cities of Didymoteichos and Adrianople. After his defeat by the Turks of Halil in Thrace he had been sent to reside in Thessalonica, where he endured a strained relationship with his stepmother Eirene. His private life was no more fortunate than his public career. The elder of his two sons, Andronikos, was crowned as co-Emperor in February 1316 when he was 19. In this way the senior Emperor Andronikos II, like Michael VIII before him, hoped to secure the dynastic succession for two generations to come, through his son Michael IX and his grandson Andronikos III. But it was not to be.

The young Andronikos was brought up in the palace by his grandfather together with his younger brother Manuel. He was at first a great favourite with the old Emperor. But he began to kick over the traces in his adolescence. He developed into a reckless and extravagant youth, keeping company with undesirable associates and running up debts even with the Genoese in Galata. He was ambitious, but he felt that he would hardly live long enough to benefit from the elaborate plans that had been made for his eventual succession to the throne. His elders and betters arranged for him to marry a well-connected German lady in the hope of settling his restlessness. She was Adelaide, or as the Byzantines called her, Eirene of Brunswick, daughter of Henry, Duke of Brunswick-Grubenhagen. The wedding was in October 1317. Eirene bore one son who died in infancy. But she seems to have failed to reform her husband. Andronikos began to toy with the idea of taking over a principality of his own, in Armenia, where his mother had come from, or in the Morea or one of the Aegean islands. His father and grandfather were disappointed at the way the young man was turning out.

The ill-feeling in the family came to a head after a particularly tragic incident. Andronikos III became infatuated with a lady in Constantinople who was nobly born but notoriously free with her affections. He laid an ambush one night for one of his rivals near the lady's house. The night was dark. The first person to pass that way chanced to be his own brother Manuel. The hired assassins mistook their victim, and Manuel was murdered. The news of this latest scandal proved too much for Michael IX. He was still in mourning for the recent death of his daughter Anna, wife of the Despot of Epiros. He was in poor health and the shock sent him into a decline from which he never recovered. He died at Thessalonica on 12 October 1320. The senior Emperor then declared that he could no longer tolerate his grandson Andronikos and disinherited him. His place in the line of succession was to be taken by the Despot Constantine, brother of the late Michael IX, or rather by his bastard son Michael Katharos. These were the events that precipitated the first of the series of civil wars of succession which were to bring the Empire to the verge of ruin in the fourteenth century.[4]

The Byzantine historians of the time report the outbreak of war between Andronikos II and his grandson Andronikos III almost entirely in terms of a personal vendetta. No one can doubt that there was a clash of temperaments. But that was not the only cause of conflict. By 1321 Andronikos II had been on the throne for nearly 40 years. He was over 60 years of age. Things seemed to have gone from bad to worse during the latter years of his reign. Byzantine Asia Minor was as good as lost to the Turks, and the few remaining cities could not hold out much longer on their own. Thrace had been devastated by Catalans and Turks. Constantinople could neither feed nor accommodate the refugee population. Its trade and even its food supply were at the mercy of the Italians.

Yet those who still had land, wealth and comparative security were taxed beyond endurance to raise money simply to maintain the status quo. Most of the revenue coming into the imperial treasury was being paid out in annual tributes or subsidies to the Empire's enemies and neighbours. The landowners in northern Thrace and in Macedonia, who had so far escaped the full horrors, bitterly resented having to pay increased taxes merely to buy off the Catalans or the Turks or to subsidize the Italians. They did not believe that this form of appeasement was the only alternative to the expense of equipping an army and a navy. They regarded it rather as the alternative to any positive or constructive policy on the part of their government. The old Emperor was defeated by events. Perhaps it was time for the younger generation to take over.

About 1320 Andronikos II announced a further increase in taxation. It was imposed with such severity that, for a time, the economy of the Empire appeared to revive. The Emperor's tax-collectors, writes Gregoras, vied with each other in the lucrative business of serving the Emperor's interests as well as their own. So that in a short while, although the boundaries of the Empire were continually shrinking, the revenue brought into its treasury went up by thousands and thousands. With the proceeds the Emperor proposed to build a fleet of 20 warships to patrol the seas and coastal districts threatened by his enemies, and to maintain a standing force of 1000 cavalry in Bithynia and 2000 in Thrace and Macedonia. The remainder was to be spent on embassies and subsidies to the surrounding nations and on the other myriad expenses of the administration. 'But since God, for his inscrutable reasons, willed otherwise, everything was suddenly turned into confusion as by the throw of a die.'[5]

The die was cast when the young Andronikos III and his supporters declared war on his grandfather. The family tragedy and misunderstanding following the death of Michael IX and the disinheritance of Andronikos III provided the occasion for a planned revolt of the younger generation of the aristocracy. Some of them banded together round Andronikos III to support his claim to the throne. Perhaps they were justified. But the old Emperor put up a long and obstinate resistance, and it was the wrong moment for Byzantium to become involved in civil war. War was declared to right the wrongs done to Andronikos III, and his principal champions were members of the landed nobility. This was no uprising of the oppressed and overburdened peasants or citizens against their incompetent government. But it is significant that one of the first things the rebels did was to proclaim freedom from taxation for all the towns and villages of Thrace. There was no surer way of gaining their support. All of them from the suburbs of Constantinople to as far west as Christoupolis were at once up in arms and eager to fight for the young Emperor against his grandfather. The tax-collectors then going their rounds in Thrace were arrested and tortured without mercy, and the money that they had gathered was seized and diverted to the rebel cause.[6]

The leaders of the rebellion were mainly of an age with Andronikos III. But their motives were varied, and not all were primarily interested in saving the state. The three most directly concerned in the affair were John Cantacuzene or Kantakouzenos, Syrgiannes Palaiologos, and Theodore Synadenos. John Cantacuzene was about 25 years of age in 1320. He came of a rich and well established family. His father had been governor of the Byzantine province in the Morea. His mother Theodora, who brought him up as an only child, was related to the imperial family of Palaiologos. John was the heir to vast estates in Macedonia, Thrace and Thessaly. He had been a childhood friend of the young Andronikos III; he was his most intelligent and influential supporter in the civil war, and he was to become the leading figure or the power behind the scene for much of the rest of the fourteenth century. He was also the author of his own memoirs, written in retirement later in his career, and this has put him at unfair disadvantage. For it has been perhaps too often assumed, at least by latter-day historians of Byzantium, that John Cantacuzene's object in writing the history of his own time was to present his own shortcomings in the most favourable light. Scholars have therefore tended to magnify his shortcomings to give themselves the satisfaction of pointing out where Cantacuzene has concealed or excused them; and between the lines of some of the clearest and simplest literary Greek style written in the Byzantine period they have discerned the workings of a devious and dishonest mind. Cantacuzene's memoirs are undoubtedly in some sense an apologia. But the statements that he makes in his own favour are often justified, for none of his contemporaries had the same measure of talents as a soldier, an administrator, or a writer. In 1320, however, he held only a minor position at court.[7]

Syrgiannes was a less stable character. He may have been of Mongol descent on his father's side, but his mother was a cousin of the Emperor Andronikos II and related to the Cantacuzene family. He had earned a reputation for rebellion during a spell as a military governor in Macedonia. Syrgiannes was unscrupulous and ambitious; but he was, or he made out to be, a devoted friend of Andronikos III. Theodore Synadenos was rather older and had been a friend of the late Michael IX. Like John Cantacuzene he belonged to the military and landed aristocracy. He held a command in Thrace until 1320 when the old Emperor, sensing what was in the wind, posted him to the Serbian frontier. There was a fourth party to the conspiracy who came from a very different background. His name was Alexios Apokaukos. He could lay no claim to noble birth or landed property. He was an upstart, one of the nouveaux riches thrown up by the unsettled conditions of the time; and he owed what fortune and position he had to John Cantacuzene, who had befriended and trusted him. Shameless and resourceful, Apokaukos was in the plot only for what he could get out of it. To begin with he was content to get little.[8]

These were the men who rallied round Andronikos III when he was disowned by his grandfather in 1320. John Cantacuzene and Syrgiannes prepared the ground for action on his behalf by bribing the authorities to give them commands in Thrace where discontent was rife, and where the names of Michael IX and his son were perhaps more respected than that of the old Emperor. By exploiting the grievances of the overtaxed population and appropriating the revenues they were able to raise armies to fight for the overthrow of Andronikos II. Cantacuzene presents in his memoirs an almost blow by blow account of what then took place. For him it was a spontaneous uprising on behalf of a wronged prince who was also his personal friend. Gregoras, whose account is less charged with emotion, interprets the affair as a deliberate plot to dethrone Andronikos II. Both versions are true. To be successful the business had to be planned in advance, as Cantacuzene readily admits. But there was also a general feeling that there was a wrong to be righted, and there was a hope that the younger Emperor who had suffered that wrong might be able to save the Empire that his grandfather had nearly ruined.

When word of the plot reached Andronikos II, he had his grandson arrested and interrogated before the Patriarch, the hierarchy and the senators. But at Easter 1321 the young Andronikos slipped out of Constantinople with a party of followers on the pretext of going on a hunting expedition. He made his way to the camp near Adrianople where his friends John Cantacuzene and Syrgiannes were waiting for him. In Thrace he was hailed as Emperor and excited a fervour of loyalty by lavish promises and donations. The old Emperor was rightly anxious that the spirit of revolt would spread to Constantinople. He blustered and threatened. He made the Patriarch excommunicate the conspirators and demanded an oath of allegiance from his own officials. But when news came that Syrgiannes was leading an army on the capital he gave in. On 6 June 1321 an agreement was reached, partly through the mediation of the mother of Syrgiannes who went out to meet her son near Selymbria. The Empire was to be partitioned between the two Emperors Andronikos. They were to rule as colleagues, Andronikos III in Adrianople, Andronikos II in Constantinople. So far no blood had been shed.

There is little doubt that popular opinion was mainly on the side of Andronikos III. But for various reasons his supporters could not agree among themselves. Syrgiannes was upset by the young Emperor's evident partiality for John Cantacuzene and claimed in addition that his wife's honour had been slighted. In December 1321 he changed sides and encouraged Andronikos II to renew the conflict. The old Emperor was ready enough to teach his grandson a lesson and to protest that he had violated their agreement. War broke out, and for some six months there was fighting in Thrace. Andronikos III was soon desperately short of money to pay his mercenaries and afraid of losing popularity if he reimposed the taxes that he had abolished. John Cantacuzene and his mother came to his rescue, however, and Cantacuzene paid his own mercenaries from his private fortune. But the young Emperor's cause continued to win support. Thessalonica declared for him, and then the island of Lemnos.[9]

In July 1322 a second settlement was reached between the two Emperors. The experiment of partitioning the Empire was now scrapped, and Andronikos reluctantly conceded that his grandson should rule as his colleague over the whole Empire and be nominated as his heir. He was to receive an annual stipend of 36,000 *hyperpyra* and his troops were to be provided for by the state. But no amount of formal language could conceal the mistrust that existed. Andronikos II remained senior in authority; and so long as this was the case the young Andronikos and his advisers could never introduce any new domestic or foreign policies for the Empire's benefit. For all that he was now accepted as Emperor in the capital, Andronikos III preferred to reside in the Thracian city of Didymoteichos. For five years the two Emperors spied on each other's movements while presenting a façade of collaboration.[10]

The letter of their agreement was honoured. On 2 February 1325 Andronikos III was crowned as Emperor in St Sophia. In October 1326 he obeyed his grandfather's wishes by taking as his second wife Giovanna or Anne, the daughter of Count Amadeo V of Savoy. A superficial calm prevailed, but there was little real trust or confidence; the partisans of either side in the late civil war, as well as the protagonists, seemed to be so immersed in intrigue that they had little time to attend to the Empire's welfare or protection. Syrgiannes, whose own schemes were upset by the reconciliation between the two emperors, was caught plotting to murder Andronikos II and seize the throne. He was tried and condemned to perpetual imprisonment. The state of paralysis was fully exploited by the Empire's enemies. About 1324 Andronikos II in desperation had granted a pardon to Alexios Philanthropenos, the general who had been convicted of treason in Asia Minor nearly 30 years before, and sent him to relieve the Turkish blockade of the city of Philadelphia. Philanthropenos was blind and elderly; though he took an oath of loyalty the Emperor would not trust him with an army under his own command. But to the Turks in Lydia his name was still a legend, and the news of his return to the scene of his former triumphs is said to have sent them scattering from Philadelphia. But no one seemed able to prevent bands of Turkish pirates from raiding the coast of Thrace. John Cantacuzene, who was appointed Grand Domestic or commander-in-chief by both Emperors jointly, did what he could under the circumstances. He helped Andronikos III to hold the pass in the north against renewed attacks by the Bulgars and by the Mongols of the Golden Horde. He was praised to the skies by one of his correspondents for a campaign that he fought and won against the Turks across the Hellespont. But it was in April 1326 that the Osmanlis forced the citizens of Brusa to surrender; and no Byzantine army seems to have been there to relieve the siege.[11]

At that time the minds of both emperors were distracted by a new development in the western provinces. The governor of Thessalonica, John Palaiologos, a nephew of Andronikos II, seceded from the Empire and declared his independence. He was supported by the commanders of two of the Macedonian fortresses on the Serbian frontier; and the King of Serbia, Stephen Dečanski, was waiting to help him establish an autonomous principality in Thessalonica. John gave his daughter in marriage to Dečanski. His rebellion caused great anxiety in the Empire for a short while, though it came to an end when he died in 1327. But he had succeeded in arousing the interest of Serbia in Byzantine politics, and this was a development fraught with trouble for the future.[12]

The third and final stage of the civil war between Andronikos II and his grandson opened in the autumn of 1327. It was characterized if not instigated by the intervention on opposing sides of the rulers of Serbia and Bulgaria. The Bulgarian tsar Michael Šišman had married the widow of his predecessor Svetoslav in 1323. She was a sister of Andronikos III. In May 1327 Andronikos spent a week with his new brother-in-law on the Bulgarian frontier and made a treaty with him. The terms were that he would help Šišman in war against the Serbs if Šišman would support him in war against his grandfather. Almost at the same moment Andronikos II was negotiating an alliance of his own with Stephen Dečanski of Serbia. It was a dangerous precedent to invite the foreign enemies of the Empire to take sides in its domestic disputes. But the way had now been shown.

In October 1327 Andronikos III and his court moved down from Didymoteichos to Selymbria. They were met by messengers from the old Emperor telling them to stay clear of Constantinople since Andronikos had violated his agreements. For two months rude messages were passed back and forth between the Emperors. Andronikos II sent a deputation of bishops, monks and senators to reason with his grandson and to lay various charges against him. Some of the charges were probably valid, but the purpose of the exercise was simply to give the old Emperor just cause for questioning yet again his grandson's right to the throne. The Patriarch Esaias was asked to excommunicate Andronikos III. He refused to do so and was confined to a monastery. The old Emperor had lost his sense of proportion, and by 1327 he had lost the confidence of all but his lifelong friends. His Grand Logothete Theodore Metochites remained faithful to the end.

In the winter of 1327 feeling in favour of Andronikos III rose high in the Empire and even in Constantinople. He saw to it that the flames were fanned by propaganda, by still more promises of a new deal under a new Emperor, of lower taxes for the people and higher pay for the troops. John Cantacuzene and Theodore Synadenos, who were both with him in Thrace, advised him strongly that the moment had now come to put an end to the business by open war. In January 1328 the city of Thessalonica surrendered to him. Various other cities and fortresses in Macedonia followed the lead set by Thessalonica. The King of Serbia preferred to hover on the sidelines and did nothing to honour his alliance with the Emperor in Constantinople. Michael Šišman of Bulgaria, on the other hand, now offered to change sides.

The offer, made in secret, was gladly accepted by Andronikos II, and 3000 Bulgarian cavalry arrived to take up their positions outside the walls of Constantinople. In the spring of 1328 Andronikos III hurried his army towards the capital to forestall any further movement of Bulgarian troops to its defence. He persuaded the commander of the Bulgarian cavalry to withdraw, and sent a stiff note to Michael Šišman to remind him of the terms of their alliance. The way was clear for his entry into Constantinople.

The population in the capital in May 1328 were ready for almost any form of relief from their distress. For some weeks a Venetian fleet of 40 ships had been blockading Galata and the Bosporos by way of reprisal against the Genoese. The control that the Italians exercised over the life of Constantinople had never been more graphically demonstrated. While civil war was raging over the Byzantine throne, Venice and Genoa continued with bland unconcern to fight out their own private quarrels in the Bosporos. With no supply ships coming in the food shortage in the city was acute. Andronikos III tried to turn the situation to his own profit by secretly offering the Venetian admiral a sum of money to withdraw. But the Venetians were only interested in getting their pound of flesh from the Genoese.

On the night of 23 May, however, Andronikos III, Cantacuzene and Synadenos, who had already contacted their supporters inside the city, made their way into Constantinople by bribing one of the guards. A rope ladder was let down from the walls by the gate of St Romanos, and the first men over opened the gate from within. The young Emperor marched into the city at the head of a force of some 800 troops. But they had orders to make no disturbance and to offer no violence to any person or property. Andronikos III, like his great-grandfather Michael VIII (67 years before), wished it to be thought that God alone had granted him possession of the city. The old Emperor, who had been roused from sleep by the uproar in the streets, was understandably fearful for his safety. But he was treated with courtesy and humanity. Although now obliged to abdicate in favour of his grandson, he was permitted to retain his imperial insignia and to go on living in the palace, and he was provided with a pension. The Patriarch Esaias, who had boldly refused to excommunicate Andronikos III, was now brought out in triumph from the monastery where he had been confined. A strange scene took place which perhaps expressed some of the people's relief from tension. The Patriarch was led back to his palace in one of the imperial carriages. On his way a procession accompanied him not of bishops and priests but of musicians and dancing girls, one of whom, riding her horse like a man, reduced the Patriarch and the rest of the company to helpless laughter by her antics and her bawdy nonsense.[13]

Despite the Emperor's orders there was some looting of property by the troops and people, particularly of the wealthier houses. Nikephoros Gregoras claims to have been a victim. But the only house that was thoroughly plundered and destroyed was that of the Grand Logothete, Theodore Metochites. He was held responsible, rightly or wrongly, for the failures of his friend and master Andronikos II; and he served as a scapegoat. His very considerable fortune was partly taken over by the imperial treasury and he was sent into exile. Two years later the old Emperor was pushed into a monastery and became a monk with the name of Antonios. In his last years he went blind. He died on 13 February 1332 after dining with his daughter Simonis who, 30 years before, he had given as a child wife to Stephen Milutin of Serbia. He was in his 74th year and had reigned for almost exactly half a century. A month later his faithful counsellor Theodore Metochites also died as a monk. He had been allowed to return to Constantinople to reside in the monastery of the Chora which he had lavishly restored at his own expense. Funeral orations on both men were composed and read by Nikephoros Gregoras. The Patriarch Esaias, the last of the eight patriarchs appointed and dismissed by the pious Emperor Andronikos II, died in May of the same year. It was like the passing of an age.[14]

NOTES

The principal narrative sources are: Gregoras, I, 283-428; Cantacuzene, I, 13-306.

Modern works: The causes and events of the first civil war (1321-8) are analysed by V. Parisot, *Cantacuzène, homme d'état et historien* (Paris, 1845), 29-83; T. Florinskij, 'Andronik Mladšij i Ioann Kantakuzin', *Žurnal ministerstva narodnago prosveščenija*, CCIV (1879), 87-143; Ursula V. Bosch, *Kaiser Andronikos III. Palaiologos. Versuch einer Darstellung der byzantinischen Gesellschaft in den Jahren 1321-1341* (Amsterdam, 1965), 7-52.

1 A. Th. Papadopulos, *Versuch einer Genealogie der Palaiologen 1259-1453* (Munich, 1938), nos. 58, 59, 60. Cf. Dade, *Versuche*, 67f.; C. Marinescu, 'Tentatives de mariage de deux fils d'Andronic II Paléo-

169

logue avec des princesses latines'; and G. I. Bratianu, 'Notes sur le projet de mariage entre l'empereur Michael IX Paléologue et Catherine de Courtenay', in *Revue historique du sud-est européen*, I (1924), 59-63, 139-43.

2 Georgios Sphrantzes, *Memorii 1401-1477*, ed. V. Grecu (Bucharest, 1966), 172. Cf. Gregoras, I, 233-5.

3 Cf. C. Diehl, 'Yolande de Montferrat', in Diehl, *Impératrices de Byzance* (Paris, 1959), 265-74 (=*Figures byzantines*, II (Paris, 1908), 226-45; Hélène Constantinidi-Bibicou, 'Yolande de Montferrat impératrice de Byzance', *L'Hellénisme contemporain*, 2me série, IV, 6 (1950), 425-42; Ostrogorsky, *History*, 480-1. A. E. Laiou, 'A Byzantine prince latinized: Theodore Palaeologus, Marquis of Montferrat', *B*, XXXVIII (1968), 386-410; J. W. Barker, 'The problem of appanages in Byzantium during the Palaiologan period', *Byzantina*, III (Thessalonike, 1971), 103-22.

4 Gregoras, I, 277, 283-6. *Short Chronicle of 1352*, ed. Loenertz, part I, 333, 348. Cf. Bosch, *Kaiser Andronikos III*, 9-12.

5 Gregoras, I, 317-18.

6 Gregoras, I, 319.

7 On the antecedents and early career of John Cantacuzene, see D. M. Nicol, *The Byzantine Family of Kantakouzenos (Cantacuzenus)* (Dumbarton Oaks Studies, XI: Washington, D.C., 1968), 27-36.

8 On Syrgiannes, see S. Binon, 'A propos d'un prostagma inédit d'Andronic III Paléologue', *BZ*, XXXVIII (1938), 133-5, 377-407. On Alexios Apokaukos, see R. Guilland, 'Etudes de civilisation et de littérature byzantines, I: Alexis Apocaucus', in *Revue du Lyonnais* (1921), 523-54; A. Xyngopoulos, 'St Demetrios the Megas Doux Apokaukos' (in Greek), *Hellenika*, XV (*Festschrift S. B. Kougeas*) (1957), 122-40; S. Eyice, 'Alexis Apocauque et l'église byzantine de Sélymbria (Silivri)', *B*, XXXIV (1964), 77-104; O. Feld, 'Noch einmal Alexios Apokaukos und die byzantinische Kirche von Selymbria (Silivri)', *B*, XXXVII (1967), 56-65.

9 Bosch, *Andronikos III*, 19-25.

10 Bosch, *Andronikos III*, 26-34. It has been suggested that the double-headed eagle, which is often described as the heraldic device of the house of Palaiologos but which seems first to have been so employed by Andronikos III, was adopted in place of the single-headed eagle to symbolize this division of the imperium between the two Andronikoi in 1325. B. Hemmerdinger, 'Deux notes d'héraldique', *BZ*, LXI (1968), 304-9.

11 Nicol, *Byzantine Family of Kantakouzenos*, 39. On the marriage

of Andronikos III to Anne of Savoy, see Bosch, *Andronikos III*, 106-7; and in general, D. Muratore, *Una principessa Sabauda sul trono di Bisanzio, Giovanna di Savoia imperatrice Anna Paleologina* (Chambéry, 1906); C. Diehl, 'Anne de Savoie, femme d'Andronic III', in Diehl, *Impératrices de Byzance*, 275-95. On Philanthropenos, see Gregoras, I, 361-2; and *Correspondance de Nicéphore Grégoras*, ed. R. Guilland (Paris, 1927), no. 47, 166-73; P. Schreiner, 'Zur Geschichte Philadelpheias im 14. Jahrhundert', *OCP*, XXXV (1969), 375f.

12 Bosch, *Andronikos III*, 39-41.

13 Bosch, *Andronikos III*, 42-52; Nicol, *Byzantine Family of Kantakouzenos*, 39-40. The restoration of the Patriarch Esaias is described by Gregoras, I, 425.

14 Gregoras, I, 426-8, 460-3, 465-81. Cf. *Short Chronicle of 1352*, ed. Loenertz, part II, 40, 50-2.

Eleven

The Reign of Andronikos III
1328-41

The younger generation had triumphed, but at great cost. If the civil war between Andronikos II and his grandson had been the last of its kind, or if it had been fought in other circumstances, the Byzantine Empire might have reaped some benefit from the victory of new men with new ideas. But the war had stirred up too many rivalries and jealousies, and by the time it was over too many outside parties had discovered that there was a profit to be made by keeping those rivalries alive. In the years between 1321 and 1328 the Serbs and the Bulgars had been shown an easy way to keep a foot in the door of Constantinople; while the Italians and still more the Turks had turned the Empire's malaise to their own advantage.

Andronikos III was 31 years of age when he became undisputed master of the Empire in May 1328. At the time, although already twice married, he had no children. There was therefore as yet no question of following the precedent set by his ancestors and nominating a co-Emperor or heir to the throne. Andronikos preferred the excitement of action to the tedium of administration. He liked to lead his own men into battle, and he was usually more successful as a general than his father and always more popular with his soldiers than his grandfather, who had seldom led them in person as an Emperor. Hunting was his great delight and he is said to have maintained an establishment of 1000 huntsmen, 1000 falcons, and 1000 hounds. But he also enjoyed showing his prowess at the un-Byzantine activity of jousting, a western pastime that had been introduced to his court by the Italian entourage of his second wife, Anne of Savoy. The young Emperor found their company most congenial. To celebrate the birth of his first son John in 1332 he staged a tournament at Didymoteichos and caused great alarm by breaking lances with some of the foreigners in jousting contests.[1] His more elderly courtiers thought that such proceedings were unnecessarily risky and also degrading to an emperor. But some of the older generation were inclined on other counts to feel that the coming of Andronikos III to the throne had lowered the standards of behaviour at court. For he was none too keen on ceremonial and liked to be more accessible to his subjects than his rather aloof grandfather. Perhaps he had less to fear from them.

Those who had helped him in the civil war received their rewards when it was over. Theodore Synadenos was made Prefect of the city. Syrgiannes was released from prison and pardoned on the recommendation of John Cantacuzene, and was appointed governor of Thessalonica. Alexios Apokaukos, who had so far played his part with cautious discretion, was nominated as controller of the imperial secretariat, the treasury and the revenue. These were duties which John Cantacuzene had hitherto performed on behalf of Andronikos III, and it was he who handed them over to Apokaukos. Cantacuzene himself retained no office or title except that of Grand Domestic. But he was acknowledged to be the first minister in the new government. Almost all appointments were in his gift; almost all affairs of state passed through his hands. He sometimes made the mistake of supposing that those whose fortunes he created by promoting them to office would be loyal as well as grateful. Syrgiannes and Apokaukos were to teach him bitter lessons in this respect. But the Emperor had every confidence in him, and it was not misplaced for their friendship was proverbial. More than once Andronikos urged Cantacuzene to accept the title of co-Emperor or at least of regent. But he preferred to wield the power without the title and to support the right of the reigning Emperor.

There were several people in high places who resented the influence that John Cantacuzene had with the Emperor. The Empress Anne of Savoy felt that he had too much hold over her husband. The Emperor's mother Maria, the widow of Michael IX, was even more bitter at being pushed into the background by Cantacuzene. She was, moreover, insanely jealous of Cantacuzene's mother Theodora, whose wealth and ambition had played so great a part in her son's rise to power. Maria preferred to live in Thessalonica, which kept her out of the way. But the undercurrents of intrigue were still strong even though the civil war might seem to be over.

The new Emperor was quick to show his foreign enemies that things had changed. In June 1328 Michael Šišman of Bulgaria violated his agreements yet again by invading northern Thrace and bringing his Bulgar and Mongol army within sight of Adrianople. Andronikos III retaliated by leading his own army up to the frontier and capturing a Bulgarian fortress; and when Šišman repeated the experiment two months later the Emperor had an army drawn up ready to challenge him in battle. He preferred to negotiate, and a new treaty was signed at Adrianople. It was ratified in 1329 and the Bulgars gave no further trouble during the reign of Andronikos III. Those who had expected that the Byzantine Empire must be ruined and exhausted by civil war were surprised to find that under its new management it possessed a new vigour and a power to hit back.[2]

In Europe it might still be possible to show the flag to lesser breeds like the Bulgars. But in Asia Minor nothing could now save Byzantine prestige. Brusa had fallen to Osman in 1326. Andronikos II had mourned its loss but had not allowed his grandson to go to its rescue. Brusa became the first capital of the Osmanlis; from there Orchan, who succeeded his father in the same year, directed his warriors to the conquest of the other Byzantine cities in Bithynia, especially Nicaea and Nikomedia, which had been isolated for some years. Andronikos III and John Cantacuzene were determined at least to make the effort to save the situation by holding up the Turkish advance along the Gulf of Nikomedia towards Constantinople. In May 1329 they hurriedly collected an army of 2000 veterans from the capital and not many more from Thrace. On 1 June they were ferried across the Bosporos to Chrysopolis or Skutari by a fleet of boats which stayed on hand in case a retreat had to be sounded. The Emperor and his Grand Domestic led the army along the shore of the Gulf of Nikomedia until, on the third day of their march, they came to a place called Pelekanon. There they sighted Orchan encamped in the hills above the coast with about 8000 men. The conditions were far from favourable for the Byzantines. But on 10 June they challenged the Turks to fight. Orchan made the most of his advantage. Three hundred of his mounted archers attacked the Byzantine army in the plain while the main body of his troops waited in the hills. Towards evening two larger assaults by the Turks were driven back. But at nightfall Cantacuzene advised the Emperor that since the Turks would not come down from the hills and fight on equal terms the Byzantines should withdraw to their camp and beat an orderly retreat the following morning. During the withdrawal, however, the Turks charged the rear of the army and the Emperor was wounded in the knee. A rumour got about that his wound was fatal, and in the night the Byzantine soldiers panicked, deserted the camp and made for the coast. Cantacuzene vainly tried to restore order. The Emperor was carried on a stretcher to the port of Philokrene, where he was put on a ship for Constantinople. He reached the capital on 11 June. But meanwhile the

Turks had pursued the army in its flight to the coast, and at dawn on 11 June a battle was fought outside the walls of Philokrene. Two high-ranking officers, both relatives of Cantacuzene, were killed in the action. But Cantacuzene himself managed to rally the remnants and march them in something like order to Chrysopolis, where they had left their ferry-boats.[3]

The battle of Pelekanon was the first direct encounter on the field of battle between a Byzantine emperor and an Osmanli emir. It proved the futility of supposing that any military solution could now be provided to the Turkish problem, at least in that part of Asia Minor. The collapse of Byzantine resistance in Bithynia was rapid and total after 1329. Nicaea surrendered to Orchan on 2 March 1331. Nikomedia held out until 1337.[4] But well before that date the Emperor had sunk his pride and made terms with the Osmanlis. In August 1333 he crossed over to Asia Minor on the pretext of relieving the siege of Nikomedia, which Orchan was then personally conducting. But instead of fighting Andronikos invited Orchan to meet him and discuss the terms of a treaty. This was the first diplomatic encounter between the Emperor and the emir, and the first indication of a new Byzantine approach to the Turkish problem. It is tempting to see the guiding hand of John Cantacuzene behind this policy. But he is reticent about what the treaty entailed, for it was more humiliating to the Byzantines than his own account of it would suggest. The full terms are supplied only by one of the chronicles: the Emperor agreed to pay an annual tribute of 120,000 *hyperpyra* to the Osmanlis for the possession of the few remaining Byzantine territories in Bithynia.[5]

On the other hand, it was more realistic to make a settlement with Orchan than to pretend that the Empire was in a fit state to muster and equip an army of the strength needed to reconquer Asia Minor. And the Byzantines could always comfort themselves with the thought that this would inevitably occur in God's good time. But the Osmanlis set such a good example of pacific conquerors that they won the confidence of many of their victims. When Nicaea fell, for example, Orchan allowed all who wanted to leave the city to go, taking with them their holy relics. Few availed themselves of the chance. No reprisals were taken against those who had resisted, and the city was left to manage its internal affairs under its own municipal government. The resistance had in fact depended very largely on the strength of the walls of Nicaea, and on the lingering hope that help would come from Constantinople. After the battle of Pelekanon in 1329 the city's walls remained but the hope of relief had faded. The inhabitants surrendered not from starvation or defeat but from a calculation of their own best interests. They were quickly and willingly incorporated into the growing Osmanli nation. Only eight years after the fall of Nicaea, the Patriarch of Constantinople was shocked to learn that many of the citizens of this once great Christian city had already abjured their Orthodox faith and embraced Islam. In 1339 and 1340 he addressed encyclicals to them for the salvation of their souls, but it was too late.[6]

The capture of Nicaea and Nikomedia all but completed the Osmanli conquest of Bithynia and the north-western corner of Asia Minor. By 1336 Orchan had also taken over the emirate of Karasi in Mysia and so extended his domain along the south shore of the Sea of Marmora up to the Hellespont and as far south as Pergamon. For some years to come that was the limit of Orchan's territorial ambitions. Turkish pirates from all parts of Asia Minor, however, continued to come over on plundering expeditions to the islands and to the coast of Thrace; and the emirs of Menteshe in the south and of Aydin in the region of Smyrna were beginning to attract the notice of a wider world by their activities in the Aegean Sea. Andronikos III made it his business to rebuild the Byzantine navy and to strengthen the line of defence in the islands along the coast of Asia Minor. In the autumn of 1329 the island of Chios reverted to imperial rule. Chios had been taken over in 1304 by the Genoese adventurer Benedetto Zaccaria. It had been formally ceded to him as a fief by Andronikos II, and his successor Martino Zaccaria still held it as such in 1328. Martino was a great lord in a small but wealthy island and the Turks respected him. Philip of Taranto, who hoped for his assistance in the conquest of Constantinople, was pleased to call him 'King and Despot of Asia Minor'. But in 1329 the Greeks in the island decided that they had had enough of him and rebelled. Their uprising was led by one of their own nobles, Leo Kalothetos, who was an old friend of John Cantacuzene. It was helped by the treachery of Martino's brother Benedetto II Zaccaria. In the autumn of that year Andronikos III came to the support of the islanders with his fleet and Martino was captured and carried off to Constantinople as a prisoner. Kalothetos was appointed as Byzantine governor of Chios. The annual revenue of the island was said to be 120,000 *hyperpyra*. It was therefore a valuable economic asset. But its strategic value was even greater, as the Turks were well aware.

It was now possible for Andronikos III to re-assert Byzantine authority on the mainland opposite Chios. At the end of 1329 he sailed across to the Genoese city of New Phokaia and, in the absence of its ruler Andreolo Cattaneo, accepted the allegiance if not the surrender of his deputy. But that was not the only purpose of the Emperor's journey. For at the same time he invited the emirs of Saruchan and Aydin to come and see him and negotiate some kind of settlement. Saruchan came in person. Mehmed of Aydin was indisposed, but he sent messengers with presents for the Emperor. The event is recorded by the Turkish poet Enveri as well as by John Cantacuzene. The former saw it as the submission of the Emperor to the father of his hero Umur; the latter saw it as an agreement made for the benefit of the Byzantine Empire. Whatever the terms of that agreement it may be considered as another tentative step towards the new policy of the Byzantine government with regard to the Turks; and, as with the agreement made with Orchan a few years later, the initiative may well have come from John Cantacuzene. If Byzantium could control the principal Aegean islands with the support or at least the neutrality of the Turkish emirates in the south then it might be possible to contain the Osmanlis and encourage the other emirs to fight them. It might also be possible to prevent the Italians, and especially the Genoese, from gaining any further territory in Byzantine waters.[7]

Unfortunately the Emperor and his Grand Domestic were not to be allowed to pursue their own policies in this part of the world. The Knights of Rhodes, the Venetians, the Genoese, the French kings of Cyprus and the many lesser Latin rulers in the Greek islands all had a stake in the eastern Mediterranean. Their fate at the hands of the Turks became a matter of concern for all the Catholic powers of western Europe. As early as 1327 the Venetians were thinking in terms of the formation of a league of Christian powers against the Turks which should include the Byzantine Emperor and the Knights of Rhodes. But the initiative in organizing the league was assumed by Pope John XXII. The interested parties fell into two categories. On the one hand there were those like the Pope himself and the King of France who saw a campaign against the Turkish emirs in the larger context of a new crusade which could pass through Asia Minor on its way to the Holy Land. On the other hand there were those who were already long settled in the area. Their ideas were limited to the more immediate objective of protecting their trade or their property from the growing nuisance and danger of Turkish piracy.

It was difficult to know what part the Byzantines could or would play in this western venture. Since the restoration of Orthodoxy in 1282 there had been no communication between the Byzantine Emperor and the Papacy until in 1324 Andronikos II sent the first of a number of envoys to pay his respects to the papal court at Avignon. The question of the union of the Churches was once more in the air. The Emperor also made contact with King Charles IV of France. In 1326 the Pope and the French king sent a Dominican friar to Constantinople to seek assurances that these overtures were sincere and to see how best the Byzantines might be brought back to the fold of the Roman Church. If ever they were to be invited to join a league of Christian allies they must first become Christian in the proper sense. Schismatics could hardly be accepted as partners in a project sponsored by the Pope. Andronikos II and his Grand Logothete Theodore Metochites both wrote courteous letters to the King of France. But they were deeply pessimistic about the prospect of proclaiming the union of the Churches. The civil war was in its final phase and the old Emperor would not endanger what little popularity he retained by publicizing his interest in such an inflammatory subject.[8]

In 1332 the league of Christian powers began to take shape. The Venetian nobleman Marino Sanudo Torsello, who was related to the Duke of Naxos and had an expert knowledge of eastern affairs, performed prodigies of diplomatic and propagandist activity to rouse the Catholic west to a crusade against the Turks before it was too late. It was probably due to his influence that Andronikos III was invited to co-operate with Venice and the Knights in the formation of a maritime league in September 1332. But the Pope did not share Sanudo's comparatively sympathetic attitude to the schismatic Greeks. The anti-Turkish league as constituted at Avignon in 1334 made no allowance for Byzantine participation. Its membership was in the end restricted to the Papacy, France, Venice, Rhodes and Cyprus. The situation had become more pressing in the meantime; for in 1332 and 1333 Umur of Aydin had launched his first piratical raids across the Aegean Sea and attacked the Venetian island of Negroponte as well as the Greek mainland. The league's first military objective must clearly be the harbour of Smyrna, from which Umur conducted his operations. In the summer of 1334 a fleet of 40 ships contributed by its members sailed into the eastern Mediterranean. They had some limited success against the Turks, notably against the emir of Karasi off Adramyttion, but they failed to reach Smyrna; and at the end of the year they withdrew. In December Pope John XXII died and for a time the league went into abeyance. Its members fell out among themselves, and Umur of Aydin resumed his profitable piracy.[9]

The Byzantines were aware that the main concern of the western powers was not the defence of Constantinople but the defence of their possessions in the Aegean and off the coast of Asia Minor, which properly belonged to the Byzantine Empire. Pope John XXII and his successors tried to bring the Emperor into the picture, but always and only on condition that he would agree to renounce the schism. Andronikos III was more ready than his grandfather had been to discuss the matter with the Pope's representatives, though he did so with the greatest reserve and the minimum of publicity. But he was not willing to win the favour of the west by bullying all his people into submission, as Michael VIII had done; and he was inclined to feel that the best way to protect his empire from its nearest enemies, the Osmanlis, might be to make alliances with the other Turkish emirs against whom the league of western powers was directed.

The activities of the Genoese finally confirmed him in this opinion. In 1335 Benedetto Zaccaria, brother of Martino who had been dispossessed of Chios in 1329, borrowed some ships from his friends in Galata and tried to recapture the island. He failed; but later in the same year his action was imitated by Domenico Cattaneo, the Genoese lord of Phokaia, who revoked his allegiance to the Emperor and attacked the island of Lesbos. With ships hired from Genoa and from Rhodes, Cattaneo occupied Mitylene and most of the island. The Genoese in Galata, who had encouraged both of these enterprises, strengthened the fortifications round their settlement for fear of reprisals from the Emperor. But when the news reached the capital that the Genoese had captured Lesbos the Emperor ordered the defences of Galata to be destroyed; and he himself then set out with John Cantacuzene and a fleet for the scene of the trouble.

Andronikos III was now convinced that the Turkish emirs were rather more reliable allies than the Italians. It was against the Genoese as much as against the Osmanlis that he called on the help of the emirs Saruchan and Umur. At the end of 1335, having left some ships to blockade Lesbos, he sailed over to lay siege to Phokaia. Saruchan sent him some help and kept his troops supplied with provisions while the siege went on, until the city surrendered. Umur of Aydin, however, came to see the Emperor in person. They met at Cape Erythrea or Kara Burun, between Chios and Smyrna; and there a treaty of alliance more formal and more binding than any that had gone before was concluded between the Empire and the emirate of Aydin. John Cantacuzene, who was present at the meeting, no doubt rightly takes much of the credit for having arranged it, and he persuaded Umur to lend ships for the recovery of the island of Lesbos from the Genoese. Mitylene surrendered to the imperial forces in the winter of 1336, after the Emperor had returned to Constantinople.[10]

The Emperor's interview with Umur at Kara Burun is once again described by Enveri as well as by Cantacuzene, though their interpretations of the event are naturally different. It marked the beginning of a long friendship between John Cantacuzene and Umur. They spent four days wining and dining each other. Nikephoros Gregoras was later to compare their relationship to that between Pylades and Orestes. The treaty that came of it all was a defensive alliance of Byzantium with the emirate of Aydin against the Osmanlis as well as the Italians. It implied Byzantine recognition of the emirate as a permanent institution, and the Emperor had to pay the sum of 100,000 *hyperpyra* to Umur. But the arrangement secured peace between Byzantium and the emirates of Saruchan and Aydin at least until the death of Andronikos III in 1341; and Umur was happy to provide the Emperor with large numbers of soldiers to fight his battles in Europe. These were perhaps dangerous tactics; but they are intelligible, given the hostility of the Italians and the demands of the Papacy concerning Byzantine participation in the league of Christian powers.[11]

While these events were taking place in the east, changes were occurring in the Balkans which were to have great consequences. The peace between Byzantium and Bulgaria had not been disturbed since Michael Šišman had been pacified in 1328. But Šišman's own relations with his neighbours in Serbia were far from friendly. In 1330 war broke out, and on 28 July the forces of Stephen Dečanski destroyed the Bulgarian army in a battle at Velbužd, the modern Kjustendil. Michael Šišman was fatally wounded. His wife, Theodore, the sister of Andronikos III, was driven out of the country, and the victorious Serbian king set up a ruler in Bulgaria who was related to his own family. The battle of Velbužd brought little benefit to the Byzantines. Andronikos occupied some fortresses on the Bulgarian frontier and seized the ports of Mesembria and Anchialos on the Black Sea under pretext of avenging his sister Theodora. But he had to abandon them shortly afterwards.

The aftermath of the battle produced palace revolutions in both countries. In Bulgaria the Serbian protégé was dismissed and a nephew of Michael Šišman called John Alexander Stracimir came to the throne. In Serbia a rebellion against Stephen Dečanski broke out almost immediately after the battle. It was led by some of the nobles who felt that he should have pursued his victory. They persuaded his son to assist in his father's murder and then ascend the throne in 1331. His name was Stephen Uroš IV, but he became known as Stephen Dušan. It was he who followed up his father's victory at Velbužd, not by the destruction of Bulgaria but by a union of Bulgarian and Serbian interests which left him free to begin a systematic conquest of the Byzantine province of Macedonia. Dušan married a sister of John Alexander of Bulgaria, and under his régime the Serbs began to dream the dream that had haunted the Bulgars in the past, of making Constantinople the capital of a new form of empire in which Slavs would predominate over Greeks.[12]

The proximity of Thessalonica to the Serbian frontier was always a danger to Byzantium and a challenge to the rulers of Serbia in the fourteenth century. After the civil war Cantacuzene had appointed his friend Syrgiannes as its governor. Syrgiannes was a clever soldier but not the most trustworthy of men. He had not been long in Thessalonica when he began to intrigue with the Empress-mother Maria against John Cantacuzene. She was so taken with him that she adopted him as her son. When she died in 1333 his suspicious behaviour was brought to the notice of the Emperor, who was in the district at the time. The Emperor had just been on a remarkably successful campaign in Thessaly and had rounded it off with an equally successful interview with Stephen Dušan which had resulted in what seemed like an understanding between Serbia and Byzantium. He did not want his triumphs to be marred by a conspiracy in Thessalonica. Syrgiannes was brought to Constantinople to stand trial for treason. But the trial never took place for the prisoner escaped by night to Galata and disappeared. Later it became known that he had found his way to Negroponte and from there, by way of Thessaly, to Serbia. He presented himself as a refugee to Stephen Dušan, who supplied him with troops; and in 1334 Syrgiannes seized the town of Kastoria from its Byzantine garrison and showed the Serbian army the way to the conquest of a number of other Byzantine fortresses in Macedonia. Dušan conveniently forgot his recent understanding with the Emperor Andronikos and made full use of the ally that providence had sent him.

The presence of so talented and distinguished a defector commanding a Serbian army within striking distance of Thessalonica called for immediate counter-action. The Emperor at once prepared to lead his soldiers to the spot. But one of his officers, Sphrantzes Palaiologos, offered to go forward into Serbian territory, gain the confidence of Syrgiannes and then arrest him. He was given leave to make the attempt while the Emperor and his Grand Domestic marched to

Thessalonica. In the event Sphrantzes exceeded his orders by murdering Syrgiannes. But the crime produced the desired effect. Stephen Dušan sent envoys to the Emperor to negotiate another peace settlement, and in August 1334 Andronikos again met the Serbian king at a river not far outside Thessalonica. They agreed that the places on the frontier that had been conquered with the help of Syrgiannes were to be restored to the Empire. Dušan went back to Serbia richer by a sum of Byzantine gold, and soon afterwards he was glad to be able to call on the support of Andronikos to help defend his own northern frontier against the King of Hungary.[13]

So ended the career of Syrgiannes, one of the leading promoters and beneficiaries of the civil war that had brought Andronikos III to the Byzantine throne. Gregoras declares that murder was no more than he deserved, and characteristically compares his flight to the Serbs with the flight of Themistocles to the Persians.[14] Others have called him a Byzantine Alcibiades. Half-caste barbarian though he was, there is something peculiarly Greek or Byzantine about the character of Syrgiannes. His death cleared the air between Byzantium and Serbia, but only for a time. For the vision of Tsargrad as the future capital of a Serbian Empire was very vivid in the imagination of Stephen Dušan.

The military and diplomatic successes of Andronikos III over the Genoese, the Bulgars, the Serbs and even the Turks restored some of the lost confidence of the Byzantines in the years after 1328. But in their eyes his greatest achievement was the recovery of the provinces of northern Greece which had been detached from the Empire since 1204. The defiant local patriotism of the separatist states of Epiros and Thessaly had somewhat mellowed with the years. The direct line of succession from their founders had come to an end in both in precisely the same year. In Thessaly the young John II Doukas, who had weathered the storm of the Catalan invasion of Greece, died in 1318. He left no heir to his title, only a confusion of claimants and pretenders. Thessaly broke up into anarchy. The Emperor Andronikos II claimed it by right, since John II's widow Eirene was his daughter, and Byzantine troops from Thessalonica annexed some of the country on the northern border. Most of the southern part of Thessaly was invaded and taken over by the Catalans. Alfonso Fadrique, the Catalan Duke of Athens, marched in from Thebes in 1319 and made his headquarters at Neopatras. The Venetians moved in to occupy the harbours on the Gulf of Demetrias or Volos on the east coast; while in the central plains a number of local landowners set themselves up independently as feudal lords and resisted Catalans and Byzantines alike.

The confusion was aggravated by the arrival in Thessaly of the first wave of nomad Albanian immigrants from the north.

The north-west corner of the country, from Trikkala up to Kastoria, was ruled after 1318 by a landlord called Stephen Gabrielopoulos. He held the Byzantine title of *sebastokrator* which seems to imply that he ruled his domains by arrangement with one of the Emperors in Constantinople. But when he died in 1333 northern Thessaly was bereft of government and at the mercy of its neighbours. The reigning Despot of Epiros, John Orsini, seized the occasion to march across the Pindos mountains and instal garrisons of his own in Trikkala and other places. The Emperor Andronikos III was in Macedonia at the time. He saw a chance of restoring not merely the fief of Stephen Gabrielopoulos but the whole of Thessaly to Byzantine rule. He ordered his general Michael Monomachos to lead an army down from Thessalonica. The Emperor followed after him with his own troops, and in a matter of weeks all Thessaly as far south as the Catalan frontier had been reclaimed. The soldiers who had been sent in by the Despot of Epiros were allowed to go home. The long history of bitter rivalry and warfare between Thessaly and Constantinople was over. The surrender was complete. Even the Albanians, some 12,000 in number, sent a deputation to the Emperor asking for his protection and offering him their allegiance. Michael Monomachos was appointed governor-general of the long-lost Byzantine province of Thessaly; and the Emperor returned in triumph to Thessalonica.[15]

The incorporation of Thessaly into the Empire greatly strengthened its powers of resistance to Serbia. But the achievement would only be completed when northern Greece as a whole had been placed under the direct government of Constantinople. The reconquest of Epiros must be the next step. The opportunity did not arise for some years after 1333, but when it did the Emperor was quick to take it. In the Despotate of Epiros the last male descendant of the ruling family died in 1318. He was the Despot Thomas, the son of Nikephoros and Anna. He had married Anna, a sister of Andronikos III, only five years earlier. His own elder sister, called Maria, had married John Orsini, the Italian Count of Cephalonia, in 1294, when Thomas was only about ten years old. Where other Latin states and principalities in Greece had changed hands several times, the Italian County of the island of Cephalonia had remained remarkably stable. It had been in possession of the members of a single family, the Orsini, ever since the end of the twelfth century. Almost from the first they had been involved in the affairs of Epiros across the water. By 1300 the Counts of Cephalonia were supposed to be the vassals of the Angevin Kingdom of Naples and more particularly of Philip of Taranto, who claimed suzerainty over the Principality of Achaia and over the coastal towns of Epiros.

But in 1317 Nicholas Orsini succeeded his father John. At that moment there was no effective Prince of Achaia. Nicholas decided to defy Philip of Taranto and make himself master of the Angevin territories on the Greek mainland. In 1318 he contrived the assassination of the Despot Thomas of Epiros, married Thomas's widow, and proclaimed himself 'by the grace of God, Despot of Romania'. His title indicated that he meant to acquire the whole of Greece and not simply Epiros. But in fact his rule was confined to Akarnania or the southern portion of Epiros alone. The northern part, including the city of Ioannina, was still occupied by Byzantine troops and its inhabitants seem to have preferred to belong to the Empire. Ioannina, which Andronikos II had elevated to the status of a metropolitan bishopric, was especially favoured with privileges by the Emperor, and Nicholas Orsini at first respected its position. But when his Byzantine wife died and when civil war broke out in the Empire in 1321, he was encouraged to think that he could take over northern Epiros as well. He tried to interest the Venetians in helping him, offering to fly the banner of St Mark from all his castles. But Venice was then at peace with Byzantium and unwilling to further the ambitions of Nicholas Orsini.

Possibly it was his ambition that caused his downfall. In 1323 Nicholas was murdered by his brother John. John II Orsini may well have been supported by the growing number of people in Epiros who favoured strengthening the Byzantine connexion. To begin with he came to terms with Constantinople. The Emperor accorded him the title of Despot on condition that he governed Epiros as an imperial estate. Like his brother, John adopted the Orthodox faith; and he married Anna, a daughter of Andronikos Palaiologos, one of the Byzantine commanders in northern Epiros. But the Angevins of Naples continued to press their claim on Greece. Philip of Taranto died in 1332, leaving all his titles to his widow Catherine of Valois; and there were those in Epiros then, as there had been in the thirteenth century, who felt that co-operation with the Angevins was less humiliating than submission to Constantinople. Presumably it was their influence that caused John Orsini to send troops into Thessaly in 1333. But once Thessaly had been reintegrated into the Byzantine Empire the pro-Byzantine party in Epiros gained ground again. John's wife Anna was among its leaders.[16]

About 1335 Anna poisoned her husband and assumed the regency for her son Nikephoros, who was still a boy. She then let it be known in Constantinople that she would be prepared to recognize the authority of the Byzantine Emperor. Some months later, in 1337, Andronikos III and John Cantacuzene arrived in northern Epiros with an army partly made up of 2000 Turkish soldiers kindly supplied by their ally, Umur of Aydin. Trouble had been reported in the region of Berat and Kanina as the result of repeated attacks by the Albanians. The Albanians, as Cantacuzene remarks, were usually able to escape into their mountain hiding places when pursued.[17] But the Turks were adept at this kind of fighting and quickly put an end to the trouble. Thousands of Albanians were killed or carried away into slavery by the Turks. The citizens of Berat and the other Byzantine fortresses in the area were thankful to be relieved of the menace and also pleased to see their Emperor. For it was the first time for nearly two centuries that any Emperor had visited his most westerly province.

The Emperor's presence in Albania led to much discussion among the contending parties in Epiros. The Despot's widow Anna was for seizing the opportunity to negotiate an honourable settlement, by terms of which her son Nikephoros would in due course be entitled to succeed to the Despotate. She sent a deputation to Andronikos at Berat. The Emperor replied, however, that compromise was no longer possible. If the inhabitants of Epiros would not submit unconditionally then he was ready to lead his army against them from the north. No doubt the news had got about of the way the Turkish soldiers had treated the Albanians. Anna agreed to submit to the Emperor's demands. Andronikos then dismissed his Turkish mercenaries and sent them home by way of Thessalonica, before travelling down from Berat to Epiros with John Cantacuzene. Most of the Epirotes seem to have accepted the new situation without complaint. The Emperor visited the principal towns and encouraged the loyalty of their leading citizens by granting them honours, titles and annuities. Theodore Synadenos was appointed governor-general in Epiros with his head-quarters at Arta; and Andronikos went on his way rejoicing, as Cantacuzene says, and giving thanks to God that a large part of the Empire, which had been separated from it since the time of the Fourth Crusade, had now been restored without bloodshed.[18]

He took with him Anna and her two little daughters. They were provided with a house and lands in Thessalonica. It had also been agreed that her son Nikephoros should be betrothed to a daughter of John Cantacuzene. But when the Emperor came to leave Epiros, the young Nikephoros was nowhere to be found. Inquiries revealed that he had been abducted to Italy by some of the Epirote aristocracy who looked on him as the last remaining symbol of their independence from Constantinople. Nikephoros was taken to Taranto, to the court of Catherine of Valois, the titular Latin Empress. He was sure of a warm welcome there and perhaps also of military aid to recover his lost heritage. Towards the end of 1338 Catherine moved house to her principality in the Morea where it was easier to keep in touch with events in Epiros; and from there she did her best to stir up a nationalist rebellion against Byzantine rule, using Nikephoros as the instrument of her ambition. The revolt began in Arta. Theodore Synadenos was arrested and thrown into prison. It spread to a number of other towns, including Ioannina in the north. Nikephoros was sent across from the Morea in 1339, escorted by an Angevin fleet provided by Catherine. He established himself at Thomokastron, a castle built by his grand-uncle on the coast of Epiros, where he could maintain contact with the Morea and with Italy.

The rebellion does not seem to have had universal support in Epiros. But the arrest of the imperial governor and the active intervention of Catherine of Valois could not go unchallenged. The Emperor ordered an army to proceed to Arta from Thessalonica at the end of 1339, commanded by Michael Monomachos, governor of Thessaly, and by John Angelos, a cousin of Cantacuzene. In 1340 he arrived in Epiros himself, accompanied as before by his Grand Domestic, John Cantacuzene. Order was restored within a few months, not so much by force of arms as by the diplomacy and eloquence of Cantacuzene, who talked the rebels into surrender. In his memoirs he gives a full account of the arguments that he put to their leaders to persuade them to lay down their arms. Arta, the old capital of the Despotate, resisted longer than the other centres and was besieged by the Emperor's troops. But in the end it gave in. Synadenos was set free, and a general amnesty was declared. The Emperor was taken ill during the siege of Arta so that the final act of the drama was left to Cantacuzene alone. It was he who went to Thomokastron and induced Nikephoros to abandon the role of the young pretender. The Angevin ships sent by Catherine of Valois lay at anchor off the coast, and the supporters of the cause which Nikephoros himself was barely old enough to understand were heartened by the arrival of reinforcements. But Cantacuzene eventually persuaded them they would get a better deal by submitting to the Emperor than by allowing themselves to be used as pawns in a game of western colonial adventure. For the Latins were out to conquer Epiros for themselves and not for the benefit of its Greek inhabitants; and the Greeks did not need to be told what servitude to the Latins entailed. Thomokastron, the last centre of resistance in northern Greece, consequently surrendered, and Nikephoros was handed over. Cantacuzene left a garrison there to discourage the Angevin fleet which was still in sight and returned to the Emperor at Arta bringing Nikephoros with him.[19]

By November 1340 the campaign was over. The Emperor and his court went back to Thessalonica for the winter. Nikephoros was honoured with the title of *panhypersebastos* and betrothed to Cantacuzene's daughter Maria. Cantacuzene's cousin John Angelos was left as imperial governor at Arta. Synadenos became governor of Thessalonica. The restitution to the Empire of the provinces of northern Greece might be thought in some measure to offset the loss of Byzantine Asia Minor. It raised great expectations of the Empire's recovery as a European power. It should have added greatly to its economic and military resources. But the expectations were not realized and the resources were not exploited. Andronikos III had ascribed his achievement to providence. But the same providence that guided the hand of the Orthodox Emperor in Constantinople ordained that, only a few years later, Epiros and Thessaly should pass into the possession of another Orthodox ruler, Stephen Dušan of Serbia.

Andronikos III was a man of action rather than a statesman. But he had a vision of the Empire's possibilities of recovery which his grandfather, at least in his latter years, had lost. Andronikos II had allowed himself to be taken over by events; Andronikos III was more energetic and more determined to shape events in a mould of his own making. To win victories over the enemies of the Empire was important; but he was also eager to restore confidence in the Empire's internal government and administration. At the very beginning of his reign he had passed legislation regulating the ownership of properties that had changed hands during the upheaval of the civil war. The rule of law was to be enforced.[20] But the machinery of its enforcement had broken down during the years of anarchy. Landlords in the provinces and leading families in the towns had become used to interpreting the law to suit their own purposes. It had lost its link with the central government in the capital and its administrators were open to corruption. It was a symptom of the times that more and more people preferred to take their cases before an ecclesiastical or episcopal tribunal where they could be more certain of an impartial hearing and a just verdict.

In 1329 Andronikos introduced a thorough reform of the administration of the law. Four supreme judges were appointed with the new title of Universal Justices of the Romans. Two were laymen and two were priests. They were endowed with exceptional powers to enforce the law throughout the Empire, particularly in the matter of corruption among imperial officials and in cases of tax evasion by the great landlords. Their verdicts were to be final and irreversible. Bribery and corruption in high places was no new problem. The Patriarch Athanasios had inveighed against such practices and blamed them as a main cause of the Empire's decline. Andronikos II had attempted a reform of the law courts in 1296 by setting up a special high court of appeal composed of 12 judges selected from the higher clergy and the senators. But its activities had soon run down, as Gregoras says, like the slackening strings of a musical instrument. The fact that a prominent official like John Cantacuzene could, on his own admission, buy himself a military command in Thrace in 1320 by bribing the authorities shows the extent of corruption in the imperial administration. Theodore Metochites, though a man of the highest principles and an expert on moral philosophy, used his position as Grand Logothete to add to his fortune by trafficking in the sale of offices. The practice was endemic and infectious. Even the incorruptible Justices of the Romans were soon found to be corrupt. In 1337 three of them were brought before the Emperor and the Patriarch in a special trial in St Sophia and convicted of taking bribes. They were dismissed and sent into exile.

But others were appointed to take their place; and it is to the credit of Andronikos III that he reminded the Byzantine people that their society was still governed by the principles of Roman law as handed down, adapted and interpreted by the successors of Justinian. The institution of the Supreme Justices of the Romans endured until the last days of the Empire. It was expanded by the appointment of local justices with similar powers in such places as Thessalonica and the Morea; and it no doubt had its effect on the work of the two great academic lawyers of the fourteenth century, Matthew Blastares and Constantine Harmenopoulos. The *Syntagma* of Blastares, written in 1335, was a collection of rulings in ecclesiastical as well as civil law; the *Hexabiblos* of Harmenopoulos, compiled ten years later, was a compendium of civil and criminal law in six books. Both works were to exert a profound influence on the development of law in the countries within the orbit of the Byzantine Empire. The *Syntagma* of Blastares was translated into Serbian very soon after its publication on the orders of Stephen Dušan; and it was widely known and employed throughout the Slav world even long after the fall of Constantinople.[21]

NOTES

The main narrative sources for the reign of Andronikos III (1328-41) are: Gregoras, I, 430-568; Cantacuzene, I, 310-560.
Modern works: Ursula V. Bosch, *Kaiser Andronikos III. Palaiologos. Versuch einer Darstellung der byzantinischen Geschichte in den Jahren 1321-1341* (Amsterdam, 1965).

1 Gregoras, I, 482-3. Cantacuzene, I, 205, also comments on the Savoyard influence at the court of Andronikos III.

2 Bosch, *Andronikos III*, 69f.

3 On the battles of Pelekanon and Philokrene, see Arnakis, *Early Osmanlis*, 177-87; Bosch, 152-8. For the chronology, see the *Short Chronicle of 1352*, ed. Loenertz, part II, 39, 45-7.

4 Arnakis, *Early Osmanlis*, 187-97; Bosch, 158-63. *Short Chronicle of 1352*, ed. Loenertz, part II, 40, 49-50.

5 Cantacuzene, I, 446-8; *Short Chronicle of 1352*, II, 40, 52-4.

6 The Greek texts of the encyclicals of the Patriarch John XIV Kalekas are in *MM*, I, 183-4, 197-8.

7 Cantacuzene, I, 370-90; *Destān d'Umūr Pacha*, 55-7, lines 235-86. Cf. Lemerle, *L'Emirat d'Aydin*, 56-60; Bosch, 112-18.

8 H. Omont, 'Projet de réunion des églises grecque et latine sous Charles le Bel en 1327', and 'Lettre d'Andronic II Paléologue au Pape Jean XXII', in *Bibliothèque de l'Ecole des Chartes*, LIII (1892), 254-7; LXVII (1906), 587. A. Laiou, 'Marino Sanudo Torsello, Byzantium and the Turks: The background to the anti-Turkish League of 1332-1334', *Speculum*, XLV (1970), 374-92. There were some in western Europe who still thought in terms of a repetition of the Fourth Crusade. In 1332 a French priest who had been in the East prepared for Philip VI of France a document known as the *Directorium* (or *Advis Directif*); this was a plan for a great crusade, which was to be preceded by the conquest of Serbia and of Constantinople. See S. Runciman, *History of the Crusades*, III, 440-1; A. S. Atiya, *The*

Crusade in the Later Middle Ages (London, 1938), 96-113 (especially 103-4).

9 Lemerle, *L'Emirat d'Aydin*, 89-101; Bosch, 119-28; Laiou, *op. cit.* The victory of the Christian fleet off Adramyttion was celebrated in a thanksgiving by a local Greek writer: see V. Laurent, 'Action de grâces pour la victoire navale remportée par les Turcs à Atramyttion au cours de l'automne 1334', *Eis Mnemen K. I. Amantou* (Athens, 1960), 25-41.

10 Lemerle, *op. cit.*, 102-15; Bosch, 159-60.

11 Cantacuzene, I, 482-95; *Destān d'Umūr Pacha*, 83-5, lines 1035-84.

12 Bosch, 74-82.

13 Bosch, 91-6; Ostrogorsky, 505-6. On the chronology, see R.-J. Loenertz, 'Ordre et désordre dans les mémoires de Jean Cantacuzène', *REB*, XXII (1964), 230-1.

14 Gregoras, I, 490, 498.

15 The recovery of Thessaly is described by Cantacuzene, I, 473-4. Cf. Nicol, *Meteora*, 53-4; Bosch, 134-5; and for the chronology, see Loenertz, *op. cit.*, 229.

16 Cf. Miller, *Latins in the Levant*, 249-50; Nicol, *Meteora*, 54-5.

17 Cantacuzene, I, 496.

18 The reconquest of Epiros is described at length by Cantacuzene, I, 495-504. Cf. Gregoras, I, 536, 544-6.

19 Cantacuzene, I, 509-34; Gregoras, I, 550-4. Cf. Bosch, 135-8; Miller, *Latins in the Levant*, 273-5. For the chronology, see *Short Chronicle of 1352*, ed. Loenertz, II, 56-8.

20 Cantacuzene, I, 312, 322. Cf. Bosch, 167-8.

21 See Bosch, 168-71; Ostrogorsky, 503-4 and references; W. Ensslin, in *CMH*, IV, 2, 30.

Twelve

The Second Civil War
1341-7

In the years between 1328 and 1340 the Empire seemed to have gone a long way towards revival. It is true its rulers had admitted the loss of Asia Minor to the Turks, that Serbia and Bulgaria still threatened the northern frontiers, that central Greece was still in Catalan control, and that Italian families still held many of the Aegean islands. But northern Greece had been regained and in 1340 plans were being suggested to launch a campaign for the reconquest of the Morea from the French. If the whole peninsula of Greece could be united under Byzantine government then the Empire would once again be a homogeneous structure, able to stand up to the Serbs, the Italians and its other enemies. It would be small, but it would be a compact and manageable economic and administrative unit running from Cape Matapan to Thessalonica and Constantinople. This was the hope and the plan of John Cantacuzene, who had prompted and realized so much of the policy of Andronikos III. Even his enemies had to confess that Cantacuzene had never betrayed or abused his Emperor's trust in him. Early in 1341 his eldest son Matthew, then aged about 16, married a cousin of the Emperor, Eirene Palaiologina. The wedding took place in Thessalonica. The Cantacuzene family thus came to be more nearly related to the house of Palaiologos. But the relationship implied no right or prospect that John Cantacuzene or any member of his family would succeed to the throne in the event of the Emperor's death.

In the spring of the same year Andronikos and Cantacuzene left Thessalonica together to return to Constantinople. A few months later, on the night of 14-15 June 1341, the Emperor died after a short illness. He was in his 45th year. Both his predecessors, Andronikos II and Michael VIII, had taken elaborate precautions to ensure that the line of succession would be determined for many years to come. Andronikos III had made no such provision. He had three sons, but the eldest of them, John Palaiologos, was barely nine years old. John was the heir-presumptive to the throne, but he had not yet been proclaimed or crowned as co-Emperor. To many people it seemed right and natural that John Cantacuzene, the closest friend and counsellor of the late Emperor, should take charge of the situation and be accepted as regent. At the moment of the Emperor's death Cantacuzene himself assumed that it was his duty to see to the comfort and welfare of the widowed Empress Anne of Savoy and her children and to make arrangements for the state funeral. In the long term he confidently expected that most affairs of state would continue to be in his hands and that he would act as guardian of the boy Emperor John. He moved into the imperial palace and wrote letters to all the governors of the provinces advising them against taking any independent or revolutionary action. The tax-collectors were also warned that they were to be answerable for their accounts just as if the Emperor were still alive. Good order and calm must be maintained.

To all intents and purposes John Cantacuzene was regent of the Empire. It was unfortunate that the Emperor Andronikos had not more specifically declared this to be his wish before he died. But some could recall that when the Emperor had been seriously ill on a previous occasion, in January 1330, he had made it plain that, if he did not recover, Cantacuzene was to be regent if he declined to be proclaimed as Emperor. For at that time John Palaiologos had not been born. On several other occasions also the late Emperor had tried to induce Cantacuzene to become his colleague or co-emperor. One need not doubt the truth of these propositions because they are recorded by Cantacuzene's own pen. They are confirmed by other sources. Nor are they so flattering to his reputation as Cantacuzene may have thought, for his self-effacement and humility cloaked a sense of indecision and hesitancy. It is arguable that if Cantacuzene had seized the reins of government with a more aggressive and less nervous hand in June 1341 he might have saved the Empire from a deal of trouble.[1]

On the other hand it cannot be doubted that there was strong opposition to John Cantacuzene as a person and as the representative of the interest of a particular class in Constantinople and elsewhere. The Empress Anne was prepared to accept his protection and comfort in her bereavement. He had, after all, been her husband's nearest friend—nearer, some said, than herself; and from his death-bed Andronikos had advised her to rely upon the help and counsel of Cantacuzene. But she had never liked or trusted him. Anne was much under the influence of the Patriarch of Constantinople, John

Kalekas. Kalekas had been appointed as the Patriarch John XIV in 1334, nearly two years after the death of the Patriarch Esaias. His elevation from a humble bishopric had been sponsored by Cantacuzene.² He was not the kind of patriarch who was content to be a mere figurehead. Like his predecessors Athanasios and Arsenios he felt bound to have his say in the political as well as the spiritual affairs of the Empire; but he lacked the moral indignation of the one and the integrity of the other. He too claimed the right to act as regent for the boy Emperor John. He based his claim on the indisputable fact that the Emperor Andronikos had appointed him as regent when he left Constantinople to deal with the revolt of Syrgiannes in 1334, and that he had again acted as such when the Emperor was on campaign in northern Greece.

It ought to have been possible for Cantacuzene, the Empress and the Patriarch to come to some agreement between themselves for the management of the Empire; and indeed, if Cantacuzene is to be believed, they tried to do so, and for a time succeeded. But the man who played the role of fourth party during the first civil war now saw his way to play the same role with much greater effect. Alexios Apokaukos, by posing as the loyal servant of the interests of Cantacuzene, had acquired great power in the capital in the years since 1328 and had quietly amassed an immense fortune. He was a past master at making the most of his opportunities, and with the death of Andronikos III he sensed that there was a new tide to be taken at the flood. He had prepared for any eventuality by constructing his own castle at Epibatai on the Bosporos to which he could retreat if any of his plans went awry. Apokaukos was the creature of John Cantacuzene, without whom, for all his talents, he would never have gained the rank, the fame and the fortune that he had. Cantacuzene had only recently persuaded the late Emperor to grant Apokaukos the office of Grand Duke or High Admiral and to give him command of a fleet to guard the Hellespont against the Turks. Andronikos had disapproved of adding yet further to his power; but it was the fault of John Cantacuzene to be over-optimistic about winning the gratitude of those whom he favoured.

After the Emperor's death Apokaukos tried to induce Cantacuzene to allow himself to be proclaimed as Emperor. He might then have satisfied his own ambition by becoming the chief minister and commander-in-chief of the Empire, as Cantacuzene had been for Andronikos III. But Cantacuzene refused to consider the proposal. He saw it as his duty to protect and serve the rights and interests of the reigning house of Palaiologos. Apokaukos therefore turned against him. If he could not achieve the summit of his ambition by flattering his patron he would achieve it by ruining him. He became the leading supporter of the claims of the Patriarch and the Empress. The issue was said by both sides to be simply that of defending the rights of the legitimate heir to the throne, John Palaiologos. It was assumed that after 80 years of continuous rule the dynasty of Palaiologos had established an inalienable right to the crown. The Arsenites and the Laskarids had long since spent their force. In an earlier age the principle of hereditary succession was not always so generally accepted; though it was always desirable that an emperor should nominate his heir to prevent the possibility of a civil war for the throne. Cantacuzene says that he offered to retire from public life altogether rather than run that risk by pressing his claim to the regency or the management of the state. He held long interviews with the Empress Anne and the Patriarch. The Empress is said to have burst into tears and implored him not to desert her and her children in their hour of need; and an agreement was reached between the three parties.[3]

This arrangement might have been workable and effective if Cantacuzene had stayed on hand in Constantinople. But, as usual when the word got abroad that an Emperor had died, the enemies of Byzantium seized their chance to take advantage of the interregnum. Stephen Dušan again invaded Macedonia; the Turks of Saruchan raided the coast of Thrace; and the Bulgars threatened to attack from the north. John Alexander of Bulgaria demanded the extradition of his rival Michael Šišman who had been given asylum in Constantinople; and Cantacuzene, as Grand Domestic and commander of the Empire's defences, had to leave the capital in July 1341. Alexios Apokaukos, in his capacity as Grand Duke, was left in charge of the fleet to protect the city. In a matter of weeks Cantacuzene restored order on all the northern frontiers. The raiding parties of Turks were driven away from Thrace. Umur of Aydin, who had sent a fleet to plunder the coast, agreed to send his ships up the Black Sea to the mouth of the Danube, to frighten the Bulgars into submission. As a result John Alexander withdrew his troops and renewed his treaty with Byzantium. Stephen Dušan was also induced to make peace, while Cantacuzene completed his diplomatic triumphs by signing a treaty with Orchan, emir of the Osmanlis. The future seemed full of hope. While he was in Didymoteichos in the summer of 1341 some ambassadors arrived from the Morea offering to effect the surrender to the Empire of the French principality of Achaia.

Whatever the rights and wrongs of his position as regent there was little doubt that John Cantacuzene was master of the Empire's foreign affairs. He returned to Constantinople in September 1341, optimistic about the opportunity of reincorporating yet more of Greece under Byzantine rule. But his enemies in the capital had not been idle during his absence. Apokaukos, who had been left in charge of the fleet, had clearly let the Turks cross over to Thrace with deliberate intent. Worse still, he had tried to kidnap the young John Palaiologos to hold him as a hostage until the Empress produced a ransom. The plot had failed and Apokaukos had retreated to his castle on the Bosporos. Cantacuzene saw to it that he was kept there under guard. It would surely have been wise to make this latest adventure the excuse for depriving Apokaukos of all his powers. But, after talking the matter over with the Empress, Cantacuzene agreed to pardon the offender and to give him yet another chance. At the same time he suggested that it might help matters if the young John Palaiologos were now to be crowned as Emperor. It was also proposed that John should marry a daughter of Cantacuzene. But neither proposal was put into effect.

On 23 September 1341 John Cantacuzene left Constantinople for a second time taking his army with him to Thrace to make preparations to enforce or to accept the proposed surrender of the Morea. More than five years were to elapse before he returned to the capital. As soon as he was gone Apokaukos set himself to organize a clique of supporters who would serve his own cause and declare Cantacuzene to be a public enemy. Apokaukos knew his men. The Patriarch John Kalekas needed no persuasion to condemn his political rival. Others were bribed, flattered, or threatened according to their susceptibilities. Among them was Cantacuzene's own father-in-law Andronikos, who came of the Bulgarian family of Asen. Apokaukos used all his persuasive art to convince the Empress Anne that Cantacuzene, for all his fine words, was really plotting against her and her son. It was hard for her to discover the truth, but she was ready to believe the worst about her husband's dearest friend. She gave Apokaukos the office of Prefect of the City, which enabled him to distribute honours and titles to all the enemies of John Cantacuzene. The Patriarch openly proclaimed himself regent for the young Emperor, and there began a persecution of Cantacuzene's relatives and supporters in the city. His mother Theodora was placed under house arrest. All his property in Constantinople was either sequestered or destroyed, and some 40 of his associates escaped and fled to his camp at Didymoteichos in Thrace. The Empress signed an order for him to resign his command and disband his army. He was not even to be allowed to plead his own case.[4]

These were the circumstances in which, on 26 October 1341, John Cantacuzene was proclaimed Emperor at Didymoteichos. The Empress's refusal to negotiate gave him and his more aggressive partisans every excuse for taking action. If he had been planning to usurp the throne, which he always strenuously denied, he could have done so at the moment of the late Emperor's death. If on the other hand he felt bound to accept the title of Emperor to save the state then he did well to give his enemies the rope with which to hang themselves. For at least he could protest that they had been the first to put themselves in the wrong. Many pages of Cantacuzene's memoirs are devoted to the moral justification of his action in October 1341. They make somewhat painful reading, for they betray once more the diffidence and hesitation of one who had his decisions forced upon him by circumstances and yet desperately wanted everyone to understand that this was so. Possibly it was a wrong, or a premature, decision. The Bishop of Didymoteichos, when called upon to give his blessing to the deed, remarked that to be Emperor of the Romans was certainly something ordained by God; but those who ate figs that were not yet ripe would just as certainly suffer from swollen lips.[5] This cryptic observation could be construed to mean that John Cantacuzene had plucked the fruit of empire too soon and must suffer the consequences. The Bishop of Didymoteichos was famous for his prophetic gifts. But there were some strangely ominous events at Cantacuzene's investiture. On the day itself, when the new Emperor came to put on his imperial robes, it was found that, although they had been carefully made to measure, the inner garment was far too tight and the outer one far too loose. This led one of his familiars to predict that the beginning of his reign would be troublesome and hard to bear but that later things would become more relaxed and peaceful. The story is told by Cantacuzene himself, though at the time of writing he must have been sadly aware that the prediction had not been wholly fulfilled and that the incompetence of his tailor could not be wholly ascribed to supernatural causes.[6]

The ceremony at Didymoteichos on 26 October, the Feast of St Demetrios, was that of the proclamation and investiture of an emperor. There was no coronation. But the act of proclamation was, in the Byzantine tradition, sufficient in itself to make a man Emperor, at least in the eyes of the representatives of the church, the state and the army who proclaimed him. Cantacuzene, however, insisted on making it clear that he was still nothing more than the guardian of the rights of the legitimate heir to the throne, John Palaiologos. In the acclamation which formed part of the ceremony the names of the Empress Anne and her son John were pronounced before those of John Cantacuzene and his wife Eirene as Emperor and Empress. On the other hand, Cantacuzene now began to describe himself as a 'brother' of the late Emperor Andronikos III. He wished it to be known that he enjoyed a special relationship with the ruling house.[7]

But whatever the niceties of protocol that he observed, and whatever his reluctance to accept the imperial title, the fact of Cantacuzene's proclamation amounted to a declaration of war so far as the régime in Constantinople was concerned. No doubt the Patriarch and Apokaukos had hoped that matters would come to this pass, for it made it easier for them to denounce Cantacuzene as a professed usurper and a danger to the peace. They could now present him to the people as one who had wilfully brought the Empire to the brink of another civil war. They were confident that the war would be short. They did not foresee that it would develop into what Cantacuzene later looked back on as 'the worst civil war that the Romans had ever experienced, a conflict that destroyed almost everything, reducing the great Roman Empire to a feeble shadow of its former self'.[8]

There were many reasons why the second civil war in Byzantium proved to be so much more disruptive and destructive than the first. The intervention of foreign powers was more active and more calculated than before; the economy of the Empire almost broke down under the strain of another conflict so soon after the first. But the news that their rulers had once again declared war on each other produced in the Byzantine people a wave of hostile reaction and divided society into opposing camps in a manner that had never occurred before. Even the protagonists seem to have realized that they had unleashed social and political forces over which they had little control. Apokaukos deliberately incited the mob of Constantinople to attack and destroy the property of Cantacuzene and his followers, and so turned to his own political gain the deep resentment of the underprivileged against the aristocracy. But in other cities the ordinary people released their own tensions by taking the

197

law into their own hands. Cantacuzene represented the interests of the landowning nobility who used their wealth and influence to lord it over the urban population in the cities of Thrace and Macedonia. Bitter experience had taught people to distrust the claim of the landed aristocracy to know what was best for the Empire. Few would believe that John Cantacuzene's motives were altruistic.[9]

The glaring contrast between the riches of the few and the poverty of the many had been accentuated by the first civil war and its consequences. It did not seem likely that another civil war would help to right the balance. The vast amount of gold and silver plate, jewellery, hoards of grain and provisions discovered in the house of Cantacuzene's mother in Constantinople when she was arrested seemed to show how little the upper classes cared for the welfare of the people.[10] Apokaukos made the most of such revelations for his own propaganda purposes. The extent of the Cantacuzene property in the provinces was another such discovery. Cantacuzene admits that when his estates in Macedonia were expropriated in the civil war he lost 5000 head of cattle, 1000 draft animals, 2500 mares, 200 camels, 300 mules, 500 asses, 50,000 pigs and 70,000 sheep.[11] Peasants whose little livelihood was measured and taxed in terms of *zeugaria*, or the amount of land that could be ploughed by two oxen, and whose freedom of action and movement was determined by their status as tenant farmers on estates of such unimaginable dimensions, were bound to be sceptical about the motives of landowners like Cantacuzene. They had been taken in before by promises of the remission of taxes. They had evidence of the fortunes that some of the revenue officials had made and continued to make with the connivance of the government. One such was a man called Patrikiotes who put his accumulated riches at the disposal of Cantacuzene in 1341 for the payment of arrears to the army and for the reconstitution of properties held in *pronoia* from the Emperor. It was difficult for the people to stage a protest in the countryside. But in the towns and cities where the word of the aristocracy was also law agitation could be organized.[12]

Such were the currents of unrest that Alexios Apokaukos was able to exploit to his own political advantage. He was also quick to point out to the people that they had a constitutional right to confirm the election and proclamation of their emperor, and that that right had been flouted. The issue between Cantacuzene and the regency could thus be presented as one between the hereditary rights of the lawful Emperor in Constantinople and the wrongs of a usurper proclaimed without reference to the people of the capital. In this way Apokaukos contrived to stir the enthusiasm and secure the loyalty of the poor and the underprivileged. But the manifestations of revolt in the provincial cities were spontaneous in origin and had little to do at first with the constitutional issues.

The way was shown by the citizens of Adrianople. On 27 October 1341 the nobles of Adrianople assembled the people and read out to them a letter which had arrived from nearby Didymoteichos announcing the proclamation of John Cantacuzene as Emperor. The news was well received by the aristocracy but not by the people, some of whom openly denounced Cantacuzene and all he stood for. A few of the more outspoken were arrested and flogged. But that same night a manual labourer called Branos, with two associates of equally humble background, went round the people's houses inciting them to rebellion against their oppressors. Rioting broke out. The wealthy aristocracy who had declared in favour of Cantacuzene were attacked and their property was destroyed or seized. Many of them fled, but others were rounded up and put under guard. The crowd rampaged through the streets plundering and demolishing the houses of the rich. A revolutionary government was set up to protect the people against the forces of what now came to be described simply as 'Cantacuzenism'. To such an extent were the interests of the aristocracy identified with those of John Cantacuzene in the popular mind. The revolutionaries were quickly recognized as the lawful rulers of the city by Apokaukos and the regency in Constantinople, who saw the usefulness to their own cause of Cantacuzenism as a political slogan. Apokaukos appointed his own son Manuel as governor and representative of the regency in Adrianople.[13]

The example set by Adrianople was soon followed in the other towns of Thrace and Macedonia. The pattern of revolt varied, but in general the propertied classes declared for Cantacuzene while the rest took the law into their own hands and legitimized their actions by declaring for the Emperor John Palaiologos in Constantinople. Cantacuzene recalls how the revolution caught on. 'It spread', he writes, 'like a malignant and horrible disease, producing the same forms of excess even in those who before had been moderate and sensible men.... All the cities joined in this rebellion against the aristocracy, and those that were late in doing so made up for their lost time by excelling the example set them by others. They perpetrated all manner of inhumanity and even massacres. Senseless

199

impulse was glorified with the name of valour and lack of fellow feeling or human sympathy was called loyalty to the Emperor.'[14]

Cantacuzene made his headquarters at Didymoteichos to the south of Adrianople. It was there that he had been hailed as Emperor and there that his troops were stationed. The citizens of Didymoteichos were not given the chance or the option of revolution, though some of the villagers who lived beyond the walls of the city were later to stage an abortive uprising. It was now out of the question for Cantacuzene to carry out his plan to accept the surrender of the Morea. He spent the winter of 1341 in Didymoteichos, hopeful that a settlement might still be reached with the regents in Constantinople. But Apokaukos and the Patriarch John Kalekas kept up a barrage of propaganda against him in the capital. The Patriarch excommunicated him and, on 19 November 1341, set the imperial crown on the head of the young John Palaiologos. Cantacuzene was now condemned and outlawed by all the powers of church and state. His mother, insulted and ill-treated by the agents of Apokaukos, succumbed to an illness and died in Constantinople in January 1342. Meanwhile the spirit of revolution spread beyond the capital, and the governors of some of the provinces in Macedonia and Thessaly turned against Cantacuzene. Their instincts might have led them to side with him, but they were driven into the opposite camp by fear of reprisals being taken against their relatives or their property in Constantinople and elsewhere. The only one who declared for Cantacuzene, and that in secret, was his old friend and political ally Theodore Synadenos, then governor of Thessalonica. Synadenos offered to open the gates of the city to Cantacuzene if he would come and claim it.

The man who controlled Thessalonica might be thought to control almost half of what was left of the Empire. The chance was not to be missed. In March 1342 Cantacuzene left his wife Eirene in charge of the garrison at Didymoteichos and set out for the city with his army. But before he got there the infection of revolution had done its work in Thessalonica too. Synadenos was driven out and the supporters of Cantacuzene who would have welcomed his arrival went into hiding or fled. The revolt against the aristocracy in Thessalonica was marked by its efficient organization. Those who carried it through were not merely labourers or the rabble of the streets; they had something of the character of a political party with a programme of reform. They called themselves the Zealots, and in the early summer of 1342 they conceived and established a régime which had no real precedent or parallel in any other city in the history of the Byzantine Empire. It made Thessalonica a republic managing its own domestic and foreign affairs. The original motives of the Zealots were similar to those of the revolutionaries in Adrianople and elsewhere. They roused up the people against the aristocracy, and 'for two or three days', writes Cantacuzene, 'Thessalonica was like a city under enemy occupation and suffered all the corresponding disasters. The victors went shouting and looting through the streets by day and by night, while the vanquished hid in churches and counted themselves lucky to be still alive. When order returned, the Zealots, suddenly raised from penury and dishonour to wealth and influence, took control of everything and won over the middle class of citizens, forcing them to acquiesce and characterizing every form of moderation and prudence as "Cantacuzenism".'[15]

As elsewhere the victory of the revolutionaries was promptly acknowledged as a fact by the regency in Constantinople. Apokaukos sent an army to their support and soon arrived in Thessalonica in person with a fleet of 70 ships. Theodore Synadenos, whose wife and family were in Constantinople and likely to suffer in consequence of his actions, thought it wise to change sides; and Apokaukos appointed his own son John as imperial governor of the city, as he had made his other son Manuel governor at Adrianople. The fiction was thus maintained that Thessalonica was loyal to the house of Palaiologos; and so it was, in preference to the house of Cantacuzene. But the real rulers of the city were the leaders of the Zealot party; and for more than seven years they managed the affairs of Thessalonica as a more or less independent commune in the heart of the Byzantine Empire.[16]

John Cantacuzene was left in a critical position. He toyed with the idea of joining up with his friends in Thessaly and Epiros. But when the army and the fleet arrived from Constantinople he was almost surrounded and completely cut off from his headquarters at Didymoteichos. His only hope of escape seemed to lie in making a dash for the Serbian frontier and begging the help of Stephen Dušan. He gave his troops the option of going with him or going over to the side of his rivals. Only about 2000 chose to accompany him to Serbia. One of the many talents of Cantacuzene was an ability to make and to keep influential friends. He had met Stephen Dušan in company wth Andronikos III some years before and formed a friendly acquaintance with him. The nature of their friendship was now to be put to the test. The two men doubtless had much in common, but not even Cantacuzene could pretend that Dušan's friendship was entirely disinterested. The Serbian king jumped at the chance of intervening so directly in Byzantine affairs and readily offered his protection and assistance. Thanks to the good offices of one of the Serbian nobles, John Oliver, whom Cantacuzene had also met on a previous occasion, a meeting was arranged. Dušan came down to Priština near Skoplje and there received Cantacuzene with great honour and courtesy in July 1342. The potential value of their alliance was estimated in different terms by the two parties; and the price suggested by Dušan, the cession to him of a great part of Byzantine Macedonia, was higher than Cantacuzene was prepared to pay. But for the moment he was the honoured guest and protégé of the King of Serbia.

At the end of the summer of 1342 Cantacuzene set out with a contingent of mercenaries supplied by Dušan to fight his way back to Didymoteichos. He got no further than the city of Serres. The inhabitants of Serres refused to submit to him; the pass of Christoupolis further east along his road was reported to be held by an army from Constantinople; and his troops who were laying siege to Serres were afflicted by an epidemic, which carried off about 1500 of them. He was forced to retreat back to Serbia with not more than about 500 men. His fortunes were at their lowest ebb. The regency in Constantinople seemed certain of victory if only they could lay their hands on Cantacuzene himself. The Empress Anne, prompted by Apokaukos and the Patriarch, twice sent messengers to Stephen Dušan to bribe him into surrendering his guest. But Dušan had everything to gain by playing the part of Philip of Macedon in the squabbles of the Greeks. It suited his own purpose to keep them at war with each other. If he was going to betray Cantacuzene he would do it in his own time.[17]

Few events in late Byzantine history are as well documented as the second civil war between 1341 and 1347. Gregoras, whose sympathies were on the side of the aristocracy, strives to give an impartial account. Cantacuzene devoted the whole of the third book of his memoirs, some 600 pages in the printed text, to recalling the stages of his struggle and his ultimate victory against overwhelming odds. Like many a soldier in retirement he describes with a wealth of vivid detail every strategic setback and advance. Battles which were really no more than skirmishes between a handful of soldiers on either side take on the colour of epic conflicts when seen in the context of the object for which they were fought, the mastery of the Roman Empire. What one is tempted to condemn as a sordid struggle for power seems to acquire some redeeming dignity when dressed up in the language of Thucydides or Xenophon. But the literary style of Cantacuzene and Gregoras cannot disguise the fact that the war was really directed, fought and won by the common enemies of both sides, the Serbs and the Turks. For when the dust had settled after all the years of fighting it was seen that the wounds from which the Byzantine Empire was suffering were not all self-inflicted.

By the end of the year 1342 Cantacuzene's situation was desperate. Without the protection of Dušan he could hardly have held out. The first turn in his fortunes came with the voluntary submission to him of the province of Thessaly, whose leading men sent a deputation to him in Serbia. The landowners of Thessaly were naturally favourable to the cause of one of their own kind, and Cantacuzene and his family were not unknown in their province. They had heard what had happened to the aristocracy in Thessalonica, and looked to John Cantacuzene to preserve them from a similar fate. He replied by appointing his loyal cousin John Angelos, formerly governor of Epiros, as his deputy in Thessaly and governor general of the province for life. John Angelos soon managed to extend his authority over Epiros as well, so that the whole of northern Greece with the exception of Macedonia was behind Cantacuzene. The civil war took on the aspect of a conflict between the Greek provinces of the Empire, which Cantacuzene had done so much to recover, and the older imperial provinces of Macedonia and Thrace, which were dependent on Constantinople. But the loyalty of Thessaly and Epiros brought Cantacuzene little substantial benefit; and the city of Thessalonica, whose acquisition would have tipped the scale in his favour, preserved its autonomy if not its neutrality under the government of the Zealots.[18]

Cantacuzene's situation was desperate enough, but that of his wife and the garrison that he had left at Didymoteichos was even more so, for they were isolated and surrounded by troops from Constantinople. Cantacuzene tried once more to fight his way back to join them but again he was forced to withdraw to Serbia. Stephen Dušan was still content to support him, though the extent of his support was nicely calculated to suit the interest of Serbia. But Cantacuzene had other and more generous friends. He contrived to get in touch with Umur, the Turkish emir of Aydin, at Smyrna, with whom he had made friends seven years before. Umur was a man of his word and no shifty barbarian. Gregoras declared that he was in many ways a Hellene, which was high praise indeed.[19] He had supplied soldiers for the campaigns of Andronikos III in Albania. For the sake of his friend John

Cantacuzene he was willing to come to Europe in person at the head of his army. In the winter of 1342 he went to the relief of Didymoteichos, sailing up to the mouth of the Marica river with a fleet and then leading his troops up the valley. This was the first large-scale Turkish intervention in the civil war, and such was the reputation of Umur's soldiers that many people hoped it would be the last. Umur stayed only long enough to see to the defence of Didymoteichos and to leave a garrison there before returning to Smyrna. He had hoped, and indeed tried, to march west and make contact with Cantacuzene. But his men were not equipped to survive the rigours of an exceptionally severe winter in Thrace. The fact that he had come at all, however, was a great diplomatic victory for Cantacuzene.

The thought that they might henceforth be faced with repeated devastation by the Turks was highly alarming for the people of Thrace and the regents in Constantinople. The Empress Anne appealed to the conscience of the western world to save her Empire from the infidel. At the time Pope Clement VI was known to be engaged in reorganizing the anti-Turkish league of Christian powers. As before, the league's object was to defend western colonial interests in Asia Minor and particularly to recapture Smyrna from Umur of Aydin. But the fact that Constantinople was now ruled by an Italian Empress, Anne of Savoy, made it much more likely than before that the Byzantine Empire too might be thought worthy of the league's protection. Anne did her best to foster this likelihood. In the summer of 1343 she sent one of her Savoyard knights to Avignon with letters declaring her own submission to the Holy See and also that of her son John, of Alexios Apokaukos and even of the Patriarch John Kalekas. Her son was barely old enough to have a mind of his own on the subject. But nothing seems less probable than the conversion to Catholicism of Apokaukos and the Patriarch. At the same time, however, the Empress solicited more practical help from the west, first from Genoa and then from Venice. Both expected to be rewarded for any assistance that they might provide. But the economy of the Empire, shattered by civil war and revolution, could not now stretch to the payment of subsidies. Confiscations of property from the Cantacuzene family and their adherents had added something to the treasury, and Apokaukos was far from being a fool in the matter of managing what money there was. But in August 1343 the Empress resorted to the desperate measure of pawning the Byzantine crown jewels to the Republic of Venice. Her son John had been properly crowned as Emperor. If things went well the jewels would not be needed again for another generation, by which time the money would have been found to buy them back and to pay the interest on the loan. The Venetians paid her the sum of 30,000 ducats, which was a welcome windfall for the regency. But the crown jewels were never redeemed and were to become the cause of much contention between Venice and Constantinople in succeeding years.[20]

In April 1343 some of the towns in southern Macedonia followed the lead of Thessaly and declared John Cantacuzene as their Emperor. His luck began to change. But the change cost him the support of Stephen Dušan, who recalled the troops that he had lent him. Apókaukos, who had for long hoped that Dušan would betray his friend, arrived at Thessalonica with a fleet, and Cantacuzene was blockaded in Macedonia and almost stranded. But he still had the loyalty of the Thessalians behind him; and he could still strike terror into his enemies by summoning his Turkish ally. Once again Umur of Aydin came to his rescue, sailing into the Gulf of Thessalonica at the head of a fleet of about 200 ships. Apókaukos and his navy disappeared back to Constantinople as soon as they heard that the Turks were on their way. But not even with the help of Umur and his 6000 soldiers could Cantacuzene succeed in breaking the resistance of Thessalonica. The walls were too strong to be breached; and the Zealots made sure that none of the Cantacuzenists in the city should be allowed to raise a finger in support of their hero.[21]

Umur's intervention, however, made it possible for Cantacuzene at long last to make his way back to his headquarters at Didymot-eichos. Thereafter the war was fought not as a cat and mouse affair between the regency in Constantinople and the usurper on the run in Macedonia, but as a more direct encounter between opposing forces over the well-worn battlefields of Thrace. Cantacuzene left his younger son Manuel in command at Berroia to the west of Thessalonica. But eastern Macedonia was simply abandoned to the mercies of Stephen Dušan, and Thessalonica alone maintained a tenuous line of communication with Constantinople. The Turkish troops of Aydin helped Cantacuzene to subject or to win over many of the towns of Thrace. But the price that they exacted for their services was heavy. The Turks never returned to Asia empty-handed and much of Thrace was again reduced to the condition of a 'Scythian desert'. The Empress in Constantinople expected great things from Stephen Dušan as well as from John Alexander of Bulgaria. But since both of these allies were primarily intent on gaining permanent territorial advantages for themselves, she was not so well served as Cantacuzene, whose Turkish friends, for all their depredations, showed as yet no inclination to make lasting conquests of their own in Europe.

As Cantacuzene slowly strengthened his hold on Thrace his rivals began to feel the pinch. Food was scarce in Constantinople, not only because the Turks were devastating the Thracian countryside, but also because some of the harbours and markets on the Black Sea were temporarily closed. The Genoese, whose cargo ships kept the capital supplied with the necessities of life, were engaged in warfare with the Mongols of the Golden Horde over the possession of their colonies in the Crimea. It was, as Gregoras sententiously observes, an age of civil wars, revolutions and disturbances in every corner of the globe, in the Republic of Genoa, in Egypt, in Spain and in Asia. He had even heard the news from the more distant west that 'the Britons had sent their fleet over to the mainland of the Celts and that a great war was being waged'. It may be comforting to know that the Battle of Crécy did not pass unnoticed in Constantinople, insignificant though it seemed when compared with the civil war in which the Byzantines themselves were embroiled at the time; but they saw it as another symptom of the unrest which was, by the will of God, afflicting the whole world.[22]

When the tide began to turn in Cantacuzene's favour even some of the most loyal officers of the regency began to desert the cause. John Vatatzes, who was related by marriage to the Patriarch as well as to Apokaukos, and who held a command in Thrace, defected to the camp of Cantacuzene in 1344. Even the son of Apokaukos, Manuel, the governor of Adrianople, abandoned his post and changed sides. The citizens of Adrianople held out a little longer. But the spirit of revolt had waned, and early in 1345 they gave up the struggle and surrendered to Cantacuzene.[23]

Apokaukos began to see his power slipping away from him. To nip the reaction in the bud he posted proscription lists in Constantinople naming all those known or suspected to be against him. There was another round of arrests, especially of the rich. Apokaukos protected himself with a military bodyguard and kept a warship ready in the Golden Horn in case of emergencies. He gave orders for a new dungeon to be constructed in the so-called Palace of Constantine near his own residence to accommodate the growing number of his political prisoners, and when the work was nearing completion he went to inspect it. The high-ranking prisoners were allowed to take exercise in the courtyard of the palace. They were astonished to see the man who had condemned them to life imprisonment enter the courtyard without his bodyguard. One of them snatched up a block of wood and struck him down. The others picked up tools and materials that the builders had left to hand and joined in the murder. They hacked off his head with an axe and hung it on a pole from the palace walls.

The prison guards who had been waiting outside the courtyard scattered in terror when they saw what had happened. But the prisoners made no attempt to escape. They confidently expected to be hailed as heroes who had delivered the city from a tyrant. They had miscalculated. The Empress was shocked at their action and not at all gratified to be thus brutally deprived of her most capable first minister and commander. She allowed the servants of Apokaukos and the Gasmouli who had served him as sailors to wreak their own vengeance on the murderers of their master. Nearly all the prisoners, most of them innocent of the deed, were massacred, to the number of about 200. Some took refuge in the nearby monastery of Nea Moni, but they were struck down just the same and the sanctuary ran with blood. Alexios Apokaukos was dead, but he brought many of his victims to ruin with him.[24]

The date of his murder was 11 June 1345. It was not the end of violence, bloodshed and horror in the Empire; but it may be said to mark the beginning of the end of the civil war. Cantacuzene was at the time trying to prevent the capture of the city of Serres by the army of Stephen Dušan. He hurried to Constantinople when he heard the news, only to be frustrated on discovering that the Empress and the Patriarch had restored order and taken command of the situation. But the murder of Apokaukos removed the main protagonist of the war and set off a chain reaction in other places. In Thessalonica his son John Apokaukos, the nominal governor of the city, had for long been trying to assert his authority over the Zealot party. He organized a plot to have their leader assassinated; and when word reached him of his father's death in June 1345 John openly declared for Cantacuzene and offered to hand over the city. The Cantacuzenists who had been lying low in Thessalonica came out in his support, and a message was sent to Cantacuzene's son Manuel in Berroia. But the Zealots moved swiftly. Before Manuel or his father could take any action to assist the counter-revolution, John Apokaukos and his partisans had been rounded up and massacred. There was an orgy of bloodshed at the end of which the Zealots were more firmly in control of Thessalonica than ever before. Their revolutionary ideals had been somewhat tarnished; their régime had become more like mob rule, and though they continued to protest their allegiance to the house of

Palaiologos, they governed the city in their own interests.[25]

Events in Thessalonica had passed beyond the control of either side in the civil war. The regency in Constantinople had lost its organizer with the death of Apokaukos. But the Empress and the Patriarch still commanded a considerable following and refused to think in terms of surrender. Cantacuzene on the other hand was gradually surrounding them and beginning to make plans for forcing his way into the capital. After 1345 his friend Umur, who had so greatly advanced his cause, was less able to offer the same generous help. For the league of western powers sponsored by Pope Clement VI had finally succeeded in destroying his fleet and seizing the harbour of Smyrna in October 1344. Umur still held the upper part of the city, and he even found time to take an army to Thrace in 1345. But in the following years he became more and more preoccupied in defending his own territory, and he was killed fighting at Smyrna in 1348.[26] The Empress Anne was well aware that Cantacuzene could no longer rely on Umur's help, and she tried by various means to take advantage of the fact. Several attempts were made on Cantacuzene's life by agents from Constantinople who got into his camp. But Umur of Aydin was not the only friend that he had among the Turks. Saruchan, the emir of Lydia, had also sent troops to help him. But in 1345 he made contact with Orchan, the emir of Bithynia and leader of the Osmanlis. Orchan was within comparatively easy reach of Thrace and only too happy to be invited to take sides in the Byzantine dispute. The work begun on Cantacuzene's behalf by the soldiers of Umur was completed by the Osmanli troops supplied by Orchan.

Historians have expressed much pious horror about the manner in which John Cantacuzene invited the Turks to Europe. Even he himself felt bound to apologize for having done so. The westerners and the popes were particularly scandalized, for they were more inclined than the Byzantines to regard negotiation or alliance with the infidel as shameful. Early in 1345 Cantacuzene explained his attitude to two Franciscans sent to his camp by the Genoese of Galata. One of the friars came from Savoy and was connected with the family of the Empress Anne. Cantacuzene rather hoped that they would act as mediators to bring an end to the fighting. But he had to explain to them that his alliance with the Osmanlis was purely a matter of military necessity; and he could, and did, point out to them that he had not been the first to call on the help of the Turks. The Empress had vainly tried to win the alliance of Orchan and also of the emir of

Karasi. The Turks were flattered to be so much in demand. They could make their own decisions as to which side to join.[27]

Nor could anyone pretend that this was the first occasion on which Turks of one kind or another had been employed as soldiers on European soil. The Catalans had shown the example in that respect. Andronikos II had engaged Turkish mercenaries in the first civil war, though not with any marked success. But in the second civil war both sides were inclined to regard the Turkish emirates as valuable sources of manpower. The fact that Cantacuzene's offers to them were more attractive than those coming from Constantinople was probably due to his excellent personal relationships with their leaders, especially with Umur and Orchan. He did not need to be told that their warriors did terrible things. He was conscious that they were barbarians in the technical sense and that their ghazis were committed to the idea of holy war against the Christians. But he had come to appreciate that their leaders were intelligent and not unreasonable beings, and he took the trouble to acquire a knowledge of their language, or so at least he claimed.[28]

His friendship with Umur was of long standing, and he mourned the loss of a true friend when Umur died in 1348, as Gregoras reports.[29] His friendship with Orchan was a later development, but it quickly grew to the point at which Cantacuzene was prepared to accept him as a son-in-law. In 1346 he gave his second daughter Theodora in marriage to Orchan. The Turkish poet Enveri records, correctly, that Cantacuzene had three daughters, all as lovely as houris. One of them, perhaps Theodora, is said to have been offered as a bride to Umur at an earlier date. At all events their beauty was renowned; and, if Gregoras is to be believed, Orchan fell passionately in love with Theodora Cantacuzene, and begged or blackmailed her father into letting him marry her, promising thereafter to serve him as a vassal with his whole army. The ceremony took place at Selymbria on the European side of the Sea of Marmora, and it was attended by all the members of Theodora's family. It was not, of course, a union blessed by the church, but all the ritual customary at the wedding of a Byzantine princess was in other respects scrupulously observed. Nor did Theodora become a mere odalisque in the emir's harem. She continued to practise her Orthodox faith and brought much solace and relief to the poor and to the Christian slaves in her husband's principality.[30]

Moralists have thrown up their hands in horror at this allegedly callous sacrifice of Cantacuzene's daughter to a barbarian chieftain.

But in principle it was no more worse than the marriage of Andronikos II's five-year-old daughter Simonis to Stephen Milutin of Serbia, even though Milutin was supposed to be a Christian. No one had been greatly shocked at the marriage of the daughters of Michael VIII to the Mongol khans or at that of Andronikos II's daughter to the Khan of the Golden Horde, Tokhtu, in 1297. John Vatatzes, who went over to Cantacuzene's side in 1344, had given his daughter in marriage to the emir of Karasi, though his other children were married to a son of Alexios Apokaukos and a daughter of the Patriarch John Kalekas.[31] It is true that Byzantine standards in such matters had fallen since the great days when even the Christian princes of western Europe were not thought good enough to marry a Byzantine princess. But things in Constantinople could still compare favourably with the standards in Trebizond, where the Emperor Alexios II, who died in 1330, had married no less than three infidel wives, and where the Emperor Basil who succeeded him gave two of his daughters as brides to local emirs. The Empire of Trebizond was only able to survive by making arrangements of this kind with its neighbours. The Empire of Constantinople had not yet reached that stage.[32]

During the last months of the civil war, while Cantacuzene was in Thrace preparing the way for his entry into Constantinople, the Serbians were left free to encroach still further on Byzantine Macedonia. The strongly fortified city of Serres, which had hitherto resisted all comers, was finally taken by Stephen Dušan on 25 September 1345. He saw the encirclement and conquest of Thessalonica as his next step. Before the end of the year 1345 Dušan had begun to style himself Emperor of the Serbs and Greeks. By so doing he declared his intention to conquer not only Thessalonica but also Constantinople and to make himself master of the Roman Empire. On Easter Sunday, 16 April 1346, he had himself crowned Emperor at Skoplje by the Archbishop of the Serbian Church whom he had elevated to the rank of Patriarch. The coronation of Stephen Dušan was a direct challenge to both of the Byzantine claimants to the imperial title. For it meant that there were now three Emperors in a world where God had ordained that there was room only for one.[33]

A few weeks later, on 21 May 1346, Cantacuzene fulfilled the promise of his proclamation as Emperor five years before by allowing an imperial crown to be placed on his head. Neither he nor his contemporaries suggested that he was influenced to take this step by the known fact of Dušan's coronation in April. But it seems a probable inference. According to his own account the idea occurred to him spontaneously. The Patriarch of Jerusalem had recently fled to his camp as a refugee from Constantinople, and this was an added incentive. It was he who performed the coronation ceremony at Adrianople. No one could question the authenticity of an emperor who had received his crown from one of the five patriarchs. However, although Cantacuzene now permitted himself to take the crown as well as the name of Emperor of the Romans, he sternly resisted the proposal that he should at the same time proclaim his eldest son Matthew as his co-Emperor. It was still his firm intention to uphold the rights of the house of Palaiologos. John Palaiologos and not Matthew Cantacuzene would therefore become co-Emperor as soon as victory had been achieved.[34]

That victory was almost in sight in the summer of 1346. It was greatly desired by many, not least by the inhabitants of Thrace, whose will to rebel and to hope for better things had been stifled by the devastation of their land and even of their towns by the Turks. The Empress Anne had at last managed to secure the help of a Turkish army for her own cause. The emir Saruchan sent her 6000 soldiers who plundered what was left to plunder in Thrace and the environs of Constantinople, and carried their operations north into Bulgaria. Both sides were reaching the point of exhaustion and bankruptcy. Cantacuzene could expect little more from the impoverished and apathetic people of Thrace. The Empress was reduced to selling ornaments from the icons in the churches of Constantinople and to bullying and harassing those who were hoarding their wealth. Many of them fled to take refuge with the Genoese in Galata. Gregoras gives a sombre description of the poverty and misery of the Byzantines in the capital at this time. In his view their sufferings might have ended more quickly had not Cantacuzene wasted so many of his opportunities by delaying and procrastinating. He would have done better to model himself on one of his great predecessors like Alexios Komnenos instead of adopting so humble and apologetic an attitude to his opponents. But Gregoras also felt that much of their misfortune was due to the corruption of Christian principles caused by the war. A sure sign of this was the fact that the cathedral of St Sophia was allowed to fall into a state of disrepair until, on the night of 19 May 1346, a part of the eastern end of the building collapsed altogether. It was a memorable tragedy and a terrible omen. Repairs were soon carried out by willing armies of workers, rich and poor, men and women alike. But it was the kind of event that often signalled a change in God's purposes to the Byzantine mind. And one may wonder whether the news of this too may have helped John Cantacuzene to decide to take the crown less than two days later. At all events, the day that he chose, 21 May, was auspicious, for it was the Feast of St Constantine and his mother Helena.[35]

In the latter months of 1346 Cantacuzene left his son Matthew in charge of affairs in Thrace and pitched his camp at Selymbria where he could keep in touch with developments inside the city of Constantinople. As the winter drew on the party in favour of admitting him into the city as Emperor gathered strength. A conspiracy was formed to consider how this could be achieved, for the Empress still stubbornly refused to negotiate a settlement. Two more attempts were indeed made to have Cantacuzene assassinated by spies sent to his camp. The agent of the conspirators was one Phakeolatos who managed to get word to Cantacuzene that, if he presented himself at the Golden Gate on a certain night, his entry into Constantinople would be arranged.

The gate had been walled up. But the conspirators were as good as their word, and on the night of 2 February 1347 John Cantacuzene was admitted into the city through a breach made in the wall. He had with him an army of about 1000 men. They met with no resistance, and by break of day on 3 February he had drawn up his troops outside the walls of the Blachernai Palace. The Empress had done her best to anticipate the event by being conciliatory towards the Cantacuzenists in the city. Only the day before she had presided over a synod of her bishops at which the Patriarch John Kalekas had been deposed. But she had been led to believe such terrible things about Cantacuzene's intentions to her and her son that she was reluctant to surrender now that the moment had come. The Genoese sent two ships over from Galata to rescue her, but they were sighted and forced to turn back. Cantacuzene tried to reason with her through ambassadors whom he sent to pay his respects. But the palace gates remained barred. Finally some of his officers lost patience and anticipated their orders by setting fire to one of the gates and storming their way into the fortified area of the palace. The Empress then at last submitted and sent representatives to make peace. On 8 February 1347 a settlement was worked out. Its terms were such that they might well have been reached six years earlier. It was agreed that John Cantacuzene and the young John Palaiologos, now about 15 years old, should reign together as co-Emperors, the former being recognized as senior Emperor for the space of ten years, after which they would rule as equal colleagues. Cantacuzene promised to take no reprisals against any who had fought

212

against him and to bear no grudge against the Empress and her son. All political prisoners were to be released and the immediate past was, so far as possible, to be forgotten.[36]

Many people who were alive at the time remarked on Cantacuzene's clemency and generosity towards his late enemies. Demetrios Kydones, who was to become his first minister and a leading statesman of Byzantium for the remainder of the fourteenth century, composed two orations for the occasion. For him the fact of Cantacuzene's victory was less significant than the fact of his kindness and tolerance towards those who had so lately been thirsting for his blood. Kydones saw, or claimed to see, the civil war as a conflict between truth and falsehood, between justice and injustice, humanity and savagery, good and evil; and its outcome proved that the good and true will always prevail in the end. He spoke as one born into the aristocracy, whose father had been a close associate of Andronikos III and Cantacuzene, and whose family and property in Thessalonica had suffered grievously as a result. He hoped to be rewarded for his loyalty to the aristocratic cause. The language of his orations is stiff with rhetorical artifice and hardly an advertisement for the prevalence of truth over falsehood. But he is surely to be believed when he commends Cantacuzene for his desire to put an end to slaughter and bloodshed, and when he reports the spontaneous relief of the people at the news that the fighting was at last over.

Kydones vividly recalls that memorable night when the Emperor, John Cantacuzene, suddenly appeared in the city with his army, and the trumpets signalled the bad news for his unsuspecting enemies. 'Before the light of day had dawned', he writes, 'everyone in the city poured out into the streets to see the Emperor as though he were a long-lost friend, to grasp his feet and embrace him with joy; and the Emperor, though grieved to see how they had been changed by so many misfortunes, shared in the general happiness. But his resolve was not affected by the magnitude of his success; and although the populace followed him up to the acropolis clamouring for the blood of the wild beasts who had shut themselves up inside, he thought in terms of negotiating a settlement rather than committing murder, and he promised to spare the lives of those who were already dead from fear.... At the end he pardoned all those who had so gravely wronged him, even when he had them at his mercy by right of conquest.... So, all you who have been weighed down by the burden of your sufferings ... and are now restored to life, you have your Emperor and you have your happiness. Rejoice for this day, as the Egyptians rejoiced for the flight of the phoenix, which should be the symbol of your better fortune.'[37]

NOTES

The principal narrative sources for the second civil war (1341-7) are: Cantacuzene, II, 11-615; Gregoras, II, 576-779.
Modern works: The events are described and documented by: Parisot, *Cantacuzène* (1845), 153-221; Florinskij, 'Andronik Mladšij ...', *Žurnal min. narod. prosveščenija*, CCIV (1879), 219-51; Nicol, *Byzantine Family of Kantakouzenos*, 44-63.

1 On the rights and wrongs of Cantacuzene's claim to the regency, see Bosch, *Andronikos III*, 176-93; F. Dölger, 'Johannes VI. Kantakuzenos als dynastischer Legitimist', in *PARASPORA* (Ettal, 1961), 194-207.

2 The Patriarch Esaias died on 13 May 1332; John Kalekas of Apros was appointed Patriarch in February 1334. Gregoras, I, 496; Cantacuzene, I, 431-5. Cf. *Short Chronicle of 1352*, ed. Loenertz, part II, 40, 41, 50-2, 54-5.

3 Cantacuzene, II, 25-52. Cf. Gregoras, II, 576-86. Nicol, *Byzantine Family of Kantakouzenos*, 44-5.

4 Nicol, *op. cit.*, 45-7.

5 Cantacuzene, II, 169.

6 Cantacuzene, II, 167-8.

7 The ceremony at Didymoteichos is fully described by Cantacuzene himself, II, 165-9.

8 Cantacuzene, II, 12.

9 The most recent and detailed study of the Byzantine ruling class and society in this period is that by G. Weiss, *Joannes Kantakuzenos—Aristokrat, Staatsmann, Kaiser und Mönch—in der Gesellschaftsentwicklung von Byzanz im 14. Jahrhundert* (Wiesbaden, 1969). See also P. Charanis, 'Internal strife in Byzantium during the fourteenth century', *B*, XV (1940-1), 208-30.

10 Cantacuzene, II, 164-5.

11 Cantacuzene, II, 185. Cf. Zakythinos, *Crise monétaire*, 56-7; Weiss, *op. cit.*, 21-2.

12 G. Ostrogorsky, *Pour l'histoire de la féodalité byzantine* (Brussels, 1954), 101f.

13 Cantacuzene, II, 175-9; Gregoras, II, 620-2. Cf. Charanis, *op. cit.*, 209-10; and especially Weiss, *op. cit.*, 70-85.

14 Cantacuzene, II, 178.

15 Cantacuzene, II, 234-5.

16 The following are among the most important modern contributions to the study of the Zealot revolution at Thessalonica: O. Tafrali, *Thessalonique au XIVe siècle* (Paris, 1913), 225-72; P. Charanis, *op. cit.*, B, XV (1940-1), 208-30; R. Browning, 'Kommunata na Zilotite v Solunu (1342-1350)', *Istoričeski Pregled*, VI, 4-5 (Sofia, 1950), 509-26 I. Švečenko, 'The Zealot revolution and the supposed Genoese colony in Thessalonica', *Prosphora eis St. P. Kyriakidin* (Thessalonike, 1953), 603-17; and 'Nicholas Cabasilas' "Anti-Zealot" Discourse: A reinterpretation', *DOP*, XI (1957), 79-171; E. Werner, 'Volkstümlicher Häretiker oder sozial-politischer Reformer? Probleme der revolutionären Volksbewegung in Thessalonike 1342-1349', *Wissenschaftliche Zeitschrift Universität Leipzig*, VIII (1958-9), 45-83; V. Hrochová, 'La révolte des Zélotes à Salonique et les communes italiennes', *BS*, XXII (1961), 1-15; C. P. Kyrris, 'Gouvernés et gouvernants à Byzance pendant la révolution des Zélotes (1341-1350)', in *Gouvernés et Gouvernants* (1968), 271-330; M. J. Sjuzjumov, 'K voprosu o kharaktere vystuplenija zilotov v 1342-1349 gg.' (On the question of the character of the Zealot uprising in 1342-9), *VV*, XXVIII (1968), 15-37; Weiss, *Joannes Kantakuzenos*, 88f., 94-101. Cf. Ostrogorsky, *History*, 515-16. On Synadenos, see Lj. Maksimović, 'Poslednie godine protostratora Teodora Sinadina' (The last years of the protostrator Theodore Synadenos), *Zbornik Radova*, X (1967), 177-85.

17 Nicol, *Byzantine Family*, 50-2.

18 Nicol, 52-3, and 147-8 (for Cantacuzene's cousin, John Angelos).

19 Gregoras, II, 648-9, where Gregoras also compares Umur's friendship for Cantacuzene to that of Pylades for Orestes.

20 On Anne of Savoy's dealings with the papacy and with Venice, see J. Gay, *Le Pape Clément VI et les affaires d'Orient (1342-1352)*, (Paris, 1904), 33-4; N. Jorga, 'Latins et grecs d'Orient et l'etablissement des Turcs en Europe (1342-1362)', *BZ*, XV (1906), 185, 188-9. For documents concerning the pawning of the Byzantine crown jewels to Venice in 1343, see Dölger, *Regesten*, V, no. 2891; T. Bertelè, 'I gioielli della corona bizantina dati in pegno alla repubblica veneta nel sec. XIV e Mastino della Scala', *Studi in onore di A. Fanfani*, II: *Medioevo* (Milan, 1962), 90-177.

21 Nicol, *Byzantine Family*, 54-6.

22 Gregoras, II, 687-9.

23 Nicol, 57-8.

24 Cantacuzene, II, 541-5; Gregoras, II, 729-41; Doukas (Ducas),

Istoria turco-byzantina, ed. V. Grecu (Bucharest, 1958), 43-7; *Short Chronicle of 1352*, ed. P. Schreiner, part III, in *OCP*, XXXI (1965), 338, 358-60.

25 Cantacuzene, II, 568-81; Gregoras, II, 740-1. Cf. Tafrali, *Thessalonique au XIVᵉ siècle*, 239-49; Charanis, *op. cit.*, 214-15. See below, pp. 234-6.

26 Lemerle, *L'Emirat d'Aydin*, 180f., 218f. and references.

27 Cantacuzene, II, 502-24.

28 Cf. E. Werner, 'Johannes Kantakuzenos, Umur Paša und Orhan', *BS*, XXVI (1965), 255-76.

29 Gregoras, II, 835.

30 On Theodora Cantacuzene and her marriage to Orchan, see Nicol, *Byzantine Family*, 134-5.

31 Gregoras, II, 741-3; Cantacuzene, II, 475.

32 For Trebizond, see below, pp. 425-33.

33 Gregoras, II, 746-7; Cantacuzene, II, 551-2. Cf. Ostrogorsky, *History*, 523 and references.

34 Gregoras, II, 762; Cantacuzene, II, 564-8. Nicol, 61.

35 Gregoras, II, 748-55. The collapse of part of St Sophia is also recorded in several of the Short Chronicles and was the subject of an essay by Alexios Makrembolites, now edited with a commentary by St. I. Kourousis, in *EEBS*, XXXVII (1969-70), 211-50.

36 Nicol, 62-3 and references.

37 G. Cammelli, 'Demetrii Cydonii orationes tres, adhuc ineditae: Ad Ioannem Cantacuzenum imperatorem oratio I', *BNJ*, III (1922), 67-76; and 'Oratio altera', *BNJ*, IV (1923), 77-83. The quotation is from the latter.

Thirteen

The Reign of John VI Cantacuzene—1347-54

John Cantacuzene is generally designated, at least by modern historians, as the sixth Byzantine Emperor of that name. John Palaiologos, the son of Andronikos III and Anne of Savoy, is called John V. The numeration tells something of the relationship between the two emperors, for John VI claimed and was accorded seniority over John V, but not precedence. As the 'spiritual brother' of the late Andronikos III he stood as it were *in loco parentis* to the junior Emperor, at least until such time as John V attained his majority. The special affinity with Andronikos III and his family which Cantacuzene claimed in 1341 was written into the settlement of 1347 by which John VI and John V became co-Emperors. It was given greater reality for the future by the announcement made very shortly after that settlement that Cantacuzene's daughter Helena was to marry John V.[1]

There were precedents for such an arrangement in Byzantine dynastic history. The most celebrated case was that of the usurper Romanos Lekapenos in the tenth century. He had made himself regent for the boy Emperor Constantine VII Porphyrogenitus in 919, ostensibly in the interest of the Macedonian dynasty whose right to the throne he claimed to uphold and protect. Romanos gave his daughter in marriage to Constantine and, at the end of 920, was crowned as co-Emperor. He thus became the imperial father-in-law, or *basileopator*, of the reigning emperor. Cantacuzene gives no hint that he had the example of Romanos Lekapenos in mind, and he preferred to describe his relationship with John V in more spiritual and less definitive terms than that of *basileopator*. But the constitutional position of the two men, as senior emperors guarding the rights of the hereditary successor, is strikingly similar.[2]

The arrangement was disliked by a number of parties for a variety of reasons. Many of the supporters of the Palaiologos family continued to look on Cantacuzene as a usurper and a hypocrite, for all his protestations. Many of his own supporters thought that he was overplaying the part of the magnanimous victor. They felt that he should now seize his chance to establish a new dynasty in place of that of the Palaiologi; and they refused at first to take the oath of allegiance to both emperors that was required of them. Lastly there was Cantacuzene's eldest son Matthew who was John V's senior by several years and who might justly expect to inherit the throne that his father had won. Matthew was a dutiful son, but he found it increasingly irksome to be made to play second fiddle to John V, and he had many sympathizers among the more outspoken Cantacuzenists who saw their hopes of gain or office being thwarted by his father's attitude.

John VI did his best to steer a middle course between these factions. The important thing was to give the Empire and its people a period of peace and a time to heal the wounds of civil war and contention. It was to this end that he declared a general amnesty for all his political opponents. Only one exception was made. The Patriarch John Kalekas, his arch-enemy who had excommunicated him in 1341, refused to forgive or to be forgiven. Cantacuzene tried to bring about a reconciliation, but the Patriarch's pride, of which he had plenty, had been hurt by recent events. He had been relieved of office by the Empress and her synod of bishops just before Cantacuzene entered the city in February 1347. He had also been anathematized *in absentia* by an assembly of bishops at Adrianople at the time of John VI's coronation in 1346. He thus stood condemned by both parties. Kalekas was no great theologian, but the reasons for his condemnation were in neither case purely political.[3]

In the last years of the reign of Andronikos III the Byzantine church had become involved in a theological controversy which threatened to be as divisive as the Arsenite schism of the previous century, or even as dangerous to the state as the iconoclast crisis of an earlier age. The dispute concerned the precepts and practices of a small group of monks, mainly on Mount Athos, known as the hesychasts. Their reputation and their influence were quite out of proportion to their numbers. The hesychasts concentrated upon perfecting a method of prayer which gave the dedicated mystic a greater awareness of the divine light. Nothing, it might be thought, could be more recondite or more remote from the political rivalries of a civil war. But theology and politics were always inextricably connected in Byzantium. The motives of the hesychasts were beyond question. All of them were monks, and their technique of meditation was best practised in solitary places as far as possible from the temptations and distractions of the world and the flesh. But there were some churchmen who suspected that their theology was questionable; there were some of their own number who only half understood what they were about; and their method of prayer, which called for the mystic to regulate his breathing and adopt curious physical postures, was all too easy for a sceptic to ridicule.[4]

The first to make mock of the hesychasts was a Greek monk from Calabria in south Italy called Barlaam. He was a scholar and his erudition was much esteemed by John Cantacuzene who in the 1330s had secured him an appointment to teach in the University of Constantinople. Barlaam's Orthodoxy appeared to be impeccable. The Emperor Andronikos III had even sent him on a secret mission to Pope Benedict XII at Avignon in 1339 to explain the Byzantine point of view on the matter of the union of the churches.[5] But he was not a native Byzantine and his claim to know more about Orthodoxy than the Orthodox themselves was soon resented. Nikephoros Gregoras was able to pick holes in his philosophy in a public debate. But the man who challenged Barlaam's theology was the monk Gregory Palamas, a leading exponent of the doctrine of hesychasm on Mount Athos. And it was on this account that Barlaam took to attacking and making fun of the hesychasts and their practices. He condemned the theology implicit in their claim to be able to apprehend the divine light, and he denounced them as heretics to the Patriarch John Kalekas. Gregory Palamas rushed to their defence and composed a manifesto approved and signed by all his colleagues on Mount Athos. It was an impressive advertisement of solidarity on the part of the largest and most influential monastic settlement left in the Byzantine Empire. John Cantacuzene, though he admired the scholarship of Barlaam, believed the doctrine and theology of the hesychasts to be perfectly consonant with Orthodox tradition; and he helped to convince the Emperor Andronikos III that a council of the church should be convened to decide whether this was so. The Patriarch rather reluctantly acquiesced, and on 10 June 1341 Barlaam of Calabria and all his works were damned at a council in St Sophia. Palamas, who had presented his own case before the bishops, was declared to be Orthodox. The president of the council was the Emperor himself who had just returned to the capital from Thessalonica. He had been ill the previous year, and the worry and exertion of the affair coming so soon after his journey is said to have hastened his death only five days later. Barlaam retired from the Byzantine scene and returned to his native Italy, where in due course he went over to the Roman Church.

But the affair was by no means ended. For Barlaam's accusations against the doctrine of the hesychasts were upheld by some reputable native Byzantine theologians, notably the monk Gregory Akindynos, who was an old friend of Palamas. The Patriarch Kalekas was not keen to have a theological quarrel on his hands. But passions had been roused, and in August 1341 a second council was held in Constantinople at which Palamas was once again commended and Akindynos was condemned. There was no Emperor to preside over the council, but the chair was taken by John Cantacuzene. From this circumstance the issue became tainted by the political rivalry between Cantacuzene and the Patriarch. For Kalekas was naturally loth to uphold the rulings of a council that had been directed by his rival for the regency. His inclination to make political capital out of it was stirred by Gregory Akindynos who was ably supported by a number of others who suspected Palamas of deviation or heresy, among them Nikephoros Gregoras. The Empress Anne was hardly able to master the subtleties of Orthodox mystical theology, though she admired Palamas. But she was dominated by the will and the personality of the Patriarch.[6]

Gregory Palamas, who was in Constantinople at the time of Andronikos III's death, was an unashamed advocate of the rights of John Cantacuzene to act as regent of the Empire. But his prestige and his moral influence were too great for the Patriarch to dare to do anything to silence him, and for some time Palamas was allowed to live in a hermitage attached to a monastery on the Bosporos. In 1343, however, the Patriarch, supported by Akindynos and by others whose theological objections to Palamite doctrine provided respectable cover for the deed, had Palamas arrested and put in prison. In November 1344 the Patriarch's synod excommunicated him and proposed the preferment of his opponent Akindynos, though he had been condemned as a heretic by the council in August 1341.

It is sometimes implied that the hesychasts or Palamites were all on the side of Cantacuzene and the anti-Palamites all on the side of the regency during the civil war. But the lines were not so simply drawn. Certainly Cantacuzene's cause benefited from the loyalty to it of Gregory Palamas and so of most of the monks of Mount Athos. But several intelligent men such as Nikephoros Gregoras, whose politics were Cantacuzenist, felt bound to oppose Palamas and the hesychasts on religious grounds. Others like Demetrios Kydones and Nicholas Kabasilas, both close friends of Cantacuzene, remained non-committal on the theological question during the war. Even Alexios Apokaukos took issue with the Patriarch over the imprisonment of Palamas; and the Empress Anne became increasingly aware that the Patriarch was exploiting the Palamite controversy as a means to strengthen his own temporal authority, and thus alienating many who had hitherto supported the regency. It was in order to win back those who were inclining towards Cantacuzene as the champion of Palamas that the Empress convened the synod of bishops at the beginning of February 1347. They accused the Patriarch of flouting the decisions of previous councils and deposed him from office. Palamas was again vindicated and released from prison. As a last minute gesture to win over the Palamite supporters of John Cantacuzene the Empress had left it too late. For on the following day Cantacuzene entered the capital with his army. But one of the mediators that she sent to him from the palace was Gregory Palamas himself, for no one could accuse Palamas of ever having sought anything but peace.[7]

It seems probable that, without the circumstances of the civil war, the controversy that Barlaam of Calabria raised over the doctrine of hesychasm would not have divided Byzantine society in the way that it did. The Patriarch Kalekas has much to answer for in this respect. For it was he who gave free rein to Gregory Akindynos, a man already condemned by the church, to pour out anti-Palamite propaganda; and it was he who tried to stamp the stigma of Cantacuzenism on the doctrine of Palamas and the hesychasts to achieve his own political aims. How misleading the identification of Cantacuzenists with Palamites was may be judged from one particular case, that of Eirene Choumnaina. Eirene was the daughter of the late Nikephoros Choumnos and had married the Despot John Palaiologos, son of Andronikos II. After her husband's death in 1308 she had become a nun with the name of Eulogia. She was extremely pious and famously rich and well-connected. She had received her religious instruction from Theoleptos, the Bishop of Philadelphia, who, though he died before the hesychast dispute broke out, had greatly contributed to the revival of Byzantine spirituality and was in some sense a forerunner of Palamas himself. Eirene's breeding and her wealth might have inclined her to the side of John Cantacuzene; her religious upbringing and her piety might have persuaded her to adopt the hesychast cause. But Eirene defied all such categorization. During the civil war she chose Gregory Akindynos as her father confessor, protected him and encouraged him to disseminate his anti-Palamite literature. Her convent became a centre of political activity directed against Cantacuzene. The case of Eirene Choumnaina demonstrates equally the error of supposing that all the wealthy aristocracy ranged themselves on the side of John Cantacuzene during the civil war, and the error of identifying the Cantacuzenists with the Palamites.[8]

It would be no less misleading to conclude that Cantacuzene championed the cause of hesychasm from purely political motives or simply to gain the backing of the powerful moral and spiritual forces of Mount Athos and the monks. Cantacuzene certainly needed all the supporters he could find in the early stages of the war. But he was a sincerely religious man and his theological convictions were more a matter of conscience than of policy. He was himself much attracted by the monastic vocation and was to become and remain a monk for the last 30 years of his life after his abdication. He also wrote dogmatic treatises in defence of Palamas and the doctrine of the hesychasts which show that he had considered and understood the theological arguments on both sides. But in February 1347, when he entered Constantinople and was accepted as senior Emperor, he had to decide what could be done in the case of the Patriarch John Kalekas who had, for his own purposes, tried to drive the theologians into opposing political camps.

The Patriarch declined to discuss any form of reconciliation and refused to attend a synod to state his own case. The synod, which was presided over by Cantacuzene and the Empress later in February 1347, therefore reaffirmed that John Kalekas had been condemned and deposed in his absence. Its findings were published in an imperial decree issued by John VI as Emperor in March and confirmed a few weeks later at yet another assembly attended by the Patriarch of Jerusalem and the other bishops who had been at Cantacuzene's court in Adrianople. John Kalekas was thus thrice condemned and the doctrine of Palamas thrice proclaimed as Orthodox within a matter of weeks in the year 1347. Gregory Akindynos, who had also been censured yet again, fled from the city and died in exile soon afterwards. In May of the same year Isidore Boukharis was elected Patriarch of Constantinople in place of Kalekas, who was exiled to Didymoteichos. Isidore was a hesychast monk and a friend of Palamas who had suffered for his convictions. There were some Palamites who felt that the choice was not a good one. But his election was ratified by both Emperors, and Isidore proceeded at once to appoint a number of new bishops, among them Palamas himself, who was raised to the see of Thessalonica.

It was Isidore who annulled the excommunication laid on Cantacuzene by John Kalekas, and it was he who had the distinction of performing the second coronation of Cantacuzene in the church of the Virgin by the palace of Blachernai. The date was 21 May 1347, a year to the day after his first coronation at Adrianople. It was a grand occasion attended by three empresses as well as the two emperors, and there were processions and banquets. But it was a mark of the Empire's poverty and depression that the ceremony could not be held in St Sophia because of the dilapidated state of the building; and the onlookers sadly observed that the crown jewels were made of glass and that the plate for the banquets was made of pewter and clay. The real crown jewels were still in pawn to Venice, and the Empress had sold most of the gold and silver plate from the palace to make ends meet during the war. About a week later the wedding of John V to Helena Cantacuzene was celebrated in the same church, and John then crowned her as his Empress according to Byzantine custom.[9]

These things augured well for the future. But there were many wrongs yet to be righted and many wounds to be healed. The reconciliation between the house of Palaiologos and the house of Cantacuzene symbolized by the marriage of John V to Helena was superficial. Neither side had yet laid down their arms. The Empress Anne's supporters were not content to be allowed to live on the sufferance and forgiveness of John Cantacuzene. There were rumours of plots to beguile her son John into continuing the fight from Galata. Some of Cantacuzene's supporters on the other hand whispered into the ear of Matthew Cantacuzene that he should fight for his right to the succession before it was too late and set himself up independently at Adrianople. There was a real danger that the civil war would be perpetuated by the next generation. But for the time being Cantacuzene eased his eldest son's frustrations by allotting him an appanage in eastern Thrace running from Didymoteichos to the suburbs of Christoupolis on the coast. From here he could guard the Empire's western frontier against the Serbs. He was given no title but invested with the insignia of a rank and dignity more exalted than those of a despot yet below those of an emperor. It was an awkward compromise. Cantacuzene's second son Manuel, who had taken refuge in Thessaly when driven out of Macedonia by Stephen Dušan, was recalled to Constantinople in 1347 and honoured with the rank and title of Despot. He was better off than his brother Matthew.[10]

The reign of John VI might well have turned the Byzantine Empire to better state. He had justified his claim to the regency in 1341 by emphasizing his long experience of administration and defence and his plans for the restoration of the Empire's former wealth and prestige. Once installed as Emperor in Constantinople he was in a position to apply his experience and to implement his plans. There can be little doubt that he had workable schemes of reform and restoration in mind. Even Nikephoros Gregoras admits that, if only Cantacuzene had not lapsed into the heresy of Palamas, he would have been one of the greatest of all Byzantine Emperors.[11] Theology apart, it might be truer to say that, although John VI was not bereft of ideas, he lacked the firmness of purpose to put them fully into action, and almost everything seemed to militate against his best intentions.

As if the ravages and casualties of civil war and the Scythian deserts created by the Turks were not enough, Constantinople and other parts of the Empire were visited by the Black Death in the very first year of John VI's reign. It is remarkable how little the Byzantines have to tell about the progress and the effects of this most celebrated and deadly epidemic of the middle ages. They were accustomed to regard such pestilences and catastrophes as visitations from God. There was therefore little point in complaining about them. But the Black Death was a visitation of exceptional severity. A western chronicler has it that eight-ninths of the population of Constantinople died.[12] This is doubtless an exaggeration, but the Byzantine historians and chroniclers themselves provide no statistics. Cantacuzene gives a highly literate account of the symptoms of the disease and the distress of the victims. But his eye when writing it was fixed on the text of the description given by Thucydides of the plague at Athens in the time of Pericles. Byzantine authors expected praise rather than blame for plagiarizing a classical model. There had been a plague in fifth-century Athens. Fourteenth-century Byzantium could not presume to have produced a better one.[13] Gregoras, however, rightly records that the infection was brought to Constantinople from the Scythian or Tartar country of Lake Maiotis or the Sea of Azov and the estuary of the Don. The classic western account links the spread of the epidemic with the Mongol siege of the Genoese colony of Caffa in the Crimea in 1346. The disease was carried from there by Genoese ships. It reached Trebizond in September 1347, but it had by then already swept through Constantinople, and it had travelled as far west as Marseille by the end of that year.[14]

The Black Death did its deadliest work in the towns. Demetrios Kydones in one of his letters describes its horrors in Constantinople.[15] But there seems to be no record of its effects on the other cities such as Thessalonica or Adrianople, nor of its progress in the Turkish emirates in Asia Minor. Historians of the Ottoman Empire have assumed that the depopulation that it caused in Europe helped to open the way for the Osmanlis into Thrace and Macedonia. But they do not explain how the Turks themselves came to be immune to the disease. The half is not told of the effects of the Black Death on the Byzantine Empire. Both of the historians who were alive at the time thought it worth mentioning that Cantacuzene's youngest son Andronikos died of it in Constantinople in 1347. But otherwise they write only in general terms of the deaths of innumerable men, women, children and animals. One is left to conjecture what the real consequences were, both material and psychological. There was evidently much nervous apprehension that the plague would return, as it did, though in less virulent form, on several occasions in the next 100 years.[16] But the epidemic of 1347 must have added very greatly to the sense of hopelessness and apathy which the Byzantines experienced at the end of two civil wars. The people in the cities, who had once had such high hopes of bettering their condition by revolution, had watched the victory of the aristocracy with sullen resignation. The Black Death reduced the survivors to fatalistic despondency. They were glad that the fighting was over. But it would be very hard to recreate in them a feeling of optimism about the future of their society; and it would be almost impossible now to realize the plan that Cantacuzene had envisaged in 1341, of reconstituting a compact and integrated Empire consisting of the Greek provinces, added to those of Macedonia and Thrace.

The territory that remained under Byzantine rule in 1347 was made up of isolated towns and provinces. Thessalonica was still controlled by the Zealots who ignored or defied all orders sent from Constantinople and refused to allow Gregory Palamas to take up his appointment as their bishop. They would rather do business with Stephen Dušan of Serbia than with John Cantacuzene. But Dušan, who already held all the surrounding country in Macedonia, wanted Thessalonica on his own terms; and the fact that his troops were occupying the city of Serres made it impossible for the Emperors in Constantinople to approach Thessalonica except by sea. Cantacuzene tried in vain to persuade Dušan to withdraw to his agreed

225

boundaries, and then threatened him with the horrors of attack by a Turkish army. In the spring of 1348 his son-in-law Orchan supplied Cantacuzene with a large army commanded by his eldest son Suleiman. They were to join forces with another army marching on Serbia under Matthew Cantacuzene. But the Turks got no further west than Christoupolis where they indulged in an orgy of plunder before going home with a vast amount of booty. Later in the same year two Serbian armies descended on Greece from Macedonia. Cantacuzene's cousin John Angelos, the Byzantine governor of Thessaly and Epiros, had died of the plague. The province was open to the new invader, and before the end of the year the whole of northern Greece was under Serbian domination. The greatest of the achievements of Andronikos III had been undone in the space of a few months; and the dominions of the Serbian Emperor, which now stretched from the Danube to the Adriatic and the Gulf of Corinth, were many times larger than those of the Emperors in Constantinople.[17]

The Serbian conquest of Thessaly and Epiros narrowed the Byzantine Empire down to its smallest measure. The nucleus was now Constantinople and Thrace, with the vitally important cities of Didymoteichos and Adrianople. But the coast of Thrace was constantly being raided by Turkish pirates; and even in the interior of the country there were marauding bands of Turks at large who seemed to have lost the urge to go back home with their plunder. Cantacuzene, when on his way through Thrace in 1348, encountered a force of 2000 Turkish horsemen and only just escaped with his life. Across the water in Asia Minor a few isolated coastal fortresses still held out against the Turks; and the city of Philadelphia alone of all the inland cities maintained a lonely and precarious independence. Smyrna was still held by the Latins. But the island of Chios, which Andronikos III had reclaimed in 1329, had fallen again to the Genoese during the civil war in 1346. One possible centre of recovery was the Morea, a large part of which was still in Greek hands; and John VI still cherished the hope that the whole of southern Greece might yet be won and provide the base for the reconquest of the rest of the Balkan peninsula.

But even without the calamities of the Black Death and the Serbian invasion of Greece, the resources of the Empire had been fatally weakened and the spirit of its inhabitants corrupted by the civil war. Some of Cantacuzene's plans for restoring its lost territory and prestige were to be realized during his brief reign.

But neither the way nor the will was there to put them all into practice. The people of Byzantium, rich and poor alike, showed a new reluctance to co-operate in the venture of imperialism. The treasury of the Empire contained nothing, according to Gregoras, except the atoms of Epicurus.[18] Cantacuzene had spent or lost his entire private fortune in the war. The Empress Anne had put Constantinople heavily in debt to the Venetians and the Genoese. Trade had virtually ceased, and the agricultural land of Thrace had been rendered almost totally unproductive by the fighting and devastation, especially of the Turks. Even the capital was falling into ruins and no money could be found for repairs. For the repair of St Sophia a sum was in fact subscribed by Symeon, the Grand Duke of Moscow, who fancied himself as the protector of Orthodoxy. But his generous contribution had to be diverted to pay for the hire of Turkish mercenaries.[19]

There was evidence of poverty, neglect and falling standards on every side. But there was too a general feeling of relief in Constantinople and elsewhere that the war was ended; and Cantacuzene was wise to foster it by granting pardon to his late enemies. Even the common people, who had been encouraged by the regency to think of Cantacuzene as the agent of aristocratic oppression, seemed ready to give him a chance to show whether he could put things right. The class conflict which had marked the second civil war died down for a while, though it was to break out again when it became clear that Cantacuzene had failed to fulfil his promises. The poor at least enjoyed the respite from fighting, even though they might not trust their new masters. The people who were least co-operative were those who had made a profit out of the crisis or had contrived to salvage some of their own wealth from the common wreckage of fortunes. Cantacuzene was aware that such wealth existed and that, whereas the provinces might be impoverished, the capital city had escaped the worst material damage of the civil wars. But he was naïve in thinking that those who still had riches would willingly part with them when asked to do so for the good of the Empire.

In 1347 he took the unusual step of summoning a general assembly of all classes of citizens in Constantinople, merchants, sailors, craftsmen, abbots of monasteries and leaders of the church, as well as the people. He addressed them at some length, apologizing for his part in the late war and not least for the damage done by his own Turkish allies; and he exhorted them now to pool what resources they still had to help set the state on its feet again. Some of the leading citizens who had lost their all as a result of the war agreed that a voluntary contribution to a common fund was a reasonable request and the only way of securing the Empire's defences. But the profiteers, and particularly the bankers and money-lenders, stoutly refused to offer any of their wealth. They protested that John Cantacuzene had already ruined the provinces and was now proposing to repeat the process in the capital. Their influence and their arguments carried the day and Cantacuzene's appeal to the conscience of the rich thus achieved nothing.[20]

It would be interesting to know how many of them were in the habit of banking their money with the Genoese in Galata. The Genoese had taken no active part in the civil war, but they had given asylum to wealthy refugees from Constantinople and their sympathies lay with the Empress Anne and her family. Phakeolatos, the man who had engineered Cantacuzene's entry into Constantinople, had enraged them in 1346 by sinking one of their cargo ships in a sea battle, and for a time they suspended deliveries of wheat to the city. The Genoese, as Cantacuzene well knew, could almost hold the capital to ransom at any moment by cutting off supplies of food from the Black Sea. They did not like doing it because it lost them valuable trade. But high on the Emperor's list of priorities was the reconstruction of a native Byzantine navy of merchant ships as well as warships. For so long as the trade and the food supply of Constantinople remained at the mercy of the Genoese there could be little hope of real recovery. Gregoras estimated that the annual revenue of Galata derived from tariffs and customs dues was almost seven times that of Constantinople, though its population was only a fraction the size.[21]

The Genoese began to see that the comfortable monopoly that they had been allowed to establish over the last few years was likely to be broken by the new Emperor in Constantinople. They had hoped to be given permission to extend their settlement by acquiring more land in Galata. Instead they found themselves subjected to new restrictions; and the rumour that Cantacuzene was proposing to rebuild the Byzantine navy made them fear that their commercial interests were in danger. Their anxiety was increased when the Emperor deliberately lowered the tariffs payable by ships unloading their wares in Constantinople, thus diverting traffic and revenues from Galata. A number of incidents occurred which aggravated the state of tension, until in August 1348 the Genoese brazenly sailed across the Golden Horn and for several days coasted along the

Byzantine shore, burning all the cargo ships that were lying at anchor as well as the few warships that were still on the stocks. They chose their moment well, for the Emperor was away in Didymoteichos and was reported to be seriously ill. The city was defended by the Empress Eirene. It must have reminded her of the early days of the civil war when she had been left in charge of Didymoteichos. Her counsellors and people whom she consulted voted unanimously for war rather than negotiations with the Latins; and her son Manuel and her son-in-law Nikephoros, though still young, did valiant service in defending the walls and gates of the city against repeated attacks by the Genoese, and retaliated by setting fire to their warehouses outside the walls of Galata.[22]

The Genoese were surprised to meet such strong resistance and alarmed when the Byzantines constructed catapults for hurling rocks across the water into their town and on to their ships. 'But such was the feeling in the air in Constantinople', writes Gregoras, 'that everyone helped in its defence, bringing out weapons and horses. Builders, tailors, metal workers, all took to arms; and labourers and navvies who enlisted as mercenaries found themselves handling oars and taking to the sea. Even slaves were given weapons by their masters and taught themselves the use of bows and arrows. For the unexpected crisis goaded everyone on to eagerness.'[23] The Genoese seemed to have endless supplies of men and materials. Reinforcements were sent to them from Chios, and some of their biggest ships, which had been out to sea, returned to harbour. They used two of these as platforms on which to build catapult machines of their own; and on a third ship they built a great turret protected with a covering of shields and tall enough to surmount the sea walls of the city. The erection was conveyed across by nine supporting warships, and a battle of heroic dimensions took place at the walls. The defenders directed a hail of stones and arrows against the protective shields until the whole edifice collapsed, and the Genoese had to withdraw with many casualties.

Deceived of their hope of an easy victory the Genoese sent ambassadors to treat for peace. But the Byzantines were now in no mood to talk the matter over. They knew that right was on their side. They had evidence that God was with them. Alexios Makrembolites composed what might, in contrast to the more polished accounts of Gregoras and Cantacuzene, be described as a journalist's report on the causes and events of the war between Byzantium and Galata. He knew that the Genoese catapults had fired rocks at the church of the Virgin in Blachernai and at the monastery of Christ the Saviour. But people had seen the rocks sliding harmlessly off the lead roofs of the buildings. Makrembolites had seen the Genoese at the end retire from the walls 'like defeated fighting cocks, leaving the Romans to sing paeans of praise to the Mother of God for her miraculous intervention'. But he also knew that they had vented their spleen on some of the more defenceless Byzantine towns in the neighbourhood, burning their ships and even selling thousands of their inhabitants into slavery.[24]

On 1 October 1348 the Emperor John Cantacuzene, though still unwell, returned to Constantinople from Thrace. He immediately gave orders for more ships to be built. By now the people needed no telling that they had left it late in the day. But the Emperor drove the lesson home by calling them together again and reminding them that they were the authors of their own misfortunes. If they had only pooled their resources and built ships in the previous year the Latins would never have dared to attack them. 'At these words', says Gregoras, 'everyone with one voice denounced the Latins and condemned their own neglect and improvidence, all wanting to contribute their goods for the common cause; and great was the zeal for manufacturing ships and catapults large and small, as also for recruiting troops both for the infantry and for the navy. Where money was needed it was levied from the citizens of Constantinople. Some of it was given willingly, but most of it with a very bad grace; and tax-gatherers were also sent out to the cities of Thrace.'[25] The collection of taxes for shipbuilding was entrusted to a special commissioner called Constantine Tarchaniotes, who did his work with impartial efficiency. But the timber for the ships had to be hauled overland by oxen from the mountains of Thrace since the Genoese controlled the sea routes.

The Genoese meanwhile made their own preparations for what was evidently going to be a war on a larger scale. They strengthened their fortification walls and began to build a tower near the summit of the hill of Galata. More than once they asked for a chance to negotiate, but the Emperor's answer was always that they must dismantle their fortifications. The Knights Hospitallers sent a ship from Rhodes and offered to mediate. But the Genoese in Italy were having their own domestic troubles and could provide no help. By the spring of 1349 the new Byzantine fleet was ready. There were nine large warships and about 100 smaller vessels, including a number of craft equipped and armed by wealthy citizens at their own expense. The command of the fleet was given to Phakeolats and the Grand Duke Tzamplakon. The plan was for them to engage the Genoese in a sea battle while an army marched round to lay siege to Galata from behind. But the captains and crews of the ships had little knowledge of seafaring. Some of them were stationed at the head of the Golden Horn. The rest of the ships were to sail round from the dockyard on the south of the city where they had been built. On the evening of 5 March they won a surprise victory by capturing and setting fire to one of the largest of the Genoese ships which was sailing up from the Sea of Marmora. But that was the beginning and the end of the Byzantine triumph.

Cantacuzene had given orders for the main attack to be launched at daybreak on 6 March. Day dawned with a misty breeze blowing, which damped the ardour of the Byzantines and gave encouragement to the Latins. The fleet came into sight rounding the promontory of Constantinople where the currents are notoriously treacherous. The ships fared badly because they had not enough sand in their keels to act as ballast; and the captains, instead of waiting to draw up in line facing the Genoese, moved slowly forward prow to stern hugging the shore until they were all in full view of the enemy. If they had then sailed on to the head of the Golden Horn they might, as Gregoras says, have joined up with the rest of the fleet and doubled back in good order. But suddenly they were seized with panic. Not a shot had been fired. But the Genoese, whose ships were drawn up outside the harbour of Galata, were astonished to see the Byzantine soldiers and sailors leaping pell-mell into the sea. Those who could swim threw away their weapons and managed to reach the shore. But most of them sank under the weight of their armour, floundering in the water like fishes and crabs; and some who were washed over to the enemy side were hunted down by the Genoese like frogs or animals cowering in the sea. 'And of this great fleet', writes Makrembolites, 'there was not so much as a bubble to be seen; it came and went with the speed of a lightning flash.'[26]

The Genoese admiral, witnessing this extraordinary spectacle from his flagship, not unnaturally suspected that it must be some form of trickery or play-acting. But when he gave the order to advance nearer he found that the Greek ships were in fact empty, and all he had to do was to tie them up and drag them all over to Galata. The captains of the other Byzantine warships could not understand what was happening when they saw their colleagues plunging headlong into the sea and their ships being hauled away empty of men. But the panic and terror spread to those standing on the beach and on the walls of Constantinople. 'For every spot both inside and outside the walls and the gates was packed with people. A trumpeter or a drummer might have inspired a little fighting spirit in them. But they stood like corpses, until suddenly they turned and stampeded in flight, trampling over each other while the enemy watched in amazement and wonder, commiserating with the disaster rather than exulting in their victory; for they felt that some evil genius must have been at work to cause men so freely to sacrifice their lives when there was no one in pursuit.'[27] The soldiers who had been sent round to attack Galata from behind also took fright when they saw what had happened to the fleet. Throwing away all their equipment they fled like mad things and did not stop running until they were back within reach of the walls of Constantinople.

Various reasons were put forward for this manifestation of divine displeasure to the Byzantines. Gregoras makes a number of moral reflexions on the theme that no good can come from evil; and he castigates the government for bringing disaster by despoiling widows and orphans to find the means for building ships. But John Cantacuzene and Alexios Makrembolites both speak of a great gale that rose just when the new Byzantine fleet was moving into position. For the former it seemed to be a punishment from God; for the latter it was an apotropaic wind that blew out the light of victory above their heads and suffused their faces with shame and disgrace.[28] And although Gregoras fails to mention it, nothing seems more likely than that the Byzantine sailors, most of whom had hardly been to sea before, were thrown into confusion and panic when their boats were blown about in a sudden gust of wind. Once the hysteria had set in it proved to be uncontrollable and infectious; and for all that Makrembolites may have to say about the treachery, wrongheadedness and wickedness of the Byzantine commanders, they clearly had not been trained in mob psychology.

On the following day the Genoese fleet sailed along under the sea walls in sight of the Blachernai palace with their ships dressed overall and dragging the imperial standards in dishonour. They then sent messengers to the Emperor demanding a settlement on their own terms. But a few days later a ship arrived from Genoa bringing ambassadors from the Republic who were empowered to conclude a proper treaty. The Byzantines were lucky. It was agreed that the Genoese should now restore the land that they had occupied beyond their boundaries on the hill of Galata; they were to pay an indemnity to the Emperor for the cost of the war to a total of more than 100,000 *hyperpyra*; and they were to swear that they would never again attack Constantinople. Gregoras compares what he calls this 'shameful peace' with the Peace of Antalkidas signed between the Peloponnesians and the Persians in 386 BC, dictated as it was by the Persian King to the detriment of Athens. But the comparison is not very apt, and the Byzantines came out of the affair better than they can have hoped.[29]

So far as Cantacuzene was concerned the catastrophe seemed to spur him on to greater efforts to make Constantinople self-sufficient in the way of commerce and defence. But it was a hard road. Many of the citizens were in uproar over the manner in which, they alleged, the Emperor's commissioner Constantine Tarchaniotes had collected the money to pay for the ships that were now lost. It was said that he extorted immense sums from the people. A public inquiry was instituted at which Tarchaniotes was called to render an account. It was shown that the taxes that he had collected had yielded quite a modest sum, all of which had been spent on the fleet. The sad truth was that, whereas the citizens were ready to co-operate in their own defence when driven to it by an imminent and common danger, their patriotism waned as soon as the danger passed. The lesson that Cantacuzene learned from the war with Galata was that the Byzantines would no longer subscribe of their own free will to the upkeep and defence of their capital city. The means must be extracted from them by law.

He therefore introduced a new programme of taxation designed to give fresh life to the Byzantine economy by protecting the home market against foreign competition and by diverting tariffs from the Italians. The taxes took forms that had no precedent in the Empire, but they were levied from those who could best afford to pay, and they might have helped to improve the balance of trade in Constantinople. The duty payable by merchants bringing their goods there rather than to Galata was lowered from 10% to 2% of the value of the goods, though a slight extra duty was imposed on every bushel of wheat bought abroad. A tax was also laid on the export of wine, which was still one of the most lucrative businesses in the Empire. The wine producers were to pay one *hyperpyron* on every 50 measures sold; but the middlemen who made an effortless profit from their deals were to pay double this amount in duty to the treasury.[30]

These measures were highly unpopular. But from his experience as controller of the finances under Andronikos III, Cantacuzene had acquired a realistic view of the economic problems of the Empire. With the proceeds of his new taxes he proposed to rebuild a merchant fleet as well as a navy for the defence of Constantinople and Byzantine waters, and before long he had nearly 200 ships at his disposal, or so he claims. Later in his reign he had the ancient harbour of Heptaskalon on the southern shore of the city dredged and cleared to provide a naval base for operations against the Turkish pirates who were in the habit of crossing over by way of the Sea of Marmora.

The Genoese saw that the Emperor meant business despite his recent defeat and they tried to improve relationships by making amends for their behaviour. In 1349 Cantacuzene sent envoys to Genoa to negotiate the return to the Empire of the island of Chios, which the Genoese had reoccupied during the civil war. It was agreed that Chios should revert to Byzantine rule after a period of ten years, until which time the Latin residents there should pay an annual rent of 12,000 *hyperpyra* to Constantinople. The Byzantine flag was to fly in the city, an Orthodox archbishop was to be appointed, and the names of the two Emperors were to be acclaimed in the island every Saturday. The Greek residents in the rest of the island would be governed by a Byzantine official. The Genoese lord of Chios, Simone Vignosi, resented these terms and force had to be employed to impose them. Vignosi was killed in the fighting; but the harbour of Phokaia on the mainland passed into Byzantine hands, and Leo Kalothetos, who had administered Chios in the time of Andronikos III, was now reappointed as governor of Phokaia and of the Greek parts of the island.

At the same time the Venetians, who had already recognized John Cantacuzene as co-Emperor with John V, saw fit to renew their treaty with Byzantium. It had last been signed by John V and the Empress Anne in March 1342. On 9 September 1349, after discussions with an ambassador from Venice, it was renewed for a period of five years on terms agreed and signed by both Emperors jointly and singly. In this way Cantacuzene may have thought that he was assuring the Empire of protection against both of the Italian republics. What he did not foresee was that by so doing he would involve the Empire more deeply than ever before in the rivalry between the Venetians and the Genoese.[31]

Such diplomacy illustrated Cantacuzene's determination to restore the prestige and reputation of Byzantium in the eyes of the rest of the world. Where fortune or circumstances played into his hands he was quick to seize the opportunities offered. In 1350 he succeeded in reuniting Thessalonica to his Empire. After the abortive attempt of John Apokaukos to hand the city over to Cantacuzene in 1345 and the consequent murder of his followers, Thessalonica passed into the control of the most extreme faction of the Zealots. The people organized their own municipal council and acknowledged as their revolutionary leaders two men of obscure origin, Andrew Palaiologos and

234

George Kokalas. Neither was able to restrain the fury of the rabble, who took hideous vengeance on the upper-class citizens who had supported the counter-revolution. Very few survived the massacre. Among them was Nicholas Kabasilas; but the tragedy prompted Demetrios Kydones, whose family suffered irremediable losses, to compose a celebrated lament on those who fell at Thessalonica.[32]

Cantacuzene's victory in 1347 had stiffened the defiance of the Zealots. Their leaders still protested their allegiance to the house of Palaiologos, but they would have nothing to do with the usurper John VI. Gregory Palamas, appointed as metropolitan of Thessalonica, was turned away from the city and unable to take over his charge. The Zealots made propaganda out of burning in public all orders coming from Constantinople; they even threatened to surrender their city to the protection of Serbia. Their overtures, whether sincere or not, were music to the ears of Stephen Dušan, who sent an army to blockade Thessalonica. It was this event more than any other that lost the Zealots the unanimous support of the people. In 1350 dissension among their own leaders led to the expulsion of Andrew Palaiologos in favour of Alexios Metochites, who claimed to represent the interests of the imperial government in Constantinople. He was a son of that pillar of the old establishment Theodore Metochites. Cantacuzene chose the moment to send an army and a fleet to the relief of Thessalonica. The army was led by his son Matthew, but its ranks were mainly filled by a corps of 20,000 cavalry commanded by Suleiman, the eldest son of the Osmanli leader Orchan.

Cantacuzene himself went by sea, taking with him his son-in-law and co-Emperor John V. It was his intention to install John as Emperor in Thessalonica as soon as he had gained control of the city, despite the protests of John's mother, the Empress Anne. The expedition was nearly a failure, for the Turkish cavalry led by Suleiman were recalled to Asia Minor before reaching their destination, and Matthew Cantacuzene had too few men to be able to continue the march on his own. However, the Emperor was lucky enough to secure the help of a Serbian officer who turned traitor, and of 22 Turkish pirate ships that happened to be anchored at the mouth of the Strymon river. Their services enabled him to force his way into Thessalonica. The Zealot revolution had by then run its course and most of the inhabitants of the city welcomed Cantacuzene as Emperor, not least because he had brought with him the young man whose imperial title they claimed to recognize. He summoned an assembly of the citizens to address them and explain the new situation to them. His speech was designed to paint the Zealots in what he considered to be their true colours, as destructive revolutionaries and traitors rather than as loyalist patriots. The arrest of the remaining Zealot leaders seems to have followed without protest. Some were deported to Constantinople to stand trial; the rest were sent into exile.[33]

The official interpretation of the evils of the Zealot régime was reinforced soon afterwards when Gregory Palamas arrived at Thessalonica to take possession of his see. In the sermon that he preached in the church of St Demetrios three days after his arrival Palamas roundly condemned the rebel leaders, little better than wild beasts, who had made Thessalonica like a city under enemy occupation, who had plundered and pillaged its houses and property, and insulted and murdered its citizens without pity or humanity. But, like his Emperor, he called now not for revenge or recrimination but for peace and concord, for all that he had a deeper awareness than the Emperor of the social injustices that had helped to precipitate the revolution.[34]

The great city of Thessalonica was now once again the second capital of the Empire from which it had been to a greater or lesser degree detached for eight years or more. The Serbs had failed to take it either by force or by intrigue, and it could now be used as a base from which to dislodge the Serbian garrisons that had occupied some of the neighbouring towns. Late in 1350 Cantacuzene contrived to recapture Berroia, helped by the Turkish pirate ships, which sailed up river to support his troops. The city was well fortified and stoutly defended by a contingent of German mercenaries in the service of Stephen Dušan. But it surrendered almost without a fight. Cantacuzene then proceeded to the even more impregnable fortress of Edessa which had successfully resisted the armies of Dušan for 11 years. Edessa soon capitulated too, and as the news went around, other towns and fortresses in the area acknowledged Cantacuzene as Emperor. The castle of Servia on the borders of Thessaly was defended by one of Dušan's ablest generals, Gregory Preljub, and defied capture. But offers of surrender came even from places well within the borders of the Serbian Empire, and some Serbian officers deserted Dušan in favour of Cantacuzene.[35]

The Byzantine recovery in Macedonia, however, was more apparent than real. It is doubtful if it could have been accomplished if Dušan had been on the spot with his much greater military resources. At the time he was engaged in war with Hungary at the other end of his dominions. But the news of Cantacuzene's victories brought him hurrying south to protest at what he chose to interpret as a violation of the Serbian-Byzantine treaty and of the bond of friendship that united him with the Byzantine Emperor. A conference was arranged and the two rulers, each accompanied by a bodyguard, met near Thessalonica to discuss their differences. There was little chance that they could resolve them. The elaborate account of their talks which Cantacuzene records not unnaturally puts all the right on his own side. But it is hard to believe that Stephen Dušan had been driven to such a pitch of anxiety that he could no longer sleep at night, or that he had courted the favour of Venice to the extent that the Republic had enrolled him among its citizens and senators only out of fear of Cantacuzene. The fact was that Dušan had offered the Venetians possession of Galata and of the whole of Epiros if they would help him become Emperor in Constantinople.[36] Cantacuzene made much of the patriotic principle of 'liberating' the Greek cities enslaved by the Serbs, for which purpose he would perforce have to employ Turkish troops, offensive though it might be to turn barbarians against a people who were, after all, of the same religion as the Greeks. In the end an arrangement was worked out and, if Cantacuzene is to be believed, a treaty was signed between the two parties stipulating a new partition of territory and a new Serbian frontier in Macedonia. Epiros and Thessaly were to be restored to Byzantine rule. This agreement, if it was ever made, was violated almost at once. Dušan led his army straight from Thessalonica to lay siege to Edessa, which fell soon afterwards; and early in 1351 Cantacuzene returned to Constantinople after an absence of nearly three months. He left Thessalonica nominally in the care of his junior Emperor John V, an act calculated to appease the remnants of the Zealot sympathizers. In practice, however, the government of the city was placed in the hands of Cantacuzene's father-in-law, Andronikos Asen.

To leave the young John V in Thessalonica was perhaps an unwise move, given the known partiality of the inhabitants to the house of Palaiologos and the proximity of the scheming Serbian Emperor. Within a matter of months Dušan had managed to incite some of John's supporters to rebellion. But Cantacuzene seems to have believed that the surest way of co-ordinating the scattered fragments of imperial territory was to allot them as appanages to individual members or relations of the imperial family. It was a system which the Emperor Andronikos II had refused to adopt for the benefit of his sons at an earlier period, and it was one which was as likely to further the disintegration of the Empire as to promote its unity. But from the short-term point of view at least it had advantages, and in one particular instance it worked remarkably well.

Cantacuzene had three sons. The youngest, Andronikos, died during the epidemic in Constantinople in 1347. His middle son Manuel had early shown promise as a soldier and administrator, first as governor of Berroia until driven out by Dušan in 1347, and then in the defence of Constantinople during the Genoese war. As soon as that war was over his father sent Manuel out to take over the administration of the Byzantine province in the Peloponnese. He arrived there in October 1349. He was still only in his early twenties, but he quickly brought order to what had been an unruly province and asserted his authority over the rebellious Greek landlords of the Morea, besides making favourable alliances with the Latin rulers of the northern part of the peninsula. Manuel remained as Despot at Mistra until his death in 1380; and under his régime the so-called Despotate of the Morea prospered and grew into the most successful offshoot of the Byzantine Empire in its latter years. Manuel found in his appanage the career that suited his talents.[37]

His elder brother Matthew was less fortunate. His portion of Empire consisted of part of western Thrace with its headquarters at Didymoteichos. But his father continued to deny him the right to any official designation or title that might be interpreted as nominating him to the succession; and it was a question of how long, in these circumstances, Matthew would remain the loyal servant of his father's cause. A third beneficiary of the apportionment was Cantacuzene's son-in-law Nikephoros of Epiros. He too had been granted the title of Despot in 1347, and in 1351 he was made governor of the Thracian cities on the Hellespont with his headquarters at the seaport of Ainos.[38]

With his sons-in-law John V and Nikephoros designated as co-Emperor and Despot respectively, with his son Manuel as Despot in the Morea and his son Matthew in Thrace, it must have seemed that the remaining cities and provinces were firmly linked together under the control of the senior Emperor. He could also derive comfort from the thought that his daughter was married to the Osmanli emir Orchan and his relative Theodora to the Emperor Alexios III of Trebizond.[39] But to run the Empire as a family concern was to make himself something much less than an absolute monarch of the earlier Byzantine style. Surrounded as he was by ambitious relatives and by a clique of aristocratic supporters of his own class, John VI was more of a *primus inter pares* than an autocrat. The old tradition of Byzantine autocracy had perhaps died with the abdication of Andronikos II. He had in any case found it hard to maintain. His successors had a more modest and less demanding conception of their role. Nor did Cantacuzene ever for long command the respect or the loyalty of the ordinary people, a fact of which he was uncomfortably conscious. Their sympathies lay almost exclusively with the family of Palaiologos and they gave only grudging recognition to the father-in-law of their legitimate ruler, John V.

The deposition of the Patriarch John Kalekas in 1347 and the election in his place of a hesychast monk, Isidore, had not fully resolved the controversy over the doctrine and practice of hesychasm in the Byzantine Church. The opposition of the Zealot party in Thessalonica to the appointment of Gregory Palamas as their bishop was based more on political than on religious grounds, for the Zealots encouraged the belief that Palamas was the creature and the protégé of Cantacuzene. But there were still theologians who objected to Palamite doctrine. After 1347 it might be true to say that the controversy was conducted at a more intellectual and less emotional level than before, though it was still argued with passion and was a divisive force in society. With the exile and death first of John Kalekas and then of Gregory Akindynos in 1348, the leading spokesman of the anti-hesychasts became Nikephoros Gregoras, the scholar and historian. In politics he was a Cantacuzenist, though he had stayed in Constantinople during the civil war and was often received at court. But his objection to the theology of Palamas bordered on the fanatical. In 1346 the Empress Anne had encouraged him to make his first public statement on the matter in an anti-Palamite tract. The views of Gregoras found favour with some prominent churchmen, notably the Bishops Matthew of Ephesos, Joseph of Ganos, and Arsenios of Tyre. But his judgment was swayed by personal considerations. His respect for John Cantacuzene was the fruit of a long friendship. He was correspondingly hurt and disappointed when his friend espoused what he thought to be heresy. His dislike of Palamas on the other hand was no less subjective. It was to some extent the hostility of a scholar to a mystic who openly declared his belief in the uselessness of scholarship.[40]

In 1351, soon after his return from Thessalonica, Cantacuzene decided that the matter should be resolved once and for all by the heads of the church. A council must be held to examine and to reaffirm the decisions taken at the synods of 1341 and 1347, at which hesychast theology had been vindicated and its opponents declared to be in error if not in heresy. The council was convened by order of John Cantacuzene as Emperor and by the Patriarch Kallistos, who had been appointed in June 1350 after the death of Isidore. Kallistos himself was an Athonite monk and a noted hesychast and friend of Palamas. The outcome of a council held under such auspices might have appeared to be a foregone conclusion. But Cantacuzene ensured that the anti-Palamite representatives, among them Gregoras, should be free to voice their opinions at length. The proceedings opened on 28 May 1351 in a room in the Blachernai palace whose walls were appropriately decorated with paintings of earlier councils of the Church. Cantacuzene presided, and the laity were represented by his brother-in-law Manuel Asen, who held the rank of *sebastokrator*, and by other members of the aristocracy and senate. His co-Emperor John V was still in Thessalonica. The number of bishops was not large, but the majority of them were known to be favourable to hesychasm; Gregory Palamas was there in person to defend his own doctrine. On 9 June, at the last of four sessions, the rulings made by the councils of 1341 and 1347 and the condemnations then pronounced against the anti-Palamites, were read out. The Patriarch Kallistos wound up the business by once again calling on the dissidents to recant. They refused, and the Patriarch then declared the Bishops of Ephesos and Ganos to be deposed. Their supporters were put in prison or under house arrest.

A few days later, in July 1351, another council was convened at the same place. But this time the anti-Palamites were not invited. Six points of Palamite theology were examined. Each member of the council was then asked his opinion. Cantacuzene was the last speaker and pronounced the final verdict: Gregory Palamas was fully Ortho-dox in his beliefs and his doctrine was in full conformity with the traditions of the Fathers. The Tomos or declaration setting forth these decisions and excommunicating the dissidents was prepared by Phil-otheos, Metropolitan of Herakleia. Finally, on 15 August, at a cere-mony in St Sophia, John Cantacuzene presented the document, signed by his own hand, to the Patriarch, and its contents were read out three times. As a document of state the Tomos of 1351 required the assent and signature also of the co-Emperor John V. He subscribed his name to it when he was next in Constantinople, in February or March 1352, though Gregoras would have us believe that he did so only under pressure from his father-in-law.

It was an exaggeration to claim that the council of 1351 was œcumenical in nature. Gregoras was quick to point out that it was not, and that such weighty matters affecting all Christians could not be resolved by so small and unrepresentative a body. But the bishops there present, though relatively few in number, seem to have spoken with the voice and authority of almost the whole Byzantine Church; and the decisions embodied in the Tomos of 1351 were soon accepted as binding by all the communities of the Orthodox faith. There was at first some opposition in Russia and also in the Patriarchate of Antioch where Arsenios, Bishop of Tyre, who had managed to escape imprisonment, had his following. But by the end of the fourteenth century the doctrine of Palamas had been absorbed into the generally accepted teaching of the Orthodox Church.[41]

Nikephoros Gregoras, however, never ceased to campaign against what he believed to be a heretical doctrine forced upon his Church by a robber council. He took monastic vows and devoted himself to exposing the enormities of the Palamites in tracts and pamphlets. The affair poisoned his friendship with John Cantacuzene. He was at first confined to his house and then to the monastery of the Chora, which had been restored by his late master Theodore Metochites. Cantacuzene tried to reason with him, but he seemed determined to suffer martyrdom and was obsessed beyond reason with the justice of his own theology. After 1354 he was again allowed his freedom. He resumed his preaching and denunciation of heresy and even conducted a debate with Palamas in person, of which he has left a far from objective account. It occupies two of the 16 books of the third volume of his History. The remainder of the volume is largely devoted to the same theme. It is disappointing that Gregoras the philosopher and historian should have degenerated into a ranting polemicist in his declining years. He had at least the satisfaction of recording the painful, lingering death of his enemy Palamas, before dying himself about 1360. He would have been appalled to learn, had he lived longer, that Gregory Palamas was canonized and enrolled among the saints of the Orthodox Church in 1368. But, if we may believe the account of one of his own anti-Palamite circle, John Kyparissiotes, the hesychasts showed a most unchristian bitterness to their arch-opponent after his death by dragging his corpse through the streets of Constantinople.[42]

In the field of theology the Byzantines were still able to fight their own battles without fear of foreign intervention. The Turks were not interested in the niceties of Palamite doctrine. The westerners found it to be yet another distressing symptom of deviation on the part of the Orthodox, but they were not disposed to intervene. There were a few

Byzantines, such as Demetrios Kydones, who were inclined to a favourable view of Latin theology; but in his own relationship with the Roman Church, Cantacuzene showed that he was not prepared to compromise the Orthodox faith for political or military advantages. Early in his reign he took the initiative by suggesting to Pope Clement VI that a council might be held to discuss the differences that divided their Churches and offering to join his forces with the Pope's crusade against the infidel. The Pope was interested in winning over the Byzantines as partners in his anti-Turkish league whose activities at Smyrna had caused the death of Umur of Aydin in 1348. But the ultimate object of the league was the recovery of the Holy Land, which must have seemed a very remote and unrealistic prospect to the Byzantines; and the Pope was uncomfortably aware also that Cantacuzene, besides being an intractable schismatic, was on very good terms with Umur and with other Turkish leaders. Moreover, the popes could never understand the Byzantine insistence on holding a council of the Church to debate ways and means of healing the schism. They took the simple view that matters of faith and doctrine which had been decided once and for all by the authority of the See of Rome admitted of no further discussion. The Greeks must therefore be persuaded to humble their pride and 'return' to the fold of Rome. So long as they held to their errors and heresies they could hardly be counted as Christians at all, let alone as potential participants in a crusade or as the beneficiaries of military aid from the western world. Alliance and co-operation between Byzantium and the Papacy would have been advantageous to both parties in the middle of the fourteenth century. Negotiations and exchanges of ambassadors between Cantacuzene and Clement VI continued intermittently until the Pope's death in 1352. But nothing came of them. For the Emperor bargained with the Pope not as a suppliant but as one convinced of the dignity and strength of his own Church and faith. He would not be shifted from the traditional Byzantine view that matters affecting the whole Church could only be resolved by an œcumenical or fully representative assembly of bishops from all over the Christian world; and he stubbornly but politely refused to play the part of Michael VIII by bullying his people into submitting to the requirements of the Papacy. Under his guidance the Byzantine Church retained its integrity and independence from foreign intervention.[43]

In political and economic affairs, however, for all the safeguards taken by John Cantacuzene, Byzantium was increasingly at the mercy of those foreigners who had a stake in the Empire's fortunes. While he was in Thessalonica at the end of 1350 Cantacuzene had been approached by an envoy from Venice seeking his support in the Venetian conflict with Genoa which had broken out in August of that year. The Emperor had no wish to become involved in the perennial dispute between the Italian republics. But it was hard to remain neutral when the subject of the dispute was the control of Byzantine waters and when the Genoese were so firmly entrenched in their commercial colony at Galata next door to Constantinople. In May 1351, after a Venetian fleet had attacked Galata, both sides solicited the Emperor's active support. When he declined to commit himself the Venetians withdrew their representative from Constantinople by way of reprisal. The Genoese from Galata then attacked the city by catapulting rocks over the walls. Once again Cantacuzene had become the victim of circumstances. He recalled the Venetian ambassador and reluctantly agreed to declare war on the Genoese. His supposed allies did little to whet his enthusiasm, for the Venetian admiral abandoned his attack on Galata as soon as he learnt that a fleet was on the way to its relief from Genoa. The Byzantines were left on their own to fight out a war which they had neither planned nor wanted. Their navy was defeated by the Genoese on 28 July 1351.

In October the fleet of some 60 ships that was on its way to Galata from Genoa put in at the Thracian port of Herakleia, ostensibly to collect supplies. Fighting broke out between the Italian sailors and the inhabitants, and the city was captured and pillaged by the Genoese. The incident and its tragic consequences were vividly described by the Bishop of Herakleia, Philotheos. He was absent at the time, but he returned to his see shortly after the event and persuaded the Emperor to grant the surviving inhabitants freedom from taxation. Herakleia had been taken unawares. But Constantinople was well prepared. Cantacuzene had given orders for the sea walls to be repaired and for all his own ships to be brought into the harbour of the Heptaskalon on the southern shore of the city. The citizens had gathered behind the walls and the army had been recalled from Thrace. Orders had also gone out to the cities on the Black Sea to look to their own defences. The Genoese were thus unable to do much more damage. Their ships sailed up the Bosporos, however, and attacked Sozopolis, the only Byzantine city which had disobeyed the Emperor's warning. It was captured by the Italians in November 1351.

Meanwhile a newly equipped Venetian fleet had set sail from Italy commanded by the admiral Niccolò Pisani. At Messina it was joined by 26 Spanish ships supplied by King Peter of Aragon, with whom both the Venetians and the Byzantines had been in diplomatic contact. The Venetian and Aragonese ships were delayed by storms and it was not until February 1352 that they reached Constantinople where they joined forces with the Byzantine fleet commanded by Constantine Tarchaniotes. The Genoese, whose ships had been sheltering under the walls of Pera, sailed out to offer battle to the allies on 13 February. There was fierce fighting until nightfall. The sea was seen to be strewn with wrecks and corpses in the morning. But neither side had won a decisive victory. The greatest casualties were suffered by the Aragonese ships whose captains had no knowledge of the local reefs and currents. The Catalan sailors who survived were cared for by the Byzantines and eventually sent home, though some 300 of them elected to stay in Constantinople and to serve the Emperor as mercenaries. The Venetian admiral declined to attempt another engagement and, after procrastinating for several weeks, sailed off home with his ships. The Genoese on the other hand were encouraged to continue the struggle. They approached Orchan of Bithynia who sent them a contingent of Turkish troops to help defend Galata. Once again the Byzantines, deserted by their allies, were left either to fight it out or to make what terms they could with the enemy. On 6 May 1352 Cantacuzene, convinced that the Venetians had broken their agreement with him, made a treaty of his own with the Genoese.[44]

The sea battle of February 1352 was only one incident in one chapter of the prolonged struggle between Venice and Genoa. The rest of that chapter was enacted in a series of skirmishes in western waters and concluded in stalemate in 1355. The next chapter began after a short interval, and the issue once again involved the Byzantines. The sequence seemed inevitable, since the dispute between the Italian republics was largely concerned with control of the Hellespont, the Bosporos and the markets of Constantinople and the Black Sea; and what they could not achieve by warfare they soon learnt to attempt by political intrigue among the Byzantines. To have an emperor on the throne in Constantinople who was favourable or indebted to either side would clearly be a great advantage. That such manœuvres would tend to provoke further civil war among the Byzantines was of small account when the stakes were so high. The Venetians soon offered to subsidize the young John V in war against his father-in-law by tendering a loan of 20,000 ducats, in return for which they were to receive the little island of Tenedos which controlled the entrance to the Hellespont. At the time John V was in Thessalonica. The rebellion which his supporters were encouraging was to be assisted also by

244

Stephen Dušan of Serbia who, like the Venetians, saw the Byzantines as pawns in his game of power politics. The news was brought to Constantinople by Andronikos Asen in the summer of 1351. The Emperor could not leave the city at that juncture, but he sent the dowager Empress Anne of Savoy to Thessalonica to reason with her son and to negotiate with Stephen Dušan. It was due to her efforts that the danger of war was averted. Dušan withdrew his offer of help, and nothing more was heard, for the moment, of Venetian intervention. The Genoese, however, who were then on their way to Constantinople, are said to have offered their services and protection to the Empress if she should require them.[45]

Anne of Savoy never returned to the capital thereafter. She lived and reigned as Empress over her own portion of the Empire in Thessalonica until her death about 1365. Her son John V was persuaded to leave for Constantinople early in 1352, and he accepted the offer of an imperial appanage in Thrace. To prevent another outbreak of civil war it seemed that John Cantacuzene had made generous concessions to the Palaiologos faction, dividing the Empire between himself, his son-in-law and the Empress Anne. His own eldest son Matthew again had cause to feel that he had been left out of account. The appanage allotted to John V was to include Didymoteichos and a large part of Matthew's principality in Thrace. In exchange Matthew was to have the city and district of Adrianople. The deal was technically in his favour, but his patience was nearly exhausted by what he and several others felt to be his father's partiality to John V. The rivalry between the two princes was almost bound to lead to trouble when they were such near neighbours in Thrace, and it was not long in breaking out. Matthew's mother, the Empress Eirene, did her best to reconcile them, but neither party would commit anything to writing.

In the summer of 1352 John V invaded Matthew's territory and laid siege to the citadel of Adrianople. The encouragement that he received from the inhabitants showed where their sympathies lay. The Emperor, who had just concluded his account with the Genoese, had to hurry north with an army of Turkish troops and fight his way into Adrianople to relieve his son. Order was restored in Matthew's principality by allowing the Turks to plunder and terrorize the nearby cities. John V retaliated by calling on the help of the Serbs and Bulgars. In October the Venetians agreed to subsidize him, and Stephen Dušan supplied him with a contingent of 4000 cavalry. The Patriarch Kallistos tried to mediate, but matters had gone too far, for the emir Orchan had answered the Emperor's call by sending over a further 10,000 or 12,000 horsemen under the command of his own son Suleiman. The Byzantine war of succession had entered a new phase. It was being fought out almost independently of the protagonists by their respective allies. It was the Turks who proved superior, crushing the Serbian and Bulgarian armies in battle on the Marica river in the winter of 1352. It was the Turks who secured Matthew's position at Adrianople before returning to Asia Minor with their booty.

These tactics and their consequences did little to stimulate popular enthusiasm for the cause of the Cantacuzene family. The Emperor later claimed that he had been forced to call in the Turks by the unreasonable demands and actions of his son-in-law. Matthew Cantacuzene, as the slighted and injured party, still commanded much support. But while the use of Turkish mercenaries might be justified in the circumstances, no one could excuse their employment as agents of terrorism. John V was aware that the tide of popularity was now turning decisively in his favour. Early in 1353 the Emperor had obliged him to leave Thrace and to move with his wife and family to the island of Tenedos, though whether as a reigning prince or as a political prisoner it was hard to say. In March he made a desperate bid to fight his way into Constantinople, sailing over from Tenedos by night with a small flotilla. The attempt was thwarted and he returned to his island exile. But before long it was reported that John V had arrived in Thessalonica, to be advised and comforted by his mother, the Empress Anne.[46]

It became increasingly difficult for John Cantacuzene to maintain the principle or even the fiction that he was the protector of the legitimate right of John V to the throne. The ordinary people of Constantinople, as he himself readily admits, were by now mainly on the young Emperor's side. But the aristocracy were divided in their loyalties, and the Cantacuzenists among them saw no good reason why their leader should not now publicly renounce the rights of John V and nominate his own son Matthew as co-Emperor and successor to the throne. Cantacuzene found it hard to make the decision. He consulted the Patriarch Kallistos. The Patriarch was horrified to think that Cantacuzene might go back on the agreement that he had sworn to observe in 1347 and threatened to resign if Matthew were proclaimed Emperor. He was soon put to the test, for the deed was done at a ceremony in the palace in April 1353. It was decreed that thenceforth the name of Matthew Cantacuzene should be commemorated in place of that of John Palaiologos in the ritual of the court and the Church. But at the same time the names of the Empress Anne and even of John V's son Andronikos were still to be remembered. The culprit had been singled out. The principle of upholding the legitimate succession had not been abandoned.[47]

By compromises of this nature, to which he was prone, Cantacuzene seldom satisfied anyone but himself. In the torrent of justification for his action which he includes in his memoirs the Emperor again betrays his own inability to make resolute decisions.[48] He pleads the provocation of his son-in-law; he argues that the unanimous insistence of his senators and officers gave him no option; he obscures his own motives by laying all the blame on others. He could not bring himself to admit that he was using the situation to replace the dynasty of Palaiologos by the dynasty of Cantacuzene. The change might have been acceptable and might have brought benefit to the Empire, had it been put into practice several years before. But by 1353 the moment had passed, for by then Cantacuzene had lost whatever popular sympathy he may have had in 1347. In any event it would be very hard to keep John V permanently isolated from his supporters, whether confined on Tenedos or elsewhere, when his own mother was reigning as Empress in Thessalonica.

Several months elapsed before the seal was set on the proceedings by the coronation of Matthew Cantacuzene as Emperor. The Patriarch Kallistos refused to perform the ceremony and retired to a monastery. A synod of bishops was convened to accept his enforced resignation, though not before he had pronounced sentence of excommunication on the man who had brought him to this pass. The bishops then elected a new patriarch, being instructed by Cantacuzene to adhere strictly to the correct procedure. Three names were duly submitted to him and his choice fell on Philotheos, Bishop of Herakleia, who was consecrated as Patriarch of Constantinople in November 1353. He was, as might be surmised, a known supporter of Cantacuzene and a noted disciple and admirer of Gregory Palamas. The unfortunate Kallistos soon escaped to Galata to take refuge with the Genoese. They helped him to get to Tenedos where he was welcomed and rewarded for his loyalty by John V, who had by then returned to the island from Thessalonica. In February 1354 Matthew Cantacuzene had his wife Eirene come to the capital from Adrianople for their coronation. It was performed by the new Patriarch, assisted by Matthew's father, in the church of the Virgin in Blachernai, though Matthew placed the crown on his wife's head with his own hands according to Byzantine custom. A panegyric was composed for the occasion by Nicholas Kabasilas, one of the three who had been short-listed for the patriarchate. It hinted at the patience and forbearance of a son who might well have been embittered by his father's treatment. At the same ceremony Matthew, now as Emperor, appended his signature to the Tomos or declaration of Orthodoxy drawn up by the hesychast council of 1351.[49]

The line of succession through the Cantacuzene family now seemed to be established for generations to come. Matthew was about 30 years old and had two sons of his own. The fact that Andronikos Palaiologos, the infant son of John V, was still counted among the Emperors was no anomaly, for Andronikos was the child of Helena Cantacuzene and so a grandson of the Emperor John VI. The dynasty looked well on paper. But the people who were supposed to acclaim its establishment thought less about the manœuvrings in the palace than they thought about the devastation of their farms and properties by the Turkish brigands who were in the pay of its founder.

For some years past the Osmanlis had been employed by all the parties who could afford to pay them in the conflicts that raged over the throne or the trade of Constantinople. They had seemed to provide a convenient and almost limitless supply of fighting men whose services could be engaged at a moment's notice and who could be relied upon to go home to Asia Minor at the end of each campaign. They had been happy enough to help the Genoese against the Venetians in 1352. Indeed the Genoese had offered Orchan not only money but also a place of honour in the roll of benefactors to their senate and republic. John V had invoked the help of the Turks in his first attack on Matthew Cantacuzene in Thrace, while Matthew's father had obtained thousands of Turkish cavalry for the relief of Adrianople in the same year. They were commanded by Orchan's son Suleiman; and their victory over the Serbian and Bulgarian allies of John V at the Marica river showed that the Turks had learnt to act independently of their Byzantine paymasters. Suleiman's operations were not simply those of a guerrilla chieftain in charge of a raiding party, prepared to return to his base as soon as each mission was accomplished.

It was inevitable that the Osmanlis would come to know the lie of the land and to make themselves at home on European territory. Cantacuzene placed much confidence in his son-in-law Orchan. Orchan was a man of his word; but his son and heir-presumptive Suleiman did not feel bound to the Byzantine Emperor by ties of personal friendship. He may well have mistrusted his father's alliance with the Emperor as implying a threat to his own position. At all events it was he who first began to make things awkward for Cantacuzene. During the campaigns of 1352 his troops had occupied a number of places in the Thracian Chersonnese, among them being the fortress of Tzympe near Gallipoli. When the fighting was over they refused to leave. Suleiman claimed possession of Tzympe by right of conquest. Cantacuzene offered him 10,000 *hyperpyra* by way of compensation for the surrender of his prize and took the matter up with Orchan. Negotiations were still in progress when an event occurred that foredoomed them to failure.

On the night of 2 March 1354 the whole coastline of Thrace was devastated by an earthquake. Some places simply disappeared into the ground. Others were totally destroyed and depopulated or left defenceless and insecure by the collapse of their walls. Cantacuzene describes how the survivors in the stricken towns fled in the night with all their belongings to take refuge in the cities that had been spared. The disaster was accompanied by blizzards and torrents of rain. Many, especially the women and children, died of exposure; many more were taken captive by the Turkish soldiers who descended on the ruins of the shattered towns at break of day. Gallipoli, the largest city in the peninsula, was almost completely destroyed, though the inhabitants managed to get away by sea, and the captain of a Greek ship on its way to the Morea collected a boatload of survivors and made back for Constantinople. Suleiman was at Pegai on the Asiatic shore of the Hellespont when he heard the news of the earthquake. At once he crossed over to Thrace, bringing with him a great crowd of Osmanlis with their wives and children to take possession of the deserted towns and villages. Before long they had repaired the damage and restored the fortifications in many places. Special attention was given to Gallipoli. A large Turkish garrison was stationed there, the walls were rebuilt, and the city was repopulated by settlers or colonists of all classes from across the water.[50]

Gallipoli controlled the passage over the Hellespont from Asia to Europe. Its loss was a catastrophe for the Byzantines. Its capture was a triumph for the Osmanlis and opened up new vistas of conquest and settlement on European soil. Legend had it in later years that Suleiman had been inspired by a dream in which the crossing from one continent to another had been illuminated for him by the light of the moon. The Venetians put it about that the Turks had been ferried over to Gallipoli on Genoese ships.[51] What is certain is that they were now beyond being bribed or bullied into relinquishing what they had won. To the formal protests of the Byzantine Emperor Suleiman replied that he could not hand back what providence had delivered to him.

His troops had merely taken over a number of places that had been deserted by their Greek inhabitants. Gallipoli had fallen to him by the will of God and not by force. In desperation the Emperor offered Suleiman four times the amount of compensation that he had previously proposed, and he arranged a conference with Orchan to discuss the situation. They were to meet near Nikomedia. But when Cantacuzene had sailed to the appointed place he was met by a messenger who reported that Orchan was ill and unable to travel. The Emperor returned empty-handed to Constantinople. He was near the end of his resources, and the thought of resigning his worldly cares in favour of the religious life was much in his mind.[52]

In the summer of 1354 he sailed over to Tenedos in the hope of settling his differences with his other son-in-law John V. But nothing came of it. The islanders of Tenedos were aggressively loyal to their imperial guest and even refused to allow Cantacuzene's ships to draw water. John V made no move either to negotiate or to fight. He knew by now that circumstances had played into his hands. The time was ripe for him to make another attempt to enter and take possession of Constantinople. He could be certain of support once he was inside the city, but he would have to surprise the guards at the gates if he were not to be repulsed or arrested. On 21 November he stole out from Tenedos with a few ships. It was a dark, stormy night and he managed to reach the harbour of the Heptaskalon undetected. A much later account has it that he was accompanied by a Genoese buccaneer called Francesco Gattilusio who had recently offered him his services. Gattilusio is said to have fooled the guards at Constantinople by hurling empty oil jars from his ship against the sea walls to attract their attention. He then gained entrance by pretending to be the master of an innocent cargo vessel in danger of shipwreck. Once inside the gates he raised the cry of 'Long live the Emperor John Palaiologos', until at dawn the people gathered in the Hippodrome to acclaim John V as their sovereign. It is a colourful tale but not substantiated by either of the historians who were alive at the time.[53]

With or without his Genoese accomplice, however, John V succeeded in entering Constantinople in the early hours of 22 November. The word of his arrival quickly spread and by dawn there was uproar in the city. Cantacuzene held a hurried consultation with his wife Eirene and his minister Demetrios Kydones. The more militant of his advisers persuaded him to make at least a show of resistance, and he sent urgent orders to his son Matthew and to other commanders in Thrace to rush reinforcements to the city.

Meanwhile crowds of people had flocked into the streets to show their support for John V. Some took to destroying and plundering the houses of Cantacuzene's relatives and friends. Others seized control of the imperial arsenal in the harbour and armed themselves to join in the fight. Encouraged by the popular reaction John V advanced on the palace precincts and encamped in the so-called Palace of Porphyrogenitus. The crowd enthusiastically helped in storming the fortifications of the Blachernai district, though at first they could make little headway against Cantacuzene's Catalan mercenaries, who drove them back and set fire to some of the houses in front of the palace. In the thick of the confusion the Patriarch Philotheos fled into hiding in a secret alcove in the cathedral of St Sophia. He had sensed which way the wind was blowing and he was justifiably afraid of the angry mob who would condemn him as a usurper and clamour for the reinstatement of his predecessor Kallistos.

On 24 November, the third day after his entry into Constantinople, John V sent a messenger to Cantacuzene proposing terms on which they might work out a settlement. Cantacuzene, who had no desire to prolong the fighting, risked the displeasure of his military advisers by surrendering. It was now his firm intention, or so he claims, to bring the matter to an end and abdicate. The agreement, to which each Emperor bound himself by oath, provided for a general amnesty and for their joint rule as colleagues. John V as junior Emperor was to respect the precedence of his father-in-law, but otherwise the government, the resources and the revenue were to be shared. Matthew Cantacuzene was to remain as independent Emperor over his own province of Adrianople until his death, and John V swore not to make war against him. Finally it was agreed that Cantacuzene should hand over to John V the fortress at the Golden Gate of the city which he had recently renovated and refortified, and which was guarded by a regiment of his Catalan mercenaries. After the treaty had been signed in the palace, John V retired to take up residence in the house of Theodore Metochites. The orders that had been sent out to Matthew Cantacuzene and the other armies in Thrace were now countermanded, although a band of Turks, who had come of their own accord to help Cantacuzene when they heard of events in Constantinople, were only induced to withdraw when the Emperor showed himself to them from the ramparts of the city.[54]

When order had been restored the two Emperors held a council of state with the senators and leading officials in the house of Metochites. The most urgent problem facing the Empire was that of the settlement of the Turks in Gallipoli and Thrace. Opinions were divided as to whether the problem should be dealt with by force or by negotiation. Cantacuzene argued strongly that the Empire's military and economic resources were quite inadequate for a campaign which, once started, would develop into total war against all the barbarian hordes of Asia. His speech, as reported in his own words, might be read as a damning indictment of his own administration, which had allowed the Empire's strength to fall so low. But it presents a realistic assessment of the situation. 'I do not suggest', he said, 'that we should tamely submit to all the wrongs done to us by the Turks. But we should not have the confidence of fools. What we need is money and the help of some foreign ally or army equivalent in strength to that of our enemy.... Further, we need a fleet to control the sea and to prevent the enemy from getting help; for if they succeed in mastering the sea routes then we shall have to fight not merely Orchan and his men in Thrace but also all the barbarians in Asia who will come to his aid. For their arch-heretic [Mahomet] promised the prize of immortality to such of their warriors as fall in battle against us.... It would be wiser to send ambassadors to them to confirm our existing treaties and to try to persuade them to relinquish their conquests in Thrace by negotiation, for this is still a possibility. Once we have thus driven them beyond our frontiers it will be easier to make war upon them, provided always that we have the ships to control the sea.'[55]

The Emperor's words were not well received. Some of the younger and bolder of the aristocracy reproached him with evading the issue of a confrontation with the Turks because of the fact that his own daughter was married to Orchan. John V expressed no opinion. But the majority seemed to favour action rather than diplomacy, and Cantacuzene dismissed the meeting without further elaborating his plans. Three days later he went with the young Emperor to hand over his fortress at the Golden Gate as he had agreed to do. It should have been a simple enough transaction, but the Catalan garrison inside the fortress at first refused to obey the order to lay down their arms. Their commander, Juan de Peralta, who had served Cantacuzene with unswerving loyalty throughout the civil war, protested that his men were well equipped and eager to fight. They were under the mistaken impression that Cantacuzene was being forced into surrendering the fortress and that by resisting they would be doing him a great service. Only by threatening to write to their own king in Spain denouncing them all as mutineers did Cantacuzene ultimately persuade them to apologize and yield up the keys of the castle. He was then able to honour his agreement with John V, who dismissed the Catalans and installed a garrison of his own, until such time as the fortress was demolished and deserted.

Conditions in the city were still far from settled. There were rumours of plots to assassinate John Cantacuzene. One morning, while the two Emperors were in council in the house called Aetos to which John V had moved, there was a violent demonstration by his supporters, who surrounded the building and made off with the horses belonging to Cantacuzene's men. The incident brought matters to a head. On the following day Cantacuzene invited his son-in-law to move into the Blachernai palace and announced his own intention of abdicating. The plan had been forming in his mind for some time. Given the evident hostility to him of the people of Constantinople there was now no point in postponing the moment or in attempting to prolong the unworkable experiment of a shared imperial authority. On 4 December 1354, at a ceremony in the palace, John VI Cantacuzene divested himself of all his regalia and adopted the habit of a monk. His wife and Empress, Eirene, took the veil as a nun with the name of Eugenia. Thereafter, for the remainder of his long life, Cantacuzene was to be known by his monastic name of Joasaph or, as a mark of deference, as 'the Emperor and monk Joasaph Cantacuzene'. He retired at first to the monastery of St George of the Mangana in Constantinople, his wife to the convent of Kyra Martha.[56]

It was widely believed at the time and it has been repeatedly stated since that Cantacuzene was forced into abdicating his throne by John V. The fact that he himself strenuously denies this charge and emphasizes the voluntary nature of his abdication has, like so many of his confessions, been turned against him.

'He asserts in his history (does he hope for belief?)', writes Gibbon, '... that, in free obedience to the voice of religion and philosophy, he descended from the throne and embraced with pleasure the monastic habit. So soon as he ceased to be a prince, his successor was not unwilling that he should be a saint.'[57] John Cantacuzene was a man of many interests, talents and qualities, as a soldier, statesman, man of letters, linguist (he was acquainted with Turkish as well as western languages), and theologian. He was at the same time

253

curiously irresolute by nature. He should perhaps have abdicated as soon as John V entered Constantinople in November 1354. He ought perhaps never to have accepted the imperial title at all. But he is surely to be believed when he defends his son-in-law against the charge of having committed perjury by forcing him into retirement in defiance of their sworn agreement. It was characteristic of him that he should look for compromises and postpone his decision until he had become the victim of circumstances. He was aware that he had always represented the interests of a ruling class of landed aristocracy. He was not alone in feeling that the expertise of that class gave its members a prescriptive right to govern, however unpopular they might be. But the lessons of the revolutions in Adrianople and Thessalonica seemed to have been lost on him and on his class. They regarded these unhappy events as temporary manifestations of 'ochlocracy' or the rule of the mob which once repressed would not occur again. They did not see them as symptoms of a much deeper and less curable malaise in their society. The uprising of the people of Constantinople against Cantacuzene in 1354 pained if it did not surprise him. But he seems hardly to have appreciated the fact that their mistrust was aggravated by the suspicion that he had brought the barbarian Turks into Europe to defend the interests of his own privileged class rather than the interests of the Empire. The Byzantines, who were irremediably conditioned to the idea of a society ruled by an emperor in Constantinople, naturally saw the antidote to this poison in the person of the rival emperor John V. But it was not he who constrained Cantacuzene to abdicate. His abdication was forced upon him by what in modern times would be called the pressure of public opinion and popular demonstration against the unholy alliance of the feudal aristocracy with the godless Turks.[58]

It was not unnatural that, when he came to write his memoirs after his abdication (they were completed by 1369), the ex-Emperor should try to justify his action by emphasizing his continual reluctance to accept or to retain the imperial title. It is easy to detect the note of special pleading. But one need not therefore condemn the plaintiff outright as a hypocrite. His intention to resign from public affairs was evidently connected with his desire to enter the religious life. As early as 1341 he had been attracted to the idea of withdrawing to Mount Athos and had bought a plot of land for his retirement from the monastery of Vatopedi. His friend the Patriarch Philotheos confirms that Cantacuzene had often thought of retreating to a monastery with a group of his friends. The plan was much in his mind in the year 1350 when he discreetly endowed the city monastery of St George of the Mangana; and it was to that monastery that he retired as the monk Joasaph in December 1354. The sincerity of Cantacuzene's monastic vocation, and of his religious beliefs, have been as much criticized and ridiculed as the voluntary nature of his abdication. His critics have perhaps too readily assumed that his theology was dictated by political considerations. No doubt it was to his advantage to support and to endow the great monasteries of Athos and elsewhere whose inmates were feudal landowners on a large scale. No doubt also that his political cause was well served by the moral support of saints like Gregory Palamas and his followers. But it is invidious to propose that Cantacuzene favoured the causes of hesychasm and monasticism simply and solely for political ends. He was himself a deeply and sincerely religious man; his interest in and understanding of faith and doctrine are attested by his own writings; and he lived the last 30 years of his life as a respected and blameless monk. Not even his friend Nikephoros Gregoras, who became embittered by his own religious bigotry, can find fault with Cantacuzene's moral character, except in so far as he allowed himself to be led into the 'heretical' doctrine of Palamas which he then forced upon the Orthodox Church.

Like many able men John Cantacuzene was ambitious. But much of his ambition was for the Empire over which he saw himself presiding and which he had such high hopes of restoring; and like many ambitious rulers he was perhaps too confident that he had a clearer vision of what was best for his people than they had themselves. To a lesser degree he was guilty of that capital error which J. B. Bury imputed to Justinian, 'the theory that the expansion of a state and the exaltation of its prestige and honour are ends in themselves, and valuable without any regard to the happiness of the men and women of whom the state consists'. His own explanation of his action in 1354 is that, having persevered as Emperor against his better judgment, he chose the first real opportunity to abdicate, 'as one who despaired of the Romans ever being able to think or to act intelligently or in their own best interests'. It is the none too modest apologia of one born into a ruling class but rewarded with ingratitude for all his sacrifices.[59]

After some weeks in the Mangana monastery Cantacuzene thought of retiring to Mount Athos, as he had earlier planned to do. But John V realized that he might yet need the support and advice of his father-in-law and persuaded him to stay in Constantinople. He moved into the smaller monastery of the Virgin called Nea Peribleptos, also known by the name of its founder Charsianites. John Charsianites had been a faithful friend and supporter of Cantacuzene, who had granted an imperial charter to his foundation. Like many others he had suffered for his Cantacuzenism during the rioting in November 1354. The mob had looted and destroyed his town house and forced him to seek asylum in St Sophia. His monastery had suffered also, for John V had at first sequestered some of the property made over to it by Cantacuzene. The monks, however, were pleased and flattered to welcome their former emperor as a resident and gave him preferential treatment fitting to his dignity by making over the abbot's house for his use. In due course the imperial monk contributed handsomely to the renovation of the monastery of Charsianites, and it may well have been there that he completed his memoirs and composed his theological treatises.[60]

John V had been right to dissuade his father-in-law from leaving the capital so long as the intentions of Matthew Cantacuzene remained uncertain. It had been agreed that Matthew should continue to reign as Emperor in Adrianople, but with no right to pass on the title to his own sons. For a while this arrangement was respected by both sides. But Matthew, who had so often been made to play second fiddle to his younger brother-in-law, was restive, and John V was soon convinced that a permanent solution could only be effected by force. In the spring of 1355 the first shots were fired in the final act of the drama of dynastic conflict between the families of Cantacuzene and Palaiologos. After some fighting in Thrace a new settlement was reached. Both men were to retain the title of Emperor, but Matthew was to relinquish his portion of Empire in Thrace and employ his title in the Morea. His brother Manuel, who had been governor of the Morea since 1349, was to be compensated with the gift of the island of Lemnos.

But at the end of the year fighting broke out again, and early in 1356 Matthew, supported by Orchan and an Osmanli army, marched on Constantinople. The Serbian governors of the towns in western Thrace also offered him their services. But, as had happened before, the Serbs and the Turks fell to fighting among themselves; and Matthew, deserted by his Greek and Turkish troops, was taken captive by the Serbs. His captor was Vojihna, Serbian commander of the city of Drama, who hoped to obtain a substantial ransom for so eminent a prisoner. John V was pleased to offer the price, though he was horrified at Vojihna's proposal to put out Matthew's eyes. Matthew was thus delivered unharmed to his brother-in-law. He was held for a time on the island of Tenedos, but in 1357 he was moved with his wife and family to custody on Lesbos. The tale was not quite ended, for while Matthew was on Lesbos a plot was hatched in Constantinople to seize the palace on his behalf and to hold John V's family as hostages for his release. But the conspirators were rounded up. In the end, mainly due to the intervention of his father, Matthew reluctantly agreed to renounce his imperial title. In December 1357 a solemn ceremony was enacted at Epibatai on the Bosporos in the presence of the Emperors and Empresses, the Patriarchs of Constantinople and Jerusalem, and an assembly of senators and bishops. Matthew Cantacuzene called them all to witness his oath of allegiance to John V. He was no longer Emperor in any sense, though he was to enjoy precedence over all the imperial family except for the heir-apparent Andronikos Palaiologos, and his sons John and Demetrios were honoured with the titles of Despot and *sebastokrator* respectively.[61]

The ceremony at Epibatai marked the close of an era that had begun with the death of Andronikos III sixteen years before. Neither Matthew nor any other member of the Cantacuzene family ever again aspired to the imperium. In 1361, when Constantinople was again afflicted by an epidemic of the plague, Matthew's father accompanied him with all his family to the Morea to join his brother Manuel the Despot at Mistra. There Matthew remained in comparative obscurity until his death some thirty years later, assisting his brother in the administration of the province and composing a number of philosophical and religious works, some of which he was pleased to dedicate to his eldest daughter Theodora. His father returned to Constantinople in 1363, though he seems to have paid several later visits to the Morea; and it was at Mistra that he died at an advanced age in 1383.[62] But after the settlement of 1357 his family resigned all claim to the throne that he had occupied in Constantinople for seven years, nine months and twenty-two days. The right of the house of Palaiologos to provide the Emperors of the Romans was never again challenged or disputed until the Empire finally succumbed to the Turks in 1453.

NOTES

Narrative sources: Cantacuzene, III, 8-365; Gregoras, II, 780-1079; III, 3-567.

Modern works: Parisot, *Cantacuzène* (1845), 221-312; Florinskij, 'Andronik Mladšij ...', *Žurnal*, CCV (1879), 1-48; CCVIII (1880), 327-34; Nicol, *Byzantine Family of Kantakouzenos*, 64-103; Weiss, *Joannes Kantakuzenos*, passim. General accounts of the period 1347-54 will be found in: Ostrogorsky, *History*, 520-33; Diehl, *L'Europe orientale*, 310-26; Bréhier, *Vie et Mort*, 357-64.

1 Cf. Dölger, 'Johannes VI. Kantakuzenos als dynastischer Legitimist', in *PARASPORA* (Ettal, 1961), 194-207.

2 Cf. Ostrogorsky, *History*, 264.

3 Nicol, *Byzantine Family*, 64-5.

4 The most authoritative account of the hesychast movement and doctrine is that by J. Meyendorff, *Introduction à l'étude de Grégoire Palamas* (Paris, 1959) (English translation: Meyendorff, *A Study of Gregory Palamas*, translated by G. Lawrence (London, 1964)). The theology of the hesychasts is described by: V. Lossky, *The Mystical Theology of the Eastern Church* (London, 1957); J. M. Hussey and T. A. Hart, in *CMH*, IV, 2, 198-205; S. Runciman, *The Great Church in Captivity* (Cambridge, 1968), 128-58. Cf. Ostrogorsky, *History*, 511-14.

5 The Latin text of Barlaam's address to the Pope in 1339 is in *PG*, CLI, 1331-42. Cf. D. M. Nicol, 'Byzantine requests for an oecumenical council in the fourteenth century', *Annuarium Historiae Conciliorum*, I (Amsterdam, 1969), 76-81.

6 Meyendorff, *Introduction*, 65-94; Weiss, *Joannes Kantakuzenos*, 103-22.

7 Meyendorff, 95-128.

8 On Eirene Choumnaina, see especially V. Laurent, 'Une princesse byzantine au cloître. Irène Eulogie Choumnos Paléologine', *Echos d'Orient*, XXIX (1930), 29-61; and 'La direction spirituelle à Byzance', *REB*, XIV (1956), 48-86. J. Verpeaux, 'Notes prosopographiques sur la famille Choumnos', *BS*, XX (1959), 256-7; Meyendorff, 125; Weiss, 118-19.

9 Nicol, *Byzantine Family*, 82.

10 Nicol, 109-10, 123.

11 Gregoras, II, 589.

12 *Chronicon Estense*, in L. A. Muratori, *Rerum Italicarum Scriptores*, XV, 448.

13 Cantacuzene, III, 49-52.

14 Gregoras, II, 797-8. For other references, see Nicol, *Byzantine Family*, 129 note 3.

15 Demetrios Kydones, *Correspondence* (ed. by R.-J. Loenertz, *Démétrios Cydonès, Correspondance*, 2 vols (Vatican City, 1956, 1960)), I, 122, no. 88.

16 The Short Chronicles record eight later outbreaks of the plague, in 1361-2, 1373-4, 1381-2, 1391-2, 1398-9, 1409-10, 1417-18, 1422-3. See R.-J. Loenertz, 'La Chronique brève Moréote de 1423', in *Mélanges E. Tisserant*, II (Studi e Testi, 232 : Vatican City, 1964), 399-439.

17 Nicol, *Meteora*, 58-9.

18 Gregoras II, 790: 'There was nothing in the imperial treasury but air and dust and, as you might say, the atoms of Epicurus.'

19 Gregoras, III, 198-200.

20 Cantacuzene, III, 33-42.

21 The annual revenue from customs at Galata in 1348 was reckoned at 200,000 *hyperpyra* compared with 30,000 *hyperpyra* at Constantinople. Gregoras, II, 842. In 1352, when the Genoese withheld their supplies, the price of wheat in Constantinople doubled within a few days. Gregoras, III, 92.

22 The war against Galata in 1348-9 is described in detail by Cantacuzene, III, 68-80; Gregoras, II, 841-67; Alexios Makrembolites, in A. Papadopoulos-Kerameus, *Analekta Hierosolymitikes Stachyologias*, I (1891), 144-59. Cf. Nicol, *Byzantine Family*, 69 and references.

23 Gregoras, II, 850-1.

24 Alexios Makremobolites, *op. cit.*, 152-3.

25 Gregoras, II, 855-6.

26 Makrembolites, 157-8.

27 Gregoras, II, 864-5.

28 Gregoras, II, 862-3; Cantacuzene, III, 76-7; Makrembolites, 153.

29 Gregoras, II, 866.

30 Gregoras, II, 869-70; Cantacuzene, III, 80-1. This passage of Cantacuzene has been differently interpreted by, e.g. Zakythinos, *Crise monétaire*, 94-5, and Ostrogorsky, *History*, 528.

31 Nicol, *Byzantine Family*, 70-1.

32 *Demetri Cydonii Occisorum Thessalonicae Monodia*, in PG, CIX, 639-52.

33 Cantacuzene, II, 568-82; III, 104-5, 108-18; Gregoras, II, 876-7. Cf. Tafrali, *Thessalonique*, 239-54.

34 Gregory Palamas, *Homilies*, I, in *PG*, CL, 12. Cf. Meyendorff, *Introduction*, 139.

35 Cantacuzene, III, 118-60. Cf. Nicol, 73-4.

36 Cantacuzene, III, 152. Cf. Jorga, 'Latins et grecs ...', *BZ*, XV (1906), 206 and references.

37 On Manuel Cantacuzene's career, see Nicol, *Byzantine Family*, 122-9.

38 Nicol, 108f., 130f.

39 Nicol, 143f.

40 On Nikephoros Gregoras, see R. Guilland, *Essai sur Nicéphore Grégoras* (Paris, 1926), especially 28-33.

41 Meyendorff, 141-53; Weiss, 123-37.

42 Guilland, *Essai*, 38-54. For the later career and canonization of Palamas, see Meyendorff, 155-70. John Kyparissiotes, in *PG*, CLII, 736.

43 Cantacuzene, III, 53-62. Cf. J. Gay, *Le Pape Clément VI et les affaires d'Orient* (Paris, 1904), 94-118; Nicol, 67.

44 Nicol, 76-9.

45 Cantacuzene, III, 200-9; Gregoras, III, 147-50. Matteo Villani, *Croniche*, ed. A. Racheli, II (Trieste, 1858), xxviii, xxxiv, 65-68. For the Venetian loan to John V, see Cantacuzene, III, 247; Dölger, *Regesten*, V, no. 3005.

46 Nicol, 79-81.

47 Nicol, 81-2.

48 See especially Cantacuzene, III, 261-9.

49 Nicol, 113-14.

50 Cantacuzene, III, 276-9; Gregoras, III, 220-2. The earthquake is also recorded by some of the Short Chronicles.

51 Gibbons, *Foundation of the Ottoman Empire*, 100f.

52 Cantacuzene, III, 279-81.

53 See D. M. Nicol, 'The abdication of John VI Cantacuzene', *Byzantinische Forschungen*, II (*Polychordia. Festschrift F. Dölger*, 1967), 269-83.

54 Cantacuzene, III, 284-94; Gregoras, III, 241-4, 247. Nicol, *Byzantine Family*, 83-4.

55 Cantacuzene, III, 295-9.

56 Nicol, 85-6, where the date of John's abdication is given as 10 December. But see now A. Failler, 'Note sur la chronologie du règne de Jean Cantacuzène', *REB*, XXIX (1971), 293-302.

57 E. Gibbon, *The History of the Decline and Fall of the Roman Empire*, ed. J. B. Bury, VI (London, 1898), 505.

58 Cf. E. Frances, 'Narodnie dviženija osenju 1354 g. v Konstanti-

nopole i otrečenie Joanna Kantakuzina', *VV*, XXV (1964), 142-7.

59 J. B. Bury, *A History of the Later Roman Empire* ... (*A.D. 395-565*), II (London, 1923), 26. Cantacuzene, III, 308.

60 Nicol, 376.

61 Nicol, 115-18.

62 On the political role of John Cantacuzene after his abdication, see Lj. Maksimović, 'Politička uloga Jovana Kantakuzina posle adbikacije (1354-1383)', *Zbornik Radova*, IX (1966), 119-93.

Part Four

Byzantium as a Vassal of the Turks: The Last Hundred Years—1354-1453

Narrative sources: No Byzantine historian living at the time felt inspired to narrate the unhappy events of the second half of the fourteenth century. Where Gregoras and Cantacuzene left off at about 1360, no contemporary took up the tale. The last Greek historians all lived in the fifteenth century, after the fall of Constantinople to the Turks. Doukas, who died in the 1460s, takes the year 1341 as the starting-point of his history, but not until the year 1389 does his work become detailed. The Chronicle of George Sphrantzes, who served the three last Byzantine emperors as a secretary and ambassador and died after 1477, only covers the period 1401-77 in its original form (*Chronicon Minus*). A much expanded version (Pseudo-(S)Phrantzes, *Chronicon Maius*) was made in the sixteenth century and deals somewhat erratically and unreliably with the period 1285-1481. The Athenian Laonikos Chalkokondyles was writing about 1480; and, though he begins with a survey of world history, his main theme is the Turkish conquest of the Byzantine Empire and its replacement by the Ottoman Empire. Part of his history covers the fourteenth century, but not in systematic form. The events of the second half of that century have therefore to be reconstructed from other sources, among which the letters of the statesman Demetrios Kydones and the meagre offerings of the Short Chronicles are particularly informative. The following are the most recent editions: Doukas (Ducas), *Istoria Turco-bizantina, 1341-1462*, ed. V. Grecu (Bucharest, 1958); Georgios Sphrantzes, *Memorii 1401-1477*, ed. V. Grecu (Bucharest, 1966); Chalkokondyles: *Laonici Chalcocandylae Historiarum Demonstrationes*, 2 vols, ed. E. Darkó (Budapest, 1922-7); Kydones: *Démétrius Cydonès, Correspondance*, ed. R.-J. Loenertz, 2 vols (Studi e Testi, 186, 208: Vatican City, 1956, 1960).

Fourteen

The Reign of John V
Palaiologos—1354-91

The year 1354 may be taken to mark the point of no return for the Byzantine Empire. As an institution, or as the shadow of such, it was to endure for another 99 years. But they were the years of the running down process of a great machine which had exhausted its fuel and lost its driving force. They were the years too of transition from one form of universal empire to another. The last century of the Byzantine Empire was a prelude to the history of the Ottoman Empire that was to take over its provinces and finally its capital in 1453.

In terms of military strength and resilience the greatest power on the scene in 1354 was neither Greek nor Turkish. It was the Serbian Empire of Stephen Dušan which then covered more of eastern Europe than the Byzantines themselves had controlled for many a year. It is commonly said that Dušan was the only man in the middle of the fourteenth century who could have checked the further progress of the Turks. But his sights were set on Tsargrad or Constantinople, and his ambition was to create a Serbian ascendancy over the Byzantine world. He divided his realm and his conquests into 'Serbia' and 'Romania'. He allowed his son Uroš V to reign as King over the Serbian portion. But he retained for himself the title and authority of Emperor of 'the Greek lands of Romania', or the portions of the Byzantine Empire that he had acquired in Macedonia and northern Greece; and he took pains to woo the Greek inhabitants of these provinces. The code of law, or Zakonik, which he published in 1349 proclaimed the equality of Greeks and Serbs in all his dominions and confirmed the charters and privileges bestowed on Greek cities by the Byzantine emperors of the past whom Dušan was pleased to regard as his imperial predecessors. His administrators were adorned with the Byzantine titles of Despot, Caesar and *sebastokrator* and his court was a model of that in Constantinople. He minted a silver coinage in the Byzantine style; and churches and monasteries in the Slav as well as the Greek provinces of his Empire were decorated by artists of the best Byzantine school.[1]

Dušan came very close to realizing that dream which had haunted so many of the Slav rulers of the past, of making the city of Constantinople the centre of a Slav Empire. His foreign policy, which he conducted in the grand manner, was directed to this end. He tried to tempt Venice into lending him ships for an attack on the city. He gave the Pope to understand that he was interested in plans for a crusade against the Turks and that if he could be appointed as its leader the Serbian Orthodox Church might see its way to union with the Church of Rome. A papal legate, Peter Thomas, was sent to Serbia in 1354, and only his missionary zeal can have blinded him to the facts that the laws of Serbia defined Roman Catholics as heretics and second class citizens and that Dušan's interest in the Pope's plans was prompted only by the thought that as a crusader he could pose as the 'liberator' of Constantinople from the Turkish peril. In the event, neither Constantinople nor Thessalonica fell victim to Serbian imperialism. Stephen Dušan, who had played cat and mouse with the Byzantine emperors for many years, died in December 1355. Serbian legend quickly canonized the drama of his passing at the very moment when he seemed poised for the conquest of the imperial city. Yet it is questionable whether the Byzantine Empire in Europe would have revived under the management of a Serbian Emperor in its capital. Even the Greek cities in Macedonia, such as Berroia and Edessa, had been ready enough to revert to their Byzantine allegiance when the occasion offered in 1350. In Constantinople or Thessalonica not even a diplomat as practised as Dušan could have overcome the aversion of the Greeks to the Serbs as a people barely one generation removed from barbarism.[2]

Dušan like Alexander the Great had not expected to die, and like Alexander he had a multitude of successors but no real heir. The empire that he had created promptly disintegrated into its component parts when his controlling hand was gone. His son Uroš V was unable to hold it together. His half-brother Symeon Uroš, whom he had made Despot in Epiros, staked his claim to the title of Emperor of the Serbs and Greeks in northern Greece with his capital at Trikkala in Thessaly. Others of his relatives or officers set themselves up as independent princes elsewhere: Vukašin ruled as Despot over the district between Prilep and Ochrida, his brother John Uglješa held the town of Serres, while the brothers Dragaš and Constantine Dejanović controlled the area of Strumica and Velbužd.[3]

The Byzantines were relieved to hear of the passing of Dušan. Cantacuzene noted with satisfaction that the nobility of Serbia were divided into 10,000 factions, and lamented that his own people were unable to take advantage of the fact.[4] But the Turks saw in the collapse of the Serbian Empire a chance to extend their own conquests in Europe; and the Turks were now securely lodged at Gallipoli, on the doorstep of Thrace. It is hard to believe that their leaders contemplated any attack on Constantinople as yet, but their ghazi warriors could see almost limitless fresh fields for plunder, and they were eager to send troops to the help of Matthew Cantacuzene in 1356. The abdication of Matthew's father and the change of dynasty in Constantinople had naturally affected their relations with Byzantium. Their emir was after all a son-in-law of the deposed Emperor and in Orchan's less sophisticated view of things a wrong had been done to his relative. He made a secret offer to have John V assassinated. There had been trust and understanding of a kind between John Cantacuzene and the Osmanlis, but the trust depended too much upon a personal relationship, and it had been severely shaken by Suleiman's refusal to surrender Gallipoli. The new Emperor John V looked for a new and different solution to the problem of the Turkish presence in Europe.

John V Palaiologos was in his 23rd year when he became sole Emperor in December 1354. He had been crowned when he was only nine; and if one dates his years as Emperor from the moment of his coronation in November 1341 his reign may be counted the longest of any of the Byzantine Emperors since the foundation of Constantinople—longer than the 46 years of his great-grandfather Andronikos II (1282-1328) or the 46 years of Constantine VII (913-59). Even if one computes his reign from 1354 it will still be seen to cover all but 37 years, an equal span with the reigns of Alexios I and Manuel I (1081-1118 and 1143-80), for he died in February 1391. It is true that affairs were taken out of his hands on two occasions —by his son Andronikos IV (1376-9) and by his grandson John VII (1390). But he held the throne for the best part of half a century, and one might have expected that so long a period of single government would have produced a consistent policy and a stable administration. The melancholy truth is that John V was far from being equal to the situation that he inherited and that there was less to show at the end of his long career than at the beginning.

He believed, as his father-in-law had believed, that his empire stood in need of the help of foreign allies. But he was too confident that the settlement of the Turks in Europe would awaken the western world to the plight of the Christian East. Salvation, in his view, was to come not from appeasement or understandings with the Turks, but from alliances and negotiations with the western powers which might inspire something in the nature of a Christian league against the Osmanlis like that which had operated against Umur of Aydin. Abandoning all hope of being able to succeed alone, John V early made over portions of his empire to westerners. In the summer of 1355 he gave his sister in marriage to the Genoese adventurer Francesco Gattilusio and made him Lord of Mitylene or the island of Lesbos. In the same year he formally relinquished possession of the island of Chios to the Genoese, in contravention of the treaty which Cantacuzene had arranged with them in 1349. Chios, with its lucrative trade in alum and mastic, was thereafter, and until the middle of the sixteenth century, administered by a mercantile company of Genoese shareholders. They came to be known as the Maona of the Giustiniani family and their operations have been fairly compared to those of the East India Company of a later age. But their profits were not shared with Byzantium. By making over two such valuable islands to the Genoese, John V had within a few months reversed the whole policy of his predecessor towards those whom he had regarded as the prime subverters of the Byzantine economy.[5]

Through his Italian mother Anne of Savoy, John V was related to various prominent families in western Europe. But, like Michael VIII before him, he supposed that the most influential figure in the west was the Pope, since the Pope alone could authorize a crusade against the infidel. Whether or not this belief was justified in the circumstances of the Babylonian captivity of the papacy at Avignon is another matter. But it must have been known in Byzantium that Pope Innocent VI had in mind to reconstitute the league of Christian powers against the Turks which Clement VI had organized for the defence of Smyrna. John V was not alone in thinking that the survival of Byzantium depended upon co-operation with the west for a small but powerful group of his political supporters were of the same mind. They included his uncle Thomas Palaiologos, Prefect of the City, and the three sons of the late Theodore Metochites: Alexios, who had once been governor of Thessalonica, and had now been promoted to the rank of Grand Domestic; Nikephoros, now Grand Logothete; and Demetrios Metochites, now *megas stratopedarches*. One who was later to become a most outspoken and eloquent advocate of friendship with the west and indeed of union with the Roman Church was Demetrios Kydones, the former prime minister of John Cantacuzene. But the abdication of his friend and master in 1354 caused Kydones to lie low for a while in his retreat in the monastery of the Mangana. It was there that he completed his translation of the *Contra Gentiles* of Thomas Aquinas on 24 December 1354. His growing admiration for Latin theology and scholarship was already producing in him that crisis of conscience which was to lead him from Orthodoxy to Roman Catholicism.[6]

John V himself was no great theologian. He seems to have taken no part in the debates over the rights and wrongs of hesychasm. He found no difficulty in accepting the fact that any approach to the Pope for help must be backed by an offer to submit the Byzantine Church to the authority of the See of Rome. In this respect as in so many others his opinions and his policy ran counter to those of his father-in-law John Cantacuzene who had consistently if courteously refused to deal with the Papacy on any but equal terms, or to discuss the union of the Churches except in the arena of an œcumenical council. John V wore his Orthodoxy more lightly. Like many Byzantine Emperors before him he saw the union of the churches as a powerful bargaining factor in negotiations with the popes. He was a young man and he was led to hope that great things would come from a great gesture.

On 15 December 1355 he put his signature and golden seal to a letter addressed to Pope Innocent VI at Avignon. He asked the Pope to arrange for the dispatch to Constantinople of reinforcements to the extent of 15 transport vessels, 5 galleys, 500 knights and 1000 infantry. These auxiliaries would serve under the Emperor's command in warfare not only against the Turks but also against his own Greek adversaries for a space of six months. During this period a papal legate would reside in Constantinople and see to the appointment of ecclesiastical dignitaries favourable to the cause of the union of the Greek and Latin Churches. That cause could hardly fail to be advanced by the arrival in the capital of material assistance from the west. Indeed the Emperor forecast the spontaneous and almost instant conversion of his grateful people. The proposal was backed by a number of elaborate guarantees. The Emperor's second son Manuel, then only five years old, was to be sent as a hostage to the Curia at Avignon; and there he would stay, to be educated and married according to the Pope's wishes, if his father failed to honour his obligations. It was even suggested that the Pope, in his role of Manuel's adoptive father, should have control of the Byzantine Empire until such time as his ward attained his majority. The Emperor's eldest son and heir-presumptive, Andronikos, was to receive special instruction in Latin language and literature, and three colleges were to be founded for the promotion of Latin studies among the sons of the Byzantine aristocracy. In the event of the Emperor's total default the Pope was given written authority to indemnify himself by arranging the seizure of a stipulated quantity of imperial property. If on the contrary, all went well, the Emperor reserved the right to request further and more substantial help against his enemies in the form of a great Christian army which would drive the Turks out of the places that they had conquered. It would fight under the supreme command of the Emperor who wanted to be known as 'captain-general and standard bearer of Holy Mother Church'. One last possibility was foreseen. It might transpire that the Emperor, for all his good intent, could simply not prevail upon all his people to co-operate in the fulfilment of his promises. In that case he pledged himself to make his own submission to the Pope in person.[7]

It is this final clause which seems to be the most realistic proposition in an otherwise rather unrealistic document; although the Emperor had taken care to preface his proposals by reminding the Pope how difficult it would be to change the deeply-rooted traditions and beliefs of a whole people. On the other hand no other Byzantine Emperor had ever offered so many pledges of his good faith in the matter of submitting his Church to the authority of Rome; and no Pope could fail to be impressed by an Emperor's offer to pay a visit *ad limina*. It is not without significance that the document was composed with the help and advice of a western bishop who understood the Orthodox mentality and the Byzantine political situation at the time. Paul, Latin Archbishop of Smyrna, happened to be in Constantinople in 1355 and knew both John V and the ex-Emperor John Cantacuzene. Like Barlaam of Calabria, who had put the point well to the Pope in 1339, Paul of Smyrna realized that the Byzantines would more readily sink their religious prejudices against the West if they were treated in advance to some material evidence of western sympathy and support.[8]

The letter was taken to Avignon by Paul in company with the Byzantine ambassador Nicholas Sigeros, who was in favour of the project and had served on earlier embassies to the Pope. It reached its destination in June 1356. Pope Innocent VI had exchanged letters with John Cantacuzene, but he had had no dealings with John V. Reports that he had heard about the change of emperors must have made him feel that political affairs in Constantinople were unpredictable and unstable. He was not disposed to take the requests and promises of the new Emperor too seriously. His reply, written in July 1356, was confined to generalities and expressions of delight that the Greeks seemed willing to return to the fold of true Christians under the one shepherd. He passed over in studious silence all the detailed proposals, promises and guarantees that the Emperor had made. There was no question of his entertaining the Emperor's son as a hostage, and no question of his organizing military and naval reinforcements for Constantinople. Clearly the proposition that excited him most was that of the personal conversion of John V; and to see that this was followed up the Pope announced that he was sending two legates to Constantinople. One was the Carmelite bishop, Peter Thomas, who had recently been on a similar mission to the late Stephen Dušan in Serbia; the other was a Dominican, William Conti, who had just been created Latin Bishop of Sozopolis. Paul of Smyrna, who had helped to draft the Emperor's letter to the Pope, was not included in the embassy. Peter Thomas and his colleague reached Constantinople in April 1357. Their brief was to make propaganda for the union of the Churches, and above all to work for the conversion to the Roman faith of the Emperor and as many members of the Byzantine court as possible.[9]

Almost all that is known about the mission of Peter Thomas comes from the biography, or rather hagiography, of him composed by the Chancellor of the French Kingdom of Cyprus, Philippe de Mézières.[10] If we are to believe this account, Peter Thomas gave instruction in the faith to the Emperor and received him into the Roman Church, although the Emperor protested that he could not force the idea of union with Rome on his people for fear that they would rise up in rebellion against him. The nature of John V's 'conversion' in 1357 is debatable. His Church and people knew nothing of it, and not even the popes seem to have been clear about it. The Patriarch of Constantinople at the time was Kallistos who had been reappointed when Cantacuzene's friend Philotheos resigned in 1354. Like Philotheos he was a fervent hesychast and temperamentally unsympathetic to Latin theology. He was not averse to exploring the possibilities of union through the medium of an œcumenical council. But he had strong views on the doctrinal errors of the Roman Church and on the exalted status of his own patriarchate; and he expressed them in a letter that he wrote to the Archbishop of Bulgaria at the very moment when his Emperor was putting forward his own project to the Pope. The Patriarch Kallistos represented the feelings of all those devout Byzantines who were liable to rebel against their emperor if he tampered with their faith.[11]

Peter Thomas, though empowered as a last resort to direct an inquisition against the unrepentant Greek heretics, soon lost heart and made his way to Cyprus. The Pope's horizons were once again limited to the formation of a league of western powers against the Turks. Its ultimate ideal might be the liberation of the Holy Land, but its practical aim was the defence of the colonial and commercial interests of Cyprus, Venice and the Knights of Rhodes in the south-eastern Mediterranean. The league was reconstituted at Smyrna in 1357. Two years later Peter Thomas, now designated as apostolic legate in the East, made heroic efforts to expand its activities to the proportions of a crusade. In the summer of 1359 he even managed to organize a raid against the Turks at Lampsakos on the Hellespont. But this was far from being the kind of assistance envisaged by the Byzantine Emperor in his proposals to the Pope. He had asked to be given overall command of a general crusade against the Turks. He found himself left out of account. His last communication with Innocent VI was dated 7 November 1357. It was never answered. Innocent died in 1362 and direct negotiations between Byzantium and the Papacy were not resumed until 1364. Nothing had come of John V's extravagant proposals.[12]

In the meantime, however, his own position had somewhat improved. Matthew Cantacuzene had resigned his claim to the throne. Stephen Dušan of Serbia had died, and the tsar of Bulgaria had been pleased to give his daughter in marriage to the Emperor's eldest son Andronikos. The Genoese in Galata, as well as those in Lesbos, Chios and elsewhere, were loyal partisans of John V; and even the Venetians, who had preferred his predecessor, finally agreed, in October 1357, to renew for a further five years the treaty with Byzantium which they had last signed in 1349. The Turks remained a constant danger. But in the spring of 1357 an incident occurred which gave John V the chance to render a slight service to the Osmanlis. Orchan's youngest son Halil was kidnapped by Greek pirates from Phokaia. The Emperor offered to intervene with the governor of Phokaia, Leo Kalothetos, to secure the boy's release. It proved an expensive business, for Kalothetos, a lifelong Cantacuzenist, refused to co-operate until the Emperor paid him a ransom of 100,000 *hyperpyra*. Halil was then returned to his father, and early in 1358 John V sailed to an island rendezvous to negotiate a settlement with Orchan.[13]

But it was in Thrace that the pressure from the Turks was felt most acutely. More and more territory fell into their grasp as they advanced inland from the Thracian Chersonnese. The Osmanlis provided a base there and a rallying point for numerous other bands of roving Turkish warriors who had originally come over to Europe in the service of Umur of Aydin, of the emirs of Saruchan or Karasi, or independently as pirates. Hadji Ilbeg, who had first come over with Umur, joined forces with Orchan's son Suleiman. Other ghazi chieftains raided and plundered Thrace on their own account. The concerted Ottoman advance into eastern Europe had hardly begun in the years between 1354 and 1360. The situation in Thrace was more confused than the history books generally suggest. But communications broke down and Greek farmers gave up the unequal struggle and withdrew behind the walls of their nearest towns. The Florentine chronicler Matteo Villani reports that the Turks had reached the walls of Constantinople in 1359. In the same year the city of Didymoteichos was temporarily taken, and in November 1361 it fell permanently into Turkish hands. But it is impossible to say with certainty that the 'Turks' who took it, or those who were seen outside Constantinople, were Osmanlis.[14]

It was in these circumstances and in this part of the world that Peter Thomas led his raid against the Turks at Lampsakos in 1359; and it was here in Thrace, not in Smyrna or in Cyprus, that a crusading army was needed. Suleiman, the architect of the Gallipoli enterprise, died in 1359. His father Orchan died in 1362. But by then the Turks had taken Didymoteichos, the second largest city of Thrace, and pressed on up the Marica valley. Here their attack is said to have been led by Suleiman's comrade-in-arms Lala Shahin who captured Philippopolis (Plovdiv) in 1363 and made it his headquarters. He is supposed to have been rewarded with the title of Beglerbeg or governor of Rumelia, for such was the name given by the Turks to the Roman or Byzantine provinces in Europe.[15]

Orchan was succeeded as emir of the Osmanlis by his son Murad. For some years Murad was occupied in securing his own position in Asia Minor against his rivals. The Turkish raids in Thrace, however, continued. One Byzantine historian has it that John V was obliged to make a treaty with the Turks in Europe as early as 1362.[16] But their offensive lacked central direction and a well-organized counter-attack might still have proved effective. The difficulty was to inspire a sense of common danger and common purpose in the various interested parties. John V almost succeeded in bringing the Venetians and the Genoese to co-operate in patrolling the straits between Europe and Asia. He reaffirmed his treaty with Venice in 1363. He looked to the Serbs to provide reinforcements by land. The Patriarch Kallistos went on a diplomatic mission to Dušan's widow who was residing at Serres. But he died there with nothing achieved in 1363; and the rumour that he had been poisoned did not help the cause of Byzantine-Serbian friendship. The Bulgars too, who had advertised their goodwill to Byzantium by a royal marriage only a few years before, chose to regard the Turkish depredations in Byzantine Thrace as no concern of theirs. The Emperor had to make representations to their tsar to prevent him from collaborating with the Turks; and in 1363 the few military and naval resources available to the Byzantines had to be employed in a campaign against the Bulgars. They were a more familiar and a more tractable problem than the Turks. It was easier to attack the Black Sea ports of Bulgaria from the sea than it was to face the armies of the real enemy by land.[17]

When he got back from Bulgaria in 1363 the Emperor heard news from the west that preparations were in hand for a new and more impressive crusade. The initiative came from Pope Urban V who had been elected two years earlier. The leaders were to be the Catholic rulers of Cyprus and Hungary. John V had been disappointed in his hopes before: plans for crusades seldom seemed to take the Byzantine Emperor into account. But he felt that the new Pope might be more helpful than his predecessor, and he had no doubt discovered that one of the most enthusiastic participants in the venture was his own cousin, Amadeo, Count of Savoy. He made some tentative approaches to the Curia at Avignon. The Pope responded cautiously at first and then with greater interest in April 1365, even proposing a plan for turning his crusade against the Turks in the Byzantine Empire. Undoubtedly Urban V was influenced towards a certain sympathy with the Byzantines through his contact with a number of the distinguished minority of Latinophiles and converts to Catholicism in Constantinople. Among these was Demetrios Kydones who seems to have emerged from his retirement by 1364 and to have resumed his political career as first minister at the court of John V. But the plan was never put into practice. The crusade assembled not at Constantinople but at Rhodes. Its leader was not the Emperor but King Peter I of Cyprus, and its destination was Egypt. The affair was of no further concern to Byzantium. It ended in a wild and disastrous raid on Alexandria in October 1365.[18]

King Louis the Great of Hungary had stayed out of it in the end. His piety moved him instead to conduct a holy war of his own against his Christian neighbours in Bulgaria. In 1365 Hungarian troops occupied the frontier province of Vidin and took prisoner its prince Stracimir, son of John Alexander. Louis of Hungary seems to have believed that it was more important that the Orthodox should be converted and rebaptized than that they should be given encouragement to drive back the Turks. The army that he sent into Bulgaria was quickly followed by Franciscan missionaries who conducted mass baptisms of the humiliated schismatics. John V, however, retained a naïve hope that the King of Hungary might still be moved to help him. He was the nearest Catholic neighbour of Byzantium and he had, after all, been willing to take the Cross against the infidel. After the fiasco of the crusade to Alexandria John V therefore took the unprecedented step of leaving his capital to pay a visit to a foreign monarch. It was without precedent because no former Byzantine Emperor would have sunk his pride or demeaned his dignity to such an extent. It had always been assumed that it was the part of lesser princes to pay their respects to the one true Emperor in Constantinople. But times had changed, and once the precedent had been set it was to be followed on several future occasions.

The Emperor set out in the depth of winter, sailing up the Black Sea to the Danube. A small retinue went with him, as well as his two younger sons Manuel and Michael. His eldest son Andronikos seems to have been left in charge of Constantinople. The Pope had been informed of what was afoot and thoroughly approved of a meeting which must surely benefit the cause of Christian union; but he agreed with King Louis' order of priorities, that conversion must come before rescue; and he privately expressed to the King his doubts about the honesty of the Greeks. The Byzantine view of the Hungarians was expressed at the same time by Demetrios Kydones. It was equally straightforward. They were a cruel people, said Kydones; but the Emperor would not have undertaken so long and tiring a journey without some hope of reward.[19]

The hope was cruelly deceived. No clear record remains of what took place at Buda. But it is a measure of the Hungarian King's mistrust that he obliged the Emperor to leave his son Manuel as a

275

hostage. The Emperor set off for home empty-handed. But he got no further than the Bulgarian frontier post of Vidin, which the Hungarians had occupied in the previous year. The Bulgars refused to allow the Emperor to enter their territory and he was unable to continue his journey. The Bulgarian tsar may reasonably have suspected that an alliance between Byzantium and Hungary, such as the Emperor had been seeking, was not in his own best interest. The Emperor's son Andronikos, who was married to the tsar's daughter and who might have intervened on his father's behalf, seems to have been in no hurry to do so. And so it came about that the one true Emperor of the Romans, despised, mistrusted and far from home, found himself the captive of his Christian neighbours. It is no wonder that the Turks found the going easy in eastern Europe.[20]

But there was one man who had taken to heart the Emperor's appeal to the western world. Moved partly by a sense of family loyalty and partly by his active crusading spirit, Amadeo, Count of Savoy, had organized his own expedition to Constantinople. Amadeo VI of Savoy, known as the Green Count, was a cousin of the Emperor John V. His father Aimon had been a half-brother of the Empress Anne of Savoy and his mother was of that branch of the Montferrat family which claimed the name of Palaiologos. He had intended to take part in the Pope's crusade together with Peter of Cyprus and Louis of Hungary, and he had taken the Cross in 1363. But through all the muddles and delays that bedevilled that expedition, Amadeo never lost sight of the possibility of going either by way of Hungary or by way of Constantinople in order to give his cousin some support against the Turks. The crusade for Egypt finally left without him. But by May 1366 he had assembled a fleet of 15 ships and some 1500 or 1800 soldiers to go to Constantinople. The Pope gave his blessing to the venture on condition that Amadeo would do all in his power to bring the Byzantine Emperor and his people over to the Roman Church. Most probably Amadeo expected a contingent of troops from Hungary to join forces with him at some stage. Certainly when he left Venice in June 1366 he had no knowledge that his cousin John V was virtually a prisoner on the border between Hungary and Bulgaria.[21]

Amadeo's little armada reached the Hellespont in August. There it was joined by Francesco Gattilusio, the Genoese lord of Lesbos who was John V's brother-in-law, and by some Greek forces. Doubtless acting on their advice Amadeo made the recapture of Gallipoli from the Turks his first objective. The resistance was fierce and the fighting went on for two days. But finally the Turks withdrew, and on 23 August Amadeo and his men entered and occupied the city. Gallipoli had been the main beachhead of Turkish operations in Thrace since 1354. Its recovery was a major triumph for the Christian cause. It was an example of the kind of practical support that was more likely to win the hearts and overcome the prejudices of the Byzantines than any number of papal legates. Even so there were those in Constantinople who, when the news of Amadeo's approach was announced, would have closed the gates of their city to a western army. They were overruled by the eloquence of Demetrios Kydones who spoke out in favour of receiving the help of the Latins with gratitude. On 2 September 1366 Amadeo entered Constantinople.[22]

By then he must have known the plight of his cousin the Emperor. He applied himself to the business of mounting a rescue operation. In October, after a month of preparations, Amadeo sailed with his army up the Black Sea coast to terrorize the Bulgars into allowing the Emperor to cross their territory. He attacked and occupied the Bulgarian ports of Mesembria and Sozopolis and laid siege to Varna. From here an embassy was sent to the tsar John Alexander at Trnovo, and shortly before Christmas the Emperor was at last permitted to cross the Bulgarian frontier and made his way to join his cousin at Mesembria on the coast. They spent the winter together at Sozopolis and returned to Constantinople in April of the following year.

It may seem strange that the Emperor, who had been absent from his capital for so long, should have delayed his return for another four months. No doubt he had to recover from his bitter experiences in Hungary, and he may have had reason to wonder what kind of reception he would get in Constantinople from his son Andronikos who had been acting as regent. But those months were not wasted, for Amadeo of Savoy had other work to do. He had by now very nearly exhausted his finances. There was the question of his expenses to be settled. The garrisons of soldiers posted in the cities that he had captured, not least in Gallipoli, were very costly to maintain and dissipated the collective strength of his army for any further campaigns against the Turks in Thrace. But the purpose of his coming to Byzantium had not been entirely military. The Pope had laid it on Amadeo's soul that he must also pursue the matter of the union of the Churches; he had brought with him as the Pope's emissary Paul, late Bishop of Smyrna, who had helped the Emperor draft his proposals in 1355. Paul had now been elevated to the dignity of

Latin Patriarch of Constantinople and his brief was to secure the conversion of the inhabitants of that city to the Roman faith.

The discussions which began in Sozopolis were continued in Constantinople after Easter 1367. Whatever Peter Thomas and Pope Innocent VI may have thought ten years earlier, it is clear that neither the Latin Patriarch Paul nor Pope Urban V considered the Emperor John V to be a fully professed member of the Roman Church. Paul, who was well acquainted with the Byzantine scene, cannot have been surprised that the Orthodox Patriarch of Constantinople refused to meet or to talk with him. John V himself was quite prepared to make the necessary confessions of faith and promises, but he knew that he could do so only on his own account and not on behalf of his Church and people. In default of the Patriarch someone had to be produced who could conscientiously put the Byzantine case to the Pope's representative. The Emperor therefore invited his father-in-law, the Emperor-monk Joasaph or John Cantacuzene, to hold an interview with Paul. They met in a hall of the palace in June 1367. Among the audience were the Empress Helena, two of her sons, and three Greek bishops. The Patriarch Philotheos, who had been reinstated after the death of Kallistos in 1363, declined to attend and was content to leave the defence of Orthodoxy in the capable hands of his old friend Cantacuzene.

A detailed report has survived of the dialogue that took place in the palace.[23] Its subject was simply the ways and means of achieving a true reunion of the divided parts of the Church. What John Cantacuzene had to say was an amplified and elaborated version of what he had said to the legates of Pope Clement VI in 1350. He affirmed his sincere wish for unity among Christians but he complained that the Church of Rome had never sought to re-establish that unity on equal terms through common discussion of the differences in a common council of bishops of both sides. Such a council, to be truly œcumenical, would have to be attended not only by the Pope but also by the Patriarch of Constantinople and all his subordinate archbishops, as well as by the Patriarchs of Alexandria, Antioch and Jerusalem, and the heads of the Orthodox Churches in Serbia, Bulgaria and Georgia. He made a caustic reference to the activities of the Christian King of Hungary who had such a warped opinion of the Orthodox Church in Bulgaria that he considered its members to be in need of a second baptism; and he cited the example of the tyranny of Michael VIII to show how futile it was to imagine that any emperor could impose union with Rome by force. The Latin

Patriarch Paul, for all his understanding of the Byzantine mentality, had still to be disembarrassed of the common western misapprehension that Byzantine emperors, being 'Caesaropapists', claimed control over the souls as well as the bodies of their subjects and that the Orthodox faith could therefore be adjusted for the faithful by a simple imperial decree. In the end, however, if the Greek report of the interview is correct, Paul was won round to agreeing that an œcumenical council should be held in Constantinople some time within the next two years. Unexpected though this conclusion may appear, there can be no doubt that it was accepted as binding by the Byzantine Church. The Patriarch Philotheos at once began to send out invitations to the council. The Patriarchs of Alexandria and Jerusalem gave their approval. Representatives of the secular and monastic clergy in Constantinople were appointed to go to Italy with Amadeo of Savoy to pay their respects to Pope Urban V. The prospect of a union of the Churches inspired by religious and not by political motives had never seemed more hopeful.[24]

But what the Pope's legate may have been induced to say in Constantinople was not the word of the Pope in Avignon or Rome. While he and the ex-Emperor were striving to reach agreement at the most idealistic level, John V and Amadeo of Savoy were engaged in arranging what was by comparison a sordid and materialistic transaction. Amadeo, who was now about to leave for home, succeeded in convincing the Emperor that the only way to elicit further help from the west was to make his own submission to the Pope in person. They could travel to Italy together. The Savoyard chronicler of these events goes so far as to say that when John complained that his people might depose him Amadeo threatened to restore Gallipoli to the Turks and to unleash his soldiers on the Byzantine Empire. He was satisfied in the end by the handing over of some jewels and other substantial securities in cash. These he was to hold in Italy or in pawn with the Genoese at Galata as pledges against the promised visit of the Emperor. Having thus exercised a form of moral blackmail, Amadeo felt free to return to Italy. He took with him the Latin Patriarch Paul as well as the Greek ambassadors to the Pope. The Emperor was to follow as soon as he felt the moment to be opportune. When he did, and when he had been received as a penitent convert by the Pope, he could then retrieve his securities.[25]

The Byzantine embassy to the Pope reached Italy in October 1367. It was the most imposing delegation of its kind for almost a century. Its eight members included personal representatives of the Emperor, of the eastern patriarchs, of the monks and of the citizens of Constantinople. Pope Urban received them at Viterbo and allowed them to accompany him on his entry into Rome on 16 October. They were there for four weeks. They might as well have stayed at home. On 6 November the Pope signed 23 letters addressed to all concerned with the union of the eastern and western Churches, among them John Cantacuzene, the Empress and her sons, Demetrios Kydones and Francesco Gattilusio, as well as to the clergy and people of Constantinople and to the Catholic princes of the east. The Byzantine delegates to Italy went with high hopes of discussing the plan for convening a council of the whole Church. The Pope's letters reveal how sadly they must have been disillusioned. Not one of them so much as mentions the possibility of summoning a council. The letters do no more than express pious generalizations about the benefits that must come to the Greeks from 'returning' to the fold of the Roman Church, while reminding them that their emperor had promised to come to Rome in person, preferably accompanied by the eastern patriarchs. The man appointed to deliver this unwelcome and disappointing message to Constantinople was the Latin Patriarch Paul. He had an unenviable task. But the Pope assured him that his work for the reunion of Christendom under Rome was God's work and that he would get his reward in heaven if nowhere else.[26]

By now the urgent question of co-operation between East and West to expel the Turks from Thrace had got lost in a fantasy world of ecclesiology. The Byzantines too, it seemed, must look to heaven for their reward after they had confessed the errors of their inherited faith. For Pope Urban V was in truth quite unable to put in motion any form of crusade for the rescue of Constantinople. Nevertheless, Byzantine morale had risen as a result of the practical help brought by Amadeo of Savoy. Gallipoli remained in Greek control for some ten years, and the Turks were hindered from sending further reinforcements or settlers across from Asia Minor. But the Byzantines seem to have had neither the will nor the strength to make the most of this advantage. The Turks who were already established in Thrace and in possession of Didymoteichos and other towns displayed a vigour and enthusiasm which were more than a match for the fatalistic apathy and entrenched conservatism of the Byzantines. In 1367 John V proposed to increase the size of his army by appropriating some landed property in the country between Constantinople and Selymbria on which to settle soldiers and their families. But the property belonged to the Church, and the Patriarch and his synod flatly refused to offend against canon law by releasing it. John V, whose dealings with the Pope did not endear him to his own Patriarch, was not the man to defy his bishops or to point out to them that, unless they co-operated in the defence of the Empire, their church might soon be at the mercy of rulers of the Muslim faith.[27]

In 1369 the Emperor was at last persuaded to fulfil his promise to go to Rome. His arrival in Italy was heralded by the papal legate Paul, who had done most to bring it about, and by Demetrios Kydones, who had seen to the translation of the document of submission that the Emperor was to make to the Pope. It was in every detail the declaration that Urban V had required in 1366. The Emperor knew in advance that he must accept the Roman doctrine without any conditions or reservations and must acknowledge the primacy of the See of Rome over the Church universal. Before leaving he appointed his eldest son Andronikos, already designated as the Emperor Andronikos IV, as regent in Constantinople and his second son Manuel as governor of Thessalonica. With him on his long journey went Demetrios Kydones, his brother-in-law Francesco Gattilusio, and a number of other Greeks who were in favour of union with Rome. But it was a different kind of embassy from that which had set out for Italy with such high hopes in 1367. The people of Constantinople were not represented and not a single member of the Byzantine hierarchy could be persuaded to join in.

The Emperor reached Naples early in August and after a short stay there as the guest of the Queen of Sicily he sailed on to Rome. The Pope entered the city a few weeks later and there, on 18 October, the cardinals who had been selected for the task received the Emperor's declaration of faith and prepared the definitive document which had been drawn up in Greek and in Latin and to which the Emperor now appended his signature and his golden seal. Three days later, on Sunday 21 October, a more brilliant ceremony was enacted. The Pope, surrounded by all his cardinals, sat on a throne at the top of the steps of St Peter's to receive the humble submission of the 'Emperor of the Greeks'. When the Emperor had genuflected three times and kissed the Pope's feet, hands and mouth, the Pope rose and recited the *Te Deum*. They then entered the cathedral together and the Pope celebrated mass in the presence of the Emperor and all his retinue. The day ended with a dinner at which all the cardinals were present.[28]

John V stayed in Rome for about five months. His immediate reward for his trouble came when the Pope ordered the Genoese and Count

Amadeo of Savoy to hand back the financial and other securities that he had lodged with them. He needed them to help pay the cost of his journey. The Pope advised Amadeo that his imperial cousin was now a full Catholic and therefore fully deserving of assistance. In November he made the same recommendation to all Catholics and voiced the hope that many other schismatics would follow the lead that their emperor had set, just as numerous pagans had once followed the lead set by Constantine the Great. To clear up any possible ambiguities in his declaration the Emperor issued a second chrysobull in January 1370 affirming that the faith which he now professed was that of the 'Holy Roman Church' and of its supreme pontiff Urban. Soon afterwards the Pope granted him permission to have a portable altar, on condition that it was never used by one who was not a Latin priest celebrating according to the Roman rite.

This privilege served to underline the fact that John V's conversion was a purely personal matter. No one, not even Pope Urban, pretended that a 'union of the Churches' had resulted. The best that the Pope could say was that the Emperor had set an example. The Patriarch Philotheos had warned Amadeo of Savoy that the Byzantine people would almost certainly depose their Emperor if he bartered their faith to the Bishop of Rome. But as a private individual he could follow his own conscience, and neither the Patriarch nor his father-in-law John Cantacuzene reproached him for doing so. There was, of course, no further talk of convening an œcumenical council. When in February 1370 Pope Urban wrote to the clergy of Constantinople and Greece exhorting them to imitate the action of their emperor, he expressed some surprise that there were still people who advocated that such a gathering should be held. In his view no good could come from debating the truths of the faith that had long since been established by the authority of the See of Rome. The only way in which the Greeks could save themselves from the Turks was by joining the communion of western Christendom. These were fine words. But, as John V must have come to realize while he was in Rome, the western Christians were far from being in communion with each other. They were in no mood and in no position to give any combined help to Constantinople even if all the Greeks were to become their brothers in the faith. King Peter of Cyprus, who had always been the main champion of a league against the Turks, had been assassinated in 1369. King Louis of Hungary had lost any enthusiasm that he may ever have had for a crusade in Europe. The Pope was powerless to stir the Knights of Rhodes or the Genoese to any action beyond their own immediate horizons. The Venetians alone seemed interested in doing business with the Byzantine Emperor; but they preferred to do it their own way.[29]

Before John V left Constantinople the Venetians had sent an envoy to Constantinople to demand payment of the money which the Republic still claimed in compensation for damage done to their property in the capital. The claim was for the sum of 25,663 *hyperpyra*. Of this amount the Emperor had been bullied into paying 4500 *hyperpyra* in 1368. But added to this there was still the matter of the loan of 30,000 ducats made to Anne of Savoy in 1343 on the security of the Byzantine crown jewels. These were still held in pawn in the Treasury of St Mark's at Venice, and the interest on the loan was steadily mounting. The Venetian envoy to Constantinople in 1368 had rudely hinted that the jewels would have to be sold on the open market if they were not quickly redeemed. To make matters worse he had instructions to negotiate with the Osmanli emir Murad for the lease of an entrepôt at Skutari on the Bosporos opposite Constantinople, which would become the Venetian equivalent of the Genoese colony at Galata.

Neither of these threats had yet materialized. But the Emperor felt that it would be as well to try to settle his accounts with Venice while he was on the spot. He wrote to the Doge from Naples almost as soon as he landed in Italy. The reply came to him in Rome, and after much haggling his treaty with Venice, which had lapsed in 1368, was renewed for a further five years on 1 February 1370. The terms allowed for some concessions to be made because of the unhappy state of the Empire. The crown jewels were to remain in Venice and the outstanding balance of the claim for damages was to be payable in annual instalments. John was encouraged to go round by Venice on his journey home. In March 1370 he finally left Rome on the ships that had brought him there. After another stay at Naples he sailed up the Adriatic first to Ancona and then to Venice. It might have been a glorious occasion of pomp and ceremony. No Byzantine Emperor had visited Venice before. But the Doge was not disposed to spend much on a visitor who was already in his debt. It soon transpired that the Emperor had not even enough money to pay for his return voyage to Constantinople.[30]

He had, however, an offer to make which the Venetians found most attractive. He proposed to make over to them the island of Tenedos which they had long coveted. Tenedos lies at the entrance to the Hellespont; its possession would compensate for their failure to secure

283

Skutari from the Turks. In return for so valuable a property the Venetians promised to return the Byzantine crown jewels and to supply the Emperor with six warships and 25,000 ducats in cash, 4000 of which were made over as an advance in July. All might have been well had the deal gone through. But the Emperor's son Andronikos IV, who was acting as regent in Constantinople, refused to obey the order to hand over the island. His refusal was almost certainly prompted by the Genoese, who had no wish to see their commercial rivals installed at the mouth of the Hellespont. The Emperor was put in a most embarrassing and humiliating position. He had neither money nor credit. He was to all intents and purposes detained at the Doge's pleasure as an insolvent debtor. He appealed to his son to raise the money for his release by selling some of the treasures of the Byzantine Church. Andronikos piously rejected the suggestion. In the end he was saved by his second son Manuel who hurried to Venice from Thessalonica in the middle of winter bringing with him the means not only to bail his father out but also to provide security for a further loan. Negotiations were then resumed, and in March 1371 the Emperor was at length enabled to continue his homeward journey. He left Venice the richer by a new loan of 30,000 ducats. The advance of 4000 that he had already spent was written off, and he was given provisions for his voyage. Manuel received a personal gift of 300 ducats, but he was required to stay in Italy for some months as a hostage of Venice.[31]

The Emperor did not reach Constantinople until October 1371. He had been away for almost two years. He had set out with great expectations of the rewards that would follow once he was accepted as a member of Catholic Christendom. He returned weary and disenchanted. Demetrios Kydones, who had travelled with him, had been predisposed to admire the cities of Rome and Venice. He had not been disappointed in the sights he saw and the scholars he met. But he shared his master's disillusionment at the outcome. It had all been, as he wrote to a friend, a waste of labour which had brought no benefit to the Empire.[32]

Kydones parted company with the Emperor at some point and reached Constantinople before him. He was there when an envoy from the emir Murad came to the capital to negotiate the return of Gallipoli to the Turks. Kydones may have been discouraged that his friends in the west could not be more co-operative. But he had no doubts about the wisdom of holding on to what they had helped the Byzantines to recover. It was most probably at this time that he composed his oration against the surrender of Gallipoli, the text of which survives.[33] As a Latinophile Kydones had a greater faith than most of his countrymen that the Pope would eventually arrange the means to help them. But he emphasized the point that the whole of western Europe would be shocked and resentful if the Byzantines willingly restored to the enemy a vital fortress which western chivalry had reconquered. In his view they would do better to collaborate with their neighbours in Serbia against the common enemy. The proposal of an alliance between Byzantium and some of the Serbian princes seems to have been in the air at the time. The Orthodox Church and the Patriarch Philotheos naturally favoured it as a union of eastern Christians. It was sponsored by John Uglješa who ruled the fragment of Dušan's Empire centred upon the city of Serres in Macedonia. He was willing to recognize the authority of the Byzantine Patriarch over the Serbian Church and even to subsidize the Empire; and there was a strong presumption that his brother Vukašin, lord of the area around Prilep, Skoplje and Ochrida, would join in.[34]

Kydones won his case about Gallipoli. But the idea of a Byzantine-Serbian alliance took no root. The situation in Constantinople in the summer of 1371 was too unsettled to permit any concerted or decisive action. There were too many conflicting opinions and too many factions. The Emperor John V was still abroad. His son and regent Andronikos IV seems to have favoured appeasement rather than resistance to the Turks. He had already defied his father's orders, and he was the friend of the Genoese whose trade would surely suffer if warfare were to break out on a large scale. So long as a Byzantine garrison controlled Gallipoli the Osmanlis and their leader Murad himself could hardly enter Europe. But the Turks who were already there in very large numbers seemed to win their victories without need of reinforcements. The chronology of these victories is far from easy to determine. But it appears that in 1369 a mixed force of Turks, most of them probably not Osmanlis by origin captured Adrianople, the chief city of Thrace. The loss of Adrianople, following on that of Didymoteichos six years before, may well have caused many Byzantines to feel that the Turks had come to stay. Better to come to terms with them than pretend that Constantinople or its allies could ever muster enough strength to reverse the process.[35]

But the Serbians had more spirit or less prudence. Once masters of Adrianople the Turks began to penetrate westward towards Serbian Macedonia. The Despot of Serres, John Uglješa, wasted no more time on persuading the Byzantines to co-operate. He and his brother Vukašin joined forces to fight their own defensive war against the invaders.

In September 1371 they led their combined armies along the road to Adrianople. The Turkish ghazi warriors fought best when they encountered stiff resistance. They met the Serbs about 20 miles west of the city. There at Črnomen on the Marica river, on 26 September, the first really decisive battle in the Turkish conquest of eastern Europe was fought and lost by the Christians. The much later Ottoman chroniclers have it that there were 60,000 Serbian soldiers to a mere 4000 of their own. But whatever the figures, it is hard to maintain that this was a victory for the Osmanlis. Murad was not there. The Turks were led by Hadji-Ilbeg and by Lala Shahin. Their troops were a mixed bag. On the other hand it was a catastrophic defeat for the Serbs and for the whole cause of eastern Christendom. Both of the Serbian princes, Uglješa and Vukašin, were killed in the battle and their men were slaughtered in such numbers that the river ran red with their blood.[36]

The battle on the Marica in 1371 had perhaps more far-reaching consequences than any other Turkish victory before 1453. The gateway to Macedonia, to Serbia, to Greece was now open to the Turks. The surviving Serbian princes, among them Vukašin's son Marko, were now bound as vassals to their Turkish masters, forced to pay tribute and to fight alongside them with their feudal levies when called upon to do so. The pattern was set of Christian vassalage to the Turks. Marko Kraljević was allowed to reign over his little kingdom of Prilep. He became the most storied hero of all Serbian folklore, the Odysseus or the Digenis Akrites of Balkan Legend. He reappeared to lead the Serbian army when they expelled the Turks from Prilep in 1912. But Marko was really a Turkish vassal dependent for his survival on fighting for, rather than against, his nation's enemies. After 1371 the same was soon to be the case with other Christian princes in the Balkans, and even with the Byzantine Emperor himself.[37]

The Emperor arrived back in Constantinople by 28 October, almost exactly a month after the battle on the Marica. The significance of the event had by then made itself felt. Even if there had been any prospect of a crusading army coming from the west in the Emperor's wake it would now have had to fight its way through miles of enemy territory. The city of Constantinople was already all but cut off from western Europe by land. The tense situation and the uncertainty in the capital seem to be reflected in the tantalizing statement of a Byzantine chronicler that the Emperor John V ordered a number of arrests to be made as soon as he arrived. Those arrested were all persons of distinction, some former partisans of the Cantacuzene dynasty. It seems likely that they had also encouraged the Emperor's son Andronikos to defy his father's commands. Andronikos himself was very soon to fall out of favour.[38]

The only Byzantine leader who reaped any advantage from the battle of the Marica was the Emperor's younger son Manuel, who had returned to Thessalonica from Venice. Manuel seized the moment of the defeat and death of John Uglješa to occupy the city of Serres in November 1371 and to recover some long-lost ground in the district which had been held by the Serbs since 1345. The Turks were quick to retaliate. They laid siege to Serres and attacked Thessalonica also in April 1372. But for the time being they were driven off. Manuel, confirmed in possession of his appanage by imperial decree, showed more courage than his father. Braving the displeasure and hostility of the Church, he did what John V had failed to do four years before by laying his hands on ecclesiastical property. Half of the monastic estates in his principality were appropriated for use as soldiers' land, and the monks found themselves deprived of their many immunities and subject to payment of taxes on their pastures and produce to help pay for their defence.[39] It may well have been this bold and unprecedented measure which prompted Nicholas Kabasilas, himself a Thessalonian, to compose his well known discourse against those who presumed to expropriate for Caesar's purposes that which belonged to God.[40]

Barely a year elapsed after his return to Constantinople before the Emperor John V bowed to what he now believed to be the inevitable and made his peace with Murad and the Osmanlis. Only the historian Chalkokondyles, writing in the fifteenth century, speaks of a formal treaty between Emperor and Sultan in 1372-3. The meagre evidence of the sources renders it difficult to be certain or clear about the Emperor's motives. Various reasons have been suggested. Pope Gregory XI, who succeeded Urban V in January 1371, had toyed with the idea of holding a summit conference at Thebes early in 1372 to see what could be done about organizing collective resistance on Greek soil. But nothing had come of it. The Emperor had been led to despair of any practical help ever coming from the west for all the sacrifices he had made. The only alternative was to seek peace with the enemy. Perhaps it was in his mind to forestall the intrigues of his son Andronikos with the Turks. Perhaps it was a simple case of being unable to beat them and therefore joining them. But it is conceivable that John V felt that Murad was the only person who could exercise proper control over the multifarious bands of Turks in Thrace and Macedonia.[41]

Murad, who now liked to be known as Sultan, knew that he held the upper hand. There was no question of a personal understanding between Greek and Turk such as had existed between John Cantacuzene and Orchan. The relationship was defined by Murad as being that between a vassal and his lord, and by early 1373 John V was to be found at the Sultan's camp in Asia Minor fighting for a master to whom he was now bound to pay tribute. Byzantium was rapidly becoming a vassal state of the Turks. By 1374, if not sooner, the Pope and the Venetians were aware that the Emperor, though now a Catholic prince, was a party to what the Pope described as 'an impious alliance' with the infidel.[42]

While he was away from the capital John V again left his son Andronikos IV in charge. But this time Andronikos expressed his defiance and discontent in open rebellion. The circumstances give much food for thought about relationships between Byzantines and Turks at this time. The Sultan Murad also had a disgruntled son called Saudži Čelebi who turned against his father. Early in May 1373 Andronikos abandoned his charge in Constantinople to join forces with the Turkish rebel, who was supported by a crowd of Greek and Turkish adherents, and for a short while the 'impious alliance' of Christian and infidel was given a new meaning by the younger generation. John V managed to make his son surrender by the end of May. But Saudži was not brought to heel by his father until the end of September 1373. The Sultan was furious at this example of insubordination. He had his own son blinded and cruelly murdered and insisted that John V should put out the eyes of Andronikos and of his infant son John. Such inhumanity was not to the Emperor's taste, but he had no choice. Andronikos and his son, the future John VII, were blinded, though the operation was so performed that both retained or regained their sight to a greater or lesser degree. But they were held as prisoners in Constantinople, and the Emperor now at last made it quite clear that Andronikos had risked his father's displeasure once too often. He was formally disinherited, and on 25 September 1373 his younger brother Manuel, summoned from Thessalonica, was crowned as Emperor and heir-presumptive.[43]

The truth of this curious joint rebellion of sons against fathers lies buried in the confused accounts of the fifteenth-century historians. But its consequences gave new scope for the Turkish and Italian enemies of Byzantium to achieve their objects by fostering the feuds and jealousies between the members of the Byzantine family of Palaiologos. Andronikos IV and his son John VII lived to see their way, however blindly, to stage yet more determined rebellions; and the Turks, as well as the Genoese and the Venetians, found it profitable to encourage a state of perennial civil conflict among those whom they wished to conquer or exploit. In October 1374 a delegation from Pope Gregory XI arrived in Constantinople to outline yet again a plan for a crusade which would be joined by the Knights Hospitallers, by Louis of Hungary, by Venice, Genoa and the Kingdom of Sicily. The project was foredoomed to failure. The rulers of Hungary and Sicily seem not even to have answered the Pope's appeal, while the Italian republics were already sparring with each other in preparation for the Venetian-Genoese war that was to occupy all their attentions for close on ten years. In December an envoy from Constantinople had to explain the true situation to the Pope. The Byzantine Emperor had been driven to accepting the terms of the Turks and to putting out the eyes of his own son and grandson. These were the harsh realities. It was idle for the Pope to repeat his warning that salvation could only come if all the Byzantines were to join the communion of the Roman Church.[44]

The bone of contention between Venice and Genoa was the island of Tenedos. John V had promised to cede it to Venice in 1370. In March 1376 ten Venetian ships sailed into Constantinople to conclude the deal. The possession of Tenedos would have meant much to Venice and the terms were accordingly generous. The Emperor was to receive a further 30,000 ducats as well as the Byzantine crown jewels. The Greek inhabitants of the island would remain under the jurisdiction of the Patriarch of Constantinople and the Emperor's standard would continue to fly alongside that of St Mark. The Genoese at Galata quickly discovered what was afoot and took action to prevent it. In July they engineered the escape from prison of Andronikos IV. He was whisked over to Galata. From there he made contact with Murad who lent him a force of cavalry and infantry. Some say that the Tsar of Bulgaria John Šišman III, and the Serbian prince Marko Kraljević also gave Andronikos some encouragement. But it was to the Genoese and to the Turks that he was most deeply indebted. With their active help he laid siege to Constantinople. On 12 August 1376 he fought his way into the city, arrested his father the Emperor and his two brothers Manuel and Theodore and threw them all into prison. Less than a fortnight later he assigned the island of Tenedos to his benefactors, the Genoese.[45]

Andronikos was now master of Constantinople and Emperor in his own right. He had successfully defied the convention that one who had been blinded could never become Emperor. Indeed the Genoese had given him medical treatment which had alleviated much of his disability. He appointed his own Patriarch, Makarios, who placed the imperial crown on his head on 18 October 1377. His little son was crowned as the co-Emperor John VII. It is possible to discern some consistency of purpose in the machinations of Andronikos IV other than a crude lust for power and an ingrained bitterness against his father. He mistrusted the Venetians. He had refused to make over Tenedos to them six years before. He was against bringing the colonial interests of Venice, who already dominated the western Aegean and the Ionian islands, any nearer to Constantinople. He made a point of arresting a number of Venetian merchants in the city and appropriating their property. Perhaps he was right. But to accomplish his *coup d'état* Andronikos had put himself heavily in debt not only to the Genoese but also to the Osmanlis. Both parties now expected their reward.

For the Genoese the reward was to be the disputed island of Tenedos. They sent an expedition to take it over. But the Byzantine governor and his garrison, loyal to John V, would not surrender their charge, and the Venetians, seeing the need for prompt action if they were not to lose it altogether, occupied the island with the co-operation of its governor in October 1376. Demetrios Kydones, who was in Constantinople at the time and who refused to have anything to do with the rebel Andronikos, vividly describes the situation in one of his letters. 'The Emperor', he writes, 'promised Tenedos to the Genoese when he was with them, after his escape from prison. But the Venetians have forestalled him by seizing the island; and now, having fortified it and its citadel with walls, provisions, men, arms and everything that makes a fortress impregnable, they have left a garrison there and gone home. They expect to come back in the spring with a great number of ships. But the Genoese cannot rest while their rivals occupy the island of Tenedos, for they feel that they will be deprived of access to the sea and of their maritime trading profits, a prospect more awful for them than if they were to be forcibly ejected from their own country. Wherefore they are planning to blockade the island with ships and engines of war of all kinds; and they are obliging the Emperor to co-operate with them, for otherwise, so they say, he would connive at the robbery of the Venetians and take their side. To clear himself of this suspicion the Emperor has agreed to be their ally, and now, for all our poverty, he is making ready weapons and munitions and ships and is compelled to hire soldiers, a thing which is for him more difficult than flying. But even these evils, grave though they are, can be accounted tolerable when compared to our domestic ills. For the Emperor's father and brothers are still held in prisons from which there is no escape.... Each evening men expect the dawn to bring some new development, and every day they fear the night will bring some terrible calamity. It is like a storm at sea where we are all in danger of going down.'[46]

The squabble over the possession of Tenedos, in which the Byzantines had now become unwillingly involved, proved to be the starting-point of a war on a much larger scale between Venice and Genoa. A Venetian fleet from the island attacked Constantinople in July 1377, and in November Andronikos IV was obliged to co-operate with the Genoese in an act of retaliation. The Venetians held on to Tenedos, however, and contrived to capture Phokaia from their rivals and to plunder the Genoese colony of Chios in 1378. But the theatre of war then shifted to Italian waters, where each side fought itself to exhaustion by 1381.[47]

The reward which the Osmanlis exacted for their services to Andronikos was the surrender of Gallipoli. It was a predictable demand. Murad had made it in 1371 and possibly several times since. If the Turkish conquests in Thrace and Macedonia were to be linked to the Turkish territories in Asia Minor under his rule then the port of Gallipoli must be his. Andronikos had no hesitation in relinquishing it. He went in person to see Murad to arrange the transfer, and he agreed to pay a yearly tribute and to ensure that Turks living within the walls of Constantinople should be guaranteed protection. By 1377, if not sooner, Gallipoli was once again in Turkish control after some ten years of Byzantine occupation. Murad celebrated the occasion by crossing over to Thrace and taking formal possession of the city of Adrianople. It was thenceforth to be the first European capital of the Ottoman Empire. 'The Turks', wrote Kydones, 'command everything and we must submit to them in everything or pay the penalty for our disobedience. To such a height of power have they risen, to such a depth of servitude have we fallen.'[48]

The brief reign of Andronikos IV is not well documented. But it could hardly last. Andronikos could do no more to control the course of events than his father. The politics, the security, the economy, even the food supply of Constantinople were now at the mercy of the Italian republics and the Ottoman Turks; and the members of the imperial family who held or aspired to hold the throne were little more than the agents of Italian avarice or Ottoman imperialism. For nearly three years after 1376 there were in fact no less than four crowned Emperors living in the capital city, Andronikos IV and his son John VII, and John V and his son Manuel. But two of them were in prison. The later Greek historians hint that Murad advised Andronikos to put them out of the way, but this seems unlikely. It was to the Sultan's interest that there should be more than one contender for the Byzantine throne. Andronikos could neither murder his father and brothers nor set them free. As it was, the Venetians seem to have made more than one attempt to effect the release of John V. Manuel in later years was to recall the sufferings that they endured in the dungeons of the tower of Anemas from which, at the time, they saw no hope of ever gaining their freedom.[49]

The moment came, however, about June 1379. The circumstances are obscure, but whether through the agency of the Venetians or on their own initiative, John V and his sons escaped and crossed over by boat to Skutari, whence they made their way straight to the court of Murad. There was really nowhere else that they could go. The Sultan must have enjoyed being thus put in the position of kingmaker. The story goes that he consulted the opinion of the people of Constantinople by messenger. But the agreement that John V made with him was sufficient to swing the balance of Turkish support in his favour and away from his son Andronikos. For John promised, when restored to his throne, to pay a larger tribute to the Sultan than ever before, to provide auxiliary troops whenever required, and also, it appears, to hand over the last remaining Byzantine possession in Asia Minor, the city of Philadelphia. The Venetians, who had their own reasons for wishing to be rid of Andronikos IV, lent ships for an assault on Constantinople. The Turks supplied an army; and on 1 July 1379 John V and Manuel re-entered the city. There was strong opposition from a garrison of Genoese soldiers. But Andronikos made his escape across to Galata, taking with him as hostages his mother the Empress Helena, her sisters and her now elderly father John Cantacuzene.[50]

But the matter was not yet settled. For more than a year there was a civil war of a new kind, fought between the cities of Constantinople and Galata. John V was supported by the Venetians and the Turks on one side of the Golden Horn; Andronikos was supported by the Genoese on the other. John and his allies laid siege to the fortress of Galata. The defenders were short of food, disease broke out, and the imperial hostages suffered much in their imprisonment. The fighting went on until April 1381, and in May the contending parties reached a settlement. Andronikos was to be forgiven and reinstated as heir to the throne. The succession was to pass through him to his son John

VII. He was granted an appanage in Thrace with his headquarters at Selymbria. There was little else left for him to govern in the neighbourhood of Constantinople. This arrangement was more or less forced upon John V. The moral victory had gone to Andronikos. But the settlement was made at the expense of his younger brother Manuel who had been led to expect the imperial inheritance for some ten years. History does not record Manuel's reaction nor what his compensation was to be. He seems to have been in Constantinople in the summer of 1382. But shortly thereafter he left the capital in circumstances that suggest haste and secrecy, and before the end of the year he was back in Thessalonica, the city that he had governed and defended before. This time, however, he was to reign there as Emperor in his own right, no longer as the loyal son and unquestioning agent of his father's policy towards the Turks. For almost five years Manuel struggled to make Thessalonica a new rallying-point of resistance and the capital of a restored Byzantine province in Macedonia and Thessaly.[51]

The only other hopeful outcome of the settlement of 1381 was the appointment of John V's fourth son Theodore Palaiologos as governor or Despot of the Morea. Manuel Cantacuzene, who had administered the Byzantine territories in southern Greece with growing success since 1349, had died in April 1380. He had no children to succeed him. His elder brother, the former Emperor Matthew Cantacuzene, seems to have taken over his duties for a while. But clearly the moment had come for the Emperor in Constantinople to reassert the prescriptive right of the house of Palaiologos to govern this important outpost of the Empire, which had for so long been under the authority of the Cantacuzenes. He therefore nominated his son Theodore to proceed to Mistra and take over the Despotate of the Morea. The aged John Cantacuzene, who had just been released from prison in Galata, seems to have approved of the arrangement, and he himself elected to take the opportunity of getting away from the unhealthy atmosphere of Constantinople to live out his last years in the relatively restful air of the Morea. The old emperor and monk died at Mistra on 15 June 1383 at the age of 78. But the arrangement was bitterly resented by one of his grandchildren, a son of Matthew Cantacuzene, who regarded the Morea as an appanage of his family. For nearly two years he enlisted the help of the Turks as well as the Latin princes of Greece to fight for his rights against the newly-appointed Despot. Not until 1383 was Theodore Palaiologos firmly established as governor at Mistra.[52]

On paper therefore it seemed that by 1383 the fragments of the Byzantine Empire were once again held by members of the same ruling family. John V reigned as Emperor in Constantinople. His son Andronikos IV and his grandson John VII both with the name of Emperor reigned over the northern coast of the Sea of Marmora. His other sons Manuel and Theodore reigned respectively as Emperor in Thessalonica and as Despot in the Morea. But each was to a greater or lesser degree a puppet of the Italians and the Turks who expected to gain more by encouraging them to quarrel than by helping them to co-operate. The Italians had their hands free again to intervene in Byzantine politics. The long conflict between Venice and Genoa which had erupted over the possession of Tenedos finally petered out in 1381. A treaty was arranged at Turin in August of that year through the good offices of Count Amadeo of Savoy. The Venetian fortifications on Tenedos were to be demolished and the island was declared to be neutral ground under the supervision of Amadeo. In expiation for their behaviour the Venetians and the Genoese alike promised to work for the conversion of the Byzantine Emperor and his people to the Catholic faith and to do their best to foster the reconciliation between John V and his son Andronikos.

Two Genoese ambassadors arrived in Constantinople in the summer of 1382 to see what could be done to further these high ideals. Long discussions took place. They culminated in a formal treaty signed in the palace on 2 November. It is an instructive document. The contracting parties were the two Emperors John and Andronikos on the one hand and the Genoese of Galata on the other. John V undertook not to make war on Andronikos or his son and to respect their territorial rights in Thrace, and he promised to come to their aid against all aggressors except Murad and the Turks. The Genoese for their part agreed to support John V in case of attack by his son; and they promised to come to his aid against all aggressors except Murad and the Turks. The terms of this treaty put the case in a nutshell. Both sides were obliged to make exception of the Sultan Murad, for both sides were in some sense dependent upon the Sultan for their survival; and the two Emperors, being as they were the sworn vassals of Murad, had forfeited their independence of action. The treaty made no mention of Manuel Palaiologos. But it was while it was being negotiated that Manuel slipped away to Thessalonica to take upon himself the initiative that his father had long since resigned. It was a heroic gesture, but it came too late. The surrender of Gallipoli had ensured that the initiative lay no longer with any of the claimants to the Byzantine crown but with the Sultan.[53]

All through the years of the reign of Andronikos IV and of the civil war between Constantinople and Galata, from 1376 to 1381, Murad was free to consolidate the previous Turkish conquests on European soil. This may be seen as the time when the foundations were truly laid of the Ottoman Empire in the Balkans. Murad had spent the early years of his reign mainly in establishing and extending his authority over the other Turkish princes in Anatolia. This he had done as much by alliance as by conquest. His dominions had come to include Ankara as well as the harbour of Attalia (Antalya) in the south of Asia Minor, and he had made peace with the emirs of the Germiyan and of the still more powerful Karamans by diplomatic marriages. The Ottoman state began to assume the character of a well-organized oriental despotism. Those who were conquered or surrendered, whether in Asia or in Europe, were assimilated into the Osmanli people, Greeks, Slavs and Turks alike. The Balkans were deliberately populated with Turkish immigrants and colonists, and the newly-won territory was divided into fiefs (ziamet or timar) among the soldiers, or into feudal estates (khāss) among the officers. Murad was also responsible for a radical development in the shape of the Ottoman army. The infantry was henceforth to be reinforced by the recruitment of prisoners of war, one-fifth of whom constituted a special regiment assigned to the Sultan's personal use. This private army of the Sultan represented the first step towards the formation of the janissaries or 'new troops' (yeni cheri), young men between the ages of 15 and 20, who were later to play such an important role in the history of the Ottoman Empire.[54]

Murad's generals had for the most part been brought up in the ghazi tradition and regarded their campaigns in Europe as holy wars against the infidel. Outstanding among them were Ghazi Evrenos Beg and Murad's vizier Hayr ad-Din Pasha, the 'Torch of the Faith'. But after the battle on the Marica in 1371 the Sultan also had at his disposal numerous levies of troops that he could summon from his Christian vassals in Serbia, Bulgaria or Constantinople. Murad's methods of conquest and assimilation were so thorough and so effective that with the best will in the world it would have been immensely difficult for the Christian peoples of the Balkans to unite against him. But the will was not there. Demetrios Kydones and others lamented the comfort given to the enemy by Greek collaborators, sympathizers and racketeers, many of whom did profitable business with the Turkish quartermasters and would even inform on cases of anti-Turkish activities among their own people. It was well known too that the law of Islam allowed for the plunder and destruction of a city only if the inhabitants put up resistance. Surrender therefore had much to commend it. Many property owners in Thrace and Macedonia accepted conversion to the Muslim faith as the safest means of preserving their wealth. But many of the country folk who had no property left to preserve fled in terror to the Greek islands.[55]

From his administrative and strategic headquarters at Adrianople, Murad was able to co-ordinate and direct the operations of his armies which penetrated into what remained of Byzantine Macedonia, Serbia and Bulgaria. They advanced systematically and in good order, following the lines of the river valleys. In Serbia, Uroš V, the son of Dušan who claimed the title of Emperor, died in December 1371, and with him died the last vestige of centralized government in the Serbian territories. A struggle for power broke out among those Serbian nobles who were not yet vassals of the Sultan. The work of conquest was made easier for the Turks. Coming up the Vardar valley they entered Ochrida and Prilep in 1380 and from there moved into Albania. At much the same time other Turkish troops were advancing up the Marica valley and beyond. Sofia fell in 1385 and Niš in 1386. The doors were closing even tighter on the overland routes from western Europe to Byzantium. Murad considered that the city of Constantinople was already virtually under his control. Its conquest could wait. He may have been displeased to learn that the agreement between John V and Andronikos had broken down early in 1385 when Andronikos tried to enlarge his appanage by appropriating a fortress near Constantinople. It is no great credit to either of them that father and son were able to muster enough soldiers to fight a pitched battle. Doubtless it would not have been the last. But on 28 June of the same year Andronikos IV died after an illness.[56]

As Demetrios Kydones wrote at the time, this sorry episode would never have occurred if John V's other son Manuel had been in the capital. It was this very squandering of the Empire's resources in civil war which had driven Manuel to set himself up independently at Thessalonica to organize resistance against the real enemy. His presence there was annoying to the Sultan, who saw Manuel as one who had broken the oath of vassalage. Thessalonica was a strongly fortified city with access to reinforcements and supplies from the sea. This made it difficult for the Turks to encircle since they had so few ships. But Murad knew that Manuel's action did not have the approval of his father in Constantinople. In 1383 he ordered his general Hayr ad-Din Pasha to capture Thessalonica and bring the rebel to him. Even for so experienced and successful a soldier it was not an easy assignment. The first step was the conquest of Serres which Manuel had taken over as long ago 1371. It lay on the route to Thessalonica, and it fell after a siege on 19 September 1383. The Turks plundered the city and carried off many of its citizens, including the bishop, to slavery. Soon afterwards they appeared outside the walls of Thessalonica. From then onwards, until April 1387, the city was under siege by Hayr ad-Din.[57]

Kydones sent a letter of comfort to his friend Manuel reminding him that many great cities such as Babylon, Rome and Athens had in the past closed their gates to barbarians and passively witnessed the devastation of their fields and the ruin of their markets. History, he wrote, was full of cases of successful resistance to long and troublesome sieges.[58] It is sadly evident, however, that the Emperor Manuel did not command the whole-hearted support of the citizens of Thessalonica in his heroic stand. Hayr ad-Din issued an ultimatum to them after he had captured Serres. They were given the choice of paying tribute to the Sultan or of being massacred. A few days later, on 26 October 1383, the Metropolitan of Thessalonica, Isidore Glabas, preached a sermon in the cathedral. It was the feast of St Demetrios, the patron of the city, who had so often in the past protected it from its enemies. The bishop warned his flock that their saint seemed slow to work a miracle again only because of the multiplicity of their sins. The Turkish ultimatum, to which he referred, had put them in a fearful dilemma, and he urged them all to respect and obey the defender and counsellor whom providence had appointed for them in the person of their Emperor Manuel. Manuel had already given his counsel to the people after receiving the ultimatum. He had summoned them all to an assembly in the city square and regaled them with a long speech urging them to hold out, to defy the threats of the barbarian, and to hope that an honourable peace treaty might yet be negotiated. As a literary and rhetorical *tour de force* Manuel's speech is noteworthy. He was so pleased with it himself that he sent a copy to Kydones in Constantinople. But the Thessalonians were not so impressed. Many of them criticized his policy; some publicly declared their preference for surrendering to the Turks.[59]

The outside world took little notice of the fate of Thessalonica in these crucial years. King Louis the Great of Hungary, who might have been concerned, had died in 1382. The Venetians, to whom Manuel applied for military and economic help in 1385, rejected his appeal. The Roman Pope, Urban VI, to whom he sent an embassy in the same year, made the diplomatic blunder of posting a legate to Constantinople where he was coldly received by Manuel's father, who continued to denounce his son as a rebel. The legate found his way to Thessalonica in 1386, but all he had to offer was the spiritual benefit of union with the Roman Church. There is, however, some evidence of collaboration between Manuel and his brother Theodore in Mistra; and the Greek or Greco-Serbian world of Macedonia and northern Greece was naturally interested in his activities. The province of Thessaly, whose people had always looked to Thessalonica as their metropolis, had by 1381 reverted from Serbian to Greek rule. Symeon Uroš, Dušan's half-brother who had reigned at Trikkala as Emperor, had died about 1371, leaving his little realm to his son John. John Uroš, however, soon renounced his throne in favour of the monastic life; and, as the monk Joasaph, he became the father-figure of the largest of the monasteries of the Meteora, whose immense rocks tower above the nothern end of the plain of Thessaly. His place was taken by a Greek called Alexios Angelos, to whom he was related by marriage. Alexios sported the Byzantine title of Caesar. The chances are that it was bestowed on him by the Emperor Manuel, to whom he certainly owed allegiance at Thessalonica in the years between 1382 and 1387. In Epiros, across the Pindos mountains from Thessaly, the Serbian Despot Thomas Preljubović who had inherited this remnant of Dušan's empire in 1367, also recognized the Emperor Manuel as his lord and took care to have his Byzantine title of Despot ratified at Thessalonica. Manuel therefore exercised some jurisdiction over Epiros and Thessaly and might have reunited northern Greece under Byzantine rule.[60]

But it was not to be. In his own reflexions on the matter Manuel laid most of the blame for his failure on the selfish, quarrelsome, treacherous and obstructive citizens of Thessalonica. On 6 April 1387 he left them to their own devices and sailed away from the city. On 9 April the Turkish soldiers marched in through the gates which had in the end been freely opened to them. The inhabitants were therefore spared the horrors of massacre and pillage with which they had been threatened. Manuel and his followers made their way first to Lesbos, where his cousin Francesco Gattilusio only reluctantly entertained him, and thence to the deserted island of Tenedos. In the summer of the year he was to be found at the camp of the Sultan Murad at Brusa. As with his father when he escaped from Constantinople in

1379, there was nowhere else that he could go. The Sultan held the whip hand. He might have vented his wrath on Manuel, but he received him as a guest and not as an abject suppliant. The evidence suggests that he had invited him to Brusa. Now that Thessalonica had submitted almost without bloodshed, Manuel must be persuaded of the advantages of accepting the status of a vassal. Having reconciled him to this idea, Murad despatched him to his father in Constantinople. John V could hardly now refuse to have him. But as a form of chastisement he relegated Manuel to exile or retirement on the island of Lemnos, and there for some time he languished in disagreeable inactivity. Demetrios Kydones tried to console him by writing to say that, in spite of appearances, his father still intended that Manuel should succeed him on the throne.[61]

In the last years of Manuel's reign in Thessalonica there had in fact been a lull in the process of Turkish conquest elsewhere in the Balkans. In 1386, after the capture of Niš, Murad had been forced to return to Asia Minor to defend his frontiers there against an invasion by the emir of Karamania. This might have been the occasion for a united counter-attack by the Christian rulers of eastern Europe. But the Byzantine Emperors and other princes who were the vassals of the Sultan made no move. Once again the only decisive effort was made by the Serbs. It was led by prince Lazar, who had emerged as the dominant figure in Serbia after 1371. Lazar organized a coalition of his Serbian colleagues, notably Vuk Branković, ruler of the district of Kossovo. It was joined by the prince of Bosnia, Tvrtko I, whose lands had not yet felt the full shock of invasion by the Turks. They scored some encouraging victories in 1386 and again in 1388, when a Turkish attack on Bosnia was driven back. The news inspired symptoms of a more general revolt in the Balkans. The Bulgars felt emboldened to proclaim their independence from the Sultan; and the Wallachians across the Danube from Bulgaria were ready to fight.

Murad dealt with the problem in characteristically methodical fashion. The Bulgars were the first to be punished. Early in 1389 Trnovo and then Nicopolis were forced to submit, and the whole country up to the Danube was systematically overrun by Turkish troops. The Bulgarian Tsar John Šišman was reduced once more to being the Sultan's vassal, though he was allowed to retain a corner of his kingdom for the time being. Murad had meanwhile arrived in Europe himself to lead his combined armies to Serbia. Their objective was Kossovo, the headquarters of Vuk Branković. The Sultan demanded levies and contingents from his various Christian vassals

299

along his route, among them being the Serbian princes Constantine of Kjustendil and Constantine Dragaš, who held Serres as a fief. Lazar with his Serbian and Bosnian troops met the Turks on the plain of Kossovo, the field of blackbirds, on 15 June 1389.

The battle of Kossovo very soon became a part of Serbian national folklore and heroic legend. It is difficult now to sort out the facts from the fantasies spun around the event. But it is clear that Lazar and his allies were in disagreement on the very eve of the battle; there was treachery in their ranks, there was gloom and despair among their troops. One can scarcely believe the conflicting accounts given by the Serbian and Turkish sources of the numbers on either side. But it is a fair assumption that the Serbs and their allies were outnumbered; and it is certain that they were outclassed by their opponents in discipline, confidence and morale. To begin with, however, they seemed to have luck on their side. Lazar broke through the Ottoman lines. But his advance was held by Murad's son Bajezid; and at the critical moment, so the story goes, Vuk Branković deserted the field with about 12,000 men. The most sensational episode was the death of Murad himself killed in the heat of the battle. One version had it that he was murdered by Lazar's son-in-law Miloš Kobilić who was intent on clearing himself of a charge of treachery. Posing as a deserter of noble rank, he is said to have been led into the Sultan's presence and then to have plunged a dagger into his heart. There are other versions of the event. But the fact is established : Murad was killed at Kossovo. It made little difference, for the command of his armies was immediately assumed by his son Bajezid, who led them on to a complete and devastating victory.

Lazar was captured and executed. He was not the only casualty. Serbian legend at least set the number of their dead at 77,000 as against 12,000 of the Turks. But of those many must have been the victims of the massacre of Serbian nobles and people that Bajezid ordered after the battle. Lazar's ally Tvrtko of Bosnia escaped before the final catastrophe, and his report of the murder of Murad had some strange consequences in western Europe. The death of the great Sultan, it was supposed, must surely signify a great Christian victory over the infidel. When the first news from Kossovo reached Florence the people assembled for a *Te Deum* in their cathedral. In Paris King Charles VI gave thanks to God in the church of Notre Dame; and Philippe de Mézières solemnly recorded the death not only of Murad but also of his son, and proclaimed the total defeat of the Turkish army.[62]

The record was soon to be rectified when the whole truth became known. For the Serbians the outcome was immediately clear. The battle of Kossovo was their last defiant gesture as a nation. It closed the final chapter of the heroic annals of their history which had opened with the accession of Stephen Dušan half a century before. It was the complement to the battle fought and lost on the Marica river in 1371. It could never be repeated. The new Sultan Bajezid made quite sure of this. The Serbian nobles that were allowed to survive had each and singly to swear their loyalty to him as vassals, to pay him tribute, and to do military service for him. On these terms Lazar's son Stephen Lazarević (1389-1427) was taken to be the successor to Serbia, and these terms Lazarević conscientiously fulfilled to the end of his days. His mother Milica did much to mitigate the horrors of the Turkish conquest and gave her youngest daughter Olivera in marriage to Bajezid. The whole country was now subject to the Turks. Every non-Muslim inhabitant was bound to pay the Ottoman capitation tax or *haradj* for the privilege of his existence. This imposition was quickly extended to all the Balkan and Byzantine territories under Turkish control. No exemptions were made, whatever immunities an individual or an institution might have enjoyed under the previous dispensation. Landowners who employed large numbers of peasants were hit particularly hard, for they were held responsible for any defaulters. The church and especially the monasteries which had landed estates suffered greatly. The monastries of Mount Athos had fallen directly under the Sultan's jurisdiction in 1386. The monks had prudently made their submission while the going was good. Their autonomy was respected. But they had to pay the *haradj* not only on their own account but also on account of the landed property which they owned far beyond the confines of the Holy Mountain. If they defaulted the ruler of the country in which that property was situated was obliged to pay up on their account.[63]

The Serbian defeat at Kossovo completed the isolation of Constantinople from the west. Resistance to the Turks was now more effectively shattered in Europe than it was in Asia Minor. But the new Sultan Bajezid was determined to make his word law throughout Anatolia as well. His policy was to incorporate the remaining Turkish principalities into his dominions not, as his father had done, by diplomacy and alliances, but by outright conquest. Bajezid engaged in war against the Karamans and deliberately dispossessed the emirs of Aydin, Saruchan, Menteshe and others, making their lands subject to his empire. If Murad had been the architect of the Ottoman Empire, Bajezid was its first Emperor. Murad had adopted the title of Sultan. Bajezid assumed the name of legitimate 'Sultan of Rum', the ancient title held by the Seljuq princes of Asia Minor. For him the conquest of Constantinople was a logical and pre-ordained eventuality. The murder of Murad, which had caused many Christians to give thanks to God, had left the way open for a Turkish ruler whose ideas were still closer to those of an oriental potentate, and who meditated on the conquest not simply of the Balkans but of the whole Christian world. Bajezid had the reputation of moving like lightning from one spot to another, which earned him the nickname of Yildirim or Thunderbolt. The Byzantines were to discover that the name described not only the speed of his actions but also his temper.[64]

Bajezid was even more adept and ruthless than his father at weakening Byzantine resistance by setting one member of the ruling family against another. The death of Andronikos IV in 1385 had eliminated one candidate for the throne. But his son John VII, who had been constitutionally proclaimed and crowned as Emperor, had been brought up to distrust his grandfather John V and his uncle Manuel. The Genoese seem to have befriended him as they had befriended his father, and about 1389 he was actually in Genoa soliciting support for his claim to the throne. But the Sultan Bajezid was a more powerful friend and evidently regarded John VII as more useful to his own purposes than Manuel. When John returned from Genoa early in 1390 Bajezid provided him with the necessary troops to force his way into Constantinople and drive out his grandfather. The Sultan posed as the defender of the legitimate Byzantine Emperor, and in April 1390 John VII was enabled to seize the palace. A Russian archimandrite, Ignatios of Smolensk, happened to be on pilgrimage in Constantinople at the time and has left a first hand account of these exciting days. He observed that the crowds that lined the streets to shout long life to the son of the Emperor Andronikos did so mainly from fear of the drawn swords of the soldiers.[65] John's triumph was not complete, however, for his grandfather barricaded himself into the fortress by the Golden Gate of the city and from there made contact with his son Manuel. Otherwise, for about four months, John VII was in control of Constantinople. Bajezid had played his first trick skilfully. The Venetians expected that he himself would arrive any day to take possession of the city, and they gave orders to their agents to act accordingly. But in the summer Manuel answered his father's call and sailed to his rescue with a small fleet, including two ships supplied by the Knights of Rhodes. At the third attempt he managed to reinstate his father as Emperor. John VII escaped and fled to the Sultan, who appointed him to return to his charge in Selymbria, though now as a Turkish vassal.[66]

This was not what Bajezid had wanted. John V and Manuel had to pay dearly for upsetting his plans. The dust had hardly settled in the palace when they were faced with a number of peremptory demands from the Sultan. The customary tribute was to be paid to him at once, and Manuel was to proceed as a hostage to Anatolia, taking soldiers to help in the campaign for the aggrandisement of the Ottoman Empire in Asia. By the time Manuel reached the Sultan's camp, his nephew John VII had received a like summons. Two of the rival claimants to the Byzantine throne were thus safely under the Sultan's wing. In the autumn of 1390 both were required to assist him in laying siege to Philadelphia, the one Byzantine city in Anatolia which had consistently refused to surrender and which had remained a Greek island in the surrounding sea of Turkish conquest. The fifteenth-century historian Chalkokondyles ruefully or cynically observed that the two 'Emperors of the Hellenes' distinguished themselves by being the first over the walls when the last surviving Hellenic city in Asia was taken by the infidel.[67] They had no option. Shortly afterwards the Sultan delivered an ultimatum to the old Emperor John V in Constantinople. He too had no option but to obey. Anxious that the Turks would assault the city, John had strengthened the fortifications of the castle by the Golden Gate. He was now commanded to demolish them. If he disobeyed his son Manuel would be imprisoned and blinded.[68]

The shocks and humiliations inflicted upon him by Bajezid took their toll of John V's declining strength. He shut himself up in his palace and died on 16 February 1391. He was not yet 60 years of age. It is hard to make a satisfactory assessment of John V's career. No historian in his own time felt bold enough to describe the process of disintegration of his world and society. Nor did John, like his father-in-law, commit any of his own thoughts to writing. As an Emperor, therefore, he is known only from the bald statements or ritual flatteries of official documents, from the sparing entries in a few annals and chronicles, and from the letters of several of his contemporaries and friends, particularly Demetrios Kydones. The later Greek historians accuse him of having led a dissolute youth and a lecherous old age. The latter charge at least seems to be unfounded. He had, it is true, one illegitimate son. But Emperors more pious and more prudent than he had done the same. He suffered from gout. But it is not quite fair to say, as one modern historian has said, that 'gout and debauchery rather than grief and humiliation ended his ignoble life'.[69]

At the end of 1354 John V inherited a situation that called for the combined qualities of a Justinian and a Belisarius. But his inheritance had not come to him by chance. He had wanted to become sole Emperor, he had much popular support, and he was prepared to throw the Byzantine world into another civil war to fulfil his ambition. Thereafter, for the space of 37 years, no one succeeded in permanently unseating him from his throne. His son Andronikos won his favour rather than his wrath for trying to do so. His second son Manuel, on the other hand, who twice loyally rescued him from the consequences of his own follies, and who might have earned some gratitude for his brave stand at Thessalonica, got little thanks. His policies were too often dictated by circumstances or contrived on the spur of the moment. A greater or a better-informed statesman would never have set out for the court of Hungary on a sudden impulse and in the depth of winter; nor would he have gone out of his way to visit Venice without considering whether he had the money to get home again. The popes and princes of the western world whose friendship and help he hoped to obtain were not much impressed by such undignified proceedings. When they failed him, as they did, John turned to seeking an accommodation with the enemy. The defeat of the Serbs in 1371 drove him to the conclusion that appeasement was the only way left to deal with the Turks; and to give him his due he pursued this policy with unimaginative consistency for the remaining 20 years of his life.

But one may ask why there were no Byzantine soldiers fighting on the Serbian side at the Marica or, for that matter, at Kossovo 18 years later. All too frequently there seemed to be native troops or mercenaries available to fight on one side or the other in the petty squabbles for the throne between John V and his sons and grandson, or to provide auxiliaries for the Sultan's army. The answer must be that it was the senior Emperor who lacked the initiative and the courage to inspire a spirit of resistance in his people; nor had he the vision to apply his moral authority as the one true Orthodox Emperor to the task of organizing a collective will to survive among the Christians of the Balkans. He would have done well to take a leaf from the book of his Patriarchs Kallistos and Philotheos who had successfully reimposed the authority of the See of Constantinople over most of the once separatist Orthodox Churches of eastern Europe. Towards the end of his reign, when his hierarchy seem to have forgiven or forgotten his error of conversion to the Roman faith, John was given the chance to reassume effective leadership of the Byzantine Church. A comprehensive document was drawn up defining in detail the constitutional rights of the Emperor over the Church as defender of the faith. But John V could neither see nor grasp the opportunity that was there to unite the Orthodox Christian world in common defiance of the infidel. The hope of restoring the Byzantine Empire even in its European provinces was beyond the limits of his horizons. For him it was simply a matter of saving what could be saved without testing the recuperative powers of his own people; and for this purpose he had but two remedies: either to beg help from the west, or to beg mercy from the Turks. He was a small and mediocre man overwhelmed by the greatness and the tragedy of events. His wife Helena, daughter of the late Emperor and monk John Cantacuzene, survived him. She became a nun in the convent of Kyra Martha in Constantinople where her own mother Eirene and her sister Maria had retired. Her religious name was Hypomone, or Patience, a virtue which she had learnt to practise to perfection. She died at the end of 1396.[70]

NOTES

Modern works: The most important study of the long reign of John V Palaiologos remains that of O. Halecki, *Un Empereur de Byzance à Rome. Vingt ans de travail pour l'union des églises et pour la défense de l'Empire d'Orient, 1355-1375* (Warsaw, 1930). General accounts of the period from 1354 to 1391 may be found in: Ostrogorsky, *History*, 533-49; Bréhier, *Vie et Mort*, 365-79; Diehl, *L'Europe orientale*, 326-44.

1 Ostrogorsky, *History*, 523-5 and references; *CMH*, IV, 1, 537-40. There is an English translation of the Zakonik of Stephen Dušan by M. Burr, in *Slavonic and East European Review*, XXVIII (1949-50), 198-217, 516-39. Cf. Obolensky, *The Byzantine Commonwealth*, 253-6, 319-20.

2 On the mission of Peter Thomas to Serbia, see J. Smet, *The Life of Saint Peter Thomas by Philippe de Mézières* (Rome, 1954).

3 Cantacuzene's son-in-law Nikephoros seized the occasion of Dušan's death to return to his hereditary principality in Epiros. But he was killed fighting the Albanians in 1359. See Nicol, *Byzantine Family*, 131-2; R. Mihaljčić, 'La bataille d'Acheloos', *Zbornik filosofskog fakulteta*, XI (Belgrade, 1970), 271-6.

4 Cantacuzene, III, 314-15.

5 W. Miller, 'The Gattilusij of Lesbos (1355-1462)', in Miller, *Essays on the Latin Orient* (Cambridge, 1921), 313-52; G. T. Dennis, 'The Short Chronicle of Lesbos, 1355-1428', in *Lesbiaka*, V (1965), 3-24. P. Argenti, *The Occupation of Chios by the Genoese*, II (Cambridge, 1958), 173-7.

6 Halecki, *Empereur*, 47-8, R.-J. Loenertz, 'Démétrius Cydonès. I : De la naissance à l'année 1373', *OCP*, XXXVI (1970), 55-6.

7 Halecki, *Empereur*, 31f.; Ostrogorsky, 535. For editions of the text of John V's chrysobull, see Dölger, *Regesten*, V, no. 3052.

8 On Paul of Smyrna, see Halecki, 36-8; and especially J. Meyendorff, 'Projets de concile oecuménique en 1367', *DOP*, XIV (1960), 152-3.

9 Halecki, 53-9.

10 ed. J. Smet, *The Life of St Peter Thomas*, 74-80.

11 Halecki, 50-2.

12 Halecki, 60-73.

13 Gregoras, III, 504-9; Cantacuzene, III, 320-2.

14 Ostrogorsky, 536 and references. But cf. Irène Beldiceanu-Steinherr, 'La conquête d'Andrinople par les Turcs', *Travaux et Mémoires*, I (1965), 439-61.

15 Ostrogorsky, 537.

16 Chalkokondyles, I, 23 (ed. Darkó). Cf. Gibbons, *Foundation of the Ottoman Empire*, 122.

17 Cantacuzene, III, 360-3 (the 50th and last chapter of the last book of Cantacuzene's memoirs). Cf. Ostrogorsky, 537; Halecki, 77-8.

18 Halecki, 79-88; Runciman, *History of the Crusades*, III, 441-9.

19 Demetrios Kydones, in *PG*, CLIV, 1000, 1004.

20 Halecki, 111-37; Meyendorff, 'Projets de concile ...', 153-6; Gy. Moravcsik, 'Vizantijskie imperatory i ich posly v g. Buda', in Moravscik, *Studia Byzantina* (Amsterdam, 1967), 341-58.

21 On Amadeo of Savoy, see E. L. Cox, *The Green Count of Savoy: Amadeus VI and Transalpine Savoy in the Fourteenth Century* (Princeton, 1967). His crusade of 1366 is described by Halecki, 138-62; A. S. Atiya, *The Crusade in the Later Middle Ages* (London, 1938), 379-97.

Cf. P. Schreiner, *Studien zu den Brachea Chronika* (Munich, 1967), 145-51.

22 Demetrios Kydones, *De admittendo Latinorum subsidio*, in *PG*, CLIV, 961. Cf. Loenertz, in *OCP*, XXXVI (1970), 64.

23 Meyendorff, 'Projets de concile . . .', 170-7 (Greek text).

24 Meyendorff, 'Projets de concile . . .', 159. Cf. Nicol, 'Byzantine requests for an oecumenical council in the 14th century', *Annuarium Historiae Conciliorum*, I (1969), 89-91; Halecki, 152-4, 235f.

25 Halecki, 149-50, 158-62.

26 Halecki, 163-75.

27 The act of the synod of Constantinople declining to surrender any property is in *MM*, I, 506-7. It has been translated by P. Charanis, 'The Monastic Properties and the State in the Byzantine Empire', *DOP*, IV (1948), 115.

28 Halecki, 188-99.

29 Halecki, 199-212.

30 F. Thiriet, *Régestes des Délibérations du Sénat de Venise concernant la Romanie*, I (Paris-The Hague, 1958), nos 459, 461, 480, 482. Cf. Halecki, 222-7, 371-8.

31 See especially R.-J. Loenertz, 'Jean V Paléologue à Venise (1370-1371)', *REB*, XVI (1958), 217-32; J. Chrysostomides, 'John V Palaeologus in Venice (1370-71) and the Chronicle of Caroldo: a reinterpretation', *OCP*, XXXI (1965), 76-84. Cf. Ostrogorsky, 539-40.

32 Demetrios Kydones, *Correspondence*, ed. Loenertz, I, no. 37.

33 Demetrios Kydones, *De non reddenda Callipoli*, in *PG*, CLIV, 1009-36. The dating of this speech has been much disputed. Loenertz, *op. cit.*, in *OCP*, XXXVI (1970), 68, dates it to 1371 rather than 1376 or 1377. But cf. J. W. Barker, *Manuel II Palaeologus* (New Brunswick, N.J., 1969), 16, 460 and references; and P. Charanis, 'The Strife among the Palaeologi and the Ottoman Turks, 1370-1402', *B*, XVI (1942-3), 297.

34 Ostrogorsky, 540-1.

35 See Beldiceanu-Steinherr, *op. cit.*, in *Travaux et Mémoires*, I (1965), 139f.; E. A. Zachariadou, 'The Conquest of Adrianople by the Turks', *Studi Veneziani*, XII (1970), 211-17.

36 Ostrogorsky, 540-1. C. J. Jireček, *Geschichte der Serben*, I (Gotha, 1911), 438-9; Barker, *Manuel II*, 16 and references.

37 Cf. H. W. V. Temperley, *History of Serbia* (London, 1917), 97-8.

38 *Short Chronicle*, no. 47, in Sp. Lambros, *Brachea Chronika*, ed. K. I. Amantos (Athens, 1932-3), 81 lines 32-4.

39 Ostrogorsky, 541 and references.

40 I. Ševčenko, 'Nicolas Cabasilas' "Anti-Zealot" Discourse: a reinterpretation', *DOP*, XI (1957), 155-79. The suggestion that this discourse, formerly supposed to be directed against the Zealots in Thessalonica, might have been directed instead against Manuel II seems first to have been made by G. T. Dennis, *The Reign of Manuel II Palaeologus in Thessalonica* (Rome, 1960), 90-1.

41 Chalkokondyles, I, 34 (ed. Darkó). Halecki, 254-60.

42 G. Ostrogorsky, 'Byzance, état tributaire de l'empire turc', *Zbornik Radova*, V (1958), 49-51; Dennis, *Manuel II*, 35.

43 Ostrogorsky, *History*, 542 and references; Charanis, 'Strife among the Palaeologi and the Ottoman Turks', 295-6; Barker, *Manuel II*, 19-23.

44 Halecki, 289-319.

45 Halecki, 319-22. F. Thiriet, 'Venise et l'occupation de Ténédos au XIVᵉ siècle', *Mélanges d'archéologie et d'histoire*, LXV (1953), 219-45; Barker, *Manuel II*, 25-9.

46 Demetrios Kydones, *Correspondence*, ed. Loenertz, I, 38-9, no. 167. Cf. Dennis, *Manuel II*, 37-9.

47 Thiriet, *op. cit.*, 227-8; Barker, *Manuel II*, 30-1.

48 Kydones, *Correspondence*, I, 38, no. 167. On the final surrender of Gallipoli and its consequences, see Beldiceanu-Steinherr, *op. cit.*, and Barker, *Manuel II*, Appendix IV, 458-61.

49 Manuel Palaiologos, *Funeral Oration for his brother Theodore*, in *PG*, CLVI, 201.

50 Barker, *Manuel II*, 31-5; Ostrogorsky, 543.

51 Dennis, *Manuel II*, 41-51 and 52f.; Barker, *Manuel II*, 35-46.

52 Dennis, *Manuel II*, 114-16; Nicol, *Byzantine Family of Kantakouzenos*, 91-2, 119, 157-9.

53 Dennis, *Manuel II*, 46-7, 50-1; Barker, *Manuel II*, 40-2.

54 Cf. H. Inalcik, 'Ottoman methods of conquest', *Studia Islamica*, II (1954), 103-29; S. Runciman, *The Fall of Constantinople 1453* (Cambridge, 1965), 35-6; *CMH*, IV, 1, 763-4.

55 Demetrios Kydones, in *PG*, CLIV, 1004-5; and *Correspondence*, ed. Loenertz, I, 156, no. 81. Cf. A. E. Vacalopoulos, *Origins of the Greek Nation, 1204-1461* (New Brunswick, N.J., 1970), 73-7; S. Vryonis, 'The Byzantine Legacy and Ottoman Forms', *DOP*, XXIII-XXIV (1969-70), 253-308.

56 Ostrogorsky, 544-5.

57 Dennis, *Manuel II*, 73-6.

58 Kydones, *Correspondence*, II, 216-18, no. 299.

59 Isidore's sermon is the first of the five published by B. Laourdas,

in *Hellenika*, section 5 (Thessalonike, 1954), 19-32. Manuel's discourse to the people is also edited by B. Laourdas, in *Makedonika*, III (1955), 290-307. There is an English summary and analysis of it in Dennis, *Manuel II*, 78-85.

60 Dennis, *Manuel II*, 103f., 132f.; Barker, *Manuel II*, 54-7. On John Uroš and his successors in Thessaly, see Nicol, *Meteora*, 63-9.

61 Dennis, *Manuel II*, 151-9; Barker, *Manuel II*, 57-66.

62 On the battle of Kossovo, see Jireček, *Geschichte der Serben*, II, 119-21; Gibbons, *Foundation of the Ottoman Empire*, 173-8; Temperley, *History of Serbia*, 99-105; Ostrogorsky, *History*, 546-7.

63 Ostrogorsky, 'Byzance, état tributaire ...', *Zbornik Radova*, V (1958), 53-6; Ostrogorsky, *History*, 547.

64 Cf. Gibbons, *op. cit.*, 180f., *CMH*, IV, 1, 765.

65 *Le Pèlerinage d'Ignace de Smolensk*, ed. B. de Khitrowo, in *Itinéraires russes en Orient* (Geneva, 1889), 127-57 (especially 140-2).

66 F. Dölger, 'Johannes VII. Kaiser der Rhomäer', *BZ*, XXXI (1931), 21-36; G. Kolias, 'The revolt of John VII against John V Palaiologos' (in Greek), *Hellenika*, XII (1951), 36-64; P. Wirth, 'Zum Geschichtsbild Kaiser Johannes' VII. Palaiologos', *B*, XXXV (1965), 592-600. Cf. Ostrogorsky, *History*, 547-8; Barker, *Manuel II*, 68-78.

67 Chalkokondyles, I, 77 (ed. Darkó).

68 Barker, *Manuel II*, 78-80. Cf. P. Schreiner, Zur Geschichte Philadelpheias im 14. Jhdt. (1293-1390)', *OCP*, XXXV (1969), 375-431.

69 Gibbons, *Foundation of the Ottoman Empire*, 198.

70 On John V's concordat with the church, see V. Laurent, 'Les droits de l'empereur en matière ecclésiastique. L'accord de 1380-1382', *REB*, XIII (1955), 5-20. Cf. Runciman, *Great Church in Captivity*, 71. On the last years of the Empress Helena, see Nicol, *Byzantine Family of Kantakouzenos*, 137-8.

Fifteen

The Reign of Manuel II.
The First Crisis—1391-1402

Manuel was at Brusa when he heard the news of his father's death. At once he slipped out of the Sultan's camp by night and hurried to Constantinople before his nephew John VII could forestall him. His arrival seems to have been welcomed by the citizens, and by March 1391 he had come at long last into his full inheritance as the Emperor Manuel II. The elderly Demetrios Kydones who, like Michael Psellos in an earlier age, had watched the emperors come and go, hailed the succession of the long-awaited philosopher-king.[1] The description certainly fitted Manuel better than his father. He was already 40 years old. His character was formed and tried by experience. In appearance he was a handsome, bearded figure who impressed even the Sultan with his regal bearing. He was blessed with a strong constitution and great resources of physical and mental energy. His patience made him his mother's rather than his father's son; and indeed Manuel was in many ways more the grandchild of John Cantacuzene than the child of John V, though he had been a faithful son. From his grandfather he inherited a taste for theology and literature as well as an aptitude in warfare. But his love for literary and rhetorical composition was probably implanted in him by his friend and mentor Demetrios Kydones, to whom he liked to send copies of the works that often whiled away his hours of depression or of enforced leisure. For, though Manuel was a greater man and a greater emperor than his father, he was often at a loose end and seldom able to exercise all his talents because of the restricted and inhibited empire that had been left to him.

The Sultan flew into a rage when he found that Manuel had escaped from his camp. The opportunity to make a new emperor of his own choice had been snatched from him. It is quite possible that he would have selected Manuel and not John VII. But Bajezid did not like being outwitted. He had too much on hand to be able to cross over to Europe at that moment, but he sent his orders to Constantinople without delay. The Byzantines were now to submit to a number of extra humiliations and impositions. They were to admit a resident agent of the Sultan in the city who would serve as arbiter or *kadi* of all affairs concerning the Muslim inhabitants, and they were to provide a special quarter in Constantinople for Turkish merchants. The tribute payable to the Sultan which, in the words of Kydones, was now so heavy that not even all the revenue of the Byzantine treasury could meet it, was to continue; and the Emperor, though now no longer his hostage, was still the Sultan's vassal. 'If you do not accept my orders and do as I command,' said Bajezid, 'then shut the gates of your city and govern what lies behind them; for everything beyond the gates belongs to me.'[2]

Only three months later Manuel was summoned to return to the Sultan's camp in Asia Minor. He could only tremble and obey. He left his mother Helena as regent in Constantinople and set out on 8 June 1391. He was not free to return until the following January. The misery and unhappiness that he experienced during those months is reflected in a number of letters that he wrote to his friends in the capital. Bajezid's campaign, which Manuel had to endure in company with his nephew John VII, penetrated deep into the heart of Anatolia and far along the Black Sea coast to Kastamuni and Sinope. The army marched, as Manuel writes, through wild and deserted country whose inhabitants had fled into the forests and mountains to escape the already legendary horrors of the Turkish scimitar. So ruined and devastated was some of the land that Manuel was unable to tell where he was. The depopulated and nameless ruins of once flourishing towns along the route saddened him. No one could now remember what they had once been called. And it was a source of particular grief to Manuel's antiquarian turn of mind to come across still recognizable ancient Greek cities whose names had been changed into something foreign and barbarous.[3]

Part of his unhappy sojourn in Anatolia, however, was passed in the comparative comfort of Ankara. While there, in the winter of 1391, he held a number of discussions with a Muslim theologian about the doctrines and faith of Christianity and Islam, with special reference to the claims of Mahomet to have been a prophet. The evident success of the prophet's followers when compared with the dismal decline of the Christians gave the Muslim apologist a head start in the debate. The Christians were visibly suffering the consequences of having rejected God's later revelation through Mahomet, just as the Jews had suffered for having spurned his revelation through Christ. There was naturally no accord between the disputants, but there was tolerance on either side. Manuel subsequently elaborated their discussions into a series of 26 Dialogues, the text of which he presented to his younger brother Theodore at Mistra. He seems to have returned to Constantinople in January 1392.[4]

A month later he married Helena, daughter of the Serbian prince of Serres, Constantine Dragaš. Although then 42 he had not taken a wife before. He may have thought of the political motive of uniting the interests of two Orthodox peoples, though it was late in the day for such alliances, since both Manuel and his father-in-law were vassals of the Sultan. It turned out to be a happy as well as a fruitful marriage. Helena was to bear him six children. The wedding was celebrated on 10 February 1392. The next day the Emperor was crowned by the Patriarch Antonios in St Sophia and placed a crown on the head of his Empress Helena. The ritual of the coronation ceremony was observed to the last detail. The Russian archimandrite from Smolensk who was still in Constantinople at the time witnessed it and describes the pageantry in tones of rapturous awe. The gorgeous vestments of the clergy, the iron-clad guards of the Emperor, the solemnity of the occasion and the beauty of the singing left him almost speechless with delight. As a pilgrim and tourist in the city Ignatios of Smolensk obviously did not feel a pervading sense of doom or wonder whether, in the circumstances, the masquerade of an imperial coronation was justified. The Genoese and Venetian representatives, who attended in their bejewelled velvet finery, may have had other ideas. But there is no doubt that the Emperor Manuel and his Patriarch Antonios were set upon putting up a brave show. An anonymous Byzantine account of the coronation fills in some of the more recondite details of procedure which escaped the wondering eyes of the Russian pilgrim. When it was over the Emperor and Empress rode from the church to the palace. The reins of their horses were held by the despots, *sebastokrators* and caesars. In the palace a platform carpeted in red had been prepared and here the Emperor and Empress sat on their thrones. When a curtain was thrown back they were revealed to the assembled people who shouted the customary acclamations. The curtain was then drawn over. The imperial couple withdrew to change their robes before sitting down to a dinner served to them by the highest dignitaries. The *protobestiarios* then distributed the ritual largesse to the people, and on the next day there was a holiday and a banquet in the palace attended by all the leading men of the city.[5]

The show was not all superficial. The real crown jewels, so far

312

as anyone knows, were still in the treasury of St Mark's at Venice. But the pomp and ceremony of Manuel's coronation expressed an underlying and still living conviction in the Byzantine myth. It was felt and voiced more perhaps by the church than by the state. It was put into forceful words by the Patriarch Antonios IV who performed the coronation. In 1393 the Patriarch took it upon himself to re-enunciate the case for the universal sovereignty of the Byzantine Emperor over all lesser kings and princes. The Grand Duke of Moscow, Basil I, had presumed to forbid commemoration of the Emperor's name in his churches. He did so not because he had lapsed from the Orthodox faith but because he felt that the Emperor had forfeited his right to be considered head of the Orthodox Church. 'We have a Church,' he said, 'but no emperor.' It was to this interpretation of affairs that the Patriarch of Constantinople took exception. The authority of the Great Church of Constantinople over the church of Russia and the other Orthodox churches of the Slav countries was still respected. But in the Byzantine view it was inconceivable that the authority of the Church and the authority of the Emperor could be divided into separate compartments. The œcumenical Church postulated an œcumenical emperor. The one could not exist without the other.

The Patriarch answered the Grand Duke's objections with a long letter setting out the Byzantine myth in all its beautiful simplicity. It was as if nothing had changed since the days of Photios or of Basil II. The Empire might be reduced almost to the area of the city of Constantinople. The enemy might be hammering at its gates. But the Emperor was still the paterfamilias of all other Christian princes, anointed by God and acknowledged as God's vicegerent on earth by all patriarchs, bishops and people of the Orthodox faith. It may be, wrote the Patriarch Antonios, that the Turks are now encircling the Emperor's residence, but it does not follow that Christians should despise him. When Peter, prince of the apostles, said 'Fear God and honour the king', he made it quite clear that, as there is only one God, so there is only one universal king, the Emperor of the Romans. All the other so-called Christian kings who have assumed for themselves the name of Emperor have violated the natural and legal order of things by so doing. The significance of this famous document lies not so much in the fact that it states what were to most Byzantines still eternal truths, but that those truths were set forth by the Patriarch of Constantinople. The Byzantine Church had shown greater powers of resilience than the state in all the catastrophes and humiliations of the Turkish conquest. The Patriarch of Constantinople commanded a deeper respect among the rest of the Orthodox people than the Emperor himself. It was the respect accorded to the Patriarch and the resilience of the Church that made it possible for the Byzantine spirit to survive among eastern Christians when, only 60 years after the letter of Antonios, they had in fact a Church but no emperor.[6]

After his coronation in February 1392 the Emperor Manuel seems to have been allowed a respite from his military duties as the Sultan's vassal. But the Turkish grip was all the while closing tighter on the Balkans. Bajezid was aware that the King of Hungary might yet be persuaded to come to the rescue of Constantinople. In 1393 John Šišman of Bulgaria, encouraged by his neighbours in Hungary, rebelled and tried to shake off his enforced dependence on the Turks. The Sultan was in Anatolia at the time, but the rebellion was not allowed to spread. A Turkish army captured the Bulgarian capital of Trnovo on 17 July 1393; Šišman was taken prisoner at Nicopolis and executed two years later. Bulgaria became the first properly constituted province or *pashalik* of the Ottoman Empire in Europe. The Bulgars were now no longer the vassals of the Sultan; they were his subjects. Only at the very western extremity of the country, at Vidin on the frontier with Hungary, was a native prince permitted to rule for a little longer. He was Stracimir, Šišman's half-brother, who had kept out of the rebellion. But in the rest of the country all political and ecclesiastical autonomy was at an end. Bulgaria set the pattern of administration for the other Turkish provinces in Europe.[7]

It was probably after the conquest of Bulgaria that Bajezid, who had left Anatolia for the purpose, decided to show the remaining Christian rulers in the Balkans who was master of the situation. In the winter of 1393-4 the Sultan summoned them all to his presence at Serres where he was holding court. The summonses were issued separately to each individual, so that none knew of the others' invitation. Those who answered the call, and none dared refuse, were the Emperor Manuel II, his brother Theodore the Despot of the Morea, their nephew the Emperor John VII, Manuel's father-in-law Constantine Dragaš, and Stephen Lazarević of Serbia. They were astonished to meet each other in such strange circumstances and not unnaturally concluded that the Sultan had rounded them all up to murder them. Manuel later described their apprehensions in these words: 'The tyrant (Bajezid) thought the moment favourable to accomplish the massacre which he had for so long contemplated, so that, in his own words, having cleared the ground of thorns (meaning us), his own people would be able to dance on Christian soil without scratching their feet.... He therefore ordered his general, a eunuch, to kill us all in the night, threatening him with death if he disobeyed. But God stayed the hand of the assassin; and the Sultan, far from punishing his disobedience thanked his servant for delaying the execution of his command. But this dark soul could not entirely wash away the blackness of his character. He vented his rage on some of our officers, putting out their eyes and cutting off their hands.' The Sultan was evidently verging on paranoia. His mood abruptly changed from maniacal anger to sweet reasonableness, and he tried to placate Manuel with presents 'as one tries to calm a child's cries with sweets after one has beaten it'.[8]

As an exercise in psychological warfare this assembly at Serres was a great success, for it struck terror into those who had been summoned. But at the end of the charade the Sultan's vassals were allowed to go free, save for the Despot Theodore. He was destined to accompany Bajezid on his projected campaign into Thessaly, though he managed to escape and get back to the Morea. The Emperor Manuel returned to Constantinople as quickly as his heels would carry him. His mind was now made up that he could never have any rational dealings with a man like Bajezid. Even their relationship of lord and vassal had ceased to carry any guarantee of security. The alternative was to sit it out patiently in Constantinople until help arrived from somewhere else. Only a miracle could revive the Empire. But so long as its capital city remained in Byzantine hands the Ottoman Empire could not be said to have replaced it. Of this fact the Sultan was very conscious. But Manuel had the courage of his convictions that the walls of Constantinople were still too strong to be breached and that the western world would surely now see the imminent danger and send help. The next time Bajezid summoned him to his presence Manuel took no notice.

Bajezid was not a man to be trifled with. In the spring of 1394 he sent a vast army to burn and depopulate the outskirts of Constantinople and to blockade the city. The blockade was to last, with varying intensity, for about eight years. Everything beyond the city walls was destroyed and rendered uninhabitable; no one could enter or leave the gates; the fields could not be cultivated; the inhabitants were reduced to desperation by the shortage of corn, wine, oil and other necessities of life. To bake what bread they could the bakers

315

were driven to tearing down houses to use the beams for firewood; there was no other source of supply. In Italy, in May 1394, the Venetian Senate passed a vote of sympathy for the plight of the Emperor Manuel and his subjects. The senators counselled him to hold out and to address appeals for help to the Pope and the Christian rulers of western Europe. As the blockade continued, however, they offered him the means of escape by sea and a place of asylum in Venice. More realistically, and more helpfully, they sent a shipment of grain to Constantinople at the end of the year to feed his hungry people. It was still possible to beat the Turkish blockade by sea. It remained to be seen whether it could be beaten by land.[9]

The conquest of Bulgaria followed by the news that Constantinople was besieged had caused a belated wave of reaction in the neighbouring countries of Hungary and Wallachia. The prince of Wallachia, Mircea the Elder, supported by Sigismund of Hungary, went into battle with the Turks at Rovine on 17 May 1395. Fighting as vassals on the Turkish side were the Serbian princes Stephen Lazarević, Constantine Dragaš, and Marko the son of Vukašin. Dragaš and Marko were killed in the battle. The military outcome was indecisive, but the political consequence was that Mircea of Wallachia too accepted the status of a vassal of the Sultan. The Turks occupied the Dobrudja and posted troops to guard the crossings over the Danube. At the same time another Turkish army had been penetrating into northern Greece. The invasion of Thessaly had begun in 1393, led by the veteran general Evrenos Beg. Trikkala, but recently the capital of a Greco-Serbian principality, fell in 1395 and became the headquarters of Turachan Beg, the first of a long line of pashas of Thessaly. Before long the Turks had reached Athens.[10]

The situation in central and southern Greece was such as to tempt an invader. In the years since 1383, when Manuel's brother Theodore had taken over the Byzantine Despotate of the Morea, there had been almost constant fighting among the foreign claimants and contenders for the rest of the country. The French principality of Achaia had broken up into numerous fragments. Corinth and district had passed to a Florentine, Nerio Acciajuoli, whose forebear had come there as an agent of the Latin Empress Catherine of Valois 50 years earlier. The city of Patras had for a while been held by the Knights Hospitallers of Rhodes, who were on the look out for an alternative base for their operations. The Catalan duchy of Athens and Thebes had been taken under the protection of the crown of Aragon. But everything had been thrown into further confusion when, shortly before 1380, an army of professional mercenaries known as the Navarrese Company had arrived in Greece. Like the Catalan Company before them they were in search of employment and lands to conquer. Some of the Navarrese accepted a commission from the Angevin claimant to the principality of Achaia. Others attacked the Catalans in central Greece and captured Thebes in 1379, though Athens fell to Nerio Acciajuoli. Between them the Navarrese had accounted for the downfall of the Catalan régime and had already assumed control of much of Achaia when Theodore Palaiologos became Despot in the Morea. To contend with their perpetual hostility on the northern border of his province, Theodore had enlisted the help of Nerio Acciajuoli, taking his beautiful daughter Bartolomaea in marriage. Almost all the contending parties in Greece, Greek as well as Latin, had at one time or another, invited the Turks to champion their cause. When Nerio died in September 1394 his estate passed not to Theodore but to his other son-in-law Carlo Tocco, the Italian Count of Cephalonia, who claimed the inheritance of his grandfathers, the Orsini, in Epiros. Carlo called on the Turks to help him take possession of his legacy against the opposition of his brother-in-law Theodore.[11] Therefore, when the Turks arrived, they knew what to expect. They need fear no united resistance. Having sacked Athens, Evrenos Beg led his men over the Isthmus of Corinth and, with the enthusiastic support of the Navarrese, entered the Despotate of the Morea and subjected the two Byzantine fortresses of Akova and Leontarion in the very heart of the peninsula. This was a punitive raid and not a definitive conquest; the Turks withdrew almost at once. But it was a foretaste of things to come. It opened the eyes of the foreigners in Greece, and their anxious messages to their relatives and friends back home added substantial weight to the feeling in western Europe that some action must be taken against the infidel.[12]

King Sigismund of Hungary was the first to take steps to organize a counter-offensive in the Balkans. His was the kingdom most nearly threatened. He appealed to all the crowned heads of Europe. The support of both Popes, Boniface IX in Rome and Benedict XIII in Avignon, translated the venture into a crusade. The chivalry of France responded with enthusiasm. Their contingent of 10,000 men was led by John, Count of Nevers, son of the Duke of Burgundy. Another 6000 were supplied by Germany. The Venetians waited to see which way the trade winds would blow, but finally agreed to lend some ships to patrol the Hellespont. The Genoese of Lesbos and Chios and the knights of Rhodes agreed to guard the Black Sea coast and the mouth of the Danube. The western armies converged on Buda in July 1396. Mircea of Wallachia had already arrived there with some 10,000 soldiers, and Sigismund himself had assembled an army of about 60,000 Hungarians. Smaller units from Poland, Bohemia, Italy, Spain and England made the crusading host up to nearly 100,000 men. No earlier crusade had reached such proportions. The news that it was gathering in Hungary at once prompted Bajezid to muster his forces and march to the Danube. Constantinople was relieved of the full force of the Turkish blockade.

In August the crusaders set out down the Danube valley. Their leaders had already disagreed about the plan of campaign. Sigismund was for caution and defensive action. The French, nurtured on tales of the great crusades of yore, wanted to beat the Turks out of Europe and carry all before them until they reached the Holy Land. Sigismund had to yield to their romanticism. At Vidin the Bulgarian prince Stracimir broke his oath to the Sultan and opened the gates of his fortress to the crusaders. At Rahova, the next stop down the Danube, they fought their way in past the Turkish garrison and massacred the inhabitants. By September they had reached Nicopolis, where the Turks were even more strongly entrenched. It was while they were laying siege to the fortress of Nicopolis that the main Ottoman army, led by the Sultan, caught up with them. Once again there was a fatal division of opinion between Sigismund and his allies about the strategy proper to the occasion. On the morning of 25 September 1396 the French knights charged up the hillside some three miles away from Nicopolis where all that could be seen of the Turkish army was a small troop of light cavalry. The rest of the Turkish horsemen, together with a squadron led by Stephen Lazarević, lay hidden behind the hill. The French were first lured on and then driven back in a welter of bloodshed. Only a few of the knights survived or were spared because of their rank, among them their leader John of Nevers. When the rest of the crusaders saw that the French had been routed they too turned to flight. Sigismund made a gallant effort to advance, but his men were forced back by the Turks and he too chose to make his escape. The battle was over.

The Sultan followed up his victory by ordering the massacre of all his Christian prisoners, except for a number of their leaders whose birth or fortune made them worth holding to ransom. Stracimir of Vidin, who had fought on the allied side, was finally dismissed, and the last vestige of Bulgaria's independence was erased. Sigismund of Hungary got away on a Venetian ship down the Danube. It was a measure of the Turkish impotence by sea that he was able to stop off and visit the Emperor Manuel in Constantinople. Nor could the Turks prevent him from sailing through the Hellespont; though, as if to prove the point that they were masters by land, they stationed their prisoners along the banks of the straits to shame him as he sailed by.[13]

The crusade of Nicopolis was the last of the international crusades on the grand scale. Its organization and its consequences had rather more to do with western Europe than with Byzantium. Its leaders had hardly consulted the Byzantines. It is true that Manuel II had been in touch with Sigismund of Hungary and had asked him to put the Byzantine case to the western powers. But they had not taken Manuel much into account in their preparations. Their immediate aim had been the protection of Catholic Hungary and the expulsion of the infidel from Europe. The liberation of the Holy Land was perhaps a secondary objective in some of the crusaders' minds, but the rescue of Constantinople was not explicitly mentioned. The battle of Nicopolis was the first real trial of strength between the nations of the west and the Ottoman Empire, and what was at stake was the fate of Hungary and the Balkans, not the survival or reconstitution of the Byzantine Empire. The only beneficial effect on Constantinople was that the Sultan had to relax the blockade of the city for a while. We are assured that the Emperor Manuel was more downcast than ever when the news of the battle reached him. But his only clear reference to the event in any of his writings expresses simply the pious horror of a Byzantine at the barbarity of the western soldiers— 'a numerous army made up of Paionians, Celts and western Galatians, whose names alone make one shudder, so barbarous are they.'[14]

As soon as the coast was clear Bajezid returned to Constantinople and made ready to take the city by assault. The blockade turned into a full-scale siege. The troops that he now had to spare he sent to invade the Morea. Led as before by Evrenos Beg an army of 50,000 men stormed into Greece from Thessaly. Athens was taken, though not yet permanently. The Despot Theodore appealed to Venice, offering to sell them the city of Corinth, but in vain. In June 1397 the Turks captured and sacked Argos with calculated savagery. The city was razed to the ground. The inhabitants that survived massacre (perhaps as many as 30,000) were taken away to slavery in Asia Minor. A few weeks later the Despot's army was beaten in battle near Leontarion. The Turks overran the Morea as far south as the Venetian ports of Modon and Coron before returning to Thessaly.[15]

The Venetians now realized that the danger to Byzantium and to their own interests was greater than ever before. Towards the end of 1396 they authorized payment for the maintenance of a fleet to protect Constantinople. The Genoese also, whose colony at Galata was already under fire, agreed to contribute ships of their own. The Sultan angrily demanded that the city should surrender. But the Emperor and his people, still hoping, as their historian puts it, that God would pardon their sins and bring relief, refused to give in. Before long they could see from their walls that work had begun on the construction of a great castle over on the Asiatic side of the Bosporos. It came to be called Anadolu-Hisar, and its ruins still stand some six miles from the city. From here the Sultan planned to direct the capture of Constantinople. At the same time he held out the threat of recognizing John VII, who was still his hostage, as the rightful Emperor, a move that would have been welcomed by those who were beginning to despair of Manuel's policy of passive defiance. The people of Constantinople, penned behind their walls, short of food and the means to procure it, were living on their nerves. Many died of starvation; others fled either to the west or to the Turks. Some felt that almost any change would be for the better. 'A bushel of grain', writes Doukas, 'cost more than 20 gold pieces, and where was the gold to be found?' It was the same with wine and all other commodities. Their privations were driving people to disloyalty and treachery; and their Emperor at every hour of every day that passed offered up this prayer: "Lord Jesus Christ, let it not come about that the great multitude of Christian peoples should hear it said that it was during the days of the Emperor Manuel that the City, with all its holy and venerable monuments of the faith, was delivered to the infidel." '[16]

The pressure of the siege was somewhat relaxed in 1397 after the impetus of the first assault. The Emperor Manuel had kept his head. His nerve had not broken. The Venetians kept assuring him that further help would soon be on its way from the west, though privately they had taken to issuing double sets of instructions to their agents, depending on whether Constantinople was or was not yet 'in the hands of the Sultan'. They urged the Emperor to continue addressing appeals to other Christian rulers, and Manuel took their advice. In 1397 and 1398 he sent deputations to the Pope and to the Kings of France, England and Aragon, as well as to the Grand Duke of Moscow. The Patriarch Antonios meanwhile begged the King of Poland, who had consulted him about the union of the Churches, to join his forces with those of the King of Hungary for another crusade. But Sigismund of Hungary, for all his hopes and promises, never took the cross again.[17]

The Roman Pope, Boniface IX, however, was moved to call upon the Catholic princes of the west to contribute either to a crusade or to a defence fund for the protection of Constantinople. He offered the usual indulgences to all who contributed and ordered that collecting boxes be set up in the churches. One such coffer was installed in St Paul's cathedral in London, for Manuel had sent two delegations to King Richard II of England. Richard had certainly no soldiers to spare, but he was not averse to advertising his generosity in the matter of comforting the Christians of the east. His Privy Council voted that a sum be allocated for this purpose, and every bishop and lord of the realm was instructed to subscribe according to his means. Richard even conferred knighthood on one of the Byzantine ambassadors at an investiture at Lichfield. The sum of 3000 marks or £2000 sterling was earmarked by the king for the relief of the Emperor Manuel. The money got no further than the office of a Genoese broker.[18]

The court of France responded to the Emperor's appeal in a more practical manner. King Charles VI of France had acquired a greater interest in the fate of Constantinople since becoming, in 1396, overlord of the Republic of Genoa and so of the Genoese colonies in the Byzantine world. There was even a rumour that John VII had, through Genoese intermediaries, offered to sell his title to the Byzantine crown to the French king in 1397.[19] Certainly the French knights who had been taken at Nicopolis, whose enormous ransom money was not paid over until nearly a year after the battle, returned to their country with a dreadful tale to tell. Among them was Jean le Meingre, known as Marshal Boucicaut, who had fought with more courage than prudence at Nicopolis. He was eager to go back to battle with the infidel and willing to serve as Charles VI's ambassador to the Emperor Manuel, whom he had already met. Early in 1399 he was authorized to take a body of 1200 soldiers to Constantinople by sea. Like Count Amadeo of Savoy 33 years earlier, Marshal Boucicaut fought his way through the Turkish blockade of the straits and disembarked his little army at Constantinople in the summer. He was given a great welcome by the harassed citizens. The Emperor gave him the title of Grand Constable and joined him in a number of raids on the enemy beyond the city walls and even on some of the towns on the coast of Asia Minor. But this was only nibbling at the problem. As a practised soldier,

Boucicaut could see that a much larger force and a much greater effort were needed. He came to the conclusion that the Emperor had better go back with him to the west so that he could reinforce this opinion and state his own case to the French king.[20]

It might be uncharitable to think that Manuel jumped at the chance thus offered him to escape from the prison of his city. But he did not delay his going. The only difficulty was to find someone to take charge of affairs while he was away. The obvious person was his nephew John VII, but he was not on speaking terms with his uncle. Marshal Boucicaut, however, displayed a talent for diplomacy unusual in a soldier. He went to talk to John at Selymbria and persuaded him to come to Constantinople and be reconciled with his uncle. If he had done nothing else the Marshal could have congratulated himself on bringing together the two parties of a family feud that had gone on for a generation. The reconciliation between John VII and Manuel II eased the tension between their respective supporters in Constantinople and made it possible for Manuel to leave the city and travel as his own ambassador to western Europe. John VII thus became Emperor-regent in Constantinople, and the Marshal detailed his lieutenant Jean de Chateaumorand to stay behind with 100 men-at-arms. History does not record how the Sultan Bajezid reacted to this gambit which seemed to cut the strings of his control over both of the Byzantine Emperors.[21]

Manuel set out with Boucicaut from Constantinople on 10 December 1399. It was to be more than three years before he returned. He took with him his wife Helena and her two little sons; for though now officially reconciled with his nephew John he felt that his family would be safer in other keeping. They disembarked at Modon in the Morea, where they were left in the custody of the Emperor's brother, the Despot Theodore. From Greece the Emperor and his party sailed on to Venice, where he landed in April 1400. Marshal Boucicaut went ahead to Paris to arrange for Manuel's reception there, while the Emperor followed at a more leisurely pace by way of Padua, Vicenza, Pavia and Milan. Here he was handsomely entertained by Gian Galeazzo Visconti, who sent him on his way to France with guides and gifts and bodyguards. Some say that Manuel also saw Pope Boniface IX during his journey through Italy. The evidence is slender, but there is no doubt that the Pope was inspired to renew his call for a crusade or for contributions in May 1400.[22]

Manuel must many a time have heard his father's tales of his bitter and humiliating experiences in the west. His own warm welcome in the cities of Italy must therefore have surprised as well as cheered him. Things had changed since John V had visited Rome and Venice. It was not only that the danger from the east had become much more real. There was also the fact that, even in those 30 years, the appetite of educated westerners for classical Greek learning had become almost insatiable. It had become fashionable to cultivate Byzantine Greeks as the purveyors of that learning. In 1396 the Emperor's friend Manuel Chrysoloras, a pupil of Demetrios Kydones, had been appointed to teach Greek at Florence. By 1400 he had moved to Milan to spread the new culture, and the Emperor was overjoyed to meet him there when he passed through on his way to France. Manuel himself was an urbane and scholarly man with a finer and more commanding presence than his father. He was a good advertisement for many of the qualities which the *literati* of Italy expected to find in a Greek. He came to western Europe at a moment when people were receptive to, and eager for the influence of Greek culture. His journey was likely to stimulate their interest still further. It was therefore a very different kind of journey from that made by his father. Manuel may have come to the west as a beggar, but he did not behave as one, and he did not look like one. Nor did he offer as an incentive the conversion of himself or his people to the Roman Church. He asked only for the unconditional help of fellow Christians in the defence of a worthy cause of which he was a worthy representative.[23]

He reached Paris in June 1400. Charles VI went out of his way to welcome and entertain his distinguished guest, and promised to supply another expeditionary force under the command of Marshal Boucicaut. In the course of the summer in Paris Manuel got in touch with the Kings of Castile and Aragon and began to sound the possibilities of visiting England. Since last he had corresponded with the English court, Richard II had been deposed by Henry IV. There seemed a chance that Henry might know what had become of the money promised but never delivered to Manuel by his predecessor. Manuel made some discreet enquiries through the agency of a prior of the Hospitallers, Peter Holt. In September he moved to Calais in anticipation of crossing the English Channel. There was little he could do in Paris at the time, for King Charles VI had just succumbed to one of his periodic fits of lunacy. In December, as soon as word came that King Henry IV was back from his campaign in Scotland and was willing to receive him, the Emperor sailed across to Dover. After a short stay at Canterbury as the guests of the Prior of Christ Church, Manuel and his suite pressed on to London. On 21 December Henry IV met them at Blackheath and escorted them to the city.

The Emperor attracted much attention in London. The simple dignity of his style of dress contrasted with the fripperies of the current English fashions, of which he is said to have disapproved. The long beards and hair styles of the Orthodox chaplains who accompanied him were objects of wonder, as was the piety and attention to daily communion of the Emperor and his party. He won much sympathy as 'a great Christian prince from the East' who had been driven by the infidel to seek help in a foreign land. For Christmas Henry IV took Manuel to his new palace at Eltham, where a tournament was staged in his honour. The aldermen of the city of London later arranged a mummery or masquerade for his entertainment. Manuel was so impressed by his reception that he seems to have become over optimistic. In a letter that he wrote from London to his friend Chrysoloras he dwells on the virtues and the generosity of the magnanimous King Henry, who is going to provide an army and a fleet for the rescue of Constantinople. These were vain hopes. No brigade of English bowmen, no flotilla of the British navy followed the Emperor when he returned to the continent in February 1401. He was, however, richer by the sum of 3000 marks, and for this he expressed his gratitude to the Kingdom of England in a letter addressed to all Christians. It was no more than the amount that had been promised him by Richard II. It is doubtful whether Henry added anything to this sum. For several years afterwards he and his treasury officials were trying to trace the money which was supposed to have been collected in the churches for the Pope's defence fund. But what they recovered was put to reimbursing the exchequer for the payment of 3000 marks or £2000 to the Emperor Manuel. Neither Manuel nor the Pope saw a penny more of it from England.[24]

Manuel got back to Paris at the end of February 1401 and settled down in France as the guest of King Charles VI. He conducted some negotiations with other Christian princes, with the Kings of Portugal and of Aragon, as well as with the Pope at Avignon; and he continued to hope, against all the evidence, that his visit to England would bear substantial fruit. From Paris he wrote to his friend Euthymios, later to become Patriarch, to the effect that preparations were already being made in Europe for the assembly of a great army, to which the Britons as well as other generous allies would provide contingents. He forecast that when he came back to Constantinople he would soon be followed by an international crusade which would accomplish and exceed all his hopes. In another letter written to Demetrios Chrysoloras he announced that many sovereigns of Europe were busily recruiting troops and that Marshal Boucicaut was going to lead them to Constantinople. But it was all an illusion. Gradually the truth of the matter began to dawn on Manuel. All the crowned heads of western Europe had other things on their minds. The Popes were incapable of action. The Venetians would only act if assured that other nations would play their part. Marshal Boucicaut, far from buckling on his armour for another crusade, had left to take up his appointment as French governor of Genoa in 1401.[25]

Early in 1402 Manuel sadly sent word to his nephew in Constantinople to advise him that King Henry of England, for all his good intentions, was not in a position to provide any help in the way of troops or money. By that time Manuel had been in Paris for more than a year. It almost looked as if he could not face the prospect of going home to his unhappy city. During the intervals in his protracted negotiations he passed some of his time in literary exercises of the type that he so much enjoyed. One of his essays which survives is a light-hearted description of a tapestry hanging in the Louvre.[26] Another, more serious composition was a theological treatise in 156 chapters on the subject of the procession of the Holy Spirit and the primacy of the See of Rome. It was written in answer to a little tract presented to him by a French priest who had put to him the Latin view of these matters.[27] Manuel's treatise was uncompromising in its Orthodoxy. For although a stranger in a strange land, engaged in delicate political bargaining, he refused to consider sacrificing his Orthodox faith for the hope of material advantage. The King of France at least seems to have admired his constancy and indeed caused some offence to his own subjects by inviting the Emperor to attend mass with him in the church of St Denys.

While Manuel was killing time in Paris, his nephew John VII was holding the fort in faraway Constantinople, gallantly assisted by the French soldiers of Jean de Chateaumorand. The city was still in a state of siege. Anonymous accounts recall how the Sultan Bajezid arrogantly gazed on its buildings from afar and allotted them to his officers in anticipation of his victory. The great church of St Sophia was to be reserved for his own use as a palace. The Byzantines were apt to describe their survival and their ultimate deliverance almost solely to the protection and intervention of the Mother of God.[28] Not one of their writers mentions the contribution made to their defence by Marshal Boucicaut or by his lieutenant. But the Marshal's biography gives a vivid account of what it was like in the city in these critical years. One can readily believe that the Seigneur de Chateaumorand 'did all that was demanded of him in his task, as a God-fearing man and as the valiant warrior that he was ... although, after the Emperor had left, there was such great famine that people were driven by hunger to let themselves down at night by ropes from the walls and to go over to the Turks.' Chateaumorand would lead his men out from time to time to forage for food when the Turks were off their guard, and by these and other means the citizens were kept alive. The sea lanes were still open since the Turks were afraid of having their own ships sunk by the Venetians and Genoese. 'And thus', says the Marshal's biographer, 'for the space of three years Chateaumorand defended the city against the might of the Saracens.... Through him and his good Frenchmen the noble and ancient city of Constantinople was saved from total destruction. Which thing is no doubt very agreeable to God and a great honour to the King of France and to the French who there proved their virtue, and also a great benefit to Christendom.'[29]

Little is known of the activities of the Emperor John VII. There are doubtful reports of attempts that he made to come to a settlement with Bajezid in the summer of 1401. There was a rumour that the Genoese in Galata had agreed to pay a yearly tribute to the Sultan. Treachery was bred by despair. Even the Patriarch Matthew was suspected of secret dealings with the enemy, though he was quick to deny the charge in an encyclical castigating the moral degradation of the people and the need for them to repent if they were to be saved from their miseries.[30] It is known that John VII wrote on his own account to Henry IV of England in June 1402, asking for aid and paying flattering tribute to the several English noblemen then active in the defence of Constantinople. But otherwise the silence in the city was like the silence before a storm. The storm broke in the summer of 1402.[31]

Even while Manuel was still in London, in February 1401, reports were reaching England of encouraging new developments in the distant east. Merchants arriving in London told how the leader of the Turks had been killed in battle by a great king of the Orient who had been converted to Christianity together with 60,000 of his people. The English chroniclers of the time took up the tale and magnified it to suitably miraculous and fantastic size. The rumours and reports were garbled and extravagant, but they were founded on a measure of fact. The great king of the Orient was the Mongol, Timur-lenk, later to be known to the English as Tamburlaine. In August 1400 Timur had made his first appearance and scored his first victory on the eastern extremities of Bajezid's Empire in Asia.[32]

Timur was by then already 64 years old and a legendary figure in the further east.[33] He claimed descent from Genghis Khan, though he was more Turk than Mongol. About 1369 he had begun the process of reconstructing the great Mongol Empire of the thirteenth century. Using Samarkand as his fixed capital he extended his dominions in all directions. On the south and east his armies overran the territory of the Mongol Ilkhans of Persia, driving into Afghanistan and India. On the north they fought against the Mongols of the Golden Horde in Russia, advancing as far as Moscow. Their campaigns were famous for their savagery; they indulged in indiscriminate massacre and devastation, and they were said to leave nothing but deserts in their wake. About 1390, when he had conquered Georgia and Armenia, Timur first came into direct confrontation with the Ottoman Turks. On these eastern limits of the Ottoman world there were still several independent Turkish emirates that had not been swallowed up in the Empire of Bajezid. Some of them were in alliance with the emperors of Trebizond, who had long since learned that the way to preserve their outpost of Byzantine civilization was to seek friends among their enemies. Alexios III of Trebizond, who died in 1390, had married off his four daughters to the Turkoman emirs in the mountainous hinterland of his empire. One of his sons-in-law was Tahartan, or Zaratan, the emir of Erzindjan (Arsinga). To save himself from Bajezid, Tahartan had become a vasal of Timur. Thus when, about 1399, Bajezid demanded tribute from Erzindjan and threatened to invade the emirate, Timur interpreted the threat as an affront to himself. In 1400 his army entered Erzindjan and from there attacked Sivas, the former Greek city of Sebaste, on Ottoman territory. Bajezid ordered his son Suleiman to defend it with reinforcements, but the city fell to Timur, who slaughtered its inhabitants and destroyed it. This was simply by way of a warning to the Sultan. Timur withdrew from Anatolia and turned south to attack Syria. But it was the news of this first encounter between Bajezid and one greater than himself that reached England in the summer of that year.[34]

The news caused a more restrained excitement in Constantinople. The presence of Timur as a potential ally on the eastern flank of the Ottoman Empire had been known for some years. The Emperor Manuel may even have made contact with him before leaving for Italy in 1399. In the western world, ever since the day of Genghis Khan, there had been a pious hope that the Mongols would turn out to be the allies

327

of the Christians against the infidel. The western missionary orders, especially the Dominicans, were eager to act as agents for the realization of this hope. Charles VI of France had been in direct communication with Timur as early as 1396 through Dominican emissaries. Correspondence had been exchanged between Samarkand and Paris; a commercial agreement, even a treaty of peace, had been suggested. The French interest in the commerce of the east had greatly increased with the takeover of Genoa. Timur is known to have exchanged embassies also with the Genoese of Galata. But the Byzantines too hoped for great things from the Mongols. In August 1401 John VII sent a Dominican friar as his envoy to Timur to pay his respects and to propose that, if the Mongols defeated Bajezid, the Byzantines would pay to Timur the tribute that they had formerly paid to the Turks.[35]

Bajezid had been stung into furious action by the Mongol sack of Sivas. He boasted that no one, least of all an upstart like Timur-lenk, could so lightly tempt the wrath and vengeance of the lord of the universe. In the winter of 1401 taunts and insults passed in messages between the Turk and the Mongol. Timur took up the challenge with deadly deliberation. He planned a massive invasion of Anatolia from the east. He sent word to the Genoese in Galata to use their ships to prevent the Turks from escaping to Europe. The Emperor of Trebizond, who had prudently acknowledged Timur as his lord, was required to provide 20 ships for the same purpose. The Venetians were also approached; and it is said that the enthusiasm of the Genoese was so great that they took to flying the Mongol standard from the walls of Galata. In the spring of 1402 the storm broke. Timur began his march westward into Ottoman territory, by way of Sivas to Caesarea. The decisive battle was fought at Djibukabad near Ankara on 28 July 1402. Bajezid had brought up a vast army. The commander of its right wing was the Serbian Stephen Lazarević, of the left the Sultan's eldest son Suleiman. Bajezid himself held the centre and rear with his other sons, commanding his private regiment of 10,000 janissaries. The Ottoman troops fought heroically, but they were conscious that they were fighting a Muslim and not a non-believer, and the fire was not in them. 15,000 Turks and Christians are said to have fallen in the attempt to break the Mongol lines. When the rest had fled, Bajezid and his rearguard continued to resist far into the night until they were overwhelmed. Bajezid was caught trying to escape. He was taken handcuffed to Timur's tent. Four of his sons contrived to get away. But the great Sultan himself became the prisoner of his conqueror. Legend had it that he was kept in chains at night and carried about in an iron cage by day. It is certain that he had to endure the sight of Timur roaming at will through his empire. He died of shame, perhaps by his own hand, on 9 March 1403, though Timur saw to it that he was given honourable burial in the mosque at Brusa.[36]

The battle of Ankara shattered the Ottoman Empire in Asia. The Mongol hordes swept through it, raping and pillaging as they went. Soon after the battle Timur turned against the only remaining Christian city in Asia Minor, Smyrna, which was still defended by the Knights of Rhodes. Its great fortifications had held off repeated attacks by Bajezid, but in December 1402, after a long siege, it fell to Timur who massacred those who had the misfortune not to get away by sea. He spent the winter in Ephesos. Timur's policy, if so it may be called, was to make sure that the shattered fragments of the Ottoman Empire were not reunited. The non-Ottoman emirs, whose principalities had been deliberately and forcibly assimilated by Bajezid, and who had in many cases taken refuge with the Mongols, were now encouraged to return. The emir of Saruchan was back in Magnesia by August 1402. The emirates of Menteshe, Aydin and others were restored to their original lords or to their heirs. The Karamans in particular gained greatly from the Sultan's defeat and quickly rose again to become the chief rivals of the Osmanlis in Anatolia. As to the sons of Bajezid, Timur encouraged their natural propensity to dispute the succession, holding out to each the hope that he would recognize his claim to the Sultanate. The eldest of them, Suleiman, forestalled his brothers by getting across to Europe. He arrived in Gallipoli on 20 August 1402, and before long had made his own arrangements with the Byzantines and had set up house at Adrianople. The youngest, Mehmed Čelebi, retained control of the north-eastern part of the Ottoman dominions in Asia Minor, as the vassal of Timur. All that was left of the rest of the Empire was the area around Brusa; and here authority was disputed between the two other sons of Bajezid, Isa and Musa.[37]

But Timur soon began to tire of the game of Turkish puppets and in the spring of 1403 he abandoned Asia Minor and the prospect of further conquest in the unfamiliar west and led his armies back to Samarkand. Two years later he died on his way to conquer China. Those who had been submerged in the huge flood of his conquests quickly rose to the surface again after he was gone. Nowhere except in India did Timur succeed in establishing anything more permanent than a legend and a nightmare memory of the savagery of his soldiers.

Historians are fond of saying that the moment of the Mongol victory at Ankara in 1402 was the moment which the whole Christian world might have seized to complete the overthrow of the stricken Ottoman Empire. Another crusade of Nicopolis might at this juncture have crushed the Turks for ever. This seems unlikely. The great Sultan Bajezid the Thunderbolt was no more; but the troops that he had led to so many victories over the Christians in Europe were still in Europe in large numbers. The battle of Ankara had broken the structure and the strength of the Ottoman Empire in Asia; but the European provinces were still as firmly held as ever. They had in fact received a great new influx of Turkish soldiers and families fleeing as refugees from the Mongols. For in the confusion after the battle no one was to know whether Timur might turn his armies on Europe; and the Genoese, who were supposed to be guarding the straits on his account, combined business with policy by ferrying thousands of the Turkish refugees across to Thrace. They were assisted by the Venetians and even the Byzantines. If the Mongols were going to invade Europe it would be no harm to have as many soldiers as possible on the spot. For some months after July 1402 fear of the Mongols was more widespread than fear of the Turks. With the gift of hindsight it is easy to say that this fear was unjustified; and in any case it soon dawned on the Byzantines and their Christian allies that the really important outcome of the battle of Ankara was that the Ottoman Empire was now divided: Rumelia, its European portion, was completely cut off from its Asiatic provinces. Their hope of survival lay in keeping things that way; and for a while it proved possible to do so. At the time, however, in August 1402, they were inclined to count their blessings. The blockade of Constantinople, which had lasted for eight years, was lifted; and the very fact of the Ottoman defeat and the humiliation of the Sultan were such unexpected events that Christians unhesitatingly ascribed them to the intervention of God and his Mother. The hoped for miracle had occurred. The future was in God's hands.[38]

NOTES

Narrative sources: Doukas; Chalkokondyles; Sphrantzes.
Modern Works: J. W. Barker, *Manuel II Palaeologus (1391-1425): A study in late Byzantine statesmanship* (New Brunswick, N.J., 1969), 84-216. Cf. the older work of J. Berger de Xivrey, *Mémoire sur la vie et les ouvrages de l'empereur Manuel Paléologue* (Paris, 1853). Ostrogorsky, *History*, 549-57; Bréhier, *Vie et Mort*, 379-89; Diehl, *L'Europe orientale*, 344-57.

1 Demetrios Kydones, *Correspondence*, II, 386, no. 430.

2 Kydones, *Correspondence*, II, 407, no. 442; Doukas, 77 (Grecu). Cf. Ostrogorsky, 'Byzance, état tributaire . . .', 52-3.

3 Barker, *Manuel II*, 87-97 (where parts of Manuel's letters are translated).

4 Edited by E. Trapp, *Manuel II*. *Palaiologos, Dialoge mit einem "Perser"* (Vienna, 1966). Cf. C. J. G. Turner, 'Pages from the late Byzantine philosophy of history', *BZ*, LVII (1964), 348-52.

5 *Pèlerinage d'Ignace de Smolensk*, ed. B. de Khitrowo, 143-7. The anonymous Byzantine account of the coronation has been edited by J. Verpeaux, *Pseudo-Kodinos, Traité des Offices* (Paris, 1966), Appendix VI, 351-61; and by P. Schreiner, 'Hochzeit und Krönung Kaiser Manuels II. im Jahre 1392', *BZ*, LX (1967), 70-85.

6 The text of the Patriarch's letter is in *MM*, II, 188-92. There are partial translations in E. Barker, *Social and Political Thought in Byzantium*, 194-6; and in J. W. Barker, *Manuel II*, 106-9. On its date, see Barker, *Manuel II*, 109 note 31. See also Runciman, *Great Church in Captivity*, 71-6; Ostrogorsky, *History*, 553-4; Obolensky, *Byzantine Commonwealth*, 264-6.

7 Ostrogorsky, *History*, 550-1; *CMH*, IV, 1, 545.

8 Manuel II, *Funeral Oration for his brother Theodore*, in *PG*, CLVI, 221-8. Cf. Barker, *Manuel II*, 112-18; Ostrogorsky, *History*, 549 and references.

9 Doukas, 79 (ed. Grecu). Barker, *Manuel II*, 123-6.

10 Ostrogorsky, *History*, 551. On the Turkish conquest of Thessaly, cf. Nicol, *Meteora*, 68-9; Vacalopoulos, *Origins of the Greek Nation*, 164-6.

11 Longnon, *L'empire latin*, 339-47; *CMH*, IV, 1, 419-23.

12 D. A. Zakythinos, *Le Despotat grec de Morée*, I (Paris, 1932), 155-6; Ostrogorsky, *History*, 550.

13 See especially A. S. Atiya, *The Crusade of Nicopolis* (London, 1934), *passim*, and *The Crusade in the Later Middle Ages* (London, 1938), 435-62. Cf. Runciman, *Crusades*, III, 455-62.

14 Manuel, *Funeral Oration*, in *PG*, CLVI, 261; *Letters*, ed. Legrand, 39-44, no. 31.

15 Zakythinos, *Despotat*, I, 156-7.

16 Doukas, 85 (Grecu). Cf. Barker, *Manuel II*, 137-41.

17 Barker, *Manuel II*, 142-54.

18 D. M. Nicol, 'A Byzantine Emperor in England. Manuel II's visit to London in 1400-1401', *University of Birmingham Historical Journal*, XII, 2 (1971), 204f.

19 See P. Wirth, 'Zum Geschichtsbild Kaiser Johannes' VII. Palaiologos', *B*, XXXV (1965), 592-600. Cf. Barker, *Manuel II*, 164.

20 The adventures of Marshal Boucicaut are narrated by his biographer in *Le Livre des faicts du Bon Messire Jean le Meingre dit Boucicaut, Mareschal de France et Gouverneur de Gennes*, in *Collections complètes des Mémoires relatifs à l'histoire de France*, VII-IX (Paris, 1825); also edited by J. A. C. Buchon (Paris, 1836). Cf. Barker, *Manuel II*, 160-4.

21 Barker, *Manuel II*, 165 and Appendix XIV, 490-3.

22 The fullest account of Manuel's visit to western Europe is that by A. A. Vasiliev, 'Putešestvie vizantijskago imperatora Manuila II Paleologa na zapadnoj Evrope (1399-1403 g.)', in *Žurnal ministerstva narodnago prosveščenija*, XXXIX (1912), 41-78, 260-304. See also G. Schlumberger, *Un Empereur de Byzance à Paris et à Londres* (Paris, 1916); Barker, *Manuel II*, 167-99; Nicol, 'A Byzantine Emperor in England ...', 204 note 1, for reference to other accounts.

23 On Manuel Chrysoloras, see G. Cammelli, *I dotti bizantini e le origini dell'umanesimo*, I : *Manuele Crisolora* (Florence, 1941); J. Thomson, 'Manuel Chrysoloras and the Early Italian Renaissance', *Greek, Roman and Byzantine Studies*, VII (1966), 63-82.

24 Nicol, 'A Byzantine Emperor in England ...', 211-19.

25 Barker, *Manuel II*, 181-91 (with translations of Manuel's letters); G. T. Dennis 'Two unknown documents of Manuel II Palaeologus', *Travaux et Mémoires*, III (1968), 397-404.

26 Greek text in *PG*, CLVI, 577-80.

27 This treatise, unpublished, exists in two manuscripts in the Vatican Library. Cf. Barker, *Manuel II*, 192-3, 434, 437.

28 P. Gautier, 'Un récit inédit du siège de Constantinople par les Turcs (1394-1402)', *REB*, XXIII (1965), 100-17.

29 *Le Livre des faicts*, chapter XXXVI. Cf. G. Schlumberger, 'Jean de Chateaumorand', in Schlumberger, *Byzance et Croisades* (Paris, 1927), 282-336.

30 Text in *MM*, II, 463-7; translation in Barker, *Manuel II*, 208-11.

31 The Latin text of John VII's letter to Henry IV has been reprinted in Barker, *Manuel II*, 500-1; translation, 213-14.

32 Nicol, 'A Byzantine Emperor in England ...', 219-22.

33 On Timur, see Ahmed ibn Arabshah, *Tamarlane or Timur the Great Amir*, translated by J. H. Sanders (London, 1936); Gibbons, *Foundation of the Ottoman Empire*, 243f.; L. Bouvat, *L'Empire mongol, deuxième phase* (*Histoire du monde*, VIII, 3 : Paris, 1927); H. Hookham, *Tamburlaine the Conqueror* (London, 1962); Runciman,

Crusades, III, 463; Ostrogorsky, *History*, 556-7.

34 This is the account of the Spanish ambassador Gonzales de Clavijo, 129-36 (translated by G. Le Strange, London, 1928). See below, 336-7.

35 Cf. Barker, *Manuel II*, Appendix XVIII, 504-9.

36 For the date of the battle of Ankara, see Marie-Mathilde Alexandrescu-Dersca, *La Campagne de Timur en Anatolie* (Bucharest, 1942). Cf. Gibbons, *Foundation of the Ottoman Empire*, 249-57.

37 P. Wittek, *Das Fürstentum Mentesche* (Istanbul, 1934), 88f. The date of Suleiman's arrival at Gallipoli is given by the *Short Chronicle*, no. 41, ed. Lambros-Amantos, 68.

38 See the Thanksgiving to the Virgin, in P. Gautier, 'Actions de Grâces de Démétrius Chrysoloras à la Théotokos pour l'anniversaire de la bataille d'Ankara (28 juillet 1403)', *REB*, XIX (1961), 340-57. Manuel II himself composed two *opuscula* expressing his relief at the news of the battle of Ankara: one, in the form of an address to the Sultan Bajezid, is entitled 'What the lord of the Persians and Scythians (i.e. Timur) may have said to the tyrant of the Turks'; the other, in the manner of a Psalm, is a prayer of thanksgiving to God for delivering his flock from the infidel Thunderbolt. There are translations of both with references, in Barker, *Manuel II*, Appendix XX, 513-18.

Sixteen

The Last Reprieve—1402-25

The good news from Ankara reached the Emperor Manuel in Paris in September 1402. The Seigneur de Chateaumorand returned to France that month bringing a first-hand account. The news had reached Venice at about the same time. On 22 September the Venetian Senate discussed what measures should be taken for the defence of their interests in Constantinople. On 9 October they wrote to Manuel in Paris offering him their congratulations on his deliverance and urging him to get home as soon as he could. The Venetians were anxious to play their full part in any new settlement with the Turks, and they would rather the arrangements were made by Manuel than by John VII, whom they rightly suspected of favouring their Genoese rivals.

Manuel left Paris at the end of November 1402, encouraged by the gift of a small annual pension from Charles VI and escorted by a troop of 200 soldiers commanded by Chateaumorand. He went by way of Genoa, where he was royally received by Marshal Boucicaut in January 1403. He was in Venice by the end of March. But he seemed to be in no great hurry to go back to Constantinople. The Venetians did all they could to speed the Emperor on his way. But he declared that he wanted to break his journey for about a month in the Morea to settle affairs there. No doubt Manuel was apprehensive about the welcome he might get from his nephew John VII after so long an absence. The Venetians fitted out three warships to take him and his suite of 40 people to the Morea and from there on to Constantinople; and Manuel finally left Venice on 5 April 1403. He was expected to call at Ragusa on his way down the Adriatic. Great preparations had been made to receive him, but his ships sailed by without stopping until they reached the Venetian harbour of Modon in the Morea. There the Emperor rejoined his wife and family and discussed the internal state of the province with his brother Theodore. Towards the end of May he resumed his journey, first to Gallipoli and thence to Constantinople, where he arrived on 9 June.[1]

Nearly a year had passed since the battle of Ankara and it had taken Manuel ten months to reach his capital since the news of the battle had come to him in Paris. It is not surprising that those on the spot in the east, the Emperor John VII, the Venetians and the Genoese, had during those months made their own accommodations to the changed circumstances. They could not wait for Manuel to make his leisurely way back from France. In August 1402 Suleiman, the eldest son of Bajezid, had arrived in Gallipoli hopeful of taking over Rumelia. It was with Suleiman that negotiations had to take place. Suleiman was not made in the image of his father. He was effeminate and self-indulgent by nature, inclined more to tolerance than to aggression. He had little to fear from the Christians in eastern Europe, but he knew that he must reach an amicable settlement with them, partly because Rumelia was now cut off from Asia Minor, and partly because he was even more anxious than they about the next move that Timur and his Mongols might make. A summit conference was held, apparently at Gallipoli. It went on for more than three months. In January or early February 1403 a treaty was drawn up. It was signed by Suleiman, by John VII, by the representatives of Venice, Genoa and Rhodes, and by Stephen Lazarević who, like Suleiman, had escaped from the battlefield of Ankara. The terms were unbelievably favourable for Byzantium and the Christian powers. The Byzantines were relieved of the tribute which they had paid to Bajezid and of the burden of vassalage to the Turks. The city and district of Thessalonica, together with Mount Athos, were to be restored to them, as well as a long stretch of the Black Sea coast from Constantinople up to Mesembria or Varna, and the Aegean islands of Skiathos, Skopelos and Skyros. Suleiman furthermore undertook to become the vassal of the Emperor, in terms graphically described by the historian Doukas. Falling at the Emperor's feet he declared: 'I shall be as a son to you if you will be my father. From now on let there be no rivalry or difference between us. Only proclaim me lord of Thrace and the other lands which I have inherited from my ancestors.'[2]

It was almost too good to be true. Suleiman departed to take up his residence in Adrianople, while the Byzantines eagerly looked forward to taking over Thessalonica and the other concessions from their Turkish garrisons. The tables were turned. The Byzantines, it seemed, from being the subjects of the Turks, were now their overlords. The Italians and the Serbs too had profited in various ways, but it was the Byzantines who had most blessings to count. The treaty had been the work of John VII. The Emperor Manuel knew nothing of it until he got to Venice in March 1403. It was partly for this reason that the

Venetians wanted him to continue his journey without delay, so that he could validate the treaty with his own signature. But Manuel took his own time about it. Not until May did he reach Gallipoli. John VII was there to meet him. Suleiman may also have been present, and there or in Constantinople he signed another version of the same treaty in June 1403. Perhaps at the same time he strengthened the new alliance by giving his neice as a bride to Suleiman. She was an illegitimate daughter of his brother Theodore.[3]

It was John VII who had done duty in Constantinople during his uncle's long travels. It was he who had seized the moment to make the most favourable terms possible in the circumstances, both with the Mongols and with the Turks. His reward was less than he had a right to expect. He was promised the governorship of Thessalonica. In the summer of 1403 his uncle sent him to the island of Lemnos, to wait there until such time as he could take over the city from the Turks by terms of the treaty. John got tired of waiting; or else a suspicion formed in his mind that he had really been sent into exile. In September he got in touch with the Genoese lord of the neighbouring island of Lesbos, Francesco II Gattilusio, and persuaded him to co-operate in seizing Thessalonica by force. Francesco was John's father-in-law. The threat of force may have been enough to clear the air, for there is no evidence that John and his Genoese friends ever attacked Thessalonica. But there are many mysteries still to be resolved in this matter. It was not in keeping with Manuel II's character to act so shabbily towards his nephew, unless he had good reason. It is far from clear how deeply the Genoese, who had always supported John VII, may have been implicated in a plot. Nor is there any record of the reaction to Manuel's return of the Byzantine faction which had once preferred his nephew. It has even been suggested that John VII had an infant son, Andronikos V, whom he had nominated if not crowned as his heir during his uncle's absence, thereby staking his claim to the imperial succession.[4]

In October 1403 a Spanish ambassador who was on his way to Samarkand put in at the island of Lesbos. Ruy Gonzalez de Clavijo was one of a delegation sent by Henry III of Castile to the great Timur, and he composed a celebrated diary of his journey between the years 1403 and 1406. It is to him that we are indebted for the only account of the supposed collaboration between John VII and Francesco Gattilusio to take Thessalonica by force. Clavijo met both parties on Lesbos. The tale told to him was that the old Emperor Manuel had lost his temper with his nephew when he discovered that a secret agreement had been made before the battle of Ankara. John VII had promised to make over Gallipoli to the Sultan Bajezid in the event of his victory over Timur. On this account Manuel had banished his nephew to the island of Lemnos. This story too may contain an element of truth. The full facts may never be known. But everything suggests that Manuel's return to his empire had at once revived the tension between himself and his nephew which Marshal Boucicaut had so diplomatically resolved four years earlier. Whether for political, dynastic, or simply temperamental reasons, Manuel II and John VII could not live together in the same city.[5]

Before the end of the year they had sunk their differences sufficiently to come to an arrangement. John VII was officially appointed to govern Thessalonica with the title of 'Emperor of all Thessaly'; and there he stayed until his death five years later. The city of Thessalonica had been in Turkish hands since Manuel abandoned it in 1387. It has sometimes been alleged that the Greeks recovered it for a while, either in 1391 or in 1394; but the fact is hard to substantiate.[6] The first of its 16 years of foreign occupation seem to have been tolerable for its inhabitants. Its bishop, Isidore Glabas, who had left his charge during the siege but returned when the Turks had taken over, remarked on the special favours that had been granted to its citizens by the Sultan Bajezid. In 1393 the city was still to some extent administered by Byzantine officials and magistrates. There may also have been some exemption from tax and tribute to the Sultan. At all events, the Bishop Isidore in his sermons suggested that his people ought to give thanks to God that their plight was not a great deal worse. On the other hand it is from him that we hear for the first time of the forcible recruitment by the Turks of Christian boys for service in the Sultan's janissary corps—the *devshirme* or child-tribute that was to become such a distressing burden on Christian families under Turkish rule thereafter. Isidore died in 1396. His successor as Bishop of Thessalonica, Gabriel, seems to have won the respect of the Turks and, by personal appeal to Bajezid, to have secured yet further privileges for his flock, so that they had at least what his biographer describes as 'a more tolerable slavery'.[7] Now, in 1403, the slavery was over. The people of Thessalonica, like those in Constantinople, had a Greek Emperor once again. 'In like manner', writes Doukas, 'in all the other cities and towns the Emperor (Manuel) appointed illustrious Greeks as governors, and all of them were taken over and the Turks were expelled. And in the province of Thrace there was utter peace and untroubled tranquillity. But in the east there was total confusion and continual change of rulers in all the provinces.'[8]

It is a fair generalization about the condition of the Byzantine and Turkish worlds at the beginning of the fifteenth century. The death of Bajezid and the disappearance of Timur the Mongol were followed by ten years of intermittent civil war among the Turks. The Emperor Manuel in Constantinople was at first the favoured suzerain or 'father' of Suleiman, the 'Sultan' in Rumelia, then in danger of reprisals from Suleiman's brother Musa, who supplanted him at Adrianople; then again the protector and friend of a third contender in the Ottoman family, Mehmed I, who with Byzantine help, made himself Sultan in 1413. During these years of crisis for the Ottoman Empire it was possible for Manuel to manipulate Turkish affairs to the advantage of the Byzantines, much as Murad and Bajezid had manipulated Byzantine affairs to their own benefit. For once the initiative to act as arbiter or mediator lay with the Byzantine Emperor.

To begin with, Manuel's chief concern was to secure the restitution of the towns and territories ceded to him by Suleiman. His grandfather John Cantacuzene had once dreamed of reuniting the Greek portions of the Empire in Europe. Now that Thessalonica and much of Thrace had reverted to Byzantine rule, it might prove possible to reunite them with the Despotate of the Morea. But Manuel hoped that the fragments of his empire could be welded together under a centralized government in Constantinople. This ideal came nearer to being realized when John VII died in September 1408. He had no heir to perpetuate the family feud, for his reputed son had predeceased him. Manuel was therefore able to nominate his own son Andronikos as Despot in Thessalonica. Some months before, in 1407, his brother Theodore had died in Mistra; and here too the succession devolved upon a son of Manuel, Theodore II, who became Despot in the Morea. But since Theodore was barely eight years old, and Andronikos even younger, the remaining provinces of the Empire seemed to be firmly under the control of the father-Emperor in Constantinople. Manuel was less diffident than his father had been in the way of exercising his supreme authority, and emphasizing to all his subordinates that it was he who invested them with their offices, dignities and titles. But he had no illusions that his entente with the Turks could last. He never ceased to look for allies; and above all he was aware, as his grandfather had been, that mastery of the seas was the ultimate strategic advantage that the Byzantines had over the Turks.

The first round in the fratricidal war between Bajezid's sons was soon over. Isa, who had for a time been given refuge in Constantinople by John VII and had then returned to Asia Minor, was killed by his brother Mehmed, who thus became the dominant member of the family in Anatolia. But in 1404 Musa, no longer content to be Mehmed's underling declared war on Suleiman. At first Suleiman held the upper hand, but the conflict was to drag on for six more years.[9] It confirmed Manuel's view that he could not always count on the friendship of a Turkish Sultan at Adrianople. He must make sure that his acquaintances in the western world were kept alive to the true state of affairs in the east. In 1404 he sent ambassadors to the Kings of Aragon and France. In 1406 he renewed his treaty with Venice. In 1407 he wrote to the Venetians imploring them 'as good Christians' to come to terms with the Genoese and co-operate against the Turks. At the end of 1409, when it looked for a horrible moment as if Suleiman was about to be defeated by Musa, Manuel wrote again to the Venetians in more urgent tones, asking them to help keep the two Sultans divided by sending some warships to hold the crossing of the Hellespont. Their answer to this request is instructive of Venetian ambiguity. On 10 January 1410 their senate decided that, whereas it was a good idea to keep the Turks apart and patrol the straits, they were not prepared to act on their own. Other western nations must be made to play their part. The Emperor had complained that Venetian ships were actually transporting Turks back and forth across the Hellespont. The senators replied that they could not prevent this. It was up to Manuel to supervise the sea traffic more efficiently. They also pointed out that the captains of Venetian ships were empowered to take on board any members of the imperial family who wanted to leave Constantinople, but the passengers would have to pay their fares. Given the prevarication of the Venetians one is not surprised to hear that several of their people had been involved in brawls with the Greeks in the streets of Constantinople.[10]

Meanwhile Manuel tried again to capitalize on his personal friendship with the King of France and to elicit some of the help, financial or otherwise, that had been promised him. As his ambassador he chose his friend Manuel Chrysoloras, who already enjoyed a reputation in the west as a man of letters and an exponent of Greek culture. He had only recently come back to Constantinople from one of his periodic visits to Italy. He was to become Manuel's ambassador at large and plenipotentiary in western Europe. He reached Paris by way of Venice early in 1408. He took with him as a present from the Emperor a magnificent manuscript of the works of Dionysios the

Areopagite, bound in gold and ivory, richly illuminated, and containing a splendid portrait of Manuel himself with his Empress Helena and their three eldest sons. The gift was intended for the library of the abbey of St Dionysios or St Denys in Paris which the Emperor knew well. It was a pleasing gesture and much appreciated by King Charles VI. Chrysoloras also crossed over to England, where he visited London and Salisbury, and later went on to Spain on his master's business. But no one had much to offer him, and any money that may once have been collected in these countries for the defence of Constantinople seemed to have evaporated. He reported his disappointments back to the Emperor about 1410. Manuel replied saying how discouraging it was to get nothing but promises. 'What you tell me,' he wrote, 'of the way in which all this business has been organized does more to lower than to raise our hopes.'[11]

In 1408, however, Manuel felt that conditions were settled enough for him to pay another call on his outlying province in southern Greece. He set great store by the Despotate of the Morea, and he wanted to make certain of its security and of its links with Constantinople. His brother, the Despot Theodore, had died in 1407. Manuel's purpose in going to Mistra was partly to install his own infant son as successor. While he was there he felt moved to compose a long funeral oration for his late brother. The evidence suggests, and the prolixity of the work surely confirms, that he never in fact delivered the oration at Theodore's tomb, at least in its extant form. But, as with other of his literary works, the Emperor was sufficiently proud of it to send copies to his friends.[12] The Despot Theodore deserved to be so commemorated. He had ridden the storms of Latin aggression and Turkish invasion more or less single-handed. After the terrible plunder of the Morea and the sack of Argos in 1397 he had almost despaired. Communications between Mistra and Constantinople were hampered by the Turkish blockade. After great deliberation he had agreed, with his brother's consent, to sell Corinth to the Knights of Rhodes. The deal was concluded in 1400. The Knights then bullied him into parting with more territory. But the local inhabitants fought bitterly against this sell-out to the Latins; and the Turks, thinking it to be a dangerous development, made representations about it. Further negotiations resulted in his redeeming Corinth from the Knights in 1404. He gained the support of Carlo Tocco in successful warfare against the Navarrese in Achaia, and in the last years of his life he was able to devote himself to the organization and administration of the Despotate without the constant fear of attack from the north. His death was a great loss to the Byzantine cause in Greece. Manuel was so encouraged by the improved condition of the Morea that he instructed Manuel Chrysoloras to bargain with the Venetians about the return to the Empire of some of their acquisitions there. Needless to say, Venice would not entertain any such idea. But the proposal shows how much importance the Emperor attached to the Morea.[13]

He was still there when he heard of the death of John VII in Thessalonica in September 1408. This was an occasion for thanksgiving rather than mourning. The Emperor hurried north to the city that he had once called his own, to install as its governor Andronikos, the third of his infant sons. While he was there he took the opportunity to examine the state of the monasteries of Mount Athos which had so recently been liberated from Turkish supervision. The monks were now no longer obliged to pay the *haradj* to their Ottoman masters, and many of their confiscated landed properties had been restored to the Empire. But, in his precarious economic state, the Emperor could not see his way to restoring to them all their previous immunities. Only two-thirds of their property was given back to the monasteries, and they, like other landowners in Macedonia, were in future to pay to the treasury in Constantinople one-third of the amount of tax that they had been paying to the Sultan. The fact that the name *haradj* was still to be used for this tax did not make it any more palatable. But at least the monks of Athos and the people of Macedonia were a little better off than they had been under the Turks.[14]

When he got back to Constantinople the Emperor found that the second round in the Ottoman struggle for power was already under way. In July 1410 Suleiman was surprised at Adrianople by his brother Musa. For a while he held out with Byzantine support. But his own soldiers were against him, and in February 1411 they deserted him. He was strangled by his brother. The Byzantines feared that the worst had happened. The Ottoman Empire of Europe and Asia seemed to have been reunited, and under a Sultan who was dedicated to punishing all those who had given comfort to his rival. Musa was a different character from the easy-going Suleiman. He owed his victory in part to a reaction of the ghazi, warrior element in the Ottoman army against his brother's mild policy towards the Christians. Once established in Adrianople, Musa took his revenge. First he humiliated Stephen Lazarević of Serbia who had fought for his brother. Then he announced his intention of taking back from the

Byzantines all the concessions made to them by Suleiman in 1403. He led his troops to Constantinople, burning and devastating the country on his way, and laid siege to the city by land and sea. More of his regiments were sent to besiege Thessalonica. They swarmed into the Strymon valley and down into Thessaly.

But Manuel had foreseen these possibilities. Constantinople was well prepared for a siege. The people had withdrawn behind the walls and there were ample stocks of provisions. The Byzantines were even able to hit back. Musa had to keep his distance, while his ships were triumphantly driven off by a fleet commanded by a brother of the Emperor. Musa then demanded payment of an enormous tribute. But Manuel had a better idea. He got in touch with Mehmed, the only other surviving son of Bajezid, at Brusa, offering him the means of transport across the Hellespont if he would come and deal with his brother. Mehmed was tempted; and early in 1412 Manuel went over to Skutari to meet him, escorted him back to Constantinople and entertained him there for three days. On the fourth day Mehmed set out from the city with his 15,000 men to do battle with his brother Musa. He was defeated and returned to Asia Minor. Manuel, however, persuaded him to prepare a larger expedition, which would be assisted by Byzantine troops as well as the Serbian army of Stephen Lazarević. Mehmed's second attack was no more successful. But at the third attempt he and his allies drove Musa and his men back to Adrianople and then pursued them far into the Balkans. The final decisive engagement was fought at Camurlu, in Serbia, on 5 July 1413. Musa was captured and strangled. Mehmed I became Sultan of Rumelia and of Rum.[15]

Mehmed Čelebi was a cultivated and intelligent man. He was also a man of his word. He did not forget the help that the Byzantines and their allies had given him to overcome his brother. The Emperor had played his cards well. His reward was a treaty by which the new Sultan restored to him all the territory and other privileges that Suleiman had granted ten years earlier. The messengers that Manuel sent to him after his victory were commanded to go back to their master with these words: 'Go and say to my father the Emperor of the Romans that, with the help of God and the co-operation of my father the Emperor, I have recovered my hereditary dominions. From this day forth I am and shall be his subject, as a son to his father. For he will find me neither unaware nor ungrateful. Let him order me to do his bidding and I shall with the greatest of pleasure execute his wishes like a servant.' The ambassadors from Serbia, Bulgaria, Wallachia and Greece, who waited upon Mehmed were received in like manner. He feasted them all at his table and sent them away saying: 'Tell your masters that I offer peace to all and accept peace from all. He who maliciously disturbs this peace, may the God of peace be against him.' Such at least is the account of the Greek historian Doukas.[16]

Mehmed's triumph heralded the last period of such peace that the Byzantines were ever to know. Its existence once again was guaranteed only by a personal relationship between a Sultan and an Emperor. It was not likely to survive the death of the one or of the other. Of this fact, to give him his due, Manuel was fully conscious. The future was still in God's hands. Providence had wrought great mercies. But it was the Byzantines who were ultimately dependent upon the goodwill of the Turks and not the other way about. If anything were to be made of this welcome respite therefore it must be done quickly and energetically. Manuel was now in his sixties. He had married late and though his eldest son John was about 20 in 1413, the rest of his sons were too young to be of much practical help to their father. Yet he himself still had much of the energy that he had shown at Thessalonica when he was 30 years younger; and in the years after 1413 he applied it to making the most of what had been gained and strengthening the ties between Constantinople and the provinces, so that when the wind changed his Empire might have a stronger and more united will to survive.

On 25 July 1414 Manuel set out on a tour of his dominions. He left Constantinople in charge of his son John VIII. Thessalonica was his first objective, but on his way there he took occasion to reassert his authority over the island of Thasos which was being contested by a son of Francesco Gattilusio of Lesbos. In September he sailed on to Thessalonica, where he spent the winter with his young son the Despot Andronikos. In the spring of 1415 he left for the Morea.[17] He went by way of the island of Negroponte, where he was courteously received by the Venetian governor, and reached Kenchreai on the Saronic Gulf not far from Corinth on 29 March. In a letter that he wrote to some friends in Thessalonica Manuel had mentioned a plan that was already much in his mind for the protection of the Morea against invasion from the north. That plan was now to be put into practice. A wall was to be built across the six-mile neck of land from the Saronic Gulf to the Gulf of Corinth. It would make the Morea, which was now largely in Greek control, a Byzantine island, rendering it defensible against any Turkish attacks by land and self-sufficient by sea. The plan was not new. Such a wall across the Isthmus of Corinth had been built more than once in antiquity, and in the sixth century Justinian had given it the permanence characteristic of his engineering works. Manuel's wall, the Hexamilion, was erected on the solid foundations laid down by Justinian's architects. It had to be done quickly before the Turks got to hear of it; and it is said to have been completed in 25 days. It was fortified with 153 towers and there was a castle at either end. The Venetians, when Manuel informed them of the project, congratulated him on his enterprise, though they fought shy of his suggestion that they might contribute to the cost of it. The cost was heavy. To find the money and the labour the Emperor had in fact to levy special taxes on the inhabitants of the Morea, which the local landlords bitterly resented. Some of them organized a rebellion, but Manuel took up the challenge and crushed the revolt near Kalamata in July 1415. The ringleaders were captured and removed to Constantinople. The Emperor spent the rest of the year at Mistra, returning to his capital in March 1416.[18]

The Hexamilion wall was a solid advertisement for the truth about Byzantine-Turkish relationships. The Emperor and the Sultan were officially at peace. But Manuel took no chances. A time of peace was a time to make ready for war. He was fortunate in the fact that most of the Sultan Mehmed's reign was taken up in restoring order to the chaos in the Asiatic sector of his empire. Mehmed was involved first in war against the rebellious emir of Aydin, Djuneid, and then against the Karamans. He had to contend with two uprisings of a religious nature; and about 1416 his position was threatened by the revolt of one Mustafa, who claimed to be a long-lost son of Bajezid who had been lying low since the battle of Ankara. In this affair the Byzantines became implicated. The pretender Mustafa was at first supported by the Venetians to whom he had appealed. They seem to have engineered his crossing to Europe, where he found a ready ally in Djuneid who had been deported from Smyrna by the Sultan. But, as a rival claimant to the Sultanate, he was of interest also to the Byzantines. The Emperor Manuel even plotted on his behalf with Stephen Lazarević and with the emir of the Karamans. Mehmed's newly built fleet which attempted to intervene was sent to the bottom of the sea off Gallipoli by the Venetians in May 1416.

But the pretender Mustafa with his friend Djuneid were soon

cornered by the Sultan's army in Thessaly. They fled to Thessalonica where the Byzantine governor, in the name of the Despot Andronikos, gave them asylum. It was an unfriendly act in view of the treaty existing between the Byzantine government and the lawful Sultan, and Mehmed appealed to the Emperor in Constantinople. Manuel politely refused to hand over his political refugees; but he promised to hold them as prisoners for the rest of their lives if the Sultan would provide an annual pension for their maintenance. Mehmed agreed to these terms. Mustafa was put on the island of Lemnos, Djuneid was confined in a monastery in Constantinople. The affair illustrated the precarious nature of the relationship between Emperor and Sultan. They had a gentleman's agreement. But neither was sufficiently confident of his own strength to wish that agreement broken by an outright act of war. Mehmed realized perfectly that the Emperor now had in his hands a pretender who might one day prove very useful. It was a clever stroke. But the two men understood each other, and the incident did strangely little harm to their understanding.[19]

One valuable by-product of it was the destruction of the new Turkish fleet by the Venetians in 1416. This was a severe blow to Mehmed's hopes of reviving his continental Empire. But it seems to have occurred as much by accident as by design. The Venetians still coyly refused to give unilateral aid to Constantinople. They must be assured in advance that other European powers were involved. The Emperor Manuel nexer relaxed his diplomatic approaches to those powers despite the lull in hostilities with the Turks. But since 1402 Venice had been at war with Hungary, and the two western powers that were most capable of helping Byzantium, by sea and by land, were otherwise occupied.[20] The Pope, immersed as he was in the problems of his own divided Church, was quite unable to give a lead. Manuel Chrysoloras, the Emperor's roving ambassador in the west, followed Pope John XXIII around on his unhappy peregrinations and was actually present when the Council met at Constance in November 1414 to resolve the conflicts in the western Church. Chrysoloras, who had himself become a Roman Catholic, died of a fever at Constance in April 1415. But the convocation of the Council, instigated largely by King Sigismund of Hungary, gave Manuel new hope that here was a gathering which could be influenced towards helping him. While he was in the Morea he sent ambassadors to Constance offering to act as a mediator between Hungary and Venice and to put forward proposals for the union of the Churches. But the Council of Constance had far more pressing business in hand, and by the time the new Pope Martin V could turn his mind to the Byzantine proposals it was almost too late.[21]

There were two curious consequences of the Byzantine embassy to Constance. One was the granting by Pope Martin of indulgences to all Christians who subscribed to the building of the Hexamilion wall in Greece. The other was his permission for marriages of some of the Emperor's family to Catholic princesses as a gesture towards improved relations between the Churches. Suitable brides were selected for Manuel's sons John and Theodore and brought to Constantinople from Venice in 1420. Theodore, the Despot of the Morea, who was then about 25 years old, married Cleope Malatesta, the daughter of the Count of Rimini. John, Manuel II's heir, married Sophia of Montferrat. The wedding took place in St Sophia on 19 January 1421, and it was followed by John's coronation as co-Emperor with his father. John had been married before, to Anna, daughter of the Grand Duke Basil I of Moscow. But Anna had died in 1418 at the tender age of 15 and after barely four years of marriage. His second marriage was a failure from the outset. Sophia of Montferrat was pathetically unattractive. Her figure was said to be like Lent in front and like Easter behind. John was so disgusted with her that he kept her out of his sight in a remote corner of the palace. The poor girl fled back to Italy in 1426.[22]

The wedding and coronation ceremonies at the beginning of 1421 were formal announcements to the world that John VIII was to inherit the throne. Manuel had made sure that there should be none of the uncertainty about the succession that had dogged his own early career. He had groomed and trained his son John for the tasks that lay ahead. He had composed edifying tracts and tedious treatises for him on the proper education and moral conduct of a prince.[23] He had given him a taste of power as regent while he was away in Greece, and in 1416 he had sent him to gain practical experience of provincial administration with his brother Theodore in the Morea for almost two years. Now, in 1421, the Emperor Manuel, who was 71 and in poor health, felt that the time had come to withdraw from the limelight and let his son John VIII take over.

There were those of John's generation who had been waiting for this moment in order to put forward their plans for a more aggressive policy towards the Turks. It was no secret that the Sultan had gained as much if not more than the Byzantines from his entente with the Emperor Manuel. Some felt that time was running out, that the days of gentleman's agreements were over, and that action was needed. In 1421 Mehmed asked leave of Manuel to cross over from Europe to Asia by way of Constantinople. A rumour got about that he meant to settle his affairs in the east preparatory to launching an attack on the city. Some of Manuel's advisers concluded that here was a heaven-sent opportunity to seize the Sultan and murder him. But Manuel declined to be the first to break his oath. He sent out an escort to meet Mehmed, sailed alongside his ship across the straits, and dined with him in his tent at Skutari. The Emperor had behaved with honour, but the gesture was differently construed by many of his own people. The Sultan returned to Adrianople without mishap. A few days later, however, he died, on 21 May 1421. Reports vary as to whether he died in a hunting accident, by poison, or from dysentery. But even the fact of his death was not known to the outside world for some weeks, for his vizir deliberately concealed it so that his son Murad should have time to get to Adrianople and claim the succession.[24]

The news of Mehmed's death aggravated the current division of opinion in Constantinople. The Emperor Manuel was for recognizing Murad II as the lawful heir to the Sultanate. Murad would have been content to be so recognized. But the co-Emperor John VIII thought it would be a clever move to play off against him the pretender to the Sultanate, Mustafa, who was still in Byzantine custody. John's view was shared by his brothers and by some others of their generation. The late Sultan had, in his will, made Manuel the guardian of his two last born sons, aged seven and eight. But when messengers were sent to Murad's court to collect them the new Sultan's vizir is said to have refused to hand them over on the ground that it was not lawful for Muslim boys to be brought up by infidels.[25] This incident, if true, must have strengthened the voice of those in Constantinople who hoped for action. The Emperor Manuel was too old and tired to do more than try to dissuade his son John from a precipitate and dangerous plan. But in the end he washed his hands of the affair and resigned responsibility, as he had already resigned the government, to his co-Emperor.

In the autumn of 1421 Mustafa was brought out of his confinement in Lemnos and put up as the Byzantine favourite for the Sultanate. He was made to promise certain concessions in the event of his victory; but victory was never within his reach. For a few weeks he seemed to control Rumelia. But in January 1422 Murad brought an army over from Anatolia and redressed the balance. Mustafa was captured and hanged. The whole scheme had been ill-conceived. Even if the pretender had been successful the Byzantines would have been the losers. For Mustafa was too shifty a character to honour his promises. Murad, now undisputed Sultan of Europe and Asia, was furious. He had no time for the Greek ambassadors who were sent to mollify him. He made immediate preparations to attack Constantinople. In June he arrived on the scene to direct the siege of the city. Simultaneously another Turkish army was dispatched to blockade Thessalonica. Once more the tables had been turned on the Byzantines. Now it was clear to them that their days of peace were over and that they were back where they had been before the Sultan Mehmed I came to his throne in 1413.[26]

The siege of Constantinople in 1422 was no mere punitive gesture against those who had offended the Sultan. Murad employed every means at his disposal to break the resistance of the inhabitants and take their city by assault. An eye-witness of the siege, John Kananos, tells how the Sultan built an immense rampart of earth from the Sea of Marmora to the Golden Horn. From this his troops discharged volleys of fire and stones from catapults against and over the land walls. The Turkish camp was full of slave-traders and dervishes, come to collect the booty and the slaves that had been promised after the capture of the city. A much revered imam called Seid-Bokhari, who claimed descent from the Prophet, had foretold that Constantinople would fall on 24 August. The main assault was therefore made on that day. There was a long and bitter battle for possession of the walls. But suddenly the Turks panicked, burnt their encampments and beat a retreat, leaving only a small body of men behind. In the eyes of John Kananos the Byzantine victory was due partly to the heroic defence of the city walls directed by the Emperor John VIII, in which men and women alike participated. But the abrupt withdrawal of the Turks and the salvation of the city were due, as they had been 20 years before, to the miraculous intervention of its protectress, the Mother of God.[27]

The more professional historians of the time, however, suggest that the old Emperor Manuel also had a hand in his city's deliverance. Of the two little boys for whom Mehmed had made him guardian, one had already been strangled by his elder brother Murad, who thus set an unfortunate precedent for later Ottoman rulers. The other, however, whose name was Mustafa, had some support from Murad's rivals in Anatolia. In the course of the siege of Constantinople, Manuel contrived to get word to little Mustafa's tutor at Brusa that he would champion his claim to the Sultanate. Mustafa was indeed proclaimed Sultan across the water. This challenge to his authority meant, as Manuel had intended it should, that Murad had to abandon his siege operations. He took his army with him from Constantinople on 6 September 1422. It was the last time that the Byzantines were given a chance to play off one Ottoman prince against another. Mustafa was quickly rounded up and strangled. But Murad's temper was not sweetened by this further evidence of Byzantine double dealing. Nor did his withdrawal from Constantinople mean that the Turks relaxed their efforts in other parts of Europe. The blockade of Thessalonica continued, and in 1423 Ottoman armies invaded Albania and attacked the Morea from Thessaly. The Hexamilion wall at the Isthmus, of which Manuel had been so proud, proved no obstacle to the Sultan's general Turachan and his soldiers who ravaged the peninsula.[28]

Things had gone from bad to worse. Thessalonica was cut off by land. At any moment Murad might elect to resume the siege of Constantinople. John VIII, now more than ever in practical charge of affairs, decided to make one more attempt to rouse the conscience of the western world by a personal approach. Venice and Hungary had at length stopped fighting in 1420. But they were not on speaking terms. The Venetians were seriously alarmed by the Turkish invasion of Albania and the possible danger to their security in the Adriatic. Sigismund of Hungary was the man most likely to be able to organize military aid for Constantinople. John VIII therefore made for Venice and for Hungary. In November 1423 he set sail for Venice. He stayed there for more than a month. The response to his appeals was courteous but familiar: the Venetians would gladly co-operate in the defence of Byzantium if there was anyone with whom to co-operate. But they would not go it alone, except in so far as to defend their own maritime interests in Negroponte, the Morea and the Greek islands. John went on to Hungary by way of Milan. If he had thought that he would have any real influence as a mediator between Hungary and Venice he was sadly mistaken. Nor had King Sigismund anything to offer the young Emperor except the blessings which would accrue to the unhappy Greeks if they would accept union with the Church of Rome.[29]

John got back to Constantinople on 1 November 1424. His mission had not been fruitful. But by that time his father Manuel or his advisers had worked out a new settlement with the Sultan. After various exchanges of embassies, in which the historian Sphrantzes took part, a new treaty had been fixed on 22 February 1424. It gave peace to Constantinople. But it was of a very different nature from the peace that had prevailed in the first years of the fifteenth century. The Empire was now reduced almost to the suburbs of its capital, and its Emperor was reduced to renting his throne from the Sultan for a tribute of 100,000 ducats a year. Almost nothing was left to him of the territories that he had regained by his treaties with Suleiman and Mehmed I.[30]

There was one exception, and that was the city of Thessalonica. It had been under siege since 1422. Its defence was in the hands of the Despot Andronikos but, like Constantinople, its survival depended on the strength of its walls and on the fact that communications were still open to it by sea. The conditions inside the walls, however, soon became intolerable. Cut off from food supplies and from all contact by land with the surrounding country, the inhabitants began to suffer from famine. The port, though precariously open, was idle. Commerce had stopped. Many people packed their belongings and fled from the city, and the population was reduced perhaps to a mere 25,000. In these desperate circumstances, with no prospect of help forthcoming from any other quarter, Andronikos looked for a desperate remedy. He was only 23. He was crippled by elephantiasis. He was saddled with a responsibility far beyond his competence. In 1423 he offered his city to the care of the Venetians. It was not a sale, nor was it a surrender. The transaction was proposed and carried through in a most business-like manner with every regard for the welfare of the city and its Greek inhabitants.[31]

Andronikos did not deal directly with Venice but with the Venetian authorities in Negroponte. He sent an envoy to them declaring the desperate state of Thessalonica; and in his name and in that of all its citizens he offered the city to the management of the Republic of Venice, on condition that they would defend it against its enemies, allow the people their own municipal government, and respect their property and their Church. The offer was at once passed on to the Senate in Venice. During the first week of July 1423 the senators deliberated the matter and interrogated a number of merchants who knew the situation. They decided to accept the offer and wrote to Andronikos accordingly.[32] Instructions were then sent to their governor in Negroponte and also to the baillie in Constantinople, who was to inform the Emperor what was afoot. The whole affair was transacted with the full knowledge and assent of Manuel II. The Turks too were officially informed of the takeover, with an assurance that Venice wished to live at peace with the Sultan. They were told that Venice wanted to secure Thessalonica 'for fear lest the city might fall into the hands of other Christians'.[33] Two Venetian deputies were appointed to take formal possession of the city. They arrived in September 1423 bringing six ships with stores and provisions for the hungry inhabitants. They were welcomed as saviours and at once planted the banner of St Mark in the square and on the ramparts of Thessalonica.

The conditions of the agreement had allowed that the Despot Andronikos should be granted an annual subvention by way of rent for his property. There was no mention of a sum of money being paid for the purchase of the city. Andronikos left as soon as he decently could and went with his infant son John to the Morea, where he hoped that the climate would be better for his health. He died there as a monk only four years afterwards. A later Venetian report unkindly suggested that Andronikos made a counter-attack on Thessalonica in alliance with the Turks and had to be arrested by the Venetian governors and sent into exile. But there is no truth in it. Early in 1424, acting on instructions from Venice, the governors of the city sent a representative to the Sultan at Adrianople to arrange a treaty. But Murad threw him in gaol. No amount of Venetian diplomacy would make him accept their presence in Thessalonica. The Turkish blockade of the city was not lifted.[34]

On 21 July 1425 the Emperor Manuel II died at the age of 75. He had been paralysed by a stroke three years before and had lived out his last months as a monk with the name of Matthew. We are told that his passing was mourned more deeply and more sincerely than that of any of his predecessors. He was buried in the monastery church of the Pantokrator in Constantinople. Bessarion of Trebizond, the future Bishop of Nicaea, pronounced his funeral oration.[35] Manuel had been popular with his subjects if for no other reason than that he had for over 30 years preserved them from their enemies without making any unnecessary concessions to the Latin West. He had visited the West and he had entertained western ambassadors and legates. But he had never sold his dignity for cheap rewards, and he had never lost face or compromised the dignity of his church and people to gratify a pope or curry favour with a Catholic king. There had been little talk of bowing to the superiority of the See of

351

Rome, as his father had done, to win a crumb of comfort from the Latins. In September 1422 an apostolic legate from Pope Martin V had arrived in Constantinople in the person of Antonio da Massa, Provincial of the Franciscans. He brought a nine-point plan for the reunion of the Greek and Latin Churches.

There are some who say that the Byzantines were so lost in the clouds of their own mystique that they could never discern or face up to the realities of their situation. One may wonder whether the popes and their legates were any more realistic. Antonio da Massa reached Constantinople only four days after the Turkish Sultan had withdrawn his army from the walls. It is surprising that the Emperors and the Patriarch could find the time or the patience to listen to his proposals at all. If they had expected to hear anything new they were disappointed. Pope Martin, through his nuncio, blandly promised immediate help for Constantinople from the King of Aragon—but only after the Greeks had 'returned' to the flock of Rome and had been instructed in the true faith by a selected team of bishops and doctors of theology. Antonio had to wait until November for a reply. The old Emperor Manuel was stricken with paralysis in October; John VIII had others matters to attend to. But the reply, when it did come, was undoubtedly influenced if not phrased by Manuel. The legate was told to inform his master the pope that the only way in which a proper and lasting union of the Churches could be realized was through the medium of a general council. It should be convened not in the west but in Constantinople, at a time when political conditions permitted. It was hinted that the Pope might like to defray the expenses of all the eastern bishops and patriarchs attending the council and also provide for the defence and security of the city in advance. Such was the message that Antonio da Massa delivered to the Council that was meeting at Siena in April 1423. The Council regretfully decided that no progress could be made in the matter of union with the Greek Church and that they had better confine themselves to problems nearer their own doorstep.[36]

The words spoken to the papal legate in November 1422 might equally well have been spoken by the Emperor Manuel's grandfather John Cantacuzene. For they stated the same view and the same truth, that where their immortal souls were concerned the Byzantines were the equals of all other Christians. The order of priorities was still the same on either side. It is well expressed by Edward Gibbon: 'the Greeks insisted on three successive measures, a succour, a council, and a final reunion, while the Latins eluded the second, and only promised the first as a consequential and voluntary reward of the third.'[37]

The historian and courtier Sphrantzes records a conversation that he overheard in the palace between Manuel and his son John. On the subject of the union of the churches Manuel advised his son in the following words: 'The infidels are very worried that we might unite and come to agreement with the Christians of the west; for they sense that if this occurred it would be very harmful to their own interests. Therefore my advice with regard to the holding of a council is this: go on studying and investigating the project as long as you can, especially when you have need of something to frighten the Turks. But do not really try to put it into practice; for in my opinion our people are not in the frame of mind to discover a way of uniting with the Latins or to put themselves out to create an atmosphere of peace, concord and mutual understanding, unless it were through the hope that the Latins would revert to the position in which we all found ourselves originally. But this is a virtual impossibility; and I fear that if we are not careful a worse schism may come about and then we shall be left defenceless before the infidel.' John VIII is said to have retired pensive and in silence after hearing his father's advice. Manuel turned to Sphrantzes and said: 'My son thinks himself a great Emperor. Perhaps he has the stuff in him. But he is not really of his age, for he expects things of this age which it cannot supply him. What the Empire needs today is not a good Emperor but a good manager.'[38]

NOTES

Narrative sources: Doukas; Chalkokondyles; Sphrantzes.
Modern works: Barker, *Manuel II*, 216-385; Ostrogorsky, *History*, 557-60; Bréhier, *Vie et Mort*, 389-98.

1 Barker, *Manuel II*, 218-38; B. Krekić, *Dubrovnik (Raguse) et le Levant au moyen âge* (Paris-The Hague, 1961), 44-5.

2 G. T. Dennis, 'The Byzantine-Turkish treaty of 1403', *OCP*, XXXIII (1967), 72-88; cf. Barker, *Manuel II*, 225. Doukas, 111 (ed. Grecu).

3 Dennis, *op. cit.* Papadopulos, *Versuch einer Genealogie der Palaiologen*, no. 85.

4 Barker, *Manuel II*, 238-45. G. T. Dennis, 'An unknown Byzantine

353

Emperor, Andronicus V Palaeologus (1400-1407?)', *Jahrbuch der österreichischen Byzantinischen Gesellschaft*, XVI (1967), 175-87; cf. N. Oikonomides, in *Thesaurismata*, V (Venice, 1968), 23-31.

5 *Narrative of the Embassy of Ruy Gonzalez de Clavijo to the Court of Timour, at Samarkand, A.D. 1403-6*, translated by C. R. Markham (London, 1859), 22-5; translated by G. Le Strange (London, 1928), 51-3.

6 See G. T. Dennis, 'The second Turkish capture of Thessalonica 1391, 1394 or 1430', *BZ*, LVII (1964), 53-61; A. Vakalopoulos, 'Zur Frage der zweiten Einnahme Thessalonikis durch die Türken 1391-1394', *BZ*, LXI (1968), 285-90. Cf. Ostrogorsky, *History*, 546.

7 Vacalopoulos, *Origins of the Greek Nation*, 124-5 and references. Cf. S. Vryonis, 'Isidore Glabas and the Turkish "devshirme"', *Speculum*, XXXI (1956), 438-42.

8 Doukas, 113 (ed. Grecu).

9 P. Wittek, 'De la défaite d'Ankara à la prise de Constantinople', *Revue des études islamiques*, XII (1938), 1-34; *CMH*, IV, 1, 767-8; Barker, *Manuel II*, 248 and references.

10 F. Thiriet, *Régestes des Délibérations du Sénat de Venise concernant la Romanie*, II (Paris-The Hague, 1959), no. 1362. Cf. Barker, *Manuel II*, 255-61, 268-9.

11 *Lettres de l'empereur Manuel Paléologue*, ed. E. Legrand (Paris, 1893), no. 56. Cf. Barker, *Manuel II*, 261-8 and references.

12 Manuel II, *Funeral Oration*, in *PG*, CLVI, 181-308; ed. by S. P. Lambros, *Palaiologeia kai Peloponnesiaka*, III (Athens, 1926), 11-119. On the date, see Barker, *Manuel II*, Appendix XXII, 525-7.

13 Zakythinos, *Despotat grec de Morée*, I, 157-65; Barker, *Manuel II*, 273-8.

14 Barker, *Manuel II*, 278-80. Manuel's son Andronikos, being only about 13, was no more than titular Despot of Thessalonica. Its effective governor, until 1415, was the Emperor's right-hand man Demetrios Laskaris Leontaris. See B. Ferjančić, 'Despot Andronik Paleolog u Solunu', *Zbornik Radova*, X (1968), 227-35. Ostrogorsky, 'Byzance, état tributaire ...', 54-8; N. Oikonomides, 'Le haradj dans l'empire byzantin du XVᵉ siècle', *Actes du Iᵉʳ Congrès international des études balkaniques et sud-est européennes*, III (*Histoire*) (Sofia, 1969), 681-8.

15 Wittek, 'De la défaite d'Ankara ...', 18-23; Barker, *Manuel II*, 280-9.

16 Doukas, 133 (ed. Grecu).

17 Barker, *Manuel II*, 298-301; Ferjančić, *op. cit.*

18 Zakythinos, *Despotat*, I, 167-72; Barker, *Manuel II*, 301-17.

19 N. Iorga, *Geschichte des osmanischen Reiches*, I (Gotha, 1900), 366-73; Barker, *Manuel II*, 340-4.

20 F. Thiriet, *La Romanie vénitienne au moyen âge* (Paris, 1959), 367-8.

21 Barker, *Manuel II*, 321-5. J. Gill, *The Council of Florence* (Cambridge, 1959), 20-1.

22 Zakythinos, *Despotat*, I, 188-90; Gill, *Council of Florence*, 23-4; Barker, *Manuel II*, 344-50. F. Dölger, 'Die Krönung Johanns VIII. zum Mitkaiser', *BZ*, XXXVI (1936), 318-19. On Sophia of Montferrat, see C. Diehl, *Figures byzantines*, II (Paris, 1908), 273-5; cf. Papadopulos, *Versuch einer Genealogie der Palaiologen*, nos 90, 91. The rude comment on Sophia's figure is retailed by Doukas, 137 (ed. Grecu). On Cleope Malatesta, see Gudrun Schmalzbauer, 'Eine bisher unedierte Monodie auf Kleope Palaiologina von Demetrios Pepagomenos', *Jahrbuch der österreichischen Byzantinistik*, XX (1971), 223-40.

23 Manuel II, *Praecepta educationis regiae*, and *Orationes ethicopoliticae*, in *PG*, CLVI, 313-84, 385-557. Cf. Barker, *Manuel II*, 344-5.

24 Barker, *Manuel II*, 350-4.

25 Doukas, 173 (ed. Grecu).

26 Iorga, *Geschichte des osmanischen Reiches*, I, 379-80; Barker, *Manuel II*, 354-60.

27 The account of John Kananos (Cananus) is edited by I. Bekker in the *CSHB* volume of (S)Phrantzes (Bonn, 1838), 457-79. Other accounts of the siege of 1422 are given by Doukas, Sphrantzes, Chalkokondyles, and the *Short Chronicle* no. 47; cf. Schreiner, *Studien zu den Brachea Chronika*, 172-5.

28 Barker, *Manuel II*, 361-71.

29 Barker, *Manuel II*, 374-9.

30 Dölger, *Regesten*, V, nos 3412-14. Barker, *Manuel II*, 379.

31 The tale that Andronikos formally sold the city to Venice for 50,000 ducats derived from the much later account of Pseudo-Sphrantzes, *Chronicon Maius*, ed. Grecu, 260. The truth of the transaction is found in the Venetian documents published by K. Mertzios, *Mnemeia Makedonikes Istorias* (Thessalonike, 1947), 34f. See especially P. Lemerle, 'La domination vénitienne à Thessalonique', *Miscellanea G. Galbiati*, III (=*Fontes Ambrosiani*, 27: 1951), 219-25. Andronikos had been paying tribute to the Turks at least since 1415; see M. Spremić, 'Harač Soluna u XV veku', *Zbornik Radova*, X (1967), 187-95.

32 Thiriet, *Régestes*, II, nos 1891, 1892.

33 Thiriet, *Régestes*, II, no. 1898.

34 Thiriet, *Régestes*, II, nos 1929, 1931. See J. Tzaras, 'La fin d'Andronic Paléologue, dernier despote de Thessalonique', *Revue des études sud-est européennes*, III (1965), 419-32; Barker, *Manuel II*, 372-4.

35 Greek text in Lambros, *Palaiologeia kai Peloponnesiaka*, III, 284-90; Latin translation in *PG*, CLXI, 615-20. Cf. Barker, *Manuel II*, 381-5.

36 Gill, *Council of Florence*, 33-6; Barker, *Manuel II*, 327-9.

37 Gibbon, *Decline and Fall of the Roman Empire*, ed. J. B. Bury, VII, 97.

38 Pseudo-Sphrantzes, *Chronicon Maius* (ed. Grecu), 320.

Seventeen

The Ottoman Revival and the Reign of John VIII Palaiologos—1425-48

Manuel II left six sons; but the extent of his empire and his fortune was barely enough to sustain so many princes. His eldest son John VIII, now about 30, was already Emperor in Constantinople. Constantine, the fourth of the family, was nominally in charge of the towns of Mesembria and Anchialos on the Black Sea, by favour of the Sultan. But he was soon to join his brother the Despot Theodore II in the Morea. Andronikos, the third son, had already fled there from Thessalonica; and Thomas, the youngest of the family, was also at Mistra. The fifth son, Demetrios, had as yet no responsibilities. The fact that four of Manuel's family were congregated in the little province of southern Greece indicated that it was there that security was to be found and there alone that recovery might be possible.

Manuel had been right to devote so much attention to the Despotate of the Morea. It was defended by a stout wall across the Isthmus; it was protected by the sea on all sides. Its ruler had established good terms with the Venetians, and had gained the upper hand over the remaining Latin lords. It should have been the springboard of a Byzantine restoration. But there was something about the character of its inhabitants and the nature of the Peloponnese itself that made it hard to reintroduce a government which everyone would obey. Anarchy and rebellion seemed to be endemic. Manuel had lamented the fact himself on his last visit to Mistra in 1415. In a letter to his friend Euthymios he wrote: 'It seems to me that it is the fate of the Peloponnesians to prefer civil war to peace. Even when there appears to be no pretext for such war they will invent one of their own volition; for they are all in love with weapons. If only they would use them when they are needed, how much better off they would be. In the midst of it all I spend most of my time trying to reconcile them with each other.'[1]

Part of the trouble stemmed from the fact that the Byzantine

Despots, first Manuel Cantacuzene and then the two Theodores of the Palaiologos family and their successors, were in a sense foreigners in the country. They and their staff were imported from Constantinople as a ruling ascendancy with an increasing amount of autonomy as communications with the capital became more and more tenuous. The local Greek nobility, the landed gentry of the Morea, resented the interference of the despots and administrators from Byzantium. They had lost the habit of living under a centralized administration. But the geography of the country, with its natural divisions of mountains and valleys, promoted separatism and, as in ancient times, feuds between rival clans.

The prosperity of the Morea depended upon agriculture. The few cities that were left, like Mistra, Corinth, Patras and Monemvasia, were on a small scale. The economy was not urban. It was based on agricultural units where the land was cultivated by tenant farmers and slaves, each with its own *kastron* or keep where the local lord resided. The Albanian immigration into the Morea had much increased in the latter part of the fourteenth century. Theodore I had encouraged the Albanians to come, for they were valuable as farmers and as soldiers. Their numbers had risen to 30,000 by the fifteenth century. The army in which many of them served was vital to the continuing independence of the Despotate. It may have numbered about 20,000 men, and its recruitment formed a connecting link of sorts between the Byzantine administrators and the native landlords. The navy, which in earlier times, had successfully operated from the harbour of Monemvasia, had long since ceased to exist. What people feared was not an invasion from the sea but an attack from the north by land, from the Turks coming down through Thessaly and Attica. The Hexamilion wall was supposed to be the Hadrian's wall of the Morea. The protection of the Despotate by sea was left to the Venetians, who tended to regard the Greek coast and islands as the last line of defence against the Ottomans. The islands of Negroponte and of Crete were the bases from which their navies operated, whether to patrol the Hellespont or to defend their Greek colonies.

But it was Venetian ships also which kept the Despots of the Morea in contact with Constantinople, and it was Venetian merchants who very largely controlled the trade of the Despotate. The harbours of Modon and Coron had been in their hands since the time of the Fourth Crusade. After the end of her war with Genoa in 1381, Venice had made great efforts to acquire more harbours in Greece.

Monemvasia had nearly changed hands in 1384; Nauplia had become a Venetian possession in 1388. Through these ports passed most of the exportable commodities of the Morea, notably wine, raisins, salt and the silk manufactured from the worms of the mulberry tree that gave the country its name. But there was a confusion of aims between the Venetians who felt that they alone had the means to defend Greece from the Turks, and the Byzantines who regarded it as their own country and their own responsibility and were therefore opposed to the annexation by Venice of any more of its coast and harbours.[2]

The capital city of Mistra, perched on a spur of Mount Taygetos overlooking the plain of Sparta, had by 1400 become something much more than an administrative and strategic centre. It might be described as a late Byzantine version of an ancient Greek city state. Within the narrow compass of its walls were churches, monasteries, palaces, schools and libraries. Here flourished the kind of intellectual, religious and artistic life that had characterized the city of Constantinople in the early fourteenth century. Writers and philosophers congregated at Mistra. Its architects and artists evolved their own variations of Byzantine styles and techniques. The earliest of its churches, that of St Demetrios, was built and decorated with frescoes at the expense of the local Bishop of Sparta about 1310. The two churches of the Brontocheion, dedicated to St Theodore, and to the Hodegetria, known as the Aphentiko, were built soon afterwards. The latter houses the mortuary chapel of the Despot Theodore I who died in 1407, as well as an inscription recording a number of endowments made by chrysobull of the Emperors Andronikos II and Michael IX between the years 1312 and 1322.

From later in the fourteenth century date the churches of the Peribleptos and of the Pantanassa, sometimes attributed to the Despot Manuel Cantacuzene. The wall-paintings in these two churches are among the most striking examples of later Byzantine art. In those of the Peribleptos the traditional style of the Constantinopolitan school is fused with a new liveliness and attention to realistic detail; but at the same time the more contemplative scenes, such as the Nativity, have a mystical and ethereal quality that bespeaks something of the spirit of hesychasm. The paintings in the Pantanassa illustrate the last phase of Byzantine art at Mistra. They were done at the time of the restoration of the church in 1428; and here the realism as well as the colouring are taken far beyond the limits traditionally imposed upon Byzantine artists. Italian influence there may have been, but it was surely not sufficient to explain the kind of liberation from conventional restraint that is to be seen in such productions as the pictures of the raising of Lazarus or the entry into Jerusalem in the Pantanassa. There is a rediscovery here of the art of late antiquity, as well as an attempt to relate the Christian message to contemporary humanity.[3]

The culture that flourished at Mistra, especially in the early fifteenth century was, like that in fourteenth-century Constantinople, a mixture and sometimes a blend of monastic asceticism and medieval humanism. The court in the palace of the despots attracted monks as well as scholars and men of letters from Constantinople and Thessalonica. Works of classical antiquity as well as Christian theological and historical works were there transcribed for their libraries. The intellectuals of Mistra were without doubt a tiny minority, living on an island of culture in what they themselves described as a sea of barbarism and ignorance. The Emperor Manuel, who was partial to scholarship, fostered and patronized the development, particularly after his son Theodore II had been enthroned as Despot in 1408. In the last half century of Byzantine civilization, Mistra was to number among its luminaries the monk Isidore, later Bishop of Kiev, who was to become a cardinal of the Roman Church; Bessarion, Bishop of Nicaea and also to become a cardinal; and George Scholarios, the future Gennadios II, first Patriarch of Constantinople under Turkish rule. But the most arresting personality and the most original scholar of all was the platonist George Gemistos Plethon. As Theodore Metochites had been in fourteenth-century Constantinople, so was Plethon in fifteenth-century Mistra. Indeed he was in many ways the intellectual successor and heir of Metochites.[4]

In 1409 the funeral oration which Manuel had composed for his brother Theodore I was pronounced at Mistra by the monk Isidore. Plethon had the honour of delivering an introductory speech.[5] It was his first known public appearance in Greece. He was then about 50 and already a much respected philosopher. He became the counsellor of the young Theodore II, the adviser of Manuel on the problems of the Morea, and ultimately a figure of international renown. Plethon, more than any other Byzantine scholar, developed the theory or the conceit that the Byzantines were in some sense the descendants of the Hellenes of antiquity. The idea was not new. But no one had previously constructed on it so elaborate a hypothesis. Mistra, lying in the heart of Greece, near to the site of ancient Sparta, inspired in Plethon's mind the fancy that Hellenism might be reborn on Hellenic soil. 'No country', he wrote, 'can be found which is more intimately and closely connected with the Greeks than is the Peloponnese ... It is a country which the same Greek stock has always inhabited, as far back as human memory goes: no other people had settled there before them, nor have immigrants occupied it subsequently ... On the contrary, Greeks have always occupied this country as their own, and while they have emigrated from it, owing to the pressure of population, and have occupied other and not inconsiderable territories, they have never abandoned it.'[6]

But Plethon's ideas were not limited to romantic evocations of ethnic continuity. In a series of memoranda addressed to the Emperor Manuel and his son Theodore between 1415 and 1418 he elaborated a thorough scheme for the reform of the administration, the economy, the social structure, and above all the defence of the Morea. The Peloponnese, as he said, was at once an island and a continent, an ideal testing-ground for sociological innovations. His remedy for the separatism of the local landlords and the consequent tendency to anarchy was to create a strongly centralized monarchy empowered to impose what amounted to a system of martial law. Plato was the source of much of Plethon's social and political ideology. At the court of the Despot in Mistra he fancied himself in the role that Plato had played at the court of Syracuse; but the schemes that he proposed to Theodore II were no more practicable than those that Plato had propounded to the tyrant Dionysios II. This is not to say that he had not studied and considered the problems of the Morea more attentively than most of his contemporaries. Nor were all his plans unrealistic. But no free society could sustain the all-embracing authoritarian régime envisaged by Plethon. The proximity of Mistra to Sparta, and the preference of Plato for the Spartan system of government, seem to have had much to do with the solutions that Plethon worked out for the salvation of the Morea.

The first necessity, as he saw it, was the creation and maintenance of a standing army made up not of mercenaries but of native Greeks. The economy must be geared to supporting such an army. Society was therefore to be divided into two categories: the soldiers and the tax-payers, the latter being exempt from military service so that they could support the former who would be exempt from taxation. This contented military élite, maintained by the mass of contentedly loyal citizens, paying their taxes in kind and not in cash, were to be governed under the Despot by a council of trained and educated men of moderate means; they would be drawn neither from the aristocracy nor from the commons, and they would set standards of temperance, dedication and moderation for all to imitate. Plethon's ideas about the ownership of land must have appeared even more revolutionary. He proposed that all land should be common property. A man could freely cultivate, build upon, or plant any piece of land he chose. The cultivation of waste or virgin land was to be particularly encouraged. But he must recognize that it was not his own property and that he must, if of the tax-paying class, render one-third of his produce to the common funds. Socialistically utopian though it might seem, this part of Plethon's reforms was based upon the experience of history. He could see around him the results of years of an agrarian economy dictated by the interests of great landowners who were usually in conflict with the government either of Mistra or of Constantinople. His proposed redistribution of property would at least ensure that all the land available would be intensively exploited for the benefit of all the community. Plethon also had proposals for reforming the currency and for protecting and stimulating home produce by regulating the import and export trade. His plans were comprehensive. It can rightly be objected that, in the form we know them, they were full of ambiguities and contradictions and largely unworkable; and if they had been applied they would have produced an unpleasant mixture between a philosopher kingdom and a socialist military dictatorship, for everything was to be subordinated to the state and regulated in the interests of the state. But one has to admit that George Gemistos Plethon was almost the only person in all the last centuries of Byzantium who proposed that the state could be saved by any means other than by tentative adaptations or modifications of inherited ideas and traditional institutions.

The Emperor and his son listened patiently to their philosopher's words of wisdom. They thanked him with honours and commendations. But there is no evidence that they tried to put any of his plans into practice. The Byzantine world was too old and tired, too conservative of the past and too apprehensive of the future, to stir itself into revolutionary action. Far more widespread than any theory of social reform was the belief that the survival of the state and its possible regeneration depended upon God and his providence. At its worst this was manifested as a blind resignation to the will of God; at its best by the continual pronouncements of Byzantine bishops and monks that salvation could only come through

362

an inward reformation of morals and attitudes. Plethon would have agreed that a change of heart was needed if the Byzantines were to live up to the high ideal of Hellenes. But his thoughts led him further and further away from any expectation that this could come about through the medium of the Christian faith. Not until towards the end of his life did he commit these thoughts to writing in a treatise called *On the Laws*. In this he was to advocate a total rejection of Christianity in favour of a new 'Hellenic' religion, incorporating the pantheon of ancient Greek gods and based on a theological and ethical system derived mainly from Plato but also from Zoroaster. Little is known of this work, for it was consigned to the flames as an atheistical and dangerous tract by Plethon's friend George Scholarios, after he had become Patriarch. But it marks out Plethon still more as a dreamer of dreams. He was not really even a man before his time. As a Byzantine he was an odd man out. As an academic philhellene and as a Platonist he was to be much esteemed in Florence, but as a prophet in his own country he was without much honour.[7]

The realities were very different from the romantic ideas of Plethon. At about the time that he was composing his memoranda for the Emperor and the Despot a satirical pamphlet was published under the title of *The Sojourn of Mazaris in Hades*. The author describes, in imitation of Lucian, the descent into the underworld of one Mazaris, who had just died of the plague in Constantinople. Among the dead he meets Manuel Holobolos, but recently a secretary of the Emperor Manuel, and gives him a scurrilous account of life at the Byzantine court and of the jostling for position among the courtiers. The second scene of the work takes place in the Morea, to which Mazaris has returned from the dead. It contains a series of scandalous sketches of the leading men of the Morea who come before Mazaris in a dream. Almost without exception they are castigated for their selfish, unpatriotic and unscrupulous behaviour. The labours of the Emperor Manuel to complete the Hexamilion wall across the Isthmus are praised. But there is a scathing denunciation of the local nobles who did everything in their power to obstruct the Emperor, so that he was forced to go to war against them and to spend his valuable time and resources on defeating the treacherous intrigues and rebellion of a crowd of deceitful and grasping yokels. The picture is clearly exaggerated, its accuracy is often questionable, and many of the personal allusions remain enigmatic. But the dreams of Mazaris declare rather more of the truth than the dreams of

Plethon.[8]

Nevertheless, Plethon was justified in thinking that the Morea was the only part of the Byzantine Empire that had a future. The Turkish invasion led by Turachan in 1423 had been devastating enough, but it had not led to the permanent occupation of the country by Ottoman troops. The Despots found it possible to repair the damage and to consolidate their hold on the Morea still more firmly. In 1426 the new Emperor John VIII took personal command of a campaign against Carlo Tocco, the ruler of Cephalonia and Epiros, who had seized control of Clarentza on the west coast of the Morea. Tocco's ships were routed in a sea battle at the entrance to the Gulf of Patras in 1427. He was forced to relinquish his claims in southern Greece and gave his niece in marriage to the Emperor's brother Constantine. In 1429 Constantine besieged and captured the city of Patras which for some years had been governed by its Latin archbishop. The Venetians loudly protested, but the Sultan Murad was persuaded to give his sanction to the reoccupation of Patras by the Greeks. At the same time Constantine's brother Thomas campaigned successfully against the Navarrese prince of Achaia, Centurione Zaccaria. Like Carlo Tocco, Zaccaria was made to surrender and gave his daughter in marriage to Thomas with the title to almost all of his possessions as dowry. He died two years later. By 1430, therefore, the Byzantine Despotate had been extended to cover most of the mainland of the Morea. The Venetians still controlled the vital harbours of Modon, Coron and Nauplia. But the Greeks no longer had to live under the constant threat of border warfare with the Latin princes of Achaia. They could concentrate on putting their own house in order and on maintaining the Morea as the last bastion of the Byzantine inheritance or the first breeding-ground of medieval hellenism.[9]

It was soon to be proved, however, that the province was not large enough to satisfy the ambitions or meet the needs of all the progeny of the late Manuel II. The brothers Theodore, Constantine and Thomas became themselves infected by the Peloponnesian plague of feud and faction which their father had lamented as a disease endemic to the country. Each had his portion or appanage, Theodore at Mistra, Thomas at Clarentza, Constantine at Kalavryta. But as they grew older and the question of the succession loomed larger they found it ever harder to co-operate. For as the years went on it became clear that their brother the Emperor John VIII, who had married for a third time in 1427, was never going to produce an heir to the throne; and when the Despots took to quarrelling over their rights and fighting over their possessions, the Turks were pleased to assist them in accomplishing their own ruin.[10]

The new dawn of the Byzantine cause in the Morea was darkened by events in northern Greece. For in 1430 the city of Thessalonica had fallen again into Turkish hands. Seven years earlier the Venetians had taken it over. They had been hailed as saviours by the inhabitants. They had boasted that they would turn Thessalonica into a second Venice. But everything had turned sour. 30,000 Turkish soldiers continued to blockade the city. The Greeks had chafed under the rule of Italian governors who failed to honour their agreements. They lodged formal and detailed protests to the Doge in Venice about the disrespect to their rights and property. Tension rose so high that the Venetians became fearful that the inhabitants would open the gates of their city to the Turks, and they took to deporting upper-class Greeks to the islands or to Venice, on the plea that the food shortage would be eased if the population were reduced. Far from becoming a second Venice, Thessalonica had become a liability for the Italians. They made several vain attempts to negotiate a settlement with the Turks. In 1427 a treaty of sorts was arranged by which the Venetians were to pay a yearly tribute to the Sultan. But in 1428 the tribute had to be doubled. The Sultan Murad was merely playing for time. Famine was causing more and more people to leave the city. In 1429 the citizens drew up another long list of complaints, to which the Venetians responded rather testily, re-marking on the 'endless expense' of defending Thessalonica which was then costing them about 60,000 ducats a year. Things went from bad to worse. The Venetians had lost heart in the enterprise. They had even let the fortifications fall into disrepair, and many of the Greeks openly said that they would rather surrender than risk the sack of the city which they knew would follow if they resisted. The Bishop Symeon, who had done his best to relieve the suffering, died towards the end of 1429. His death was taken to be a sign from God presaging the fall of Thessalonica to the Turks.[11]

In March 1430 word went around that the Sultan Murad was on his way to direct operations with an army of 190,000 men. Three Venetian ships put in to the harbour to give encouragement to the terrified people and add some weight to their defences. On Sunday, 26 March, the Sultan's army could be seen approaching. It was not yet in battle order, for Murad hoped that the city would surrender without a struggle. But the messengers that he sent to announce his offer to the inhabitants were greeted by a hail of arrows from the walls. Murad was not to be deterred. His heart was set on capturing Thessalonica. In later years a Turkish legend told how God had appeared to the Sultan in a dream holding out to him a rose of exquisite beauty and scent. It was the symbol of Thessalonica. God had told him it was his for the plucking, since destiny had decreed that it should be his to enjoy. A local Greek legend, on the other hand, tells of the treachery of the monks of the monastery of the Vlattades, which still stands at the northern end of the city. The monks are said to have advised the Sultan to cut the pipes that supplied the city's water and so drive the people to give in from thirst.[12] He gave them one more chance to consider his offer, but the Venetian governors made sure that it would not be accepted. The night before the attack some Christians from Murad's camp came up to the walls to persuade the guards to accept the Sultan's terms before it was too late. But the guards were answerable to the governors, who redeployed their troops to meet the situation. Some thought that the Venetians were preparing to escape. Panic swept through the city; and those who were not manning the walls crowded into the churches to spend the night in prayer.

The Turkish assault began before sunrise on 29 March. It was led by Sinan Pasha, the *beglerbeg* or governor-general of Rumelia. His front-line soldiers rushed at the walls from all sides, yelling their war cries as they came. Others brought up battering rams, siege engines and scaling ladders, under the covering fire of a hail of arrows from archers in the rear who shot down the guards on the battlements with deadly accuracy. The wall on the eastern side of the city took the main brunt of the wave upon wave of attackers. It was the most dilapidated section of the circuit. Here the Sultan took command in person. The defenders did their best, but they suffered enormous casualties from the rain of Turkish arrows. They were heavily outnumbered and many lost their nerve and deserted their posts. Shortly after nine o'clock in the morning a Turkish soldier scaled the wall at its least protected point and tossed down from the battlements the severed head of a Venetian guard. It was the signal for his comrades to follow him. They poured over and through the walls and, brandishing their swords, tore through the streets like a hurricane. The inhabitants fled in terror to take shelter in houses, churches, sewers and graveyards. But when the Turkish cavalry and the rest of the infantry came storming in from all directions there was no hope of escape. A few lucky souls managed to get away by boat. But large numbers of the people, men, women and children, were rounded up, shackled together and dragged out to the Turkish camp as slaves.

A Greek eye-witness tells how the heavens rang with the noise, the yells of the Turks mingling with the screams and tears of children torn from their parents, friends from their friends and families from their kinsmen. He estimated that 7000 were carried off to slavery. For three days the buildings and churches were ransacked and pillaged. Such was the treatment allowed by the law of Islam for cities that resisted conquest. When the Sultan called a halt to the plundering there was scarcely a stone left unturned. But it was not his intention that Thessalonica should become an empty ruin. Once he had taught the Greeks their lesson Murad set about restoring their confidence and rehabilitating their city. His soldiers were made to evacuate the houses in which they had quartered themselves and restore them to their owners. He paid from his own funds the ransom money for many of the well-to-do citizens who had been captured. Several of them at once adopted the Muslim faith to show their relief and gratitude. To mark his own gratitude to the God of his victory, Murad transformed the ancient church of the Virgin Acheiropoietos into a mosque. An inscription on one of the columns of the church still records how, in the year of the Muslim era 883, the Sultan Murad captured Thessalonica. The Venetian governors of the city had managed to make their escape in the confusion. They sailed to Negroponte. They were charged with having neglected the defences and put in prison for a while.[13]

The Byzantines had looked on Thessalonica as the second city of their empire. The Venetians had tried and failed to turn it into a second Venice. Now, in March 1430, it was the second prize for the Turks in Europe. The first prize, Constantinople, was still to be won, but it would not be long withheld from them.

As soon as he had restored order in Thessalonica, Murad turned his army loose on Epiros and Albania. The city of Ioannina had for long been the capital of the northern part of the old Despotate of Epiros, first under the Serbs and then under the Italian Counts of Cephalonia. In 1429 it had just passed to a nephew of Carlo Tocco. Carlo II was not given much time to enjoy its possession. When the citizens of Ioannina heard of the approach of Sinan Pasha, *beglerbeg* of Rumelia, and his army they sent him a delegation led by their bishop to offer their surrender on certain conditions. They had no wish to share the dreadful fate of Thessalonica. Their offer was gladly accepted. Ioannina capitulated to the Turks on 9 October 1430. But its church and its people were protected in advance by a charter written in Greek and known as the Decree of Sinan Pasha. The governor-general therein promised that no one would lose his freedom, no children would be abducted, no churches would be destroyed or turned into mosques. The metropolitan bishop was to retain all his prerogatives and privileges; the nobles would keep their estates. All rights of heredity, property and personal possessions were to be guaranteed. All reasonable requests were to be granted. Many copies of the decree were produced. It was the charter of the freedom of the Greeks of Ioannina under Ottoman rule for centuries to come. It was also good propaganda for the tolerance of the Turkish conquerors. The people of Constantinople would hear what had happened in Thessalonica in March and what had happened in Ioannina in October 1430. The Sultan hoped that they would draw the right conclusions and make the right choice.[14]

For the Byzantines the choice was between two evils. In 1430 there cannot have been many who would have opted for the surrender of Constantinople. But some were already expressing the view that to give in to the Turks might be a lesser evil than to survive under a burden of indebtedness to the Latins. The loss of Thessalonica had caused a stir in western Europe. The Venetians had suffered damage to their prestige as well as to their material interests, and they were alarmed by the Turkish penetration into Albania and towards the Adriatic coast. The last line of resistance to the Turks in Europe had been pushed further and further back, until the King of Hungary, from being the ideal if reluctant champion of the Christian cause, had been forced into real if desperate action. In 1427, when Stephen Lazarević of Serbia died, his nephew and successor George Branković swore an oath of loyalty to King Sigismund of Hungary. For a moment it seemed that Hungary and Serbia together might hold the line. George Branković was granted the title of Despot by the Emperor John VIII in 1429, and in 1430 he built the vast fortress of Smederevo on the Danube near Belgrade. It became the last capital of medieval Serbia, and it betokened a will to resist stronger than that shown by George's uncle Lazarević. But even at the time of its construction, Branković had been compelled to accept the fact that he was in principle a vassal of the Turkish Sultan.[15]

Now that Venice and Hungary were more directly affected than ever before, the Emperor John VIII concluded that an appeal to the western world to save Constantinople from extinction might

368

really be answered. Heedless of his father's advice, he resumed negotiations with the Pope. In 1430 he proposed to Pope Martin V that a council might be convened to resolve the schism between the churches. It was at this stage still possible for the Emperor to make his point that the council should be held in Constantinople. But Martin V died in February 1431, and his successor Eugenius IV proved more difficult to deal with. Just before his death Pope Martin had summoned the Council at Basel at which, among other things, the mounting disagreement over the question of authority in the Roman Church was to be aired. The tug of war in the western church between the Pope and the conciliarists was really of little concern to the Byzantines. But the supporters of the conciliarist movement were somewhat of the same mind as the Byzantines on the ways and means of achieving union. For they too rejected the idea that matters affecting the whole church could be decided simply by the authority of the Bishop of Rome. There was therefore a body of opinion in western ecclesiastical circles favourable to the Orthodox view of these affairs; and the Emperor John VIII probably thought that he might get a better hearing as a consequence.[16]

The new Pope Eugenius IV, who received John's ambassadors in 1431, had hopes of winning the first round in his conflict by transferring the Council from Basel to Italy. But the Council refused to budge. The fathers at Basel, however, rather hoped that the Byzantines would address their appeals to them instead of to the Pope. They invited the Emperor to send delegates to their Council. They pointed out that they and not Pope Eugenius represented the church universal, that they had the support of Sigismund of Hungary and of all the princes of Europe, and that in the matter of resolving the schism their authority was greater than that of a pope. It is far from certain that John VIII or his advisers fully understood the quarrel in the western church. But in 1433 he and his Patriarch both agreed that the invitation to Basel should not be turned down. Three Byzantine legates were appointed to go there. They were held up by a series of mishaps and did not reach Basel until July 1434. Thereafter the matter developed into something approaching a race between the Pope and the Council to win the favour of the Greeks for reasons of prestige. Both parties sent their own ambassadors to Constantinople and the Emperor, in growing bewilderment, dispatched his own legates to both in return. For more than three years the question of summoning a council to promote the union of the churches was discussed as a side issue to the debate between the conciliarists and the Pope. But the advantage that the Byzantines gained in the end was one that no pope had ever before allowed them. All parties to the negotiations between 1433 and 1437 were agreed that the schism could only be mended through the medium of a council of the whole church.

The Byzantines were doubtless relieved that Pope Eugenius was finally able to make an offer to hold a council on his own ground. They would have preferred it to take place at Constantinople, hazardous though this might have been in the political circumstances. But their experience of dealing with the contentious fathers at Basel had confirmed them in their view that after all the Pope was, and always had been, the head of the western Church. Once Eugenius had won over a minority party of the conciliarists and come forward with a plan to invite the Emperor and the Patriarch to a splinter council of his own at Ferrara, the Byzantines were pleased to accept. In July 1437 the Greek legates to the Council at Basel who had been won over to the minority party and had gone with it to join the Pope in Italy declared that they accepted its members as the only true council; the Byzantine Emperor and Patriarch would now be willing to come to Italy just as soon as the Pope could arrange to send ships for their transport. The Pope was quick to act. His own legates reached Constantinople to arrange the details at the beginning of September. They were followed by a fleet of Venetian ships hired by the Pope to bring the Greek delegation to a council at Ferrara. A few days later envoys arrived in Constantinople from Basel bringing a fleet of their own to transport the Byzantines to an alternative council. They had never been so sought after. But the Emperor and the Patriarch had already made up their minds. The messengers from Basel were dismissed with their ships; and at the end of November 1437 the Byzantine delegation to the Council of Ferrara embarked on the papal ships at Constantinople.[17]

It was a remarkable delegation, more numerous and more distinguished than any that had previously gone to the west. There were precedents for the visit of an emperor to Italy, but no patriarch of Constantinople had ever before accompanied his emperor there. The Patriarch Joseph II was a kindly old man but in poor health and not equal to the rigours of theological debate. His fellow Patriarchs of Alexandria, Antioch and Jerusalem had also nominated their representatives to the Council, though without binding themselves in advance to its decisions. The most intelligent and outstanding clerical delegates were not of patriarchal status. But they included

370

some who were already intellectually predisposed towards a liking for western culture and even for Latin theology. Bessarion, lately made Bishop of Nicaea, was one confirmed advocate of union with the Roman Church. As a young man he had come from his native Trebizond to pursue his education in Constantinople. There he had met the Italian humanist Francesco Filelfo, who had himself been inspired to study at Constantinople after attending the classes of Manuel Chrysoloras in Italy. Through Filelfo, Bessarion had learnt of the exciting new intellectual developments in the revival of classical learning in the west. He had moved to Mistra to sit at the feet of George Gemistos Plethon. But, like Demetrios Kydones a century before, Bessarion was in love with Italy before he even got there.

Another pro-unionist was Isidore, abbot of the monastery of St Demetrios in Constantinople, who was promoted to the See of Kiev and All Russia in 1436. Isidore had been among the Byzantine legates to the Council of Basel. His latinophilia was perhaps more theological than cultural. On the other side of the fence stood Mark Eugenikos, a monk who had just been raised to the See of Ephesos. Nothing could persuade him of the truth of Latin doctrine, nor was he any great admirer of Latin culture. But in many ways, and for all his limitations, Mark Eugenikos obeyed the voice of his Orthodox conscience with greater sincerity than any of his colleagues. The lay delegates were if anything even more remarkable and on the whole more learned than the clerics. They were led by the Emperor John VIII and his brother Demetrios. But their most illustrious member was the elderly Gemistos Plethon from Mistra. By that time Plethon's philosophy had already developed to the point at which he had outgrown Christianity, whether eastern or western. He went with his emperor to the Council partly out of a sense of duty and partly for the ride to Italy, for he had no objections to bridging the cultural gap between Greeks and Latins. But he was bored by the proceedings and attended few of the sessions. His friend George Scholarios had been appointed as a delegate not least because of his thorough knowledge of Latin. Scholarios was trained as an academic lawyer, as well as being a theologian and philosopher. The subtleties of Latin theology, particularly as expounded by Thomas Aquinas, greatly appealed to him. He was therefore an excellent choice for a gathering at which much Latin theology was bound to be aired. But he was also a great admirer of Gregory Palamas and of the Orthodox doctrine of hesychasm; and he argued with Plethon about the merits of Aristotelianism over Platonism. The other leading lay delegates were the philosophers George Amiroutzes and George of Trebizond, the first a Platonist, the second an Aristotelian in the controversy that deflected the minds of their contemporaries from the realities of life in Constantinople.[18]

The realities were becoming less and less tolerable. It is true that in 1437 the Turks were not actually blockading the city. The Emperor had even found occasion to repair some of the damage to the land walls and to clean the silt and débris out of the moat that protected them. But what lay within those walls presented a depressing picture of emptiness, neglect and ruin. The city had always been noted for its open spaces of parks and gardens. But now there were more spaces than ever. The Spanish ambassador Clavijo at the beginning of the fifteenth century had commented on the unhappily desolate state of the once magnificent palaces, churches and monasteries. Another Spanish traveller, Pero Tafur, who paid his first call on Constantinople in 1437, remarked on the sparsity of the population. There had been yet another outbreak of plague in 1435. He observed that the church of the Blachernai, the scene of so many imperial ceremonies in the past, was a burnt-out shell. The Emperor's palace nearby was badly in need of repairs. The people in the streets had an air of misery and poverty. They would not have been comforted by Tafur's arrogant conclusion that they were such a vicious, sinful lot that they deserved far worse than what they were already suffering.[19] But those who had the chance to leave the city were not reluctant to take it. They had the official excuse of leaving on an imperial mission, and many of them who were given the chance already had the inclination to visit Italy in any case. In contrast to the occasion in 1274 when the Emperor Michael VIII had tried to get together a representative delegation to go to the Council at Lyons, not many seem to have declined the invitation to accompany the Emperor John VIII to the Council at Ferrara.

What took place at that Council, first at Ferrara in 1438 and then at Florence in 1439, is more the concern of the historian of the Church than the historian of the Byzantine Empire. The Council was a long and tedious exercise in the unrealities of ecclesiology and theological hairsplitting. It is not unfair to say that it was conceived and conducted very largely for the gratification of the Roman Church, to prove the point that the popes had laboured so consistently, that the Greeks must accept the supremacy and the authority of the See of Rome before there could be any question of a material move to save them from the infidel. The fact that the Council was in the end convened at Ferrara under the auspices of Pope Eugenius IV and not at Basel was highly significant for the future of the papacy. It was a diplomatic victory that proved the death blow to the conciliarist movement. But it was an expensive victory, for the whole eastern contingent of some 700 people had to be maintained in Italy at the Pope's expense. The party of the Emperor and the Patriarch, who took with him about 30 bishops, left Constantinople on 27 November 1437, but they took more than two months to reach Italy. They put in at Venice early in March 1438. This time the Doge and people of Venice exerted themselves to entertain the Emperor in the greatest possible style. All the pomp and grandeur of Venice at the height of her glory were paraded in a wealth of pageantry. The Doge came to meet the Emperor's ship in his ceremonial state barge, its prow adorned with the Byzantine eagle flanked by two golden lions of St Mark. The richly liveried oarsmen wore caps bearing the emblems of Venice and of the imperial house of Constantinople. Trumpets sounded, the bells of the city pealed, and the gaily dressed crowds on the quays shouted out their welcome to the Emperor.[20]

After some days the party sailed on to Ferrara, completing their journey on horseback. The Emperor arrived there on 4 March in pouring rain, which somewhat marred the brilliance of his entry, but he was courteously received by the Pope. The Patriarch arrived a few days later; and it was at this point that the first unpleasantness occurred. The Emperor had sent a messenger to warn the Patriarch that, despite all that they had hoped, Pope Eugenius was going to insist that the Patriarch should bow down and kiss his foot. To the westerners this may have been nothing more than a customary salutation. But to a patriarch of Constantinople it was an unthinkable indignity and quite out of keeping with the Byzantine idea of the collegiality of bishops. The Patriarch refused to come ashore, and in the end the Pope had to yield on a point of ritual for fear of prejudicing the whole operation at the start. The incident illustrates the desire on both sides to lose no more ground than necessary. Before the Council formally opened there were agonizing deliberations about precedence, protocol and seating arrangements. Both the Pope and the Emperor were acutely sensitive about the etiquette fitting to their dignity. But finally the stage was set to the satisfaction of all, except for the Patriarch; and on 9 April 1438 the Council began its proceedings in the cathedral at Ferrara.[21]

The points of difference that had to be resolved if ever union were to be achieved were many, and they were familiar to both sides.

Some were so familiar and had been for so long debated and argued in polemical tracts and exchanges between Greeks and Latins that they were better not raised at all. Such was the view of the Emperor John VIII. He did his best to confine the agenda to the obvious points, particularly to the questions of the procession of the Holy Spirit, the primacy of the See of Rome, the use of unleavened bread in the sacrament (to which the Orthodox had always objected), and to the Roman doctrine of Purgatory (which they had never understood). It was agreed that the truth on these matters should be sought by reference to the scriptures, to the canons of former œcumenical councils, and to the writings of the Fathers, Latin as well as Greek. The Emperor worked hard to control his delegation. He knew their propensity for disputation. He appreciated their difficulties in understanding the Latin texts that were adduced by the Catholic side. The Latin delegates had the advantage of being able to present their case from a prepared position of unanimity. Their leader was Cardinal Julian Cesarini, who had originally presided over the Council at Basel. Among them were some learned Dominicans who had lived or travelled in the east and knew the Byzantine objections in advance. They were trained in Latin scholastic methods of debate, and under the guidance of the Pope they spoke with one voice. Some of the items on the agenda proved to be more tractable than others. The questions of the doctrine of Purgatory and of the unleavened bread in the sacrament were tactfully disposed of. But when it came to the question of the procession of the Holy Spirit it seemed that there would be no end to the arguments.

The Orthodox position on the western 'innovation' or addition to the Creed of the words *filioque* had not changed. The Byzantines still believed, as they had believed in the thirteenth century, that it was wrong to imply that the Holy Spirit proceeds from the Son as well as from the Father. The discussions on this point alone took more time at the Council than all the other items put together. The argumentation was abstruse. The citations from the Fathers intended to support the one view or the other were sometimes contradictory and often subject to misinterpretation. Mutual understanding was gravely hampered by the simple difficulty of interpretation between the Greek and Latin languages. There were trained theologians on either side of the debate, brandishing their bones of contention with all the passionate intensity of obsessed academics. But their common terms of reference had subtle differences of meaning in their two languages. The Greek word *ousia*, for example, did not mean quite the same as the Latin *substantia*, nor did the Latin word *persona* convey the proper meaning of *hypostasis*. The only hope of agreement was through a form of compromise. It was eventually reached, though only after many weary months. At the end of 1438 Pope Eugenius got the delegates to agree to transfer the Council to Florence. Plague had broken out at Ferrara, though the real reason for the Pope's decision may well have been financial. The cost of the Council and of supporting the Byzantine delegation had crippled his resources. At Florence he could get more funds by courtesy of the Medici family. As soon as the proceedings were resumed at Florence in January 1439 the discussions about the *filioque*, which had begun at Ferrara, continued unabated. The compromise formula was not finally accepted until the following March. It was one that had been suggested on previous occasions. It depended upon blurring the distinction between the propositions 'from' and 'through'. The Byzantines agreed that the Holy Spirit proceeded from the Father 'through the Son'. This could be taken to mean 'from the Son'. But to get them to admit this had taken many months of argument, and some were still not satisfied.[22]

At the time of the Second Council of Lyons in 1274, a Greek-born Franciscan had complained that the problem of the procession of the Holy Spirit was too eagerly seized upon by both sides to keep their differences alive: all who genuinely desired union could see that the question was one of interpretation and not of significance. Given a little goodwill it could easily be resolved.[23] This may have been true. But the Greeks at Florence were far from home, weary of it all and nostalgic. Their spokesman, Sylvester Syropoulos, who composed a full if not very impartial account of their doings in Italy, implies that they were virtually starved into submission; and what the Greeks in Constantinople could not see was why, if the differences were so slight, the Roman Church could not simply accept or at least approve the Greek point of view. Why was it always the Orthodox who had to give in? The matter was succinctly put by Mark Eugenikos, Bishop of Ephesos, in the course of the debates. 'The addition of a word,' he said, 'seems to you a small matter and of no great consequence. So then to remove it would cost you little or nothing; indeed it would be of the greatest profit, for it would bind together all Christians. But what was done was in truth a big matter and of the greatest consequence, so that we are not at fault in making a great consequence of it. It was added in the exercise of mercy; in the exercise of mercy remove it again so that you may receive to your bosoms brethren torn apart who value fraternal love so highly.'[24]

The question of the supremacy of the Pope was treated as tactfully as possible and comparatively quickly, since it was the subject of some difference of opinion in the Roman Church. It is not without interest that the issue was laid to rest at one debate by a reading of the Donation of Constantine; for it was only a year later that Lorenzo Valla published his proof that the Donation was a forgery.[25] At length the document of Union was drawn up. The Emperor questioned some points in the Greek text when it was submitted for his ratification. The Pope added some words to it by way of thanks to God for having brought to an end the schism that had lasted for 437 years. The Orthodox bishops and abbots signed the document on Sunday, 5 July 1439. The Patriarch Joseph, who had been ill during the latter stages of the Council, had died three weeks earlier. But on the day before his death he had prepared a signed profession of his own submitting to everything that 'the Catholic and Apostolic Church of our lord Jesus Christ of the elder Rome understands and teaches'.[26] It was found among the papers on his desk. The only Byzantine prelate who refused to append his signature to the document was Mark Eugenikos of Ephesos. Of the lay members of the delegation only the Emperor was required to sign. The Latins then signed the decree in the presence of Greek witnesses, the Pope's name taking pride of place. On 6 July the Union of the Churches was formally proclaimed and celebrated. A public holiday was declared in Florence so that the people could crowd into the cathedral and assemble in the piazza outside to watch the ceremony. After the Pope had said mass and blessed the congregation, the decree of Union was recited from a pulpit near his throne, first in Latin by Cardinal Cesarini and then in Greek by Bessarion of Nicaea. The opening words, 'Laetentur caeli', called on the heavens to rejoice that the wall dividing the eastern and western Churches for so long had now been demolished and that peace had been restored.[27]

Most of the Byzantine delegation left Florence about a fortnight after the event, though the Emperor's brother Demetrios with Gemistos Plethon and George Scholarios had already gone. The Emperor John stayed on for about a month and then left for Venice where his party were to take ship for home. Their return was much delayed, and their journey was hampered by bad weather. Not till February of the following year did the Emperor reach Constantinople.

He was greeted by the news that his third wife had died a few days before. His homecoming was a mournful affair without that added tragedy. For most of the clergy and the people of the capital had already made up their minds that the Union of Florence was a shameful business. The men who had signed it found themselves denounced and shunned as traitors who had sold their souls to the Latins. Mark Eugenikos may have been in a minority of one at Florence. But once back in Constantinople he quickly discovered that he was a hero and a confessor for the faith. It was necessary to appoint a patriarch to replace Joseph. But it was not easy to find a suitable candidate for the unpopular position of a unionist patriarch. In May 1440 Metrophanes, Bishop of Kyzikos, was finally elected, and for the first time for many years the name of the Pope was commemorated in the liturgy in St Sophia. Mark Eugenikos at once left the capital for his See at Ephesos. Other bishops did likewise. The papal nuncio in Constantinople reported back to the Pope that the Emperor was not being firm enough in silencing the opposition and enforcing the Union. The Pope was trying to prepare an army and a fleet for the defence of the now Catholic Christians of the east. It was to be ready by the beginning of 1441. But the news of the Emperor's prevarication did not incline him to hurry his arrangements.[28]

The 'peace' that had been restored at Florence caused storms and bitterness in the Orthodox world. As early as 1441 some of those who had signed the decree of Union publicly repudiated their action in a manifesto. The Emperor's brother Demetrios, who resided as Despot at Mesembria, tried to seize the throne with the support of the anti-unionists who looked on him as the protector and restorer of Orthodoxy. He attacked Constantinople with the help of the Turks in the summer of 1442, only to be taken prisoner and put under house arrest.[29] But, as always in Byzantium, what divided the Church divided the state and society as well. In the same year Mark Eugenikos came back to Constantinople and began a campaign of anti-unionist propaganda which found a ready audience. The Emperor was in a difficult position. Mark Eugenikos was commonly thought to be the only honest man among those who had gone to Florence. He was a clever controversialist, but he was also highly respected for his sincere piety and his impeccable holiness of life. To obstruct or silence his activities would have been construed as a flagrant example of imperial interference in the affairs of the Church. To persecute him would merely have made him still more of a martyr with a still greater following, as Michael VIII had proved by persecuting the anti-unionists after the Council of Lyons. Michael VIII had perhaps been more fortunate in having a theologian like John Bekkos to back him up. The prominent unionists in the fifteenth century, such as Bessarion of Nicaea and Isidore of Kiev, were too out of touch with the mass of the clergy, monks and people to be able to sway their emotions. Bessarion was so disappointed by their opposition that he left Constantinople to return to Florence at the end of 1440. He had already been created a Cardinal of the Roman Church. He never returned to his native land. Isidore, whom the Pope had also made a Cardinal, discovered for himself that the hostility to the Union was no less fierce in the Orthodox world beyond the Byzantine frontiers. When he went back to Moscow as apostolic legate in 1441 he was denounced by the people and condemned by the Grand Duke Basil II as a ravening wolf preying upon his innocent flock. He was deposed and arrested. He too escaped to Italy. The Orthodox Patriarchs of Antioch, Alexandria and Jerusalem disowned the signatures of their representatives at Florence and also rejected the Union. George Scholarios alone showed any sign of rising to the bait of Mark Eugenikos in polemical literature. But it was not long before he too changed his mind and withdrew his support from the Union of Florence; and when Eugenikos died in 1444 his mantle as leader of the anti-unionist party fell on the shoulders of Scholarios. The Patriarch Metrophanes conscientiously laboured to make the Union effective. But he died in August 1443, and for more than a year there was no patriarch to give any kind of guidance or direction to the cause.[30]

The Emperor John VIII, his patriarch, his bishops and his philosophers had gone to Italy in 1437 on the understanding that, if and when the union of the churches was accomplished, they and their people would be the beneficiaries of a crusade against the Turks in which all their brethren in western Christendom would happily participate. The Union was achieved in 1439. In October of that year Pope Eugenius outlined his proposals for the promised crusade. From some points of view the moment was propitious. The Turks had made further headway in Serbia. The fortress of Smederevo, built by the Despot George Branković, had surrendered to the Sultan Murad II in 1439 after a three-month siege. Belgrade had resisted an even longer siege in 1440; but most of the rest of northern Serbia had been overrun by the Turks, and in 1441 they invaded Transylvania. Branković had taken refuge in Hungary, and it was here that the resistance seemed to be crystallizing. The Kingdom of Hungary had been united with that of Poland under the young Polish King Ladislas III. The coalition had been supported by the Hungarian general John Hunyadi, formerly in the service of King Sigismund. Ladislas rewarded him with the governorship of Belgrade and the title of *voivode* of Transylvania. Hunyadi had already fought valiantly against the Turks at Smederevo and with even greater success in Transylvania. He was a brilliant soldier and he had the kind of courage that the situation demanded. Pope Eugenius looked to him and to his sovereign Ladislas to provide the troops and the inspiration for his crusade. Cardinal Cesarini was appointed to take charge of arrangements and to stimulate support for the enterprise. The Hungarians and Serbs were joined by the Prince of Wallachia. The Pope, the Venetians and the Duke of Burgundy were to provide a fleet of ships. The preparations took longer than expected, but by June 1444 all was ready.[31]

By that time the moment was even more favourable for war against the Turks in Europe, for the Sultan had been called away to Anatolia to suppress a dangerous rebellion of the Karamans. There were also signs and symptoms of defiance and revolt elsewhere. In northern Albania a renegade Muslim called George Kastriotes was gathering round him a number of local chieftains and their tribes to fight for their independence. Kastriotes had been taken by the Turks as a hostage while he was still a boy and brought up in the Muslim faith. The Sultan had been so impressed with his prowess that he gave him the name of Iskender or Alexander, with the title of *beg*, a name which the Albanians were to translate into Skanderberg. By 1444 Skanderberg had escaped from the Turks and was busily organizing revolt from his fortress of Kroia in the mountains of Albania.[32] Meanwhile, in the Morea Constantine, the brother of the Emperor John VIII, had optimistically rebuilt the Hexamilion wall and even extended his authority into central Greece. From the safety of Rome, Cardinal Bessarion wrote to the Despot Constantine to congratulate him on refortifying the Isthmus of Corinth, and outlined a scheme, not unlike that of Plethon, for reforming the army and the economy of the Morea before it was too late. In 1444 Constantine took over the city of Athens and forced its duke, Nerio II Acciajuoli, to pay to him the tribute that he had hitherto been paying to the Sultan.[33] The Sultan must have thought that his suspicions about the outcome of the Council of Florence, which the Emperor had assured him was a matter that affected only the Church, were being justified.

In these promising circumstances the Pope's crusade, the reward to the Byzantines for their submission at Florence, set off from Hungary in July 1443. The plan of campaign was to be much the same as in the crusade of Nicopolis in 1396. While the army of about 25,000 men moved down the Danube valley, the fleet, which had gone ahead, would sail up river from the Black Sea. From Belgrade the allied army, led by Cesarini, George Branković and John Hunyadi, marched on Niš and then on Sofia. Both places surrendered to them before the end of the year. These were notable victories. But the onset of winter prevented the allies from continuing their march and they withdrew the way they had come. They had shown what they could do. In June 1444 Ladislas III, Branković and Hunyadi sent ambassadors to the Sultan at Adrianople. Murad II was alarmed. He elected to play for time. A truce was arranged for a period of ten years. Its terms were ratified by King Ladislas at Szegedin in July in the presence of the Sultan's envoys. Murad was able to return to Anatolia in the belief that all was well in Rumelia. He had made certain concessions to the Christians but only for a limited period of time. He expected that, being Christians, they would abide by their oaths.

George Branković, who had been restored to his dominions in Serbia by the treaty, felt bound to observe it. But among the other leaders of the Christian army there was disagreement. Cardinal Cesarini in particular was saddened by the thought that the crusade which he had done so much to organize might now have to be disbanded. There are conflicting reports and interpretations of what happened. The Cardinal is said to have absolved King Ladislas from the oath that he had sworn to the infidel Murad, and by September 1444 the crusade was on its way again. Its numbers were smaller, since Branković and his Serbian contingent stayed behind. But the Prince of Wallachia supplied an army, and this time the crusade succeeded in fighting its way right down through Nicopolis and Bulgaria to the coast of the Black Sea near Varna. The Sultan was horrified at the perfidy of the Christian leaders. But he rushed back from Anatolia. The allied fleet prevented him from crossing the Hellespont, but they failed to hold the crossing of the Bosporos. In November Murad arrived at Varna with an army of between 80,000 and 100,000 men. The crusaders, outnumbered three to one, barely had a chance of victory. But they fought heroically until first Ladislas and then Cesarini were killed. Their army was almost totally annihilated. Of its leaders only John Hunyadi managed to get away, taking some of the Hungarian troops. And so, on 10 November 1444, ended the last attempt at a crusade against the Turks in eastern Europe. The crusade of Varna had involved the Byzantines rather more nearly than the crusade of Nicopolis. Its main objective had in fact been Constantinople. But it never reached there, and many of the city's inhabitants were not sorry that it had failed. For its failure seemed to point the moral that no good could come to them from those who had forced them to tamper with the faith of their fathers. They would rather hope for a miracle of divine intervention than expect a material reward for perpetuating a union which was so displeasing in the sight of God.[34]

The Sultan had gone into battle at Varna with the text of the broken treaty pinned to his standard. The Emperor John VIII had to greet him and congratulate him after his victory. The Venetian fleet was not there, either to help the Christian prisoners escape or to prevent the Sultan and his army crossing back over the Bosporos. The ships provided by the Pope and the Duke of Burgundy made some raids on Turkish installations in the Black Sea and up the Danube before sailing back to Constantinople in 1445. But the Venetians made their own arrangements and in February 1446 signed a peace treaty with Murad II. Perhaps they were wise. They could see that the collapse of the crusade at Varna and the deaths of its leaders meant that it would be a long time before another campaign of the same kind could be mounted.[35] The impetus provided by the Council of Florence had spent its force. Moreover, the Sultan quickly took his revenge on those who had assisted the crusade or chosen the moment to rebel. In the winter of 1446 he took command of his own army to invade Greece. It is immaterial that he was invited by his vassal Nerio Acciajuoli of Athens, who had been dispossessed by the Despot Constantine of the Morea. Murad would have taken action in any case to put a stop to Constantine's ephemeral victories. The Turks first re-established Acciajuoli in Athens and then overran the northern shore of the Gulf of Corinth where Constantine had recently asserted control. The Venetians were not disposed to help the Greeks who had appropriated much of what they considered to be the property of Venice. They withdrew their fleet.

In November 1446 therefore the Byzantines of the Morea had to face the vengeance of the Sultan on their own. The Despots Constantine and Thomas took their stand at the Hexamilion wall at the Isthmus. The Sultan ordered it to be demolished without delay. An ambassador whom Constantine sent to parley with him was held prisoner; he was the father of the future historian Laonikos Chalkokondyles. Murad meant business. He had brought with him a number of long cannons as well as an array of conventional machines for destroying and surmounting battlements. The Greeks and their Albanian soldiers had no means of countering a bombardment by artillery. They resisted as best they could. But they were disorganized and by no means wholly loyal, and on 10 December 1446 the Sultan's troops mastered the Isthmus wall. One of his janissaries, a Serbian by birth, is said to have been the first over the top. Many of the defenders were massacred or captured. The two Despots made their escape. But the way was open for yet another Turkish invasion of the Morea.

The Sultan split his forces. Turachan led one army to Mistra. Murad himself led the other along the southern shore of the Gulf of Corinth, burning, plundering and destroying as they went. When they reached Patras they found the city almost empty. Most of its inhabitants had fled across the water to Naupaktos or Lepanto, which was still in Venetian hands. But the 4000 or so who had barricaded themselves behind the walls of the acropolis of Patras beat off the assaults of the janissaries. The Sultan pursued his murderous journey to Clarentza and then joined up with Turachan's forces before withdrawing from the Morea. Again it had been only a punitive raid. The Morea was still not beaten into the status of a sandjak or pashalik of the Ottoman Empire. But the punishment had been more severe than ever before. The province was ruined and depopulated. The Greek and Italian sources independently estimated the number of prisoners as 60,000. These were the ones taken away to the slave markets of Turkey. Those that were left were the captives of their own misfortune. The Despots Constantine and Thomas had to bind themselves under oath to the Sultan and pay tribute as his vassals. Yet life went on. It was in the year after Murad's invasion that the Italian antiquarian and traveller Ciriaco of Ancona paid his second visit to Greece. He observed that some parts of the country at least were still well-planted with fruit-trees, vineyards and olives; and at Mistra, where he was received by the Despot Constantine, he found that intellectual and cultural activities had not ceased. Plethon was still there; and Ciriaco also met there the future historian Chalkokondyles, then a young man, who seems to have translated into Greek an Italian sonnet that Ciriaco composed while meditating upon the ruins of ancient Sparta. In the circumstances of the time it was stretching even poetic licence rather far to compare the Mistra of Constantine with the Sparta of Lycurgus.[36]

Having reduced the Morea to a tributary province, the Sultan turned to settling his accounts with John Hunyadi, the only leader of the Varna crusade who had eluded him. Hunyadi had now become regent of Hungary. He had not given up hope that a crusade could yet be organized. He looked for the co-operation of Skanderbeg of Albania. But the matter was not entirely in his hands. George Branković of Serbia seemed content to honour his contract with the Turks and would not take kindly to the passage of an anti-Turkish crusade through his territory. But a new factor had been introduced by the ambitious schemes of the King of Aragon, Alfonso V, who had moved his capital to Naples in 1443. Alfonso had dreams of resurrecting the Latin Empire of Constantinople, to which he felt that he had a claim through his hereditary title to parts of Greece, and a title through his claim to the Angevin crown of Naples. Pope Eugenius IV, the architect of the Council of Florence, died in 1447. His successor Nicholas V seemed eager to promote and subsidize the plans of Alfonso of Aragon and Naples. The Venetians on the other hand resolutely opposed him. Skanderbeg of Albania, who was ready to join Hunyadi of Hungary on his crusade, was seduced by Alfonso into making war on Venice. The Venetians thereupon invited the Turks to invade Albania. The Christian powers were hardly united in their purpose. Nevertheless, Hunyadi set off with his own army of Hungarians, Wallachians and other mercenaries in September 1448, in the belief that Skanderbeg would catch up with him. He got as far as the plain of Kossovo, the battlefield on which, nearly 80 years before, the Serbs had gone down fighting against the Turks. There Murad II waited for him. For three days the battle raged, from 17 to 20 October, until the Hungarians and their allies were routed. The Albanians never arrived. John Hunyadi escaped the Turks only to fall into the hands of George Branković, who held him prisoner until he promised to pay compensation for the damage his army had done to Serbia.[37]

The damage was as much political as material. George Branković of Serbia was determined to show the Turks that he was a neutral party in the squabbles of the Christians and loyal to the agreements that he had made with the Sultan. His own instincts and background made him lean more to the Orthodox east than to the Catholic west. He held the Byzantine title of Despot, officially conferred upon him by the Emperor John VIII, and he was married to a princess of the Cantacuzene family. In 1429 he and his wife covenanted an annuity to the monastery of Esphigmenou on Mount Athos. The deed of gift, in the form of a Byzantine chrysobull, bears portraits of George Branković and his wife and five children wearing the robes and headgear proper to their exalted status of a Byzantine Despot, his *basilissa*, and their royal offspring.[38] His youngest son Lazar married a daughter of the Despot Thomas of the Morea in 1446 and was himself granted the rank of Despot by John VIII. He was not wholly in sympathy with international ventures against the Turks organized by the west, nor with the heroics of a Hunyadi or a Skanderbeg. As early as 1435 he had given his daughter Mara in marriage to the Sultan Murad. The Sultan had a deep respect for her. His son Mehmed II, though not the child of Mara, inherited that respect and often took her advice. Two of her brothers, however, had been blinded by Murad shortly after he had captured Smederevo in 1439. The experience had taught their father his lesson. Thereafter George Branković preferred to show willing to the Sultan. He had his reward. Smederevo was restored to him because he had opted out of the crusade to Varna. A Serbian folksong recalls how Branković was once told by John Hunyadi that he would impose the Latin faith on the Serbs if he rescued them from the Turks. The Sultan on the other hand promised that, if the Turks conquered Serbia, he would build a church near every mosque and allow everyone the freedom to practise his own faith.[39] Branković may not have had to suffer all the humiliations that his uncle Stephen Lazarević had once suffered as a vassal of the Sultan Bajezid. But he had learnt a lot about how to handle and to live with the Turks.

The battle at Kossovo in 1448 did not mean the end of Hungary. Hunyadi was soon back in the kingdom as its captain-general. But he had been beaten twice in four years, and his thoughts now turned more to defence than to attack. Skanderbeg of Albania, however, was still defiant; and it was against Albania that Murad turned after his victory at Kossovo. Albania was vitally important to the security of the Ottoman dominions in the Balkans. It bordered on the Adriatic Sea and thus on the preserves of Venice. But its coast-line was seen by King Alfonso of Aragon and Naples as the beach-head for a campaign that would place him at the summit of all eastern Christendom as Latin Emperor. It was the same dream that had very nearly been realized by Charles of Anjou in the thirteenth century and that had haunted his descendants. There was not a chance of it coming true in the fifteenth century. But the Pope was very taken with the idea. For a while Skanderbeg was allowed to fight his own skirmishes with the Turks, bravely driving off repeated attacks on his mountain fortress of Kroia. But the more successfully he fought, the more he became an object of interest to Alfonso and to the Pope as the last-ditch Christian hero east of the Adriatic.[40]

More and more the Ottoman conquest of the Byzantine Empire was coming to be accepted as a *fait accompli* in western Europe. The line might be held at the borders of Hungary and in the mountains of Albania. Pious hopes might be held out for the protection of the great Christian city of Constantinople. But the country between Hungary and the Black Sea, as well as Macedonia, Thessaly, and the city of Thessalonica, seemed to have been written off as lost. The early victories of John Hunyadi and the first campaign of the crusade of Varna had shown that the Turks were not immovably entrenched. But after the disasters at Varna in 1444 and at Kossovo in 1448 no one had the strength or the nerve to try again. Those who were in the battle line had already begun to transfer their assets and even their families to western or neutral countries, to Ragusa on the Dalmatian coast which had kept its neutrality by paying an annual tribute to the Sultan, to the Venetian colonies of Crete or Corfu, or further afield. Even George Branković made provision for his family in Hungary against the day when his arrangements with the Turks might break down. Constantinople was isolated and seemed very far away from the front line. No one could any longer regard it as the capital of an empire. It was an island of Christian culture around whose walls lapped the waters of Islam. Its emperor had become a poor and tragic relative of the Catholic community of the west. He had seen the light and joined their Christian flock. Therefore he was to be pitied and comforted. People deluded themselves with the thought that Constantinople was so well fortified as to be impregnable. But few really believed that the flood waters of Islam could be turned back as far as the Bosporos. The Union of Florence had served in the end to isolate the Byzantines still further from the western world both spiritually and physically. In the years after the crusade of Varna the records of diplomatic exchanges between the Emperor John VIII and his friends are sparse. He seems to have had dealings with Pope Nicholas V. He sent an ambassador to Alfonso V at Naples in 1447. But at the end of the day he concluded that his only potential allies who knew what they were doing were the Venetians. In April 1448 he signed yet again the time-honoured Byzantine treaty with Venice.[41]

A few months later, on 31 October 1448, John VIII died. He may be remembered as the Emperor who went to the Pope's Council at

385

Florence. He was so remembered, with some bitterness, by most of his subjects. But in other respects he was not in the tradition of those emperors in Constantinople who had influenced the course of events. Perhaps it was too late for such an emperor. Perhaps his father Manuel II had been right: what the Empire needed was not a great emperor but a good manager. John VIII, for all his qualities as a person, was neither. He had not even been able to manage his own brothers. His younger brother Demetrios had his eye on the throne. But his eldest surviving brother Theodore not unnaturally considered himself to have prior claim. In 1443 Theodore had agreed to exchange the Despotate of Mistra, which he had governed for 36 years, for the appanage of Selymbria in Thrace. The arrangement put an end to the feud that he had been waging with his younger brother Constantine in Greece. It also put Theodore that much nearer to Constantinople to move into the palace when the moment came. But he was never given the chance, for he died in June 1448, four months before the Emperor. The tragic fact that John VIII had no children of his own was compounded by the jealousy among his brothers. Before he died, however, John officially nominated one of them as his successor. He chose the Despot Constantine. From every military and political point of view it was the wisest choice.[42]

NOTES

Narrative sources: Doukas; Chalkokondyles; Sphrantzes.
Modern works: J. Gill, *The Council of Florence* (Cambridge, 1959); J. Gill. 'John VIII Palaeologus: a character study', in Gill, *Personalities of the Council of Florence* (Oxford, 1964), 104-24. Ostrogorsky, *History*, 561-567; Bréhier, *Vie et Mort*, 398-415.

1 *Lettres de Manuel Paléologue*, ed. E. Legrand, no. 51, 77-8. Cf. D. A. Zakythinos, *Les Despotat grec de Morée*, I, 174.

2 D. A. Zakythinos, *Le Despotat grec de Morée*, II: *Vie et Institutions* (Athens, 1953), *passim*; A. Bon, *La Morée franque. Recherches historiques, topographiques et archéologiques sur la principauté d'Achaie (1204-1430)*, I (Paris, 1969), 282f.; F. Thiriet, *La Romanie vénitienne au moyen âge*, 355-71.

3 For the monuments and the art of Mistra, see e.g., Bon, *La Morée franque*, I, 533-684; II (Plates); D. Talbot Rice, *Byzantine Painting. The Last Phase* (London, 1968), 177f.

4 See especially F. Masai, *Pléthon et le platonisme de Mistra* (Paris,

1956); Zakythinos, *Despotat*, I, 175-80; II, *passim;* E. Barker, *Social and Political Thought in Byzantium* (Oxford, 1957), 196-219; B. Tatakis, *La Philosophie byzantine* (=E. Bréhier, *Histoire de la Philosophie,* fasc. suppl. II: Paris, 1959), 281-306; S. Runciman, *The Last Byzantine Renaissance* (Cambridge, 1970), 77-8, 100-1; Vacalopoulos, *Origins of the Greek Nation,* 126-35.

5 Cf. Barker, *Manuel II,* Appendix XXII, 525-7.

6 Address to Manuel II, in Lambros, *Palaiologeia kai Peloponnesiaka,* III, 247-8; translated in E. Barker, *Social and Political Thought in Byzantium,* 198-9. Most of the works of Plethon are contained in *PG,* CLX and CLXI, and in Lambros, *op. cit.,* III and IV. Several passages are translated in E. Barker, *op. cit.,* 198-218. For the late Byzantine view of the ethnic continuity of the Hellenic stock, see Runciman, *Last Byzantine Renaissance,* 17-23 and references; Vacalopoulos, *Origins of the Greek Nation, passim.*

7 The fragments of the treatise *On the Laws* are edited by C. Alexandre, *Pléthon, Traité des Lois* (Paris, 1858). Cf. E. Barker, *op. cit.,* 212-19; Zakythinos, *Despotat,* I, 365-76.

8 The work of Mazaris is edited by J. F. Boissonade, *Anecdota Graeca,* III (Paris, 1831), 112-86; and, with a German translation, by A. Ellissen, *Analekten der mittel- und neugriechischen Litteratur,* IV (Leipzig 1860), 187-314. There is a Russian translation by S. P. Kondratjev, with a commentary by T. M. Sokolov, in *VV,* XIV (1958), 318-57.

9 Zakythinos, *Despotat,* I, 199-210.

10 John VIII's third wife was Maria, daughter of the Emperor Alexios IV of Trebizond. She died childless in 1439. See Nicol, *Byzantine Family of Kantakouzenos,* 171-2.

11 On the Venetian occupation of Thessalonica, see Lemerle, 'La domination vénitienne à Thessalonique', *Miscellanea G. Galbiati,* III (1951); and A. E. Vacalopoulos, *A History of Thessaloniki,* translated by T. F. Carney (Thessalonike, 1963), 65-70.

12 Vacalopoulos, *op. cit.,* 74-5.

13 This account of the Turkish siege and capture of Thessalonica derives from the eye-witness account and *Monodia* of John Anagnostes, in the Bonn edition of (S)Phrantzes (*CSHB,* 1839), 483-534. Cf. Vacalopoulos, *op. cit.,* 71-5.

14 For the Decree (or *Horismos*) of Sinan Pasha, see Vacalopoulos, *Origins of the Greek Nation,* 148-9.

15 *CMH,* IV, 1, 553. On George Branković, see the bibliography in Nicol, *Byzantine Family of Kantakouzenos,* 184-5.

16 J. Gill, *The Council of Florence*, 42-5.

17 Gill, *Council of Florence*, 46-84.

18 See J. Gill, *Personalities of the Council of Florence*; S. Runciman, *The Great Church in Captivity* (Cambridge, 1968), 103-5. On Bessarion, see also Runciman, *The Last Byzantine Renaissance*, 80-4 and references; Vacalopoulos, *Origins of the Greek Nation*, 172-8, 241-5, 257-8. On Scholarios, see C. J. G. Turner, 'The Career of George-Gennadius Scholarius', *B*, XXXIX (1969), 426-55.

19 Ruy Gonzales de Clavijo, *Embassy*, ed. G. Le Strange, 87f.; Pero Tafur, *Travels and Adventures 1435-1439*, ed. M. Lewis (London, 1926), 145. Cf. Vasiliev, *History*, 678-9.

20 Gill, *Council of Florence*, 85-103.

21 Gill, *Council of Florence*, 104f.

22 On the proceedings and theological debates at Ferrara and Florence, see Gill, *Council of Florence*, 115-269; Runciman, *The Great Church in Captivity*, 105-9; D. J. Geanakoplos, 'The Council of Florence', in Geanakoplos, *Byzantine East and Latin West* (Oxford, 1965), 84-111; Ostrogorsky, *History*, 562-3 and references.

23 John Parastron, quoted by Pachymeres, I, 371-2.

24 Mark Eugenikos, cited by Gill, *Council of Florence*, 163. The *Memoirs* of Sylvester Syropoulos were edited by R. Creyghton under the title of *Vera Historia Unionis non Verae* (The Hague, 1660); for the new, definitive edition by V Laurent (Paris, 1971), see Bibliography below, 448.

25 Gill, *Council of Florence*, 279-80.

26 Gill, *Council of Florence*, 267.

27 Gill, *Council of Florence*, 270-96.

28 Gill, *Council of Florence*, 296-304, 349f.; Runciman, *Great Church in Captivity*, 109-10.

29 Gill, *Council of Florence*, 353; S. Runciman, *The Fall of Constantinople 1453* (Cambridge, 1965), 49. This event is also recorded in the *Short Chronicle of Mesembria*; cf. Schreiner, *Studien zu den Brachea Chronika*, 167-70.

30 Gill, *Council of Florence*, 354-65; Obolensky, *Byzantine Commonwealth*, 267-71.

31 Gill, *Council of Florence*, 327-30; *CMH*, IV, 1, 553-4.

32 On Skanderbeg, see J. Radonić, *Djuradj Kastriot Skenderbeg i Albanija u XV v.* (Belgrade, 1942); A. Gegaj, *L'Albanie et L'invasion turque au XVᵉ siècle* (Paris, 1937); G. C. Soulis, in *EEBS*, XXVIII (1958), 446-57.

33 Zakythinos, *Despotat*, I, 226-31. Bessarion's letter of advice to

the Despot Constantine is in Lambros, *Palaiologeia kai Peloponnesiaka*, IV, 32-45. Cf. Vacalopoulos, *Origins of the Greek Nation*, 172-8.

34 The most thorough modern account of these events is that by O. Halecki, *The Crusade of Varna. A Discussion of Controversial Problems* (New York, 1943); but several of his conclusions have been challenged. See also Runciman, *Crusades*, III, 465-6; Runciman, *Fall of Constantinople*, 46; Gill, *Council of Florence*, 329-33; Ostrogorsky, *History*, 565-6 and references.

35 On the attitude of Venice to the crusade of Varna and its aftermath, see Thiriet, *La Romanie vénitienne au moyen âge*, 377-9.

36 Zakythinos, *Despotat*, I, 232-6. For Ciriaco's visit to Greece, see E. W. Bodnar, *Cyriacus of Ancona and Athens* (Brussels, 1960).

37 On the oriental policy of Alfonso V, see Ostrogorsky, *History*, 568 and references. Runciman, *Fall of Constantinople*, 46-7; *CMH*, IV, 1, 554-91; F. Babinger, *Mahomet II le Conquérant et son temps (1432-1481)* (Paris, 1954), 70, 80, 90.

38 See Nicol, *Byzantine Family of Kantakouzenos*, 187 and references; Plates 11-14.

39 Temperley, *History of Serbia*, 111. On Mara Branković, see Nicol, *op. cit.*, 210-13.

40 Gegaj, *L'Albanie et l'Invasion turque*, 61f.; Babinger, *Mahomet II*, 88-90.

41 Dölger, *Regesten*, V, nos 3512, 3516. The Greek text of this, the last of the many Byzantine treaties with Venice, is in *MM*, III, 216-24. For the Latin text, see Lambros, in *Neos Hellenomnenon*, XII (1915), 153-70.

42 Zakythinos, *Despotat*, I, 226-40. On the death of Theodore II at Selymbria, see Schreiner, *Studien zu den Brachea Chronika*, 175-7.

Eighteen

Constantine XI and Mehmed II: The Fall of Constantinople—1448-53

At the moment of the Emperor's death in October 1448 Constantine was in the Morea. It was there that he had shown the qualities that made him best fitted to take over the management and defence of Constantinople and its suburbs, for such was now the extent of the Byzantine Empire. Constantine liked to be known by his mother's surname of Dragaš or Dragases, which she inherited from her Serbian father. His mother lived on as a widow and a nun until March 1450; and it was her firmness that ultimately assured that Constantine should wear the crown.[1] For early in November 1448 his brother Demetrios had already hurried to the capital from Selymbria to claim the succession; and his other brother Thomas was on his way there from the Morea. Demetrios was, or represented himself to be, the champion of the anti-unionist party. He was accepted as such by George Scholarios, and he assumed charge of the city's defence. But the mother of them all, the Empress Helena, overruled him and asserted her right to act as regent until the eldest of her surviving sons arrived from Greece. In December she sent George Sphrantzes to the Sultan Murad to ask that he would recognize Constantine as the new Emperor. Constantine himself wrote to the Venetian governor of Crete announcing the fact of his father's death and asking for safe conduct from the Morea to Constantinople. Meanwhile two leading courtiers had been sent from the capital to Mistra bearing the imperial regalia; and on 6 January 1449 they performed the coronation of the new Emperor Constantine at Mistra. It was unusual but not unprecedented for an emperor to be crowned in a provincial city. The founder of the dynasty of Palaiologos, Michael VIII, had been crowned at Nicaea; John VI Cantacuzene had been crowned at Adrianople. But in all such cases in the past it had been thought desirable to repeat the ceremony in Constantinople. In the case of Constantine there was no second coronation. To be crowned in the capital by a unionist patriarch would only have inflamed the existing religious discord. The times were too hectic and too short. He reigned for only four years and five months. He was the last Byzantine Emperor.[2]

Constantine entered Constantinople on 12 March 1449. Almost at once he sent an ambassador to Murad to pay his compliments and to ask for a treaty of peace. The Sultan might have preferred to see Demetrios Palaiologos on the throne, for he distrusted the union of the Greeks with the Latins which Constantine supported and which Demetrios renounced. But he did not hesitate to acknowledge the prior claim by heredity of the Emperor Constantine. The Emperor's brothers were invested with the government of the Despotate of the Morea. After long deliberations it was decided that the province should be partitioned between them. Thomas was to have the north-western section with Achaia and the towns of Patras and Clarentza; Demetrios was to govern the rest from Mistra. They swore solemn oaths in the presence of their mother Helena and their brother the Emperor that they would respect each other's boundaries, and they left for Greece in the summer of 1449. The arrangement resolved a constitutional crisis and perhaps averted a dynastic war in Byzantium, but only at the expense of its last remaining province. For the two Despots began to quarrel within a matter of months; each in his turn called on the Turks for help, and both fell foul of Venice. Constantine intervened to patch up their differences for a time at the end of 1450. But he must have been disheartened to see the resources of the Morea, which he had done so much to preserve, being dissipated in fratricidal war.[3]

Constantinople too was a divided city. The Union of Florence, which Constantine was determined to uphold as the last frail link with the world from which help might come, was increasingly unpopular. No one had yet dared to celebrate it in St Sophia. Men of the world, however, realized that the moment was too critical for such luxuries as religious or even political differences. The civil servants and officers who served the Emperor Constantine did so with a loyalty that rose above their divergent allegiances in other matters. Two of them were members of the Cantacuzene family: Andronikos, the Grand Domestic, who was a brother-in-law of George Branković, and John, who had been the Emperor's faithful servant and friend in the Morea and moved with him to Constantinople in 1449. Both were noted unionists. John's son, Constantine Cantacuzene, who carried on his father's career in Greece, even earned the title of a Count Palatine of the Lateran from the Pope. The Emperor's first ministers were another member of the same family, Demetrios Cantacuzene, and Loukas Notaras, who held the title, for by the fifteenth century it was little more than a title, of Grand Duke or High Admiral. Of these the latter at least opposed the idea of union with the Roman Church; but he was prepared to put up with the practice of it for appearance's sake and for fear that the Latins would totally abandon Constantinople to its fate. George Scholarios, on the other hand, who for all his change of heart on the subject had continued to serve John VIII as secretary and judge, saw no future in serving Constantine. He retired to a monastery and in 1450 became a monk with the name of Gennadios.[4]

But among the bishops, priests and monks, and among the ordinary people of the city, ambiguous attitudes were not possible. The Patriarch of Constantinople, Gregory III called Mammas, did his best to pour oil on the troubled waters. But the leading anti-unionist clergy refused to pray for their emperor in their churches. The Emperor tried to bring them to be more reasonable. But Scholarios and John Eugenikos, the brother of the late Mark of Ephesos, poured out literature in defence of the traditional Orthodox position and continually decried the folly of those in authority who put their hope of salvation not in God but in human and alien hands. The tension in ecclesiastical circles was so intolerable that the Patriarch Gregory abandoned his charge in disgust or despair and went to Rome in August 1451. For the last two years of its independent existence the See of Constantinople was widowed. There was a Church but no Patriarch. There was an Emperor but no Empire. The Pope, Nicholas V, was distressed by the reports from Constantinople and urged Constantine to take repressive measures against the opponents of union. He must be made to understand that there was a limit to prevarication. There were already Catholics in Rome protesting that the Greeks had been given rope enough with which to hang themselves and suggesting that Constantinople could look after its own problems. The Pope insisted that the Patriarch Gregory must be reinstated and that the Union of Florence must be proclaimed and celebrated in the cathedral of St Sophia. In May 1452 the cardinal Isidore of Kiev was appointed apostolic legate to see that this was done.[5]

It was almost too late for such celebrations. In February 1451 the Sultan Murad II died at Adrianople. He had in fact resigned in favour of his son Mehmed six years before; but he had been forced to come out of his retirement to take vengeance on the Hungarians and the Greeks. Mehmed II, known to history as Fatih or the Conqueror, was 19 years old in 1451. He had spent his childhood in obscurity in Adrianople until, by the death or murder of his two brothers, he had become heir to the Sultanate at the age of 12. His father then saw to it that he had the education and upbringing fitting to his destiny. Naturally intelligent and perceptive, gifted with impulsive energy and an aptitude for learning, Mehmed quickly and eagerly absorbed what his masters had to teach him of philosophy, science and languages, and what his father taught him of administration and of war. Now that the storm of the last crusade was over in Europe, and with the peace that his father had established in Asia, Mehmed II could expect to inherit a well-ordered and flourishing Ottoman Empire, complete but for the city of Constantinople. That inheritance was his in February 1451 when Murad died; and from that very moment Mehmed planned the conquest of Constantinople as his main objective and his overriding obsession. But the Byzantines were slow to recognize that so young and inexperienced a ruler presented them with a danger more formidable than any Sultan since the great Bajezid. For to begin with Mehmed seemed ready to be their friend, even to the point of making certain guarantees and small concessions. Among other things, he allowed his stepmother Mara Branković to return in safety to her home in Serbia.[6]

If the Byzantine Empire were ever to have a future there must be an heir to the throne. Constantine's advisers therefore urged him to find a wife before it was too late. He had been married twice already. His first wife, a niece of Carlo Tocco, had died in 1429. His second wife, daughter of Dorino Gattilusio of Lesbos, had died in 1442. Neither had borne him any children. It was thought that his third marriage, if it came about, should be arranged with an eye to business. A lady must be found who would bring a substantial dowry to her impoverished husband and also the benefit of a political and military alliance. The matter provoked much diplomatic activity. Imperial ambassadors were sent to look for an empress in places as far apart as Italy and Georgia. At Naples they inquired about the daughter of the King of Portugal, who was a nephew of Alfonso of Aragon. In Venice the daughter of the Doge Francesco Foscari was considered. In Taranto the name of a lady of the Orsini family was mentioned. But the Emperor's closest friends felt strongly that he would do better to marry into some family nearer home. George Sphrantzes was entrusted with the delicate task of visiting the courts of Georgia and of Trebizond to find a suitable bride. The

King of Georgia, George VIII, quickly put himself out of the running by proposing that the hand of his daughter should be worth a large sum of money. The Emperor John IV of Trebizond, however, had more conventional ideas about arranging a dowry which might go with the hand of one of his daughters.

It was while he was in those parts that Sphrantzes heard of the death of Murad and the accession of the Sultan Mehmed II. In his own account of his diplomatic missions he tells how the Emperor of Trebizond greeted him with the good news of the old Sultan's death in 1451, and of how he warned the Emperor not to be over optimistic. The new Sultan, he said, was young and dedicated to the destruction of Christians; the news of *his* death would indeed be an occasion for rejoicing since he was the only surviving son of his father, and if he died there would be discord among the Turks. The Emperor of Trebizond was deeply impressed by the Byzantine ambassador's cautious and statesmanlike appraisal of the situation.[7]

But word must very soon have reached Trebizond that the widow of the late Murad, Mara Branković, had been allowed to go home to her father in Serbia; for she was a niece of the Emperor John IV. The idea at once occurred to George Sphrantzes that she of all people was best fitted to become the bride and Empress of his master Constantine. Diplomatically this may have been so. Mara Branković was closely related to the courts of Serbia and Trebizond, she was rich, she was a Byzantine princess and an Ottoman Sultana in her own right, and as the respected stepmother of the new Sultan she might have been a great influence for peace. But she was already about 50 years old and unlikely to be able to produce an heir to the throne. Constantine, however, was quite taken with the idea when Sphrantzes put it to him. Mara's father, George Branković, was also naturally in favour of it. The Emperor's advisers were divided in their opinions. But the lady herself would have none of it. She soon let it be known that she had taken a vow that, if she were ever released from her marriage to the infidel Sultan, she would live out the rest of her days in chastity and devotion to charitable works. Nor would she alter her resolution, not even for the Emperor of the Romans. The Emperor therefore instructed his ambassador to pursue negotiations with the King of Georgia. They were long drawn out, and by the time that a marriage contract had been drafted it was too late. The last Byzantine Emperor was fated to die without a wife and without an heir.[8]

The Byzantines were not alone in underestimating the strength of the new Sultan. People in the western world comforted themselves and salved their consciences with regard to the Christian east by the thought that not much harm could come while the Ottoman Empire was in the hands of one so young. The illusion was fostered by the known facts that Mehmed II had made treaties with John Hunyadi of Hungary and with George Branković of Serbia, and that he had expressed his goodwill to the prince of Wallachia, to the Knights of Rhodes, and to the Genoese lords of Chios and Lesbos. But the illusion was shared also by the Karamans, the inveterate enemies of the Ottomans in Asia. In the autumn of 1451, while the young Sultan was still in Europe, the Karamans organized a rebellion aimed at reconstituting the local principalities which had formerly existed under the emirs of Aydin, Menteshe and elsewhere. They soon discovered their mistake. The revolt was crushed just as soon as Mehmed arrived on the scene. It was now the turn of the Byzantines to be shown that they too were mistaken.[9]

The Emperor Constantine had thought to take advantage of the Sultan's embarrassments in Asia by making certain representations. The only known member of the ruling Ottoman house apart from Mehmed was a grandson of the late Sultan Suleiman called Orchan who lived in exile at Constantinople. Mehmed had agreed to continue paying an annuity for his maintenance. The Emperor now sent a formal complaint to the Sultan's vizir at Brusa that the annuity was not sufficient; and he suggested that in the person of Orchan the Byzantines had a pretender to the Ottoman Sultanate whom they might feel obliged to let loose. The game had been played before. It was in the best traditions of Byzantine diplomacy. Constantine's father Manuel II had played it with varying success in the years after 1402. But it was risky, and in any case the obscure Orchan could have been no match as a rival to Mehmed II. Mehmed's vizir, Halil Pasha, was appalled by the ineptitude of Constantine's threats and suggestions. He lost his temper with those who had brought the message. 'You stupid Greeks,' he exclaimed, 'I have known your cunning ways for long enough. The late Sultan was a lenient and conscientious friend to you. The present Sultan Mehmed is not of the same mind. If Constantinople eludes his bold and impetuous grasp, it will only be because God continues to overlook your devious and wicked schemes. You are fools to think that you can frighten us with your fantasies and that when the ink on our recent treaty of peace is barely dry. We are not children without strength or sense. If you think that you can start something, do so. If you want to proclaim Orchan as Sultan in Thrace, go ahead. If you want to bring the Hungarians across the Danube, let them come. If you want to recover places that you lost long since, try it. But know this: you will make no headway in any of these things. All that you will do is lose what little you still have.'[10]

The Sultan's own reply to the proposals was more terse. He promised simply to examine them and to act upon them with justice and honour as soon as he returned to Adrianople. This he did with the minimum of delay. He made a truce with the emir of the Karamans and crossed the Bosporos in the winter of 1451. The small concessions that he had made to the Byzantines earlier in the year were now revoked and in defiance of his treaty with them, which in his view they had already broken, he gave orders for the encirclement of Constantinople to begin. The first step was the construction of a fortress on the European shore of the Bosporos over against that which Mehmed's grandfather Bajezid had built. Workmen and masons were assembled for the task. When the Emperor saw what was happening he sent messengers to protest. He even arrested all the Turkish residents in the city. But the Sultan took no notice. The work on the castle began in April 1452. The Turks called it Boghaz-kesen, the cutter of the channel. It came to be known as Rumeli-Hisar, the European fortress, in contrast to the Asiatic fortress of Anadolu-Hisar. It took four months to complete; and the Byzantines watching the work from their walls now felt that all the prophecies about the end of their world and the coming of the antichrist were about to be fulfilled.[11]

Constantine had sorely misjudged his enemy. The only practical measure that he could take was to lay in all the provisions he could find and to see to the repair of the city walls. He was old enough to remember the siege of Constantinople in 1422 and knew what to expect. He made sure that the fields in the neighbourhood were harvested well in advance, and he bought or begged all the supplies that could be shipped from the islands and from Venice, Genoa and Naples. In particular he tried to keep the Venetians informed of the state of affairs, alerting them to the fact that Constantinople was about to be cut off by sea as well as by land and that there were now no doubts about the Sultan's intentions. But the Venetians seemed to have lost interest in Constantinople. They still had their commercial quarter in the city, and its privileges had been renewed by the Emperor in 1450. But they had made their own very promising arrangements with the Turks. The Emperor was aware that their merchants were doing a brisk trade in the markets of Adrianople and that their Doge was on excellent terms with the Sultan. In September 1451 he had signed a treaty with Mehmed II reaffirming that which had been made with Murad in 1446. The Venetians were not going to risk interfering with the Sultan's plans in the Bosporos.

There was a remote chance that the news of an impending siege of Constantinople might awaken some reaction in other quarters of the west. The Emperor made desperate appeals to Ragusa, offering their merchants special privileges in Constantinople, to the cities of Italy, and to the Pope. He was lavish in his promises of reward for anyone who would bring help. To John Hunyadi he promised the city of Mesembria; to King Alfonso of Aragon he offered the island of Lemnos. But in vain. The Genoese, whose colony of Galata was in the thick of it, behaved with the same cautious ambiguity as the Venetians. The governors of Galata and of Chios received orders to act on their own initiative but not to become unnecessarily involved in warfare with the Turks. Constantinople might well fall to the Sultan Mehmed, but that did not mean that the opportunities for trade in the Black Sea ports and the islands would cease. They might indeed improve.[12]

The castle of Rumeli Hisar was finished in August 1452. In October Cardinal Isidore, who had been appointed papal legate, arrived in Constantinople. He brought with him a company of 200 archers from Naples, and he was accompanied by Leonardo, Genoese Archbishop of Chios. Two hundred men would not go far against the might of Mehmed II. But they were better than nothing; and Isidore was warmly welcomed by the Emperor. His mission, however, was not military but religious. He had come to save the souls of the Byzantines by proclaiming the union of the churches in their midst. How such a proclamation was supposed to affect the material circumstances does not seem to have been seriously considered. The Union of Florence had so far brought the Byzantines little comfort. Those who favoured it may have felt that to have it celebrated in their own cathedral would set the seal on their spiritual affinity with their Catholic brethren in the west. But it was not likely now to stir those brethren into a frenzy of last-minute action. Those who opposed the Union deplored its celebration in their most holy church as the ultimate affront to their faith and their traditions. Scholarios, now the monk Gennadios, was passionate in his denunciations. He harangued the people on the betrayal of their faith. He nailed a declaration on the door of his cell, bearing witness before God that he would sooner die than forswear the Orthodoxy that was his heritage. The Union was an evil thing. It portended the ruin of those who had turned their backs on God.

The Grand Duke Loukas Notaras tried to keep tempers cool. But the words of Gennadios struck an answering chord in the minds of the people. Isidore was sympathetic but firm. He had experienced the full blasts of anti-unionist emotion in Russia. In the absence of a patriarch it fell to the Emperor to summon the dissenting clergy and listen to their objections. There was a meeting in the palace on 15 November 1452, at which the anti-unionists signed a document of protest. But the sound of Turkish guns firing in the Bosporos beyond the city walls was more effective than the tirades of Gennadios. At the end of November he retired from the fray and pledged himself to desist from embarrassing his emperor any further. Finally, on 12 December, a concelebration of the Catholic and Orthodox liturgy took place in St Sophia. The Emperor and his court were present. The names of Pope Nicholas V and of the absent Patriarch Gregory III were commemorated. The decrees of Union as recited at Florence were read out. The heavens may have rejoiced, as they are said to have done at Florence. But the ceremony brought little joy to the people of Byzantium. It seemed that in the end, when their backs were to the wall, they had allowed the Latins to win the last round in the battle of wits that had begun with the Fourth Crusade.[13]

At the moment when the final siege of Constantinople was about to begin there must surely have been those who thought that it would be better to surrender than to resist. It was common knowledge, and common experience from the fate of other Byzantine cities, that resistance, if unsuccessful, brought a terrible retribution from the Turks. There were certainly those who felt and perhaps said that they would prefer to see the Sultan's turban in their city than the Latin mitre. The remark was attributed to Loukas Notaras; and although it seems to be out of character, he may well have been goaded into uttering it by the insensitivity of some of the unionists.[14] But surrender was not much spoken of. Constantinople was unique. It was the nerve centre of a whole way of life. Even in its surrounding provinces that were now irretrievably under Turkish domination the currents of thought and faith that had emanated from it over the centuries were still flowing. Omens and prophecies about the ultimate fate of the city had been heard for many years. The Byzantines were given to bouts of fatalistic gloom and pessimism.

It was widely believed that the end would come in the 7000th year from the Creation, in 1492, which meant that there were still forty years to run. But still, when the moment came, as it seemed to come in the long winter of 1452, there were few who felt that their Queen of Cities was not worth defending. To rate their motives at the meanest level one may suppose that the business of preparing the defences afforded some relief from the suspense and anxiety of waiting for the Turks to break in. But heroes moved by higher impulses and ideals were not lacking when the storm broke.[15]

The noblest of them was the Emperor himself. Throughout that winter he exhorted his people, men and women alike, to help in repairing and strengthening the walls of the city and collecting weapons for its defence. If he was afraid that even the massive walls of Constantinople would not stand up to the new artillery of Mehmed he did not show it. He was tragically aware that he had been unable to find the money or the materials to satisfy a Hungarian engineer called Urban who had offered his services to him in the previous summer. Urban had sold his skills to the Sultan for a higher price; and already a great cannon had been erected on the ramparts of Rumeli Hisar which made it impossible for any ships to run the blockade. But rumour had it that Urban was constructing a gun of twice the size at Adrianople, and that it was to be brought to the walls of Constantinople. With the best will in the world, and even with the full co-operation of the churches, monasteries and private fortunes in the capital in raising the money, the Emperor could not find the men, materials and provisions to hold out for very long. But neither he nor his officials would admit the fact. To admit anxiety was to admit defeat; and this the Emperor Constantine would not consider.

In the hour of crisis his determination was shared by all his officers and courtiers, whatever their differences of opinion on other matters. The Grand Duke Loukas Notaras took charge of the defences along the shore of the Golden Horn, together with the Emperor's kinsman Nikephoros Palaiologos. Demetrios Cantacuzene and his son, the *protostrator*, who was a brother-in-law of Nikephoros, commanded a body of 700 men in the region of the Holy Apostles church in the centre of the city, ready to move wherever the need was greatest. His relative John Cantacuzene, the Emperor's closest confidant, was at the land walls, as also was Theophilos Palaiologos. It is sadly appropriate that, in its last months, the defence of Byzantium should have been so largely in the hands of members of the two ruling families who had guided or misguided its destinies for some 200 years. But there were others. The Venetian colony in the city, led by their baillie Girolamo Minotto, guaranteed their full support with the ships that they had in the harbour; and two visiting Venetian captains who were on their way home from the Black Sea promised to stay and fight. The exploits of the Venetians were to be recorded with pride by one of their compatriots, Niccolò Barbaro, in a diary of the siege of Constantinople.[16]

There were men from Genoa too who volunteered to join in the defence and brought their own little companies of soldiers. The most celebrated and the most heroic was Giovanni Giustiniani Longo who arrived in January 1453 bringing a contingent of 700 troops recruited from Genoa, from Chios and from Rhodes. Giustiniani was renowned for his skill in siege warfare, and the Emperor readily entrusted to him the overall command of the defence of the land walls. He had with him a sapper and engineer called John Grant whom the Greeks thought to be a German, though he may well have come from Scotland. The Genoese of Galata across the Golden Horn were in a difficult position. They had the future of their colony to think of, and it went against their grain to join forces with the Venetians in any enterprise. But many of their people came over in secret to swell the numbers. The consul of the Catalan community in the city offered the Emperor his help; and so also did the Ottoman pretender Orchan, who perhaps hoped to gain his own advantage from the defeat of Mehmed II. There were defectors. A number of Venetian ships from Crete, whose services might have helped to tip the scale, slipped out of the Golden Horn in February with several hundred Italians on board. But it was an isolated case of cowardice. When the siege began there were in all 26 battleships anchored in the Golden Horn. They stood little chance against the number of ships which the Sultan Mehmed had equipped. The number of the defenders within the walls was assessed by George Sphrantzes, who claimed to have been set to count them by the Emperor, at 4773 and about 200 foreigners. On the Turkish side he reckoned that there were as many as 200,000 men. Neither of these figures can be accepted without question. Italian sources put the number of Greeks at 6000-7000. Turkish authorities set the total of the Ottoman forces at not more than 80,000. But it is clear that the defenders were outnumbered by at least fifteen to one.[17]

Against such overwhelming odds the Byzantines had only two devices in their favour. One was a boom or chain across the entrance to the harbour of the Golden Horn which the Emperor ordered to be put in place at the beginning of April 1453. It ran on wooden floats from the Tower of Eugenios across to the wall of Galata and effectively prevented the Turkish fleet from entering the harbour to attack the sea wall of the city, as the crusaders had done in 1204. The other deterrent was the great land wall of Constantinople stretching across the four miles of country from the Sea of Marmora to the Blachernai district at the northern end of the Golden Horn. The Turks were rightly expected to direct their main attack along this line. The land wall or walls (for it was a triple line of fortification) had never been taken by assault since the time of its construction in the fifth century. To an attacker it presented first a ditch or moat 60 feet wide and 20-30 feet deep. There was next an embankment protected by a parapet leading to the outer wall, which was guarded by square towers built at intervals of 50-100 yards along its length and rising to heights of 30 feet. The last line of defence, separated from the outer wall by a space of about 50 feet, was the inner or great wall, about 40 feet in height, protected by 96 towers rising to heights of 60 feet. The land walls had always been the despair of the enemies of Constantinople. Now, in 1453, they were the last hope of the inhabitants. They were in reasonably good repair. Constantine's brother John VIII had looked after them. They could hold off any conventional attack, so long as the defenders could survive. But they had not been built to withstand bombardment by heavy artillery, and in 1453 it was a question of time before the defenders ran out of provisions and supplies. Constantinople was for once totally cut off from the rest of Europe by sea as well as by land.[18]

The Sultan had made sure of that. The Turkish fleet was stronger than it had ever been; and in case any help might come from the Emperor's brothers or the Venetians in Greece, the Sultan had ordered Turachan to lead another invasion of the Morea at the end of 1452. The Hexamilion wall had fallen yet again and the whole province, from Corinth to the south coast, had been laid waste. Whether any help, supplies or reinforcements might be able to get through from the western world depended on factors beyond the control of the Byzantine Emperor. He had done his best. He had acknowledged his indebtedness to the west in the ceremony in St Sophia in December 1452. Many of his people wondered why this public humiliation had been necessary when the credit for the debt had still to be advanced. The Pope, for all his good intentions, could do little without the Venetians. Not until February 1453 did Venice decided to send two ships to Constantinople carrying 800 soldiers, with the promise that a larger fleet would follow. But there were endless delays in getting it ready and it did not sail until April. In the same month the Pope announced that he was sending five ships to supplement a cargo of arms and supplies that he had already dispatched on Genoese vessels. The Genoese themselves had been pleased to offer one ship. But neither John Hunyadi nor Alfonso of Aragon, whose schemes were so great on paper, was available when he was most needed. Nor did any other Christian ruler, Catholic or Orthodox, rise to the occasion. George Branković of Serbia, who had contributed to the repair of the city walls in 1448, dutifully sent a body of troops to help his lord the Sultan break through them. John Hunyadi, who might have caused a diversion on the Danube, sent an embassy to the Sultan's camp in the course of the siege to announce the accession of a new King of Hungary. The announcement indicated that he himself was no longer bound by the agreement that he had made with Mehmed in 1451. But at the same time it is said that some of his envoys kindly instructed the Sultan's gunners in the more efficient aiming of their cannons at the walls of Constantinople.[19]

At the beginning of 1453 the Sultan ordered his general in Rumelia, Karadja Beg, to advance from Adrianople on the last remaining Byzantine possessions in Thrace. Epibatai and Herakleia on the Sea of Marmora were captured. Anchialos, Mesembria and other places on the Black Sea coast, which had formed one of the last imperial appanages, fell soon afterwards. On Easter Monday, 2 April, the advance guard of Mehmed's army moved up to pitch camp on the landward side of Constantinople. The inhabitants could give thanks that they had at least been allowed the comfort of their Easter ceremonies without interruption. There was no prospect of comfort ahead. It was now that the Emperor ordered the boom to be placed across the harbour entrance. Three days later the Sultan arrived with the rest of his army and encamped within sight and fire of the gate of St Romanos, midway along the land walls. He had already posted a detachment under his lieutenant Zaganos Pasha in the hills above Galata to maintain communications with the Bosporos and to keep an eye on the Genoese. The first bombardment of the walls by the Turkish cannons began on 6 April. It did considerable damage. But not until the following week were the guns deployed to the Sultan's full satisfaction.[20]

Pride of place was taken by the huge cannon constructed by the

Hungarian engineer Urban. It had been brought from Adrianople on a carriage drawn by 60 oxen and manned by 200 soldiers. When its deafening roar was first heard inside the city, people rushed into the streets in terror calling on the name of the Lord. The cannon-balls that it shot weighed 12 hundredweight; and though it was an unwieldy and complicated piece of machinery that could only be fired seven times a day, it had a deadly effect in wearing down the ancient structure and the masonry of the walls. The smaller guns added their contribution to the damage, and before many days were out a section of the outer wall had collapsed into the moat. The defenders had some primitive muskets and even heavier guns of their own. But they were short of explosives, and their cannons were too liable to shake the stonework of the walls. They fought back from the battlements of the outer wall with arrows, spears and catapults; and at night, when the Turkish guns were silent, they crept out to clear the rubble out of the moat and patch up the damage as best they could.

The daily bombardment of the walls was an unnerving experience for the inhabitants. But they were rewarded with some fleeting successes. The Turkish navy in the Bosporos was beaten off when it tried to break its way through the boom across the Golden Horn; and on 18 April, the Sultan's infantry which had launched a surprise assault against the most ruined portion of the wall was also driven back after some hours of heavy fighting. Two days later there was yet another ray of hope. Three of the Genoese ships commissioned by the Pope at last hove in sight of Constantinople. They had been joined by a large Greek cargo ship which the Emperor had sent to Sicily to load up with wheat supplied by Alfonso of Aragon. The Sultan at once commanded his admiral Balta Oglu to take action. A battle was fought under the walls on the Sea of Marmora. It was touch and go. But finally as the day's light began to fade the Genoese, who had lashed their three ships together with the Greek freighter, broke their way through the Turkish lines; and as soon as it was dark the boom was lifted to let them into the haven of the Golden Horn. These victories gave the Byzantines and their allies fresh heart to persevere with the struggle. They had inflicted many casualties on their enemy. They were the stronger by three more ships and the richer by further supplies of weapons and food; and they had proved what they had always known, that they were better seafarers than the Turks. The Turkish admiral was made to pay a heavy price for his defeat. The Sultan publicly humiliated him, stripped him of his rank, and divided his fortune among the janissaries.[21]

Mehmed now knew that he must find a way to get part of his fleet into the Golden Horn. His engineers had already begun work on building a road up and over the hill behind Galata from the Bosporos. It was now to be completed and used to transport his ships overland and down the other side, where they could be launched into the harbour. It was an immense undertaking, but the Sultan had the manpower and the materials. Wheeled trolleys were constructed to run on tracks along the road, pulled by oxen. The boats were mounted on the trolleys while still in the water and then dragged ashore to make their journey across country. The preparations were finished under a cover of gunfire directed at the boom, and on the morning of 22 April the people on the walls of Constantinople were horrified to see the Turkish ships already coming down the hill beside the walls of Galata and being lowered into the water. The Emperor at once summoned a council of war with the Venetians and Giustiniani. A scheme was proposed to set fire to the Turkish ships. But its execution was fatally delayed because of disagreements between the Venetians and the Genoese, who felt that they had not been properly consulted. Not until 28 April was the attempt made, and it failed miserably. The Sultan also had a pontoon bridge constructed across the narrowest part of the Golden Horn, on which he stationed one of his largest guns.

The effectiveness of the tiny garrison within the city was now greatly reduced. Men had to be detached from their posts at the land walls to patrol the wall along the Golden Horn. There were hardly enough troops to man the four miles of the land walls, let alone the 14 miles of the whole circuit of the city. Communications between the defenders at different points were slow and difficult. The problem of supplies was becoming acute. There was still food to be had in the city but only at inflated prices, and the rich were inclined to hoard their money against the prospect of an uncertain future. The Emperor took determined action. He ordered his officials to levy money from private houses and from the churches and monasteries, and he set up a commission to use the proceeds to buy food for distribution among the people. Church plate was appropriated to be melted down, though the Emperor promised to repay its owners four-fold when the crisis was over. Meanwhile the bombardment of the walls continued with sickening monotony. The defenders had to withdraw behind the outer wall. Before long a breach had been made big enough to expose a section of the inner wall. But still the repeated attacks of the Sultan's soldiers were driven off by the troops under Giustiniani's command. Mehmed commanded his sappers to undermine the wall at different points. But they were continually obstructed by counter-mining operations directed by the engineer John Grant. On 18 May the Turks, who had succeeded in filling in a part of the moat, tried to move up against the wall an immense wooden turret on wheels from which they could storm the battlements under cover. But the defenders managed to set it alight before it had got within striking range.[22]

The only hope left to the Emperor and his people was that the promised fleet from Venice would arrive in time before their munitions and their food supplies ran out. But the hope was dashed when a Venetian ship that had slipped out to scour the Aegean Sea returned to report that no fleet was anywhere in the offing. The morale of the people began to break. Desertions became more frequent. Food was getting scarcer, nerves and tempers were frayed. Giustiniani and Notaras took to accusing each other of cowardice and treachery. The Venetians and the Genoese quarrelled so violently that the Emperor had to remind their leaders that they were engaged in a war large enough without bringing their own conflict within the walls. The anti-unionists refused to enter the doors of St Sophia now that it had been polluted by the Latin mass. Their followers turned on the Emperor and shouted abuse at him in the streets as one who had betrayed Orthodoxy and so involved the faithful in ruin. Many must have believed them. But it was too late now to reverse the process. The just must suffer with the unjust, the innocent with the guilty. The wrath of God was turned against all his children, as it had been foretold. The end of the world seemed to be nigh.

There was an atmosphere in which coincidences were translated into the fulfilment of oracles and unusual phenomena into half-expected portents. On the night of 24 May the dome of St Sophia appeared to be suffused with a red glow that crept slowly up and round from its base to the great gilt cross at the top. The light lingered there for a moment and then went out. The crowds who saw it were in no mind to explain it as a reflection from the flames of the Turkish bonfires beyond the walls. It must be an omen. Niccolò Barbaro says that it looked like an eclipse of the moon. Had not the prophets warned that the city would fall in the days when the moon was waning? Others interpreted it as a sign that the holy light in the cathedral of the Holy Wisdom, and with it the guardian angel of the city, had gone for ever. The Virgin too, who had always been its protectress, seemed to be wavering in her affections. When the most hallowed of her icons was brought out to be paraded round the streets, it slipped off the framework on which it was being carried aloft; and almost at once a thunderstorm broke out and the city was deluged with torrents of rain and hail. Such a coincidence would have made the Byzantines anxious at the best of times. In their present state of terror and credulity it moved them to hysteria.[23]

The heavens themselves seemed to be saying that further resistance was hopeless. But still the Emperor would not contemplate surrender; and still his officers, both Greek and Italian, stayed at their appointed posts. His courtiers and some of his clergy implored him to escape while he could. The Queen of Cities might be about to fall. But so long as its Emperor lived there would be hope that one day he might retrieve it. It had happened before. They urged him to leave for the Morea, or for any place from which he could work for the recovery of his city. He was so exhausted, and so discouraged by the thought that even his bishops had lost heart, that he collapsed for a moment. But when they had revived him, he rejected any idea of abandoning his charge. If his city fell that would be by God's will. But he would not go down in history as the Emperor who ran away. He would stay and die with his people. His reply to the Sultan was the same. Mehmed sent a messenger to him offering terms on which surrender could be arranged. The Greeks could either live under his rule on payment of an annual tribute, or they could simply evacuate the city and find somewhere else to live. The Emperor and his council answered that the Sultan could have anything that he wanted except for the city of Constantinople. They would rather die than surrender that. It was the last communication between a Byzantine Emperor and an Ottoman Sultan.[24]

Mehmed had not expected any other reply. But he had covered himself. By the laws of his religion he was now at liberty to do his worst and to promise his soldiers the right of three days of plunder and a just division of the spoils in anticipation of victory. The prospect excited them still further. The bombardment of the land walls grew heavier by day. A section of the inner wall collapsed in ruins. By night swarms of Turkish soldiers and navvies laboured to fill up the moat with everything they could lay their hands on. On Monday 28 May the defenders knew that the moment of truth was upon them. There was an ominous silence from the Turkish camp beyond the walls. The Sultan had ordered a day of rest before the great assault. He spent the day haranguing his troops and giving final instructions to his officers and to his admirals in the Golden Horn and beyond the boom. He also issued a stern warning to the Genoese in Galata to remember the fact of their neutrality. In the certainty of imminent danger the defenders forgot their quarrels and sank their differences. The Emperor had the icons and relics from the city churches brought out and carried round the walls, while all the church bells rang. A procession was formed of Greeks and Latins alike, chanting hymns and prayers. After it had wound its way round the city, the Emperor addressed a gathering of his Greek and Italian officers and of the citizens, encouraging them to be steadfast in the impending hour of trial. It was, as Gibbon says, 'the funeral oration of the Roman Empire'.[25]

Towards evening the people made their way as if by instinct to the cathedral of St Sophia. The soldiers stayed at their posts on the walls. But most of the rest of the population, Latins as well as Greeks, crowded into the great church to pray together for their deliverance. Common fear and common danger worked more of a wonder than all the councils of the church. Orthodox bishops, priests and monks, who had loudly declared that they would never again set foot in their cathedral until it had been purged of the Roman abomination, now approached the altar to join their Catholic brethren in celebrating the holy liturgy. Among the celebrants was Isidore the Cardinal, whom many of the faithful had condemned and shunned as a heretic and an apostate. The Emperor Constantine came to pray and to ask forgiveness and remission of his sins from every bishop present before receiving holy communion at the altar. The priest who gave him the sacraments cannot have known that he was administering the last rites to the last Christian Emperor of Constantinople. Those who were too old or frail for active service spent the night in vigil in the church. The Emperor went back to his palace at Blachernai to say his farewells to his household, and then rode into the night for a last inspection of his soldiers at the wall.[26]

The attack began in the early hours of Tuesday 29 May. Wave upon wave of the Sultan's front-line troops charged up to the land walls, yelling their war cries and excited to frenzies of courage by the beat of drums and the blare of trumpets. For nearly two hours they hammered at the weakest section of the wall. But the breach was held by Giustiniani and his men; the Emperor was there to help, and the attackers began to fall back. Almost at once their place was taken by some of the more professional regiments of the Ottoman army. They were better armed and better disciplined, and they were supported by covering fire from the Turkish guns. But still they could not get through. At the same time the assault was being pressed on the sea wall along the Golden Horn. But here too the defenders still held the initiative. The Sultan's plan was to give the Christians no respite, to wear down their strength as his guns had worn down the strength of their walls. It was expensive in casualties, but the Sultan had the men to spare. The *coup de grâce* was reserved for his own janissaries. Before the soldiers on the land walls had had time to lick their wounds and recover from the second attack, the janissaries advanced at the double, in full battle array, fresh and eager. They closed with the defenders on the outer wall. In many places the fighting was now man to man, while some of the janissaries tried to bring up scaling ladders. Just before the break of day Giovanni Giustiniani, who had been holding the line at the critical point for more than six hours, was wounded. The Emperor hurried up to beg him to stay at his post, but he was bleeding and in pain and too weak to carry on. His bodyguard took him off down to the harbour and on to a Genoese ship.

As soon as his soldiers realized that Giustiniani was gone they lost heart. The defence wavered. The janissaries saw their opportunity. One of them, a giant of a man from Lopadion called Hasan, clambered up on to the top of the outer wall. He was struck down, but the others who had followed him up held their ground. The Emperor and his men fought with desperation, but the Genoese had left them to it; and before long some of the janissaries had battled their way through to the inner wall and scaled it. While the battle for the walls was in full swing a body of about 50 Turks had broken in through a little gate called the Kerkoporta further up the hill. It had been insecurely bolted and it yielded to their pressure. They were the first Turks to enter the city; and had it not been for the confusion on the walls they might have been discovered and slaughtered. But by now it was too late. They had already mounted the tower above the gate and flown the Ottoman standard from its summit. Their comrades had understood the signal and followed on their heels. The janissaries at the walls saw what had occurred and echoed the shouts from within that the city was taken.

The defenders fell back as more and more of the janissaries stormed the breaches in the walls or forced their way into the city through the open gate. They were seized with panic as they saw that their means of retreat from the walls was being cut off behind them. Many had in their minds the fate of their wives and children in the city. The Emperor did everything he could to rally them. Theophilos Palaiologos, who with Demetrios Cantacuzene had valiantly beaten off one assault of the enemy, could bear the shame no longer. Crying out that he would sooner die, he charged into the press of Turks sword in hand. Other commanders followed his example; some disappeared fighting hand to hand or, like animals, tooth and nail with the janissaries. The struggle was fiercest at the gate called the Gate of St Romanos. It was there that the Emperor Constantine was last seen. He had thrown away his regalia. He was killed fighting as a common soldier to stem the flood of infidels pouring into his Christian city.

As the cry went round that the Turks were inside the walls other sections of the defence also concluded that the cause was lost. Greek soldiers began rushing to their houses to defend and protect their families. The Venetians rushed to their ships. A few of the Genoese got safely over to Galata. Some of the men on the wall jumped to their death; others surrendered. The Turks were left free to open all the gates in the walls. There was little fighting along the Golden Horn. The walls there were soon mastered by Turkish soldiers put ashore from their ships. While they and the sailors who followed them were preoccupied with getting into the city so as not to miss their share of the booty, the Italian commander of the Venetian fleet sounded the opinion of the Genoese across the water before deciding to run for it. His sailors hacked at the boom across the mouth of the harbour until it snapped, and the Venetian ships, packed with refugees who had swum out from the shore, sailed away. Hard behind them came a number of Genoese vessels and a few of the Emperor's ships. They only just escaped in time, for by midday the Turkish navy was in control of the Golden Horn.[27]

The sack and plunder of the city began as soon as the first Turks broke in, and as the day wore on there seemed no end to it. The conquerors were impatient to collect the rewards of their victory. Every living thing that stood in their way was slaughtered and the streets ran with blood. The houses nearest the land walls suffered earliest. They were broken open and ransacked, the children were thrown out, the women raped or captured. The palace at Blachernai and the churches nearby were soon gutted and their treasures stolen or burnt. Books and icons were pitched into the flames after their bejewelled bindings and silver frames had been wrenched off. But rumour had it that the greatest treasures of all were to be found in St Sophia, and the janissaries were eager to be the first to get there. The church was packed with terrified people. The doors had been bolted; but the soldiers quickly broke their way in and set to work tearing down the gold and silver ornaments, murdering those who got in their way, and squabbling over the possession of the more desirable captives. For there was no means of escape. The male prisoners were tied together with ropes, the women were bound by their own veils and girdles and dragged away. The great church rang with the screams and tears of human beings so suddenly reduced to the state of tortured animals. The priests who had been celebrating the morning liturgy at the high altar when the Turks broke in were never seen again. The legend soon grew that the celebrant had been observed to disappear into the wall of the sanctuary taking the chalice with him. The wall that closed behind him will reopen for him on the day that Constantinople once again becomes a Christian city; and the liturgy so rudely interrupted on the morning of 29 May 1453 will then be resumed.[28]

Such fancies were dreamed up after the event. On the day itself men's minds were filled not with dreams of the future but with the horrors of the present. Whole families were butchered or separated one from the other as captive slaves. Their houses were wrecked and their fortunes ruined. In terms of human suffering the shock was appalling. But there were things that the Byzantines held even more dear than life itself; and to see those destroyed without a murmur of complaint from heaven was still more bewildering. The ancient icon of the Mother of God, the Hodegetria, the protectress of the city painted by St Luke, which was brought out in procession every Easter, was torn down and smashed in pieces; and the perpetrators of the crime were not struck dumb. The cathedral and numerous other churches had been desecrated; and no voice had come from heaven. Nuns had been rounded up and divided as spoil among their captors, the crucifix had been mocked; but the veil of the temple had not been rent in twain. To some such things were sure proof of the magnitude of their sins. To others they were proof that God and his Mother had deserted them because they had betrayed the faith to the Latins. For a few, and it is said that there were monks among them, the proof that God was on the other side was so strong that they declared themselves converted to Islam.[29]

The conquering Sultan entered the city in the afternoon with an escort of his vizirs, pashas, ulemas and janissaries. He rode at once to the church of St Sophia to give thanks to God for his victory. To the few priests and people still hiding in corners of the building he extended his mercy. He could afford to be merciful now. One of his priests mounted the pulpit and chanted the praise of Allah and his Prophet; and then the Sultan, the Prophet's namesake, to whom it had been given to fulfil the prophecy vouchsafed to the first Caliphs of the Arabs, made his own prayer to the God of Islam at the marble altar of the Christians.

The plundering and destruction went on for three days, but the worst was over by the end of the first 12 hours. The dead were estimated at 4000; the number of prisoners was thought to be at least 50,000. There was no hope of mercy or release for those who were not worth a ransom. But the Sultan sought out the survivors of the noblest Byzantine families. The fate of the Emperor Constantine was of particular concern to him. A search was made but, though many stories are told, the Emperor's body was never certainly identified. The important thing was to be sure that he was not still alive and that he had not escaped; and these facts at least admit of no doubt. Not even legend suggested that the last Constantine ever reappeared to lead his people back to their heritage. Of those who had fought with him or beside him in the last hours some, like Theophilos Palaiologos, had already gone valiantly to their deaths. Several of the officers and courtiers who were captured were at first honourably treated by the Sultan. Prominent prisoners were the Grand Duke Loukas Notaras, with his wife and two sons, and his son-in-law, a Cantacuzene, and the Grand Domestic Andronikos Palaiologos Cantacuzene. But five days after the conquest they were arrested with nine other notables and executed. The cause of their punishment is said to have been the Grand Duke's refusal to hand over one of his sons to the Sultan's pleasure. His children were therefore murdered before his eyes and he himself was then decapitated. His son-in-law and the Grand Domestic were also beheaded. Notaras was without doubt a brave man, but it was his treachery more than his courage that the Sultan feared. Mehmed had come round to the opinion expressed by some of his advisers that the cream of the Byzantine aristocracy would be safer dead than alive. Their widows were sent with the rest of the prisoners to Adrianople.[30]

Several of the orphaned children of the Byzantine nobility were taken off to the Sultan's seraglio to be specially educated. In later years some of them were to rise to high office in the service of the Ottoman Empire forming, like the janissaries, a separate class of servants of the Sultan. Not all the aristocracy were captured however, and in the confusion after the Turks broke in even some of the commanders who had been fighting at the walls found time to collect their wives and families and make for the ships in the harbour. A passenger list has been preserved of the refugees taken on board one Genoese ship on 29 May. It bears the names of John and Demetrios Cantacuzene, of six members of the Palaiologos family, two Lascarids, two Komneni, two of the Notaras family, and many of less distinguished birth. The ship's captain, Zorzi Doria, carried them to Chios, where some of them took refuge. Others were taken on in a Venetian ship to Crete, whence they made their different ways to the Morea, to Corfu and the Ionian islands, or to Italy.[31] It was the beginning of the Byzantine diaspora which was to send so many refugees to the Venetian-occupied islands or to Venice itself. The Greek exiles who reached Venice in growing numbers after 1453 were to find there an influential champion of their cause in the person of Anna Palaiologina Notaras, a daughter of the celebrated Grand Duke. Her father had sent her to Italy with some of the family treasures long before the fall of Constantinople. She had settled in Venice with her niece Eudokia Cantacuzene. The two ladies were still respected patrons of the Greek community in Venice 30 years later, and had been granted the exceptional privilege of having a private chapel for their Orthodox devotions.[32]

Some of the captives on whom the Sultan would have liked to lay his hands, had adventurous escapes. Cardinal Isidore eluded death by exchanging his red hat and robes for those of a beggar in the streets. The beggar was executed as a cardinal, while the cardinal was caught but ransomed for next to nothing by a Genoese merchant in Galata. The Genoese Archbishop of Chios, Leonardo, was also ransomed by his compatriots before the Turks knew who he was. He was glad to be back on Italian soil, for he had come to dislike the Greeks and was inclined to feel that they had got what they deserved. The Turkish pretender Orchan, however, was not so lucky. He had played his part in the defence of the city, more out of desperation than loyalty. He tried to get away dressed up as a monk. But he was betrayed by one of the Byzantine prisoners and promptly beheaded. His head was sent to the Sultan. The gallant Giustiniani, the mainspring of the defence at the land walls, got as far as Chios before he died of his wounds. There were those who said that he should have stayed and died at his post. They forgot that he had no moral call or patriotic duty to be there in the first place. He was one of those whose 'shoulders held the sky suspended', even if only for a few brief hours.

The hero of the Byzantine people henceforth was to be neither a soldier nor an emperor, but a monk. The Orthodox Church, which for many years had shown greater powers of survival than the Byzantine state, was now to fill the vacuum left by the removal of the secular institutions in Christian society. The Sultan wanted it to be so. He wanted the Christian *raias* to be properly organized into a *millet* or community within his Ottoman Empire under their own leader who would be answerable to him for their conduct. The Patriarch of Constantinople was the obvious leader. But in 1453 the Patriarch Gregory was abroad. Gregory was in any case a unionist, and the Sultan was suspicious of any signs of co-operation between the Greeks and the west. The man who would best suit his purpose and be most welcome to the Byzantines as their Patriarch was George Scholarios, the monk Gennadios. A search had to be made for him, since he had been dragged off to the slave market with the other monks of his monastery. He was discovered serving in the household of a Turk at Adrianople and brought to the Sultan. To be the first Patriarch of Constantinople under infidel rule was a daunting prospect. It might make or mar the future of the Orthodox Church. Scholarios was hesitant. But in the end he accepted the responsibility; and it was with him that Mehmed worked out the proposed administration of the Christian *millet* in Ottoman territory. In January 1454 Scholarios was enthroned as the Patriarch Gennadios II, not in the church of St Sophia which was now a mosque, but in the church of the Holy Apostles. The ceremony was punctiliously performed. The Sultan Mehmed handed the new Patriarch his staff of office, just as the emperors had always done in the past. The act symbolized the close relationship between Church and State. Mehmed II was pleased to see himself as the Sultan-Basileus, the heir of the Caesars and the successor of all the Constantines. It was hard for Christians to see him that way, though some tried. But they were mightily relieved to find that even though they had no Emperor they were still allowed to have their Church; and thanks to the arrangements made between Gennadios and the Sultan, their Patriarch was to become in some sense the ghost of the Christian Emperor seated upon the grave thereof. In temporal authority at least the Patriarchate of Constantinople lost nothing by the Turkish conquest.[33]

Of the heroes who had held the frontiers in eastern Europe before the conquest, George Branković died in December 1456. His Serbian

Despotate had by then been greatly reduced in size and influence by Turkish encroachments, though the Sultan's main objective was the key fortress of Belgrade, which was defended by John Hunyadi. It was at this point that the line held in Europe. Mehmed had to call off his siege of Belgrade in July 1456. But Hunyadi died shortly afterwards and, with Branković gone as well, the race of heroes was almost extinct. The sons of Branković quarrelled among themselves, though his daughter Mara, the widow of the Sultan Murad, continued to have some influence over her stepson Mehmed until her death in 1487. But the protection and control of what was left of Christian Serbia became matters of Hungarian and Bosnian politics. The inhabitants of Smederevo, the great castle that Branković had built on the Danube, opened their gates to the Turks on 20 June 1459. Surrender to the Sultan seemed a safer option than acting as pawns in the political games of their neighbours. Serbia was thus at last totally absorbed into the Ottoman Empire, whose frontiers now ran with those of the kingdom of Hungary.

The last Christian hero of all on the European front was Skanderbeg of Albania, who continued to defend his fortress of Kroia against repeated Turkish attacks and sieges until he died in 1468. The Venetians at once intervened to take over what they had long coveted. But they were unable to hold it for more than a few years. Kroia fell to the Sultan in 1478; and by the end of the fifteenth century the Turks had advanced up to the Adriatic coast, captured Durazzo and other Venetian colonies, and put an end to the Venetian intrusion in Albania. Only the little city state of Ragusa, whose people had a way of keeping out of the heroics, managed to make arrangements with the Turks calculated to ensure their own survival and continuing prosperity.[34]

NOTES

The main Greek sources for the reign of the last Byzantine Emperor and the fall of Constantinople are: Chalkokondyles; Doukas; Sphrantzes; and Kritoboulos of Imbros, ed. V. Grecu, *Critobul din Imbros, Din Domnia lui Mahomed al II-ea anii 1451-1467* (Bucharest, 1963) (English translation by C. T. Riggs, *Kritovoulos, History of Mehmed the Conqueror* (Princeton, 1954)). The other Greek, western, Slavonic, and Turkish sources for the siege and capture of the city in 1453 are listed by S. Runciman, *The Fall of Constantinople 1453* (Cambridge, 1965), Appendix I, 194-8.

Modern works: Runciman, *The Fall of Constantinople*; E. Pears, *The Destruction of the Greek Empire and the Story of the Capture of Constantinople by the Turks* (London, 1903); Ch. Mijatovich, *Constantine. The Last Emperor of the Greeks* (London, 1892); F. Babinger, *Mahomet II le Conquérant et son temps (1432-1481)* (Paris, 1954) (translated from the German edition of 1953). Cf. Ostrogorsky, *History*, 567-72; Bréhier, *Vie et Mort*, 415-28; Diehl, *L'Europe orientale*, 368-78; Vasiliev, *History*, 644-56.

1 On Helena Dragaš, see Ostrogorsky, *History*, 567 and references. There is some doubt as to whether the last Constantine should be accounted the XIth or the XIIth. B. Sinogowitz, "Über das byzantinische Kaisertum nach dem vierten Kreuzzuge', *BZ*, XLV (1952), 354-6, argued that the XIth of the name was Constantine Laskaris who was proclaimed, though never crowned, as Emperor in Constantinople in 1204. This view was tacitly accepted by V. Grumel, *La Chronologie*, 359, 365, 366, and by Dölger, *Regesten*, V, 132f., though not by Ostrogorsky, *History*; and it has been seriously questioned by I. Papadrianos, in *Zbornik Radova*, IX (1966), 217-22, and by C. M. Brand, *Byzantium confronts the West, 1180-1204* (Cambridge, Mass., 1968), 258 and 381 note 58. Gibbon, *Decline and Fall*, ed. Bury, VII, 154 and note 52, had other grounds for counting the last Constantine as the XIIth.

2 Runciman, *Fall of Constantinople*, 51-2; Gill, *Council of Florence*, 372; Schreiner, *Studien zu den Brachea Chronika*, 178-9.

3 Zakythinos, *Despotat grec de Morée*, I, 240-3; Runciman, *Fall*, 52-3.

4 Runciman, *Fall*, 53-4; Gill, *Council of Florence*, 375-6; Vacalopoulos, *Origins of the Greek Nation*, 192-3. Cf. Nicol, *Byzantine Family of Kantakouzenos*, 179-81, 192-5, 196-9.

5 Gill, *Council of Florence*, 372-6, 383; Vacalopoulos, *Origins*, 188.

6 On the youth and earlier career of Mehmed, see especially Babinger, *Mahomet le Conquérant*, 13-83; Runciman, *Fall*, 55-9.

7 Sphrantzes, *Chronicon Minus*, ed. Grecu, 74-8.

8 Sphrantzes, *Chronicon Minus*, ed. Grecu, 78-82. S. Lambros, 'Constantine Palaiologos as a husband in history and in legend' [in Greek], *Neos Hellenomnenon*, IV (1907), 417-66; cf. Runciman, *Fall*, 54-5; Nicol, *Byzantine Family of Kantakouzenos*, 211 and references.

9 Runciman, *Fall*, 61-5; Babinger, *Mahomet*, 84-91.

10 Doukas, *Istoria*, ed. Grecu, 294-5. Runciman, *Fall*, 65; Babinger, *Mahomet*, 91-3.

11 Runciman, *Fall*, 65-6; Babinger, *Mahomet*, 98-101.

12 F. Thiriet, *La Romanie vénitienne au moyen âge*, 379-81; Dölger, *Regesten*, V, nos. 3522, 3529, 3535, 3551 (embassies to Alfonso V); no. 3545 (chrysobull for John Hunyadi). Cf. Runciman, *Fall*, 67-8.

13 Gill, *Council of Florence*, 383-7; Runciman, *Fall*, 69-72; Vacalopoulos, *Origins*, 191-3.

14 The words are put into the mouth of Loukas Notaras by Doukas, 329 (ed. Grecu).

15 See, e.g., C. Diehl, 'Sur quelques croyances byzantines sur la fin de Constantinople', *BZ*, XXX (1930), 192-6; A. A. Vasiliev, 'Medieval ideas of the end of the world : West and East', *B*, XVI (1944), 462-502; P. J. Alexander, 'Historiens byzantins et croyances eschatologiques', *Actes du XIIe Congrès International des Etudes Byzantines*, II (Belgrade, 1964), 1-8; *idem*, 'Medieval Apocalypses as Historical Sources', *American Historical Review*, LXXIII (1968), 997-1018.

16 Niccolò Barbaro, *Giornale dell'assedio di Constantinopoli*, ed. E. Cornet (Vienna, 1856); English translation by J. R. Jones, *Diary of the Siege of Constantinople* (New York, 1969).

17 Runciman, *Fall*, 77-85; Babinger, *Mahomet*, 108-10; M. Klopf, 'The army in Constantinople at the accession of Constantine XI', *B*, XL (1970), 385-92. None of these authorities resolves the discrepancy in the number recorded in the texts of Sphrantzes; the *Chronicon Minus*, ed. Grecu, 96, gives the figure as 4773 Greeks and 200 foreigners; the *Chronicon Maius*, ed. Grecu, 386, gives 4973 Greeks and 2000 foreigners.

18 Runciman, *Fall*, 87-91. See especially A. van Millingen, *Byzantine Constantinople. The Walls of the City* (London, 1899).

19 Doukas, 341-2 (ed. Grecu); Sphrantzes, *Chronicon Minus*, ed. Grecu, 102. Zakythinos, *Despotat*, I, 246; Runciman, *Fall*, 79-83; Babinger, *Mahomet*, 102-4.

20 Runciman, *Fall*, 74-5; Vacalopoulos, *Origins*, 193f.

21 Runciman, *Fall*, 94-104; Babinger, *Mahomet*, 109-13.

22 Runciman, *Fall*, 104-19; Babinger, *Mahomet*, 113-15.

23 Sphrantzes, *Chronicon Maius*, ed. Grecu, 408; Kritoboulos, ed. Grecu, 119-21; Barbaro, *Giornale*, 46-8. Runciman, *Fall*, 120-2; Babinger, *Mahomet*, 116-18.

24 Doukas, 345, 351 (ed. Grecu); Chalkokondyles, II, 156-7 (ed. Darkó); Kritoboulos, 87-9 (Grecu). Runciman, *Fall*, 122-4.

25 Gibbon, *Decline and Fall of the Roman Empire*, ed. Bury, VII, 188.

26 Runciman, *Fall*, 126-32.

27 Runciman, *Fall*, 133-44; Babinger, *Mahomet*, 118-19; Vacalopoulos, *Origins*, 198-9.

28 Runciman, *Fall*, 145-8; Babinger, *Mahomet*, 120-1.

29 Vacalopoulos, *Origins*, 202-3.

30 For the fate of the Grand Domestic and the Grand Duke Notaras, see Vacalopoulos, *Origins*, 200-1; and *idem*, in *BZ*, LII (1959), 13-21; Nicol, *Byzantine Family of Kantakouzenos*, 179-81; Runciman, *Fall*, 151-2; Babinger, *Mahomet*, 122-5.

31 See document published by K. D. Mertzios, in *Actes du XIIe Congrès International des Etudes Byzantines*, II (Belgrade, 1964), 171-6; Nicol, *op. cit.*, 194 and references; Vacalopoulos, *Origins*, 201-2.

32 See D. J. Geanakoplos, *Greek Scholars in Venice* (Cambridge, Mass., 1962), 62 and references; Nicol, *op. cit.*, 230-3.

33 Runciman, *Fall*, 150-6; *idem*, *The Great Church in Captivity*, 165f.; Babinger, *Mahomet*, 129-31; C. J. G. Turner, 'The Career of George-Gennadius Scholarius', *B*, XXXIX (1969), 439f.

34 Babinger, *Mahomet*, 133-4, 153-6, 167-78, 185f.; Gegaj, *L'Albanie et l'Invasion turque au XVe siècle*, 97f.; 149f.; L. S. Stavrianos, *The Balkans since 1453* (New York, 1965), 61-5.

Nineteen

The Last Outposts of Byzantium

The Venetians, who had made most out of the Fourth Crusade and the dismemberment of the Byzantine Empire in 1204, and the Genoese, who had made most out of the Empire's restoration in 1261, were the last of the Christians to abandon their colonies in the ruins of that empire. The Genoese in Galata made their own terms with the Turks. As soon as it was certain that Constantinople had fallen they opened the gates of their fortress city to Zaganos Pasha and sent messengers to offer their congratulations and respects to the Sultan. On 1 June 1453 Mehmed issued a document setting out the terms and conditions on which Galata might be permitted to survive. The Genoese had expected better things as a reward for their neutrality. They were commanded to pull down their walls and fortifications and to hand over their weapons, and a capitation tax was to be paid by every male citizen. In other respects, although they were left in a comparatively privileged position, they were little better off than if they had simply surrendered in the first place; for they and their commercial activities were now subject to the restrictions and delays of Ottoman law. Under such conditions the Genoese found it impossible to maintain still less to expand their trade in the Black Sea. Their ships were no longer in undisputed possession of the Bosporos, and merchants from their mother city were reluctant to pay dues to the Turks or to risk their capital in the hazardous business of operating the trade routes to the Crimea or to Trebizond. Not much more than 20 years after the fall of Constantinople all the former dependencies of Galata and Genoa beyond the Bosporos had been lost.[1]

Some of the Genoese colonies elsewhere in the Byzantine world struggled on for a while longer by paying tribute to the Sultan. The Gattilusio family of Lesbos kept a precarious hold on their island until 1462, though their relatives in the smaller islands of Thasos, Imbros, Lemnos and others had by then already forfeited their possessions to the Turks. The Maona or Genoese trading company, which had run the island of Chios for over a century, had some of their acquisitions taken from them. Phokaia on the Turkish mainland was captured in 1455, and the island of Samos some 20 years later. But by faithfully fulfilling all the requirements of a succession of Sultans, the Maona contrived to make some profit out of Chios until they were forced to relinquish it in 1566. Naxos and its satellite islands in the Cyclades also remained in Christian hands until the same year. The so-called Duchy of Naxos had been usurped from the descendants of Marco Sanudo in 1383 by the Veronese family of the Crispi. They had been content to live as the vassals first of Venice and then of the Turks. But in 1566 the Sultan Selim II deposed the last Christian Duke, Jacopo Crispo, and gave control of Naxos to a wealthy Jew called Joseph Nasi.

The Venetians, who had sunk more of their capital in the Empire, did not lose heart quite so easily as the Genoese. They were even prepared to pick up some of the pieces left by other colonists. Their occupation of Negroponte, which had begun in 1205, was brought to an end by Mehmed II in 1470. But they held on to Naupaktos or Lepanto until 1499, to Coron and Modon until 1500, and to Monemvasia until 1540. The island of Cyprus, which they took over in 1489, did not fall to the Turks until 1571; the island of Crete not until 1715; while the island of Corfu remained a Venetian possession until it was assigned to France in 1797. In the other Ionian islands however, and on the mainland of Epiros, Turkish conquest came more swiftly. Ioannina had already submitted in 1430. Arta, the original capital of the Byzantine Despots of Epiros, fell to the Turks in 1449, and with it fell nearly all of the continental properties of the Tocco family. Carlo II Tocco had died the year before. His son Leonardo managed for a few more years to preserve the islands of Leukas (or Santa Mavra), Ithaka, Cephalonia and Zante, but only as a protectorate of Venice. In 1463 he had married a grand-daughter of the Despot of the Morea, Thomas Palaiologos, but when she died he took to wife a daughter of Ferdinand I of Aragon and Naples. Two years later, in 1479, he was forced to take refuge with his new father-in-law at Naples when the Turks decided to round off their conquests in this part of the Greek world. The family of Tocco, whose ancestors had acquired their island county from the Orsini, lost it to the Turks and the Venetians in 1479. The larger islands changed hands more than once over the succeeding years. But Leukas was in Turkish control for over two centuries as a dependency of the Pasha of Lepanto.[2]

The Italian colonies, however, like Serbia and Albania, were places that had long since ceased to be within the Byzantine orbit. After 1453 the only portion of Greek territory that remained in Byzantine hands was the Morea. Some may have hoped that it might become, like Nicaea or Epiros in the thirteenth century, the breeding-ground of a Byzantine Empire in exile from which the recovery of Constantinople could be plotted. But it was in no condition to do so. The latest Turkish invasion, led by Turachan in 1452, had provoked the population of the Morea to the point of revolution against the Byzantine Despots Thomas and Demetrios Palaiologos. The revolt was prompted and led by the Albanian immigrants, but they were eagerly joined by the native Greek landowners, who appointed Manuel Cantacuzene as their own Despot. He seems formerly to have been governor of Mani. The Albanians called him Ghin Cantacuzino, and one must assume that he was a descendant of his namesake Manuel, the first Byzantine Despot of the Morea. The Venetians negotiated with him over the purchase of Corinth and Patras. But the Sultan Mehmed was not keen on having the Morea under Albanian control.

In December 1453 Turachan's son Umur Pasha was sent to Greece to restore order; and in October 1454, in response to requests from Thomas and Demetrios, Turachan Beg arrived in the Morea himself. The Turks were thus called upon to act as a police force on behalf of the Byzantine authorities. They did their job efficiently. Manuel, the 'pseudo-Despot', was forced to flee the land. The rebellion was suppressed, but its underlying causes were not alleviated, nor could they be in the political circumstances. The landed gentry continued to fight their own feuds. The two Byzantine Despots continued to fight each other, and the Greek and Albanian peasantry were the losers at every turn. It is said that they even appealed to the Sultan to divide the country among them in defiance of their overlords.[3]

The Sultan was astonished at the behaviour of the Despots Thomas and Demetrios. They were his sworn vassals. He had gone out of his way to keep them in power. Yet as soon as his back was turned he heard that they were plotting with the Pope, with the Duke of Milan and with the King of France to draw the western world into a crusade. Even in this forlorn project they were unable to co-operate. Each brother did his dealings with the western powers separately. The Sultan's patience was finally exhausted. In May 1458 he crossed the Isthmus of Corinth at the head of his own army from Adrianople. Athens had already fallen to Umur Pasha in June 1456, and the last of the Florentine Dukes of the Acciajuoli family was eking out his existence as a Turkish vassal at Thebes. The Greek lord of Corinth resisted the Turks as vigorously as he had resisted the Byzantines. The Sultan left his gunners to bombard and besiege the Acrocorinth while he took the rest of his army into the interior of the country.

It was a march of conquest and destruction through the portion of the Morea nominally ruled by Thomas Palaiologos. The Turks went as far south as Tripolis and then up to Patras. As before, the citizens of Patras had mostly fled to the Venetian haven of Naupaktos across the water; but this time the garrison left in the acropolis surrendered after a few days. The Sultan saw a great future for a town and harbour so well situated as Patras. He invited the refugees to return on very favourable conditions. From there he marched back along the coast to Corinth, accepting or forcing the submission of every place on his route. The defenders of the Acrocorinth, which was still under siege, were finally persuaded to give in. The deal was done without the prior knowledge of the Despot Thomas, and it was roundly condemned by many Greeks at the time. But the Sultan had rightly made up his mind that he who controlled Corinth could control the Isthmus and so control the Morea. He would have made it his in any case sooner or later. It fell in August 1458. The result of Mehmed's campaign was the loss to the Byzantines of about one-third of the territory of the Despotate of the Morea. The north-western area, indeed most of what had been the portion of Thomas, was now directly under Turkish occupation. Its appointed governor was Umur, son of Turachan Beg of Thessaly. The Byzantine Despotate was now restricted to the rest of the Peloponnese. Thomas and Demetrios were allowed to divide it as best they could, though strictly as the vassals of the Sultan and on payment of a yearly tribute. The Sultan must have suspected that the two brothers, who had found it hard to live in peace with each other before, would find it impossible to do so when they were thrown together in an even more confined area.

On his way back to Adrianople, Mehmed spent four days at Athens, more as a tourist than as a conqueror, although his visit was made the occasion for laying the foundations of the Mosque of the Conqueror that was to stand in the middle of the city until the nineteenth century. He was intrigued and impressed by the antiquities of Athens, notably by the temples on the Acropolis, of which he had read so much. Like the Italian traveller Ciriaco of Ancona, the Sultan Mehmed was a forerunner of that long line of admirers of classical Greece who have fancied themselves to be at home with Plato and Aristotle among the ruins of Athens; and in the manner of Caesar, he was pleased to grant exceptional privileges to the Athenians 'in consideration of their great men of the past', privileges which were to stand them in good stead through nearly four centuries of Turkish rule. Not since the time of the Fourth Crusade had the Byzantines been given the option to treat the cradle of their own culture with such consideration.[4]

The last years of the last vestige of the Byzantine Empire in Greece make sorry reading. The Despots Thomas and Demetrios fell to quarrelling again almost as soon as the Sultan had left. Thomas continued to toy with the hope that the Pope might send reinforcements. Demetrios, who disliked and mistrusted the Latins, looked for Turkish support to suppress his brother. Neither had any real control over the people they were supposed to govern. The local lords were free to indulge in the anarchy which they had usually preferred. The district of the Morea that was under Turkish government was a model of order compared to the chaos that reigned in the Byzantine section. The Sultan soon decided that he must take action. The Pope had already shown some interest in the cause of the Despot Thomas; it would never do if the powers of western Christendom were to find their way back into Greece. In April 1460 Mehmed again set out for the Morea from Adrianople. This time he would complete the process by turning the whole of the Morea into a province of his empire. From Corinth he led his army down past the ruins of Argos to Mistra. Demetrios surrendered without a struggle; and on 29 May 1460, seven years to the day since the fall of Constantinople, the city of Mistra passed into Turkish hands. Perhaps it was as well that the Byzantine Sparta gave in so tamely, for otherwise it might have been reduced to the 'worthless soil' of Ovid's ancient Sparta; its churches, monuments and works of art might have been razed to the ground; and posterity would have been denied the chance to stand among, and perhaps to admire, the mortal remains of a purely Byzantine city.[5] The ghosts of George Gemistos Plethon and his cultured friends may be poor substitutes for the shades of Plato and Aristotle. But it is among the ruins of Mistra more than anywhere else that one can still sense the undiluted spirit of Byzantium.

From Mistra the Sultan turned against the dominions of Thomas in the centre and south-west of the Morea. His army had orders to terrorize the population. Where resistance was offered the local inhabitants were massacred or deported to Constantinople. Refugees flocked south to the Venetian colonies at Coron and Modon. The last known defender of the lost cause in the Morea was an otherwise obscure member of the Palaiologos family called Constantine Graitzas, who held out in his fortress at Salmenikos near Patras until July 1461. But by then the true Palaiologi, the brothers of the last Emperor, had already abandoned their charge. Thomas escaped to Corfu with a few of his nobles. From there in November 1460 he went to Rome in the hope of inciting a crusade for his restoration. He took with him as a present for the Pope the head of the apostle Andrew which he had brought with him from Patras. He was warmly received at Rome by Pope Pius II in March 1461. Cardinal Bessarion handed over the holy relic, and its presentation made such an impression that the scene was later depicted on the Pope's tomb in the church of Sant' Andrea della Valle. Thomas was rewarded with a papal honour and pensions from Pius II and his cardinals, as well as an annual subsidy from Venice. He was still pleading his case in Italy when he died in May 1465. The Pope had gone so far as to invite the princes of Christendom to prepare for the recovery of the Peloponnese. It was, he reminded them, so placed that it could become the point of departure for the salvation of the Christians of the east. Such had been the view of John Cantacuzene when he sent his son to govern it in 1349. But now it was too late. The only parts of mainland Greece still in Christian hands were the Venetian ports of Coron and Modon, Pylos or Navarino, and Naupaktos or Lepanto. The rock of Monemvasia, which Thomas had placed under papal protection, also came into their possession in 1463 when its governor, Nicholas Palaiologos, sold it to Venice for a paltry sum of money.[6]

Thomas's brother Demetrios never hoped or expected to be restored to his Despotate in the Morea. When the Turkish conquest was complete he accompanied the Sultan back to Adrianople. He was a prisoner, but a favoured one. Mehmed made over to him the islands of Imbros and Lemnos, and parts of Samothrace and Thasos, from which Demetrios, living in Adrianople, drew a substantial revenue to supplement the pension that he got from the Ottoman treasury. But about 1467 he fell out of the Sultan's favour. He was sent to exile in Didymoteichos. He died as a monk in 1470, and with him died his line; for his only daughter Helena was already dead and his wife Theodora outlived him by only a few weeks.[7]

It was through the offspring of Thomas that the imperial house of Palaiologos was perpetuated in exile after 1453. The ruling class of the Byzantine world may have lost its property and its fortune after 1453, but it made every effort to propagate its species. The surnames that Thomas's family acquired by intermarriage provide striking testimony of this fact. His wife Catherine, who bore the Bulgarian name of Asenina, was a daughter of the Genoese prince Centurione Zaccaria. Their eldest daughter Helena, who bore the name of Palaiologina, married in 1446 Lazar, the third son of George Branković of Serbia, who inherited the name of Cantacuzene from his mother. She produced three children: Maria, who married Stefan Tomasević of Bosnia; Milica, who married Leonardo Tocco of Cephalonia; and Eirene, who married the son of Skanderbeg of Albania. The younger daughter of Thomas, Zoe, became the wife of Ivan III, Grand Prince of Moscow, in 1472. The wedding was celebrated with great pomp in Rome by Pope Sixtus IV, who provided a dowry for the bride. But once in Russia Zoe quickly reverted to the Orthodox faith. The Russians called her Sophia; and the fact of this union between 'the new Constantine of Moscow', as Ivan III liked to be known, and the niece of the last Constantine Palaiologos, lent some substance to the growing myth that Moscow was the Third Rome.

The two surviving sons of Thomas were Andrew, born in 1453, and Manuel, born in 1455. They were brought up in Italy under the watchful eye of Cardinal Bessarion. The cardinal expected great things of them, and composed improving treatises for them to commit to memory. Pope Pius II provided them with pensions after their father's death in 1465, but Pope Sixtus IV found it necessary to reduce the amount. Manuel left Rome about 1476 and threw himself on the mercy of the Sultan Mehmed II, who gave him an appanage and an income. He married and had two sons: John, who died young; and Andrew, who became a Muslim and may be identified with the soldier Mesih Pasha, who took part in the abortive Turkish attack on Rhodes in 1480.

Thomas's other son, Andrew Palaiologos, being the eldest nephew of the last Constantine, was generally considered, not least by Bessarion, to be the lawful heir to the Byzantine throne as well as to the Despotate of the Morea. The Pope adorned him with the title of Despot of the Romans. But after Bessarion's death in 1472, Andrew had no one to keep him in mind of his responsibilities. He married a woman of the streets of Rome called Catherine. The Pope refused to support him for a while as a result, and he went to live with his sister in Russia. But soon he was back in Rome persuading the Pope to help finance an expedition for the recovery of the Morea from the Turks. The money was found and spent, but nothing came of the expedition. Andrew then visited France at the expense of King Charles VIII; and in 1494 he ceded to Charles all his rights over the Byzantine Empire, Trebizond and Serbia. For himself he reserved only the Despotate of the

Morea. But when Charles VIII died in 1498, Andrew was left almost penniless. In 1502 he bestowed all his titles on Ferdinand and Isabella of Castile, and in June of that same year he died as a pauper. His widow had to beg the sum of 104 ducats from the Pope to pay for the cost of his funeral. He seems to have had a son called Constantine, who was employed in Rome in 1508 as commander of the papal guard.[8]

During the Greek War of Independence in the nineteenth century a delegation from Greece was sent to Cornwall to investigate a rumour that there were descendants of the Byzantine family of Palaiologos living there. In 1817 a Cornish clergyman had published the text of an inscription on a gravestone in the parish churchyard of Landulph near Plymouth. It records the death on 21 January 1636 of one Theodore Palaiologos of Pesaro in Italy, 'descended from the imperial line of the last Christian Emperors of Greece'; and it traces the descent of Theodore through four generations from a son of Thomas Palaiologos, second brother to Constantine, the last of the line that reigned in Constantinople, called John. Theodore was married to a lady from Suffolk whose name was Mary Balls, and he had three sons and two daughters. One of his sons is said to have been killed at the battle of Naseby. Another may be the Ferdinand Palaiologos who went to sea and settled in Barbados, where he is buried. His tombstone records that he died on 3 October 1678 after serving as a vestryman of the parish for 20 years. A grandson of Theodore Palaiologos is said to have died as a sailor in the British navy in 1694. Unfortunately, the chain of descent of the Cornish Palaiologi is questionable at its first link, for there is no independent evidence that the Despot Thomas ever had a son with the name of John. His line, and so the descendants of the Emperor Michael VIII who founded the dynasty of Palaiologos, became extinct with the death of Andrew in 1502, or at latest with the death of Andrew's alleged son Constantine.[9]

The Despotate of the Morea came to its not very glorious end in May 1460. But the last pocket of Byzantine civilization lay far away from Greece and even from Constantinople, in the little Empire of Trebizond on the shores of the Black Sea. The rulers of Trebizond had been pleased to style themselves emperors since the time of the Fourth Crusade. They inherited the family name of Komnenos. Over the years they had married into the imperial houses of Palaiologos and Cantacuzene. They had too some admixture of Georgian blood. But all in all they were very Byzantine. Their brothers and sisters, however, like the people over whom they ruled, married with less care for the

purity of their stock and contributed their issue to the mixed population of their empire. Trebizond was an empire in a constitutional
rather than a geographical sense. Territorially it consisted of little
more than a long strip of coast protected from central Anatolia by the
barrier of the Pontic mountains. For a while in the thirteenth century
it held sway over a part of the Crimea. But that was the beginning
and the end of its imperialism. Its rulers, however, were sensitive about
their right to the Byzantine title of Emperor or Basileus. Michael VIII
had tried to cut them down to size in 1282, and thereafter they qualified their claims by styling themselves Emperors of all the East, including Georgia. This was a more modest title than that of the heirs of
the Caesars. But they were still emperors, with all that that implied in
the Byzantine world, and they distinguished themselves from their
imperial ancestors by adopting the name of Grand Komnenos.[10]

Early in the fourteenth century the Grand Komnenos Alexios II had
tried to shake off the burden of troublesome neighbours and merciless
exploiters to which his empire seemed to be prone. But its geographical
situation made real independence almost impossible. The Genoese and
the Venetians could not resist the lure of its harbour and its profitable
markets, through which flowed the trade coming from the east by way
of Tabriz and Erzurum, and in which were to be found such local
products as silver, iron and alum. The emperors, however, did better
out of the foreigners than their colleagues in Constantinople, since
the Italian merchants were not allowed to trade tax-free; and the
wealth from their silver mines enabled them to mint their own coinage. But just as their empire was liable to commercial exploitation
from the sea, so it was liable to foreign domination from the land;
and much of its history was dictated by the necessity of preserving a
modus vivendi with the Turks or with the Mongols in the interior.
This was achieved by timely submissions and payments of tribute, or
by well-planned marriages between the princesses of Trebizond and
their covetous neighbours. As the Byzantine historian Chalkokondyles
observed, the ruling family of Trebizond retained Greek manners and
the Greek language, but they did not hesitate to intermarry with the
surrounding barbarians in order to prevent their territory being devastated.[11] Most of the emperors were blessed with a progeny of marriage-
able daughters, and the beauty of the ladies of Trebizond was as
legendary as the wealth of their dowries. Their most persistently
troublesome neighbours were the emirs of the nomad Turkoman tribes
that for so long defied incorporation into the Ottoman Empire. But the
emirs could sometimes be tamed or coaxed into becoming the allies of

Trebizond against the Mongols or the Ottomans by the hand of a princess. The daughters of Alexios II, who died in 1330, married the emirs of Sinope and of Erzindjan; his grand-daughters married the emir of Chalybia and the Turkoman chieftain of the so-called Ak-Koyunlu, or horde of the White Sheep; his great-granddaughters, the children of Alexios III, who died in 1390, performed even greater service to the Empire. One married the emir of Chalybia, another the lord of the Ak-Koyunlu, another Tahartan the emir of Erzindjan, a fourth the emir of Limnia, while a fifth daughter married King Bagrat V of Georgia.[12]

In the middle of the fourteenth century Trebizond suffered something of the same political and social upheavals that were afflicting Byzantium and Thessalonica. Emperors and empresses came and went as a result of dynastic wars and palace revolutions. But the Empire and the dynasty survived. The Grand Komneni were never ousted or replaced, and for all their involvement in the affairs of a non-Greek neighbourhood they and their city retained an unmistakably Byzantine character. Their principal link with Constantinople was through the Church, for the See of Trebizond was content to come under the jurisdiction of the Patriarch of Constantinople. It was an important see, since a very great part of the wealth of the Empire was centred in the monasteries which controlled by far the largest landed estates. The three great monasteries of Vazelon, Peristera and Soumela were handsomely endowed by the emperors. But they also advertised their Orthodox piety to a wider world by founding the Monastery of Dionysiou on Mount Athos in 1374. This was the work of Alexios III Komnenos and his wife Theodora, a relative of the Emperor John VI Cantacuzene.[13]

The imperialist ambition of the Sultan Bajezid in Anatolia naturally affected the Empire of Trebizond. By 1400 many of the Turkoman emirates in its hinterland had been assimilated into the Ottoman dominions. Manuel III Komnenos, who succeeded his father Alexios in 1390, witnessed the defeat of his brother-in-law, the lord of the Ak-Koyunlu, by Bajezid. But it was through another of Manuel's brothers-in-law, Tahartan the emir of Erzindjan, that Bajezid first became involved with Timur the Mongol in 1400. Tahartan sought the protection of Timur to save his emirate from being absorbed into Ottoman territory. The Emperor Manuel III followed his example; and it was because his troops fought on the Mongol side against the Turks that his empire was spared after the battle of Ankara in 1402. Like the Byzantine Empire, Trebizond profited from the aftermath of that battle, from the disruption of the Ottoman Empire in Anatolia and from the dynastic feud among the sons of Bajezid.[14]

It was during this time, in April 1404, that the Spanish ambassador Gonzalez de Clavijo passed through Trebizond on his way to Samarkand. He had the honour of being received by the Emperor Manuel, whom he describes as being tall and handsome. 'The Emperor and his son', writes Clavijo, 'were dressed in imperial robes. They wore on their heads tall hats surmounted by golden cords, on the top of which were cranes' feathers; and the hats were bound with the skins of martens ... This Emperor pays tribute to Timur Beg, and to other Turks, who are his neighbours. He is married to a relation of the Emperor of Constantinople, and his son is married to the daughter of a knight of Constantinople, and has two little daughters.'[15]

The constant rivalry between Venice and Genoa caused Manuel III much trouble, and indeed he was forced into a war with the Genoese which ended with his son Alexios IV having to pay them an indemnity in 1418. But the temporary collapse of Bajezid's empire meant that the Turkoman princes in the neighbourhood of Trebizond came into their own again. The most dangerous of them were the lords of the tribes of the Black Sheep and the White Sheep, the Kara-Koyunlu and the Ak-Koyunlu. Alexios IV followed established tradition by absorbing both of them into his family through marriage. One of his daughters became the wife of Cihanshah, khan of the Black Sheep; another married Ali Beg, khan of the White Sheep. The matrimonial policy of Alexios IV reflects the international interests and ramifications of Trebizond in the early fifteenth century. His own wife was, as Clavijo observed, the daughter of a knight of Constantinople, Theodora Cantacuzene. His eldest daughter Maria became the third wife of the Byzantine Emperor John VIII Palaiologos. His fourth daughter was the first wife of George Branković of Serbia. Of his three sons, the eldest, John, married into the royal house of Georgia; the second, David, married a princess of Gotthia in the Crimea; the third, Alexander, married a lady of the Genoese family of Gattilusio of Lesbos. From Genoa and Serbia to Constantinople and Georgia the fame of the Empire of Trebizond was known. Its metropolitan bishop was given a place of honour at the Council of Florence. Yet the traveller Pero Tafur, who visited it at about that time, reckoned the population of the city of Trebizond to be not more than 4000.[16]

As a last outpost of Byzantine culture and civilization Trebizond of the fifteenth century may be fairly compared with Mistra. Its situation was different in that it looked towards the sea and was surrounded by people whom not even Plethon would have regarded as being of Hellenic stock. But within its walls it was, like Mistra, a microcosm of Byzantine Constantinople. The ruins of the Emperors' palace can still be seen on the hill in the upper part of the city, and the walls that guarded it still run down to the sea shore on either side. The Byzantine churches and monasteries within those walls are no less numerous than those of Mistra, for Trebizond too was a city whose ruling family relied heavily on the hope of divine protection. Its patron was St Eugenios, a local martyr of the third century who, like St Demetrios of Thessalonica, more than once intervened to rescue his city from its enemies. His church, built in the thirteenth century, still stands. So also does the cathedral, dedicated to the Golden-headed Virgin or Panagia Chrysokephalos, in the middle of the upper city. It was here that many of its emperors were crowned and its bishops enthroned. The best preserved and the most striking of its monuments, however, the monastery church of St Sophia, lies some two miles to the west of the city walls on a promontory overlooking the sea. The church, which dates from the thirteenth century, is essentially Byzantine in style, but it is unusually rich in sculptural decoration, and its interior is covered with wall paintings of the same period.[17]

The Emperors of Trebizond were patrons of letters as well as of art. The city is said to have boasted its own academy of sciences, founded in the late thirteenth century by the scholar Gregory Chioniades, whose interest was in astronomy and astrology. Trebizond was well placed to become a centre for the collection and translation of the astronomical and mathematical works of Persian and Arabic scientists. The studies of Chioniades in this field were continued by the monk Manuel of Trebizond, and by his more famous pupil George Chrysokokkes, who wrote treatises on medicine and geography as well.[18] None of their researches produced any startling results, however, and it is doubtful if the astronomers of Trebizond made any new observations. Among a number of lesser scholars and men of letters, the city's most distinguished son was Bessarion, later Bishop of Nicaea and Cardinal of the Roman Church, who was born there about 1395. He left Trebizond while still young, but he seems always to have retained a fondness for his native city, and later in his life he composed an Encomium of it. He also wrote no less than three laments on the death of its Empress Theodora and a consolation piece for her husband Alexios IV in 1426.[19] His contemporary John Eugenikos, the brother of the anti-unionist Mark of Ephesos, seems also to have been born in Trebizond. He wrote a description of the city, as well as a lament for the death of Alexios IV's daughter Maria, the wife of the Emperor John VIII, who died in 1439. Two of the lay delegates to the Council of Florence also came from Trebizond: George Amiroutzes the philosopher was Grand Logothete of the Empire in its last years and a man of encyclopaedic learning, who sold his talents if not his soul to the Sultan Mehmed II; the other George, whose parents came from Trebizond, was in fact born in Crete and, like Bessarion, ended his days in Rome.[20] From the viewpoint of posterity the most useful of all the *literati* of Trebizond was a man of little learning or pretensions called Michael Panaretos who, in the fifteenth century, wrote down a Chronicle of the Emperors of the house of the Grand Komneni. It covers, in simple style and in chronological sequence, the major political and ecclesiastical events in the Empire between the years 1204 and 1426. Panaretos was no great historian, but without his chronicle we should know even less than we do about the Empire of Trebizond.[21]

The last Emperors were John IV and David Komnenos. John IV, who reached the throne by contriving the assassination of his father Alexios in 1429, held it against the assaults of his neighbours, notably the Sultan Murad II, who attacked Trebizond in 1442. It was to him that George Sphrantzes was sent in 1451 to seek the hand of a princess in marriage for the Emperor Constantine Palaiologos. He was still on the throne of Trebizond when Constantinople fell two years later. Many refugees found their way to his territory. John IV sensed that his own little empire would be next on the Sultan's list. In 1456, while Mehmed II was laying siege to faraway Belgrade, the Ottoman governor of Amaseia attacked Trebizond. He failed to breach its walls, but he took a large number of prisoners and demanded a heavy tribute from the Emperor. If and when the full might of the Sultan's army was turned against the city it could not hold out for long on its own.[22]

John IV prepared for the eventuality by planning a coalition of his neighbours against the Ottomans. Foremost among them was the lord of the White Sheep, Uzun Hasan, son of that Ali Beg who had married John's sister. Hasan had more than retrieved his family's fortunes by subduing his rival, the lord of the Black Sheep, and imposing his authority over the other Turkomans from his capital at Diyarbakir in Mesopotamia. To this formidable warrior John IV gave his daughter Theodora in marriage. Her beauty was already legendary not only throughout Persia but also in Venice and the west; and Uzun Hasan promised for so rich a prize to defend the Empire of Trebizond with all his men, his money and his own person. The other neighbours on whom John IV relied for support against the Ottomans were the emirs

430

of Sinope and of Karamania, and the King and princes of Georgia. But they were not so dependable as Uzun Hasan.[23]

John IV died, however, in 1458 without having to put his allies to the test. His brother David at once ascended the throne of Trebizond. David's plans for an anti-Ottoman coalition were even more ambitious. He got in touch with Philip, Duke of Burgundy, and with Pope Pius II, giving them a somewhat exaggerated picture of the size and significance of his coalition and urging them to join in. There was even talk of liberating Jerusalem from the infidel. The Sultan, who got to hear of these wild schemes, might have been content to dismiss them as fantasy, had his temper not been roused. The Emperor David unwisely requested the Sultan to remit the tribute that he had imposed on John IV. Still more unwisely, he entrusted the negotiations to his relative and ally Uzun Hasan; for Hasan took the occasion to put in some exorbitant demands to the Sultan on his own account. It is said that it was these diplomatic blunders which finally determined Mehmed II to be done with the Greek Empire of Trebizond. He had been master of Constantinople for seven years. Mistra had just fallen to him. In the Sultan's eyes the capture of Trebizond was simply the last phase of the tidying-up process in the conquest of the Byzantine Empire.[24]

He spent the winter of 1460 preparing his army and navy for an expedition whose destination was not revealed. In June 1461 he took command of the troops that had been assembled at Brusa, to the number of 60,000 cavalry and 80,000 infantry. His first objective turned out to be Sinope on the Black Sea coast, whose emir had been invited to help in the defence of Trebizond. He surrendered as soon as he saw the size of the Ottoman forces which encircled his city by land and sea. He was deported to Philippopolis on the Danube. The Ottoman fleet then sailed on for Trebizond, while Mehmed took his army inland by forced marches through the mountains of Armenia. Koyunlu-Hisar, the frontier fortress of the White Sheep, fell before them; and Uzun Hasan thought it prudent to make a gesture of peace before worse befell his principality. The network of alliances on which the security of Trebizond was supposed to depend had already collapsed. Trebizond was isolated.

The Turkish fleet was there well in advance of the Sultan and his army. Its arrival took the Emperor David by surprise. The fields around the walls had been burnt and the city was under siege almost before the people knew what was happening. But they held out for over a month, helped by the peasants from the mountains who attacked the besiegers from behind. It was a hopeless cause, and it was seen to be as good as lost when the first regiment of Mehmed's army appeared from over the hills. The Grand Vizir Mahmud, who had command of it, sent an offer of peace with the customary terms of surrender to the Emperor. The alternative was the total destruction of the city and the enslavement or death of its inhabitants. David submitted, though not without some hesitation. He is said to have been pushed into his decision by his Logothete George Amiroutzes, who took charge of the discussions with the Sultan's ambassadors. Much has been made of the supposed treachery of Amiroutzes. Events were later to show that he himself did rather well out of the surrender of Trebizond. But, given the known practice of the Turks in the matter of cities that resisted capture, it may well appear that Amiroutzes gave good counsel to his Emperor. The surrender of Trebizond was effected about 15 August 1461.[25]

The last Emperor of Trebizond was not called upon to meet his death doing heroic deeds at the walls of his city like the last Emperor of Constantinople. He was put aboard one of the Turkish ships together with his family and a few of his officials, including Amiroutzes, and taken to Constantinople. After a while he was moved to Adrianople, where Demetrios Palaiologos from Mistra was also living in exile. The Sultan allowed him a quite substantial income from estates in the Strymon valley. But two years later he was accused of complicity in a plot and arrested. The story goes that his niece, the wife of Uzun Hasan, asked him to send one of his sons to be brought up at her court. She entrusted the message to George Amiroutzes, who revealed it to the Sultan. Mehmed did not take kindly to things being arranged behind his back. He took his revenge by having David and his family incarcerated in Adrianople. But the only safeguard against the perpetuation of the line of the Grand Komneni was to be rid of them all. On 1 November 1463 the Sultan ordered the Emperor David, his older children, and his nephew to be executed in Constantinople. Their remains were thrown outside the walls.[26]

A sixteenth-century Greek historian living in Italy, who claimed some family connexion with the Cantacuzenes and so with the Empress Helena of Trebizond, tells what he had heard of the melancholy end of the house of Komnenos. The Sultan had allowed the Empress and two of her children to survive the massacre on payment within three days of a sum of 15,000 ducats. Her friends in Constantinople contrived to raise the money within 24 hours. But Helena declined to accept the Sultan's mercy. She put on sackcloth and shut herself up in a hut outside the city walls near the unburied corpses of her husband and family. The Sultan had decreed that their bodies should become the prey of the dogs and crows. But Helena secretly dug a grave in which she buried them by night. A few days later she died of grief. It seems tragically fitting that the last woman to bear the Byzantine title of Empress should have ended her days like Antigone. Of the two surviving children of David Komnenos, George, who was three years old, was sent to the court of Uzun Hasan and there brought up in the Muslim faith. His sister Anna was sent to the harem of Zaganos Pasha, and she too became a Muslim.[27]

Ten years after the conquest of Constantinople the last Byzantine family that might produce a claimant to any part of the Roman Empire was thus liquidated. Mehmed the Conqueror need fear no Christian pretender, at least within his own dominions. He was now the undisputed Sultan-Basileus, the master of Rum and of Rumelia, of Asia and of Europe. In 1480 Lorenzo de Medici had a medal engraved as a present for the Sultan. The Sultan's portrait is there inscribed with the words: Mehmed, Emperor of Asia and Trebizond and Great Greece. On the reverse of the medal are depicted three princesses in chains. They are described as Greece, Trebizond and Asia.[28]

So great and long-lived an institution as the Byzantine Empire could not be laid to rest by the blast of a cannon or the stroke of a pen. The outward forms were gone. There were no more despots, *sebastokrators* and caesars; the Sultan's firman replaced the imperial chrysobull; the cathedral of St Sophia was no longer a Christian shrine. But people who have lived with the same inherited conceptions and prejudices for over a thousand years do not at once abandon them because their material circumstances have changed. The shock of conquest had been visited progressively between the years 1430 and 1460 on the cities of Thessalonica, of Constantinople, of Mistra, and finally of Trebizond. But other urban centres of Byzantine civilization, such as Nicaea, had felt it a hundred years earlier; and their inhabitants had long since rallied and made their own accommodations with the changed circumstances. The Ottoman Empire was not built in a day. The Byzantines had had ample time to reflect on how they would contrive to live under an alien dispensation.

And yet the loss of Nicaea or of Thessalonica set no precedents for the loss of Constantinople. Losing Constantinople was like losing a world. When it was gone, the many people of Greece, Macedonia, Thrace and Asia Minor, who had for long been living under Turkish rule, were finally deprived of their last faint hope that the old order might be restored. For Constantinople was no ordinary city. It was the centre through which God and his Mother radiated their protection of all true Christians. Without that protection and that source of divine energy there could be no chance of recovery.

The news that the Queen of Cities had fallen must have affected the inhabitants of the former Byzantine provinces rather in the way that the news of the sack of Rome in 410 affected the people of North Africa. But the Byzantines had no St Augustine to transmute their material loss into a spiritual gain. Laments on the Fall of Constantinople, mostly in popular style, were soon being composed and recited; and legends about its eventual recovery were also popularized. But they were only a substitute for hope. For those who remained as Christians within the Ottoman Empire the best that could be done was to go on living in a manner as inoffensive as possible to their Turkish masters. Those who escaped or made their way as refugees to the Venetian colonies or to Italy sometimes deluded themselves that their activities as disseminators of Greek learning would prompt a massive rescue operation from the grateful West. But very few of them had the intellectual or human qualities of such as Demetrios Kydones or Cardinal Bessarion. They were competent enough as proofreaders and editors of Greek manuscripts for the hungry printing-presses of Venice and elsewhere. But they were not compelling advertisements for the lost glories of a great civilization. And in any case the western world, full of its own preoccupations, quickly recovered from whatever shock it may have felt at the fall of Constantinople.

Our story began with the conquest of Constantinople by the crusaders in 1204. It ends some two hundred and fifty years later with the conquest of Constantinople and its outposts by the Turks. The first of these conquests might be called a non-event, for nothing was built upon it by its perpetrators and it produced no constructive consequences. The Turkish conquest on the other hand marked the culmination of a long process, the end of the transition from a Christian to a Muslim Empire which covered very much the same portion of the globe. Its positive and constructive consequence was the solid establishment of the Ottoman Empire. Under both dispensations it is possible to say that the majority of the Emperor's or the Sultan's subjects were oppressed and lived hazardous and often unhappy lives. But after 1453 there was a vital difference; for most of them, at least in the European provinces, looked back with nostalgia to the days when their oppressive landlords and taxgatherers had been Christians and not Muslims, and when their Emperor in distant Constantinople had been the elect of God and not of Allah. It was by capitalizing on this nostalgia that the Orthodox Church, with the initial support of the Sultans, was able to keep alive the Byzantine spirit through the long centuries of infidel domination. In much the same way that the Roman Church was the spiritual successor of the Roman Empire in the West during the dark ages, the Orthodox Church preserved and nourished the immortal soul of Byzantium after its body had been destroyed by the Ottomans. The mystery and glory of the liturgy recalled to the faithful the splendours that their ancestors had once known. The household icons of the Virgin, or of St Constantine and his mother, Helena, put men in mind of the Virgin Hodegetria whom the last Constantine had venerated on the last day of Christian Constantinople. The great monasteries of Mount Athos or of the Meteora, secure on their pillars of rock in Thessaly, kept the prayer wheels turning against the day when God might pardon the sins of his people and lead them back to the promised land of their New Jerusalem.

The institutions of the Empire could never be revived. Perhaps they had died of old age and decay, like the ancient tree trunk whose younger branches still put forth leaves but whose heart is hollow, so that it falls when the great gale comes. None of the Greek historians who were alive during that storm wondered how the heart of the tree had rotted away. What puzzled and interested them was why God had allowed the winds to blow. Modern historians are apt to say that the Byzantine Empire would have died in any case because of the shift in the economic and commercial balance of the world that followed the discovery of new lands and new trade routes in the sixteenth century. It may be true that Constantinople would have lost its place as a centre of world trade. But it had already sacrificed that role to the Italian republics long before 1453; and the Ottomans successfully centred their own version of a universal Empire on the same spot without setting much store by the world's markets.

One may wonder what might have happened if Byzantium had belied the predictions of some of its own prophets and survived beyond the end of the sixth millennium, which, by the Byzantine method of reckoning, was to occur in the year 1492. For the Byzantine Empire was the last Christian civilization which had its beginning, its middle and its end in the pre-Columbian era. It died before the dawning of the new age of discovery and technology, before the widening of men's horizons. Its historians, philosophers and theologians were the last of their kind who had to transmit their thoughts and ideas in

435

manuscript alone. If they had been spared to set up a Greek printing-press at Constantinople they would have found a ready and profitable market for editions of the treasures of classical literature that they had preserved through the centuries. But in other respects the Byzantines would probably not much have enjoyed or participated in the new developments in the western world. By the fifteenth century it had been amply proved that they could neither stomach their dislike of the westerners nor survive without their help. Most of them would prefer to go it alone than to sacrifice their faith as well as their fortune. They would rather submit to infidels whose ways, though unpleasant, were familiar, than prolong their agonies by soliciting the charity of foreign Christians who had never understood what it meant to be a Roman.

There was a streak of fatalism in the Byzantine mentality. They had sensed, with growing conviction, that their world would not after all endure until the Second Coming; that their Empire was something less than a pale reflexion of the Kingdom of Heaven; and that the only permanence, the only security, and the only certain happiness were to be found in the true Kingdom above and beyond this vale of tears. When the end came in 1453 they were ready for it. It is surprising that it had not come sooner. It is perhaps as well that it came when it did.

NOTES

1 Runciman, *Fall of Constantinople*, 162-3; Babinger, *Mahomet le Conquérant*, 126-7.

2 For the history of the Italian colonies in Greece and the Greek islands after 1453, see W. Miller, *The Latins in the Levant. A History of Frankish Greece (1204-1566)* (London, 1908).

3 Zakythinos, *Despotat grec de Morée*, I, 256-62; Babinger, *Mahomet*, 104, 151-3; Vacalopoulos, *Origins*, 207-8. On Manuel Cantacuzene, see Nicol, *Byzantine Family of Kantakouzenos*, 201-3.

4 Zakythinos, *Despotat*, I, 256-62; Babinger, *Mahomet*, 191-6; Vacalopoulos, *Origins*, 208-11.

5 Ovid, *Metamorphoses*, XV, 248: 'vile solum Sparte est, altae cecidere Mycenae ...'

6 Zakythinos, *Despotat*, I, 265-74, 287-90; Vacalopoulos, *Origins*, 211-16; Babinger, *Mahomet*, 210-19.

7 Zakythinos, *Despotat*, I, 285-7.

8 On the last of the Palaiologos family, see Papadopoulos, *Versuch*

436

einer Genealogie der Palaiologen, nos. 98-103; Zakythinos, *Despotat*, I, 287-97; Runciman, *Fall*, 181-5.

9 Zakythinos, *Despotat*, I, 295-7. The monumental inscriptions from Landulph and from Barbados are reproduced in T. Spencer, *Fair Greece Sad Relic* (London, 1954), 5. See also P. Leigh Fermor, *The Traveller's Tree* (London, 1950), 145-9; *idem*, *Mani. Travels in the southern Peloponnese* (London, 1958), 26-7.

10 On the Empire of Trebizond, see W. Miller, *Trebizond. The Last Greek Empire* (London, 1926); Chrysanthos, Metropolitan of Trebizond, *The Church of Trebizond* (in Greek), in *Archeion Pontou*, IV-V (Athens, 1936); E. Janssens, *Trébizonde en Colchide* (Brussels, 1969), 64-163. A. A. M. Bryer, *The Greeks of the Pontos, ca. 1100-1869*, had not been published at the time this book went to press.

11 Chalkokondyles, II, 219 (ed. Darkó).

12 Miller, *Trebizond*, 60-1. On the marriage and family of Alexios III Komnenos, see Nicol, *Byzantine Family of Kantakouzenos*, 143-6

13 F. Dölger, *Mönchsland Athos* (Munich, 1943), 96-7; Chrysanthos, *Church of Trebizond*, 507-13.

14 Miller, *Trebizond*, 71f.; Janssens, *Trébizonde*, 124f.

15 Gonzalez de Clavijo, *Embassy*, translated by C. R. Markham (London, 1859), 62.

16 On the family of Alexios IV Komnenos, see Nicol, *op. cit.*, 168-70. Pero Tafur, *Travels and Adventures*, translated by M. Letts (New York and London, 1926), 131.

17 Janssens, *Trébizonde*, 220f.; D. Talbot Rice, *The Church of Hagia Sophia at Trebizond* (Edinburgh, 1968); *idem*, *Byzantine Painting. The Last Phase* (London, 1968), 53f.

18 See Runciman, *The Last Byzantine Renaissance*, 52-3, 89 and references; Janssens, *Trébizonde*, 188.

19 Bessarion, *Encomium of Trebizond*, ed. by S. Lambros, in *Neos Hellenomnenon*, XIII (1916), 145-204. For the other works, see Nicol, *Byzantine Family of Kantakouzenos*, 169.

20 See Miller, *Trebizond*, 111-12, 120-1; Janssens, *Trébizonde*, 195f.

21 Michael Panaretos, *Chronicle of Trebizond*, ed. by S. Lambros, in *Neos Hellenomnenon*, IV (1907), 266-94; by O. Lampsides (with commentary in Greek), in *Archeion Pontou*, XXI (1958), 5-128 (also printed separately: Athens, 1958).

22 Miller, *Trebizond*, 83-8; Janssens, *Trébizonde*, 132-41.

23 Miller, *Trebizond*, 88-96; Janssens, *Trébizonde*, 141-5, and (for Theodora) 211-17.

24 Miller, *Trebizond*, 97-100; Janssens, *Trébizonde*, 145-53.

25 Miller, *Trebizond*, 100-5; Janssens, *Trébizonde*, 153-60.

26 Miller, *Trebizond*, 105-12; Janssens, *Trébizonde*, 160-2.

27 On the fate of Helena and her children, see Nicol, *op. cit.*, 189-90; cf. Janssens, *Trébizonde*, 162-3.

28 Janssens, *Trébizonde*, 163.

Glossary

(The titles of Byzantine dignitaries in the middle of the fourteenth century, most of them purely honorary, are listed in order of precedence in the handbook of court procedure entitled Pseudo-Kodinos, *De Officiis*, ed. J. Verpeaux (Paris, 1966).)

Basileus
Official title of the Byzantine Emperor, sometimes linked with the title of *autokrator*.

Caesar
Honorary title ranking its holder fourth in precedence after the emperor; reserved for members of the imperial family and for foreigners who rendered special service to the Empire.

Chartophylax
Archivist, general secretary to the Patriarch.

Chrysobull
Document of state sealed with the golden bull of the Emperor.

Despot
Title ranking its holder second in precedence after the Emperor; generally reserved for brothers or sons of the Emperor; occasionally conferred on foreigners related to the imperial family by marriage.

Grand Constable (*megas konostavlos*)
Military rank, sometimes denoting the officer in command of the Latin mercenaries.

Grand Domestic (*megas domestikos*)
Commander-in-chief of the army, elevated by Andronikos III to fifth in order of precedence after the Caesar.

Grand Duke (*megas doux*)
Commander of the imperial navy; sometimes a purely honorary title and conferred on foreigners.

Grand Logothete (megas logothetes)
First minister of the Empire, in charge of civil administration and foreign affairs.

Grand Primmikerios (megas primmikerios)
Master of ceremonies in the palace.

Grand Stratopedarches
Staff officer, nominally in charge of provisions and equipment for the army.

hyperpyron
The name given in this period to the Byzantine gold coin (*nomisma*).

Mesazon
Imperial chancellor; literally, the intermediary between the Emperor and his subjects; a descriptive title rather than a rank.

Parakoimomenos
Imperial chamberlain, though often with many other administrative duties.

Porphyrogenitus (porphyrogennetos)
Born in the purple chamber of the imperial palace; a title sometimes held by princes of the blood born after their father's accession to the throne.

Protobestiarios
One of the highest-ranking courtiers, nominally in charge of the imperial wardrobe.

Protostrator
Military rank above that of Grand Stratopedarches but below that of Grand Domestic.

Sebastokrator
The highest honorary title after those of Basileus and Despot; reserved for members of the imperial family.

typikon
Foundation charter of a monastery.

Bibliography

I. SOURCES

A. COLLECTIONS OF SOURCES

Acts of Athos
  Chilandari: L. Petit and B. Korablev, *Actes de Chilandar*, I: *Actes grecs*, VV, XVII (1911); II: *Actes slaves*, VV, XIX (1912). V. Mošin and A. Sovre, *Supplementa ad acta graeca Chilandarii* (Ljubljana, 1948).
  Dionysiou: N. Oikonomides, *Actes de Dionysiou* (Archives de l'Athos, IV: Paris, 1968).
  Esphigmenou: L. Petit and W. Regel, *Actes d'Esphigménou*, VV, XII (1906).
  Kutlumus: P. Lemerle, *Actes de Kutlumus* (*Archives de l'Athos*, II: Paris, 1945).
  Lavra: G. Rouillard and P. Collomp, *Actes de Lavra* (Archives de l'Athos, I: Paris, 1937; new edition in progress).
  Panteleimon: *Akty russkogo na svjatom Afone monastyrja ... Pantelejmona* (Kiev, 1873).
  Pantokrator: L. Petit, *Actes de Pantocrator*, VV, X (1903).
  Philotheou: W. Regel, E. Kurtz and B. Korablev, *Actes de Philothée*, VV, XX (1913).
  Xeropotamou: J. Bompaire, *Actes de Xéropotamou* (Archives de l'Athos, III: Paris, 1964).
  Zographou: W. Regel, E. Kurtz and B. Korablev, *Actes de Zographou*, VV, XIII (1907).
BARKER, E. *Social and Political Thought in Byzantium from Justinian to the last Palaeologus* (Oxford, 1957).
BELGRANO, L. 'Prima serie di documenti riguardanti la colonia di Pera', *Atti della società ligure di storia patria*, XIII (1877), 97-336.
BERTOLOTTO, G. 'Nuova serie di documenti sulle relazioni di Genova coll'impero bizantino', *Atti della società ligure di storia patria*, XXVIII (1898), 339-573.

441

BOISSONADE, J. F. *Anecdota Graeca*, 5 vols (Paris, 1829-33).

—— *Anecdota Nova* (Paris, 1844).

Corpus Scriptorum Historiae Byzantinae (Bonn, 1828-97) (=*CSHB*).

DÖLGER, F. *Facsimiles byzantinischer Kaiserurkunden* (Munich, 1931).

—— *Regesten der Kaiserurkunden des oströmischen Reiches*, part III : 1204-82; part IV : 1282-1341; part V : 1341-1453 (Munich and Berlin, 1931-65).

—— *Aus den Schatzkammern des Heiligen Berges*, 2 vols (Munich, 1948).

GOODACRE, H. *A Handbook of the Coinage of the Byzantine Empire*, 2nd edition (London, 1957).

GUILLOU, A. *Les Archives de Saint-Jean-Prodrome sur le Mont Ménécée* (Bibliothèque Byzantine, ed. P. Lemerle, Documents, 3 : Paris, 1955).

HOPF, C. *Chroniques gréco-romanes inédites ou peu connues* (Berlin, 1873).

JORGA, N. *Notes et extraits pour servir à l'histoire des croisades au XVe siècle*, 6 vols (Paris, 1899-1916).

KHITROWO, B. DE. *Itinéraires russes en Orient* (Société de l'Orient latin : Geneva, 1889).

KREKIĆ, B. *Dubrovnik (Raguse) et le Levant au moyen âge* (Paris, 1961).

LAMBROS, SP. *Palaiologeia kai Peloponnesiaka*, 4 vols (Athens, 1912-30).

LAURENT, V. *Les Régestes des Actes du Patriarcat de Constantinople*, I : *Les Actes des Patriarches*, fasc. IV : *Les Regestes de 1208 à 1309* (Paris, 1971).

Liber iurium reipublicae Genuensis, ed. H. Ricottius, 2 vols (*Monumenta Historiae Patriae*, VIII, IX : Turin, 1854-7).

MANSI, J. D. *Sacrorum conciliorum nova et amplissima collectio*, 31 vols (Florence and Venice, 1759-98).

MIGNE, J. P. *Patrologiae cursus completus. Series graeco-latina*, 161 vols (Paris, 1857-66) (=*PG*).

MIKLOSICH, F. and MÜLLER, J. *Acta et Diplomata graeca medii aevi sacra et profana*, 6 vols (Vienna, 1860-90) (=*MM*).

MURATORI, L. A. *Rerum Italicarum Scriptores*, 25 vols (Milan, 1723-51; new edition in progress).

PAPADOPOULOS-KERAMEUS, A. *Analekta Hierosolymitikes Stachyologias*, 5 vols (St Petersburg, 1891-8).

—— *Hierosolymitike Bibliotheke*, 4 vols (St Petersburg, 1891-9).

RHALLES, G. A. and POTLES, M. *Syntagma ton theion kai hieron kanonon*, 6 vols (Athens, 1852-9).

Rubio y Lluch, A. *Diplomatari de l'Orient Català (1301-1409)* (Barcelona, 1947).

Sathas, K. N. *Mesaionike Bibliotheke. Bibliotheca graeca medii aevi*, 7 vols (Venice and Paris, 1872-94).

—— *Mnemeia Hellenikes Historias. Documents inédits relatifs à l'histoire de la Grèce au moyen âge*, 9 vols (Paris, 1880-90).

Schlumberger, G. *Sigillographie de l'empire byzantin* (Paris, 1884).

Soloviev, A. and Mosin, V. *Grčke povelje srpskih vladara* (Greek documents of the Serbian rulers) (Belgrade, 1936).

Tafel, G. L. F. and Thomas, G. M. *Urkunden zur älteren Handels- und Staatsgeschichte der Republik Venedig (Fontes rerum Austriacarum*, II, xii-xiv), parts i-iii (Vienna, 1856-7).

Thallóczy, L. de, Jireček, C. J. and Sufflay, E. de. *Acta et Diplomata res Albaniae mediae aetatis illustrantia*, 2 vols (Vienna, 1913-18).

Theiner, A. and Miklosich, F. *Monumenta spectantia ad unionem ecclesiarum Graecae et Romanae* (Vienna, 1872).

Thiriet, F. *Régestes des délibérations du Sénat de Venise concernant la Romanie*, 3 vols (Paris, 1958-61); II : 1364-1463 (Paris, 1971).

—— *Délibérations des Assemblées Vénitiennes concernant la Romanie*, I : 1160-1363 (Paris, 1966).

Thomas, G. M. and Predelli, R. *Diplomatarium Veneto-Levantinum (1300-1454)*, 2 vols (Venice, 1880-99).

Vakalopoulos, A. E. *Sources for the History of Neo-Hellenism (1204-1669)* [in Greek] (Thessalonike, 1965).

Wroth, W. *Catalogue of the Imperial Byzantine Coins in the British Museum*, 2 vols (London, 1908).

Zepos, J. and P. *Jus graeco-romanum*, 8 vols (Athens, 1931).

B. INDIVIDUAL SOURCES

1. Greek

Akindynos, Gregory. *Letters*, ed. R.-J. Loenertz, in *EEBS*, XXVII (1957), 89-109, and *OCP*, XXIII (1957), 114-44.

Akropolites, George. *Historia*, ed. A. Heisenberg (Leipzig, 1903).

Anagnostes, John. *De Thessalonicensi excidio narratio*, ed. I Bekker (in (*S*)Phrantzes (*CSHB*, 1838), 481-528).

Anonymous. P. Gautier, 'Un récit inédit du siège de Constantinople par les Turcs (1394-1402)', *REB*, XXIII (1965), 100-17.

ATHANASIOS I, Patriarch. *Letters*. See R. Guilland, 'La correspondance inédite d'Athanase patriarche de Constantinople (1289-1293; 1304-1310)', *Mélanges Charles Diehl*, I (1930), 121-40 (reprinted in Guilland, *Etudes Byzantines* (Paris, 1959), 53-79); N. Banescu, 'Le patriarche Athanase Ier et Andronic II Paléologue', *Académie Roumaine. Bulletin de la section historique*, XXIII (1942), 28-56. (An edition of these letters is now in preparation.)

BARLAAM of Calabria. *Barlaam Calabro, Epistole greche*, ed. G. Schirò (Palermo, 1954) Oratio pro Unione habita, in PG, CLI, 1331-42.

CANANUS (see KANANOS).

CANTACUZENUS (see KANTAKOUZENOS).

CHALKOKONDYLES, LAONIKOS. *Laonici Chalcocandylae Historiarum Demonstrationes*, ed. E. Darkó, 2 vols (Budapest, 1922-7).

CHORTASMENOS, JOHN. H. Hunger, *Johannes Chortasmenos (ca. 1370-ca. 1436/37). Briefe, Gedichte und kleine Schriften* (Vienna, 1969).

CHOUMNOS, NIKEPHOROS. *Letters* and other works, in Boissonade, *Anecdota Graeca*, I-III, V; see also J. Verpeaux, *Nicéphore Choumnos* (Paris, 1959).

Chronicle of Ioannina (Epirotica). Ed. I. Bekker (*CSHB*, 1849); new edition by S. Cirac Estopañan, *Bizancio y España*, 2 vols (Barcelona, 1943).

Chronicle of the Morea. Ed. J. Schmitt (London, 1904); ed. P. P. Kalonaros (Athens, 1940); English translation by H. E. Lurier, *Crusaders as Conquerors* (New York, 1964).

Chronicle of the Turkish Sultans. Ed. G. T. Zoras [in Greek] (Athens, 1958).

CHRYSOLORAS, DEMETRIOS. P. Gautier, 'Actions de Grâces de Démétrius Chrysoloras à la Théotokos pour l'anniversaire de la bataille d'Ankara (28 Juillet 1403)', *REB*, XIX (1961) (=*Mélanges Raymond Janin*), 340-57.

DELEHAYE, H. *Deux typica byzantins de l'époque des Paléologues* (Brussels, 1921).

DOUKAS. *Istoria turco-bizantina 1341-1462*, ed. V. Grecu (Bucharest, 1958).

GENNADIOS, GEORGE SCHOLARIOS. *Oeuvres complètes de Gennade Scholarios*, ed. L. Petit, X. A. Sideridès, M. Jugie, 8 vols (Paris, 1928-36).

GREGORAS, NIKEPHOROS. *Byzantina Historia*, ed. L. Schopen, 3 vols (*CSHB*, 1829, 1830, 1855).

—— *Letters*, ed. R. Guilland, *Correspondance de Nicéphore Grégoras* (Paris, 1927); ed. M. Bezdeki, 'Nicephori Gregorae epistulae XC', *Ephemeris Dacoromana*, II (1924), 239-377.

HARMENOPOULOS, CONSTANTINE. *Hexabiblos*, translated by E. Freshfield, *A Manual of Byzantine Law compiled in the Fourteenth Century* (Cambridge, 1930).

HYRTAKENOS, THEODORE. *Letters*, ed. F. J. G. La Porte-du Theil, in *Notices et Extraits des Manuscrits de la Bibliothèque Nationale*, V (1798), 709-44; VI (1800), 1-48.

—— *Speeches*, ed. Boissonade, *Anecdota Graeca*, I, II, III.

ISIDORE of Thessalonica. *Homilies on the Feast of St Demetrios*, ed. B. Laourdas, *Hellenika*, section V (Thessalonike, 1954) [in Greek].

KABASILAS (CABASILAS), NICHOLAS. *Letters*, ed. P. Enepekides, *BZ*, XLVI (1953), 18-46.

—— *Panegyrics*, ed. M. Jugie, *Izvestija russkago arkheologičeskago Instituta v Konstantinopole*, XV (1911), 112-21.

—— *Treatises: Contra feneratores*, in *PG*, CL, 727-50; *On usury*, ed. R. Guilland, 'Le traité inédit "Sur l'Usure" de Nicolas Cabasilas', in *Eis Mnemen Spyridonos Lamprou* (Athens, 1935), 269-77; 'Anti-Zealot' *Discourse*, ed. I. Ševčenko, *DOP*, XI (1957), 81-171 (cf. *DOP*, XIV (1960), 179-201; *DOP*, XVI (1962), 402-6. P. Charanis, 'Observations on the "Anti-Zealot" Discourse of Cabasilas', *Revue des études sud-est européennes*, IX (1971), 369-76).

KALEKAS, MANUEL. *Letters*, ed. R.-J. Loenertz, *Correspondance de Manuel Calécas* (Studi e Testi, 152: Vatican City, 1950).

KANANOS (CANANUS), JOHN. *De Constantinopoli oppugnata* (1422), ed. I. Bekker, in (S)Phrantzes (*CSHB*, 1838), 457-79.

KANTAKOUZENOS (CANTACUZENUS), JOHN. *Historiae*, ed. L. Schopen, 3 vols (*CSHB*, 1828-32).

KODINOS (see PSEUDO-KODINOS).

KRITOBOULOS of Imbros. *De rebus per annos 1451-1467 a Mechemete II gestis*, ed. V. Grecu, *Critobul din Imbros. Din Domnia lui Mahomed al II-lea anii 1451-1467* (Bucharest, 1963); translated by C. T. Riggs, *Kritovoulos, History of Mehmed the Conqueror* (Princeton, N.J., 1954).

KYDONES, DEMETRIOS. *Letters*, ed. R.-J. Loenertz, *Démétrius Cydonès, Correspondance*, 2 vols (Studi e Testi, 186, 208: Vatican City, 1956, 1960); ed. G. Cammelli (Paris, 1930).

—— *Speeches: Occisorum Thessalonicae Monodia*, in *PG*, CIX, 639-52; *De admittendo Latinorum subsidio*, in *PG*, CLIV, 961-1008; *De non reddenda Callipoli*, in *PG*, CLIV, 1009-36; to John Cantacuzene and John Palaiologos, ed. G. Cammeli, *BNJ*, III (1922), 67-76; IV (1923), 77-83, 282-95; ed. Loenertz, *Correspondance*, I, 1-10; 10-23.

MAKREMBOLITES, ALEXIOS. *Historical Discourse on the Genoese*, ed.
A. Papadopoulos-Kerameus, *Analekta Hierosolymitikes Stachyolo-
gias*, I (1891), 144-59.
—— *Dialogue between the Rich and the Poor*, ed. I. Ševčenko, *Zbornik
Radova*, VI (1960), 187-228.
—— *On the collapse of St Sophia*, ed. S. I. Kourousis, *EEBS*, XXXVII
1969-70), 235-40.
MANUEL II PALAIOLOGOS. *Letters*, ed. E. Legrand, *Lettres de l'empereur
Manuel Paléologue* (Paris, 1893); a new edition is in preparation
by G. T. Dennis. See also G. T. Dennis, 'Four unknown letters
of Manuel II Palaeologus', *B*, XXXVI (1966), 35-40; 'Two unknown
documents of Manuel II Palaeologus', *Travaux et Mémoires, III*
(1968), 397-404.
—— *Speeches etc.: Discourse to the people of Thessalonica*, ed. B.
Laourdas, *Makedonika*, III (1955), 290-307; *Funeral Oration for his
brother Theodore*, in *PG*, CLVI, 181-307; *Praecepta educationis
regiae*, and *Orationes ethico-politicae*, in *PG*, CLVI, 313-84, 385-557.
—— *Dialogues*, ed. E. Trapp, *Manuel II Palaiologos, Dialoge mit
einem 'Perser'* (Vienna, 1966). (For Manuel's other literary works,
see Barker, *Manuel II*, 554-5).
MATTHEW I, Patriarch. H. Hunger, 'Das Testament des Patriarchen
Matthaios I (1397-1410)', *BZ*, LI (1958), 288-309.
MAZARIS. *Sojourn in Hades*, ed. Boissonade, *Anecdota Graeca*, III
(1831), 112-86; ed. A. Ellissen, *Analekten der mittel-und neugriechis-
chen Litteratur*, IV (Leipzig, 1869), 187-250 (with German transla-
tion, 251-314).
METOCHITES, THEODORE. *Essays*, ed. C. G. Müller and T. Kiessling,
Theodori Metochitae Miscellanea philosophica et historica (Leip-
zig, 1821).
—— *Poems: Dichtungen des Grosslogotheten Theodoros Metochites*,
ed. M. Treu (Potsdam Gymnasium Programm, 1890); R. Guilland,
'Les poésies inédites de Théodore Métochite', in Guilland, *Etudes
Byzantines* (Paris, 1959), 178-205.
MEYENDORFF, J. 'Projets de concile oecuménique en 1367: Un dialogue
inédit entre Jean Cantacuzène et le légat Paul', *DOP*, XIV (1960),
147-77.
—— 'Le Tome synodal de 1347', *Zbornik Radova*, VIII (1963)
(=*Mélanges Georges Ostrogorsky*, I), 209-27.
MICHAEL VIII PALAIOLOGOS. *Autobiography*, ed. H. Grégoire, 'Impera-
toris Michaelis Palaeologi De Vita Sua', *B*, XXIX-XXX (1959-60), 447-
75.

Pachymeres, George. *De Michaele et Andronico Palaeologis*, ed. I. Bekker, 2 vols (*CSHB*, 1835).

Panaretos, Michael. *Chronicle of the Empire of Trebizond*, ed. S. Lambros, *Neos Hellenomnenon*, IV (1907), 266-94; ed. O. Lampsides, *Archeion Pontou*, XXI (1958), 5-128 (printed separately as *Pontikai Ereunai*, 2: Athens, 1958).

Philes, Manuel. *Poems*, ed. E. Miller, *Manuelis Philae Carmina*, 2 vols (Paris, 1855, 1857); ed. Ae. Martini, *Manuelis Philae Carmina Inedita* (Naples, 1900).

Philotheos, Patriarch. *Historical Discourse on the siege and capture of Herakleia by the Latins (1351)*, ed. C. Triantafillis and A. Grapputo, *Anecdota Graeca e Codicibus Manu Scriptis Bibliothecae S. Marci*, I (Venice, 1874), 1-33.

Planoudes, Maximos. *Letters*, ed. M. Treu, *Maximi monachi Planudis epistulae* (Breslau, 1890).

Plethon, George Gemistos. *Addresses* to Manuel II and to Theodore Palaiologos, ed. A. Ellissen, *Analekten der mittel- und neugriechischen Litteratur*, IV, 2 (Leipzig, 1860), 41-84 (with German translations, 85-130); ed. S. Lambros, *Palaiologeia kai Peloponnesiaka*, IV (Athens, 1930), 113-35, 246-65. (Selections translated by E. Barker, *Social and Political Thought in Byzantium* (Oxford, 1957), 198-219.)

Pseudo-Kodinos. *De Officiis*, ed. J. Verpeaux, *Pseudo-Kodinos, Traité des Offices* (Paris, 1966).

Raoul, Manuel. *Letters*, ed. R.-J. Loenertz, 'Emmanuelis Raoul Epistulae XII', *EEBS*, XXVI (1956), 130-63.

Short Chronicles. Brachea Chronika, ed. Sp. Lambros and K. I. Amantos, *Mnemeia Hellenikes Historias*, I, 1 (Athens, 1932-3).

—— P. Charanis, 'An important Short Chronicle of the 14th Century', *B*, XIII (1938), 335-62.

—— *Chronicon breve thessalonicense*, ed. R.-J. Loenertz, *Démétrius Cydonès, Correspondance*, I, 174-5.

—— 'Chronicon breve de Graecorum imperatoribus, ab anno 1341 ad annum 1453 e codice Vaticano graeco 162', ed. R.-J. Loenertz, *EEBS*, XXVIII (1958), 204-315.

—— 'La chronique brève Moréote de 1423. Texte, traduction et commentaire', ed. R.-J. Loenertz, *Mélanges E. Tisserant*, II (Studi e Testi, 232: Vatican City, 1964), 399-439.

—— *Short Chronicle of 1352*, ed. R.-J. Loenertz, 'La chronique brève de 1352. Texte, traduction et commentaire', part I, *OCP*, XXIX (1963), 331-56; part II, *OCP*, XXX (1964), 39-64; ed. P. Schreiner, part III, *OCP*, XXXI (1965), 336-73; part IV, *OCP*, XXXIV (1968), 38-61.

(See also R.-J. Loenertz, 'Etudes sur les chroniques brèves byzantines', *OCP*, XXIV (1958), 155-64; P. Schreiner, *Studien zu den BPAXEA XPONIKA* (Munich, 1967); Z. G. Samodurov, 'Malye Vizantijskie Khroniki i ikh istočniki', *VV*, XXVII (1966), 153-61).

SPHRANTZES, GEORGE. *Chronicon Minus*, edited together with the *Chronicon Maius* of Pseudo-Phrantzes by V. Grecu, *Georgios Sphrantzes, Memorii 1401-1477* (Bucharest, 1966).

SYROPOULOS, SYLVESTER. *Vera Historia Unionis non Verae inter Graecos et Latinos sive Concilii Florentini* &c., ed. by R. Creyghton (The Hague, 1660); new edition by V. Laurent, *Les 'Mémoirs' du Grand Ecclésiarque de l'Eglise de Constantinople Sylvestre Syropoulos sur le Concile de Florence (1438-1439)* (Paris, 1971).

THOMAS, MAGISTER. *Speeches*, ed. F. W. Lenz, *Fünf Reden Thomas Magisters* (Leiden, 1963).

2. Western, Slavonic and Oriental

BADOER, GIACOMO. *Il libro dei conti di Giacomo Badoer (Costantinopoli 1436-1440)*, ed. U. Dorini and T. Bertelè (Rome, 1956).

BARBARO, NICCOLÒ. *Giornale dell'Assedio di Constantinopoli 1453*, ed. E. Cornet (Vienna, 1856); translated by J. R. Jones, *Diary of the Siege of Constantinople* (New York, 1969).

BOUCICAUT, Marshal. *Le livre des faicts du Bon Messire Jean le Meingre dit Boucicaut, Mareschal de France et Gouverneur de Gennes*, in *Collections complètes des Mémoires relatifs à l'histoire de France*, VII-IX (Paris, 1825), ed. J. A. C. Buchon (Paris, 1836).

BROCQUIÈRE, BERTRANDON DE LA. *Le Voyage d'Outremer*, ed. C. H. A. Schefer, in *Recueil des voyages et des documents pour servir à l'histoire de la géographie depuis le XIIIe jusqu'à la fin du XVe siècle*, XII (Paris, 1892); translated by T. Wright, *Early Travels in Palestine* (London, 1848), 283-382.

Bulgarian Chronicle from 1296-1413. Ed. J. Bogdan, 'Ein Beitrag zur bulgarischen und serbischen Geschichtschreibung', *Archiv für slavische Philologie*, XIII, 4 (1891), 526-43.

Cronaca di Morea. Ed. C. Hopf, *Chroniques gréco-romanes* &c., 414-68 (Italian version of the *Chronicle of the Morea*).

CLAVIJO, RUY GONZALEZ DE. *Narrative of the Embassy of Ruy Gonzalez de Clavijo to the Court of Timour at Samarkand, A.D. 1403-6* translated by C. R. Markham (Hakluyt Society: London, 1859); translated by G. Le Strange (London, 1928); ed. F. Lopez Estrada, *Embajada a Tamorlan* (Madrid, 1943).

Dušan, Stephen. *Zakonik (Legal Code)*, ed. S. Novaković, *Zakonik Stefana Dušana, cara srpskog* (Belgrade, 1898); translated by M. Burr, in *Slavonic and East European Review*, XXVIII (1949), 198-217; XXIX (1950), 516-39.

Enveri. *Le Destān d'Umūr Pacha (Düstūrnāme-i Enverī)*, ed. Irène Mélikoff-Sayar (Bibliothèque Byzantine, ed. P. Lemerle, Documents, 2: Paris, 1954).

Ibn Battuta. *Travels (A.D. 1325-1354)*, translated by H. A. R. Gibb (Hakluyt Society: Cambridge, 1962).

Ignatios of Smolensk. 'Le Pèlerinage d'Ignace de Smolensk, 1389-1405', ed. B. de Khitrowo, *Itinéraires russes en Orient* (1889), 127-57.

Libro de los Fechos et Conquistas del Principado de la Morea, compiled by Don Fray Johan Ferrandez de Heredia, ed. A. Morel-Fatio (Geneva, 1885) (Spanish version of the *Chronicle of the Morea*).

Livre de la Conqueste de la Princée de l'Amorée, ed. J. Longnon (Paris, 1911) (French version of the *Chronicle of the Morea*).

Muntaner, Ramon. *Cronace Catalane del secolo XIII e XIV* (Florence, 1844); *The Chronicle of Muntaner*, translated by Lady Goodenough (Hakluyt Society: London, 1921).

Pegolotti, Francesco Balducci. *La pratica della mercatura*, ed. A. Evans (Cambridge, Mass., 1936).

Mézières, Philippe de. *The Life of Saint Peter Thomas by Philippe de Mézières*, ed. J. Smet. (*Textus et Studia Historica Carmelitana*, II: Rome, 1954).

Sanudo, Marino Torsello. *Istoria del Regno di Romania*, ed. C. Hopf. *Chroniques gréco-romanes*, 99-170.

Sanuto, Marino. *Vite di duchi di Venezia*, in Muratori, *Rerum Italicarum Scriptores*, XXII, 405-1252.

Schiltberger, Johann. *Reisebuch*, ed. V. Langmantel (Tübingen, 1885); Translated by J. B. Telfer, *The Bondages and Travels of Johann Schiltberger* (Hakluyt Society: London, 1879).

Stella, Giorgio. *Annales Genuenses*, in Muratori, *Rerum Italicarum Scriptores*, XVII, 951-1318.

Stephen of Novgorod. 'Le Pèlerinage d'Etienne de Novgorod vers 1350', ed. B. de Khitrowo, *Itinéraires russes en Orient* (1889), 113-25.

Villani, Matteo. *Croniche di Giovanni, Matteo e Filippo Villani*, ed. A. Racheli, II (Trieste, 1858); and in Muratori, *Rerum Italicarum Scriptores*, XIV.

II. MODERN WORKS

AHRWEILER, HÉLÈNE. 'L'histoire et la géographie de la région de Smyrne entre les deux occupations turques (1081-1317), particulièrement au XIIIᵉ siècle', *Travaux et Mémoires*, I (1965), 2-204.

—— *Byzance et la Mer* (Paris, 1966).

ALEXANDER, P. J. 'A chrysobull of the Emperor Andronicus II Palaeologus in favor of the See of Kanina in Albania', *B*, XV (1940-1), 167-207.

ANTONIADIS-BIBICOU, HÉLÈNE. *Recherches sur les Douanes à Byzance* (Paris, 1963).

ARGENTI, P. *The Occupation of Chios by the Genoese*, 3 vols (Cambridge, 1958).

ARNAKIS, G. G. *The Early Osmanlis. A Contribution to the Problem of the Fall of Hellenism in Asia Minor* [in Greek] (Athens, 1947).

ATIYA, A. S. *The Crusade of Nicopolis* (London, 1934).

—— *The Crusade in the Later Middle Ages* (London, 1938).

BABINGER, F. *Beiträge zur Frühgeschichte der Türkenherrschaft in Rumelien (14.-15. Jahrhundert)* (Munich, 1944).

—— *Mahomet II le Conquérant et son temps (1432-1481)* (Paris, 1954).

BARKER, J. W. *Manuel II Palaeologus (1391-1425). A Study in Late Byzantine Statesmanship* (New Brunswick, N.J., 1968).

BECK, H.-G. *Theodoros Metochites. Die Krise des byzantinischen Weltbildes im 14. Jahrhundert* (Munich, 1952).

—— *Kirche und theologische Literatur im byzantinischen Reich* (Munich, 1959).

BELDICEANU-STEINHERR, IRÈNE. 'La conquête d'Andrinople par les Turcs. La pénétration turque en Thrace et la valeur des chroniques ottomanes', *Travaux et Mémoires*, I (1965), 439-61.

BERGER DE XIVREY, J. *Mémoire sur la vie et les ouvrages de l'empereur Manuel Paléologue* (Mémoires de l'Institut de France, Académie des Inscriptions et Belles-Lettres, XIX: Paris, 1853).

BERTELÈ, T. 'L'iperpero bizantino dal 1261 al 1453', *Rivista Italiana di Numismatica e Scienze Affini*, LIX (1957), 70-89.

—— 'I gioielli della corona bizantina dati in pegno alla repubblica veneta nel sec. XIV e Mastino della Scala', *Studi in onore de Amintore Fanfani*, II: *Medioevo* (Milan, 1962), 90-177.

BINON, ST. 'A propos d'un prostagma inédit d'Andronic III Paléologue', *BZ*, XXXVIII (1938), 133-55, 377-407.

BON, A. *La Morée franque. Recherches historiques, topographiques et archéologiques sur la principauté d'Achaie* (1204-1430), 2 vols (Paris, 1969).

BOSCH, URSULA V. *Kaiser Andronikos III. Palaiologos. Versuch einer Darstellung der byzantinischen Geschichte in den Jahren 1321-1341* (Amsterdam, 1965).

BRATIANU, G. I. *Etudes byzantines d'histoire économique et sociale* (Paris, 1938).

BRÉHIER, L. *Le monde byzantin*, I: *Vie et Mort de Byzance*; II: *Les Institutions de l'empire byzantin*; III: *La Civilisation byzantine* (Paris, 1969-70).

BROCKELMANN, C. *History of the Islamic Peoples*, translated by J. Carmichael and M. Perlmann (New York, 1960).

BROWNING, R. 'Kommunata na Zilotite v Solunu (1342-1350)' (The Zealot commune in Thessalonica), *Istoričeski Pregled*, VI, 4-5 (Sofia, 1950), 509-26.

CAHEN, C. *Pre-Ottoman Turkey* (London, 1968).

Cambridge Medieval History, IV: *The Byzantine Empire*. Part 1: *Byzantium and its Neighbours*; Part 2: *Government, Church and Civilisation*. Edited by J. M. Hussey (Cambridge, 1966, 1967).

CHAPMAN, C. *Michel Paléologue, restaurateur de l'empire byzantin* (Paris, 1926).

CHARANIS, P. 'An important Short Chronicle of the fourteenth century', *B*, XIII (1938), 335-62.

——— 'Internal strife in Byzantium during the fourteenth century', *B*, XV (1940-1), 208-30.

——— 'The strife among the Palaeologi and the Ottoman Turks, 1370-1402', *B*, XVI (1942-3), 286-314.

——— 'The monastic properties and the state in the Byzantine Empire', *DOP*, IV (1948), 51-119.

——— 'On the social structure and economic organisation of the Byzantine Empire in the thirteenth century and later', *BS*, XII (1951), 94-153.

——— 'Economic factors in the decline of the Byzantine Empire', *Journal of Economic History*, XIII (1953), 412-24.

——— 'Observations on the "Anti-Zealot" Discourse of Cabasilas', *Revue des études sud-est européennes*, IX (1971), 369-76.

CHIONIDES, G. C. *History of Beroia, the city and the district*, II: *The Byzantine period* [in Greek] (Thessalonike, 1970).

CHRYSANTHOS, Metropolitan of Trebizond. *The Church of Trebizond* [in Greek] (*Archeion Pontou*, IV-V: Athens, 1936).

CHRYSOSTOMIDES, JULIAN. 'John V Palaeologus in Venice (1370-1371) and the Chronicle of Caroldo: a reinterpretation', *OCP*, XXXI (1965), 76-84.

—— 'Venetian commercial privileges under the Palaeologi', *Studi Veneziani*, XII (1970), 267-356.

DADE, E. *Versuch zur Wiedererrichtung der lateinischen Herrschaft in Konstantinopel im Rahmen der abendländischen Politik, 1261 bis etwa 1310* (Jena, 1938).

DARROUZÈS, J. 'Conférences sur la primauté du Pape à Constantinople en 1357', *REB*, XIX (1961), 76-109.

DELAVILLE LE ROULX, J. *La France en Orient au XIVe siècle*, 2 vols (Paris, 1886).

DENNIS, G. T. *The Reign of Manuel II Palaeologus in Thessalonica, 1382-1387* (Orientalia Christiana Analecta, 159: Rome, 1960).

—— 'The Byzantine-Turkish treaty of 1403', *OCP*, XXXIII (1967), 72-88.

—— 'An unknown Byzantine Emperor, Andronicus V Palaeologus (1400-1407?)', *Jahrbuch der österreichischen byzantinischen Gesellschaft*, XVI (1967), 175-87.

DIEHL, C., GUILLAND, R., OECONOMOS, L., GROUSSET, R. *L'Europe orientale de 1081 à 1453* (=*Histoire Générale*, ed. G. Glotz: *Histoire du Moyen Age*, IX, 1: Paris, 1945).

DINIĆ, M. 'The Balkans, 1018-1499', *CMH*, IV, 1 (1966), Chapter XII.

DÖLGER, F. 'Johannes VII. Kaiser der Rhomäer', *BZ*, XXXI (1931), 21-36.

—— 'Johannes VI. Kantakuzenos als dynastischer Legitimist', *Seminarium Kondakovianum*, X (1938) (=*Festschrift A. A. Vasiliev*), 19-30; reprinted in Dölger, *PARASPORA* (Ettal, 1961), 194-207.

—— 'Zum Aufstand Andronikos IV. gegen seinem Vater Johannes V. im Mai 1373', *REB*, XIX (1961) (=*Mélanges R. Janin*), 328-32.

DUJČEV, I. 'Le patriarche Nil et les invasions turques vers la fin du XIVe siècle', *Mélanges d'archéologie et d'histoire*, LXXVIII (1966), 207-14.

—— *Medioevo Bizantino-Slavo*, 3 vols (Rome, 1965-70).

ESZER, A. K. *Das abenteuerliche Leben des Johannes Laskaris Kalopheros* (Wiesbaden, 1969).

EVERT-KAPPESOWA, HALINA. 'La société byzantine et l'union de Lyon', *BS*, X (1949), 28-41.

—— 'Une page de l'histoire des relations byzantino-latines. Le clergé byzantin et l'union de Lyon (1274-1282)', *BS*, XII (1952-3), 68-92.

—— 'Byzance et le Saint Siège à l'époque de l'union de Lyon', *BS*, XVI (1955), 297-317.

—— 'La fin de l'union de Lyon', *BS*, XVII (1956), 1-18.

FERJANČIĆ, B. *Despoti u Vizantiji i jugosslovenskim zemljama* (Despots in Byzantium and on South Slav territory) (Posebna Izdanja Vizantološkog Instituta, 8: Belgrade, 1960).

—— 'Sevastokratori u Vizantiji' (Sebastokrators in Byzantium), *Zbornik Radova*, XI (1968), 141-92.

FINLAY, G. *A History of Greece from its Conquest by the Romans to the Present Time, B.C. 146 to A.D. 1864*, ed. H. F. Tozer, III and IV (Oxford, 1877).

FLORINSKIJ, T. 'Andronik Mladšij i Ioann Kantakuzin' (Andronikos the Younger and John Cantacuzene), *Žurnal ministerstva narodnago prosveščenija*, CCIV (1879), 87-143, 219-51; CCV (1879), 1-48; CCVIII (1880), 327-34.

FRANCES, E. 'Narodnie dviženija osenju 1354 g. v Konstantinopole i otrecenie Joanna Kantakuzina' (The popular movement in Constantinople in the autumn of 1354 and the abdication of John Cantacuzene)', *VV*, XXV (1964), 142-7.

FRANCHI, A. *Il Concilio II di Lione* (Studi e Testi francescane, 33: Naples, 1965).

FUCHS, F. *Die höheren Schulen von Konstantinopel im Mittelalter* (Leipzig, 1926).

GAY, J. *Le Pape Clément VI et les affaires d'Orient (1342-1352)* (Paris, 1904).

GEANAKOPLOS, D. J. *Emperor Michael Palaeologus and the West, 1258-1282. A study in Byzantine-Latin relations* (Cambridge, Mass., 1959).

—— *Byzantine East and Latin West: Two worlds of Christendom in Middle Ages and Renaissance* (Oxford, 1966).

GEGAJ, A. *L'Albanie et l'invasion turque au XVᵉ siècle* (Louvain, 1937).

GIBBON, E. *The History of the Decline and Fall of the Roman Empire*, ed. J. B. Bury, VII (London, 1900).

GIBBONS, H. A. *The Foundation of the Ottoman Empire. A History of the Osmanlis up to the death of Bayezid I, 1300-1403* (Oxford, 1916).

GILL, J. *The Council of Florence* (Cambridge, 1958).

—— *Personalities of the Council of Florence and Other Essays* (Oxford, 1964).

GRUMEL, V. *La Chronologie* (Traité d'études byzantines, ed. P. Lemerle, I: Paris, 1958).

GUILLAND, R. *Essai sur Nicéphore Grégoras. L'homme et l'oeuvre* (Paris, 1926).

—— *Etudes Byzantines* (Paris, 1959).

GUILLAND, R. *Recherches sur les Institutions byzantines*, 2 vols (Berliner Byzantinische Arbeiten, 35 : Berlin, 1967).

HALECKI, O. *Un Empereur de Byzance à Rome. Vingt ans de travail pour l'union des églises et pour la défense de l'empire d'Orient, 1355-1375* (Warsaw, 1930).

—— *The Crusade of Varna. A discussion of controversial problems* (New York, 1943).

HAMMER-PURGSTALL, J. VON. *Geschichte des osmanischen Reiches*, I (Pest, 1827).

HEISENBERG, A. *Aus der Geschichte und Literatur der Palaiologenzeit (Sitzungsberichte der bayerischen Akademie der Wissenschaften, Philosophische-philologische und historische Klasse*, Abh. 10 : Munich, 1920).

HEYD, W. *Histoire du Commerce du Levant au Moyen Age*, 2 vols (Leipzig, 1936).

HOPF, C. *Geschichte Griechenlands vom Beginn des Mittelalters bis auf unsere Zeit*, in J. S. Ersch and J. G. Gruber, *Allgemeine Encyklopädie der Wissenschaften und Künste*, LXXXV, LXXXVI : Leipzig, 1867, 1868).

HROCHOVÁ, V. 'La révolte des Zélotes à Salonique et les communes italiennes', *BS*, XXII (1961), 1-15.

INALCIK, H. 'Ottoman methods of conquest', *Studia Islamica*, II (Paris, 1954), 103-29.

—— 'Mehmed the Conqueror (1432-1481) and his time', *Speculum*, XXXV (1960), 408-27.

JANIN, R. *Constantinople byzantine. Développement urbain et répertoire topographique* (Paris, 1950; revised edition, 1964).

JANSSENS, E. *Trébizonde en Colchide* (Brussels, 1969).

JIREČEK, C. J. *Geschichte der Bulgaren* (Prague, 1876).

—— *Geschichte der Serben*, 2 vols (Gotha, 1911-18); revised edition by J. Radonić, *Istorija Srba*, 2 vols (Belgrade, 1952).

JORGA (IORGA), N. *Philippe de Mézières et la Croisade au XIVe siècle* (Paris, 1896).

—— 'Latins et grecs d'Orient et l'établissement des Turcs en Europe, 1342-62', *BZ*, XV (1906), 179-222.

—— *Geschichte des osmanischen Reiches*, I (Gotha, 1908).

KALLIGAS, P. *Studies on Byzantine History from the first to the last capture (1205-1453)* [in Greek] (Athens, 1894).

KOLIAS, G. 'The revolt of John VII Palaiologos against John V Palaiologos (1390)', [in Greek], Hellenika, XII (1952), 34-64.

KREKIĆ, B. *Dubrovnik (Raguse) et le Levant au Moyen Age (Docu-*

ments et Recherches sur l'économie des pays byzantins, islamiques et slaves, V: Paris, 1961).

KRUMBACHER, K. *Geschichte der byzantinischen Litteratur von Justinian bis zum Ende des oströmischen Reiches (527-1453)*, 2nd edition (Munich, 1897).

KYRRIS, C. P. 'Gouvernés et gouvernants à Byzance pendant la révolution des Zélotes (1341-1350)', *Gouvernés et Gouvernants* (1968), 271-330.

LAIOU, A. E. 'The provisioning of Constantinople during the winter of 1306-1307', *B*, XXXVII (1967), 91-113.

—— 'A Byzantine prince latinized: Theodore Palaeologus, Marquis of Montferrat', *B*, XXXVIII (1968), 386-410.

—— 'Marino Sanudo Torsello, Byzantium and the Turks: The background to the anti-Turkish league of 1332-1334', *Speculum*, XLV (1970), 374-92.

LANGER, W. L. and BLAKE, R. P. 'The rise of the Ottoman Turks and its historical background', *American Historical Review*, XXXVII (1932), 468-505.

LASKARIS, M. *Vizantiske princeze u srednjevekovnoj Srbiji* (Byzantine princesses in mediaeval Serbia) (Belgrade, 1926).

LAURENT, V. 'La correspondance de Démétrius Cydonès', *Echos d'Orient*, XXX (1931), 399-454.

—— 'Une princesse byzantine au cloître. Irène Eulogie Choumnos Paléologine', *Echos d'Orient*, XXIX (1930), 29-61.

—— 'Les grandes crises religieuses à Byzance. La fin du schisme arsénite', *Académie Roumaine. Bulletin de la section historique*, XXVI (1945), 225-313.

—— 'Les droits de l'empereur en matière ecclésiastique. L'accord de 1380-1382', *REB*, XIII (1959), 5-20.

—— 'La direction spirituelle à Byzance. La correspondance d'Irène-Eulogie Choumnaina Paléologine avec son second directeur', *REB*, XIV (1956), 48-86.

LEMERLE, P. *Philippes et la Macédoine orientale à l'époque chrétienne et byzantine* (Paris, 1945).

—— 'La domination vénitienne à Thessalonique', *Miscellanea Giovanni Galbiati*, III (=*Fontes Ambrosiani*, XXVII: Milan, 1951), 219-25.

—— 'Le juge général des Grecs et la réforme judiciaire d'Andronic III', *Mémorial Louis Petit* (Bucharest, 1948), 292-316.

—— 'Recherches sur les institutions judiciaires à l'époque des Paléologues, I: le tribunal impérial', *Mélanges Henri Grégoire*, I (Paris, 1949), 369-84.

LEMERLE, P. 'Recherches sur les institutions judiciaires à l'époque des Paléologues, II: le tribunal du patriarcat ou tribunal synodal', *Mélanges Paul Peeters*, II (=*Analecta Bollandiana*, LXVIII (1950)), 318-33.

—— *L'Emirat d'Aydin, Byzance et l'Occident. Recherches sur 'La geste d'Umur Pacha'* (Paris, 1957).

LOENERTZ, R.-J. 'La première insurrection d'Andronic IV Paléologue', *Echos d'Orient*, XXXVIII (1939), 334-45.

—— 'Pour l'histoire du Péloponnèse au XIVe siècle (1382-1404)', *REB*, I (1943), 152-96.

—— 'Ambassadeurs grecs auprès du Pape Clément VI (1348)', *OCP*, XIX (1953), 178-96.

—— 'Jean V Paléologue à Venise (1370-1371)', *REB*, XVI (1958), 216-32.

—— 'Notes d'histoire et de chronologie byzantines', *REB*, XVII (1959), 158-67; 'Deuxième série', *REB*, XX (1962), 171-80.

—— 'Ordre et désordre dans les mémoires de Jean Cantacuzène', *REB*, XXII (1964), 222-37.

—— 'Mémoire d'Ogier, protonotaire, pour Marco et Marchetto nonces de Michel VIII Paléologue auprès du Pape Nicholas III. 1278 printemps-été', *OCP*, XXXI (1965), 374-408.

—— 'Démétrius Cydonès, I: De la naissance à l'année 1373', *OCP*, XXXVI (1970), 47-72; 'II: De 1373 à 1375', *OCP*, XXXVII (1971), 5-39.

—— *Byzantina et Franco-Graeca (Articles parus de 1935 à 1966 réédités avec la collaboration de Peter Schreiner)* [Storia e Letteratura: Raccolta di Studi e Testi, 118] (Rome, 1970).

LONGNON, J. *L'empire latin de Constantinople et la principauté de Morée* (Paris, 1949).

LUTTRELL, A. 'John Cantacuzenus and the Catalans at Constantinople', *Martinez Ferrando, Archivero. Miscelánea de estudios dedicados a su memoria* (Asociación Nacional de Bibliotecarios, Archiveros y Arqueólogos, 1968), 265-77.

MAKSIMOVIĆ, LJ. 'Politička uloga Jovana Kantakuzina posle abdikacije (1354-1383)' (The political role of John Cantacuzene after his abdication), *Zbornik Radova*, IX (1966), 119-93.

MASAI, F. *Pléthon et le Platonisme de Mistra* (Paris, 1956).

MATSCHKE, K. P. *Fortschritt und Reaktion in Byzanz im 14 Jahrhundert* (Berlin, 1971).

MERCATI, G. *Notizie di Procoro e Demetrio Cidone, Manuele Caleca e Teodoro Meliteniota ed altri appunti per la storia della teologia e della letteratura bizantina del secolo XIV* (Studi e Testi, 56 : Vatican City, 1931).

MEYENDORFF, J. *Introduction à l'étude de Grégoire Palamas* (Paris, 1959); translated as *A Study of Gregory Palamas*, by G. Lawrence (London, 1965).

—— 'Projets de concile oecuménique en 1367: Un dialogue inédit entre Jean Cantacuzène et le légat Paul', *DOP*, XIV (1960), 147-77.

—— 'Alexis and Roman : a study in Byzantine-Russian relations (1352-1354)', *BS*, XXVIII (1967), 278-88.

—— 'Society and Culture in the fourteenth century. Religious problems', *XIVe Congrès International des Etudes Byzantines, Rapports*, I (Bucharest, 1971), 51-65.

MIJATOVICH, CH. *Constantine. The Last Emperor of the Greeks* (London, 1892).

MILLER, W. *The Latins in the Levant. A History of Frankish Greece, 1204-1566* (London, 1908).

—— *Essays on the Latin Orient* (Cambridge, 1921).

—— *Trebizond. The Last Greek Empire* (London, 1926).

MORAVCSIK, GY. *Byzantinoturcica*. 2nd edition, 2 vols (Berlin, 1958).

—— 'Hungary and Byzantium in the Middle Ages', *CMH*, IV, 1 (1966), Chapter XIII.

NICOL, D. M. *The Despotate of Epiros* (Oxford, 1957).

—— *Meteora. The Rock Monasteries of Thessaly* (London, 1963).

—— 'The Greeks and the Union of the Churches : The preliminaries to the Second Council of Lyons, 1261-1274', *Medieval Studies presented to A. Gwynn, S.J.*, ed. J. A. Watt and others (Dublin, 1961) 454-80.

—— 'The Greeks and the Union of the Churches. The Report of Ogerius, Protonotarius of Michael VIII Palaiologos, in 1280', *Proceedings of the Royal Irish Academy*, LXIII, sect. C, 1 (1962), 1-16.

—— 'Constantine Akropolites. A prosopographical note', *DOP*, XIX (1965), 249-56.

—— 'The abdication of John Cantacuzene', *Byzantinische Forschungen*, II (=*Polychordia. Festschrift F. Dölger*: Amsterdam, 1967), 269-83.

—— *The Byzantine Family of Kantakouzenos (Cantacuzenus) ca. 1100-1460. A genealogical and prosopographical study* (Dumbarton Oaks Studies, XI : Washington, D.C., 1968).

—— 'Byzantine requests for an oecumenical council in the fourteenth century', *Annuarium Historiae Conciliorum*, I (1969), 69-95.

—— 'The Byzantine Church and Hellenic Learning in the Fourteenth

Century', *Studies in Church History*, V, ed. G. J. Cuming (Leiden, 1969), 23-57.

—— 'The Byzantine reaction to the Second Council of Lyons, 1274', *Studies in Church History*, VII, ed. G. J. Cuming and D. Baker (Cambridge, 1971), 113-46.

—— 'A Byzantine Emperor in England. Manuel II's visit to London in 1400-1401', *University of Birmingham Historical Journal*, XII, 2 (1971), 204-25.

NORDEN, W. *Das Papsttum und Byzanz* (Berlin, 1903).

OBOLENSKY, D. 'Byzantium, Kiev and Moscow : A study in ecclesiastical relations', *DOP*, XI (1957), 21-78.

—— *The Byzantine Commonwealth. Eastern Europe, 500-1453* (London, 1971).

OSTROGORSKY, G. *Pour l'histoire de la féodalité byzantine* (Brussels, 1954).

—— *Quelques problèmes d'histoire de la paysannerie byzantine* (Brussels, 1956).

—— 'Byzance, état tributaire de l'empire turc', *Zbornik Radova*, V (1958), 49-58.

—— 'La prise de Serrès par les Turcs', *B*, XXXV (1965) (=*Mémorial Henri Grégoire*), 302-19.

—— *Serska oblast posle Dušanove smrti* (The province of Serres after the death of Dušan) [Posebna Izdanja Vizantološkog Instituta, 9] (Belgrade, 1965); French summary by H. Miakotine, in *Travaux et Mémoires*, II (1967), 569-73.

—— *History of the Byzantine State*, translated by Joan Hussey, 2nd edition (Oxford, 1968).

PALL, F. 'Encore une fois sur le voyage diplomatique de Jean V Paléologue en 1365/60', *Revue des études sud-est européennes*, IX (1971), 535-40.

PAPADOPULOS, A. TH. *Versuch einer Genealogie der Palaiologen, 1259-1453* (Munich, 1938).

PARISOT, V. *Cantacuzène, homme d'état et historien* (Paris, 1845).

PEARS, E. *The Destruction of the Greek Empire and the Story of the Capture of Constantinople by the Turks* (London, 1903).

POLEMIS, D. I. *The Doukai. A Contribution to Byzantine Prosopography* (University of London Historical Studies, XXII: London, 1968).

RAYBAUD, L.-P. *Le gouvernement et l'administration centrale de l'empire byzantine sous les premiers Paléologues (1258-1354)* (Paris, 1968).

ROBERG, B. *Die Union zwischen der griechischen und der lateinischen*

Kirche auf dem II. Konzil von Lyon (1274) (Bonn, 1964).

RODD, R. *The Princes of Achaia and the Chronicles of Morea. A study of Greece in the middle ages*, 2 vols (London, 1907).

RUNCIMAN, S. *A History of the Crusades*, III (Cambridge, 1954).

—— *The Sicilian Vespers. A History of the Mediterranean World in the Late Thirteenth Century* (Cambridge, 1958).

—— *The Fall of Constantinople 1453* (Cambridge, 1965.)

—— *The Great Church in Captivity. A Study of the Patriarchate of Constantinople from the Eve of the Turkish Conquest to the Greek War of Independence* (Cambridge, 1968).

—— *The Last Byzantine Renaissance* (Cambridge, 1970).

SALAVILLE, S. 'Deux documents inédits sur les dissensions religieuses byzantines entre 1275 et 1310', *REB*, V (1947), 116-36.

SAULI, L. *Della Colonia dei Genovesi in Galata*, 2 vols (Turin, 1831).

SCHLUMBERGER, G. *Expéditions des 'Almugavares' ou routiers catalans en Orient* (Paris, 1902).

—— *Un Empereur de Byzance à Paris et à Londres* (Paris, 1916).

—— *Byzance et Croisades. Pages médiévales* (Paris, 1927).

SCHREINER, P. *Studien zu den BPAXEA XPONIKA* (Miscellanea byzantina monacensia, 6: Munich, 1967).

—— 'Zur Geschichte Philadelpheias im 14. Jahrhundert (1293-1390)', *OCP*, XXXV (1969), 375-431.

SETTON, K. M. *Catalan Domination of Athens, 1311-1388* (Cambridge, Mass., 1948).

—— 'The Byzantine background to the Italian Renaissance', *Proceedings of the American Philosophical Society*, 100, no. 1 (1956), 1-76.

—— *A History of the Crusades*, II: *The Later Crusades, 1189-1311*, ed. R. L. Wolff and H. W. Hazard (Philadelphia, 1962).

—— 'The Latins in Greece and the Aegean from the Fourth Crusade to the end of the middle ages', *CMH*, IV, 1 (1966), Chapter IX.

ŠEVČENKO, I. 'The Zealot revolution and the supposed Genoese colony in Thessalonica', *Prosphora eis St Kyriakidin* (Thessalonike, 1953), 603-17.

—— 'Intellectual repercussions of the Council of Florence', *Church History*, XXIV (1955), 291-323.

—— 'Nicolas Cabasilas' "Anti-Zealot" Discourse: a reinterpretation', *DOP*, XI (1957), 79-171.

—— 'Alexios Makrembolites and his "Dialogue between the Rich and the Poor"', *Zbornik Radova*, VI (1960), 187-228.

—— 'The Decline of Byzantium seen through the eyes of its intellectuals', *DOP* XV (1961), 169-86.

—— *Etudes sur la Polémique entre Théodore Métochites et Nicéphore Choumnos* (Brussels, 1962).

SHERRARD, P. *The Greek East and the Latin West. A study in the Christian tradition* (Oxford, 1959).

SKRJINSKAJA, E. 'Genueszi v Konstantinople v XIV v.' (The Genoese in Constantinople in the fourteenth century), *VV*, I (1947), 215-34.

SOKOLOV, N. P. 'Venecija i Vizantija pri pervykh Paleologakh (1263-1328)' (Venice and Byzantium under the early Palaiologi), *VV*, XII (1957), 75-96.

STARR, J. *The Jewries of the Levant after the Fourth Crusade* (Paris, 1949).

STEIN, E. 'Untersuchungen zur spätbyzantinischen Verfassungs- und Wirtschaftsgeschichte', *Mitteilungen zur osmanische Geschichte*, II (1923-5), 1-62; reprinted separately (Amsterdam, 1962).

SYKOUTRES, I. 'On the schism of the Arsenites' (in Greek), *Hellenika*, II (1929), 267-332.

TAESCHNER, F. 'The Ottoman Turks to 1453', *CMH*, IV, 1 (1966), Chapter XIX.

TAFRALI, O. *Thessalonique au XIVᵉ siècle* (Paris, 1913).

TATAKIS, B. *La Philosophie byzantine (Histoire de la Philosophie*, ed. E. Bréhier, fasc. suppl. no. II: Paris, 1959).

TEMPERLEY, H. W. V. *History of Serbia* (London, 1917).

THIRIET, F. 'Venise et l'occupation de Ténédos au XIVᵉ siècle', *Mélanges d'archéologie et d'histoire*, LXV (1953), 219-45.

—— *La Romanie vénitienne au moyen âge* (Paris, 1959).

THOMSON, J. 'Manuel Chrysoloras and the Early Italian Renaissance', *Greek, Roman and Byzantine Studies*, VII (1966), 63-82.

TURNER, C. J. G. 'Pages from the late Byzantine philosophy of history', *BZ*, LVII (1964), 346-73.

—— 'The career of George-Gennadius Scholarius', *B*, XXXIX (1969), 420-55.

TZARAS, J. 'La fin d'Andronic Paléologue, dernier despote de Thessalonique', *Revue des études sud-est européennes*, III (1965), 419-32.

VAKALOPOULOS, A. E. 'Les limites de l'empire byzantin depuis la fin du XIVᵉ siècle jusqu'à sa chute (1453)', *BZ*, LV (1962), 56-65.

—— *A History of Thessaloniki*, translated by T. F. Carney (Institute for Balkan Studies: Thessalonike, 1963).

—— 'Zur Frage der zweiten Einnahme Thessalonikis durch die Türken 1391-1394', *BZ*, LXI (1968), 285-90.

—— *History of Macedonia, 1354-1833* [in Greek] (Thessalonike, 1969).

—— *Origins of the Greek Nation, 1204-1461* (New Brunswick, N.J., 1970).

VASILIEV, A. A. 'Putešestvie Vizantijskago Imperatora Manuila II Paleologa po zapadnoj Evrope (1399-1404 g.)' (The journey of the Byzantine Emperor Manuel II to western Europe in 1399-1404), *Žurnal ministerstva narodnago prosveščenija*, new series, XXXIX (1912), 41-78, 260-304.

—— 'Il viaggio di Giovanni V Paleologo in Italia e l'unione di Roma', *Studi bizantini e neoellenici*, III (1931), 153-92.

—— 'Pero Tafur, a Spanish traveller of the fifteenth century and his visit to Constantinople, and Trebizond, and Italy', *B*, VII (1932), 75-122.

—— *History of the Byzantine Empire, 324-1453* (Madison, 1952).

VERPEAUX, J. *Nicéphore Choumnos, homme d'état et humaniste byzantin (ca 1250/1255-1327)* (Paris, 1959).

—— 'Hiérarchie et préséance sous les Paléologues', *Travaux et Mémoires*, I (1965), 421-37.

VILLER, M. 'La question de l'union des églises entre Grecs et Latins depuis le Concile de Lyon jusqu'à celui de Florence.' *Revue d'histoire ecclésiastique*, XVI (1921), 260-305, 515-32; XVIII (1922), 20-60.

VOORDECKERS, E. 'Un empereur palamite à Mistra en 1370', *Revue des études sud-est européennes*, IX (1971), 607-16.

VRYONIS, S. 'Isidore Glabas and the Turkish Devshirme', *Speculum*, XXI (1956), 433-43.

—— 'The Byzantine Legacy and Ottoman Forms', *DOP*, XXIII-XXIV (1969-70), 253-308.

VRYONIS, S. *The Decline of Medieval Hellenism in Asia Minor and the Process of Islamization from the Eleventh through the Fifteenth Century* (Los Angeles, 1971).

WÄCHTER, A. H. *Der Verfall des Griechentums in Kleinasien in XIV Jahrhundert* (Leipzig, 1903).

WALTER, G. *La Ruine de Byzance. 1204-1453* (Paris, 1958).

WEISS, G. *Joannes Kantakuzenos—Aristokrat, Staatsmann, Kaiser und Mönch—in der Gesellschaftsentwicklung von Byzanz im 14. Jahrhundert* (Wiesbaden, 1969).

WERNER, E. 'Volkstümlicher Häretiker oder sozial-politische Reformer? Probleme der revolutionären Volksbewegung in Thessalonike 1342-1349', *Wissenschaftliche Zeitschrift Universität Leipzig*, VIII (1958-9), 45-83.

—— 'Johannes Kantakuzenos, Umur Paša und Orchan', *BS*, XXVI (1955), 255-76.

—— *Die Geburt einer Grossmacht—Die Osmanen (1300 bis 1481). Ein Beitrag zur Genesis des türkischen Feudalismus* (Berlin, 1966).

WIRTH, P. 'Zum Geschichtsbild Kaiser Johannes' VII. Palaiologos', *B*, XXXV (1965) (=*Mémorial Henri Grégoire*), 592-600.

WITTEK, P. *Das Fürstentum Mentesche. Studie zur Geschichte Westkleinasiens im 13.-15. Jh.* (Istanbul, 1934).

—— *The Rise of the Ottoman Empire* (Royal Asiatic Society Monographs, 23: London, 1938).

—— 'De la défaite d'Ankara à la prise de Constantinople (un demi-siècle d'histoire ottomane)', *Revue des études islamiques*, XII (1938), 1-34.

ZACHARIADOU, ELIZABETH. *To Chronikon ton Tourkon Soultanon (tou Barberinou Ellen. Kodika 111) kai to Italiko tou protypo* (The Chronicle of the Turkish Sultans and its Italian prototype) (Thessalonike, 1960).

—— 'The Conquest of Adrianople by the Turks', *Studi Veneziani*, XII (1970), 211-17.

ZAKYTHINOS, D. A. *Crise monétaire et crise économique à Byzance du XIIe au XVe siècle* (Athens, 1948).

—— *Le Despotat grec de Morée (1262-1460)*, I: *Histoire politique* (Paris, 1932); II: *Vie et Institutions* (Athens, 1953).

ZINKEISEN, J. W. *Geschichte des osmanischen Reiches in Europa*, I (Hamburg, 1840).

Index

Joseph I, Patriarch of Constantinople (1266-75; 1282-3), 49, 58, 60, 66-7, 82, 101, 102, 111

Joseph II, Patriarch of Constantinople (1416-39), 370, 373, 376-7

Joseph, Bishop of Ganos, 239-41

Josephites, 67, 82, 104, 114

jousting at Constantinople, 172

Julian, Emperor, 85

justice, administration of, 187-9

Justinian I, Emperor, 3, 79, 255, 304, 344

Kabasilas, Nicholas, 221, 235, 247-8, 287

kadi, Turkish judge, 311

Kalamata, 344

Kalavryta, 364

Kalekas (*see* John XIV, Patriarch)

Kallistos I, Patriarch of Constantinople (1350-3; 1355-63), 240, 245-7, 251, 271, 272, 274, 278, 305

Kalojan, tsar of Bulgaria (1197-1207), 13-14, 24, 125

Kalothetos, Leo, Byzantine governor of Chios and Phokaia, 176, 234, 272

Kananos (Cananus), John, Byzantine chronicler, 348

Kanina, 185

Kantakouzenos (*see* Cantacuzene)

Kara Burun (Erythrea), 179-80

Karadja Beg, Ottoman general in Rumelia, 402

Kara-Koyunlu (Horde of the Black Sheep), 428

Karaman, Karamania, emirate, 150-1, 155, 295, 299, 301, 329, 344, 379, 395-6, 431

Karasi, emirate, 152, 176, 178, 208, 210, 273

Karia, 91, 132, 151

Karystos, 64

Kassandria, 141, 142, 143

Kastamuni, 311

Kastoria, 36, 37, 181-2

Kastriotes, George (*see* Skanderbeg)

Kastriotes, John, son of George, 424

Kavalla (Christoupolis), 141

Kaykhusraw II, Seljuq Sultan (died 1243), 27

Kelaun, Mamluk Sultan of Egypt, 86

Kenchreai, 343

Kephissos river, 143

khàss, Ottoman estate, 295

Kiev, 26, 371

Kipchak (*see* Golden Horde)

Kjustendil (Velbužd), 180, 300

Knights of St John, at Rhodes, 151-2, 155, 177, 230, 272, 282, 289, 316-7, 329, 340, 395

Kobilić, Miloš, son-in-law of Lazar of Serbia, 300

Kokalas, George, 235

Komnenos, Isaac, 9 (*see also* Alexios, Basil, David, George, John, Manuel, Theodora, Komnenos)

Kontoskalion, harbour at Constantinople, 46

Konya, 148, 150

Kopais, lake, 143

Korea, 26

Kosmas (*see* John XII, Patriarch)

Kossovo, battle at (1389), 299-301, 304; battle at (1448), 383-5

Koyunlu-Hisar, 431

Kraljević (*see* Marko)

Kroia, Albania, 379, 385, 414

Kuzin Pasha, Mongol chieftain, 135

Kydones, Demetrios, writer and statesman, 213-14, 220-1, 225, 235, 241, 250, 269, 274, 275, 277, 280-1, 284-5, 290-1, 295-7, 299, 303, 310, 323, 371, 434

Kyparissiotes, John, 241

Kyzikos, 110, 134-5, 136-7, 139, 377

Ladislas III, King of Poland and Hungary, 379-80

Lala Shahin, Turkish general, 273, 286

Lamia, 63, 143

Lampsakos, 134, 138, 272-3

land, landowners, 198f., 203, 280-1, 287, 301, 341; at Mistra, 361-2

Landulph, Cornwall, 425

Laskaris family, 35, 41, 48-9; political supporters of, 87, 89, 110-11, 131, 194 (*see also* John IV, Maria, Theodore I, Theodore II)

Lateran Council (1215), 20

Latin Empire of Constantinople (1204-1261), 10-17

Lazar, Serbian prince (1371-89), 299-300, 301

Lazar Branković, Despot in Serbia (died 1458), 384, 424

Lazarević, Stephen, Despot in Serbia (1389-1427), 301, 314, 316, 318, 328, 335, 341-2, 368, 384

Murad I, Ottoman Sultan (1362-89), 273, 283-5, 287-9, 291, 294-7, 299-300, 302, 338

Murad II, Ottoman Sultan (1421-51), 347-50, 351, 365-8, 378, 380-4, 390-2, 394, 397, 414, 430

Murisco, Andrea, Genoese captain, 120, 140

Musa, son of Bajezid I, Sultan (1411-1413), 329, 338-9, 341-2

Mustafa, son of Mehmed I, 348-9

Mustafa, alleged son of Bajezid I, 344-5, 347-8

Mykonos, island, 117

Mysia, 150, 152, 176

Namur, Philip of, 14-15

Naples, 53, 122-4, 184, 281, 283, 383, 393, 397, 419

Naseby, battle of, 425

Nasi, Joseph, of Naxos, 419

Naupaktos (Lepanto), 382, 419, 421, 423

Nauplia, 359, 364

Navarrese Company, 317, 340

navy, Byzantine, recreated by Michael VIII, 46; disbanded by Andronikos II, 114-15, 118-19, 123, 130-1; fleet of 20 ships, 162; in 1342, 201; rebuilt by John VI, 228-34, 244

Naxos, Italian Duchy of, 65, 117, 178, 419

Negroponte (Euboia), 64-5, 117, 178, 181, 343, 349-50, 358, 367, 419

Nemanja, Stephen I, of Serbia, 9

Nemanja, Stephen II, King of Serbia (1217-27), 125

Neokastra, 132

Neopatras (Hypati), 63, 67, 182

Nevers, John, Count of, 317-18

New Phokaia, 120, 176-7

Nicaea, Empire of (1208-61), 13-15, 17-19, 23-41, 48-9, 65, 84, 103, 142; in the Byzantine Empire, 48, 90, 131, 134, 148, 153-4, 390; captured by the Osmanlis (1331), 174-6, 433

Nicholas III, Pope (1277-80), 68-70

Nicholas V, Pope (1447-55), 383-5, 392, 398, 401-2

Nicholas of Cotrone, Bishop, 53

Nicopolis, 299, 314, 380

Nicopolis, Crusade of (1396), 317-19, 321, 380

Nikephoros Phokas, Emperor, 80

Nikephoros I Doukas, Despot in Epiros (c. 1268-94), 28, 30, 32, 37, 38, 48, 57, 63, 67-8, 70, 72, 121-4, 126, 145, 183

Nikephoros II, Despot in Epiros (1338-1340; 1356-9), 185-7, 229, 238

Nikomedia, 48, 119, 131, 134-5, 148, 153, 154; Turkish (from 1337), 174-176, 250

Niphon, Bishop of Kyzikos, Patriarch of Constantinople (1310-14), 110-111, 135

Niš, captured by Turks (1386), 296, 299, 380

Noah, 153

Nogaj, Khan of the Golden Horde, 73, 86, 93, 147

Normans, 3, 8, 10

North Africa, 55, 56, 434

Notaras, Anna Palaiologina, daughter of Loukas, 412

Notaras, Loukas, Grand Duke, 392, 398-9, 405, 411

Nymphaion, 38-9, 131, 132; treaty of (1261), 38-9

Nyssa, 92; Turkish, 137

Ochrida, 24, 126-7, 285, 296

Odysseus, 286

Ogerius, imperial protonotarius, 69, 84

oikoumene, 78

Öldjaitu, Mongol khan, 148, 150-1

Oliver, John, Serbian noble, 202

Olivera, daughter of Lazar of Serbia, wife of Bajezid I, 301

Orchan, son of Osman, emir of Bithynia (1326-62), 154, 174-6, 177, 194, 208-10, 226, 235, 238, 244-6, 248-50, 252, 256, 267, 272-3, 288

Orchan, grandson of Suleiman, 395-6, 400, 412

Orestes, 180

Orsini, family, Counts of Cephalonia and Despots in Epiros, 393

Orsini, John I, 123, 183

Orsini, John II, 184-5

Orsini, Nicholas, 184

Orsini, Richard, 123

Orvieto, treaty of (1281), 72, 74

Osman (Othman), emir of Bithynia, founder of Osmanli dynasty (died 1326), 134, 148, 153-5, 174

Osmanlis (Ottomans), 12, 134, 153-6, 166, 174-6, 179-80, 208, 225, 248, 267, 268, 285-6, 295 and passim

Otto de la Roche, French Duke of Athens, 12

Ovid, 422

Pachomios, monk, 93

Pachomios, village in Thrace, 93

Pachymeres, George, Byzantine historian, 74, 84-5, 89, 93, 95, 100, 101, 106, 108, 110, 114, 116, 120, 132, 134, 136, 141-2, 148, 150-1

Padua, 322

Palaiologina, Anna, niece of Michael VIII, wife of Nikephoros I of Epiros, 51, 63, 67, 121-4, 183

Palaiologina, Anna, daughter of Michael IX, wife of (i) Thomas of Epiros (ii) Nicholas Orsini, 124, 161, 183-4

Palaiologina, Anna, daughter of Andronikos Palaiologos, wife of John II Orsini, 184

Palaiologina, Eirene, wife of Matthew Cantacuzene, 191

Palaiologina, Eirene, illegitimate daughter of Andronikos II, wife of John II of Thessaly, 182

Palaiologina, Eudokia, daughter of Michael VIII, wife of John II of Trebizond, 81, 126

Palaiologina, Eulogia (Eirene), sister of Michael VIII, 40, 58, 67, 100, 121

Palaiologina, Euphrosyne, illegitimate daughter of Michael VIII, wife of Nogaj, 86

Palaiologina, Helena, daughter of Demetrios, Despot in the Morea, 358-9

Palaiologina, Helena, daughter of Thomas, Despot in the Morea, 424

Palaiologina, Maria, daughter of Eulogia, 58

Palaiologina, Maria, illegitimate daughter of Michael VIII, wife of Abaga, 86, 147-8

Palaiologina, Maria, niece of Andronikos II, wife of Roger de Flor, 136

Palaiologina, Theodora, wife of Michael VIII, 34, 41, 84, 93, 100, 103

Palaiologina, Theodora Raoulaina, daughter of Eulogia, 121

Palaiologina, Theodora, wife of Demetrios, Despot in the Morea, 423

Palaiologina, Theodora, daughter of Michael IX, wife of (i) Svetoslav

(ii) Michael Šišman of Bulgaria, 180

Palaiologina, Zoe, daughter of Despot Thomas, wife of Ivan III of Russia, 424

Palaiologina (see also Simonis)

Palaiologopolis (see Tralles)

Palaiologos, Andrew, Zealot leader in Thessalonica, 235-6

Palaiologos, Andrew, son of Despot Thomas, 424-5

Palaiologos, Andrew, son of Manuel, 424

Palaiologos, Andronikos, father of Michael VIII, 27, 34

Palaiologos, Andronikos, cousin of Michael VIII, 84

Palaiologos, Constantine, brother of Michael VIII, 51

Palaiologos, Constantine Porphyrogenitus, brother of Andronikos II, 131

Palaiologos, Constantine Despot, son of Andronikos II, 99, 159, 161

Palaiologos, Constantine Graitzas, 422-3

Palaiologos, Constantine, son of Andrew, 425

Palaiologos, Demetrios Despot, son of Andronikos II, 159-60

Palaiologos, Ferdinand, 425

Palaiologos, John, brother of Michael VIII, 36-8, 51, 64, 90-1

Palaiologos, John, nephew of Michael VIII, 84

Palaiologos, John Despot, son of Andronikos II, 108, 159-60, 221

Palaiologos, John, nephew of Andronikos II, governor of Thessalonica, 166

Palaiologos, John, son of Andronikos, 351

Palaiologos, John, son of Manuel, 424

Palaiologos, John, alleged son of Thomas, 425

Palaiologos, Manuel, son of Despot Thomas, 424

Palaiologos, Manuel Despot, son of Michael IX, 159-61

Palaiologos, Michael Despot, third son of John V, 275

Palaiologos, Nicholas, 423

Palaiologos, Nikephoros, 399

476